SQL Server Developer's Guide

SQL Server Developer's Guide

Joseph J. Bambara and Paul R. Allen

M&T Books.
An imprint of IDG Books Worldwide, Inc.

Foster City, CA ◆ Chicago, IL ◆ Indianapolis, IN ◆ New York, NY

SQL Server Developer's Guide

Published by
M&T Books
An imprint of IDG Books Worldwide, Inc.
919 E. Hillsdale Blvd., Suite 400
Foster City, CA 94404
www.idgbooks.com (IDG Books Worldwide Web site)

ISBN: 0-7645-4672-4

Printed in the United States of America

10 9 8 7 6 5 4 3 2 1

1O/QW/QT/QQ/FC

Distributed in the United States by IDG Books Worldwide, Inc.

Distributed by CDG Books Canada Inc. for Canada; by Transworld Publishers Limited in the United Kingdom; by IDG Norge Books for Norway; by IDG Sweden Books for Sweden; by IDG Books Australia Publishing Corporation Pty. Ltd. for Australia and New Zealand; by TransQuest Publishers Pte Ltd. for Singapore, Malaysia, Thailand, Indonesia, and Hong Kong; by Gotop Information Inc. for Taiwan; by ICG Muse, Inc. for Japan; by Intersoft for South Africa; by Eyrolles for France; by International Thomson Publishing for Germany, Austria and Switzerland; by Distribuidora Cuspide for Argentina; by LR International for Brazil; by Galileo Libros for Chile; by Ediciones ZETA S.C.R. Ltda. for Peru; by WS Computer Publishing Corporation, Inc., for the Philippines; by Contemporanea de Ediciones for Venezuela; by Express Computer Distributors for the Caribbean and West Indies; by Micronesia Media Distributor, Inc. for Micronesia; by Chips Computadoras S.A. de C.V. for Mexico; by Editorial Norma de Panama S.A. for Panama; by American Bookshops for Finland.

For general information on IDG Books Worldwide's books in the U.S., please call our Consumer Customer Service department at 800-762-2974. For reseller information, including discounts and premium sales, please call our Reseller Customer Service department at 800-434-3422.

For information on where to purchase IDG Books Worldwide's books outside the U.S., please contact our International Sales department at 317-596-5530 or fax 317-596-5692.

For consumer information on foreign language translations, please contact our Customer Service department at 800-434-3422, fax 317-596-5692, or e-mail rights@idgbooks.com.

For information on licensing foreign or domestic rights, please phone +1-650-655-3109.

For sales inquiries and special prices for bulk quantities, please contact our Sales department at 650-655-3200 or write to the address above.

For information on using IDG Books Worldwide's books in the classroom or for ordering examination copies, please contact our Educational Sales department at 800-434-2086 or fax 317-596-5499.

For press review copies, author interviews, or other publicity information, please contact our Public Relations department at 650-655-3000 or fax 650-655-3299.

For authorization to photocopy items for corporate, personal, or educational use, please contact Copyright Clearance Center, 222 Rosewood Drive, Danvers, MA 01923, or fax 978-750-4470.

ABOUT IDG BOOKS WORLDWIDE

Welcome to the world of IDG Books Worldwide.

IDG Books Worldwide, Inc., is a subsidiary of International Data Group, the world's largest publisher of computer-related information and the leading global provider of information services on information technology. IDG was founded more than 30 years ago by Patrick J. McGovern and now employs more than 9,000 people worldwide. IDG publishes more than 290 computer publications in over 75 countries. More than 90 million people read one or more IDG publications each month.

Launched in 1990, IDG Books Worldwide is today the #1 publisher of best-selling computer books in the United States. We are proud to have received eight awards from the Computer Press Association in recognition of editorial excellence and three from Computer Currents' First Annual Readers' Choice Awards. Our best-selling ...For Dummies® series has more than 50 million copies in print with translations in 31 languages. IDG Books Worldwide, through a joint venture with IDG's Hi-Tech Beijing, became the first U.S. publisher to publish a computer book in the People's Republic of China. In record time, IDG Books Worldwide has become the first choice for millions of readers around the world who want to learn how to better manage their businesses.

Our mission is simple: Every one of our books is designed to bring extra value and skill-building instructions to the reader. Our books are written by experts who understand and care about our readers. The knowledge base of our editorial staff comes from years of experience in publishing, education, and journalism — experience we use to produce books to carry us into the new millennium. In short, we care about books, so we attract the best people. We devote special attention to details such as audience, interior design, use of icons, and illustrations. And because we use an efficient process of authoring, editing, and desktop publishing our books electronically, we can spend more time ensuring superior content and less time on the technicalities of making books.

You can count on our commitment to deliver high-quality books at competitive prices on topics you want to read about. At IDG Books Worldwide, we continue in the IDG tradition of delivering quality for more than 30 years. You'll find no better book on a subject than one from IDG Books Worldwide.

John Kilcullen
Chairman and CEO
IDG Books Worldwide, Inc.

Eighth Annual
Computer Press
Awards ≥1992

Ninth Annual
Computer Press
Awards ≥1993

Tenth Annual
Computer Press
Awards ≥1994

Eleventh Annual
Computer Press
Awards ≥1995

Credits

ACQUISITIONS EDITOR
Debra Williams Cauley

PROJECT EDITOR
Matthew E. Lusher

DEVELOPMENT EDITOR
Terry O'Donnell

TECHNICAL EDITOR
Mark Ashnault

COPY EDITORS
Amy Eof
Robert Campbell

PROJECT COORDINATORS
Linda Marousek
Marcos Vergara

GRAPHICS AND PRODUCTION
SPECIALISTS
Jude Levinson
Michael Lewis
Ramses Ramirez
Victor Pérez-Varela
Dina F. Quan

QUALITY CONTROL SPECIALISTS
Chris Weisbart
Laura Taflinger

BOOK DESIGNER
Jim Donohue

ILLUSTRATOR
Brent Savage

PROOFREADING AND INDEXING
York Production Services

About the Authors

Joseph J. Bambara and **Paul R. Allen** of UCNY, Inc. reside in New York, New York. They have over 40 years' collective experience in developing application systems and database applications, and have also been developing with SilverStream and Java for Web development the past three years. They have taught various computer courses for CCNY's School of Engineering (Mr. Bambara) and Columbia University (Mr. Allen). They have co-authored the following books: *PowerBuilder: A Guide to Developing Client/Server Applications* (McGraw-Hill, 1995), *Informix: Client /Server Application Development* (McGraw Hill, 1997), and *Informix: Universal Data Option* (McGraw Hill, 1998). They have presented numerous courses and presentations for SilverStream and Sybase in several cities and countries, including Los Angeles, Vienna, Paris, Berlin, Orlando, Nashville, New York, Copenhagen, Oslo, and Stockholm over the past four years.

To Roseanne, Vanessa, and Michael.
— Joseph J. Bambara

To Martha, Francesca, Freddie, George, Olivia, Eden, Dakota, and Ethan.
— Paul R. Allen

Preface

In recent years, the information technology industry has been called upon to undergo a massive redevelopment effort. Large firms have been re-mediating for the year 2000 and re-engineering their existing application environment, incorporating intranet and Internet capabilities. Smaller firms are breaking away from their standalone PC applications and using them to connect to intranet and Internet applications using database servers provided by Internet Service Providers (ISV's). Now that the Y2K effort has been virtually completed, there are new development efforts underway involving Internet applications. Thankfully, there are mature technologies that can facilitate this new development. One of them is Relational Database Management Systems (RDBMS) technology. RDBMSs, for example, Microsoft's SQL Server, have dramatically improved over the last three years, with each new vendor release providing a plethora of showcased features. SQL Server has emerged as the RDBMS that is the easiest to install and use. Moreover, in terms of price/performance, it performs very well. The Transaction Processing Performance Council (TPC) lists SQL Server in all positions within its top ten list for price/performance involving databases of 100GB or less. The point is that Oracle, Sybase, and IBM DB2 database environments, although good, are not as comprehensive and easy to use as SQL Server. For these reasons, SQL Server is the choice of many development efforts. This book is intended to: A) introduce the reader to the guaranteed approach to learning SQL Server; B) educate those new to database application development with an understanding of the concepts and theories behind this paradigm; and C) present real-world techniques for object-oriented programming (OOP) and relational database access, including data definition, data manipulation and stored procedure language. This book will also help experienced developers transfer their skills from large mainframe pre-Y2K environments or standalone PC environments to Microsoft SQL Server.

What's in This Book

A roadmap for navigating the book follows.

Part I: SQL Server 7 Environment is comprised of Chapters 1 and 2. It will introduce the reader to SQL Server 7. Chapter 1, "Introduction to MS-SQL Server 7" elaborates on why the Microsoft database product is the one that database administrators and development managers are choosing more and more frequently over the higher priced and less functional DBMS products like Sybase. In addition, we review issues that developers need to know about in order to plan a development effort using the SQL Server 7 database product line. This information will prove helpful for new development efforts, especially the planning of software and hardware procurement.

In Chapter 2, "The MS SQL-Server Environment" defines the SQL Server environment. It covers the improvements over the prior release, especially with respect to the architecture, server, and development enhancements. This chapter also covers the steps that should be followed when building an application that uses a SQL Server 7 database.

Part II: Database Administration for the Developer is comprised of Chapters 3 through 6. Chapter 3, "SQL Server 7 Common Administration" provides an introduction to the common administration tasks surrounding SQL Server 7. This includes starting, pausing, and stopping SQL Server. It also includes the management of the server and/or client connectivity, as well as the tools available to monitor and diagnose the performance and activity of SQL Server 7.

Chapter 4, "SQL Server 7 Tools and Components" provides an introduction to the tools and components that enable you to move and copy data to and from a SQL Server 7 database. It also introduces and reviews software tools that enable you to execute SQL and perform basic maintenance of the server environment.

Chapter 5, "DBMS Administration Tasks" provides details on the DBMS administration tasks for backing up and recovering database data, including the capability to schedule backups automatically. This chapter also reiterates techniques used to copy data from one server to another.

Chapter 6, "Database Administration Using Enterprise Manager" describes how you can design, administer, and manage the database and database objects using the graphical administration tool known as the Enterprise Manager. It also introduces other tools that you can use to design and maintain databases.

Part III: SQL Server 7 Application Development is comprised of Chapters 7 through 15. Chapter 7, "Setting Up the Development Environment" covers the installation or upgrade procedure for SQL Server 7. It also provides insights into the planning of a project and the development of an application, including standards, guidelines, and good practices. Additionally, it provides the specifics of setting up the developer's workstation environment.

Chapter 8, "Overview of the Application Development Process" provides a detailed view of how a software team can develop an application and the prerequisites for the development environment are outlined. The importance of database design, especially the need to virtually complete the database design before full-scale development begins, is emphasized. The choice of user interface is also considered here. The "how" and "when" to build basic application components: GUI windows, data access, and basic batch processing is reviewed as a workflow.

Chapter 9, "Defining the Application" provides an overview of types of Web, client/server and object-oriented systems. This includes descriptions of the architecture, strategies, and theories associated with application development. The phases of a development effort — many will be familiar to experienced developers — are presented. The chapter goes further and drills down into the steps required for successful application development efforts. The chapter also covers the distinctions between traditional development and contemporary development.

Chapter 10, "Designing the Application" is an overview of process-modeling and data-modeling techniques. Data design and modeling tools like Erwin are showcased.

Chapter 11, "Constructing the Database" describes the data-definition language that developers use to create the application database, as well as the practical considerations that are incorporated into the definition. This chapter also looks at the processes for creating tables, creating views, and maintaining the database. Additionally, the chapter takes a brief look at utilities that help facilitate the redefinition and repopulation of a database as it is being developed.

Chapter 12, "Manipulating Data" introduces and expands upon the development and use of the relational database constructs (DML, DDL, and SPL) and components (tables, columns, indexes, etc.). After the database creation basics are mastered the text continues to drill down to the essence of the database transaction: connecting to the database, SQL: database manipulation and definition language are presented with a developer's perspective. The reader goes behind the scenes to discover how the actual database update takes place and how to control the cost of the database access. Moreover, you will learn how to construct and manipulate the SQL to provide specialized features such as ad hoc database query tools that users need to perform dynamic business functions.

Chapter 13, "Developing the User Interface" covers the components of a database application that uses the Windows graphical user interface as well as the converging of Web and client/server systems. It provides an overview of the various types of document interfaces and sub-components that are common in many of today's user interfaces.

Chapter 14, "Tuning Your Environment, primarily focuses on the server resources that affect performance of SQL Server and coverage of the hardware and operating system issues. This chapter will guide you through the various areas that may be affecting the performance of the SQL Server 7 environment, enabling you to resolve any issues problems as soon as possible.

In Chapter 15, "Debugging" discusses the fundamentals of debugging, including items to consider when attempting to locate a problem, and some of the tools that are available for the debugging process.

Part IV, Programming Languages and Tools, is comprised of Chapters 16 through 17. In Chapter 16, Building Common Database Procedures, discusses the use of stored procedures, triggers, and the enhancements to stored procedures that SQL Server 7 provides over SQL Server 6.5. In addition, it introduces the database stored procedure by using a real example to illustrate Transact-SQL statements and their integration. The stored procedure functionality may range from a simple singleton select to a complex multiple table update for an application.

Chapter 17, "C and Java with SQL", details the ability for common programming languages, such as C and Java, to access relational database. This chapter will introduce and then compare and contrast the two languages and their embedded SQL functionality.

Appendix A: "Third-Party Tools" covers the myriad of third party tools that can be used to aid the development of an application using SQL Server 7.

Appendix B: "Standards Guidelines and Maxims" provides an example of the areas that should be standardized especially when implementing large-scale enterprise wide solutions.

Note that Appendix A and B can and should be browsed early in the reader's use of the book. Their content is referenced in many places throughout the book. The reader is encouraged to jump around per their interest from chapter to chapter. An attempt was made to follow the development life cycle as a form of stepwise material presentation, especially in Chapters 7 through 17.

In conclusion, the book will not only provide an introductory treatment of SQL Server 7 development, but, it will also be useful later on as your reach each milestone in the development life-cycle as a checklist to ensure that you have considered your options. No book can satisfy all needs but this guide was written by two developers who have been implementing computer-based solutions for a period fast approaching fifty years. In any event, the authors hope you enjoy reading the book and that it improves your SQL Server 7 development abilities.

Contacting the Authors

We're always interested in feedback from readers. Contact us at:

UCNY, Inc.
30 West 21st Street
8th Floor
New York, NY 10010
+1.212.352.9372 (voice)
+1.212.352.9383 (fax)
URL: http://www.ucny.com

email:
Joe Bambara: jbambara@ucny.com   Paul Allen: pallen@ucny.com

Acknowledgments

I would like to thank Debra Williams Cauley and our agent Chris Van Buren for presenting us with the opportunity to write this book. I would also like to thank Matt Lusher, Terry O'Donnell, Amy Eoff, Robert Campbell, and all of the folks at IDG Books for their hard work and dedication in producing this book. I would also like to thank Mark Ashnault for the hard work he dedicated to thet technical editing of the book. I would also like to thank Suresh and Revi Nadesan for their contributions to the book. Thanks to CNA Insurance (Shaati Chattopadhyay, and Bill Skelton), Schroder & Company (Gary Salamone, Bill Gillen, Lester Gray, Charlie Dugan, and Vicki DiSalvo) TIAA CREF (Andrew Lavers, Harish Nautiyal, Barry Kushnir, and Peter Russo) and New York City HPD (Kamal Bherwani and Lynn Lewis) for providing us with opportunities to develop our material. Special thanks to Johnny Bauer, Morten Olsen and René Madsen at CoreBit/United Consultants for providing us with opportunities to present our materials in Europe and Scandinavia. A very special thanks to my co-author Paul R. Allen, especially for his friendship and for being a great partner no matter what we attempt.

Thanks to my dad Joseph, my mom Carmela, my brothers Vincent and Richard, my sister Patricia, my father-in-law Joseph, and the rest of my family who are always there when I need them.

Foremost, I thank my wife Roseanne and my children Vanessa and Michael who are, and have always been, patient, loving, helpful, and encouraging no matter what I pursue. Roseanne, thanks. I could not have done it without you.

Joseph J. Bambara
Greenvale, New York

I would like to thank Debra Williams Cauley and our agent Chris Van Buren for presenting the opportunity to write this book. I would also like to thank Matt Lusher, Terry O'Donnell, Amy Eoff, Robert Campbell, and all of the folks at IDG Books for their hard work and dedication in producing the book. I would also like to thank Mark Ashnault for the hard work he dedicated to the technical edit of the book.

Thanks to Schroder & Company (Gary Salamone, Bill Gillen, Lester Gray) and Lewco Securities (Charlie Dugan and Vicki DiSalvo) for the opportunity to work with them on terrific financial Web projects. Special thanks to Johnny Bauer, Morten Olsen, and René Madsen at CoreBit/United Consultants for providing us with great opportunities to present in Europe and Scandinavia. I would also like to thank Sandra & Goran Jovicic, Kailash Chanrai, Jim Burns, Peter Naughton, Sheila Ruddigan and Lenny Appleton, and Ian Stokes for their friendship and support.

Very special thanks to my co-author, Joseph J. Bambara, for his friendship, encouragement, and perseverance during the writing of this book and our other endeavors.

I would like to give special thanks to my uncles John and Roy Allen for taking care of what I hold most dear. I wish to thank Brian Holmes for his advice, counsel, and for taking good care of my mother. I would like to thank my mother, Carole and my sister Lorisa and the rest of our family, for their neverending love, optimism, and support. To my nieces Francesca, Olivia, Eden, and Dakota; and my nephews Freddie, George, and Ethan; always believe in your dreams. Foremost, I would like to thank my wife Martha for letting me get away with doing yet another book. I would like to remember my grandfather, Charles, and my father, Terence. We miss them so much, but feel better knowing that they keep a watchful eye over us all from heaven.

Paul R. Allen
New York, New York

Contents at a Glance

Contents

Part III: SQL Server 7 Application Development

Part I

SQL Server 7 Environment

CHAPTER 1
Introduction to Microsoft SQL Server 7

CHAPTER 2
The MS SQL-Server Environment

Chapter 1

Introduction to Microsoft SQL Server 7

IN THIS CHAPTER

- ◆ Why choose MS-SQL Server 7 over all other RDBMSs?
- ◆ Why you should upgrade from prior versions
- ◆ Choosing the testing and deployment server
- ◆ Finding help

THIS CHAPTER PROVIDES AN introduction to the Microsoft SQL Server 7 product. It begins with a comparison of this product's major competitors. It provides a to-do list covering what you will need to have in place to begin development with SQL Server. It will review things that you must consider before deploying a SQL Server 7–based application. Finally, the chapter will list some places where you can go to get help with SQL Server issues.

Why Choose Microsoft SQL Server 7?

If you are a new user of relational database technology, which database should you choose? Moreover, why buy SQL Server 7? Relational database technology has been in use since the mid 1980s. Since then it has matured significantly. Additionally, widespread use has caused the best of the rest, in terms of overall licenses in use, to rise to the top. In effect, the RDBMS vendor market has thinned down to three major players: IBM, Oracle, and Microsoft.

In the large organizations that have been using computers since the 1960s, IBM's DB2 remains the most popular choice because these organizations need the reliability of this platform to continue processing their voluminous transactional and "book and records" type of data. The sheer power of the mainframe makes this technology a necessity. In the past 20 years of relational database server technology, no hardware platform has been able to usurp the mainframe.

However, in the middle-tier market, where Sun Solaris UNIX servers have become commonplace, Oracle now has the most significant market share. Recently, Oracle, in conjunction with Sun Microsystems, announced plans for a new product called "Raw Iron." This product will marry a lighter (or leaner and meaner) Solaris operating system with the Oracle database kernel. This is similar to the tight coupling of the mainframe operating system and the DB2 database kernel, which is one of the biggest reasons why DB2 works so well on the mainframe. If Oracle and Sun can pull off the technology that is behind Raw Iron, they'll be in an excellent position to dominate most of the middle-tier market.

The lower- to middle-tier market has seen some evolution over the past five years. The Windows NT operating system has become the common choice for network servers for many companies, and now it also becomes the most common choice as a lower- to middle-tier database server. Both IBM and Oracle provide versions of their database server product for Windows NT, but it is Microsoft's SQL Server that is dominating the Windows NT market.

The reason why SQL Server is a very popular choice for Windows NT is that it provides functionality equal or greater to the IBM and Oracle products at a lower price. On a more technical level, like DB2 on the mainframe, SQL Server is very tightly integrated with the Windows NT operating system. This tight integration is one of the reasons why SQL Server 7 consistently yields the best performance numbers for the Windows NT platform (see the section "The Transaction Processing Performance Council" later in this chapter). SQL Server 7 is a very good product that can easily cope with departmental level data, and as Windows NT (soon to be Windows 2000) improves, it will make some headway as a database choice for the middle-tier and high-end enterprise level for many non-mainframe and non-UNIX environments.

Why Upgrade from Earlier Releases of Microsoft SQL Server?

Microsoft SQL Server 7 is a major release of SQL Server. It's major in the sense that the server architecture, development tools, and administration functions have been completely reengineered to provide new features, while maintaining ANSI and SQL Server 6.x compatibility. These new features can be divided into two sections, *server enhancements* and *administration enhancements* (see Tables 1-1 and 1-2).

TABLE 1-1 SQL SERVER 7 SERVER ENHANCEMENTS

Server Enhancement	What Does This Mean to You?
Cursor enhancements	There is enhanced support for local cursors, cursor variables, and parameters.

Server Enhancement	What Does This Mean to You?
New data types	`bigint` — an 8-byte integer for storing very large numbers in the range –2^63 to 2^63 – 1
	`sql_variant` — for storing values of all data types except `text`, `ntext`, `image`, and `timestamp` (This is similar to `Variant` data type in Visual Basic.)
	`table` — a temporary result set used for subsequent processing
Data warehousing	New algorithms have been written to improve speed of table joins for complicated queries. The storage engine and many other utilities within SQL Server have been optimized for very large database (VLDB) support.
	If you have data that is distributed across various DBMS vendors, it can be accessed (or replicated) and managed by SQL Server tools and components. There is also a parallel query engine for speeding up complex queries.
Distributed queries and updates	Support is improved for extra-server (or distributed) queries.
	SQL Server has the capability to execute distributed queries, which can access data that can be stored in multiple data sources on either the same or different computers. These data sources can be other SQL Server data sources, other relational data sources (for example, Oracle, Informix, Sybase, DB2), or nonrelational data sources via OLE DB.
Dynamic locking	Full row-level locking is supported for both data rows and index entries. The lock manager now implements dynamic locking, in which the granularity of the lock is based on the cost of the SQL operation. The default is row-level locking, where the SQL operation is changing a small number of rows, or rows scattered throughout a table. The server will dynamically escalate to a page-level lock if the SQL operation is changing many of the rows in a page. The server will dynamically escalate to a table-level lock if the SQL operation is changing many of the pages allocated to a table.
	Support for Unicode data types and increases in capacity of existing data types

Continued

TABLE 1-1 SQL SERVER 7 SERVER ENHANCEMENTS *(Continued)*

Server Enhancement	What Does This Mean to You?
	SQL Server 7 supports the Unicode data types: `nchar`, `nvarchar`, and `ntext`. These data types make it easier to store data in multiple languages within one database by eliminating the problem of converting characters and installing multiple code pages. Unicode stores character data using two bytes for each character rather than one byte. SQL Server now supports the unique identifier data type for the storage of a globally unique ID (GUID). The maximum size of character (`char`, `varchar`) and binary (`varbinary`) data types has been increased to 8,000 characters (from 255). So you don't have to use the text and image anymore to store fairly large data items; they can now be reserved for very large data items. Note that the Unicode data types (`nchar`, `nvarchar`, and `ntext`) have a maximum of 4,000 bytes, because two bytes are used for each character.
Full-text search	Now you can create indexes of words in character-based columns of tables. Extensions to the Transact-SQL language exploit these indexes to support linguistic and proximity searches. Several languages are supported. These indexes can be managed through a GUI (SQL Server Enterprise Manager) or from the command line interface (via new stored procedures).
Improved performance and data management	Pages are 8KB (up from 2KB). Rows can be as wide as 8,060 bytes. Character and binary data can be 8,000 bytes wide (up from 255). Tables can have 1,024 columns. These changes, along with the improved locking levels and associated lock escalation, significantly improve the product over prior releases in terms of performance and flexibility.
Improved DSS/OLAP services	SQL Server is now designed to support Online Analytical Processing (OLAP). These services help with reporting, analysis, modeling, and decision support system (DSS) requirements. Supports multidimensional OLAP (MOLAP), relational OLAP (ROLAP), and hybrid OLAP.
Improved backup and restore	It's basically faster, less intrusive, and easier to make a backup and restore the backup (even on a new computer).
Indexing operations	SQL Server 7 now uses index intersection and index union on a table with multiple indexes to satisfy queries.

Server Enhancement	What Does This Mean to You?
SQL access via Microsoft Proxy Server	The Windows Sockets Net-Library has been changed to work with Microsoft Proxy Server. It now provides secure access to your SQL server from outside your firewall. In other words, authenticated users can access the SQL Server via the Internet, although from an application point of view, this might be better addressed through the use of an application server that sits inside your firewall and handles all requests for data.
Microsoft Repository	Data Warehousing Alliance (Microsoft and other partners) has developed repository extensions for a common development infrastructure. This allows the sharing of information, such as database schemata, meta-data, and data transformations. These are useful when constructing data warehousing applications.
Multiple Instances	During the install, you can create default and named instances. Each instance has its own set of system and user databases. There can only be one default instance on a machine that contains multiple versions of SQL Server; for example, 6.5 and 7.0. There can be any number of SQL Server 7 named instances.
Multisite management	You can group servers into logical units, perform cross-server transactions, and create and maintain multistep jobs from a central location.

The system administrator (sa) can group servers together and name one server as a master. The master can be used to communicate and distribute jobs, alerts, and event messages to the other servers in the group. The administrator can also manage and monitor performance of any server from within a single instance of SQL Server Enterprise Manager. |
| New security model | SQL Server is now more tightly integrated with Windows NT security. Database permissions can now be assigned directly to Windows NT users. You can define SQL Server roles to include not only Windows NT users and groups but also SQL Server users and roles. |

Continued

TABLE 1-1 SQL SERVER 7 SERVER ENHANCEMENTS *(Continued)*

Server Enhancement	What Does This Mean to You?
New Transact-SQL statements	SQL Server has more powerful Transact-SQL statements, which are:
	ALTER PROCEDURE, ALTER TRIGGER, ALTER VIEW, ALTER TABLE, BULK INSERT, COMMIT WORK, DENY, RESTORE, RESTORE FILELISTONLY, RESTORE HEADERONLY, RESTORE LABELONLY, RESTORE VERIFYONLY, and ROLLBACK WORK
PivotTable service	A companion to the OLAP services, this service runs on client workstations and allows applications to access data held locally. This may be a viable solution for users who are either on the road (mobile) or happen to be detached (disconnected) from the network.
Programming interfaces	SQL Server now supports the following programming interfaces: OLE DB, ADO, ODBC, and SQL-DMO.
Reduced administrative overhead	Most of the server configuration options have been stream-lined and simplified so that the product is now a self-configuring engine. For example, it will dynamically adjust the memory and lock resource use. The database server will also automatically expand and grow a database as it fills with data. It will even shrink it if data is removed.
Replication enhancements	The publish and subscribe metaphor has been enhanced to provide three types of replication, which are:

♦ *Snapshot replication* – complete snapshot replacement on a periodic basis

♦ *Transactional replication* – incremental changes distributed in (almost) real time

♦ *Merge replication* – merging changes from autonomous database sites into one (cannot guarantee transactional consistency)

The type you may choose depends upon your application requirements for transactional consistency, site autonomy, and capability to partition the data to avoid conflicts.

Server Enhancement	What Does This Mean to You?
Trigger enhancements	A database can be configured to allow triggers to call themselves recursively. A single table can have multiple triggers of the same type. For example, a table might be set up to have a single insert trigger, three update triggers, and two delete triggers. This flexibility will enable you to implement varying business rules in separate triggers.
Upgrades	Databases can be easily upgraded from SQL Server 6.x to 7, using the upgrade utility.
	The upgrade process can be performed on the same computer, where it needs double the disk space (or a tape backup device) to perform the data transfer successfully.
	Alternatively, the upgrade can be performed on a separate machine, where the upgrade takes place using a Named Pipe connection to transfer definitions and the data. The latter technique is the more likely scenario for you.
User-defined functions	This feature enables you to define your own functions and, in effect, extend the Transact-SQL language.
All 32-bit Windows platforms	You can install the Desktop Edition on Windows 95/98 and Windows NT 4.0 Workstation (SP4 and above). By the way, you won't be able to install it on Windows 3.1, even if you have Win32s!
XML Support	This release introduces support for XML, including:

◆ Access to SQL server through HTTP via a URL

◆ The FOR XML clause in the SELECT statement to retrieve results in XML format

◆ System stored procedures for managing XML data

TABLE 1-2 SQL SERVER 7 ADMINISTRATION ENHANCEMENTS

Administration	What Does This Mean to You?
Data Transformation Services (DTS)	This is great because you'll be able to import, export, and transform data between SQL Server and any OLE DB — or ODBC-compliant data source (even a text file). This can be done either interactively or automatically on a regularly scheduled basis.
Index Tuning Wizard	Although the Query Optimizer will choose the best indexes available, your queries can also be analyzed to determine the best index mix. The Index Tuning Wizard will suggest and also implement changes to indexes (including creating new indexes) to achieve optimal query performance.
Management Console (Enterprise Manager)	This provides rich graphical management of all objects and common tasks. Uses Wizards, in part, to perform most of the common tasks. Integrated HTML-based monitoring.
SQL Server Agent	This enables unattended job execution and alert/response management; multitasking jobs in Transact-SQL, ActiveScript, or OS command files; running multischedule jobs; and running multiserver jobs (defining jobs once to be executed on multiple servers).
SQL Server Profiler	You can monitor, capture, and analyze SQL Server activity; monitor queries, stored procedures, locks, transactions, and log changes; and replay captured data on another server. Also includes a date/time filter to capture events that occur during the designated time.
SQL Server Query Analyzer	This color-coded SQL authoring tool enables you to graphically analyze the plan of a query, execute multiple queries, and choose indexes, in addition to showing you the result set of the query. Comes with the SHOWPLAN option, which documents the methods and indexes chosen by the query optimizer.
Web Assistant Wizard	You can export SQL Server data out to an HTML file, import tabular data from an HTML file, and POST to and GET from HTTP and FTP servers.

Planning for Development

Now assuming that you've made up your mind to go ahead and use MS-SQL Server 7, what are your next moves? Here's a short list of what you're going to need, or need to do next:

- ◆ Order (or start the download of) the product from Microsoft.

- ◆ Find, or buy, a suitable machine for development. See Chapter 7, "Setting Up the Development Environment," for an in-depth look at the requirements for SQL Server 7.

- ◆ Start thinking about the main and supplemental development tools and coding standards that you want to use. Even if you don't have a project yet, you can still take a glance through Appendix A, "Third-Party Tools," for more on related tools and Appendix B, "Standards, Guidelines, and Maxims," for more on standards and guidelines.

Once you have completed this process, you should not wait too long before you move on to the next stage and start thinking about what the production server will look like.

Choosing the Testing and Deployment Server

When you need to purchase suitable hardware for your SQL Server testing (quality assurance) and production environments, you will need to evaluate the various hardware vendors' offerings. For help in your evaluation, you can check the Transaction Processing Performance Council's (TPC) benchmarks for a short list of hardware vendors.

The Transaction Processing Performance Council

The TPC is a nonprofit corporation founded to define transaction processing and database benchmarks. They have defined a series of benchmarks named: TPC-A, TPC-B, TPC-C(tm), and TPC-D. Independent auditors certify benchmark results, and a full disclosure report is filed with the TPC. These reports are a great source of information about system performance and system cost. You can obtain more information and the full disclosure reports for the particular hardware that you are considering on the TPC Web site (see http://www.tpc.org/).

A rule of thumb on acquiring memory

When determining hardware for database servers, our thinking is that more is better. This is particularly true in the case of memory, or RAM, which is a critical resource. As of this writing, the maximum amount of addressable RAM in a Windows NT 4.0 server is 1GB. For Windows NT 4.0 Enterprise Server, the maximum is 2GB of RAM. (These numbers become 2GB and 4GB, respectively, for Windows 2000). We recommend that you put the maximum amount of memory that your version of Windows NT can address. This resolves two questions: The first is that memory will not be an issue (if it is, then you're probably trying to do the impossible with a poor database design in a relatively short amount of time). The second is that you won't have to schedule downtime on that server in order to add more memory.

Finding Help

Apart from the abundant help that can be found in Books Online, a help component that comes with SQL Server, you will inevitably find yourself in a situation that is not well (or at all) documented. Once you reach this point, you may want to check out the Internet resources listed in Table 1-3 for more help.

TABLE 1-3 USEFUL WEB SITES AND NEWSGROUPS ON THE INTERNET

Site	Description
http://www.swynk.com/	Stephen Wynkoop's Web site
http://www.microsoft.com/sql/	Microsoft's general SQL Server page
http://www.tpc.org/	The Transaction Processing Performance Council publishes hardware performance benchmarks for major database vendors
http://www.microsoft.com/sql/olap/	Microsoft's information on OLAP Services
http://www.microsoft.com/sql/eq/	English Query support
http://www.microsoft.com/support/	Microsoft's technical support
news://msnews.microsoft.com/	Microsoft's Usenet newsgroups

Summary

This chapter has presented some basic information describing why you should choose Microsoft's SQL Server 7 for your environment. We have also looked into the reasons you should upgrade from the prior release. We've covered some of the tasks you need to start thinking about if you want to deploy SQL Server in a production environment and where to go to get more information about the product (in addition to this book, obviously!).

Chapter 2

The MS-SQL Server Environment

IN THIS CHAPTER

◆ Defining the SQL Server environment

◆ Improvements over SQL Server 6.5

◆ Architecture, server, and development enhancements

◆ Building an application

MICROSOFT SQL SERVER 7 starts with the building blocks of a dynamic, scalable architecture and extends the capability of the relational database management system to a virtual object-relational database management system. This combination makes SQL Server one of the most comprehensive environments available for today's intranet, Internet, and extranet development. This chapter presents definitions and terminology that will be expanded upon later. If you are familiar with these ideas, then just quickly browse this chapter and move on to the next chapter.

Defining the Environment

SQL Server is a tool that provides a database server with an integrated database development environment packaged into a suite of software. We will mention most of the SQL Server components here in this chapter, but the book will concentrate on the SQL Server RDBMS, which is the second or third most widely installed database management system. As of this book's writing in 1999, the database industry is rumbling on; Oracle Corporation has disclosed plans to delay its Oracle8i database release by two months, and ex-SQL Server partner Sybase Incorporated has shaved its work force significantly. The delay brought smiles to Microsoft Corporation, which was in a race with Oracle in recent months as it readied the SQL Server 7.0 database upgrade. Version 7.0 was released on schedule at the end of 1998.

An important new option has been included in release 7. SQL Server can now run on Windows 98 (personal copy) as well as NT Workstation and Server platforms. The environment has expanded in other ways as well. Many third-party vendors have added SQL Server 7 interfaces to their products (for example, Erwin version 3.5.2, the database modeling tool and SilverStream version 2.5, the Java Web development tools). Perhaps the most significant change is the perception of NT as a bona fide server platform and SQL Server as more than just a departmental server. Table 2-1 contains Transaction Processing Council (TPC) data showing that SQL Server 7 can provide cost-effective database operation. This table depicts TPM C ratings (the top ten performers; see the "Database" column on the far right). TPMC indicates an application that contains OLTP and some decision support.

TABLE 2-1 TPM C RATINGS

Rank	Company	Configuration	Cost $ /TPMC	TPMC	Database
1	Compaq	ProLiant 7000 c/s (4-way)	$18.84	22,478.90	SQL 7 Enterprise
2	Compaq	ProLiant 5500 6/400	$21.71	17,715.90	SQL 7 Enterprise
3	Unisys	Aquanta QS/2V (4-way)	$22.11	19,118.37	SQL 7 Enterprise
4	Unisys	Aquanta QR/2V (4-way)	$22.19	19,118.37	SQL 7 Enterprise
5	Compaq	ProLiant 7000 c/s (4-way)	$22.50	19,725.10	SQL 7 Enterprise
6	HP	NetServer LH 4r	$23.10	19,050.17	SQL 7 Enterprise
7	Unisys	Aquanta QR/2 (4-way)	$23.73	18,343.17	SQL 7 Enterprise
8	Unisys	Aquanta QR/2 (4-way)	$24.83	18,154.00	SQL 7 Enterprise
9	Unisys	Aquanta QR/2 (4-way)	$25.49	18,154.00	SQL 7 Enterprise
10	IBM	Netfinity 7000 M10 (4-way)	$25.70	22,459.80	SQL 7 Enterprise

Defining a database

A database is a place to store data. The database management system — in this case SQL Server 7 — provides an interface to operating system files that store the actual data. Like the old mainframe file, a database does not present information directly to a user. The user runs an application that accesses data from the database. The application then presents the data to the user in a digestible format. Database systems based upon SQL are standardized and more powerful than file systems. Related tuples of data are grouped together in a single record or row, and relationships can be defined between these rows.

A little background on the evolution of databases and database theory will help you understand the workings of SQL. Database systems store information in every conceivable business environment. From large tracking databases such as airline reservation systems to an individual's wine collection, database systems store and distribute the data that we depend on. Twenty years ago, large database systems could be run only on large mainframe computers. These machines have traditionally been expensive to design, purchase, and maintain. However, today's generation of powerful, inexpensive workstation computers enables programmers to design software that maintains and distributes data quickly and inexpensively.

A database contains a system catalog or mapping that applications use to navigate the data. Generic database applications can use the catalog to dynamically present users with data from different databases, without being tied to a specific data format. To be usable, a database has two components: the files holding the physical database and the database management system (DBMS) software that applications use to access data. The DBMS is responsible for enforcing the database schema, including:

♦ Maintaining relationships between the entities in the database

♦ Ensuring that data has integrity, that is, that the rules defining data relationships are not violated

♦ Enabling recovery of data to a point of consistency

Defining a relational database

Different ways exist to organize data in a database, but relational databases have been the most effective over the past 17 years. Relational database systems are an application of mathematical set theory to the problem of effectively organizing data. In a relational database, data is collected into tables. A *table* represents an entity that is important to an organization. For example, a company may have a database with a table for employees, another table for departments, and another for products. Each table comprises *columns* and *rows* (attributes and tuples in relational theory). Each column represents some attribute of the object represented by the table. For example, an Employee table would typically have columns for first name, last name, employee ID, department, network user ID, and e-mail address. Each row represents an instance of the object represented by the table (for example, one row for each employee).

Using Structured Query Language (SQL)

To work with data in a database, you must use a set of commands and statements (language) defined by the DBMS software. The characteristic that differentiates a DBMS from an RDBMS is that the RDBMS provides a set-oriented database language. For most RDBMSs, this set-oriented database language is SQL. "Set-oriented" means that SQL processes sets of data in groups. That is, SQL statements work on data that is a subset or an intersection of grouped data stored in tables. You can define and manipulate data in a table with SQL commands. You use data definition language (DDL) commands to define the DBMS objects. DDL commands include commands for creating and altering databases and tables.

You can update, delete, or retrieve data in a table with data manipulation (DML) commands. DML commands include commands to alter and fetch data. The most common SQL command is the SELECT command, which enables you to retrieve data from the database.

Two standards organizations, the American National Standards Institute (ANSI) and the International Standards Organization (ISO), currently promote SQL standards to the industry. Although these standard-making bodies prepare standards for database system designers to follow, all database products differ from the ANSI standard to some degree. In addition, most systems provide some proprietary extensions to SQL that extend the language into a true procedural language. We have used various RDBMSs, so to prepare the examples in this book, we try to keep it simple to give you an idea of what to expect from the common database systems. For example, if an application working with a nonrelational flat file needs to display a list of the names of managers in New York, it must retrieve the entire employee file. If the application is working with a relational database server, it sends this command:

```
SELECT first_name, last_name FROM tb_employees
WHERE emp_type = 'Manager' AND emp_state = 'NY'
```

The relational database only sends back the subset, that is, names of the managers in New York, not all of the information about all employees. This basic form of the SELECT statement is a typical command.

Working with the database architecture

When using a database, you primarily work with the component objects such as tables, views, procedures, and users. Each SQL server has multiple databases. SQL Server has four system catalog databases (master, model, tempdb, and msdb), and each SQL server will have one or more user databases that house the application data. To control database objects, whether permanent or temporary, the common DBMS systems include catalog databases containing control information and metadata to facilitate the processing of user databases. Microsoft SQL Server has four such catalog databases. Each is described as follows:

- ◆ **The master database.** The master database records all of the system-level information for a SQL Server system. It records all login accounts and all system configuration settings. The master database records the existence of all other databases and the location of the primary files that contain the initialization information for the user databases. The master database records the initialization information for SQL Server; always have a recent backup of master available.

- ◆ **The tempdb database.** The tempdb database holds all temporary tables and temporary stored procedures, and it fills any other temporary storage needs. The tempdb database is a global resource; the temporary tables and stored procedures for all users connected to the system are stored there. The tempdb database is recreated every time SQL Server is started, so the system starts with a clean copy of the database. Because temporary tables and stored procedures are automatically dropped on disconnect, and no connections are active when the system is shut down, there is never anything in tempdb to be saved from one session of SQL Server to another.

  The tempdb database autogrows as needed. Each time the system is started, tempdb is reset to its default size. You can avoid the overhead of having tempdb autogrow by using ALTER TABLE to increase the size of tempdb.

- ◆ **The model database.** The model database is used as the template for all databases created on a system. When a CREATE DATABASE statement is issued, the first part of the database is created by copying in the contents of the model database, and then the remainder of the new database is filled with empty pages. Because tempdb is created every time SQL Server is started, the model database must always exist on a SQL Server system.

- ◆ **The msdb database.** The msdb database is used by SQL Server Agent for scheduling alerts, jobs, and recording operators.

In SQL Server version 7.0, every database, including the aforementioned system databases, has its own set of files and does not share those files with other databases. Table 2-2 shows that the default location for these files is the C:\Mssql7\Data directory.

TABLE 2-2 DEFAULT LOCATION AND SIZE FOR SYSTEM DATA

Database File	Physical Filename	Default Size, Typical Setup
master primary data	Master.mdf	7.5MB
master log	Mastlog.ldf	1.0MB
tempdb primary data	Tempdb.mdf	8.0MB
tempdb log	Templog.ldf	0.5MB
model primary data	Model.mdf	0.75MB
model log	Modellog.ldf	0.75MB
msdb primary data	Msdbdata.mdf	3.5MB
msdb log	Msdblog.ldf	0.75MB

In earlier versions of SQL Server, the master and model system databases were on a single file, known as the master device. The first 2MB allocation of tempdb also resided on the master device, as did, sometimes, the pubs sample database. The restriction of having these databases all reside in a single file sometimes caused problems with space in the master and model databases. You do not want to run out of space on the master. If you do, your DBMS will be virtually paralyzed.

In SQL Server 7.0, all of these databases have their own set of files that can grow independently of each other. This pleases DBAs. Each database in SQL Server contains system tables tracking the data needed by the SQL Server components. The successful operation of SQL Server depends on the integrity of information in the system tables; therefore, Microsoft does not support users' directly updating the information in the system tables. These tables are, as a read-only database, a great source for user database metadata.

Working with the physical database architecture

SQL Server 7 has amended the way data is stored physically. These changes are virtually transparent to SQL Server users, but they do impact the setup and administration of SQL Server databases. The SQL Server 7 organization is different from the organization of data in earlier versions of SQL Server.

The fundamental unit of data storage in any DBMS, including SQL Server 7, is the *page*. In SQL Server 7 the size of pages is 8K. This is a significant increase from prior releases, which supported the 2K page. This change was necessary because in today's applications, text and other data for document retrieval systems exceeded the 2K limitation. The start of each page contains control information consisting of a 96-byte header. This page header is used to store system information such as the type of page, the amount of free space on the page, and the object ID of the object owning the page. This obviously reduces the usable space to 8K – 96 bytes.

There are six types of pages in the files of a SQL Server 7 database (see Table 2-3). These pages support the physical data storage architecture for SQL Server.

TABLE **2-3 PAGE TYPES**

Page type	Contains
Data	Data rows with all data except text, ntext, and image data
Index	Index entries
Text/image	Text, ntext, and image data
Global allocation map	Information about allocated extents
Page free space	Information about free space available on pages
Index allocation map	Information about extents used by a table or index

Log files do not contain pages; they contain a series of log records that store "before images" of rows that have been modified. Data pages contain all the data in data rows except text, ntext, and image data. Data items defined with these data types are stored in separate pages. Data rows are placed sequentially on the page immediately after the header. A row-offset table starts at the end of the page. The row-offset table contains one entry for each row on the page, and each entry records how far the first byte of the row is from the start of the page.

The entries in the row-offset table are in reverse sequence from the sequence of the rows on the page. Rows can span pages in SQL Server. This is necessary because certain data types can be as large as 8K. In SQL Server 7, the maximum amount of data contained in a single row is 8,060 bytes, not including text, ntext, and image data. *Extents* are the basic unit in which space is allocated to tables and indexes. An extent is eight contiguous pages, or 64K. This means SQL Server 7 databases have 16 extents per megabyte.

To make its space allocation efficient, SQL Server 7 does not allocate entire extents to tables with small amounts of data. SQL Server 7 has two types of extents:

♦ *Uniform* extents are owned by a single object; all eight pages in the extent can only be used by the owning object.

♦ *Mixed* extents are shared by up to eight objects.

A new table or index is allocated pages from mixed extents. When the table or index grows to the point that it has eight pages, it is switched to uniform extents. These are used by code tables and entities used to store control data.

PHYSICAL DATABASE FILES AND FILEGROUPS

SQL Server 7 maps a database over a set of operating system files. Data and log information are never mixed on the same file because recovery in case of a failure would become virtually impossible. Moreover, individual files are used only by one database.

SQL Server 7 databases have three types of files:

◆ **Primary files.** The primary data file is the starting point of the database and points to the rest of the files in the database. Every database has one primary data file. The recommended file extension for primary files is .mdf.

◆ **Secondary files.** Secondary files comprise all of the files other than the primary data file. Some databases may not have any secondary files, whereas others have multiple secondary files. The recommended file extension for secondary files is .ndf.

◆ **Log files.** Log files hold all of the log information used to recover the database. There must be at least one log file for each database; although there can be more than one. The recommended file extension for log files is .ldf.

SQL Server 7 does not enforce the .mdf, .ndf, and .ldf file extensions, but these extensions are recommended to help identify the use of the file.

SQL Server 7 files have two names:

◆ The *logical_file_name* is a name used to refer to the file in all Transact-SQL statements. The logical filename must conform to the rules for SQL Server identifiers and must be unique to the database.

◆ The *os_file_name* is the name of the physical file. It must follow the rules for Microsoft Windows NT or Microsoft Windows 95 filenames.

Pages in a SQL Server 7 file are numbered sequentially starting with 0 for the first page in the file. Each file has a file ID number. As in most other relational database systems, uniquely identifying a page in a database requires both the file ID and page number. The first page in each file is a file header page containing information about the attributes of the file. The ninth page in a primary data file is a database boot page containing information about the attributes of the database.

Unlike previous releases of SQL Server, version 7 files can automatically grow from their originally specified size. When you define a file, you can specify a growth increment. Each time the file fills, it increases its size by the growth increment. If there are multiple files in a filegroup, they do not grow automatically until all the files are full. Each file can also have a maximum size specified. If a maximum size is not specified, the file can continue to grow until it has used all available space on the disk. This feature is especially useful when SQL Server is used as a database embedded in an application where the user does not have ready access to a system administrator. The user can let the files grow automatically to lessen the administrative task of monitoring the amount of free space in the database and allocating additional space manually. DBAs should still review space allocation to avoid physical operating system disk limitations.

DATABASE FILEGROUPS

Database files can be grouped together in filegroups for allocation and administration purposes. If you are familiar with SQL 6.5, filegroups basically obviate or replace devices. Devices are still used for backups, however. Please see Chapter 11, "Constructing the Database," for more details on this subject.

Some systems can improve their performance by controlling the placement of data and indexes onto specific disk drives. For example, data used in OLTP system should probably be separated from data used in decision support systems. Filegroups can aid this process. The system administrator can create filegroups for each disk drive and then assign specific tables; indexes; or the text, ntext, or image data from a table to specific filegroups. No file can be a member of more than one filegroup. Tables; indexes; and text, ntext, and image data can be associated with a filegroup, in which case all their pages will be allocated in that filegroup. Log files are never a part of a filegroup. Log space is managed separately from data space.

Files in a filegroup will not autogrow unless no space is available on any of the files in the filegroup. There are three types of filegroups:

- The *primary* filegroup contains the primary data file and any other files not put into another filegroup. All pages for the system tables are allocated in the primary filegroup.

- *User-defined* filegroups are any filegroups specified using the FILEGROUP keyword in a CREATE DATABASE or ALTER DATABASE statement.

- The *default* filegroup contains the pages for all tables and indexes that do not have a filegroup specified when they are created. In each database, only one filegroup at a time can be the default filegroup. Members of the db_owner fixed database role can switch the default filegroup from one filegroup to another. If no default filegroup was specified, it defaults to the primary filegroup.

The primary filegroup is important because it contains all of the system tables. If the primary filegroup runs out of space, no new catalog information can be added to the system tables. If a user-defined filegroup fills up, only the user tables specifically allocated to that filegroup will be affected. The primary filegroup only fills if either AUTOGROW is turned off or the disk holding the primary filegroup runs out of space. If this happens, either turn AUTOGROW back on or move other files off the disk to free more space.

Members of the db_owner fixed database role can back up and restore individual files or filegroups instead of backing up or restoring an entire database.

SQL Server 7 is very effective at quickly allocating pages to objects and reusing space freed up by deleted rows. SQL Server 7 introduces some significant changes to the internal data structures used to manage the allocation and reuse of pages.

SQL Server 7 will autoshrink databases that have a large amount of free space. Only those databases where the autoshrink option has been set to true are candidates for this process. The server checks the space usage in each database periodically. If a database is found with a lot of empty space and it has the autoshrink option set to true, SQL Server will reduce the size of the files in the database. You can also use SQL Server Enterprise Manager or the DBCC SHRINKDATABASE statement to manually shrink the files of a database.

Server Improvements and New Features

The main improvements in SQL Server 7 from an administrative point of view revolve around self-configuration. Do not worry, DBAs, there is still plenty to do. Many server configuration options, however, have been streamlined and simplified. For example, by default the server dynamically adjusts its memory and locks resource use. A database increases allocated resources when necessary without ever committing them and decreases the resources used when they are no longer needed. Earlier versions of SQL Server required manual adjustment of these settings. Care must now be taken to review the database as it evolves. DBAs should watch to ensure that these automatic configurations and growth adjustments do not run out of control. To separate itself from Sybase forever, Microsoft SQL Server 7 introduced the features described in this section.

Controlling administrative overhead and cost of ownership

SQL Server has added some features that obviate certain administrative tasks. The text that follows will introduce some of these features. The feature on-demand memory assists the memory manager in cooperating with the operating system to provide memory in peak periods of activity. The feature on-demand disk assists in helping files grow and shrink automatically. Auto-update statistics, statistics on nonindexed columns, and table and row sampling assist in determining when to perform recompilation. Auto recompilation of plans will take advantage of optimized access paths based on database table changes.

Additionally, configuration tasks are reduced; that is, certain settings can be allowed to automatically configure themselves. Database locking, including connections, locks, and open objects, has been problematic. SQL 7 now includes dynamic cost-based locking, by which lock escalation is performed in a cost-effective way.

Full row-level locking is the default in SQL Server 7. Locking dynamically scales to page or table locking if needed and it is determined to be efficient. Note that SQL Server 7 now supports full row-level locking for both data rows and index entries. The lock manager has been optimized to complete lock requests faster and with less internal synchronization.

Many OLTP applications can experience increased concurrency, especially when applications append rows to tables and indexes. This is because database updates to rows on the same page do not lock out different users. Where possible, however, developers and designers should avoid the use of creeping or sequential indices and keys that can cause these page contention problems. Try some randomizing schemes, such as a reversed date or sequence number. The lock manager dynamically adjusts the resources it uses for larger databases, eliminating the need to manually adjust the lock server configuration option. It automatically chooses between page locking (preferable for table scans) and row-level locking (preferable for inserting, updating, and deleting data).

Query processing for complex queries

With the introduction of multiple index operations and shared row indicators, SQL Server 7 uses index intersection and union techniques on multiple indexes to filter data before it retrieves rows from the database. All indexes on a table are maintained concurrently, and constraint evaluations are part of the query processor's execution plan. These two factors simplify and speed the updating of multiple rows of a table.

The SQL Server 7 query processor extracts information from the statistics and regathers statistics automatically, using fast sampling. This ensures that the query processor uses the most current statistics, and it reduces maintenance requirements. The query optimizer has a wide set of execution strategies. In particular, SQL Server 7 is less sensitive to index-selection issues than earlier versions, resulting in less tuning work. SQL Server 7 supports parallel execution of a single query across multiple processors. A CPU-bound query that must examine a large number of rows often benefits if portions of its execution plan run in parallel. This obviously applies to multiple CPU servers only. SQL Server 7 automatically determines which queries will benefit from parallelism and generates a parallel execution plan. If multiple processors are available when the query begins executing, the work is divided across the processors.

During query optimization, SQL Server looks for queries that might benefit from parallel execution. For these queries, SQL Server inserts exchange operators into the query execution plan to prepare the query for parallel execution. An *exchange operator* is an operator in a query execution plan that provides process management, data redistribution, and flow control. After exchange operators are inserted, the result is a parallel query execution plan. A *parallel query execution plan* can use more than one thread, whereas a *serial execution plan,* used by a nonparallel query, only uses a single thread for its execution. The actual number of threads used by a parallel query is determined at query plan execution and initialization and is called the *degree of parallelism.*

Page and row formats

As mentioned previously, all database pages are now 8K in size, which is an increase from 2K. The maximum number of bytes in a row is now 8,060 bytes, and the limit on character and binary data types is 8,000 bytes, increased from 255 bytes. Tables can now have 1,024 columns, a significant increase over the 250 columns supported previously. Additionally, SQL 7 includes mixed extents (multiple tables within one extent to save space). This feature is similar to an Oracle or DB2 table space. Filegroups replace devices to improve data placement and provide flexibility for maintenance.

Utility function improvements

Backup and restore utilities in SQL Server 7 run much faster than in earlier versions, have less impact on server operations, and have new features. An incremental backup captures only those data pages that have changed after the last database backup. Incremental backups can often eliminate much of the time the server spends rolling transactions forward. However, this method does require special care when executing the database recovery functions. A portion of the database can be restored, or rolled forward, to minimize recovery time in the event of media failure. Statements in the DBCC, that is, the database consistency utility program, have been redesigned to provide substantially improved performance. In addition, bulk copy operations now validate constraints and fire triggers as the data is loaded. DBAs must be sensitive to database relationships when loading data.

New SQL Server security model

The security architecture is further integrated with Microsoft Windows NT and provides additional flexibility. Database permissions can now be assigned directly to Windows NT users. You can define SQL Server roles to include not only Windows NT users and groups but also SQL Server users and roles. A SQL Server user can be a member of multiple SQL Server roles. This feature enables database administrators to manage SQL Server permissions as Windows NT groups or SQL Server roles, rather than as individual user accounts. Database access and permissions are now managed using Windows NT groups. New fixed server and database roles such as `dbcreator`, `diskadmin`, and `sysadmin` provide more flexibility and greater security than the system administrator login.

Additional data type support

The maximum size of character and binary data types has increased to 8,000 characters. The maximum length of the `char`, `varchar`, and `varbinary` data types is now 8,000 bytes, an increase from the limit of 255 bytes in SQL Server 6.*x*. The Transact-SQL string functions also support these very long `char` and `varchar` values. The use of text and image data types can now be reserved for very large data values. The SUB-STRING function can be used to process text and image columns. The handling of nulls and empty strings has been improved. A new `uniqueidentifier` data type is provided for storing a globally unique identifier (GUID).

Windows 95 or later support

As a full-featured RDBMS targeted for workstation and mobile applications, SQL Server 7 can execute under Microsoft Windows 95/98 or Windows NT Workstation. Mobile clients are fully supported with merge replication and conflict resolution. SQL Server 7 for Windows 95/98 is full-featured except for a few limitations imposed by the operating system. On Windows 95/98, for example, SMP, asynchronous I/O, and integrated security are not supported.

Replication options

The replication model is based on the "publish and subscribe" metaphor that was introduced in version 6.0. New replication interfaces are available for custom third-party applications.

Three major types of replication are available. The type used for an application depends upon requirements for transactional consistency, site autonomy, and the capability to partition the data to avoid conflicts.

- ◆ Snapshot replication takes a snapshot of current data in a publication at a Publisher and replaces the entire replica at a Subscriber on a periodic basis.

- ◆ Transactional replication distributes transactions to Subscribers as incremental changes are made.

- ◆ Merge replication allows sites to make autonomous changes to replicated data and, at a later time, merges changes made at all sites. Merge replication does not guarantee transactional consistency.

Replication is built directly into SQL Server 7 and SQL Server Enterprise Manager. Wizards are included for most common replication tasks. SQL Server 7 also includes Internet replication. Anonymous subscriptions and built-in support for Internet distribution simplify data replication to the Internet.

Unicode

SQL Server now supports Unicode data types, which makes it easier to store data in multiple languages within one database by eliminating the problem of converting characters and installing multiple code pages. Unicode stores character data using two bytes for each character rather than one byte. There are 65,536 different bit patterns in two bytes, so Unicode can use one standard set of bit patterns to encode each character in all languages, including languages such as Chinese that have large numbers of characters. Programming languages also support Unicode data types.

The fact that Unicode data needs twice as much storage space is offset by the elimination of the need to convert extended characters between code pages. In SQL Server, the new data types that support Unicode are `ntext`, `nchar`, and `nvarchar`. They are exactly the same as `text`, `char`, and `varchar`, except for the wider range of characters supported and the increased storage space used.

Upgrading previous SQL Server versions

Databases are easily transferred from SQL Server 6.*x* to 7.0 by using a fully automated upgrade utility. The following scenarios illustrate how to carry out the upgrade process. Depending on how servers are set up, elements may need more than one scenario, but together they cover all the requirements.

SIDE-BY-SIDE UPGRADES

Depending on the amount of disk space, the side-by-side upgrade takes place on a single computer using a disk-to-disk Named Pipes connection or a tape drive. Upgrades can be done over a direct pipeline with enough disk space. Otherwise, the SQL Server Upgrade Wizard can export the SQL Server 6.*x* catalog data, objects, and databases to a tape backup. Disk space occupied by SQL Server 6.*x* is claimed, and the SQL Server Upgrade Wizard is run again to import and upgrade the SQL Server 6.*x* catalog data, objects, and databases. When the upgrade is complete, SQL Server 7 immediately takes over as the production server.

COMPUTER-TO-COMPUTER UPGRADES

Install SQL Server 7 on one computer and then connect to another computer where the existing SQL Server 6.x is installed. The computer-to-computer upgrade takes place using a Named Pipes connection to transfer data. When the upgrade is complete, SQL Server 7 immediately takes over as the production server.

Indexing operations

SQL Server now uses index intersection and index union to implement multiple indexes in a single query. Shared row indicators are used to join two indexes on the same table. Earlier versions of SQL Server employed no more than one index per table in a query. If a table has a clustered index (and thus a clustering key), the leaf nodes of all nonclustered indexes use the clustering key rather than the physical record identifier as the row locator. If a table does not have a clustered index, nonclustered indexes continue to use the physical record identifiers to point to the data pages. In both cases, the row locator is stable. When a leaf node of a clustered index is split, the nonclustered indexes do not need to be updated, because the row locators are still valid. If a table does not have a clustered index, page splits do not occur. That is to say, data need not be in a physically ordered sequence.

Architecture Enhancements

SQL Server 7 has expanded its range to include applications that span a range of platforms, from personal systems, such as desktop and notebook computers, to high-end symmetric multiprocessing (SMP) servers with 8 to 16 processors, several gigabytes of memory, and a terabyte or more of disk storage.

Pages, rows, and columns

All database pages are now 8K in size, which is an increase from 2K. The maximum number of bytes in a row is now 8,060, and the limit on character and binary data types is 8,000 bytes, which is an increase from 255 bytes. Tables can now have 1,024 columns; this is a significant increase over the 250 columns supported earlier. The new page and row formats support row-level locking, are extensible for future requirements, and improve performance when large blocks of data are accessed, because each I/O operation retrieves more data.

Indexes

In earlier versions of SQL Server, nonclustered indexes used physical record identifiers (page number, row number) as row locators. For example, if the leaf node of a clustered index (data page) was split, many rows were moved to a new data page and thus had new physical record identifiers. All of the nonclustered indexes had to be updated with these new physical record identifiers, in a process that could require a significant amount of time and resources.

SQL Server 7 uses an improved index design. If a table has a clustered index (and thus a clustering key), the leaf nodes of all nonclustered indexes use the clustering key rather than the physical record identifier as the row locator. If a table does not have a clustered index, nonclustered indexes continue to use the physical record identifiers to point to the data pages. In both cases, the row locator is stable. When a leaf node of a clustered index is split, SQL Server 7 does not need to update the nonclustered indexes, because the row locators are still valid. If a table does not have a clustered index, page splits do not occur.

Earlier versions of SQL Server employed no more than one index per table in a query. SQL Server 7 uses index intersection and index union to implement multiple indexes in a query. SQL Server 7 also uses shared row indicators to join two indexes on the same table.

Text and image data

Storage of text and image data has been redesigned. SQL Server 7 can store more than one `text` or `image` value on a single data page. Space for small `text` or `image` values is thus used more efficiently. SQL Server 7 uses parallel retrieval of text and image data to optimize retrieval of large objects.

Row-level locking

The locking subsystem has changed significantly. Most important, SQL Server 7 now supports full row-level locking for both data rows and index entries. The SQL Server 7 lock manager has been optimized to complete lock requests faster and with less internal synchronization. Many OLTP applications can experience increased concurrency, especially when applications append rows to tables and indexes.

The SQL Server 7 lock manager dynamically adjusts the resources it uses for larger databases, eliminating the need to manually adjust the lock server configuration option. SQL Server 7 automatically chooses between page locking (which is preferable for table scans) and row-level locking (which is preferable for inserting, updating, and deleting data).

Transaction log

Before SQL Server 7, the log was a system table (syslogs) that used ordinary database pages. These log pages were allocated and deallocated just like pages of other tables, and they competed with data pages for space in the memory cache. The SQL Server 7 transaction log is significantly different. It consists of one or more log files, each containing a contiguous set of log records. The log is no longer represented as a system table.

Query processor

The SQL Server 7 query processor has been redesigned to support the large databases and complex queries found in decision support, data warehouse, and OLAP applications. The query processor includes several new execution strategies that can improve the performance of complex queries. It now uses hash join, merge join, and hash aggregation techniques. These techniques can scale to databases larger than those supported by the nested-loop join technique only. SQL Server 7 uses index intersection and union techniques on multiple indexes to filter data before it retrieves rows from the database. All indexes on a table are maintained concurrently, and constraint evaluations are part of the query processor's execution plan. These two factors simplify and speed updating of multiple rows of a table.

The SQL Server 7 query processor extracts information from the statistics and regathers statistics automatically using fast sampling. This ensures that the query processor uses the most current statistics, and it reduces maintenance requirements. The SQL Server 7 query optimizer has a wide set of execution strategies, and many of the optimization limitations of earlier versions of SQL Server have been removed. In particular, SQL Server 7 is less sensitive to index-selection issues, resulting in less tuning work. Improved costing-model and compile-time enhancements, such as predicate transitivity and constant folding, greatly improve the quality of query plans. The cost-based optimizer can be rapidly adapted for new or refined execution strategies.

To examine how the SQL Server 7 query processor executes a query, view the Plan tab of SQL Server Query Analyzer or the Transact-SQL SHOWPLAN statement output. The query processor supports new query hints, and some query limitations have been loosened or removed. For example, a single query can now reference 32 tables, and the number of internal work tables used by a query (16 in earlier versions) is no longer limited.

Server Enhancements

In SQL Server 7, changes have been made to the server configuration options and to the server utilities such as backup, restore, DBCC, and bulk copy. SQL Server 7 provides for parallel query execution, more powerful security, and improved stored procedure performance. With SQL Server 7, many advancements have been made to SQL Server replication.

Configuration options

Many server configuration options have been streamlined and simplified. For example, by default the server dynamically adjusts its memory and lock resource use. SQL Server 7 increases allocated resources when necessary, without overcommitting them, and decreases the resources used when they are no longer needed. Earlier versions of SQL Server required manual adjustment of these settings.

Backup, restore, DBCC, and bulk copy

SQL Server 7 server utilities, such as backup and restore, run much faster than before and have less impact on server operations. SQL Server 7 also includes a variety of new features designed to support the underlying database architecture and to provide more flexible system management. SQL Server 7 also includes a number of new features designed to reduce database backup and recovery times.

An incremental backup captures only those data pages that have changed after the last database backup. Many times, incremental backups can eliminate much of the time the server spends rolling transactions forward. With SQL Server 7, a portion of the database can be restored or rolled forward to minimize recovery time in the event of media failure. Restoring a backup is easy because the restore process automatically creates the database and all necessary files. SQL Server 7 supports backups using the Microsoft Tape Format, allowing SQL Server backups to share the same tape media with other backups, such as those written by the Microsoft Windows NT Backup program.

The database consistency checking utility (DBCC) statements have been redesigned to provide substantially improved performance. In addition, bulk copy operations now validate constraints and fire triggers as the data is loaded.

The bulk copy utility (bcp) uses ODBC to communicate with SQL Server and supports all SQL Server 7 data types. The SQL Server 7.0 server uses improved index maintenance strategies that make loading data into tables with indexes more efficient than in earlier versions. Bulk copy operations are also faster.

Parallel query execution

SQL Server 7 supports parallel execution of a single query across multiple processors. A CPU-bound query that must examine a large number of rows often benefits if portions of its execution plan run in parallel. SQL Server 7 automatically determines which queries will benefit from parallelism and generates a parallel execution plan. If multiple processors are available when the query begins executing, the work is divided across the processors. Parallel query execution is enabled by default.

Security

SQL Server 7 includes an enhanced security architecture that is better integrated with Windows NT and provides increased flexibility. Database permissions can now be assigned directly to Windows NT users. You can define SQL Server roles to include not only Windows NT users and groups but also SQL Server users and roles. In addition, a SQL Server user can be a member of multiple SQL Server roles. This feature enables database administrators to manage SQL Server permissions as Windows NT groups or SQL Server roles, rather than as individual user accounts. You can now manage database access and permissions using Windows NT groups. New fixed server and database roles such as dbcreator, diskadmin, and sysadmin provide more flexibility and improved security than the system administrator login.

Stored procedures

The stored procedure model has been enhanced in SQL Server 7 to provide improved performance and increased application flexibility. When a stored procedure is compiled and placed in the procedure cache, that one copy of the compiled plan is shared by all users of the stored procedure. SQL statements submitted through the ODBC SQLPrepare function and the OLE DB ICommandPrepare interface can also share plans. Deferred name resolution enables you to create stored procedures referencing objects that don't yet exist. This provides more flexibility for applications that create and then use tables as part of their processing.

Consistency and standards compliance

SQL Server 7 builds on SQL Server's compliance with the SQL-92 standard by focusing on SQL-92 as the preferred SQL dialect. SQL Server 7 addresses several inconsistencies in earlier versions of SQL Server, including several differences between actual and documented behaviors. SQL Server 7 also fixes several problems in earlier versions of SQL Server on which an application might have accidentally relied. In the small number of cases where a change in the default behavior of SQL Server 7 may affect existing applications, options have been provided to retain the pre-7.0 behavior. These options are controlled by the `sp_dboption` or `sp_dbcmptlevel` stored procedures.

SQL Server Enterprise Manager

SQL Server Enterprise Manager is based on a new common server management environment called Microsoft Management Console (MMC). This shared framework provides a consistent user interface for Microsoft server applications. Using SQL Server Enterprise Manager, you can examine and configure your SQL Server 7 system by setting server properties, database properties, remote server properties, and security properties. You can create and alter tables, views, stored procedures, rules, defaults, and user-defined data types, as well as manage alerts and operators, view error logs, create Web Assistant jobs, create and manage full-text indexes, and import and export data.

SQL Server Enterprise Manager includes full-featured job creation and scheduling. Jobs can be simple, single-step commands that are scheduled to run on a regular basis. Alternatively, they can be complex, multistep jobs that completely control flow and notification options. You can even establish multiple schedules for a single job. Job steps can be created using Transact-SQL, or operating-system commands.

SQL Server Agent

SQL Executive is now called SQL Server Agent. SQL Server Agent manages jobs, alerts, operators, and notifications, as well as replication jobs. SQL Server Agent allows multitasking, multischeduling, and multiserver and idle-time jobs.

SQL Server Service Manager

SQL Server Service Manager is now a taskbar application. SQL Server Service Manager enables you to start, stop, and pause the MSSQLServer, MSDTC, MSSearch (only start and stop are applicable), and SQLServerAgent services, and to view their status at any time. When you select SQL Server Service Manager from the Start menu, the Service Manager icon appears minimized in the taskbar by default.

Multiple instances of the Service Manager are represented by multiple icons in the taskbar.

Development Enhancements

SQL Server 7 has additional development flexibility and power as well as easier-to-use application development tools. SQL Server 7 is compatible with SQL Server 6.*x* applications and provides new and enhanced features for developers. SQL Server 7 includes internal enhancements that benefit all applications, such as increased query performance, full row-level locking, and new deadlock avoidance strategies and lock escalation policies that should reduce contention problems. SQL Server 7 now supports OLE DB as a native programming interface. Improvements to the Transact-SQL language and the ODBC programming API are also included.

Transact-SQL

Transact-SQL revolutionized the original SQL Server by enabling multiple SQL operations to be performed in response to a single user invocation. SQL Server 7 offers many new Transact-SQL features, including but not limited to:

- Unicode data types: `nchar`, `nvarchar`, and `ntext`.

- The `TOP` *n* `[PERCENT` *n*`]]` extension to the `SELECT` statement.

- Local cursors, cursor variables, returning cursors as parameters from stored procedures, additional properties for cursors declared through the `DECLARE CURSOR` statement, and functions and stored procedures for describing cursors.

- Identifiers that can now be a maximum of 128 characters, increased from the 30 characters of earlier versions. In addition, the left square bracket ([) and right square bracket (]) can be used for delimiting identifiers in addition to the SQL-92 standard double quotation mark (").

SQL Server 7 gives you complete flexibility to design and redesign tables. You can remove an existing column and its data from a table. You no longer need to export data in a separate step. Prior to SQL Server 7.0, only nullable columns could be added to a table. Now, you can add non-nullable columns without having to import data in a separate step.

SQL Server 7 includes views for the ANSI/ISO schema information tables as defined in SQL-92, providing a standard way to examine metadata of a SQL Server database.

SQL Server 7 makes revising database objects easier by enabling you to change the definition of a procedure, trigger, or view in place without disturbing permissions or dependencies.

SQL Server 7 uses deferred name resolution in stored procedures, triggers, and statement batches. For example, you can now create a procedure that references a table that does not exist when the procedure is created, providing greater flexibility to applications that create tables at run time.

You can now append multiple triggers of the same type to a single table. For example, a single table can have one delete trigger, three insert triggers, and two update triggers. This enhancement enables you to put different business rules into different triggers. A database option allows triggers to call themselves recursively.

The maximum length of the char, varchar, binary, and varbinary data types is now 8,000 bytes, an increase from the limit of 255 bytes in SQL Server 6.*x*. The Transact-SQL string functions also support these very long char and varchar values. You can reserve the use of text and image data types for very large data values. You can now use the SUBSTRING function to process text and image columns. The handling of NULLs and empty strings has been improved. SQL Server 7 also includes a new uniqueidentifier data type for storing a globally unique identifier (GUID).

The SQL Server 7 query processor uses new execution strategies and algorithms (including hash, sort, and merge iterators) to provide improved performance.

ODBC

SQL Server 7 includes an updated SQL ODBC Server 3.*x* driver that is compliant with the Open Database Connectivity 3.5 specification and a beta release of the ODBC 3.7 Driver Manager. The SQL Server ODBC driver fully supports SQL Server 7 and 6.*x* servers. It is recommended that you use ODBC for low-level development (outside of the COM environment) of SQL database applications. Use ADO for developing your business applications, and use OLE DB for developing your data access infrastructure in the COM environment.

The SQL Server ODBC driver includes a new set of SQL Server bulk copy functions that are identical to the DB-Library bulk copy functions.

Descriptors enable you to execute procedures using named parameters (earlier, only positional parameters were supported) and to share bindings between statements. Diagnostic arrays provide more detailed SQL Server error information, including the severity, state, procedure name, and line number of a SQL Server message. Quick rebinding by offset enables you to use an existing set of bindings with a new memory location, which eliminates many redundant ODBC function calls and improves performance. Connection pooling provides increased performance to applications that make and break the same connection to SQL Server. For more information, see your Microsoft ODBC 3.0 SDK documentation.

The Microsoft Server DSN Configuration Wizard makes creating and managing SQL Server data sources easier. File DSN support makes distributing data sources easier. The SQL Server ODBC driver also reveals other improvements when connecting to SQL Server 7 servers, such as establishing more efficient connections that are completed in a single round trip using default settings.

The SQL Server ODBC 3.5 driver fully supports programs using all of the MS toolset data objects including: ActiveX Data Objects (ADO), OLE DB Provider for ODBC, Data Access Objects (DAO), and Remote Data Objects (RDO). The driver also fully supports Web pages using Active Server Pages (ASP), Internet Database Connector (IDC), and third-party tools such as SilverStream application server 2.5.

SQL Server 7 includes features and enhancements specifically designed for certain types of applications. It supports data warehousing with SQL Data Transformation Services (DTS), which provide a set of COM objects based on OLE DB that let you define and execute complex data conversions between OLE DB data providers. You can use VBScript or Microsoft Jscript to create data transformation scripts. SQL 7 supports replication with programming components that include COM objects you can use to distribute data from third-party data sources. They also include Microsoft ActiveX controls that applications can use to implement distribution and merge functionality without dependence on the SQL Server Agent.

SQL 7 supports Internet and intranet applications with the SQL Server Web Assistant, which has been enhanced in SQL Server 7. In addition to exporting SQL Server data out to an HTML file, it can also import tabular data from an HTML file into SQL Server, and it can post to and read from HTTP and FTP locations. The TCP/IP Sockets Net-Library has been enhanced to work with Microsoft Proxy Server and provide secure communication across the Internet. SQL Server 7 also makes replicating your data across the Internet easy with anonymous subscriptions and built-in support for Internet distribution.

SQL Server 7 supports distributed applications, where you can use MS DTC for distributing transactions among multiple SQL servers using the two-phase commit protocol. In addition, the store-and-forward replication services of SQL Server 7 are exposed through COM interfaces, allowing your application to use the SQL Server 7 replication infrastructure to publish your data.

SQL Server 7 supports administration tools with SQL Distributed Management Objects (SQL-DMO), which have been redesigned and expanded to reflect SQL Server 7 features and architecture. SQL Server 7 SQL-DMO objects are very similar to the SQL Server 6.*x* SQL-DMO objects (with some exceptions, such as the replication hierarchy and the Device object).

Prototyping, profiling, and debugging

SQL Trace is now called SQL Server Profiler. SQL Server Profiler captures a continuous picture of server activity in real time. You pick the items and events to monitor, including Transact-SQL statements and batches, object usage, locking, security events, and errors. SQL Server Profiler can filter these events, showing only the events that you care about. You can replay a recorded trace against the same or another server, re-executing those recorded commands. By focusing on specific events, SQL Server Profiler makes monitoring and debugging SQL Server problems much easier.

ISQL/w is now called SQL Server Query Analyzer. The Plan tab of SQL Server Query Analyzer is significantly improved, showing more detail about every stage of query execution, optimization, and index usage. SQL Server Query Analyzer implements a color-coded editor, Graphical Showplan, and Help integration for checking syntax. SQL Server Query Analyzer communicates with SQL Server through ODBC.

SQL Server 7 also includes the `osql` command prompt utility, which uses ODBC to communicate with SQL Server. This utility is similar to `isql`, which uses the DB-Library interface.

Other programming interfaces

Another option available to you is the Embedded SQL for C for running batch jobs. We review the syntax and use of the simple interface later in Chapter 17, "C and Java with SQL." FastForward is a 100 percent Java implementation of the Java Database Connectivity API (also known as JDBC), the industry standard for relational database access from Java clients. FastForward provides Java clients with direct access to Microsoft SQL Server (all versions).

Building an Application

The basic steps you follow when building an application based upon the SQL Server7 DBMS are as follows. After you first set up the application development environment, you can work in any order. That is, you can define the objects used in your application in any order, as you need them. To develop an application you might:

- ◆ Create the database, which is the "hub" of the application. The database includes the description and content of all information/data required to facilitate the operation of the business.

- ◆ Create the application object, which is the entry point into the application. The application object names the application, specifies which database to use to save the objects, and specifies the application-login scripts. An example is the main index page in a Web application.

- ◆ Create windows and pages. Place controls in the windows and pages and build scripts (programs) that specify the processing that will occur when events are triggered.

- ◆ Create data access objects. Use these objects to retrieve data from the database, format and validate data, analyze data through graphs and crosstabs, create reports, and update the database.

- ◆ Create menus and navigation. Menus in your windows can include a menu bar, drop-down menus, and cascading menus. You can also create pop-up menus in an application. You define the menu items and write scripts that execute when the items are selected. Within a Web-based application, you would build HTML links to navigate between pages.

◆ Create business objects. If you want to be able to reuse components that are placed in windows or pages, define them as business objects and save them in a library. Later, when you build an HTML page or a GUI window, you can simply invoke the business object instead of having to redefine the components.

◆ Create functions, methods, and structures. To support your presentation code, you probably want to define functions or methods to perform processing unique to your application as well as data structures to hold related pieces of data.

◆ Test and validate your application. You can run your application anytime. If you discover problems, you can validate your application by setting breakpoints, stepping through your code statement by statement, and looking at variable values during execution.

When your application is complete, you prepare a release candidate executable. Then you have a dress rehearsal system test involving the user. If all goes well and the user signs off, you prepare a final executable version to distribute to your users.

Summary

This chapter has covered the way in which SQL Server 7 has obviously enhanced the development and deployment environment. With respect to scalability and performance, SQL 7 has clearly established itself as a player. We will concentrate on the database environment as well as the process of developing database applications in greater detail as we move on.

Part II

Database Administration for the Developer

Chapter 3

SQL Server 7 Common Administration

IN THIS CHAPTER

◆ Starting, pausing, and stopping SQL Server

◆ Managing servers and clients

◆ Monitoring SQL Server

THIS CHAPTER PROVIDES AN introduction to the common administration of Microsoft SQL Server 7.0. SQL Server 7 is largely self-configuring; it is manually administered via the Enterprise Manager (MMC) and Service Manager (SQLMANGR). The architecture of the server and its associated tools enable you to perform routine administrative duties, such as starting the server, shutting down, managing servers and clients, and monitoring activity and performance.

Starting, Pausing, and Stopping SQL Server

You have several ways to start, pause, and stop SQL Server 7. You can use either the visual tools or the command line tools or a combination thereof. We will first take a look at the visual tools, and then we will look at how the command line tools can be used to start, pause, and stop SQL Server 7.

Using visual tools

Two visual tools that come with SQL Server can be used to maintain the status of SQL Server 7. They are the Enterprise Manager and the SQL Server Service Manager. Please note that you can also use the Windows NT services program (in Control Panel) to start, pause, and stop SQL Server (see Figure 3-1), but you'll probably prefer to use the SQL Server visual tools.

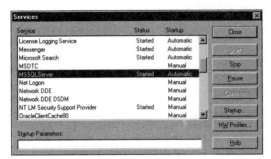

Figure 3-1: Windows NT services

USING SQL SERVER ENTERPRISE MANAGER

If your database server is either stopped or paused, you can start or continue it, by right-clicking the server name in SQL Server Enterprise Manager and choosing Start (if stopped) or Continue (if paused) from the pop-up menu (see Figure 3-2).

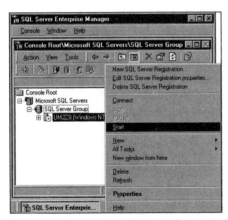

Figure 3-2: Starting SQL Server in Enterprise Manager

If your database is running, you can pause it by right-clicking the server name in SQL Server Enterprise Manager and choosing Pause from the pop-up menu (see Figure 3-3).

If your database is paused or running, you can stop it by right-clicking the server name in SQL Server Enterprise Manager and choosing Stop from the pop-up menu (see Figure 3-4).

Figure 3-3: Pausing SQL Server in Enterprise Manager

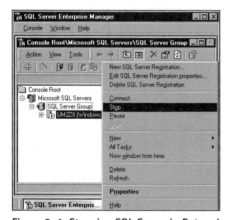

Figure 3-4: Stopping SQL Server in Enterprise Manager

USING SQL SERVER SERVICE MANAGER

If your database server is either stopped or paused, you can start or continue it by clicking Start/Continue in the SQL Server Service Manager (see Figure 3-5).

Figure 3-5: Starting SQL Server with Service Manager

If your database is running, you can pause it by clicking Pause in SQL Server Service Manager (see Figure 3-6).

Figure 3-6: Pausing SQL Server with Service Manager

If your database is paused or running, you can stop it by clicking Stop in SQL Server Service Manager (see Figure 3-7).

Figure 3-7: Stopping SQL Server with Service Manager

Using command-line tools

Several command-line tools can be used to maintain the status of SQL Server 7. They are the Service Control Manager and the Windows NT NET command. The Service Control Manager is much more advanced and can be used to maintain remote servers. The Windows NT NET command is simpler and can only be used on services running on the local machine.

USING THE SERVICE CONTROL MANAGER

The Service Control Manager is a command line utility that can start, pause, and stop SQL Server 7. The following is the syntax for calling the Service Control Manager, and Table 3-1 describes each of the parameters in the syntax.

```
scm.exe -Action action [-Server server_name] [-Pwd password]
  [-StartupOptions startup] [-Service service_name]
  [-ExePath path_name] [-SvcStartType service]
```

```
[-SvcAccount account_name] [-SvcPwd password]
[-Dependencies services]
```

TABLE 3-1 PARAMETERS FOR CALLING SERVICE CONTROL MANAGER (SCM.EXE)

Argument	Description
-Action action	1 = start, 2 = restart, 3 = is running (returns −1 if false, 1 if true)
-Server server_name	Name of the SQL Server (default is local machine)
-Pwd password	'sa' password (default is "")
-StartupOptions startup	Space-delimited startup options
-Service service_name	Name of service (default is MSSQLServer)
-ExePath path_name	Path to the service executable
-SvcStartType service	1=SERVICE_DEMAND_START, 2=SERVICE_AUTO_START
-SvcAccount account_name	Service account name
-SvcPwd password	Service account password
-Dependencies services	List of service name dependencies, separated by semicolons

USING THE WINDOWS NT NET COMMAND

The Windows NT NET command is a command line utility that is installed on Windows NT environments. It can also be used to start, pause, and stop SQL Server. Table 3-2 shows the syntax for calling the Windows NT NET command.

TABLE 3-2 PARAMETERS FOR CALLING THE WINDOWS NT NET COMMAND

Command line	Action required
net start mssqlserver	Start a stopped SQL Server
net pause mssqlserver	Pause a running SQL Server
net continue mssqlserver	Continue a paused SQL Server
net stop mssqlserver	Stop a running or paused SQL Server

Note that SQL Server can only be paused or continued if it was started as a Windows NT service. In other words, you cannot pause or continue SQL Server if it was started using the sqlservr.exe program on a command line. Also note that stopping SQL Server using this method causes SQL Server to perform a checkpoint in all databases and then a SHUTDOWN WITH NOWAIT to flush all committed data from the data cache and then stop the server immediately.

STARTING SQL SERVER DIRECTLY

SQL Server can also be started as a program directly running inside a command prompt. This can be useful in situations where you wish to quickly change some settings before restarting it as a full-blown service. Typically, this option is used if you experience problems with system databases that require repair.

The following is the syntax for starting SQL Server directly from a command prompt, and Table 3-3 describes each of the parameters in the syntax.

```
sqlservr.exe [-c] [-dmaster_path] [-f] [-eerror_log_path]
[-lmaster_log_path] [-m] [-n] [-pprecision_level]
[-sregistry_key] [-Ttrace#] [-v] [-x] [-g number] [-O] [-y number]
```

TABLE 3–3 PARAMETERS FOR STARTING SQL SERVER DIRECTLY (SQLSERVR.EXE)

Argument	Description
-c	You are starting SQL Server as a program that is independent of the Windows NT Service Control Manager. Use this to shorten the amount of time it takes for SQL Server to start. However, if you use this option, you cannot stop SQL Server by using SQL Server Service Manager or the Windows NT NET STOP command. Also, when you log off, SQL Server will be stopped.
-dmaster_path	The fully qualified path for the master database file. There is no space between -d and master_path.
-f	Minimally configured mode. The sa can specify configuration options with the sp_configure system stored procedure.
-eerror_log_path	The fully qualified path for the error log file (typically, driveletter:\Sql70\Log\Errorlog). If you do not specify this option, an error log is not written. There is no space between -e and error_log_path.

Argument	Description
-lmaster_log_path	The fully qualified path for the master database transaction log file. There is no space between -l and master_log_path.
-m	Start SQL Server in single-user mode. Only a single user can connect when SQL Server is started in single-user mode. The CHECKPOINT mechanism, which guarantees that completed transactions are regularly written from the disk cache to the database device, is not started.
-n	Do not log SQL Server events to the Windows NT application log. If you do this, use the -e option to log the SQL Server events to a file or they will be discarded.
-pprecision_level	Maximum level of precision to be supported by decimal and numeric data types. SQL Server has a default maximum of 28. You can specify values from 1 through 38. If the -p parameter is supplied but no precision_level value is supplied, it defaults to 38. There is no space between -p and precision_level.
-sregistry_key	Start SQL Server using an alternate set of startup parameters stored in the Windows NT Registry under registry_key.
-Ttrace#	Started with a specified trace flag (trace#) in effect. Trace flags are used to temporarily set specific server characteristics or to switch off a particular behavior (see Table 3-4 for a list of trace flags).
	Important: When specifying a trace flag, use -T to pass the trace flag number. A lowercase t (-t) is accepted by SQL Server; however, -t sets other internal trace flags that are needed only by SQL Server support engineers.
-v	Displays the server version number.
-x	Disables CPU statistics.

Table 3-4 provides a list of trace flags.

TABLE 3-4 TRACE FLAGS

Trace Flag	Description
106	Disables line number information for syntax errors.
107	Interprets numbers with a decimal point as float instead of decimal.
206	Provides backward compatibility for the SETUSER statement.
237	Disables the requirement for REFERENCES permissions to create a foreign key on a table that is not owned by the key creator, and, when disabled, ensures SQL-92 standard behavior. When enabled, this flag needs only SELECT permissions to ensure SQL Server behavior.
243	Provides backward compatibility for nullability behavior. When set, SQL Server has the same nullability violation behavior as that of a version 4.2 server:
*	Processing of the entire batch is terminated if the nullability error (inserting NULL into a NOT NULL field) can be detected at compile time.
*	Processing of the offending row is skipped, but the command continues if the nullability violation is detected at run time.
	The behavior of SQL Server is now more consistent because nullability checks are made at run time and a nullability violation results in the command terminating and the batch or transaction process continuing.
244	Disables checking for allowed interim constraint violations. By default, SQL Server checks for and allows interim constraint violations. An interim constraint violation is caused by a change that removes the violation such that the constraint is met, all within a single statement and transaction. SQL Server checks for interim constraint violations for self-referencing DELETE statements, INSERT statements based on a SELECT, and multirow UPDATE statements. This checking requires more work tables. With this trace flag, you can disallow interim constraint violations, thus requiring fewer work tables.
260	Prints version information about extended stored-procedure dynamic-link libraries (DLLs).
325	Prints information about the cost of using a nonclustered index or a sort to process an ORDER BY clause.
326	Prints information about the estimated and actual cost of sorts.
330	Enables full output when using the SET SHOWPLAN option, which gives detailed information about joins.

Trace Flag	Description
506	Enforces SQL-92 standards regarding null values for comparisons between variables and parameters. Any comparison of variables and parameters that contain a NULL always results in a NULL.

This flag is disabled if ANSI_NULLS is enabled with a setting of TRUE. |
1204	Returns the type of locks participating in the deadlock and the current command affected.
1205	Returns more detailed information about the command being executed at the time of a deadlock.
1609	Turns on the unpacking and checking of remote procedure call (RPC) information with the execution of sp_sqlexec in Open Data Services. This trace flag is used only when applications depend on the old behavior. The application should be changed to EXECUTE sql_string rather than sp_sqlexec.
1704	Prints information when a temporary table is created or dropped.
2701	Sets the @@ERROR system function to 50000 for RAISERROR messages with severity levels of 10 or less. When disabled, sets the @@ERROR system function to 0 for RAISERROR messages with severity levels of 10 or less.
3205	By default, if a tape drive supports hardware compression, either the DUMP or BACKUP statement uses it. With this trace flag, you can disable hardware compression for tape drives. This is useful when you want to exchange tapes with other sites or tape drives that do not support compression.
3604	Sends trace output to the client. Used only when setting trace flags with DBCC TRACEON and DBCC TRACEOFF.
3605	Sends trace output to the error log. (If you start SQL Server from the command prompt, the output also appears on the screen.)
3640	Eliminates the sending of DONE_IN_PROC messages to the client for each statement in a stored procedure. This is similar to the session setting of SET NOCOUNT, but when it is set as a trace flag, every client session is handled this way.
4022	Bypasses automatically started procedures.

Continued

TABLE **3-4 TRACE FLAGS** *(Continued)*

Trace Flag	Description
4030	Prints byte and ASCII representations of the receive buffer. This is useful if you want to see what queries a client is sending to SQL Server and if you encounter a protection violation and want to determine which statement caused it. Typically, you can set this flag globally or use SQL Server Enterprise Manager. The alternate is DBCC INPUTBUFFER.
4031	Prints byte and ASCII representations of the send buffers (what SQL Server sends back to the client). The alternate is DBCC OUTPUTBUFFER.
4032	Prints only an ASCII representation of the receive buffer. This is usually used in place of trace flag 4030 (because it's faster) when you want to see what queries the client is sending to the server.
7501	For 6.5 and earlier versions, dynamic cursors are used by default on forward-only cursors. They are faster in 7.0 and no longer require unique indexes. This disables the 7.0 enhancements and reverts to version 6.0 behavior.
7502	For 6.5 and earlier versions, disables the caching of cursor plans for extended stored procedures.
7505	Enables version 6.*x* handling of return codes when calling dbcursorfetchex and the resulting cursor position follows the end of the cursor result set.
8783	Allows DELETE, INSERT, and UPDATE statements to honor the SET ROWCOUNT ON setting when enabled.

Following is an example that turns on trace flag 8783 by using DBCC TRACEON:

```
DBCC TRACEON (8783)
```

The next example turns on trace flag 8783 at the command prompt:

```
sqlservr /dc:\mssql7\data\master.dat /T8783
```

Managing Servers and Clients

Several utilities enable you to test and manage the connectivity for SQL Server. This includes the network protocol connectivity between SQL Server and various client applications. These settings are managed using the visual tools that are installed with the SQL Server product.

Using the Server Network utility

You can use the Server Network utility (svrnetcn.exe) to manage the server network libraries. It is used to specify the network protocol stacks on which the server will listen for client requests, and it can be used to specify items such as port numbers and pipe names that SQL Server will listen to on a network address (see Figure 3-8).

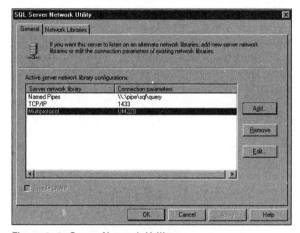

Figure 3-8: Server Network Utility

Most administrators will not need to go back and use the Server Network utility because they typically specify the server Net-Libraries on which SQL Server will listen during the installation routine. If the default network addresses are selected, clients will be able to connect to the SQL Server by just specifying the network name of the server on which SQL Server is running.

Using the Client Network utility

You can use the Client Network utility (cliconfg) to manage the client Net-Libraries and define server alias names (see Figure 3-9).

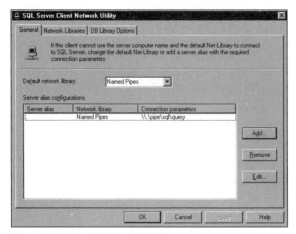

Figure 3-9: Client Network Utility

This utility can also be used to set the default options used by DB-Library applications. Most users will never need to use the Client Network utility. To connect to SQL Server, they will need to specify only the network name of the server on which SQL Server is running. If SQL Server is configured to listen on alternate network addresses and the client must explicitly specify the alternate address, a client will want to use the Client Network utility to set up an alias to specify in place of the server network name in the connection request.

Using the Version Switch utility

SQL Server 7 can be installed on the same computer that contains SQL Server 6.*x*. However, only one version can be active at a time. When the SQL Server Upgrade Wizard is complete, SQL Server 7 becomes the active version. To switch from one version to the other, use the Microsoft SQL Server-Switch application on the Programs menu, or run vswitch.exe, which is in the \Mssql7\Binn directory. Do not switch between the different versions of SQL Server if the Upgrade Wizard process is running.

The following is the syntax for the Version Switch utility, and Table 3-5 describes each of the parameters in the syntax.

```
vswitch.exe -SwitchTo {60|65|70} [-Silent {0|1}] [-NoCheck {0|1}]
```

TABLE 3-5 PARAMETERS FOR THE VERSION SWITCH UTILITY (VSWITCH.EXE)

Argument for vswitch.exe	Description
-SwitchTo {60|65|70}	Specifies which version of SQL Server to make active. Choose 60 for version 6.0, 65 for version 6.5, or 70 for version 7.
-Silent {0|1}	Specifies if no UI or messages are displayed. Choose 1 for no user interface or messages. The default is 0.
-NoCheck {0|1}	Specifies if no check for running applications is made. The default is 0.

Testing named pipes

The makepipe and readpipe utilities test the integrity of the network's Named Pipe services. You must use the version specific to the operating system on which you are testing the integrity of the named pipe. The following is the syntax for the makepipe utility, and Table 3-6 describes each of the parameters in the syntax.

```
makepipe.exe [/h] [/w] [/p pipe_name]
```

TABLE 3-6 PARAMETERS FOR THE MAKEPIPE UTILITY (MAKEPIPE.EXE)

Argument	Description
/h	Displays help.
/w	The wait time, in seconds, between a read and write. The default is 0.
/p pipe_name	The name of the pipe. The default is abc.

The following is the syntax for the readpipe utility, and Table 3-7 describes each of the parameters in the syntax.

```
Readpipe.exe /Sserver_name /Dstring [/n] [/q] [/w] [/t]
[/p pipe_name] [/h]
```

TABLE 3-7 PARAMETERS FOR THE READPIPE UTILITY (READPIPE.EXE)

Argument	Description
/Sserver_name	The name of the SQL Server running the makepipe utility. There is no space between /S and server_name.
/Dstring	A test character string. There is no space between /D and string.
/n	The number of iterations.
/q	Queries for incoming data (polling). Without /q, readpipe reads the pipe and waits for data.
/w	The wait time, in seconds, to pause while polling. The default is 0.
/t	Asks for Transact-SQL Named Pipes. This option overrides polling.
/p pipe_name	The name of the pipe. The default is abc.
/h	Displays help.

After makepipe is started, the server waits for a client to connect. The readpipe command prompt utility can then be run from other workstations. When all testing is complete, go to the screen where the makepipe utility is running and press Ctrl+Break or Ctrl+C to stop execution.

Testing ODBC

The odbcping utility tests the integrity of an ODBC data source and the capability of the client to connect to a server. The following is the syntax for the odbcping utility, and Table 3-8 describes each of the parameters in the syntax.

```
odbcping [/?] | [{ -Sserver_name | -Ddata_source }
[-Ulogin_id] [-Ppassword ] ]
```
   -Ppassword The password for *login_id.*

If the connection is successful, the odbcping utility will display the version of the SQL Server ODBC driver and the SQL Server to which it connected. If the connection attempt fails, the odbcping utility displays the error messages it receives from the SQL Server ODBC driver.

TABLE 3-8 PARAMETERS FOR THE ODBCPING UTILITY (ODBCPING.EXE)

Argument	Description
/?	Displays the command syntax.
-Sserver_name	The name of a server to connect to. The connection is made without testing any ODBC data source.
-Ddata_source	The name of an ODBC data source defined to use the SQL Server ODBC driver. It verifies that the data source is correct by using it to connect to the server named in the data source.
-Ulogin_id	The login ID for the server.

Here are some examples:

1. Connecting through a data source:

```
odbcping /Dsilvermaster3 /Udba /Psql
```

2. Connecting directly to a server:

```
odbcping /Sum2z8 /Uadministrator /Padmin
```

Monitoring Server Performance and Activity

Several utilities installed with SQL Server can be used to monitor the server and the performance of its current activity. These utilities help the database administrator determine if response is at an acceptable level.

Using the Query Analyzer utility

The Query Analyzer utility, isqlw.exe, is a graphical user interface for designing and testing Transact-SQL statements, batches, and scripts interactively. It can be called from SQL Server Enterprise Manager, or by entering **isqlw** from the command line (see Figure 3-10).

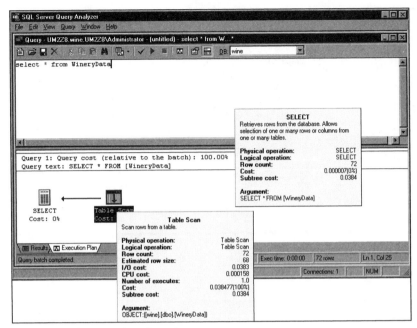

Figure 3-10: Query Analyzer in action

SQL Server's Query Analyzer has the following features:

♦ A free-form text editor for keying in Transact-SQL statements.

♦ Color-coding of Transact-SQL syntax to improve the readability of complex statements.

♦ Results presented in either a grid or a free-form text window.

♦ A graphical diagram of the showplan information showing the logical steps built into the execution plan of a Transact-SQL statement. This enables programmers to determine what specific part of a poorly performing query is using a lot of resources. They can then explore changing the query in ways that minimize resource use while still returning the desired data.

♦ An Index Tuning Wizard to analyze a Transact-SQL statement and the tables it references to see if adding additional indexes will improve the performance of the query.

Using Performance Monitor

The Windows NT Performance Monitor utility, perfmon.exe, collects information from SQL Server using remote procedure calls (RPC) (see Figure 3-11).

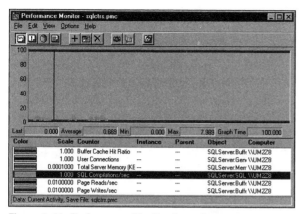

Figure 3-11: Performance Monitor in action

Any user who has permissions to run Performance Monitor can use it to monitor SQL Server.

Using the Profiler utility

SQL Server's Profiler utility, sqltrace.exe, can be used to view captured event data in a trace. The Profiler utility displays data according to defined trace properties (see Figure 3-12).

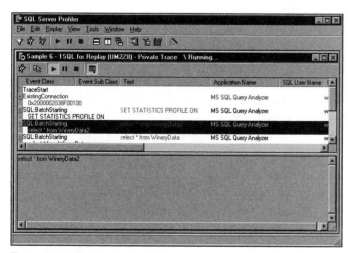

Figure 3-12: SQL Server Profiler

Each line in the trace capture data describes an event in SQL Server. One way to analyze SQL Server data is to copy the data to another program, such as SQL Server

Query Analyzer or the Index Tuning Wizard. The Index Tuning Wizard can use a trace file that contains SQL batch and remote procedure call (RPC) events and Text data columns. By specifying a server and/or database name when using the wizard, you can analyze the captured data against a different server and/or database.

Using the Index Tuning Wizard

The Index Tuning Wizard enables you to select and create an optimal set of indexes and statistics for a SQL Server database without requiring an expert understanding of the structure of the database, the workload, or the internals of SQL Server (see Figure 3-13).

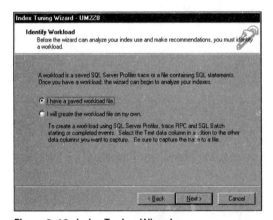

Figure 3-13: Index Tuning Wizard

To build a recommendation of the optimal set of indexes that should be in place, the wizard requires a *workload*. A workload consists of a SQL script or a SQL Server Profiler trace saved to a file or table containing SQL batch or remote procedure call (RPC) event classes and the Event Class and Text data columns. If you do not have an existing workload for the Index Tuning Wizard to analyze, you can create one using SQL Server Profiler. Either create a workload using the Sample 1 - TSQL trace definition or create a new trace that captures the default events and data columns. Once you have determined that the trace has captured a representative sample of the normal database activity, the wizard can analyze the workload and recommend an index configuration that will improve the performance of the database.

Using the Query Diagnostics utility

The Query Diagnostics utility, sqldiag.exe, gathers and stores diagnostic information and the contents of the query history trace (if currently executing) into two files, *installdrive*:\Mssql7\Log\Sqldiag.txt and *installdrive*:\Mssql7\Log\Sqldiag.trc.

These output files include the error log, the output from any `sp_configure` executions, and additional version information. If the query history trace is running when the utility is invoked, the trace file will also contain the last 100 SQL events and exceptions. The Query Diagnostics utility was originally intended to help gather information for Microsoft Support, but it is also worth a look for yourself.

The following is the syntax for the `sqldiag` utility, and Table 3-9 describes each of the parameters in the syntax.

```
sqldiag [ [-U login_id] [-P password] | [-E] ] [-O output_file]
```

TABLE 3-9 PARAMETERS FOR THE QUERY DIAGNOSTICS UTILITY (SQLDIAG.EXE)

Argument	Description
-U login_id	The login ID for the server.
-P password	The password for *login_id*.
-E	Uses a trusted connection instead of requesting a password (NT only).
-O output_file	The output filename for text and trace files. The default output filename is sqldiag (with .txt and .trc extensions).

The `sqldiag` utility gathers the following information:

◆ Text of all error logs

◆ Registry information

◆ DLL version information

◆ Output from the following:

■ `sp_configure`

■ `sp_helpdb`

■ `sp_helpextendedproc`

■ `sp_lock`

■ `sp_who`

■ `sysprocesses`

■ `xp_msver`

◆ Input buffer SPIDs/deadlock information

◆ Microsoft Diagnostics Report for the server, including the following:

  ▪ Contents of the *servername*.txt file

  ▪ Operating system version report

  ▪ System report

  ▪ Processor list

  ▪ Video display report

  ▪ Hard drive report

  ▪ Memory report

  ▪ Services report

  ▪ Drivers report

  ▪ IRQ and port report

  ▪ DMA and memory report

  ▪ Environment report

  ▪ Network report

◆ The last 100 queries and exceptions

If SQL Server is not running, the `sqldiag` utility skips gathering the input buffer SPIDs information and the diagnostics report. The `sqldiag` utility must be run on the server itself, not on a client workstation. If the `sqldiag` utility is executed on a Windows 95 or 98 system, the `-U` and `-P` options are required, which means the `sqldiag` utility must be run from a DOS prompt.

Summary

This chapter covered the routine administration aspects of Microsoft SQL Server 7.0. We covered how to manually administer the server via the Enterprise Manager and Service Manager. We also looked at the associated tools and utilities that enable you to perform routine administrative duties and to monitor the activity and performance of the database engine.

Chapter 4

SQL Server 7 Tools and Components

IN THIS CHAPTER

◆ Importing and exporting data

◆ Additional command line programs

THIS CHAPTER provides an introduction to the tools and components of Microsoft SQL Server 7. The tools and components enable you to shift data in and out of the server. There are also several tools that enable you to execute SQL and perform basic maintenance of the server environment.

Importing and Exporting Data

Data can be imported and exported from SQL Server using several tools and/or Transact-SQL statements. You can also write your own programs to import and export data using the programming models and application programming interfaces (APIs) available with SQL Server.

Methods for copying data to and from SQL Server include:

◆ Using the Data Transformation Services (DTS) Import and Export Wizards or DTS Designer to create a DTS package that can be used to import or export data. The DTS package can also transform data during the import or export process.

◆ Using SQL Server replication to distribute data across an enterprise. The replication technology in SQL Server enables you to make duplicate copies of your data, move those copies to different locations, and synchronize the data automatically so that all copies have the same data values. Replication can be implemented between databases on the same server or different servers connected by LANs, WANs, or the Internet.

- Using the `bcp` command prompt utility to import and export data between SQL Server and a data file.

- Using the `BULK INSERT` statement to import data from a data file to SQL Server.

- Using the `SELECT INTO` statement to create a new table based on an existing table. It is possible to select data from an arbitrary OLE DB provider, enabling data to be copied from external data sources into SQL Server.

- Using the `INSERT` statement to add data to an existing table.

A distributed query that selects data from another data source can also be used to specify the data to be inserted.

The best method that you should use to import or export data depends on the following requirements:

- The format of the source and destination data

- The location of the source and destination data

- Whether the import or export is a one-time occurrence or an ongoing task

- Whether you want to use a GUI utility, a Transact-SQL statement, or command prompt utility

- The performance required for the import or export operation

Table 4-1 shows the variety of methods available in SQL Server to import and export data.

TABLE 4-1 METHODS FOR IMPORTING AND EXPORTING DATA

Functionality Requirement	DTS Wizards	Replication	Bulk Copy (bcp)	BULK INSERT	SELECT INTO / INSERT
Import text data	✓		✓	✓	✓[1]
Export text data	✓		✓		
Import from all ODBC data sources	✓	✓			
Export to ODBC data sources	✓	✓			

Functionality Requirement	DTS Wizards	Replication	Bulk Copy (bcp)	BULK INSERT	SELECT INTO / INSERT
Import from OLE DB data sources	✓	✓			✓[1]
Export to OLE DB data sources	✓	✓			
GUI tool	✓	✓			
Command line interface	✓	✓	✓		
Transact-SQL scripts		✓		✓	✓
Automatic scheduling	✓	✓	✓[2]	✓[2]	
Ad hoc import/export	✓		✓	✓	✓
Recurring import/export	✓	✓	✓		
High performance			✓	✓	
Data transformation	✓				
Programmatic interface	✓	✓	✓		

[1] If you use a distributed query retrieving data from an external source supplied via an OLE DB provider
[2] If you create a job and schedule it to run via SQL Server Agent

Distributed Transaction Coordinator

The Microsoft Distributed Transaction Coordinator (DTC) is a transaction manager that allows client applications to include several different sources of data in a single transaction. DTC coordinates the commit of the distributed transaction across all the servers involved in the transaction (see Figure 4-1).

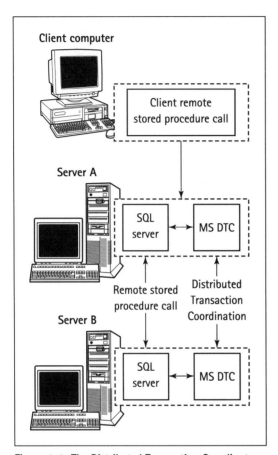

Figure 4-1: The Distributed Transaction Coordinator

The following is a list of the ways that a SQL Server can engage in a distributed transaction:

◆ Calling stored procedures on remote servers running SQL Server.

◆ Automatically or explicitly promoting the local transaction to a distributed transaction and enlisting remote servers in the transaction.

◆ Making distributed updates that update data on multiple OLE DB data sources. If these OLE DB data sources support the OLE DB distributed transaction interface, SQL Server can also enlist them in the distributed transaction.

The DTC service coordinates the proper completion of the distributed transaction to ensure that either all of the updates on all the servers are made permanent or, in the case of errors, all of the updates are rolled back.

SQL Server applications can also call DTC directly to start a distributed transaction. One or more servers running SQL Server can then be instructed to enlist in the distributed transaction and coordinate the proper completion of the transaction with DTC.

The DTC Administrative Console (dac.exe), shown in Figure 4-2, enables you to stop and start the DTC services, check on the status of current transactions, view transactions that are being traced, and check the current and aggregated DTC statistics.

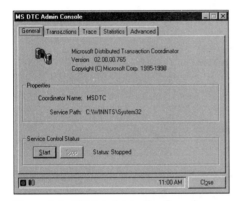

Figure 4–2: DTC Administrative Console

Data Transformation Service

The Data Transformation Service Wizard (dtswiz.exe) is a utility that enables you to start the Data Transformation Services import and export wizards (see Figure 4-3) using command prompt options. The wizards can be used to create Data Transformation Service (DTS) packages that import, export, or transform data between data sources – for example, between SQL Server and an Oracle database, ASCII text file, or any other ODBC data source.

The following is the command line syntax for calling the Data Transformation Service Wizard.

```
dtswiz [{/? | {/n | [/u login_id] [/p password]} [/f filename]
{/i | /x} {/r provider_name | [/s server_name]
[/d database_name] [/y]}}]
```

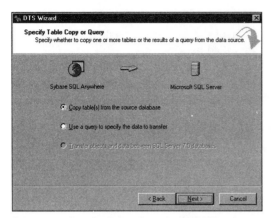

Figure 4-3: Sample dialog from the DTS Wizard

The parameters for the syntax calling the Data Transformation Service Wizard are discussed in the following list:

♦ /? – Displays the usage.

♦ /n – Specifies Windows NT Authentication, and takes precedence over /u and /p.

♦ /u *login_id* – The login ID for SQL Server.

♦ /p *password* – A user-specified password for *login_id*.

♦ /f *filename* – Saves the package created by the wizard to a COM-structured storage file. If /f is not specified, the wizard asks if you want to save the package to the SQL Server msdb database.

♦ /I – Imports to SQL Server.

♦ /x – Exports from SQL Server.

♦ /r *provider_name* – Name of the provider used to connect to the data source when importing, or the destination when exporting. Here are some examples:

Provider Name	Provider
SQLOLEDB	SQL Server
MSDASQL	OLE DB for ODBC
MSDAORA	Oracle

Provider Name	Provider
Microsoft.Jet. OLEDB.4.0	Microsoft Access/Microsoft Excel
MSIDXS	File system

- ◆ /s *server_name* — Name of the SQL server that data is to be exported from or imported to.

- ◆ /d *database_name* — Name of the SQL Server database that data is to be exported from or imported to.

- ◆ /y — Hides system databases (master, model, msdb, and tempdb) from the list of data sources or destinations.

The created DTS package can be saved either to the SQL Server msdb database, a COM-structured storage file, or the Microsoft Repository.

Replication Log Reader Agent

The Replication Log Reader Agent utility (logread.exe) configures and begins a replication log reader agent that moves transactions marked for replication from the transaction log on the Publisher to the distribution database. This syntax is used at the command prompt, and the executable file can be found in the \Mssql7\Binn directory. Listing 4-1 provides the command line syntax for calling the Replication Log Reader Agent:

Listing 4-1: Calling the Replication Log Reader Agent

```
logread [-?]
-Publisher publisher
-PublisherDB publisher_database
[-AsynchLogging]
[-Buffers number_of_buffers]
[-Continuous]
[-DefinitionFile def_path_and_file_name]
[-Distributor distributor]
[-DistributorLogin distributor_login]
[-DistributorPassword distributor_password]
[-DistributorSecurityMode [0|1]]
[-HistoryVerboseLevel [0|1|2]]
[-LoginTimeOut login_time_out_seconds]
[-MessageInterval message_interval]
[-Output output_path_and_file_name]
```

```
[-OutputVerboseLevel [0|1|2]]
[-PacketSize packet_size]
[-PollingInterval polling_interval]
[-PublisherSecurityMode [0|1]]
[-PublisherLogin publisher_login]
[-PublisherPassword publisher_password]
[-QueryTimeOut query_time_out_seconds]
[-ReadBatchSize number_of_transactions]
[-ReadBatchThreshold read_batch_threshold]
```

The parameters in the syntax for calling the Replication Log Reader Agent utility
are discussed in the following list:

- `-?` — Displays the usage.

- `-Publisher` *publisher* — Name of the Publisher.

- `-PublisherDB` *publisher_database* — Name of the Publisher database.

- `-AsynchLogging` (Uses a background thread to write history messages
  to replication monitoring tables. Defaults to false when not specified.

- `-Buffers` *number_of_buffers* (Number of buffers available for
  asynchronous transactions. Default is 2. Increasing can improve
  performance by reducing memory paging. But it will also increase
  memory reserved for paging.

- `-Continuous` — Agent will poll replicated transactions from the source
  at polling intervals even if there are no transactions pending.

- `-DefinitionFile` *def_path_and_file_name* — Path of the agent definition
  file, which contains command prompt arguments for the agent. The content
  of the file is parsed as an executable file. Double quotation marks (") can be
  used to specify argument values containing arbitrary characters.

- `-Distributor` *distributor* — Distributor name.

- `-DistributorLogin` *distributor_login* — Distributor's login name.

- `-DistributorPassword` *distributor_password* — Distributor's password.

- `-DistributorSecurityMode` [0|1] — Distributor's security mode: 0 =
  (default) SQL Server Authentication, and 1 = Windows NT Authentication.

- `-HistoryVerboseLevel` [0|1|2] — The amount of history logged during
  a log reader operation. The 0 = none or minimal output. The 1 = always
  update a previous history message of the same status (startup, progress,
  success, and so forth). If no previous record with the same status exists,
  insert a new record. The 2 (default) = insert new history records unless
  the record is for such things as idle messages or long-running job
  messages, in which case update the previous records.

- ◆ -LoginTimeOut *login_time_out_seconds* — The number of seconds before a login times out. The default is 15 seconds.

- ◆ -MessageInterval *message_interval* — The time interval used for history logging. A history event is logged if either the Transactions PerHistory value is reached after the last history event is logged or the MessageInterval value is reached after the last history event is logged. If no replicated transaction is available at the source, the agent reports a no-transaction message to the Distributor. This option specifies how long the agent waits before reporting another no-transaction message. Agents always report a no-transaction message when they detect that no transactions are available at the source after previously processing replicated transactions. The default is 3,600 (seconds).

- ◆ -Output *output_path_and_file_name* — The path of the agent output file. If the filename is not provided, the output is sent to the console. If the specified filename exists, the output is appended to the file.

- ◆ -OutputVerboseLevel [0|1|2] — The 0 = only error messages are printed; the 1 = all the progress report messages are printed, and the 2 = all error messages and progress report messages are printed (default).

- ◆ -PacketSize *packet_size* — The packet size, in bytes. The default is 4,096.

- ◆ -PollingInterval *polling_interval* — The frequency with which the log is queried for replicated transactions. The default is 10 seconds.

- ◆ -PublisherSecurityMode [0|1] — The 0 indicates Mixed Mode (default), and a value of 1 indicates Windows NT Authentication Mode.

- ◆ -PublisherLogin *publisher_login* — The Publisher's login name.

- ◆ -PublisherPassword *publisher_password* — The Publisher's password.

- ◆ -QueryTimeOut *query_time_out_seconds* — The number of seconds before the query times out. The default is 300 seconds.

- ◆ -ReadBatchSize *number_of_transactions* — The maximum number of transactions read out of the source. For the Log Reader Agent, the source is the transaction log of the publishing database. For the Distribution Agent, the source is the distribution database. The default is 500.

- ◆ -ReadBatchThreshold *read_batch_threshold* — The number of replication commands to be read from the transaction log before being issued to the Subscriber by the Distribution Agent. The default is 100.

When optional parameters are not specified, values from predefined Registry settings on the local computer are used.

If you installed SQL Server Agent to run under a local system account rather than under a domain user account (the default), the service can access only the local computer. If the Log Reader Agent that runs under SQL Server Agent is configured to use Windows NT Authentication Mode when it logs into SQL Server, the Log Reader Agent fails. The default setting is Mixed Mode.

Replication Merge Agent

The Replication Merge Agent utility (replmerg.exe) configures and begins a replication Merge Agent, which applies initial snapshots held in the database tables of the Publisher to the Subscribers. It also merges data changes made by the Publisher or Subscribers after the initial snapshot is created. This syntax is used at the command prompt, and the executable file can be found in the \Mssql7\Binn directory. Listing 4-2 provides the command line syntax for calling the Replication Merge Agent.

Listing 4–2: Calling the Replication Merge Agent

```
replmerg [-?]
-Publisher publisher
-PublisherDB publisher_database
-Publication publication_name
-Subscriber subscriber
-SubscriberDB subscriber_database
[-Continuous]
[-DefinitionFile def_path_and_file_name]
[-Distributor distributor]
[-DistributorAddress distributor_address]
[-DistributorLogin distributor_login]
[-DistributorNetwork distributor_network]
[-DistributorPassword distributor_password]
[-DistributorSecurityMode [0|1]]
[-DownloadGenerationsPerBatch download_generations_per_batch]
[-DownloadReadChangesPerBatch download_read_changes_per_batch]
[-DownloadWriteChangesPerBatch download_write_changes_per_batch]
[-ExchangeType [1|2|3]]
[-FastRowCount [0|1]]
[-FileTransferType [0|1]]
[-FtpAddress ftp_address]
[-FtpPassword ftp_password]
[-FtpPort ftp_port]
[-FtpUserName ftp_user_name]
[-HistoryVerboseLevel [1|2|3]]
[-Hostname host_name]
[-LoginTimeOut login_time_out_seconds]
[-Output]
[-OutputVerboseLevel [0|1|2]]
```

```
[-PollingInterval polling_interval]
[-ProfileName profile_name]
[-PublisherAddress publisher_address]
[-PublisherLogin subscriber_login]
[-PublisherNetwork publisher_network]
[-PublisherPassword publisher_password]
[-PublisherSecurityMode [0|1]]
[-QueryTimeOut query_time_out_seconds]
[-SubscriberDatabasePath subscriber_path]
[-SubscriberLogin subscriber_login]
[-SubscriberPassword subscriber_password
[-SubscriberSecurityMode [0|1]]
[-SubscriberType [0|1|2]]
[-SubscriptionType [0|1|2]]
[-UploadGenerationsPerBatch upload_generations_per_batch]
[-UploadReadChangesPerBatch upload_read_changes_per_batch]
[-UploadWriteChangesPerBatch upload_write_changes_per_batch]
[-Validate [0|1|2]]
[-ValidateInterval validate_interval]
```

Note that parameters can be specified in any order. When optional parameters are not specified, values from predefined Registry settings on the local computer are used. Each of the parameters in the previous syntax is discussed in the following list:

♦ -? — Displays the usage.

♦ -Publisher publisher — The name of the Publisher.

♦ -PublisherDB publisher_database — The name of the Publisher database.

♦ -Publication publication_name — The name of the publication. For both types of distribution, this parameter is valid only for immediate_sync publications. If this parameter is not specified, then the Distributor processes all the nonimmediate_sync publications in the Publisher database.

♦ -Subscriber subscriber — The name of the Subscriber.

♦ -SubscriberDB subscriber_database — The name of the Subscriber database.

♦ -Continuous — An agent will poll replicated transactions from the source at polling intervals even if there are no transactions pending.

◆ -DefinitionFile *def_path_and_file_name* — The path of the agent definition file that contains command prompt arguments for the agent. The content of the file is parsed as an executable file. Double quotation marks (") can be used to specify argument values containing arbitrary characters.

◆ -Distributor *distributor* — The distributor's name. For push distribution, the name defaults to the name of the local distributor.

◆ -DistributorAddress *distributor_address* — The network connection string for the Net-Library defined in the DistributorNetwork option. If the DistributorNetwork option is the TCP/IP Sockets Net-Library, then the connection string is in the form of 'address,socket'. This is useful for configuring connections across the Internet.

◆ -DistributorLogin *distributor_login* — The Distributor's login name.

◆ -DistributorNetwork *distributor_network* — The Net-Library (without the .dll extension) to use when connecting to the Distributor. This option is useful when configuring the Merge Agent to connect to a Distributor over the Internet.

◆ -DistributorPassword *distributor_password* — The Distributor's password.

◆ -DistributorSecurityMode [0|1] — The Distributor's security mode. The 0 = (default) SQL Server Authentication and 1 = Windows NT Authentication.

◆ -DownloadGenerationsPerBatch *download_generations_per_batch* — The number of generations to be processed in a single batch while downloading changes from the Publisher to the Subscriber. A generation is defined as a logical group of changes per article. Default for a reliable communication link is 100. Default for an unreliable communication link is 10.

◆ -DownloadReadChangesPerBatch *download_read_changes_per_batch* — The number of changes to be read in a single batch while downloading changes from the Publisher to the Subscriber. The default is 100.

◆ -DownloadWriteChangesPerBatch *download_write_changes_per_batch* — The number of changes to be applied in a single batch while downloading changes from the Publisher to the Subscriber. Default is 100.

◆ -ExchangeType [1|2|3] — Specifies the type of exchange: 1 = push, 2 = pull, and 3 = bidirectional.

◆ -FastRowCount [0|1] — The type of rowcount calculation method should be used for rowcount validation: 1(default) = fast method and 0 = full rowcount method.

- `-FileTransferType [0|1]` – The file transfer type: 0 = UNC (Uniform Naming Convention) and 1 = FTP (File Transfer Protocol).

- `-FtpAddress ftp_address` – The network address of the FTP service for the Distributor. When not specified, `DistributorAddress` is used. If the `DistributorAddress` is not specified, Distributor is used.

- `-FtpPassword ftp_password` – The user password used to connect to the FTP service.

- `-FtpPort ftp_port` – The port number of the FTP service for the Distributor. When not specified, the default port number for FTP service (21) is used.

- `-FtpUserName ftp_user_name` – The username used to connect to the FTP service. When not specified, anonymous is used.

- `-HistoryVerboseLevel [1|2|3]` – Specifies the amount of history logged during a merge operation: 1 = update a previous history message of the same status (startup, progress, success, and so forth) – if no previous record with the same status exists, insert a new record; 2 (default) = insert new history records unless the record is for such things as idle messages or long-running job messages, in which case update the previous records; and 3 = always insert new records, unless it is for idle messages.

- `-Hostname host_name` – The network name of the local computer. The default is the local computer name.

- `-LoginTimeOut login_time_out_seconds` – The number of seconds before the login times out. The default is 15 seconds.

- `-Output output_path_and_file_name` – The path of the agent output file. If the filename is not provided, the output is sent to the console. If the specified filename exists, the output is appended to the file.

- `-OutputVerboseLevel [0|1|2]` – Specifies whether the output should be verbose. If the verbose level is 0, only error messages are printed. If the verbose level is 1, all of the progress-report messages are printed. If the verbose level is 2 (default), all error messages and progress-report messages are printed, which is useful for debugging.

- `-PollingInterval polling_interval` – The frequency, in seconds, that the Publisher or Subscriber is queried for data changes. The default is 60.

- `-ProfileName profile_name` – Specifies an agent profile to use for agent parameters. If `ProfileName` is `NULL`, the agent profile is disabled. If `ProfileName` is not specified, the default profile for the agent type is used.

◆ `-PublisherAddress` *publisher_address* — The network connection string for the Net-Library defined in the `PublisherNetwork` option. If the `PublisherNetwork` option is the TCP/IP Sockets Net-Library, then the connection string is in the form of `'address,socket'`.

◆ `-PublisherLogin` *publisher_login* — The Publisher's login name. If `PublisherSecurityMode` is 0 (for Mixed Mode), then this parameter must be specified.

◆ `-PublisherNetwork` *publisher_network* — The Net-Library (without the .dll extension) to use when connecting to the Publisher. This option is useful when configuring the Merge Agent to connect to a Publisher over the Internet.

◆ `-PublisherPassword` *publisher_password* — The Publisher's password. If `PublisherSecurityMode` is 0 (for Mixed Mode), then this parameter must be specified.

◆ `-PublisherSecurityMode [0|1]` — The Publisher's security mode: 0 (default) = Mixed Mode and 1 = Windows NT Authentication.

◆ `-QueryTimeOut` *query_time_out_seconds* — The number of seconds before the query times out. The default is 30.

◆ `-SubscriberDatabasePath` *subscriber_database_path* — The path to the Jet database (.mdb file) if SubscriberType is 2. (This allows a connection to a Jet database without an ODBC DSN.)

◆ `-SubscriberLogin` *subscriber_login* — The Subscriber's login name. If `SubscriberSecurityMode` is 0 (for Mixed Mode), then this parameter must be specified.

◆ `-SubscriberPassword` *subscriber_password* — The Subscriber's password. If `SubscriberSecurityMode` is 0 (for Mixed Mode), then this parameter must be specified.

◆ `-SubscriberSecurityMode [0|1]` — The Subscriber's security mode. A value of 0 indicates Mixed Mode (default), and a value of 1 indicates Windows NT Authentication Mode.

◆ `-SubscriberType [0|1|2|3]` — The type of Subscriber connection: 0 = SQL Server, 1 = ODBC data source, 2 = Jet direct database, and 3 = OLE DB data source.

◆ `-SubscriptionType [0|1|2]` — The Subscription type for distribution: 0 = Push, 1 = Pull, and 2 = Anonymous.

◆ `-UploadGenerationsPerBatch` *upload_generations_per_batch* — The number of generations to be processed in a single batch while uploading changes from the Subscriber to the Publisher. A generation is defined as a logical group of changes per article. The default for a reliable communication link is 100. The default for an unreliable communication link is 1.

◆ `-UploadReadChangesPerBatch` *upload_read_changes_per_batch* — The number of changes to be read in a single batch while uploading changes from the Subscriber to the Publisher. The default is 100.

◆ `-UploadWriteChangesPerBatch` *upload_write_changes_per_batch* — The number of changes to be applied in a single batch while uploading changes from the Subscriber to the Publisher. The default is 100.

◆ `-Validate [0|1|2]` — Specifies whether validation should be done at the end of the merge session, and if so, what type of validation: 0 (default) = No validation, 1 = `Rowcount`-only validation, and 2 = `Rowcount` and `checksum` validation.

◆ `-ValidateInterval` *validate_interval* — The frequency, in minutes, that the subscription is validated in continuous mode. The default is 60.

If you installed SQL Server Agent to run under a local system account rather than under a domain user account (the default), the service can access only the local computer. If the Merge Agent that runs under SQL Server Agent is configured to use Windows NT Authentication Mode when it logs into SQL Server, the Merge Agent fails. The default setting is Mixed Mode.

Replication Snapshot Agent

The Replication Snapshot Agent utility (snapshot.exe) configures and begins a replication Snapshot Agent, which prepares snapshot files of published tables and stored procedures, stores the files on the Distributor, and records information about the synchronization status in the distribution database. This syntax is used at the command prompt, and the executable file can be found in the \Mssql7\Binn directory. Listing 4-3 provides the command line syntax for calling the Replication Snapshot Agent.

Listing 4-3: Calling the Replication Snapshot Agent

```
snapshot [-?]
-PublisherDB publisher_database
-Publication publication_name
[-BcpBatchSize bcp_batch_size]
[-Continuous]
[-DefinitionFile def_path_and_file_name]
```

```
[-Distributor distributor]
[-DistributorLogin distributor_login]
[-DistributorPassword distributor_password]
[-DistributorSecurityMode [0|1]]
[-FieldDelimiter field_delimiter]
[-HistoryVerboseLevel [0|1|2|3]
[-LoginTimeOut login_time_out_seconds]
[-MaxBcpThreads]
[-Output output_path_and_file_name]
[-OutputVerboseLevel [0|1|2]
[-PublisherLogin publisher_login]
[-PublisherPassword publisher_password]
[-PublisherSecurityMode [0|1]]
[-QueryTimeOut query_time_out_seconds]
[-ReplicationType [1|2]]
[-RowDelimiter row_delimiter]
```

Each of the parameters in the syntax for the Replication Snapshot Agent is discussed in the following list:

◆ `-?` — Displays the usage.

◆ `-PublisherDB publisher_database` — Name of the Publisher database.

◆ `-Publication publication_name` — Name of the publication. For both types of distribution, this parameter is valid only for `immediate_sync` publications. If this parameter is not specified, then the Distributor processes all the `nonimmediate_sync` publications in the Publisher database.

◆ `-BcpBatchSize bcp_batch_size` — Number of rows to send in a bulk copy operation. When performing a `bcp in` operation, the batch size is the number of rows to send to the server as one transaction, and also the number of rows that must be sent before the Distribution Agent logs a `bcp` progress message. When performing a `bcp out` operation, a fixed batch size of 1,000 is used. A value of 0 indicates no message logging.

◆ `-Continuous` — Specifies whether the agent attempts to poll replicated transactions continually. If specified, the agent polls replicated transactions from the source at polling intervals even if there are no transactions pending.

◆ `-DefinitionFile def_path_and_file_name` — Path of the agent definition file. An agent definition file contains command prompt arguments for the agent. The content of the file is parsed as an executable file. Double quotation marks (") can be used to specify argument values containing arbitrary characters.

♦ -Distributor *distributor* — Distributor name.

♦ -DistributorLogin *distributor_login* — Distributor's login name.

♦ -DistributorPassword *distributor_password* — Distributor's password.

♦ -DistributorSecurityMode [0|1] — Distributor's security mode: 0 = (default) SQL Server Authentication and 1 = Windows NT Authentication.

♦ -FieldDelimiter *field_delimiter* — Character or character sequence that marks the end of a field in the SQL Server bulk-copy data file. Default is \n<x$3>\n.

♦ -HistoryVerboseLevel [0|1|2|3] — Specifies the amount of history logged during a snapshot operation: 0 = none or minimal output; 1 = update a previous history message of the same status (startup, progress, success, and so forth) — if no previous record with the same status exists, insert a new record; 2 (Default) = insert new history records unless the record is for such things as idle messages or long-running job messages, in which case update the previous records; and 3 = always insert new records, unless it is for idle messages.

♦ -LoginTimeOut *login_time_out_seconds* — Number of seconds before the login times out. Default is 15.

♦ -MaxBcpThreads — Specifies the number of bulk copy operations that can be performed in parallel. The maximum number of threads and ODBC connections that exist simultaneously is the lesser of MaxBcpThreads or the number of bulk copy requests that appear in the synchronization transaction in the distribution database. MaxBcpThreads must have a value greater than zero, and has no hard-coded upper limit. The default is 1.

♦ -Output *output_path_and_file_name* — Path of the agent output file. If the filename is not provided, the output is sent to the console. If the specified filename exists, the output is appended to the file.

♦ -OutputVerboseLevel [0|1|2] — Specifies whether the output should be verbose. If the verbose level is 0, only error messages are printed. If the verbose level is 1, all the progress report messages are printed. If the verbose level is 2 (default), all error messages and progress report messages are printed, which is useful for debugging.

♦ -PublisherLogin *publisher_login* — Publisher's login name.

♦ -PublisherPassword *publisher_password* — Publisher's password.

♦ -PublisherSecurityMode [0|1] — Publisher's security mode: 0 (default) = Mixed Mode and 1 = Windows NT Authentication.

◆ -QueryTimeOut *query_time_out_seconds* – Number of seconds before the query times out. The default is 30.

◆ -ReplicationType [1|2] – Type of replication: 1 = transactional and 2 = merge.

◆ -RowDelimiter *row_delimiter* – Character or character sequence that marks the end of a row in the SQL Server bulk-copy data file. The default is \n<,@g>\n.

Replication Distribution Agent

The Replication Distribution Agent utility (distrib) configures and begins a replication Distribution Agent, which moves transactions and snapshot jobs held in the distribution database tables to Subscribers. This syntax is used at the command prompt, and the executable file can be found in the \Mssql7\Binn directory. Listing 4-4 provides the command line syntax for calling the Replication Distribution Agent.

Listing 4-4: Calling the Replication Distribution Agent

```
distrib [-?]
-Publisher publisher
-PublisherDB publisher_database
-Subscriber subscriber
[-BcpBatchSize bcp_batch_size]
[-Buffers number_of_buffers]
[-CommitBatchSize commit_batch_size]
[-CommitBatchThreshold commit_batch_threshold]
[-Continuous]
[-DefinitionFile def_path_and_file_name]
[-Distributor distributor]
[-DistributorAddress distributor_address]
[-DistributorLogin distributor_login]
[-DistributorNetwork distributor_network]
[-DistributorPassword distributor_password]
[-DistributorSecurityMode [0|1]]
[-ErrorFile error_path_and_file_name]
[-FileTransferType [0|1]]
[-FtpAddress ftp_address]
[-FtpPassword ftp_password]
[-FtpPort ftp_port]
[-FtpUserName ftp_user_name]
[-HistoryVerboseLevel [0|1|2|3]]
[-LoginTimeOut login_time_out_seconds]
[-MaxBcpThreads]
[-MaxDeliveredTransactions number_of_transactions]
```

```
[-MessageInterval message_interval]
[-NoTextInitOnSync]
[-Output output_path_and_file_name]
[-OutputVerboseLevel [0|1|2]]
[-PacketSize packet_size]
[-PollingInterval polling_interval]
[-ProfileName profile_name]
[-Publication publication]
[-QueryTimeOut query_time_out_seconds]
[-QuotedIdentifier quoted_identifier]
[-SubscriberDatabasePath subscriber_path]
[-SubscriberDB subscriber_database]
[-SubscriberLogin subscriber_login]
[-SubscriberPassword subscriber_password]
[-SubscriberSecurityMode [0|1]]
[-SubscriberType [0|1|2|3]]
[-SubscriptionTableName subscription_table]
[-SubscriptionType [0|1|2]]
[-TransactionsPerHistory [0|1|...10000]]
```

The parameters in the syntax for the Replication Distribution Agent are discussed in the following list:

◆ -? — Displays the usage.

◆ -Publisher publisher — The name of the Publisher.

◆ -PublisherDB publisher_database — The name of the Publisher database.

◆ -Subscriber subscriber — The name of the Subscriber.

◆ -BcpBatchSize bcp_batch_size — The number of rows to send in a bulk copy operation. When performing a bcp in operation, the batch size is the number of rows to send to the server as one transaction, and also the number of rows that must be sent before the Distribution Agent logs a bcp progress message. When performing a bcp out operation, a fixed batch size of 1,000 is used. A value of 0 indicates no message logging.

◆ -Buffers number_of_buffers — The number of buffers available for asynchronous transactions. The default is 2. Increasing the number can improve performance by reducing memory paging, but it will also increase memory reserved for paging.

◆ -CommitBatchSize commit_batch_size — The number of transactions to be issued to the Subscriber before a COMMIT statement is issued. The default is 100.

◆ -CommitBatchThreshold *commit_batch_threshold* – The number of replication commands to be issued to the Subscriber before a COMMIT statement is issued. The default is 1,000.

◆ -Continuous – Specifies whether the agent attempts to poll replicated transactions continually. If specified, the agent polls replicated transactions from the source at polling intervals, even if there are no transactions pending.

◆ -DefinitionFile *def_path_and_file_name* – The path of the agent definition file. An agent definition file contains command prompt arguments for the agent. The content of the file is parsed as an executable file. Double quotation marks (") can be used to specify argument values containing arbitrary characters.

◆ -Distributor *distributor* – The Distributor name. For Distributor (push) distribution, the name defaults to the name of the local Distributor.

◆ -DistributorAddress *distributor_address* – The network connection string for the Net-Library defined in the DistributorNetwork option. If the DistributorNetwork option is the TCP/IP Sockets Net-Library, then the connection string is in the form of 'address,socket'.

◆ -DistributorLogin *distributor_login* – The Distributor's login name.

◆ -DistributorNetwork *distributor_network* – The Net-Library to use when connecting to the Distributor. This option is useful when configuring the Distribution Agent to connect to a Distributor over the Internet.

◆ -DistributorPassword *distributor_password* – The Distributor's password.

◆ -DistributorSecurityMode [0|1] – The Distributor's security mode. A value of 0 indicates SQL Server Authentication Mode (default), and a value of 1 indicates Windows NT Authentication Mode.

◆ -ErrorFile *error_path_and_file_name* – The path and filename of the error file generated by the Distribution Agent. This file is generated at any point where failure occurred while applying replication transactions at the Subscriber. This file contains the failed replication transactions and associated error messages. When not specified, the error file is generated in the current directory of the Distribution Agent. The error filename is the name of the Distribution Agent with the .err extension.

◆ -FileTransferType [0|1] – Specifies the file transfer type. A value of 0 indicates UNC (Uniform Naming Convention), and a value of 1 indicates FTP (file transfer protocol).

◆ -FtpAddress *ftp_address* – The network address of the FTP service for the Distributor. When not specified, DistributorAddress is used. If DistributorAddress is not specified, Distributor is used.

◆ -FtpPassword *ftp_password* – The user password used to connect to the FTP service.

◆ -FtpPort *ftp_port* – The port number of the FTP service for the Distributor. When not specified, the default port number for FTP service (21) is used.

◆ -FtpUserName *ftp_user_name* – The username used to connect to the FTP service. When not specified, anonymous is used.

◆ -HistoryVerboseLevel [0|1|2|3] – Specifies the amount of history logged during a distribution operation. You can minimize the performance effect of history logging by selecting 1.

◆ -LoginTimeOut *login_time_out_seconds* – The number of seconds before the login times out. The default is 15.

◆ -MaxBcpThreads – The number of bulk copy operations that can be performed in parallel. The maximum number of threads and ODBC connections that exist simultaneously is the lesser of MaxBcpThreads or the number of bulk copy requests that appear in the synchronization transaction in the distribution database. The MaxBcpThreads parameter must have a value greater than zero, and has no hard-coded upper limit. The default is 1.

◆ -MaxDeliveredTransactions *number_of_transactions* – The maximum number of push or pull transactions applied to Subscribers in one synchronization – 0 = an infinite number of transactions. Other values can be used by Subscribers to shorten the duration of a synchronization being pulled from a Publisher.

◆ -MessageInterval *message_interval* – The time interval used for history logging. A history event is logged if either the TransactionsPer History value is reached after the last history event is logged or the MessageInterval value is reached after the last history event is logged. If no replicated transaction is available at the source, the agent reports a no-transaction message to the Distributor. This option specifies how long the agent waits before reporting another no-transaction message. Agents always report a no-transaction message when they detect that there are no transactions available at the source after previously processing replicated transactions. The default is 3,600 (seconds).

◆ -NoTextInitOnSync – Specifies that applications modifying text or image columns in the published table initialize pointers with some value other than NULL in the UPDATE statement.

◆ `-Output` *output_path_and_file_name* — The path of the agent output file. If the filename is not provided, the output is sent to the console. If the specified filename exists, the output is appended to the file.

◆ `-OutputVerboseLevel` [0|1|2] — Specifies whether the output should be verbose. If the verbose level is 0, only error messages are printed. If the verbose level is 1, all the progress report messages are printed. If the verbose level is 2 (default), all error messages and progress report messages are printed, which is useful for debugging.

◆ `-PacketSize` *packet_size* — The packet size, in bytes. The default is 4,096.

◆ `-PollingInterval` *polling_interval* — The frequency, in seconds, the distribution database is queried for replicated transactions. The default is 3.

◆ `-ProfileName` *profile_name* — The agent profile name. If `ProfileName` is `NULL`, the agent profile is disabled. If `ProfileName` is not specified, the default profile for the agent type is used.

◆ `-Publication` *publication* — The name of the publication. For both types of distribution, this parameter is valid only for `immediate_sync` publications. If this parameter is not specified, then the Distributor processes all the `nonimmediate_sync` publications in the Publisher database.

◆ `-QueryTimeOut` *query_time_out_seconds* — The number of seconds before the query times out. The default is 300.

◆ `-QuotedIdentifier` *quoted_identifier* — The quoted identifier character to use. The first character of the value indicates the value the Distribution Agent uses. If `QuotedIdentifier` is used with no value, the Distribution Agent uses a space. If `QuotedIdentifier` is not used, the Distribution Agent uses whatever quoted identifier the Subscriber supports.

◆ `-SubscriberDatabasePath` *subscriber_database_path* — The path to the Jet database (.mdb file) if `SubscriberType` is 2. (This allows a connection to a Jet database without an ODBC DSN.)

◆ `-SubscriberDB` *subscriber_database* — The name of the Subscriber database.

◆ `-SubscriberLogin` *subscriber_login* — The Subscriber's login name. If `SubscriberSecurityMode` is 0 (for Mixed Mode), then this parameter must be specified.

◆ `-SubscriberPassword` *subscriber_password* — The Subscriber's password. If `SubscriberSecurityMode` is 0 (for Mixed Mode), then this parameter must be specified.

♦ `-SubscriberSecurityMode [0|1]` – The Subscriber's security mode: 0 = Mixed Mode (default) and 1 = Windows NT Authentication.

♦ `-SubscriberType [0|1|2]` – The type of Subscriber connection used by the Distribution Agent.

♦ `-SubscriptionTableName` *subscription_table* – The name of the subscription table generated or used at the given Subscriber. When not specified, the `MSreplication_subscription` table is used. Use this option for database management systems (DBMS) that do not support long filenames.

♦ `-SubscriptionType [0|1|2]` – The Subscription type for distribution: 0 = push, 1 = pull, and 2 = anonymous.

♦ `-TransactionsPerHistory [0|1|...10000]` – The transaction interval for history logging. If the number of committed transactions after the last instance of history logging is greater than this option, then a history message is logged. The default is 100, and 0 = infinite.

DTS Package Maintenance

The DTS Package Maintenance utility (dtsrun.exe) enables you to retrieve, execute, delete, and overwrite a package created using Data Transformation Services. The DTS package can be stored in the SQL Server `msdb` database, a COM-structured storage file, or the Microsoft Repository.

The following is the command line syntax for calling the DTS Package Maintenance utility:

```
dtsrun [{/? | {/[~]S server_name {/[~]U user_name [/[~]P password] |
/E}
| {/[~]F filename/[~]R repository_database_name} }
{/[~]N package_name [/[~]M package_password] |
[/[~]G package_guid_string] | [/[~]V package_version_guid_string]}
[/!X] [/!D] [/!Y] [/!C]}]
```

The parameters in the syntax for the DTS Package Maintenance utility are discussed in the following list:

♦ `/?` – Displays the usage.

♦ `~` – Specifies that the parameter to follow is hexadecimal text representing the encrypted value of the parameter. Can be used with the `/S`, `/U`, `/P`, `/F`, `/R`, `/N`, `/M`, `/G`, and `/V` options.

♦ `/S` *server_name* – The network name of the server running SQL Server to which to connect.

♦ `/U` *user_name* – The SQL Server login ID.

◆ /P *password* – The password for the login ID.

◆ /E – Use trusted connection.

◆ /N *package_name* – The name of a DTS package assigned when the package was created.

◆ /M *package_password* – An optional password assigned to the DTS package when it was created.

◆ /G *package_guid_string* – The GUID Package ID assigned to the DTS package when it was created.

◆ /V *package_version_guid_string* – The GUID Version ID assigned to the DTS package when it was first saved or executed. A new version ID is assigned to the DTS package each time it is modified.

◆ /F *filename* – The name of a structured storage UNC file containing DTS packages. If *server_name* is also specified, then the contents of *filename* are overwritten with the DTS package retrieved from SQL Server.

◆ /R *repository_database_name* – Name of the repository database containing DTS packages. If no name is specified, the default database name is used.

◆ /!X – Retrieves the DTS package from SQL Server, and overwrites the contents of *filename*, without executing the package. If this option is not specified, then the DTS package is executed immediately.

◆ /!D – Deletes the DTS package from SQL Server. The package is not executed. It is not possible to delete a specific DTS package from a structured storage file. The entire file needs to be overwritten using the /F and /S options.

◆ /!Y – Displays the encrypted command used to execute the DTS package without executing it.

◆ /!C – Copies the command used to execute the DTS package to the clipboard. This option can also be used in conjunction with /!X and /!Y.

Spaces between command switches and values are optional. Embedded spaces in values must be embedded in double-quotes. To execute a DTS package saved as a COM-structured storage file, use the following syntax:

```
dtsrun /Ffilename /Npackage_name /Mpackage_password
```

To execute a DTS package saved in the SQL Server msdb database, use the following syntax:

```
dtsrun /Sserver_name /Uuser_name /Ppassword /Npackage_Name
    /Mpackage_Password
```

To execute a DTS package saved in a Microsoft Repository, use the following syntax:

```
dtsrun /Sserver_name /Uuser_name /Rrepository_name /Ppassword
   /Npackage_Name /Mpackage_Password
```

Using Transact-SQL to import and export text data

The Transact-SQL TEXTCOPY command copies a single text or image value into or out of SQL Server. The value is a specified text or image *column* of a single row (specified by the WHERE clause) of the specified *table*.

If the direction is IN (/I), then the data from the specified *file* is copied into SQL Server, replacing the existing text or image value. If the direction is OUT (/O), then the text or image value is copied from SQL Server into the specified *file*, replacing any existing file.

The following is the command line syntax for calling the Transact-SQL TEXTCOPY command:

```
TEXTCOPY [/S [sqlserver]] [/U [login]] [/P [password]]
   [/D [database]] [/T table] [/C column] [/W"where clause"]
   [/F file] [{/I | /O}] [/K chunksize] [/Z] [/?]
```

The parameters in the syntax for the Transact-SQL TEXTCOPY command are discussed in the following list:

- ◆ /S *sqlserver* — The SQL server to connect to. Default is local SQL server.

- ◆ /U *login_id* — The login ID to connect with. If this option is not specified, a trusted connection will be used.

- ◆ /P *password* — The password for *login_id*. Default is NULL.

- ◆ /D *database* — The name of the database that contains the table with the text or image data. Default is "login".

- ◆ /T *table* — The name of the table that contains the text or image value.

- ◆ /C *column* — The name of the text or image column of 'table'.

- ◆ /W "*where clause*" — The Where clause (including the WHERE keyword) that identifies a single row of table.

- ◆ /F *file* — The name of the image or text file.

- ◆ /I — Copies the text or image value into SQL Server from *file*.

- ◆ /O — Copies the text or image value out of SQL Server into *file*.

◆ /K *chunksize* — The size of the data transfer buffer in bytes. The minimum is 1,024, and the default is 4,096.

◆ /Z — Displays debug information.

◆ /? — Displays usage.

You will be prompted for any required options you did not specify.

Using the bulk copy program

The bulk copy program (bcp.exe) is a command prompt utility that copies SQL Server data to or from a data file. The bcp utility is most frequently used to transfer large volumes of data into a SQL Server table from another program, usually another database management system. The data to be transferred is first exported from the source program to a data file and then imported from the data file into a SQL Server table using bcp. Alternatively, bcp can be used to transfer data from a SQL Server table to a data file for use in other programs. For example, the data can be copied from SQL Server into a data file; from there, another program can import the data.

Data can also be transferred into a SQL Server table from a data file using the BULK INSERT statement. The BULK INSERT statement enables you to bulk copy data into SQL Server using the functionality of the bcp utility with a Transact-SQL statement rather than from the command prompt. The BULK INSERT statement cannot bulk copy data from SQL Server to a data file. It is also possible to write programs to bulk copy SQL Server data to or from a data file using the bulk-copy application programming interface (API). The bulk-copy API can be used in ODBC, OLE DB, and DB-Library-based applications.

The following is the command line syntax for calling the bcp command line utility:

```
bcp [[database_name.][owner].]table_name
{in | out | format} data_file
[-m max_errors] [-f format_file] [-e err_file]
[-F first_row] [-L last_row] [-b batch_size]
[-n] [-c] [-w] [-N] [-6] [-q] [-C code_page]
[-t field_term] [-r row_term]
[-i input_file] [-o output_file] [-a packet_size]
[-S server_name] [-U login_id] [-P password]
[-T] [-v] [-k] [-E] [-h "hint [,...n]"]
```

The parameters in the syntax for the bcp command line utility are discussed in the following list:

◆ -S *server_name* — The SQL Server to connect to. Default is local SQL Server.

♦ `database_name` — Is the name of the database in which the specified table resides. If this option is not specified, this is the default database for the user.

♦ `owner` — Is the name of the table owner. The *owner parameter* is optional if the user performing the bulk copy operation owns the specified table. If *owner* is not specified and the user performing the bulk copy operation does not own the specified table, Microsoft SQL Server 7 returns an error message, and the bulk copy operation is canceled.

♦ `table_name` — Is the name of the destination table when copying data into SQL Server (`in`), and the source table when copying data from SQL Server (`out`). When bulk copying data from SQL Server, this can also be a SQL Server view.

♦ `in | out | format` — Specifies the direction of the bulk copy. The `in` option copies from a file into the database table; the `out` option copies from the database table to a file; the `format` option creates a format file based on the option specified (`-n`, `-c`, `-w`, `-6`, or `-N`) and the table delimiters. If the `format` option is used, the `-f` option must be specified as well.

♦ `data_file` — Is the full path of the data file used when bulk copying a table to or from a disk. When bulk copying data into SQL Server, the data file contains the data to be copied into the specified table. When bulk copying data from SQL Server, the data file contains the data copied from the table. The path can have from 1 through 255 characters.

♦ `-m max_errors` — Specifies the maximum number of errors that can occur before the bulk copy operation is canceled. Each row that cannot be copied by `bcp` is ignored and counted as one error. If this option is not included, the default is 10.

♦ `-f format_file` — Specifies the full path of the format file that contains stored responses from a previous use of `bcp` on the same table. Use this option when using a format file created with the format option to bulk copy data in or out. Creation of the format file is optional. After prompting you with format questions, `bcp` prompts whether to save the answers in a format file. The default filename is Bcp.fmt. `bcp` can refer to a format file when bulk copying data; therefore, reentering previous format responses interactively is not necessary. If this option is not used and neither `-n`, `-c`, `-w`, `-6`, nor `-N` is specified, `bcp` prompts for format information.

♦ `-e err_file` — Specifies the full path of an error file used to store any rows `bcp` is unable to transfer from the file to the database. Error messages from `bcp` go to the user's workstation. If this option is not used, an error file is not created.

♦ `-F first_row` — Specifies the number of the first row to bulk copy. The default is 1, indicating the first row in the specified data file.

◆ -L `last_row` – Specifies the number of the last row to bulk copy. The default is 0, indicating the last row in the specified data file.

◆ -b `batch_size` – Specifies the number of rows per batch of data copied. Each batch is copied to the server as one transaction. SQL Server commits or rolls back, in the case of failure, the transaction for every batch. By default, all data in the specified data file is copied in one batch. Do not use in conjunction with the -h "ROWS_PER_BATCH = `bb`" option.

◆ -n – Performs the bulk copy operation using the native (database) data types of the data. This option does not prompt for each field; it uses the native values.

◆ -c – Performs the bulk copy operation using a character data type. This option does not prompt for each field; it uses char as the storage type, no prefixes, \t (tab character) as the field separator, and \n (newline character) as the row terminator.

◆ -w – Performs the bulk copy operation using Unicode characters. This option does not prompt for each field; it uses nchar as the storage type, no prefixes, \t (tab character) as the field separator, and \n (newline character) as the row terminator. Cannot be used with SQL Server version 6.5 or earlier.

◆ -N – Performs the bulk copy operation using the native (database) data types of the data for noncharacter data, and Unicode characters for character data. This option offers a higher performance alternative to the -w option and is intended for transferring data from one SQL Server to another using a data file. It does not prompt for each field. Use this option when you are transferring data that contains ANSI extended characters and you want to take advantage of the performance of native mode. -N cannot be used with SQL Server 6.5 or earlier.

◆ -6 – Performs the bulk copy operation using SQL Server 6.0 or 6.5 data types. Use this option in conjunction with character (-c) or native (-n) format. This option does not prompt for each field; it uses the default values. Use this option when using data files generated by bcp from SQL Server 6.0 or 6.5, or when data files contain values using SQL Server 6.5 formats. For example, to bulk copy date formats supported by earlier versions of the bcp utility, but no longer supported by ODBC, use the -6 parameter.

◆ -q – Specifies that quoted identifiers are required, for example, when the table name contains characters that are not ANSI characters. Enclose the entire three-part table name (which may contain embedded special characters, such as spaces) in double quotation marks (" ").

◆ -C *code_page* — Specifies the code page of the data in the data file. *code_page* is relevant only if the data contains char, varchar, or text columns with character values greater than 127 or less than 32: ACP = ANSI (ISO 1252); OEM = default code page used by the client — this is the default code page used by bcp if -C is not specified; RAW = no conversion from one code page to another occurs. This is the fastest option because no conversion occurs; and <value> = specific code page number (for example, 851).

◆ -t *field_term* — Specifies the field terminator. The default is \t (tab character). Use this parameter to override the default field terminator.

◆ -r *row_term* — Specifies the row terminator. The default is \n (newline character). Use this parameter to override the default row terminator.

◆ -i *input_file* — Specifies the name of a response file, containing the responses to the command prompt questions for each field when performing a bulk copy using interactive mode (-n, -c, -w, -6, or -N for not specified).

◆ -o *output_file* — Specifies the name of a file that receives output from bcp redirected from the command prompt.

◆ -a *packet_size* — Specifies the number of bytes, per network packet, sent to and from the server. A server configuration option can be set by using SQL Server Enterprise Manager (or the sp_configure system stored procedure). However, the server configuration option can be overridden on an individual basis by using this option. The packet_size parameter can be from 4,096 to 65,535 bytes; the default is 4,096. Increased packet size can enhance performance of bulk copy operations. If a larger packet is requested but cannot be granted, the default is used. The performance statistics generated by bcp show the packet size used.

◆ -S *server_name* — Specifies the server running SQL Server to connect to. The *server_name* parameter is the name of the server on the network. The default is the local server running SQL Server (no server name). This option is required when executing bcp from a remote computer on the network.

◆ -U *login_id* — Specifies the login ID used to connect to SQL Server.

◆ -P *password* — Specifies the password for the login ID. If this option is not used, bcp prompts for a password. If this option is used at the end of the command prompt without a password, bcp uses the default password (NULL).

◆ -T — Specifies that bcp connects to SQL Server with a trusted connection, using the security credentials of the network user. The *login_id* and *password* parameters are not required.

◆ -v — Reports the bcp utility version number and copyright.

- ◆ -k – Specifies that empty columns should retain a null value during the bulk copy operation, rather than have any default values for the columns inserted.

- ◆ -E – Specifies that identity columns are present in the file being imported. If -E is not given, the file being imported should not contain values for these columns because SQL Server automatically assigns unique values based on the seed and increment values specified during table creation. If -E is specified, SQL Server takes the values for the identity columns from the data file.

- ◆ -h "*hint* [,...n]" – Specifies the hint(s) to be used during a bulk copy of data into a table. This option cannot be used when bulk copying data into SQL Server 6.*x* or earlier. See Table 4-2 for available options.

TABLE 4-2 HINT PARAMETER OPTIONS

Hint	Description
ORDER (*column* [ASC | DESC] [,...n])	The sort order of the data in the data file. Bulk copy performance is improved if the data being loaded is sorted according to the clustered index on the table. If the data file is sorted in a different order, or if there is no clustered index on the table, the ORDER hint is ignored. The names of the columns supplied must be valid columns in the destination table. By default, bcp assumes the data file is unordered.
ROWS_PER_ BATCH = *bb*	The number of rows of data per batch (as *bb*). Used when -b is not specified, resulting in the entire data file being sent to the server as a single transaction. The server optimizes the bulk load according to the value *bb*. By default, ROWS_PER_BATCH is unknown.
KILOBYTES_ PER_BATCH = *cc*	The number of kilobytes (K) of data per batch (as *cc*). By default, KILOBYTES_PER_BATCH is unknown.
TABLOCK	A table-level lock is acquired for the duration of the bulk copy operation. This hint significantly improves performance because holding a lock only for the duration of the bulk copy operation reduces lock contention on the table. A table can be loaded by multiple clients concurrently if the table has no indexes and TABLOCK is specified. By default, locking behavior is determined by the table option table lock on bulk load.
CHECK_ CONSTRAINTS	Any constraints on *table_name* are checked during the bulk copy operation. By default, constraints are ignored.

SQL Server identifiers, including database names, table names, logins, and passwords, can include characters such as embedded spaces and quotation marks. When specifying an identifier at the command prompt that includes a space or quotation mark, enclose the identifier in double quotation marks (" "). For table names that contain embedded spaces or quotation marks, specify the -q parameter.

Here is an example showing a bulk copy of the report.txt file into the tbexprpt table in the dbexptrk database, using the allenp login with a password of apple:

```
bcp "dbexptrk copy..tbexprpt" in report.txt -c
   -Sum2z8 -Uallenp -Papple
```

Storing statistical information

When you create an index, SQL Server automatically stores statistical information regarding the distribution of values in the indexed column(s). The query optimizer in SQL Server uses these statistics to estimate the cost of using the index for a query. As the data in an indexed column changes, these statistics can become *out of date* and cause the query optimizer to make less-than-optimal decisions on how to process a query.

For example, if you create a table with an indexed column and load 1,000 rows of data, all with unique values in the indexed column, the optimizer considers the indexed column a *good* way to collect the data for a query. If you update the data in the column so that there are many duplicated values, the column is no longer an ideal candidate for use in a query. However, the query optimizer still considers it to be a good candidate based on the index's outdated distribution statistics, which were based on the data before the update.

Therefore, SQL Server automatically updates this statistical information periodically as the data in the tables changes. The sampling is random across data pages, and taken from the table or nonclustered index for the smallest index containing the columns needed by the statistics. The frequency with which the statistical information is updated is determined by the volume of data in the index and the amount of changing data. For example, the statistics for a table containing 10,000 rows may need updating when 1,000 index values have changed because 1,000 values represents a significant percentage of the table. However, for a table containing 10 million index entries, 1,000 changing index values is less significant.

The cost of this automatic statistics update is minimized by doing statistical sampling of the data. Under some circumstances, statistical sampling will not be able to accurately characterize the data in a table. You can control the percentage of data that is sampled during automatic statistics updates on a table-by-table basis by using the SAMPLE clause of the UPDATE STATISTICS statement. It is also possible to tell SQL Server not to maintain statistics for a given column or index using:

◆ The sp_autostats system stored procedure.

◆ The STATISTICS_NORECOMPUTE clause of the CREATE INDEX statement.

◆ The NORECOMPUTE clause of the UPDATE STATISTICS statement.

If you tell SQL Server not to automatically maintain statistics, you will need to manually update the statistical information using the UPDATE STATISTICS statement.

Updating statistics

The UPDATE STATISTICS statement updates information about the distribution of key values for one or more indexes in the specified table. The UPDATE STATISTICS statement is run automatically when an index is created on a table that already contains data.

The following is the syntax for the UPDATE STATISTICS statement and a table that describes each of the parameters in the syntax:

```
UPDATE STATISTICS {table}
[index | (index_or_column [, ...n])]
[WITH [[FULLSCAN]| SAMPLE number {PERCENT | ROWS}]]
[[,] [ALL | COLUMNS | INDEX]
[[,] NORECOMPUTE]]
```

The arguments for the UPDATE STATISTICS statement are discussed in the following list:

◆ *table* – The table for which statistics are being updated. Table names must conform to the rules for identifiers. The *table* is the table with which the index is associated. Because index names are not unique within each database, *table* must be specified. Specifying the database or table owner is optional.

◆ *index* – Index for which statistics are being updated. Index names must conform to the rules for identifiers. If *index* is not specified, the distribution statistics for all indexes in the specified table are updated. To see a list of index names and descriptions, execute sp_helpindex with the table name.

◆ *index_or_column* – The name of the column(s) or index(es) for which statistics are being updated. Index and column names must conform to the rules for identifiers. The index_or_column argument is required only when the INDEX or COLUMN options are specified. Columns consisting of ntext, text, image, or bit data types, and computed columns cannot be specified as statistics columns.

◆ n – A placeholder indicating that multiple index or column names can be specified.

◆ FULLSCAN – Causes SQL Server 7 to perform a full scan of the index or table when gathering statistics.

♦ SAMPLE *number* {PERCENT | ROWS} — Specifies the percentage of the table or the number of rows that are being sampled when collecting statistics for larger tables. To use the default-sampling behavior for larger tables, use SAMPLE *number* with PERCENT or ROWS. SQL Server ensures a minimum number of values are sampled to ensure useful statistics. If the PERCENT, ROWS, or *number* option results in too few rows being sampled, SQL Server automatically corrects the sampling based on the number of existing rows in the table. The default behavior is to perform a sample scan on the target table. SQL Server automatically computes the required sample size.

♦ ALL | COLUMNS | INDEX — Specifies whether the UPDATE STATISTICS statement affects column statistics, index statistics, or all existing statistics. If no option is specified, the UPDATE STATISTICS statement affects existing indexes only. When COLUMN is specified, statistics are created or updated (if they already exist) for columns that do not have preexisting statistics.

♦ NORECOMPUTE — Specifies that statistics that become out of date are not automatically recomputed. Statistics become out of date depending on the number of INSERT, UPDATE, and DELETE operations performed on indexed columns. When specified, this option causes SQL Server to never automatically rebuild statistics and disables automatic statistics rebuilding. To restore automatic statistics recomputation, reissue UPDATE STATISTICS without the NORECOMPUTE option or execute sp_autostats. Disabling automatic statistics recomputation can cause the SQL Server query optimizer to choose a less optimal strategy for queries that involve the specified table.

The UPDATE STATISTICS statement's permissions default to the table owner. Permissions are not transferable. SQL Server keeps statistics about the distribution of the key values in each index and uses these statistics to determine which index(es) to use in query processing. Query optimization depends on the accuracy of the distribution steps:

♦ If there is significant change in the key values in the index, rerun UPDATE STATISTICS on that index.

♦ If a large amount of data in an indexed column has been added, changed, or removed (that is, if the distribution of key values has changed), or the table has been truncated using the TRUNCATE TABLE statement and then repopulated, use UPDATE STATISTICS.

To see when the statistics were last updated you can use the STATS_DATE function. Some examples are shown in Table 4-3.

TABLE 4-3 UPDATE STATISTICS STATEMENT EXAMPLES

Example	Description
UPDATE STATISTICS tb_emp_exp_rpt	Creates or updates the distribution statistics for all indexes on the tb_emp_exp_rpt table.
UPDATE STATISTICS tb_emp_exp_rpt idx_exp_rpt_id	Creates or updates only the distribution information for the idx_exp_rpt_id index of the tb_emp_exp_rpt table.
UPDATE STATISTICS tb_employee(emp_last _name, emp_first_name) WITH COLUMNS, SAMPLE 50 PERCENT	Creates or updates statistics for the emp_last_name and emp_first_name columns in the tb_employee table using 50 percent sampling.
tb_employee(emp_last _name, emp_first_name) WITH COLUMNS, FULLSCAN, NORECOMPUTE	Creates or updates statistics for the emp_last_name and emp_first_name columns in the tb_employee table by forcing a full scan of all rows in the tb_employee table. It also turns off automatic statistics updating for the emp_last_name and cmp_first_name columns.

Other Essential Programs

As you can see, there are many utilities in SQL Server. We will now take a look at the remaining essential utilities. These include the ones that enable you to execute non-Unicode and Unicode SQL statements (isql.exe and osql.exe), as well as the basic maintenance utility (sqlmaint.exe) and the database consistency checker (DBCC).

Executing SQL statements

The isql utility is a command line program that enables you to enter Transact-SQL statements, system procedures, and script files; it uses DB-Library to communicate with the SQL Server. DB-Library applications do not support some SQL Server 7 features. For example, they cannot retrieve Unicode ntext data. For this reason the osql utility is also provided. It has the same user interface as isql, but it supports the full set of SQL Server 7 features. Listing 4-5 provides the syntax for both the isql and osql command line utilities.

Listing 4-5: The isql and osql Syntax

```
isql -U login_id [-e] [-E] [-p] [-n] [-d db_name] [-Q "query"]
[-q "query"] [-c cmd_end] [-h headers] [-w column_width]
```

```
[-s col_separator] [-t time_out] [-m error_level] [-L] [-?]
[-r {0 | 1}] [-H workstation_name] [-P password]  [-S server_name]
[-i input_file] [-o output_file] [-a packet_size]
[-b] [-O] [-l time_out] [-x max_text_size] [-C configuration_file]
[-D scripts_directory] [-T template_directory]

osql -U login_id [-e] [-E] [-p] [-n] [-d db_name] [-Q "query"]
[-q "query"] [-c cmd_end] [-h headers] [-w column_width]
[-s col_separator] [-t time_out] [-m error_level] [-I] [-L] [-?]
[-r {0 | 1}] [-H workstation_name] [-P password]  [-R]
[-S server_name] [-i input_file] [-o output_file] [-u]
[-a packet_size] [-b] [-O] [-l time_out]
```

The parameters in the syntax for both the isql and osql command line utilities are discussed in the following list:

◆ -U login_id — The user login ID.

◆ -e — The echoes input.

◆ -E — Uses a trusted connection.

◆ -p — Prints performance statistics.

◆ -n — Removes numbering and the prompt symbol (>) from input lines.

◆ -d db_name — Issues a USE db_name statement.

◆ -Q "query" — Executes a query and immediately exits isql when the query completes. Use double quotation marks around the query and single quotation marks around anything embedded in the query.

◆ -q "query" — Executes a query when isql starts, but does not exit isql when the query completes. (Note that the query statement should not include GO.) If you issue a query from a batch file, you can use %variables. Environment %variables% also work — For example, SET table = sysobjects and isql /q "Select * from %table%". Use double quotation marks around the query and single quotation marks around anything embedded in the query.

◆ -c cmd_end — A command terminator. By default, commands are terminated and sent to SQL Server by entering GO on a line by itself. When you reset the command terminator, do not use SQL reserved words.

◆ -h headers — The number of rows to print between column headings. The default is to print headings one time for each set of query results. Use -1 to specify that no headers will be printed. If using -1, there must be no space between the parameter and the setting.

◆ -w *column_width* — Enables the user to set the screen width for output. The default is 80. When an output line has reached its maximum screen width, it is broken into multiple lines.

◆ -s *col_separator* — A column-separator character, which is a blank space by default. To use characters that have special meaning to the operating system (for example, | ; & < >), enclose the character in double quotation marks (").

◆ -t *time_out* — The number of seconds before a command times out. If no time_out value is specified, a command runs indefinitely; the default time-out for logging into isql is 8 seconds.

◆ -m *error_level* — Customizes the display of error messages. The message number, state, and error level are displayed for errors of the specified severity level or higher. Nothing is displayed for errors of severity levels lower than the specified level. Use -1 to specify that all headers are returned with messages, even informational messages. If using -1, there must be no space between the parameter and the setting.

◆ -I — (osql only) Sets the QUOTED_IDENTIFIER connection option on.

◆ -L — Lists the locally configured servers and the names of the servers broadcasting on the network.

◆ -? — Displays the syntax summary of isql switches.

◆ -r {0 | 1} — Redirects message output to the screen (stderr). If you don't specify a parameter, or if you specify 0, only error messages with severity 17 or higher are redirected. If you specify 1, all message output (including "print") is redirected.

◆ -H *workstation_name* — The workstation name. The workstation name is stored in sysprocesses.hostname and is displayed by sp_who. If it's not specified, the current computer name is assumed.

◆ -P *password* — A user-specified password. If the -P option is not used, isql prompts for a password. If the -P option is used at the end of the command prompt without any password, isql uses the default password (NULL). Passwords are case-sensitive. The ISQLPASSWORD environment variable enables you to set a default password for the current session. Therefore, you do not have to hard-code a password into batch files. If you do not specify a password with the -P option, isql first checks for the ISQLPASSWORD variable. If no value is set, isql uses the default password, NULL. The following example sets the ISQLPASSWORD variable at the command prompt and then accesses the isql utility:

```
D:\>SET ISQLPASSWORD=gfos
D:\>isql
```

◆ -S *server_name* — The server_name to connect to.

◆ -i *input_file* — The file-containing batch of SQL statements or stored procedures. The less than (<) comparison operator can be used in place of -i.

◆ -o *output_file* — The file that receives output from isql. The greater than (>) comparison operator can be used in place of -o.

◆ -u — Specifies that *output_file* is stored in Unicode format, regardless of the format of the *input_file*.

◆ -a *packet_size* — Requests a different-sized packet. The valid values for *packet_size* are 512 through 65535. The default value for Windows NT is 8192. Increased packet size can enhance performance on larger script execution where the amount of SQL statements between GO commands is substantial. Microsoft testing indicates that 8192 is typically the fastest setting for bulk copy operations. A larger packet size can be requested, but isql defaults to 512 if the request cannot be granted.

◆ -b — Specifies that isql exits and returns a DOS ERRORLEVEL value when an error occurs. The value returned to the DOS ERRORLEVEL variable is 1 when the SQL Server error message has a severity of 10 or greater; otherwise, the value returned is 0. MS-DOS batch files can test the value of DOS ERRORLEVEL and handle the error appropriately.

◆ -0 — Specifies that isql reverts to the behavior of earlier versions. These features are deactivated:

   ▪ EOF batch processing

   ▪ Automatic console width scaling

   ▪ Wide messages

It also sets the default DOS ERRORLEVEL value to -1.

◆ -l *time_out* — The number of seconds before an isql login times out. If no *time_out* value is specified, a command runs indefinitely. The default time-out for log into isql is 8 seconds.

◆ -x *max_text_size* (isql only) — The maximum length (bytes) of text data to return. Text values longer than max_text_size are truncated. If max_text_size is not specified, text data is truncated at 4,096 bytes.

◆ -C *configuration_file* (isql only) — Uses options specified in configuration file. Other arguments explicitly specified on the command line supercede the configuration file settings.

◆ -D *scripts_directory* (isql only) — Overwrites the default saved script directory specified in the Registry or the configuration file specified with -C.

♦ -T *template_directory* (isql only) — Overwrites the default template directory specified in the Registry or the configuration file specified with -C.

♦ -D *data_source_name* (osql only) — The osql connection uses the ODBC data source specified.

All DB-Library applications, such as isql, work as SQL Server 6.5-level clients when connected to SQL Server 7. They do not support some of the new SQL Server 7 features. The osql utility is based on ODBC and does support all new SQL Server 7 features. Use osql to run scripts that isql cannot run.

The SQL Server Query Analyzer default is to save SQL scripts as Unicode files. The isql utility does not support Unicode input files. Attempting to specify one of these files in the -i switch results in a 170 error:

```
Incorrect syntax near ' '.
```

Use the osql utility to run these Unicode files. An alternative is to specify ANSI instead of Unicode in the File format list of the SQL Server Query Analyzer File/Save As dialog box.

Like most DB-Library applications, the isql utility does not set any connection options by default. Users must issue SET statements interactively or in their scripts if they want to use specific connection option settings. The isql utility is started directly from the operating system with the case-sensitive options listed here. After starting, isql accepts Transact-SQL statements and sends them to SQL Server interactively. The results are formatted and printed on the standard output device (the screen). Use QUIT or EXIT to exit from isql.

If you do not specify a username when you start isql, SQL Server checks for the environment variables and uses those — for example, isqluser=(user) or isqlserver=(server). If no environment variables are set, the workstation user-name is used. If you do not specify a server, the name of the workstation is used. If neither the -U or -P options are used, SQL Server attempts to connect using Windows NT Authentication Mode. Authentication is based on the Windows NT account of the user running isql.

The osql utility uses the ODBC API. The utility uses the SQL Server ODBC driver default settings for the SQL Server SQL-92 connection options, except for QUOTED_IDENTIFIER. The osql utility defaults to setting QUOTED_IDENTIFIER OFF. Use the -I switch to set it on.

In addition to using Transact-SQL statements within isql and osql, the following commands are also available:

♦ GO — Executes all statements entered after the last GO.

♦ RESET — Clears any statements you have entered.

♦ ED — Calls the editor.

♦ !! command — Executes an operating-system command.

♦ QUIT or EXIT( ) – Exits from isql or osql.

♦ Ctrl+C – Ends a query without exiting from isql or osql.

The command terminators GO (by default), RESET, ED, !!, EXIT, QUIT, and Ctrl+C are recognized only if they appear at the beginning of a line, immediately following the isql or osql prompt. Anything entered on the same line after any of these keywords is disregarded by isql and osql.

The GO command signals both the end of a batch and the execution of any cached Transact-SQL statements. When you press Enter at the end of each input line, isql or osql caches the statements on that line. When you press Enter after typing GO, all of the currently cached statements are sent as a batch to SQL Server.

The current isql or osql utility works as if there is an implied GO at the end of any script executed so all statements in the script execute. Some earlier versions of isql or osql would not send any statements to the server unless there was at least one GO in an input script. Any statements after the last GO would not be executed. Earlier versions of the isql utility required that GO be at the start of a line, without any blanks preceding it.

End a command by typing a line beginning with a command terminator. You can follow the command terminator with an integer to specify how many times the command should be run. For example, to execute this command 101 times, type:

```
SELECT x = 1
GO 101
```

The results are printed once, at the end of execution. With isql or osql, there is a limit of 1,000 characters per line. Large statements should be spread across multiple lines.

The user can call an editor on the current query buffer by typing ED as the first word on a line. The editor is defined in the EDITOR environment variable. The default editor is "edit" for Windows NT. You can specify a different editor by setting the EDITOR environment variable. For example, to make the default editor WordPad, enter at the operating system prompt:

```
SET EDITOR=write
```

Operating system commands

Operating system commands can also be executed by starting a line with two exclamation points (!!) followed by the command. The command recall facilities of DOSKEY can be used to recall and modify previously entered isql or osql statements on a computer running Windows NT. The existing query buffer can be cleared by typing RESET.

When running stored procedures, isql or osql prints a blank line between each set of results in a batch. In addition, the "0 rows affected" message does not appear when it doesn't apply to the statement executed.

Using isql or osql interactively

To use `isql` or `osql` interactively, type the **isql** or **osql** command (and any of the options) at a command prompt. You can read in a file containing a query (such as branch.sql) for execution by `isql` or `osql` by typing a command similar to this:

```
isql /U um2z8 /P /i expense.sql
```

or

```
osql /U um2z8 /P /i expense2.sql
```

The file must include a command terminator(s).

You can read in a file containing a query (such as reportsum1.sql) and direct the results to another file by typing a command similar to this:

```
isql /U allenp /P almonds /i reportsum1.sql /o reportsum1.out
```

When using `isql` or `osql` interactively, you can read an operating system file into the command buffer with `:r file_name`. Do not include a command terminator in the file; enter the terminator interactively after you have finished editing.

INSERTING COMMENTS

You can include comments in a Transact-SQL statement submitted to SQL Server by `isql`. Two types of commenting styles are allowed: `--` and `/*...*/`.

USING EXIT TO RETURN RESULTS IN ISQL

You can use the result of a `SELECT` statement as the return value from `isql`. The first column of the first result row is converted to a four-byte integer (long). MS-DOS passes the low byte to the parent process or operating system error level. Windows NT passes the entire four-byte integer. The syntax is:

```
EXIT(query)
```

For example:

```
EXIT(SELECT @@rowcount)
EXIT(SELECT 5)
```

You can also include the `EXIT` parameter as part of a batch file. For example:

```
isql /Q "EXIT(SELECT COUNT(*) FROM '%1')"
```

The `isql` utility passes everything between the parentheses ( ) to the server exactly as entered. The `EXIT( )` statement can span lines. If a stored system procedure selects a set and returns a value, only the selection is returned. The `EXIT( )` statement with nothing between the parentheses executes everything preceding it in the batch and then exits with no return value.

There are four EXIT formats:

◆ `EXIT` – Does not execute the batch; quits immediately, returning no value.

◆ `EXIT( )` – Executes the batch, and then quits, returning no value.

◆ `EXIT(query)` – Executes the batch, including the query, and then quits after returning the results of the query.

◆ `RAISERROR` with a state of 127 – If `RAISERROR` is used within an `isql` script and a state of 127 is raised, `isql` or `osql` will quit and return the message ID back to the client. For example: `RAISERROR(50001, 10, 127)`. This error will cause the `isql` or `osql` script to end and the message ID 50001 will be returned to the client. The return values `-1` through `-99` are reserved by SQL Server; `isql` or `osql` defines the following values:

◆ `-100` – Error encountered prior to selecting return value

◆ `-101` – No rows found when selecting return value

◆ `-102` – Conversion error when selecting return value

DISPLAYING MONEY AND SMALLMONEY DATA TYPES

The `osql` utility displays the `money` and `smallmoney` data types with two decimal places even though SQL Server stores the value internally with four decimal places. Consider the example:

```
SELECT CAST(CAST(10.3496 AS money) AS decimal(6, 4))
```

This statement produces a result of 10.3496, which indicates that the value is stored with all decimal places intact.

Using the Basic Maintenance utility

The Basic Maintenance utility (sqlmaint.exe) performs a specified set of maintenance operations on one or more databases. Use `sqlmaint` to run DBCC checks, to dump a database and its transaction log, to update statistics, and to rebuild indexes. All database maintenance activities generate a report that can be sent to a designated text file, HTML file, or e-mail account. Listing 4-6 provides the syntax for the `sqlmaint` command line utility.

Listing 4-6: Syntax for the sqlmaint Utility

```
sqlmaint.exe
[-?] |
[
[-S server]
[-U "login_ID" [-P "password"]]
{
[ -D database_name | -PlanName name | -PlanID guid ]
[-Rpt text_file [-DelTxtRpt <time_period>] ]
[-To operator_name]
[-HtmlRpt html_file [-DelHtmlRpt <time_period>] ]
[-RmUnusedSpace threshold_percent free_percent]
[-CkDB | -CkDBNoIdx]
[-CkAl | -CkAlNoIdx]
[-CkTxtAl]
[-CkCat]
[-UpdSts]
[-UpdOptiStats sample_percent]
[-RebldIdx free_space]
[-WriteHistory]
[
{-BkUpDB [backup_path] | -BkUpLog [backup_path] }
{-BkUpMedia
{DISK [ [-DelBkUps <time_period>]
[-CrBkSubDir ] [ -UseDefDir ]
]
| TAPE
}
}
[-BkUpOnlyIfClean]
[-VrfyBackup]
]
}
]
<time_period> ::=
number[minutes | hours | days | weeks | months]
```

The parameters in the syntax for the sqlmaint utility are discussed in the following list:

◆ -? – Specifies that the syntax diagram for sqlmaint be returned. This parameter must be used alone.

◆ -S *server* — Specifies the target server. If this option is not supplied, SQL Server 7 is assumed to be on the local computer. SQL Server cannot be version 6.5 or earlier. Use the 6.5 version of sqlmaint for earlier versions of SQL Server.

◆ -U "*login_ID*" — Specifies the login ID to use when connecting to the server. If this option is not supplied, sqlmaint attempts to use Windows NT Authentication. The login_ID option must be enclosed in double quotation marks (").

◆ -P "*password*" — Specifies the password for the login ID. It is only valid if the -U parameter is also supplied. The *password* option must be enclosed in double quotation marks.

◆ -D *database_name* — Specifies the name of the database in which to perform the maintenance operation.

◆ -PlanName *name* — Specifies the name of a database maintenance plan defined using the Database Maintenance Plan Wizard. The only information sqlmaint uses from the plan is the list of the databases in the plan. Any maintenance activities you specify in the other sqlmaint parameters are applied to this list of databases. You can get the plan name from SQL Server Enterprise Manager.

◆ -PlanID *guid* — Specifies the globally unique identifier (GUID) of a database maintenance plan defined using the Database Maintenance Plan Wizard. The only information sqlmaint uses from the plan is the list of the databases in the plan. Any maintenance activities you specify in the other sqlmaint parameters are applied to this list of databases. This must match a *plan_id* value in msdb.dbo.sysdbmaintplans.

◆ -Rpt *text_file* — Specifies the full path and name of the file into which the report is to be generated. The report is also generated on the screen. The report maintains version information by adding a date to the filename. The date is generated as follows: at the end of the filename but before the period, in the form *_yyyyMMddhhm*, where *yyyy* = year, *MM* = month, *dd* = day, *hh* = hour, and *mm* = minute.

If you run the utility at 10:23 A.M. on December 1, 1996, and this is the *text_file* value:

```
c:\mssql7\backup\Nwind_maint.rpt
```

The generated filename is:

```
c:\mssql7\backup\Nwind_maint_199612011023.rpt
```

The full UNC filename is required for text_file when sqlmaint accesses a remote server.

◆ `-DelTxtRpt` `<time_period>` – Specifies that any text report in the report directory is to be deleted if the time interval after the creation of the report file exceeds the `<time_period>`. It looks for files whose name fits the pattern generated from the `text_file` parameter. If `text_file` is C:\Mssql7\Backup\Nwind_maint.rpt, then `-DelTxtRpt` causes `sqlmaint` to delete any files whose names match the pattern C:\Mssql7\Backup\Nwind_maint*.rpt and that are older than the specified `<time_period>`.

◆ `-To` `operator_name` – Specifies the operator to whom the generated report will be sent through SQL Mail. The operator can be defined by using SQL Server Enterprise Manager.

◆ `-HtmlRpt` `html_file` – Specifies the full path and name of the file into which an HTML report is to be generated. The `sqlmaint` utility generates the filename by appending a string of the format `_yyyyMMddhhmm` to the filename, just as it does for the `-Rpt` parameter. The full UNC filename is required for `html_file` when `sqlmaint` accesses a remote server.

◆ `-DelHtmlRpt` `<time_period>` – Specifies that any HTML report in the report directory is to be deleted if the time interval after the creation of the report file exceeds `<time_period>`. It looks for files whose name fits the pattern generated from the `html_file` parameter. If `html_file` is C:\Mssql7\Backup\Nwind_maint.htm, then `-DelHtmlRpt` causes `sqlmaint` to delete any files whose names match the pattern C:\Mssql7\Backup\Nwind_maint*.htm and that are older than the specified `<time_period>`.

◆ `-RmUnusedSpace` `threshold_percent` `free_percent` – Specifies that unused space be removed from the database specified in `-D`. This option is only useful for databases that are defined to grow automatically. The `Threshold_percent` option specifies in megabytes the size that the database must reach before `sqlmaint` attempts to remove unused data space. If the database is smaller than the `threshold_percent`, no action is taken. The `Free_percent` option specifies how much unused space must remain in the database; it is specified as a percentage of the final size of the database. For example, if a 200MB database contains 100MB of data, specifying 10 for `free_percent` results in the final database size being 110MB. Note that a database will not be expanded if it is smaller than `free_percent` plus the amount of data in the database. For example, if a 108MB database has 100MB of data, specifying 10 for `free_percent` will not expand the database to 110MB; it will remain at 108MB.

◆ `-CkDB` | `-CkDBNoIdx` – Specifies that a `DBCC CHECKDB` or a `DBCC CHECKDB` statement with the `NOINDEX` option be run in the database specified in `-D`. A warning is written to `text_file` if the database is in use when `sqlmaint` runs.

♦ -CkAl | -CkAlNoIdx — Specifies that a DBCC NEWALLOC or a DBCC NEWALLOC statement with the NOINDEX option be run in the database specified in -D.

♦ -CkTxtAl — Specifies that a DBCC TEXTALL statement be run in the database specified in -D.

♦ -CkCat — Specifies that a DBCC CHECKCATALOG statement be run in the database specified in -D.

♦ -UpdSts — Specifies that the following statement is to be run on each table in the database:

UPDATE STATISTICS *table*

♦ -UpdOptiStats *sample_percent* — Specifies that the following statement is to be run on each table in the database:

UPDATE STATISTICS *table* WITH SAMPLE *sample_percent* PERCENT

♦ -RebldIdx *free_space* — Specifies that indexes on tables in the target database should be rebuilt by using the *free_space* percent value as the inverse of the fill factor. For example, if *free_space* percentage is 30, then the fill factor used is 70. If a *free_space* percentage value of 100 is specified, then the indexes are rebuilt with the original fill factor value.

♦ -WriteHistory — Specifies that an entry is made in msdb.dbo. sysdbmaintplan_history for each maintenance action performed by sqlmaint. If -PlanName or -PlanID is specified, the entries in sysdbmaintplan_history use the ID of the specified plan. If -D is specified, the entries in sysdbmaintplan_history are made with zeros for the plan ID.

♦ -BkUpDB [*backup_path*] | -BkUpLog [*backup_path*] — Specifies a backup action. -BkUpDb backs up the entire database. -BkUpLog backs up only the transaction log. The [*backup_path*] option specifies the directory for the backup; [*backup_path*] is not needed if -UseDefDir is also specified, and it is overridden by -UseDefDir if both are specified. The backup can be placed in a directory or a tape device address (for example, \\.\TAPE0). The filename for a database backup is automatically generated as follows:

*dbname*_db_*yyyyMMddhhmm*.BAK

where *dbname* is the name of the database being backed up. The *yyyyMMddhhmm* part is the time of the backup, where *yyyy* = year, *MM* = month, *dd* = day, *hh* = hour, and *mm* = minute.

The filename for a transaction backup is automatically generated with a similar format:

*dbname*_log_*yyyymmddhhmm*.BAK

If you use the -BkUpDB parameter, you must also specify the media by using the -BkUpMedia parameter.

♦ -BkUpMedia – Specifies the media type of the backup.

♦ DISK – Specifies that the backup medium is disk.

♦ -DelBkUps <time_period> – Specifies that any backup file in the backup directory is to be deleted if the time interval after the creation of the backup exceeds the <time_period>.

♦ -CrBkSubDir – Specifies that a subdirectory be created in the [backup_path] directory. The name of the subdirectory is generated from the database name specified in -D. The -CrBkSubDir offers an easy way to put all the backups for different databases into separate subdirectories without having to change the [backup_path] parameter.

♦ -UseDefDir – Specifies that the backup file be created in the default backup directory. UseDefDir overrides [backup_path] if both are specified. With a default SQL Server setup, the default backup directory is C:\Mssql7\Backup.

♦ TAPE – Specifies that the backup medium is tape.

♦ -BkUpOnlyIfClean – Specifies that the backup occurs only if any specified -Ck checks did not find problems with the data. Maintenance actions run in the same sequence as they appear in the command prompt. Specify the parameters -CkDB, -CkDBNoIdx, -CkAl, -CkAlNoIdx, -CkTxtAl, or -CkCat before the -BkUpDB/-BkUpLog parameter(s) if you are also going to specify -BkUpOnlyIfClean, or the backup will occur whether or not the check reports problems.

♦ -VrfyBackup – Specifies that RESTORE VERIFYONLY is run on the backup when it completes.

♦ number[minutes | hours | days | weeks | months] – Specifies the time interval used to determine if a report or backup file is old enough to be deleted; number is an integer, for example, 12weeks, 3months, or 15days. If only number is specified, the default date part is weeks.

The sqlmaint utility performs maintenance operations on one or more databases. If -D is specified, the operations specified in the remaining switches are performed only on the specified database. If -PlanName or -PlanID are specified, the only information sqlmaint retrieves from the specified maintenance plan is the list of databases in the plan. All operations specified in the remaining sqlmaint parameters are applied against each database in the list obtained from the plan. The sqlmaint utility does not apply any of the maintenance activities defined in the plan itself.

The -CrBkSubDir parameter is useful for maintaining separate directories for multiple databases when using a list of databases in a maintenance plan. If you specify -CrBkSubDir with either -UseDefDir or a [backup_path], then sqlmaint creates subdirectories in the backup directory for each database it backs up. When using a [backup_path] parameter, this feature lets you put the backup files for each database in a separate subdirectory without changing the [backup_path] parameter.

The sqlmaint utility is a SQL-DMO application, which makes it necessary to register SQL-DMO on the computer where you intend to run sqlmaint. If SQL Server or SQL Server Enterprise Manager is installed on the computer, SQL-DMO is already registered.

Type the following to register SQL-DMO at the command prompt:

```
regsvr32 c:\mssql7\binn\sqldmo.enu
```

The sqlmaint utility returns 0 if it runs successfully, or 1 if it fails. Failure is reported:

- ◆ If any of the maintenance actions fail.

- ◆ If -CkDB, -CkDBNoIdx, -CkAl, -CkAlNoIdx, -CkTxtAl, or -CkCat checks find problems with the data.

- ◆ If a general failure is encountered.

For example, sqlmaint returns 1 if SQL-DMO has not been registered:

1. Perform DBCC checks on the dbExpTrk database. Create a text report, and delete any existing reports more than three months old:

   ```
   sqlmaint -S UM2Z8 -U "sa" -P "blue42" -D dbExpTrk
   -CkDB -CkAl -CkTxtAl -CkCat
   -Rpt C:\ExpTrk\dbexptrk_chk.rpt -DelRpt 3months
   ```

2. Update statistics using a 25 percent sample in all databases in a plan. Also, shrink any of the databases that have reached 200MB down to having only 20 percent free space:

   ```
   sqlmaint -S UM2Z8 -U "sa" -P "blue42" -PlanName dbExpTrkPlan
   -UpdOptiStats 25 -RmUnusedSpace 200 20
   ```

3. Back up all the databases in a plan to their individual subdirectories in the default D:\Mssql7\Backup directory. Also, delete any backups older than three weeks:

   ```
   sqlmaint -S UM2Z8 -U "sa" -P "blue42" -PlanName dbExpTrkPlan
   -BkUpDB -BkUpMedia DISK -UseDefDir -CrBkSubDir -DelBkUps
   3weeks
   ```

USING DBCC STATEMENTS

The Transact-SQL programming language provides several administrative statements that check the logical and physical consistency of a database, check memory usage, decrease the size of a database, check performance statistics, and so on. DBCC statements are the *database consistency checker* for Microsoft SQL Server. These DBCC statements check the physical and logical consistency of a database. Many DBCC statements can fix detected problems. To ensure the logical and physical consistency of data, make periodic DBCC checks of the data. SQL Server's DBCC statements take input parameters and return values. These database consistency-checking statements are grouped into the five categories shown in Table 4-4.

TABLE 4-4 DBCC STATEMENT CATEGORIES

Statement Category	Explanation
Maintenance Statements	Perform a maintenance task on a database, index, or filegroup. The examples are: DBCC DBREPAIR DBCC DBREINDEX DBCC SHRINKDATABASE DBCC SHRINKFILE DBCC UPDATEUSAGE
Miscellaneous Statements	Perform a miscellaneous task such as enabling row-level locking or removing a .dll from memory. The examples are: DBCC dllname (FREE) DBCC HELP DBCC PINTABLE DBCC ROWLOCK DBCC TRACEOFF DBCC TRACEON DBCC UNPINTABLE
Status Statements	Perform a status check. The examples are: DBCC INPUTBUFFER DBCC OPENTRAN DBCC OUTPUTBUFFER

Statement Category	Explanation
	DBCC PROCCACHE
	DBCC SHOWCONTIG
	DBCC SHOW_STATISTICS
	DBCC SQLPERF
	DBCC TRACESTATUS
	DBCC USEROPTIONS
Validation Statements	Perform validation of a database, table, index, catalog, filegroup, system tables, or allocation of database pages.
	DBCC CHECKALLOC
	DBCC CHECKCATALOG
	DBCC CHECKDB
	DBCC CHECKFILEGROUP
	DBCC CHECKIDENT
	DBCC CHECKTABLE
	DBCC NEWALLOC
	DBCC TEXTALL
	DBCC TEXTALLOC
Help	The following returns syntax information for the specified DBCC statement:
	DBCC HELP ('dbcc_statement' | @dbcc_statement_var)
	DBCC HELP returns a result set displaying the syntax for the specified DBCC statement. Syntax varies between the DBCC statements.

All DBCC statement parameters can accept both Unicode and DBCS literals. In the next sections we will present examples of two of the most popular DBCC commands, the CHECKDB and CHECKALLOC varieties.

USING THE DBCC CHECKDB COMMAND

The DBCC CHECKDB statement checks the allocation and structural integrity of all the objects in the specified database. The following is the syntax for the DBCC CHECKDB command:

```
DBCC CHECKDB
( 'database_name'
[, NOINDEX
| { REPAIR_ALLOW_DATA_LOSS
| REPAIR_FAST
| REPAIR_REBUILD
}]
) [WITH {ALL_ERRORMSGS | NO_INFOMSGS}]
```

The parameters in the syntax for the DBCC CHECKDB statement are discussed in the following list:

◆ 'database_name' — The database in which to check all object allocation and structural integrity. If this option is not specified, the default is the current database. Database names must conform to the rules for identifiers.

◆ NOINDEX — Specifies that nonclustered indexes for nonsystem tables should not be checked.

◆ REPAIR_ALLOW_DATA_LOSS | REPAIR_FAST| REPAIR_REBUILD — Specifies that DBCC CHECKDB repair the found errors. The given database_name must be in single-user mode to use a repair option and can be one of the following:

  ■ REPAIR_FAST — Performs minor, non-time-consuming repair actions such as repairing extra keys in nonclustered indexes. These repairs can be done quickly and without risk of data loss.

  ■ REPAIR_REBUILD — Performs all repairs done by REPAIR_FAST and includes time-consuming repairs such as rebuilding indexes. These repairs can be done without risk of data loss.

  ■ REPAIR_ALLOW_DATA_LOSS — Performs all repairs done by REPAIR_REBUILD, including allocation and deallocation of rows and pages for correcting allocation errors, structural row or page errors, and for deleting corrupted text objects. These repairs can result in some data loss. The repair may be done under a user transaction to enable the user to ROLLBACK the changes made, if desired. If repairs are rolled back, the database will still contain errors and should be restored from a backup. If a repair for an error has been skipped due to the provided repair level, any repairs that depend on the repair are also skipped. After repairs are completed, back up the database.

◆ WITH — Specifies an option for the number of error messages to be returned. If neither ALL_ERRORMSGS nor NO_INFOMSGS is specified, then SQL Server 7 returns all error messages.

◆ ALL_ERRORMSGS — Displays all error messages. If this option is not specified, SQL Server displays a maximum of 200 error messages per table. Error messages are sorted by object ID, except for those messages generated from tempdb.

◆ NO_INFOMSGS — Suppresses all informational messages and the report of space used.

DBCC CHECKDB is the safest repair statement because it should catch and repair the widest possible range of errors. If only allocation errors are reported for a database, execute DBCC CHECKALLOC with a repair option to repair these errors. However, to ensure that all errors (including allocation errors) are properly repaired, execute DBCC CHECKDB with a repair option rather than DBCC CHECKALLOC with a repair option.

When you execute DBCC CHECKDB, it requires a shared lock on all tables and indexes in the database for the duration of the operation. While DBCC CHECKDB is running, it is not possible to create, alter, or drop tables. The DBCC CHECKDB statement validates the integrity of everything in a database. There is no need to run either DBCC CHECKALLOC or DBCC CHECKTABLE if DBCC CHECKDB either is currently or has been recently executed. For each table in the database, DBCC CHECKDB checks the following:

◆ Index and data pages are correctly linked.

◆ Indexes are in their properly sorted order.

◆ Pointers are consistent.

◆ The data on each page is reasonable.

◆ Page offsets are reasonable.

The DBCC CHECKDB statement checks the linkages and sizes of text, ntext, and image pages for each table and the allocation of all the pages in the database. Errors indicate potential problems in the database and should be corrected immediately.

The NOINDEX option of DBCC CHECKDB decreases the overall time of execution because it does not check nonclustered indexes for user-defined tables. The NOINDEX option has no effect on system tables. The DBCC CHECKDB statement always checks all system table indexes. The DBCC CHECKDB statement performs the same checking as if both a DBCC CHECKALLOC statement and a DBCC CHECKTABLE statement were executed for each table in the database.

USING THE DBCC CHECKALLOC COMMAND

The DBCC CHECKALLOC statement checks the allocation and use of all pages in the specified database. The following is the syntax for the DBCC CHECKALLOC command:

```
DBCC CHECKALLOC
( 'database_name'
[, NOINDEX
|
{ REPAIR_ALLOW_DATA_LOSS
| REPAIR_FAST
| REPAIR_REBUILD
}]
) [WITH {ALL_ERRORMSGS | NO_INFOMSGS}]
```

The parameters in the syntax for the DBCC CHECKALLOC command are discussed in the following list:

◆ 'database_name' — The database for which to check allocation and page usage. If this option is not specified, the default is the current database. Database names must conform to the rules for identifiers.

◆ NOINDEX — Specifies that nonclustered indexes for nonsystem tables should not be checked. This is for backward compatibility. All indexes are checked when executing DBCC CHECKALLOC.

◆ REPAIR_ALLOW_DATA_LOSS | REPAIR_FAST | REPAIR_REBUILD — Specifies that DBCC CHECKALLOC repair the found errors. The given database_name must be in single-user mode to use one of these repair options and can be one of the following:

  ■ REPAIR_FAST — Performs minor, non-time-consuming repair actions such as repairing extra keys in nonclustered indexes. These repairs can be done quickly and without risk of data loss.

  ■ REPAIR_REBUILD — Performs all repairs done by REPAIR_FAST and includes time-consuming repairs such as rebuilding indexes. These repairs can be done without risk of data loss.

  ■ REPAIR_ALLOW_DATA_LOSS — Performs all repairs done by REPAIR_REBUILD and includes allocation and deallocation of rows and pages for correcting allocation errors, structural row or page errors, and for deleting corrupted text objects. These repairs can result in some data loss. The repair may be done under a user transaction to enable the user to ROLLBACK the changes made, if desired. If repairs are rolled back, the database will still contain errors and should be restored from a backup. If a repair for an error has been skipped due to the provided repair level, any repairs that depend on the repair are also skipped. After repairs are completed, back up the database.

◆ WITH — Specifies an option for the number of error messages to be returned. If neither ALL_ERRORMSGS nor NO_INFOMSGS is specified, then SQL Server 7 returns all error messages.

◆ ALL_ERRORMSGS - Displays all error messages. If this option is not specified, SQL Server displays a maximum of 200 error messages per object. Error messages are sorted by object ID, except for those messages generated from tempdb.

◆ NO_INFOMSGS — Suppresses all informational messages and the report of space used.

It is not necessary to execute DBCC CHECKALLOC if DBCC CHECKDB has already been executed. The DBCC CHECKDB command is a superset of DBCC CHECKALLOC and includes allocation checks in addition to checks of index structure and data integrity.

The DBCC CHECKDB command is the safest repair statement because it should catch and repair the widest possible range of errors. If only allocation errors are reported for a database, execute DBCC CHECKALLOC with a repair option to repair these errors. However, to ensure that all errors (including allocation errors) are properly repaired, execute DBCC CHECKDB with a repair option rather than DBCC CHECKALLOC with a repair option.

When executing DBCC CHECKALLOC:

◆ The DBCC CHECKALLOC command's messages are sorted by object ID, except for those messages generated from tempdb.

◆ The DBCC CHECKALLOC command validates the allocation of all data pages in the database, whereas DBCC CHECKDB validates the page information used in the storage of data in addition to validating the allocation information. There is no need to run DBCC CHECKALLOC if DBCC CHECKDB is used.

The DBCC CHECKALLOC command acquires a schema lock to prevent schema modifications while DBCC CHECKALLOC is in progress. The DBCC CHECKALLOC command may report errors for tempdb work tables that are created or dropped for user queries while the DBCC CHECKALLOC is running, these can be ignored.

Summary

This chapter has covered the tools and components of SQL Server 7. These tools and components enable you to shift data in and out of the server. We have also covered the most popular tools that enable you to execute SQL and perform basic maintenance of the server environment.

Chapter 5

DBMS Administration Tasks

IN THIS CHAPTER

◆ Introducing backup and recovery methods

◆ Backing up databases

◆ Scheduling automatic backups

◆ Restoring databases

◆ Copying databases

THIS CHAPTER PROVIDES details on the DBMS administration tasks for backing up and recovering database data, including the capability to schedule backups automatically. This chapter also covers the how to copy data from one server to another.

Backup and Recovery

Backing up and restoring databases is useful for nonsystem problems, such as moving or copying a database from one server to another. By backing up a database from one computer and restoring the database to another, you can quickly and easily make a copy of a database.

Backing up a database makes a copy of a database that can be used to restore the database if it is lost. Backing up a database copies everything in the database, including any needed portions of the transaction log.

We are now going to look at the specific syntax for the commands that perform backup and restore operations. We will also provide examples of the various options that you might consider for your site. The syntax for the BACKUP command is:

```
BACKUP DATABASE {database_name | @database_name_var}
TO <_device> [, ...n]
[WITH
[BLOCKSIZE = {blocksize | @blocksize_variable}]
[[,] DESCRIPTION = {text | @text_variable}]
```

```
[[,] DIFFERENTIAL]
[[,] EXPIREDATE = {date | @date_var}
| RETAINDAYS = {days | @days_var}]
[[,] FORMAT | NOFORMAT]
[[,] {INIT | NOINIT}]
[[,] MEDIADESCRIPTION = {text | @text_variable}]
[[,] MEDIANAME = {media_name | @media_name_variable}]
[[,] [NAME = {backup_set_name | @backup_set_name_var}]
[[,] {NOSKIP | SKIP}]
[[,] {NOUNLOAD | UNLOAD}]
[[,] [RESTART]
[[,] STATS [= percentage]]
```

The following is a sample database backup command:

```
BACKUP DATABASE dbExpTrk
TO DISK = N'E:\MSSQL7\BACKUP\dbExpTrkbk'
WITH NOINIT , NOUNLOAD ,
NAME = N'dbExpTrk backup', SKIP , STATS = 10, NOFORMAT
```

Protecting databases from system problems

The backup and restore component of SQL Server provides an important safeguard for protecting critical data stored in SQL Server databases. Back up and restore a database to accomplish the complete restoration of data over a wide range of potential system problems:

◆ **Media failure.** If one or more of the disk drives holding a database fail, you are faced with a complete loss of data unless you can restore an earlier copy of the data.

◆ **User errors.** If a user or application either unintentionally or maliciously makes a large number of invalid modifications to data, the best way to deal with the problem may be to restore the data to a point in time before the modifications were made.

◆ **Permanent loss of a server.** If a server is permanently disabled, or a site is lost to some natural disaster, you may need to activate a warm standby server or restore a copy of a database to another server.

The transaction log is a serial record of all the modifications that have occurred in a database, and which transaction performed each modification. The transaction log is used during recovery operations to roll forward completed transactions, and to roll back (undo) uncompleted transactions.

Backing up a transaction log backs up only the changes that have occurred in the transaction log since the transaction log was last backed up. A backup operates like a fuzzy snapshot taken of a database or transaction log:

♦ A database backup records the complete state of the data in the database at the time the backup operation completes.

♦ A transaction log backup records the state of the transaction log at the time the backup operation starts.

Analyzing backup requirements

When developing a backup plan, you will need to consider your requirements. To do this more insightfully, take a look at the following questions. Your answers may help you to choose the appropriate SQL Server backup methods for your environment.

♦ **How big is the database?** Very large databases are notoriously difficult to manage. The backup and restore processes may take a long time to execute. Always keep in mind the window of time that is available for batch processing such as backing up and restoring.

♦ **How frequently does the data change?** The frequency of data changes has a direct relationship to how often you need to execute a backup on the database in question.

♦ **If data is lost, how vital is your database to the daily operation of the enterprise?** If you back up every day, any crash of the database can easily be restored from the previous day's backup. It is vital that a good plan be in place for the rotation of the daily backup tapes. It is a good idea to have preventive measures in place at all times. In case of loss or damage of online data, production can be restored quickly with minimal or no loss of data.

♦ **How important is it to never lose a change?** In an ideal scenario, we do not want to lose any changes made during that business day. A disaster recovery plan must be in place. This ensures that quick recovery is possible from system failure. For this, a database and transaction log backup plan can be implemented.

♦ **How easy would it be to re-create lost data?** Some data is not possible to re-create, for example a Web transaction, whereas other data is very easy to re-create, for example a list of regions or state codes, because there are many sources of the data available beyond your server.

♦ **What is your critical production window?** The larger the window, the more chance for potential breakdown and therefore the more elaborate the solution required.

◆ **When is the database used most frequently?** For example, a particular database may experience peak use from 8:30 a.m. to 10 a.m. and again from 3 p.m. to 4:30 p.m.

◆ **Is your database used heavily for specific time periods (monthly, quarterly, or specific days or hours)?** In a typical business calendar, certain periods are reserved for heavy transaction processing, for example, payroll processing.

◆ **Will users access the database during backup operations?** It's a good idea that no one should be able to access the database during backup operations, as this may result in inconsistency in data and delay in the backup process.

◆ **How long can you go between transaction log truncations?** This period can optimized once you have gathered statistics during a evaluation period.

◆ **Do you keep a rotating series of backups (grandfather, father, son)?** This approach enables you to restore some data if a backup is lost, or let you restore farther back in time if a problem is not detected for some time after it occurs.

◆ **Is your SQL server in a cluster environment or a multiserver environment?** The time it takes to run backup and restore operations depends partly on the speed of the physical devices (tape or disk) used to store the backups. Backup device vendors can supply performance information to help calculate the approximate time required to back up an entire database. However, the best method for determining the time it takes to run backup and restore operations is to perform realistic tests on the production, or a duplicate, system. For example:

  ▪ Create a database backup of the real system (or a copy of the real system) and time the operation.

  ▪ Create a transaction log backup, after typical transactions that occur in production have been performed, and time the operation.

  ▪ Restore a database backup and time the operation.

  ▪ Apply the transaction log backup and time the operation.

Backing Up Databases

After analyzing your backup requirements, you use the analysis to decide which method of backup will best meet those requirements. Typically, there are three methods most likely to be used for backing up databases:

- Using database backups

- Using database and transaction log backups

- Using database and differential database backups

The method that you choose depends on how much recoverability you need, how quickly you want to back up and restore the database, what size the database is already, and how easy you would like the backup and restore to be. All backups are created on *backup devices*, such as disk or tape media. SQL Server allows you to determine how you want to create your backups on backup devices, such as by overwriting existing backups, or by appending new backups to existing backups (thereby creating a history of backups). These options help you to implement your backup and restore strategy.

The combination of complete database, differential database, and transaction log backups can be used to minimize the recovery time and the amount of potential data loss due to failure.

Creating database backups

If you create database backups and choose not to take separate transaction log backups, the only recovery procedure necessary is to restore the last backup of the database. This re-creates the database as it was when the backup operation completed. However, there is no way to recover any modifications made to the database after the most recently completed database backup.

Some of the characteristics of a system for which you would consider using just database backups include these:

- The importance of the data is low enough that losing any modifications made after the last backup can be tolerated, because it is more efficient to endure the loss and possibly re-create the data manually than to use transaction log backups. For example, a test database used in the development of a database application can tolerate lost data because the data is not vital and can be re-created easily.

- You can easily re-create the data, for example, from batch loads that take place nightly and replace the contents of most of the database.

- You need to implement simple maintenance procedures, for example, because you do not have a database administrator. Maintenance procedures can be simplified further by using the Database Maintenance Plan Wizard.

- Database changes are infrequent, such as to a read-only database.

Backing up a database backs up all the data in the database regardless of whether it changed after the last database backup was created. This means that the entire database backup is self-contained and does not rely on any other backup medium to be restored. But, with a database that is growing in size, it also can mean that the database backup will use more storage space per backup, and consequently take more time to complete with each successive backup operation, compared to using transaction logs and differential database backups.

> When you are creating only database backups, it is recommended that you set the transaction log to be truncated automatically every time a checkpoint occurs in the database by setting the `trunc. log on chkpt.` database option to TRUE. This can help prevent that transaction log from becoming full and having to be manually truncated.

Creating differential backups

A differential database backup saves only the changes that have been made to the database since the last complete database backup. A differential database backup is smaller and takes less time to complete than a database backup.

A differential database backup only allows a database to be restored to the point in time that the backup was created. Typically, this type of backup is augmented by creating frequent transaction log backups after a differential database backup is created.

Creating transaction log backups

If you create both database and transaction log backups, you will be able to restore a database to the exact point of failure, and to minimize, or in some cases eliminate, any loss of data. Transaction log backups generally use fewer resources than complete or differential database backups, so they can be created more frequently than database backups. This frequency of backup reduces the window of time in which a failure could occur after the last successful backup operation was performed, thus drastically reducing the amount of data that could be potentially lost.

Backing up to disk, tape, and named pipe devices

SQL Server backs up databases, transaction logs, and files to backup devices. Backup devices include disk, tape, and named pipe devices.

DISK DEVICES

Disk backup devices are files on hard disks, or other disk storage media, and are the same as regular operating system files. Referring to a disk backup device is exactly the same as referring to any other operating system file. Disk files can be defined on a server's local disk or on a remote disk on a shared network resource, and they can be as big or as small as needed. The maximum file size is equivalent to the free disk space available on the disk.

If the backup is to be performed over the network to a disk on a remote computer, use the universal naming convention (UNC) name in the form *Servername\Sharename\Path\File,* or use a locally redirected drive letter, to specify the location of the file. As with writing files to the local hard disk, the appropriate permissions needed to read or write to the file on the remote disk must be granted to the user account used by SQL Server.

Because backing up data over a network can be subject to error, verify the backup operation after completion.

> Backing up to a file on the same physical disk as the database is not recommended; if the disk device containing the database fails, there is no way to recover the database, because the backup is located on the same failed disk.

TAPE DEVICES

You can use tape backup devices in exactly the same way as disk devices, with two exceptions: 1) the tape device must be physically connected to the computer running SQL Server. Backing up to remote tape devices is not supported. And 2) if a tape backup device is filled during the backup operation, but more data still needs to be written, SQL Server prompts for a new tape and continues the backup operation.

To back up SQL Server (or Microsoft Windows NT) data to tape, use a tape backup device or tape drive supported by Windows NT. Additionally, use only the recommended tapes for the specific tape drive (as suggested by the drive manufacturer). For information on installing a tape drive, see the documentation for Windows NT.

Using media for the first time

When creating a backup on a tape backup device for the first time, SQL Server needs to initialize the backup medium before the backup can be created. Initializing (or formatting) the medium causes a media header (containing information about the medium) to be written and deletes any existing media header, effectively deleting the previous contents of the tape. When the tape has been initialized, previous information on the tape cannot be retrieved.

Initializing disk media only involves the backup device file(s) specified by the backup operation. Other files on the disk are unaffected. When using backup devices for the first time, SQL Server will automatically create the file(s) needed by the backup device(s) for the backup operation. Reinitializing disk backup devices overwrites the contents of the files used by the backup devices and writes a new media header.

Overwriting media

In overwriting backups on media, the existing contents of the backup set are completely overwritten with the new backup and therefore are no longer available. For disk backup media, only the files used by the backup device(s) specified in the backup operation are overwritten; other files on the disk are unaffected. When backups are overwritten, the existing media header can be preserved, and the new backup is created as the first backup on the backup device. If there is no existing media header, a valid media header with an associated media name and media description is automatically written. If the existing media header is invalid, the backup operation aborts.

By default, SQL Server performs some checks to help prevent backup media from being accidentally overwritten. Backup media are not overwritten if either of the following conditions is met:

◆ The expiration dates for the existing backups on the medium have not expired. The expiration date specifies the date the backup expires and can be overwritten by another backup. You can specify the expiration date when a backup is created. By default, the expiration date is determined by the *media retention* option set with `sp_configure`.

◆ The *media name*, if provided, does not match the name on the backup medium. The media name is simply a descriptive name given to easily identify the medium.

However, these checks can be explicitly skipped if you are sure you want to overwrite the existing medium, for example if you know that the backups on the tape are no longer needed.

Appending backup sets to existing media

Backups from the same or different databases, performed at different times, can be stored on the same medium. Additionally, data other than SQL Server data – a foreign backup set, for example – can be stored on the same medium, such as Microsoft Windows NT file backups. When a new *backup set* is appended to an existing medium, the previous contents of the medium remain intact, and the new backup is written after the end of the last backup on the medium. By default, SQL Server appends new backups to media.

When creating a database backup, the backup operation copies only the data in the database to the backup file; it does not copy unused space in the database. Because the database backup only contains the actual data in the database, not any empty space, the database backup is likely to be smaller than the database itself.

If you are only producing database backups, the backup interval should be long enough to keep the backup overhead from impacting production work, yet short enough to prevent the loss of significant amounts of data. Databases that do not contain critical data and have few modifications can be backed up on a weekly or biweekly basis. Data that is more critical or more volatile may need to be backed up daily, or even more frequently. Some databases that are usually read-only may only need to be backed up after a periodic refresh with new data.

It is also prudent to have more than one backup of the database. Have a rotating series of backup media, such that you have two or more versions of the database you can restore. This enables you to address situations where a user may make some incorrect modifications that are not detected for some time, or to fall back to an earlier backup if the backup media are damaged.

Recognizing backup restrictions

Using SQL Server, backup operations can occur while the database is online and in use. However, the following operations are not allowed during a database backup operation:

◆ Creating or deleting database files

◆ Creating indexes

◆ Conducting nonlogged operations

◆ Shrinking a database

If a backup operation is started when one of these operations is in progress, the backup operation aborts. If a backup operation is already in progress and one of these operations is attempted, the operation fails and the backup operation continues.

Implementing a backup

The following is a list of backup operation issues that you need to consider when implementing a backup scheme:

◆ Creating a backup device

◆ Backing up to tape

◆ Transaction log backup

◆ Using differential database backups with transaction log backups

CREATING A BACKUP DEVICE
Here is an example of a Transact-SQL script that creates a backup device:

```
USE master
EXEC sp_addumpdevice
 'disk', 'BackupDev1',
'E:\MSSQL7\Backup\BackupDev1.dat'
```

You can create backup devices by using SQL Enterprise Manager or by using the `sp_adddumpdevice` stored procedure. There are two ways to access the Create New Backup dialog box in SQL Enterprise Manager. You can create a backup device (see Figure 5-1), while managing backup and restoration, from the Database Backup/Restore dialog box of SQL Enterprise Manager, or you can create a backup device directly from the Management folder by selecting the backup device folder and right-clicking it.

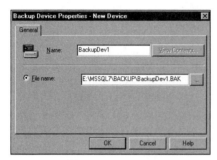

Figure 5-1: SQL Server's Backup Device Properties — New Device

You need to provide:

◆ A device name (the logical name that follows the rules for identifiers and is no longer than 30 characters — longer names are truncated)

◆ The device path (the physical name with full path for file location)

BACKING UP TO TAPE
Here is an example of a script that makes a backup to a tape device:

```
USE dbExpTrk
GO
BACKUP DATABASE dbExpTrk
TO TAPE = '\\.\Tape0'
WITH FORMAT,
NAME = 'Full Backup of Expense Tracking (dbExpTrk)'
GO
```

BACKING UP THE TRANSACTION LOG
To back up the transaction log, you can use the following sample script:

```
USE master
EXEC sp_addumpdevice 'disk', 'BackupDev1',
'E:\MSSQL7\Backup\BackupDev1.dat'
Backup LOG dbExpTrk TO BackupDev1
```

You will need to select the appropriate device type – disk or file. For a tape device, you have the option to skip headers. When the Skip Headers option is selected, SQL Server ignores any existing ANSI tape labels on the specified tape device. The ANSI label of a tape can provide warning information about the expiration date of the tape as well as enforce write permission. When a backup device is added, its logical and physical names are entered in the `sysdevices` tables in the `master` database.

USING SQL ENTERPRISE MANAGER

You can use either SQL Enterprise Manager or the `DUMP` statement to back up your database. (SQL Enterprise Manager cannot be used to back up to floppy disks. You must use the `DUMP` statement.)

You can access the SQL Server Backup dialog box shown in Figure 5-2 by choosing Backup Database from the Tools menu in SQL Enterprise Manager. (Remember to select a server from the Server Manager windows first.)

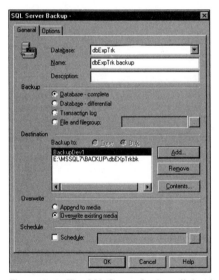

Figure 5–2: The SQL Server Backup dialog box

You can provide or change the following information:

◆ The device type that you want to use for your backup (disk or tape).

◆ The database you want to back up.

◆ Whether SQL Server should back up the complete database (including the transaction log), the changes since the last backup (known as differential), the transaction log, or a file or filegroups. Note that you can only back up the transaction log when it is on a different device from its database.

- ◆ Whether to append to an existing backup or write over the existing data and initialize the backup device.

- ◆ Whether SQL Server should read or skip existing ANSI tape labels.

- ◆ Whether SQL Server should rewind and unload the tape when finished.

- ◆ Whether to set an expiration date for the backup.

- ◆ Whether to execute the backup immediately or schedule it for later execution.

USING DIFFERENTIAL DATABASE BACKUPS WITH TRANSACTION LOG BACKUPS

Using database, differential database, and transaction log backups together can significantly reduce the amount of time it takes to restore a database back to any point in time after the database backup was created. Additionally, creating both differential database (see Figure 5-3) and transaction log backups can increase the robustness of backup procedures in the event that either a transaction log backup or a differential database backup becomes unavailable, for example, due to media failure.

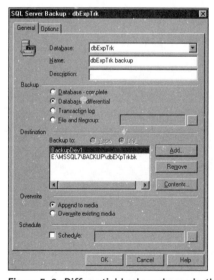

Figure 5-3: Differential backup chosen in the SQL Server Backup dialog box

Here's are excerpts from differential backup scripts:

```
/*Create a full database backup first.*/
BACKUP DATABASE dbExpTrk TO BackupDev1 WITH INIT
GO
```

```
/*Time elapses; you then create a differential
database backup, appending the backup to the same
backup device containing the database backup.*/
BACKUP DATABASE dbExpTrk TO BackupDev1 WITH DIFFERENTIAL
GO
```

Typical backup procedures using database, differential database, and transaction log backups are to create database backups at longer intervals, differential database backups at medium intervals, and transaction log backups at shorter intervals. For example, create database backups weekly, differential database backups daily, and transaction log backups hourly.

If a database needs to be recovered to the point of failure, for example, due to a system failure:

1. Back up the currently active transaction log if the transaction log files for the database are accessible.

2. Restore the last database backup created.

3. Restore the last differential backup created since the database backup was created.

4. Apply all transaction log backups, in sequence, created after the last differential backup was created, finishing with the transaction log backup created in Step 1.

If the active transaction log is not accessible, or the conditions for backing up the active transaction log are not satisfied, it is only possible to restore the database to the point when the last transaction log backup was created.

Using differential database and transaction log backups together to restore a database to the point of failure, the time taken to restore a database is reduced because only the transaction log backups created since the last differential database backup was created need to be applied. If a differential database backup was not created, then all the transaction log backups created since the database was backed up need to be applied.

A mission-critical database system requires that a database backup is created each night at midnight, a differential database backup is created on the hour, Monday through Saturday, and transaction log backups are created every 10 minutes throughout the day. For example, if the database needs to be restored to its state at 5:19 A.M. on Wednesday:

1. Restore the database backup created on Tuesday night.

2. Restore the differential database backup created at 5:00 a.m. on Wednesday.

3. Apply the transaction log backup created at 5:10 a.m. on Wednesday.

4. Apply the transaction log backup created at 5:20 a.m. on Wednesday, specifying that the recovery process only apply transactions that occurred before 5:19 a.m.

Alternatively, if the database needs to be restored to its state at 3:04 a.m. on Thursday, but the differential database backup created at 3:00 a.m. on Thursday is unavailable:

1. Restore the database backup created on Wednesday night.

2. Restore the differential database backup created at 2:00 a.m. on Thursday.

3. Apply all the transaction log backups created from 2:10 A.M. to 3:00 A.M. on Thursday.

4. Apply the transaction log backup created at 3:10 A.M. on Thursday, specifying that the recovery process only apply transactions that occurred before 3:04 A.M.

Scheduling automatic backups

To ensure that your database and logs are regularly backed up, you can use SQL Enterprise Manager to schedule backups. Scheduled backups can be set to occur one time or on a recurring basis. Recurring backups can be set to occur hourly, daily, weekly, or monthly.

To schedule a backup, click the Schedule button in the SQL Server Backup dialog box. This displays the Edit Schedule dialog box shown in Figure 5-4.

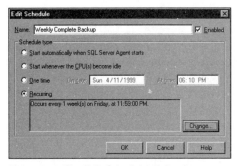

Figure 5-4: The Edit Schedule dialog box

You can provide or change the name for your scheduled backup task and when to execute the task. This can be either when the SQL Server Agent starts, when the CPU(s) become idle, once at a specific date and time, or on a recurring basis.

If you choose Recurring, you will need to decide:

◆ Whether you want to execute your backup with daily, weekly, or monthly frequency. Then you select the number of times the task will execute for the chosen frequency. For example, you can choose to execute the backup every five hours, every day, every three days, once a week on Sunday, once every week on Saturday, once a month on the first day of the month, and so on.

◆ When you would like to start your recurring backup schedule and when you would like to stop it. You can leave the End Date blank to set an unlimited duration.

MONITORING, MODIFYING, OR CREATING A SCHEDULED BACKUP

Using SQL Enterprise Manager, you can schedule a backup for one-time or recurring execution at the time you define in the Database Backup/Restore dialog box. SQL Enterprise Manager then creates a scheduled backup task. Once you do this, the scheduled backups cannot be monitored, modified, or canceled from the Database Backups/Restore dialog box. You must use the Task Scheduling window.

When using the Task Scheduling window, be aware that this window displays all tasks that are defined on the server — not just backup tasks. By default, SQL Enterprise generates the name of a backup task using the following form:

```
BACKUP - database_name
```

The user who scheduled the backup could have changed this name from the default. Also, a backup task has a type of TSQL, which indicates that the task is a scheduled execution of a Transact-SQL statement.

RESTORING A DATABASE BACKUP

Restoring a database backup returns the database to the same state it was in when the backup was created. When restoring a database, SQL Server automatically re-creates the database and all of its associated files by performing these steps:

1. All of the data from the backup is copied into the database; the rest of the database is created as empty space.

2. Any incomplete transactions in the database backup (transactions that were not complete when the backup operation originally completed) are undone (rolled back) to ensure that the database remains consistent.

This process ensures that the restored database is a copy of the database as it existed when the backup operation completed, except that all incomplete transactions have been rolled back. This is required to restore the integrity of the database.

Additionally, to prevent unintentionally overwriting a database, the restore operation can automatically perform a safety check. The restore operation fails if:

◆ The database already exists on the server and the database name does not match the database name recorded in the backup set.

◆ The set of files in the database does not match the set contained in the backup set, excluding any difference in file size.

These safety checks can be disabled if the intention is to overwrite another database.

INTERRUPTING BACKUP AND RESTORE OPERATIONS

If a backup or restore operation is interrupted, it is possible to restart the backup or restore operation from the point it was interrupted. This can be useful if very large databases are automatically restored onto other servers. If this automatic process fails, a system administrator can restart the restore operation from where it left off, rather than restarting the restore process from the beginning.

To restore a specific backup set, specify the position number of the backup set you want to restore. For example, to restore the second SQL Server backup set, the fourth backup set on the medium, specify 4 as the backup set to restore.

Restoring Databases

Restoring a database backup returns the database to the same state it was in when the backup was created. Any incomplete transactions in the database backup (transactions that were not complete when the backup operation originally completed) are undone (rolled back) to ensure that the database remains consistent.

Restoring a transaction log backup reapplies all completed transactions that are in the transaction log to the database. When applying a transaction log backup, SQL Server first reads forward through the transaction log, rolling forward all of the completed transactions in the transaction log. When SQL Server reaches the end of the transaction log, it has re-created the exact state of the database at the time the backup operation started. The restore operation then rolls back all transactions that were incomplete when the backup operation started.

Analyzing restore requirements

Before you need to recover data from a backup, you should take the time to develop a restore procedure. Don't forget that restore procedures are needed for normal day-to-day operations and for recovery from data loss. When creating a plan, consider the following:

◆ Should backup media be stored onsite or offsite? How will this affect the time taken to recover from failure?

◆ What are the probable effects of losing a backup set or backup medium, such as a tape? Are other recovery procedures in place to eliminate or minimize the effects of losing backup media?

◆ How do you recover from data loss?

◆ How long does it take to restore the full database and apply any applicable transaction logs?

RESTORING A DATABASE AND ITS LOG

When restoring a database from a backup and its transaction log, keep in mind the following:

◆ When a database is restored from a backup, that database must not be in use. Any data in the specified database is replaced by the restored data.

◆ If you are restoring a database because of media failure, you must first drop the damaged database. You can use the DROP DATABASE command, DBCC, or the sp_dbremove system procedure. Then re-create the database and restore it from a backup.

◆ Restoring a transaction log results in re-execution of the changes it contains and in rolling back any transactions that were uncommitted when the transaction log was backed up.

◆ Backups of the transaction log must be restored in the sequence in which they were made. SQL Server checks the time stamps on each backed-up database and transaction log to see that the sequence is correct.

◆ Transaction logs can be restored through a date and time that you specify. Transactions committed after the date and time will be rolled back. Point-in-time recovery applies to transaction log restores only (not to full database or table restore).

◆ If you create a database using the FOR LOAD option and then restore the database backup, the database status will still be set to dbo use only. Therefore, before your users can access the database, you must turn off the dbo use only option.

AUTOMATIC RECOVERY

Automatic recovery is, as its name implies, automatic. It is initiated every time SQL Server is started and checks to see if any recovery is necessary.

Automatic recovery ensures that all transactions completed before a system crash are physically written to the database and that the effects of all uncommitted transactions are removed from the database. A system crash refers to the system losing power (the medium remains intact). Automatic recovery cannot be turned off. Whenever SQL Server is restarted, recovery is performed automatically on each database. This does the following:

♦ Rolls back uncommitted transactions, those that were ongoing at the time SQL Server was shut down or when the system failed.

♦ Checks the transactions that had been committed between the last checkpoint and the failure and then rolls them forward.

In each database, the automatic recovery mechanism looks at the transaction log. If the log has committed transactions not yet written out to the database, it performs those transactions again. This action is known as rolling forward.

Automatic recovery begins with the `master` database, goes on to `model`, clears out the `tempdb` temporary database, recovers `msdb`, recovers `pubs`, recovers `distribution` (if the server is configured as a replication distributor), and, finally, recovers the user database. Users log into SQL Server when the system database has been recovered, but they cannot access a user database while recovery is in progress.

Two configuration options are relevant to automatic recovery:

♦ The recovery flags option, which determines what information SQL Server displays during recovery

♦ The recovery interval option, which controls the maximum time required to recover a database by setting the interval at which SQL Server decides whether to run an automatic checkpoint

These two options are set by using SQL Enterprise Manager or the `sp_configure` system procedure.

You can restore a database using SQL Enterprise Manager or the `LOAD` statement. If you restore a database from floppy disks, you must use the `LOAD` statement.

To restore a database using SQL Enterprise Manager:

1. In the left side of the Console Root dialog box, expand a server group, expand a server, and expand Databases.

2. Right-click the database, point to All Tasks, and then click Restore Database. This will display the dialog box seen in Figure 5-5.

3. On the General tab, in the Restore as database field, select the name of the database to restore if different from the default displayed. To create a new database and restore the database to this new one, enter the new name for the database.

4. Select Database.

5. In the First backup to restore list, select the backup set to restore.

6. In the Restore list, you can select the database backup to restore.

7. On the Options tab, in Restore as, enter the new name or location for each database file in the database backup.

8. Click OK.

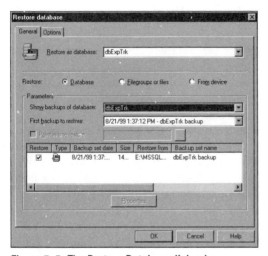

Figure 5–5: The Restore Database dialog box

To restore a database using the LOAD statement, use the following command syntax:

```
LOAD DATABASE dbname
    FROM dump_device[, dump_device2 [...,dump_device32] ]
[WITH options]
```

To load a transaction log:

```
LOAD TRANSACTION dbname
    FROM dump_device[, dump_device2 [...,dump_device32] ]
```

To load a table:

```
LOAD [ [database. ]owner.]table_name
    FROM dump_device[, dump_device2 [...,dump_device32] ]
    [WITH options]
```

To load header information:

```
LOAD HEADERONLY FROM dumpdevice
```

Identifying a backup set to restore

Each backup set on media, including foreign backup sets such as Windows NT file backups, is numbered, enabling you to easily reference the backup set you want restored. To restore a specific set, specify its position number on the medium. For example, to restore the third backup set on the medium, specify 3 on the restore.

Restoring the master database

Because so much of SQL Server activity is controlled by the `master` database, a database corruption or the loss of the `master` database can be devastating. This makes the `master` database a good candidate for mirroring.

A damaged `master` makes itself known either through an inability to start SQL Server, by segmentation faults or input/output errors, and/or in a report from the Database Consistency Checker (DBCC).

The procedure used to recover a damaged `master` database is different from the procedure used to recover user databases. If the `master` database becomes unusable, it must be re-created using SQL Setup and restored from a previous backup. Any changes made to the `master` database since the last backup are lost when the backup is restored, and therefore they must be reapplied.

To recover a damaged `master` database:

1. Use the SQL Setup program to rebuild the `master` database. You must rebuild the `master` database using the same character set and sort order as in the `master` database backup that will be restored. You must also use the same SQL Server installation path and location, name, and size of the existing `MASTER` device.

2. Add a backup device (unless the backup will be restored from floppy disks).

3. Restart SQL Server in a single-user mode.

4. Restore the `master` database from the most recent backup.

Copying Databases

The backup and restore features of SQL Server enable you to easily duplicate a database locally or remotely. The duplicated database can be used for testing, standalone application software development, or running reports. These duplicate databases could also be used to reduce contention for the single copy of the database by having duplicate databases copied to other SQL Server machines and being accessed by resource-intensive processes.

Although this technique is no substitute for full data replication, it can be very useful for creating standby servers or for copying production databases to a test or development environment.

Be aware that the server-to-server copy feature is only possible if the following criteria are satisfied:

◆ The code page/character set, sort order, Unicode collation, and Unicode locale used by SQL Server on both computers are the same.

◆ The database backup is from SQL Server version 7.

Other methods for copying data from one server running SQL Server to another include using:

◆ The Data Transformation Services import and export wizards to copy and modify data between any ODBC, OLE DB, or text data source and SQL Server

◆ The bcp utility to copy data between SQL Server and a data file, using native, character, or Unicode mode

◆ The INSERT statement, using a distributed query as the select list to extract data from another data source

The following is a list of steps required to copy a database from one server to another server:

1. Make sure that both SQL Servers are using the same code page/character set, sort order, Unicode collation, and Unicode locale.

2. Back up the database from the source SQL Server.

3. Create backup devices, if necessary, at the destination SQL Server.

4. Copy the backup devices from the source server to the destination server.

5. Restore the database backup to the destination server using the backup devices, if necessary.

When a database is restored to another server, the SQL Server login or Windows NT user who executes the restore operation by default becomes the owner of the new database. This can be changed once the database is restored.

Re-creating database files

When restoring a database, the process automatically creates all of the files needed to restore the data. No files or databases need to be created beforehand. By default, the files created by SQL Server during the restore use the same name and path as the backup files from the original database server. So it is useful to know in advance what files will be automatically created by the restore operation, because:

◆ The filenames may already exist on the server. This will cause an error.

- ◆ The directory structure or drive mapping may not exist on the server. For example, the backup contains a file that it needs to restore to e:\ mssql7\data\orderdb, but the destination server may not have this directory or it may not even have drive e:!

- ◆ If the database files are allowed to be replaced, then any existing database and files with the same names as those in the backup are overwritten, unless those files belong to a different database.

If you find that the database backup cannot be easily restored onto the destination server because of these reasons, then you can move the files to a new location as they are being restored. For example:

- ◆ It may be necessary to restore some of the database files in the backup to a different drive because of configuration or capacity differences.

- ◆ When creating a copy of an existing database on the same server, you will notice that the database files for the original database already exist, so different names need to be specified when the database copy is created during the restore operation.

Changing the database name

You can change the actual name of the database when the database is restored to the server, without having to restore the database first and then change the name manually. For example, you can change the database name from OrderEntry to OrderEntry2 to indicate that this is a second copy of an existing database.

The database name explicitly supplied when restoring a database is automatically used as the new database name. Because the database name does not already exist, a new one is created using the files in the backup.

Copying databases from earlier versions

Unfortunately, it is not possible to directly restore a database backup from earlier versions of SQL Server. The backup format from SQL Server 6.5 or earlier is incompatible with SQL Server 7. But to convert a database from SQL Server 6.5 or earlier to SQL Server 7.0, you can consider one of the following alternatives:

- ◆ Use the bcp utility to copy data from SQL Server 6.5 or earlier to a data file, and then copy the data from the data file into SQL Server 7.

- ◆ Use the Data Transformation Services import and export wizards to copy data from one SQL Server directly to another.

- ◆ Upgrade SQL Server to 7. Any databases are automatically upgraded. New backups from the upgraded server running SQL Server can now be restored into another server running SQL Server 7.

Summary

This chapter has covered the DBMS administration tasks of performing the most common of the backup procedures: complete backup, differential backup, and transaction log backup. The chapter has covered the various ways to restore data from a backup and how to recover from a corrupted `master` database. The chapter has also covered how to copy data from one server to another, and how these common DBMS tasks can be scheduled to run automatically.

Chapter 6

Database Administration Using Enterprise Manager

IN THIS CHAPTER

- ◆ Creating and maintaining an application database using Enterprise Manager
- ◆ Application database components
- ◆ Database dictionaries and SQL Server catalogs
- ◆ Basic application database administration

THE HUB OF THE TYPICAL application is the database. Before we move on to technical material, let's look briefly at the administrative issues. Most organizations have several database administrators, who design, implement, and manage data on one or more DBMSs. Responsibilities of the database administrator include design and construction of database objects, performance monitoring, tuning, and data security. This chapter describes how you can design, administer, and manage the database from within Enterprise Manager as well as introducing other tools that you can use to design and maintain databases.

Data Administration

In the 1980s, a new organizational role emerged within information services; it was commonly known as *data administration*. Analysts who are primarily concerned with modeling the business conduct data administration. Despite the similarity of names, this activity is quite different from database administration. Database administration addresses the physical components of the database: tables, indices, and any other physical database devices. The data administrator does not focus on a specific database and DBMS. The emphasis is on early life-cycle phases (analysis) and a global view of data. Responsibilities include naming standards, data models that cut across organizational boundaries, and long-range planning. Nowadays, most large organizations have a data administration function, perhaps under a different job title. We address functions of both data administration (analysis) and database administration (design, construction, and maintenance). As you saw in our discussion of the development life cycle, all these activities are related and covered by the term "database design."

Dictionaries and System Catalog Tables

Both data administrators and database administrators rely on a *dictionary* to document their designs and models. A dictionary stores data about your data: table specifications, columns, indexes, and even specifications for application software and hardware. Difficulties with early data dictionaries involved problems in translating the dictionary meta-data into usable development objects (for example, a data definition language). Because the dictionary database is one level above the humble operational database, it is sometimes called a meta-database or system catalog. Some CASE (computer aided software engineering) tools bridge the translation gap. SQL Server has its own System Catalog Tables, which are a form of dictionary database. They can be populated from CASE-like vendor tools such as ERwin (entity-relationship modeling in Windows) and PowerDesigner (a database modeling tool from Sybase). These catalog tables augment the RDBMS system catalog tables to provide data that can describe rules for editing, validating, and displaying database table and column information.

There are many alternate terms for a dictionary. Vendors of CASE tools often refer to the internal CASE dictionary as an encyclopedia or repository. "Repository" is more or less synonymous to "encyclopedia." RDBMSs have an internal catalog that contains limited but critical data about user tables, columns, indexes, and security. Although these terms differ in some respects, they all maintain meta-data, which is data about your data. If you are using a tool such as ERwin or LBMS, you can use the logical model to create the DDL to define the database.

Dictionaries may either be online or offline to development and production systems. A dictionary that is actively referenced during data entry is *dynamic*. One that is offline and used strictly for documentation is *passive*. An *active* dictionary is online to development, but not to production systems. For example, SilverStream uses a relational database to store all application components, even the Java Source, for an application. For the past few years, the technology has been moving toward active dictionaries.

Now what do we do with this data dictionary meta-data? In basic relational design, we convert data dictionary entities, relationships, and attributes to physical database tables, foreign keys, and columns. Our goal is simply to move from the language of analysis suitable for client interviews to the language of relational databases demanded by the computer. If the tools and methods used do not produce this result, this fact will severely impact the development. Ensure that proper target SQL Server translation is possible before proceeding with a particular data dictionary tool. Otherwise, all the analysis work will amount to a lost effort and a waste of time and resources.

Physical Database Objects

For the purposes of this discussion, we will assume that you have a dictionary of some kind. This is your database for the development effort: It stores all information about your emerging design. Once we start to get physical, the application's database will consist of the following components:

◆ **Tables and columns.** These are the basic building blocks of a database. They should be grouped by usage and named in a standard way. For example, all tables referring to employees should be placed in close proximity in a large model, and they should have a name like TBEMP_xxx. They start off as entities and attributes in the logical model, where they are arranged to satisfy the business processes. Development of a large application will usually begin with a CASE tool that will be used to develop the entity-relationship diagram whose entities and attributes will be converted to physical tables and columns. Conversion to the physical model requires an understanding of the target Microsoft SQL Server. ERwin, a third-party tool, can convert a logical model into any one of fifteen physical DBMSs, including but not limited to Microsoft SQL Server as well as Sybase, Oracle, DB2, and Informix.

◆ **Indexes.** These, as the name implies, provide a way to search and sometimes control the data rows within a table. One or more columns can be grouped to form an index. Most tables should have a unique index that can serve not only as a search mechanism but also as a control to avoid duplication. For example, a table containing employee information should use a unique index to ensure that information about a particular employee is not entered twice. An index may also be *clustered* to establish the physi-cal placement of inserted rows in a specified order. For example, at a television station an acquired television series will include one or more episodes. A clustered unique index for the episode table might be series_code and episode_code concatenated together. This would group all of a series' episodes on database pages stored in close proximity, which would speed up any access involving all of the episodes within a series.

◆ Keys (primary and foreign). Keys are indexes that provide for database integrity. For example, a network television station showing *Leave It to*

Beaver reruns might have a `series` table. The `series` table would have a "primary" key of `series_code`. The primary key is typically a unique table row identifier. It also establishes the first part of the key in any dependent table — for example, episodes belong to and depend on a series. The `episode` table would have a "foreign" key of `series_code` to connect the episode to the series and also to ensure that a series cannot be deleted if any episodes belonging to the series exist. Design tools such as ERwin can be used to define the database logical model and also create the physical components, including the referential definitions required to enforce database integrity.

◆ **Views.** The name *view* describes its object's function: to provide a particular view of base tables. Views are virtual tables, which are made up of columns from one or more tables that are usually joined by the same key or keys that they share in common. Views facilitate access to the data. They can provide security as well. For example, you may restrict the selection of employee column data, such as salary. Views containing columns from more than one table are not updatable.

Of particular importance are the data types that are supported by each DBMS. The database design and physical manifestation must consider which data types are available in the target DBMS. For example, date and time data types vary widely from DBMS to DBMS. We will review data types in detail later in Chapter 11, "Constructing the Database," which discusses data definition language.

Microsoft SQL Server Enterprise Manager

Database administrators had been waiting for a comprehensive database administration and maintenance software interface for a long time. In the last two or three years, a plethora of menu- and GUI-based software has provided help. Tools such as Embarcadero's DB Artisan go a long way in facilitating database administration. It provides a point-and-click capability for performing database maintenance and backup. Microsoft is also strong in GUI interfaces, and SQL Server's GUI administration tool, Enterprise Manager, a forerunner of DBArtisan, has been one of the big reasons for SQL Server's emergence as the second most popular RDBMS after Oracle.

The Microsoft SQL Server Enterprise Manager is a graphical tool that provides for easy, enterprise-wide configuration and management of Microsoft SQL Server and SQL Server objects. Using Enterprise Manager (see Figure 6-1), you can easily manage databases across the servers of your enterprise. Providing a fairly intuitive and simple-to-use graphical interface, Enterprise Manager enables you to add, list, monitor, modify, expand, and drop databases and perform management actions for the associated transaction logs. Notably, databases can also be managed using Transact-SQL statements and system procedures.

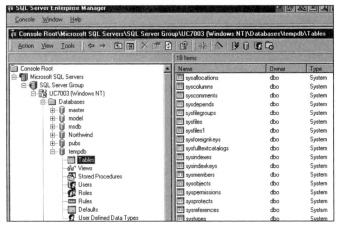

Figure 6-1: The SQL Server Enterprise Manager

SQL Server Enterprise Manager provides:

◆ A scheduling engine

◆ Administrator alert capability

◆ Drag-and-drop control operations across multiple servers

◆ A built-in replication management interface

You can also use SQL Server Enterprise Manager to:

◆ Manage logins, permissions, and users

◆ Create scripts

◆ Manage databases

◆ Back up databases and transaction logs

◆ Manage tables, views, stored procedures, triggers, indexes, rules, defaults, and user-defined data types

Enterprise Manager provides many enhanced features. You can restore data in a database to a specified point in time. You can easily transfer objects from one server to another. External tools can be added to the Enterprise Manager toolbar. Enterprise Manager for SQL Server 7 also administers SQL Server 6.0 and 6.5

servers. (Enterprise Manager for SQL Server 6.5 cannot administer SQL Server 7 servers. To connect to a SQL Server 7 server, you must upgrade to a SQL Server 7 client installation.)

Building a Physical Database

In Enterprise Manager, depending upon your level of permission, you are able to create, maintain, and monitor all of the objects that make up the organization's SQL Server environment. This includes databases, tables, indices, users, filegroups, and stored procedures. This chapter will step you through the development lifecycle to illustrate some of this functionality.

Creating and maintaining a database

Before you create a SQL Server database, review the application and perform tasks such as the following:

◆ Size the database by calculating how much physical storage will be required in the first year of database use.

◆ Choose a standard name: Use the local site's naming convention to name your database; see Appendix B, "Standards, Guidelines, and Maxims," for some examples.

◆ Specify the name and path of the database you are creating.

MS SQL databases in prior releases resided on database devices. Microsoft SQL Server version 7.0 maps a database over a set of operating system files. Data and log information are never mixed on the same file, and individual files are used by only one database. SQL Server 7.0 databases have three types of files:

◆ **Primary data files.** The primary data file is the starting point of the database and points to the rest of the files in the database. Every database has one primary data file. The recommended file extension for primary data files is .mdf.

◆ **Secondary data files.** Secondary data files comprise all of the data files other than the primary data file. Some databases may not have any secondary data files, whereas others have multiple secondary data files. The recommended file extension for secondary data files is .ndf.

◆ **Log files.** Log files hold all of the log information used to recover the database. There must be at least one log file for each database, although there can be more than one. The recommended file extension for log files is .ldf.

SQL Server 7 does not enforce the .mdf, .ndf, and .ldf file extensions, but these extensions are recommended to help identify the use of the file. SQL Server 7 files have two names:

♦ The *logical_file_name* is a name used to refer to the file in all Transact-SQL statements. The logical filename must conform to the rules for SQL Server identifiers and must be unique to the database.

♦ The *os_file_name* is the name of the physical file. It must follow the rules for Microsoft Windows NT or Microsoft Windows 95/98 filenames.

Each database has an associated *transaction log*. This log is a storage area reserved by SQL Server to keep track of transactions made to the database. The transaction logs for SQL Server are *write ahead,* which means that the commands sent to SQL Server are recorded in the log before any of the data in the database is changed. This guarantees that we can recover if there is a failure in the main database write. The transaction log is actually another System Catalog Table, *syslogs,* but you should not directly query or modify it. The transaction log competes with data for space on a database device. It is fairly common knowledge among DBAs that to improve performance you put the transaction log on a separate database filegroup from the database.

DATABASE SETUP ISSUES

Database files can be grouped together in filegroups for allocation and administration purposes. Some systems can improve their performance by controlling the placement of data and indexes onto specific disk drives. Filegroups can aid this process. The system administrator can create filegroups for each disk drive and then assign specific tables; indexes; or `text`, `ntext`, or `image` data from a table to specific filegroups. No file can be a member of more than one filegroup. Tables; indexes; and `text`, `ntext`, and `image` data can be associated with a filegroup, in which case all their pages will be allocated in that filegroup. Log files are never a part of a filegroup. Log space is managed separately from data space. Files in a filegroup will not autogrow unless no space is available on any of the files in the filegroup.

There are three types of filegroups:

♦ **Primary.** The primary filegroup contains the primary data file and any other files not put into another filegroup. All pages for the system tables are allocated in the primary filegroup.

♦ **User-defined.** User-defined filegroups are any filegroups specified using the `FILEGROUP` keyword in a `CREATE DATABASE` or `ALTER DATABASE` statement.

♦ **Default.** The default filegroup contains the pages for all tables and indexes that do not have a filegroup specified when they are created. In each database, only one filegroup at a time can be the default filegroup.

Members of the db_owner fixed database role can switch the default filegroup from one filegroup to another. If no default filegroup was specified, choice defaults to the primary filegroup.

SQL Server 7 can work quite effectively without filegroups, so many systems will not need to specify user-defined filegroups. In this case, all files are included in the primary filegroup and SQL Server 7 can effectively allocate data within the database. Filegroups are not the only method that can be used to distribute I/O across multiple drives.

Members of the db_owner fixed database role can back up and restore individual files or filegroups instead of backing up or restoring an entire database.

CREATING A DATABASE

You add a database using Enterprise Manager or the CREATE DATABASE statement. This chapter describes the use of SQL Enterprise Manager. For information about using CREATE DATABASE and other statements, see Chapter 11, "Constructing the Database."

Creating a database allocates storage space for the database on a filegroup. When you create a database, a transaction log is also created to record all transactions performed on that database. Store the transaction log on a different filegroup from the database to simplify recovery and to improve performance. If you do not specify a different device, the log is created as part of the database.

To create a database using Enterprise Manager:

1. From the Server Manager window, select a server; then from the toolbar, choose the Databases button. Right-click, and a pop-up menu appears.

2. Choose the New Database button. The New Database window appears (see Figure 6-2).

3. In the Name box, type a name for the database. The name must comply with the SQL Server rules for identifiers.

4. From the list in the Filegroup box, select a database filegroup on which to place the data. When you open the New Database window, the Data Filegroup box is automatically filled with the name of the first PRIMARY filegroup. If you do not change the entry, that filegroup is used.

5. In the Maximum File Size box, either accept the default or click the Restrict file growth radio button and then type in the amount of space, in megabytes, to allocate on that filegroup for the database. If the size you request is unavailable, Enterprise Manager displays a message showing how much space is available.

Figure 6-2: Create a new database.

6. In the Maximum File Size box, you can also choose to have SQL Server "grow" your database for you by choosing the default "Unrestricted File Growth." See the group box on the bottom of Figure 6-2.

7. Click OK. The database is added.

As all of the attributes of the newly created database are stored in the master database, it is important that you back up the master database each time you create a database. This makes recovery of application databases easier and safer in case the master database is later damaged.

In addition to storing attributes in SQL Server's master database, the physical database is initialized, which means the database's physical storage is formatted by SQL Server. Part of the storage is reserved by SQL Server's internal procedures to track allocation and capacity. When a database is created and the space allocation is specified for the database, SQL Server initializes every bit in the database to 0 (except for the allocation page for each 256-page block). However, if a filegroup has not previously contained data, then the filegroup will not be reinitialized, and database creation time is significantly reduced.

The creation of a new database is recorded in the System Catalog Table, *sysdatabases*. In Figure 6-3, notice that the database DBMSDETS has a database ID of 7 as well as other attributes. Entries are also made in the System Catalog Table, *sysusages,* which keeps track of the space allocated to databases.

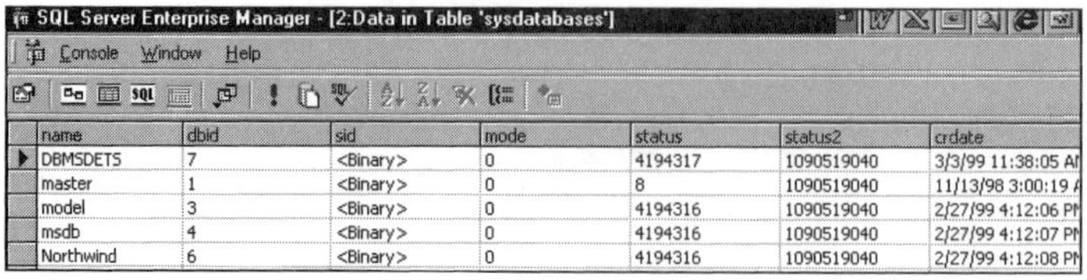

Figure 6-3: The new database as a row in the catalog table

Creating a table

Once your database has been created, you can begin to add the tables and columns that will house your application data. The Enterprise Manager provides graphic as well as batch interfaces for creating the tables and columns. We will step through the basic tasks that precede the table definition.

ANALYZING THE DATA

Your organization may use the entity-relationship approach to data analysis. Entity-relationship has two major advantages. First, it is very close to natural language. An entity is like a noun, a relationship is like a verb, and an attribute is like a prepositional phrase. This makes it easy to convert information gleaned in an interview with the user into a data model. Second, most CASE tools have adopted this approach. Learning entity-relationship is good preparation for CASE. An entity is a person, place, object, concept, activity, or event of interest to your organization. You can determine entities within an application by listening for important nouns during interviews with the users.

An entity type is a set of objects. TV Series and Episode are each different entity types. An entity instance is an element of the set. The series, *Leave It to Beaver* and the episode, "Beaver Flunks Math" are instances of entity types.

Entity types usually become tables in relational design. Entity instances usually become rows. However, entities and tables are not identical. You may split an entity into several tables for better performance. Alternatively, you may merge several entities in one table. Occasionally, entities are listed merely for documentation and disappear in relational design.

DESIGNING TABLES

The formal definition of a table according to relational godfathers, E.F. Codd and C.J. Date, consists of two parts: a heading and a body. The *heading* is the specification for the table and does not change in time. The *body,* or contents of the table, is a time-varying set of rows. Each row is a set of column-value pairs.

This definition has three important consequences. Most significantly, a table is defined as a set of rows, and each row is defined as a set of column-value pairs. Because elements of a set are not ordered, the rows and columns of a table have no logical order. It is impossible to refer to the "fourth row" of a table in SQL, for example, or the "second column." Of course rows and columns are ordered internally on storage media, but this physical order is always invisible to the user in a relational DBMS. This is called *physical data independence.*

In addition, sets may not contain duplicate elements. Consequently, tables may not contain duplicate rows or column names, in theory. In practice most systems allow unstructured tables with duplicate rows, but this is not particularly useful. After all, it is impossible to distinguish duplicate rows. One could not delete the "first" duplicate and retain the "second," because rows have no logical order. In practice, as well as in theory, tables should have unique primary keys and therefore cannot have duplicate rows.

Third, the definition implies that each row-column cell contains exactly one value, not several. This point is fundamental to database design. It means that plural attributes are harder to implement than singular attributes. Sometimes a column is denormalized into a repeating value, that is, an array for performance purposes. Natural arrays are the best because they do not change in time. For example, there will always be seven days in a week, and twelve months in a year. A table with seven columns, each representing a day of the week, may reduce the physical I/O by 84 percent. This means you get all the data in one access instead of seven. Moreover, it may reduce the physical storage required as well.

Besides naming a column and choosing its data type, we must decide if the column is a required field for our application. If it is not required, then it can be null. A concept of the relational data structure is the *null value.* A null is a special symbol that means either *unknown* or *inapplicable.* These two meanings are different – a null social security number for an employee means *unknown,* presumably, but a null commission for a salesperson means *inapplicable.* Regardless of meaning, null is always represented as the same symbol, NULL. This symbol is the same regardless of data type – NULL is used for integers and characters alike. With null values, a new arithmetic and logic is necessary. What is the value of the expression 10 + null? In SQL the answer is null, or unknown. What about 10 > null? Again, the answer is null. In fact, any arithmetic or comparative expression involving null evaluates to null.

CREATING THE TABLE WITHIN ENTERPRISE MANAGER
Although, in a large environment, a central database administration group does table definition, we will review the process using Enterprise Manager. This exercise will also give developers (new to SQL) a sense of how database objects are created and maintained. You can create permanent tables or temporary tables. SQL Server supports two types of temporary tables: local and global. A *local temporary table* is visible only to the connection that created it. A *global temporary table* is available to all connections. Local temporary tables are automatically dropped at the end of the current session. Global temporary tables are dropped at the end of the last session using the table (normally, this is when the session that created the table ends).

When you create a table, you name its columns and supply a data type for each column. You also specify whether or not a particular column can hold null values.

In SQL Enterprise Manager's Server Manager window, select the database in which you want to create the table, select Tables or Objects, click the right mouse button, and then choose New Table (see Figure 6-4).

You can also use the CREATE TABLE statement. See Chapter 12, "Manipulating the Data," or use the INTO option of the SELECT statement to copy data from an existing table into the newly created table.

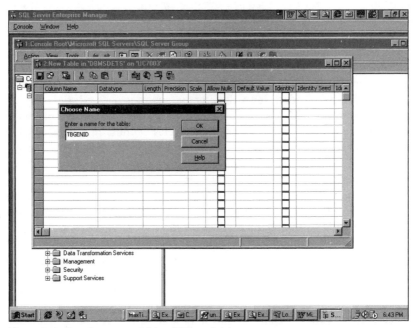

Figure 6-4: Creating a new table within a database

You can define up to 1,024 columns per table. Table and column names must follow the rules for identifiers; they must be unique within a given table, but you can use the same column name in different tables in the same database. You must define a data type for each column. See Figure 6-5, which includes a column for each of the more popular data types. For details on choosing data types, see Chapter 11.

Column Name	Datatype	Length	Precision	Scale	Allow Nulls	Default Value	Identity	Identity Seed	Idı
gen_id	int	4	10	0			✓	1	1
gen_char	char	16	0	0	✓	(joe bambara)			
gen_dte	datetime	8	0	0	✓	(12/31/1999)			
gen_dec_num	decimal	13	28	0	✓	(100000)			
gen_nchar	nchar	4000	0	0	✓				
gen_varchar	varchar	8000	0	0	✓				
gen_ts	timestamp	8	0	0					
gen_image	image	16	0	0	✓				

Figure 6-5: Creating columns in a table

Creating indices

Data in tables has both a relational order and a physical order. The relational order of values is the usual arithmetic sequence for numbers, or dictionary sequence for character data. The physical order of rows in a table is the combination of the sequence of pages on the disk drive and the sequence of rows within each page. Of course, disk drives are not serial devices; pages are spread across tracks and around sectors.

A table is *clustered* on a column when the physical order of rows matches the relational order of values in the column. For example, SERIES is clustered on SERIES_CDE. In some database systems, clustering can be imperfect – a table is considered clustered even when some rows are on the wrong page. Some databases maintain a cluster ratio or the percentage of rows that are clustered.

An *index* on a column is a list of column values, with the associated pointers to the location of the row containing each value. A *composite index* is defined over several columns. A *clustering index,* sometimes called a *primary index,* is defined on a clustering column, ideally a column that has a uniform distribution of values with which to group rows together for common or fast access. A *nonclustering index,* sometimes called a *secondary index,* is not defined on a clustering column. A *dense index* contains one entry for each row of the table. A *nondense* index contains one entry for each page of the table containing both a low and a high index value for the particular page. Nondense indexes are possible only on clustered columns, and they have a great advantage over dense indexes because they have far fewer entries and therefore occupy fewer pages. As a result, they are more efficient. In Microsoft SQL Server, for example, clustering indexes are nondense. In some other database systems, rows may be out of sequence, so a clustering index must be dense.

How does this structure handle insertions and updates? SQL Server places a new row on the correct page according to its clustering column. If this page is full, it splits in two to create free space, and a new entry is inserted at the bottom level of the index. If this index page is full, it splits in two to create more space, and a new entry is necessary in the bottom level of the index. If this index page is full, it splits to create more space, and another entry is necessary at the next higher level of the index. In the worst case, these splits propagate all the way through the top of the index, and a new level is created. Because the new level is created at the top of the index, all branches of the index tree are always the same length. Consequently, this kind of index is often called a B-tree. The "B" stands for "balanced." In theory, the system could reverse the process when rows are deleted, merging pages and reducing the index. However, Microsoft and other vendors do not support this because deletions are less frequent than insertions.

When a table does not have a clustering index, new rows are inserted at the end of the table. When a row is deleted, the empty slot is not reused until the table is physically reorganized. Because there is no clustering index, rows remain in order of initial load or insertion. Because no meaningful order is maintained, this structure has limited utility. It is useful for tables of five pages or less; after all, if a table is small, the system can scan it quickly without an index. It is also useful for archival or temporary tables.

A table can have only one clustering index, but any number of nonclustering indexes. Nonclustering indexes are necessarily dense. When and how can nonclustering indexes accelerate queries? A critical factor is the percentage of rows selected by a query, variously known as the *hit ratio,* filter factor, or selectivity. When the hit ratio is high, nonclustering indexes are useless. For example, suppose we set up a nonclustering index on the holiday column within the TV EPISODE table. The holiday column contains a code that lets us know which episodes have a holiday theme (for example, Halloween). Suppose we select all episodes not associated with a holiday. The hit ratio is quite high; most or all pages contain qualifying rows because most days are not holidays. It is faster to ignore the index and scan the entire table. In contrast, if we select all episodes associated with Halloween, the hit ratio is low. Less than five percent of episodes qualify. A nonclustering index on HOLIDAY quickly locates the few pages of interest.

In the Enterprise Manager workspace, you can create as many single- or multi-valued indexes for a database table as you need and can drop indexes that are no longer needed. As we mentioned, indices can facilitate integrity rules; they are also added for performance. An index and a table work like a book's index. Rather than scanning the entire table's data looking for a particular piece of information, the DBMS looks for the value in the index and follows a page pointer directly to its location. Well-designed indices can save I/O and processing time because the DBMS SQL optimizer will use the indices to quickly access the database rows. The choices developers make in designing indices determine how well the database will perform.

USING ENTERPRISE MANAGER'S DATABASE PAINTER

SQL Server automatically creates an index for the PRIMARY KEY and UNIQUE constraints. If you want other indexes, you must create them. To create an index, in Enterprise Manager's Server Manager window, select the appropriate table, click the right mouse button, and then choose All Tasks/Manage Indexes (see Figures 6-6 and 6-7).

Figure 6-6: The Manage Indexes dialog box

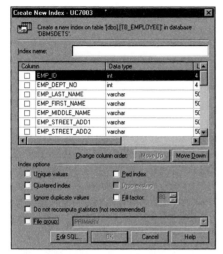

Figure 6-7: The Create New Index dialog box

You can also use the CREATE INDEX statement. See Chapter 11, "Constructing the Database."

For example:

```
CREATE UNIQUE CLUSTERED INDEX x1emp ON TB_EMPLOYEE (emp_id)
```

creates an index on the emp_id column of the TB_EMPLOYEE table to enforce uniqueness. For details on choosing indices, see Chapter 11.

Creating primary and foreign keys

There are several kinds of keys in relational theory, but only two are of practical importance: primary and foreign keys. The *primary key* of an entity identifies and distinguishes instances. The primary key must always be unique; that is, two instances should never have the same value. It must also be known and available at all times. The instance SOCIAL_SECURITY_NUMBER, for example, might make a bad primary key in an EMPLOYEE table because it may be unavailable for foreign employees. Not always, but most of the time, the primary key and the clustering index are one and the same in content.

To make matters simple, primary keys must always be unique and known. If possible, primary keys should have four additional characteristics. First, they should be stable. A changing primary key leads to confusion and errors. Second, they should not contain descriptive information such as color or size. If the color changes, the primary key is unstable. Third, short and simple alphanumeric codes or integers are best, because they are easy to input and unambiguous. Finally, users should be familiar with the primary key, so they can enter it in database queries.

Names may change and are prone to data entry errors, so they usually make bad primary keys. If you cannot find a good primary key, develop an artificial one, either an integer (a random number) or a short alphanumeric code. To discover the primary key of an entity, ask the user how the entity is identified. If you cannot determine a primary key, reconsider the entity. Perhaps it represents data, not a thing, or it is not important to your organization, or it is poorly defined.

A key is not the same as an index. *Keys* are logical; they identify rows. Indexes are physical; they locate rows. A *foreign key* is a column (or group of columns) that matches the primary key of some table. For example: SERIES_CDE in the EPISODE table is a foreign key to the SERIES table. A *join* is a SELECT statement that combines information from two related tables into one result set. Most joins compare a foreign key to its matching primary key. This is the case in our example join. Such a join is called a *primary and foreign key join*. Because primary and foreign keys are frequently compared, they must be comparable. In other words, they must be defined over the same data type.

So far we have discussed two rules for relational databases. Primary keys must be unique and nonnull. The rule "primary keys must be nonnull" is sometimes called *entity integrity*. Another rule, called *referential integrity,* governs foreign keys. Referential integrity requires that a foreign key must either be null or match some value of its primary key. It makes sense to allow a null foreign key.

Referential integrity (RI) is easy to state and important for error-free database management. It is hard to enforce, however, unless you are using a tool for generating triggers; for example, ERwin or the DBMS can enforce them with a declarative style of RI. Foreign key rules specify how to preserve referential integrity when foreign keys are inserted or updated and then primary keys are updated or deleted. In this section we examine alternative foreign key rules. First we discuss deletion of a primary key value.

OPTIONS FOR DELETING KEYS

There are four options for primary key deletion. When the database administrator specifies the *restrict* option, the primary key value may not be deleted as long as there are any matching foreign key values. The data-entry user must first change or delete all matching foreign keys. The second option is *cascade*. When a primary key is deleted, all rows containing matching foreign keys are also automatically deleted. This can be dangerous. Deletes automatically trigger deletes, which in turn trigger other deletes. If you specify this rule often, you may find that a single deletion may cause an entire database to disappear.

The third and fourth options are *nullify* and *set default*. These automatically set all matching foreign keys to null or default when a primary key value is deleted. Technically, there is another option and that is to simply allow violations of referential integrity; this is not usually recommended. This option will invariably lead to disaster when the orphans and broken links between database entities cause errors in the application components. Even application-enforced integrity is better than nothing. Rely on your DBA staff, if you have a large database with lots of lineage, or many relationships.

Similar options apply when a primary key is updated. For example, the cascade option automatically propagates the new primary key value to all matching foreign keys. However, updates to primary keys are strongly discouraged, because primary keys should be stable. For this reason, the options for primary key updates are not as important as deletes. Similar options also apply when a foreign key is inserted or updated. Usually, the restrict option is specified – new foreign key values may not be entered unless a matching primary key value already exists.

If your DBMS supports primary and foreign keys, you can work with the keys in Enterprise Manager. When you open a table with keys, Enterprise Manager gets the information from the DBMS and displays it in the painter workspace. If your DBMS supports them, use primary and foreign keys to enforce the referential integrity of your database. If you use keys, you can rely on the DBMS to make sure that only valid values are entered for certain columns instead of having to write code to enforce valid values.

For example, say you have two tables, SERIES and EPISODE. The EPISODE table contains the column series_code, which holds the name of the series. You want to make sure that only valid series are entered in this column. That is, the only valid values for series_code in the EPISODE table are values for series_code in the SERIES table. To enforce this kind of relationship, you define a foreign key for series_code that points to the SERIES table. With this key in place, the DBMS disallows any value for series_code that does not match a series in the SERIES table.

In the Enterprise Manager you can do the following:

◆ Create keys

◆ Alter keys

◆ Drop keys

For the most part, you work with keys the same way for each DBMS that supports keys. But there are some DBMS-specific issues. When you open and expand a table containing primary and/or foreign keys, Enterprise Manager displays the keys in the workspace. The keys are shown as icons with lines connected to the table. When working with tables containing keys, you can easily open related tables.

DEFINING PRIMARY KEYS

You can use PRIMARY KEY constraints to enforce entity integrity as well as referential integrity. A PRIMARY KEY constraint ensures that no duplicate values are entered, that NULL values are not allowed, and that an index is created to enhance performance. To create a PRIMARY KEY constraint, in Enterprise Manager's Server Manager window, double-click the appropriate table, and click the columns you want to include in the primary key (see Figure 6-8).

You can also use the CREATE TABLE or ALTER TABLE statement. See Chapter 11, "Constructing the Database."

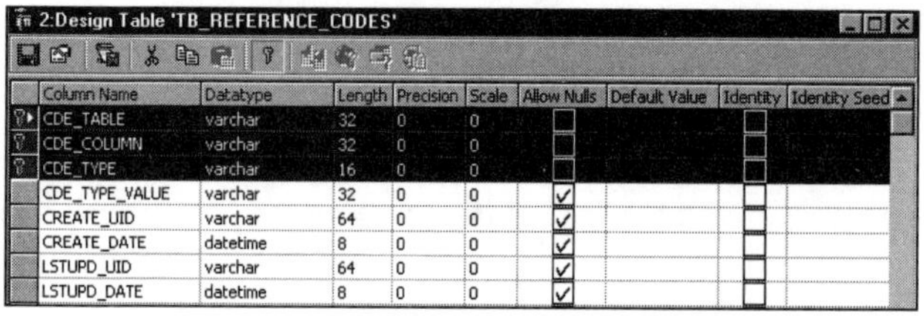

Figure 6-8: Create a primary key.

For example, the statement

```
ALTER TABLE TBEMPLOYEE
ADD
CONSTRAINT PK_emp_id PRIMARY KEY CLUSTERED (emp_id)
```

adds a PRIMARY KEY constraint on the emp_id column.

DEFINING FOREIGN KEYS

The FOREIGN KEY constraints work in conjunction with PRIMARY KEY or UNIQUE KEY constraints to enforce referential integrity among specified tables. To create a FOREIGN KEY constraint using a database diagram:

1. In Enterprise Manager's Server Manager window, open a database diagram (see Figure 6-9).

2. If you have not already defined a PRIMARY KEY or UNIQUE constraint in the foreign key table, do so now.

3. In the foreign key table, create a column.

4. Click the primary key columns that you want to copy to the foreign key table.

5. Copy the columns from the primary key table to the foreign key table.

You can also use the CREATE TABLE or ALTER TABLE statement. See Chapter 11, "Constructing the Database."

For example, the statement

```
ALTER TABLE TB_EMP_EXP_DTL
ADD
CONSTRAINT FK_TB_EMP_EXP_RPT FOREIGN KEY (EXP_RPT_ID)
   REFERENCES TB_EMP_EXP_RPT (EXP_RPT_ID)
```

adds a FOREIGN KEY constraint to the TB_EMP_EXP_DTL table on the EXP_RPT_ID column.

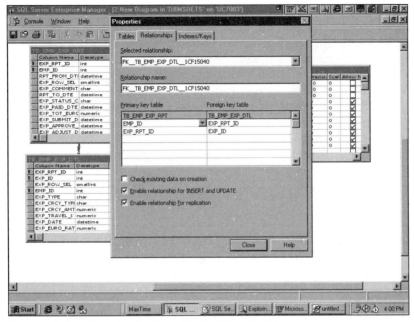

Figure 6-9: Creating a foreign key with the Enterprise Manager

Creating database views

So far in this chapter, we have discussed only base tables. A *base* table is stored on disk drives. A *view* table is not stored. It is really just a query; the rows of the view are derived by executing the query. When you construct a view with the CREATE VIEW statement, the definition is recorded in the catalog. When you run a query against the view, the system merges your query with this definition and executes the merged query. As you can see, views do not significantly affect performance; they are used primarily for convenience.

About Databases, Keys, and Indices

It is probably easier in most cases to use a tool like ERwin to build a complex database with many entities and relationships. The interaction can be planned, analyzed, and designed. These ER tools also have comprehensive schema generation to provide database triggers and DDL. We have mentioned index and key creation for completeness, but we warn against its casual use. Relationships and their update ramifications must be clearly thought out before definition.

Views are quite useful. Sensitive information such as salaries can be stored in a base table but excluded from a view. By giving users access to the view but not the base table, you secure the salary data. Views are also used like macros, as a way of packaging complete queries in the guise of a table. Views can be used to present data in a format requested by the user, without affecting your database design.

Unfortunately, views have one major limitation. The SELECT statements work well against views, but inserts, updates, and deletes may not. Suppose a view contains all the table columns except the primary key. Insertions to this view might create a null primary key and will be rejected. If you have specified NOT NULL, updates and deletions may be ambiguous, because the primary key is not available to positively identify rows.

You can define and manipulate views in Enterprise Manager. Typically you use views for the following reasons:

♦ To give names to frequently executed SELECT statements.

♦ To limit access to data in a table. For example, you can create a view of all the columns in the Employee table except Salary. Users of the view can see and update all information except the employee's salary.

♦ To combine information from multiple tables for easy access.

A VIEW is a set of columns that can be chosen from one or more tables. Views are typically not updatable but are used to provide a simple way to access natural database table joins or to provide for securing sensitive database data. In Enterprise Manager, you can create single- or multiple-table views and can use a view to create a new view. You can create a view with Enterprise Manager or by using the CREATE VIEW statement.

To create a view, from the Manage menu in SQL Enterprise Manager, choose Views, and then select New from the Views drop-down list (see Figure 6-10).

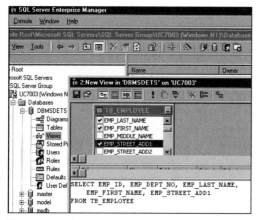

Figure 6-10: Creating a view using the Enterprise Manager

You can also use the CREATE VIEW statement.
For example, the statement

```
CREATE VIEW V1EMPLOYEE
AS
SELECT emp_id , emp_lname, emp_start_date FROM TBEMPLOYEE
```

creates a simple view called V1EMPLOYEE, consisting of the EMP_ID, EMP_LNAME, and EMP_START_DATE columns from the TBEMPLOYEE table. You'll receive a message stating that the command did not return any data, and that it did not return any rows. This is fine. The view has been created.

Before you create a view, consider the following guidelines:

- You can create views only in the current database.

- View names must follow the rules for identifiers and must be unique for each user.

- You can build views on other views and on procedures that reference views.

- You cannot associate rules, defaults, or triggers with views.

- You cannot build indexes on views.

- You cannot create temporary views, and you cannot create views on temporary tables.

- You do not need to specify column names with the CREATE VIEW statement. SQL Server gives the columns of the view the same names and data types as the columns referred to in the select list of the SELECT statement. The select list can be a full or partial list of the column names in the base tables.

- You can specify column names; you *must* specify column names in the CREATE VIEW statement for every column in the view if:

  - Any of the view's columns are derived from an arithmetic expression, a built-in function, or a constant.

  - Two or more of the view's columns would otherwise have the same name (usually because the view definition includes a join and the columns being joined have the same name).

  - You want to give any column in the view a name different from the column from which it is derived. (You can also rename columns in the SELECT statement.) Whether or not you rename a view column, it inherits the data type of the column from which it is derived.

Exporting Database Objects

You can export the syntax for a table or view to the log. This feature is useful when you want to create a backup copy of the table or view before you alter it or when you want to create the same object in another DBMS. SQL Server's Enterprise Manager includes a transfer management interface that you can use to transfer some or all objects from one database to another.

The transfer management interface eases migration of databases between servers. With the transfer management interface, you can:

◆ Copy all types of objects, or only some types.

◆ Copy all objects of a specific type, or only some objects of a specific type.

◆ Transfer schema and data, only schema, or only data.

◆ Append or replace existing data.

◆ Drop destination objects before copying schema.

◆ Include the objects that depend on a transferred object.

◆ Use default scripting options, or customize the scripts that are used to copy objects and security information.

◆ Execute a transfer immediately, or schedule the transfer to execute one time or on a recurring basis.

The destination server must be a Microsoft SQL Server 7 server. The source server can be a Microsoft SQL Server 4.*x* or 6.5 server or a SYBASE server. See Figures 6-11, 6-12, and 6-13 for a visual example.

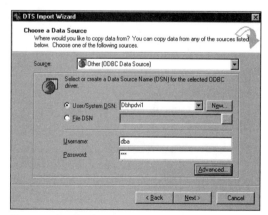

Figure 6–11: The Choose a Data Source page of the DTS Import Wizard

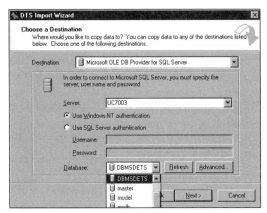

Figure 6-12: The Choose a Destination page of the DTS Import Wizard

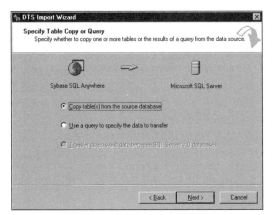

Figure 6-13: The Specify Table Copy or Query page of the DTS Import Wizard

Manipulating Data

Now we turn to the second part of the relational model, the operators used to manipulate tables. In his 1970 paper, "A Relational Model of Data for Large Shared Data Banks," E.F. Codd defined eight operators, namely: *restrict, project, join, union, difference, intersect, product,* and *divide*. Of these eight, only five are necessary. Join, difference, and divide can be derived from the other five. Additional operators can be defined, such as *outer join*. Thus, the original eight operators are a useful but somewhat arbitrary collection.

The operators act on tables just as arithmetic operators act on numbers. When an operator is applied to one or two tables, the result is another table. Consequently, we have an algebra of tables, just as we have an algebra of arithmetic. Codd called this the relational algebra. In this section we examine the three most important operators, *restrict, project,* and *join,* and we learn how they are implemented in SQL.

Let's begin with restrict. Restrict eliminates rows from a single table. In the example query, we select comedy shows. The query result conforms to the definition of a table, although it does not physically exist. In SQL, the result of every query is another table; this principle is known as *closure.*

```
SELECT SERIES_CDE, SERIES_NAME
FROM SERIES
WHERE GENRE_CDE = "COMEDY"
```

The project operator eliminates columns from a single table. In the example, we select only SERIES_CDE and SERIES_NAME.

Most SQL queries combine restrict and project. The operator that best characterizes relational database management is join. Join combines two tables by comparing one column from each. The comparison here uses "=" and is called an *equijoin.* Joins involving > or < are possible but less common. An *equijoin* results in a table with two identical columns. For it to conform to the definition of a table, one of these columns must either be eliminated with a project operator or renamed. An equijoin that eliminates the duplicate column is called a *natural join.* The example that follows is a natural join, with additional columns eliminated for clarity.

```
SELECT    episod.series_cde, pgmtrk.track_datetime,
   episod.episode_cde, episod.episode_name,
episod.eps_desc_txt,episod.eps_quest_star_txt
FROM pgmtrk, episod
WHERE ( episod.episode_cde = pgmtrk.episode_cde )
   and ( episod.series_cde = pgmtrk.series_cde )
   and  (pgmtrk.track_datetime between
       '1994-02-01 00:00' AND '1996-0401 23:59:00')
ORDER BY  episod.series_cde ASC,  pgmtrk.
       track_datetime ASC;
```

As you work on the database, you will often want to look at existing data or create some data for testing purposes. Also, you will want to test display formats, validation rules, and edit styles on real data. Enterprise Manager provides a number of query tools to examine data.

Retrieving and manipulating database information

Microsoft Query Analyzer (within the Enterprise Manager under Tools) provides a query interface to relational databases. This replaces the ISQL interface from prior releases. Using this tool, you can enter a SQL statement, execute it, and view the results.

Importing and exporting data

Outside of the Enterprise Manager, perhaps the most useful tool when creating new databases is the bulk copy program. We will discuss the bulk copy program in greater detail in Chapter 4, "Overview of SQL Server 7 Tools and Components," but it is useful to load flat-file data extracts into SQL Server tables.

With the bulk copy program (bcp), you can easily import data from other applications or export data to those applications. For example, you can import flat data from a mainframe extract, or you can export a view based on several tables for use in other SQL Servers or for analysis in Microsoft Excel.

The bulk copy program (bcp) copies SQL Server data to or from an operating-system file in a user-specified format. See Chapter 4, "Overview of SQL Server 7 Tools and Components."

The bulk copy or bcp utility is most frequently used to transfer data into a SQL Server database from another program, usually another database management system. The data to be transferred must be put into an operating-system file or onto a floppy disk with a backup facility provided by the old program.

The bcp utility is also used for temporary transfers of data for use with other programs – for example, with spreadsheet programs. The data is moved from SQL Server into an operating-system file or onto a floppy disk; from there the other program can import the data.

SQL Server can accept data in any ASCII or binary format as long as the terminators (the characters used to separate columns and rows) can be described. The table structures need not be identical. Data copied into SQL Server is appended to any existing contents of a table; data copied to a file overwrites any previous contents of the file.

To use bcp, a user must have a SQL Server login account and the appropriate permissions on the database tables, views, and operating-system files.

Summary

This chapter covered application database administration using SQL Server 7's Enterprise Manager. Enterprise Manager is a good tool for working on specific day-to-day changes to your database. The larger tasks, those that involve changes to many or most of the database tables, are usually scripted and performed in a bulk/batch fashion. This scripting technique will be discussed in the Chapter 11, "Constructing the Database."

Part III

SQL Server 7 Application Development

Chapter 7

Setting Up the Development Environment

IN THIS CHAPTER

- Installing SQL Server 7
- Upgrading from SQL Server 6.5
- Planning the development project
- Configuring developers' workstations

THIS CHAPTER IS DIVIDED into two sections. The first covers the installation or upgrade procedure for SQL Server 7. The second covers the areas concerning the development of any application, including the specifics of setting up the development workstation environment.

Installing or Upgrading to SQL Server 7

Before you install or upgrade to Microsoft SQL Server 7, you will need to take some precautionary steps. This section deals with these prerequisites, as well as the installation process.

Important! Read this first!

Before installation or upgrade, you should do the following:

- If you are upgrading, make a backup of all of the current 6.*x* databases.
- Stop all services dependent on SQL Server, including any service that is currently using ODBC, such as Internet Information Server (IIS) or SilverStream Application Server.

◆ Close any instances of the Event Viewer (eventvwr.exe) and the Registry Editor (regedit.exe or regedt32.exe).

◆ Windows NT only: Create a domain user account to assign to the MSSQLServer, SQLServerAgent, and MSDTC services if you plan to perform any server-to-server activities.

◆ Log into the system under a user account that has local administrative privileges.

Installation types

SQL Server Setup offers three installation types:

◆ **Typical.** Installs all of SQL Server using the default installation options.

◆ **Minimum.** Installs the minimum configuration necessary to run SQL Server.

◆ **Custom.** Installs SQL Server, enabling you to change the default options.

The typical and custom installation types use the same default options; but in the custom installation you are able to change these defaults. See Table 7-1 for the default values for the installation options. If you install SQL Server on Windows NT, the following options are offered for all installation types:

◆ Login accounts for SQL Server and SQL Server Agent

◆ The option to start SQL Server and/or SQL Server Agent automatically when the computer is rebooted

Also note that you can back up and change your selections at any time before the setup begins.

TABLE 7-1 DEFAULTS FOR THE INSTALLATION OPTIONS

Installation Option	Minimum	Typical & Custom
Database server	Yes	Yes
Upgrade tools	No	Yes
Replication support	Yes	Yes
Full-text search (Microsoft Search)	No	No

Installation Option	Minimum	Typical & Custom
Client management tools	None	All
Client connectivity	Yes	Yes
Online documentation	No	Yes
Development tools	None	None
Code samples	None	None
Character set	1252 – ISO	1252 – ISO
Sort order	Dictionary, case-insensitive	Dictionary, case-insensitive
Unicode collation	General, case-insensitive	General, case-insensitive
Network protocols (95/98)	TCP/IP and multiprotocol	
Network protocols (NT)	Named Pipes, TCP/IP, and multiprotocol	

Databases created during install

See Table 7-2 for a list of the database and log files that are created in the \mssql7\data\ directory during installation.

TABLE 7-2 DATABASES CREATED DURING INSTALLATION

Database Name	Database Filename	Log Filename
Master	master.mdf	mastlog.ldf
Model	model.mdf	modellog.ldf
Msdb	msdbdata.mdf	msdblog.ldf
Northwind	northwnd.mdf	northwnd.ldf
Pubs	pubs.mdf	pubs_log.ldf
Tempdb	tempdb.mdf	templog.ldf

The `master`, `model`, `msdb`, and `tempdb` databases are system databases. `Northwind` and `pubs` are example databases that you can use as learning tools. The majority of the examples in the SQL Server documentation are based on either the `Northwind` or `pubs` database.

Installing SQL Server 7

To install SQL Server, do the following:

1. Insert the SQL Server compact disc into your CD-ROM drive. If setup does not start automatically, run Autorun.exe in the root directory of the compact disc.

2. Click Install SQL Server 7.0 Components.

3. Click Database Server - Full Product or Database Server - Desktop Edition.

4. Select the type of installation (see the preceding step) to perform. Click Next.

5. If you chose the custom installation:

   a. Select components to install.

   b. Select a character set, sort order, and Unicode collation.

   c. Select the network libraries to configure.

6. If you are installing on a server running Windows NT, enter a username and password for the SQL Server service or select Use the local system account. The SQL Server Agent service defaults to the same account entered for the SQL Server service unless you specify another account.

7. When you are finished specifying installation options, the Setup program will install the product.

Upgrading from SQL Server 6.x

You can upgrade SQL Server 6.*x* to 7.0 using the SQL Server Upgrade Wizard (see Figure 7-1). The SQL Server Upgrade Wizard does not support consolidation of databases from multiple SQL Server 6.*x* installations. If you need to upgrade SQL Server 6.*x* databases from multiple servers, consolidate all of the SQL Server 6.*x* databases on one server and then run the wizard to upgrade the consolidated server.

When the upgrade process is complete, two separate installations of SQL Server, including two separate sets of the same data, exist. The SQL Server 6.*x* and SQL Server 7.0 installations are independent of each other from that point forward.

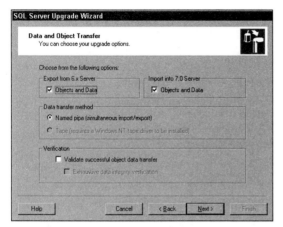

Figure 7-1: SQL Server's Upgrade Wizard

The SQL Server Upgrade Wizard does not remove SQL Server 6.*x* from the computer, although it can optionally remove the 6.*x* devices to save disk space (we do not recommend this option, which is only available if you are using a tape backup to perform the upgrade).

EXPANDING THE SIZE OF TEMPDB ON 6.X
Before you attempt the upgrade, you will probably have to expand the size of your `tempdb` database on the SQL Server 6.*x* server. To do this:

1. Calculate how much bigger you want `tempdb` to be. The Upgrade Wizard will tell you by how much more it needs to be expanded.

2. Choose a name and a location for the new device to be created.

3. From either ISQL/w or SQL Query Tool (in Enterprise Manager) enter the following. (The following example creates a 25MB device and allocates it all to the `tempdb` database.)

```
DISK INIT name='moretempdb1',
physname='d:\mssql\data\moretempdb1.DAT',
vdevno=101,
size=12800
GO
ALTER DATABASE tempdb ON moretempdb1 = 25
GO
```

THE SQL SERVER UPGRADE WIZARD

To perform the version upgrade using a direct pipeline technique:

1. In the Start the SQL Server Upgrade Wizard, click Next after the welcome screen.

2. Select Named pipe (simultaneous import/export), and then click Next.

3. In Export server (6.*x*), in the Server name box, enter the name of the computer with the SQL Server 6.*x* database.

4. In the Administrator password (sa) box, enter the sa password for SQL Server 6.*x*, and then click Next. (Note that this will stop and restart the MSSQLServer service on both the 6.*x* and 7.0 servers!)

5. Choose the code page (default is 1252 for 7.0).

6. Move any databases you do not want upgraded at this time to the Exclude list and click Next.

7. For Database Creation: Select Use the default configuration or edit the default (click Edit to examine and make changes to the proposed disk configuration within the layout utility). Press Accept to return to the SQL Server Upgrade Wizard) and click Next.

To estimate the disk space required for an upgrade: Click Advanced, and click an object in the Proposed 7.0 database layout box to view details in the Object details box. The Drive Summary box shows the estimated size of all SQL Server 7 data files and the free disk space left on all of the local fixed disks. On the Options menu, select Freespace includes 6.*x* files to view the free space that would exist if the SQL Server 6.*x* data files were deleted.

8. On the System Configuration page, set the following options, and click Next:

    ◆ **Server configuration.** Login and remote login registrations and relevant server configuration options are transferred.

    ◆ **Replication settings.** All articles, subscriptions, and publications of each selected database, plus the distribution database, if any, are transferred and upgraded.

    ◆ **SQL Executive settings.** All tasks scheduled by SQL Executive are transferred and upgraded so that they can be run in SQL Server Agent.

In ANSI Nulls, select:

♦ *Off*, if ANSI nulls should not be used when stored procedures are created.

♦ *On*, if ANSI nulls should be used when stored procedures are created.

In Quoted identifiers, select:

♦ *Mixed* (or *don't know*), if some of your objects were created with QUOTED_IDENTIFIER set to ON and some with it set to OFF.

♦ *Off*, if all objects should be compiled with QUOTED_IDENTIFIER set to OFF.

♦ *On*, if all objects should be compiled with QUOTED_IDENTIFIER set to ON.

9. Review the summary of warnings (if any) and choices. Click Finish when you are ready.

Clicking Finish will start the process of upgrading according to the script that is built through the preceding choices. See Figure 7-2 for a sample dialog box displayed by the Upgrade Script Interpreter.

Figure 7-2: A sample dialog box from the Upgrade Script Interpreter

When the upgrade is started, the following operations take place in sequence:

♦ Updates ODBC and SQL-DMO components on SQL Server 6.*x*.

♦ Exports replication settings (if any).

♦ Exports server settings from the master database.

- ◆ Exports logins.

- ◆ Exports database owners.

- ◆ Exports SQL Executive objects and settings from the `msdb` database.

- ◆ Exports database objects for all databases chosen.

- ◆ Modifies export/import scripts accordingly.

- ◆ Starts SQL Server 7.

- ◆ Imports server settings to the master database.

- ◆ Creates databases.

- ◆ Modifies SQL Executive (`msdb`) objects and settings to SQL Server 7 formats.

- ◆ Imports logins.

- ◆ Imports database objects.

- ◆ Simultaneously exports data from 6.*x* and imports it into SQL Server 7. (You'll be locked out of the 6.*x* server at this time.)

- ◆ Imports modified SQL Executive objects and settings into SQL Server 7.

- ◆ Imports replication settings (if any).

- ◆ Examines SQL Server 7 databases to verify that the upgrade is successful.

- ◆ Sets database options in SQL Server 7.

- ◆ Marks server and databases as moved (for subsequent runs of the wizard).

- ◆ Drops temporary `tempdb` files.

- ◆ The SQL Server 6.*x* catalog data, objects, and databases are upgraded and converted so that they are compatible with SQL Server 7.

- ◆ The SQL Server 7 service is stopped.

When the upgrade is complete, a 7.0 duplicate copy of the 6.*x* database server will be ready for testing.

Planning and Setup

The plan that follows makes the assumption that the following list of hardware and software resources are, or are soon to be put, in place:

- ◆ One or more database servers (for example, Sequent, IBM/RS6000, Sun, or an IBM-Compatible PC running Windows/NT or OS/2)

- ◆ Database management software (for example, Informix, Oracle, SYBASE, or DB/2)

- ◆ Shared file servers, with the necessary connections (for example, routers, bridges, and gateways) and software installed

- ◆ Client machines for all developers (for example, workstations with file space and memory)

- ◆ A plan for source management (for example, SourceSafe, PVCS, and MKS)

Development team

Projects require the bringing together of a range of skills to complete the development of an application successfully. The skill sets you'll typically need for most development projects are shown in Table 7-3.

TABLE 7-3 COMMON SKILL AREAS FOR DEVELOPMENT

Skill Area	Involves
Project management	Ability to make decisions within a short period of elapsed time, scheduling of team tasks, coordination in and between projects
End-user representation	Understanding of what users want the application to do and how they want to interact with it
System architecture	Designing of the application to meet its requirements and to fit well in the computing environment where it is intended to operate
Database administration	Development and management of test and production databases
Network administration	Configuration and monitoring of server computers and the networks that connect client computers to them
Standards control	Establishment and enforcement of conventions and standards for such things as user-interface design, coding style, documentation, and error processing
Object management	Administration of the application components that developers create (with particular attention to facilitating the reuse of these components in multiple applications)

Continued

TABLE 7-3 COMMON SKILL AREAS FOR DEVELOPMENT *(Continued)*

Skill Area	Involves
Application development	Creation and maintenance of application components (which includes painting them and coding logic for them), proficiency with SQL, familiarity with the client computer's operating system and any other programs to be accessed from the application
Documentation	Writing of comments, documents, or online Help about the application for reference by developers or end users
Multimedia artistry	Creation of pictures, sounds, or other multimedia elements to be used in the user interface of the application
Quality assurance	Testing and debugging of the application

DIVIDING THE WORK

In a large project, the Application Development can typically be broken down into subsystems, with three to four developers per subsystem. It is still important to coordinate the overall project and keep the channels of communication open at all times, particularly when changes in one of the subsystems affects any of the others. It's a good idea for changes to be published, through memos or e-mail, in advance, so that anybody who is affected will be aware and can subsequently make the necessary adjustments when appropriate.

CODE REVIEW AND WALKTHROUGH

It's a good idea to institute an ongoing code review and walkthrough session during the development of an application. This can be especially helpful on large projects that have several developers with varying SQL Server proficiency. For example, when a particular window or large section of functionality is coded, the code review meeting can be scheduled. At the review meeting, preferably in a conference room, the developer brings multiple copies of all of the scripts and the original design specification for the particular window or section of functionality. If possible, a quick demonstration of the code is given while the group refers to the original design specification to note any differences in functionality. If the group comes across any differences, a decision must be made as to whether to change the specification or to change the code. If the functionality of the code is wrong, then it must be changed and a meeting rescheduled. If there are no differences, or very minor differences, then the group proceeds to look at each piece of the code in detail. There are several purposes to this scrutiny:

◆ To check that the code appears to work per the specification

◆ To examine any new techniques and transfer the knowledge to the whole group

◆ To make sure that the code is in line with the accepted conventions

For this kind of code review to work requires that the team check their egos at the door so that they don't take the criticism personally. The idea is to improve the quality of the product that is being developed. Once the code has passed through this kind of review, it is no longer the responsibility of the original programmer; it is now owned by the review team. In the event of a problem arising later on, this change in responsibility will help prevent either the "not-invented-here" or the "Oh, it was John who developed that object" responses.

DEVELOPERS' TOOLS

It's also important to make sure that the developers have adequate hardware (for example, high-end PCs with print capabilities); the appropriate software to produce documentation (for example, Word, Excel, and PowerPoint); access to database administration tools (for example, Enterprise Manager, Query Analyzer, and Profiler); and CASE tools for modeling (for example, ERWin, How, and Rational). In addition to the documentation that is provided with these tools, very often developers need to access the wealth of information available electronically through either the Internet or bulletin board systems. These services provide many newsgroups, forums, and libraries that can be scanned for possible solutions to issues that arise during development.

Sample planning chart

The sample planning chart (see Table 7-4) shows columns for task and subtask descriptions, including any prerequisites and comments. To use this in your environment, you might add columns for human resources, scheduled completion dates, a status, or anything else pertinent to your environment.

TABLE 7-4 SAMPLE PLANNING CHART

Task	Subtask
Establish system environment	Acquire copies of the chosen development tool(s)
	Acquire local or shared disk space for development tool(s)
	Set up shared directory structure (Source, Documentation, and Class)
	Set up backup and recovery procedures
	Establish source control procedures
	Provide copies of development tool and documentation developer
	Prepare basic startup document for new developer
Install chosen development tool(s)	Run setup routine for each product on developer workstation
	Test the database connectivity (where applicable)
Configure development tool(s)	Establish project directory structures
	Establish and publish standards and naming conventions
	Establish and publish guidelines document

Standards, guidelines, and best practices

When you need to create standards for your organization, or just guidelines or best practices for projects, begin by developing a framework document that can be easily adapted and amended as time passes. One of the biggest mistakes you can make is trying to come up with the ultimate standards guide before publishing it. It's unlikely that you'll be able to create this beforehand, but make a start and keep the document current. These standards, guidelines, and best practices really help with productivity, especially if you have developers who are new to the development tools that you have chosen. After all, not everybody can, off the top of his or her head, remember the best technique for every situation.

The payback for this up-front administration normally comes much sooner than you may expect. The thought process will naturally slow the project down to begin with, but, too often, surging ahead with what first comes to mind can come back to haunt you later on! Here are some thought-provoking questions for you to ponder early on:

◆ What can be leveraged from the organization's current standards?

◆ What existing resources can be leveraged?

◆ How is version control to be implemented?

◆ What are the source code and database naming conventions?

◆ What standard user and technical documentation is required?

◆ What are the database resources and requirements?

Shared file server access

If you are in, or plan to be in, a network environment, take some time to plan the directory structures and user groups that will access these directories on the shared file server. You may want to separate the project into coders, testers, and integrators and grant access rights accordingly. You can start of with a fairly simple directory structure, such as the one shown in Figure 7-3.

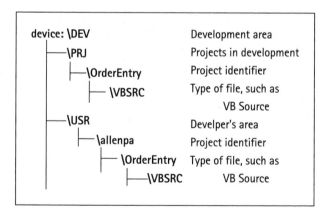

Figure 7-3: Sample directory structure

You may want to establish a review committee, which is responsible for, and meets periodically to discuss, any modifications to the directory structure.

Database server access

You can use roles (such as database owner or database administrator) to govern the access to the data tables. Create the tables, views, and so forth using the owner's login, and develop any application code using a regular developer database login. This will ensure that the correct prefix for any database table is included in a fully qualified reference for that table, which will prevent any problems of determining table identity during the run-time execution of the application.

There will be several database servers to consider:

♦ Development (default)

♦ System or Integration Test

♦ Quality Assurance

♦ User Acceptance

♦ Production

Backup and recovery procedures

No environment is immune to hardware failure and accidents, so design backup and recovery procedures for the following:

♦ File Server (Development tool objects)

♦ Data Server (Database objects and data)

Once the procedures are in place, make a point of testing them on a regular basis — that is, once a month or more frequently — so that you can determine if the recovery procedures actually work and continue to work on an ongoing basis. Catching problems before they become nightmares is the goal here. Remember to store the backups off-site, so that if the building goes up in flames, you can still operate with an emergency replacement installation.

Development preferences

Several more development considerations must be covered, such as the developer workstation configurations, the steps necessary to migrate objects through the development life cycle, the check in and check out procedures, establishing and maintaining object class libraries, the placement of the development tools, and the testing strategies. Now let's cover these considerations in more detail.

DEVELOPER WORKSTATIONS

The developer workstations are a critical factor in the development process. If the machines are configured incorrectly or inefficiently, then the possibility of delay increases.

WORKSTATION CONFIGURATION

With the geometric advances in the speed and capacity of computers, so-called "high-end" workstations become "middle of the road" machines within six months (although it feels like overnight sometimes), but your basic hardware and software setup should be as follows:

◆ The fastest processor (Pentium III 550MHz or 600MHz processor)

◆ 128MB of RAM (but more is always better!)

◆ 12GB hard disk drive

◆ CD-ROM drive for installation and access to CD-based material

◆ 3.5" high-density disk drive, necessary for floppy disk installation only

◆ Network card (assuming you're developing in a group situation)

◆ Windows NT 4.0 or Windows 2000

APPLICATION INITIALIZATION FILES

Most application initialization parameters are now stored in the Windows Registry, but if you are still using application initialization files (those with the extension .INI), they are typically found in one of the two following locations:

◆ The Windows directory (most often)

◆ The directory of the application (less often)

If you do not specify a path for the initialization file, most application development tools functions will look for an .INI file in the following locations:

◆ The current directory

◆ The directory where Windows is installed (for example, Windows or Winnt)

◆ The System subdirectory for Windows (for example, System32)

◆ The application's working directory, if not the current directory

◆ Sequentially through each directory listed in the Path statement

Administration of libraries

The migration of objects between libraries should be tightly controlled by either a version control system or a set of well-defined procedures. The version control system (or your procedures) must allow an administrator to determine which objects in the development libraries have changed and therefore need to be promoted and applied to the next level, that is, for testing.

These libraries or files include the following types of objects:

- ◆ Projects (for Visual Basic, PowerBuilder, Java, and SilverStream)

- ◆ User interface components (for example, windows, menus, and so on)

- ◆ Problem domain (for example, nonvisual functions, Java or C programs, stored procedures, and triggers)

- ◆ Operating system objects (for example, NT batch and command files)

- ◆ Database data manipulation and definition language (DML/DDL SQL)

Check in/out procedures

In multideveloper environments, where teams with many members are involved with the coding and testing of objects and libraries, version control is an important consideration. Several third-party version control systems are available with interfaces to many different development tools.

To provide the team with greater security throughout the development life cycle, version control systems provide check-out and check-in functionality for the source code; it is suggested that you take advantage of these capabilities.

Use of the check-out and check-in functionality also includes other features designed for the protection of the development environment. An object that has been checked out cannot be checked in when an application using that object is currently being executed. Although this feature helps to maintain the integrity of the development library, it can be frustrating trying to find out who is running the executable and asking them to stop the application so that you can check in your work. In addition, it is recommend that you set up separate and discrete library environments for unit test (DEV), system test or quality assurance (SYS or QA), and user acceptance test (UAT), as well as a shadow copy of what will ultimately be migrated to production (PRD). Following is an example of the how an environment could be set up.

Assuming that the following drive letters are mapped and the directories exist on the network:

N:\   This would be *distinct* for each developer.

P:\QA   This would be *common* to all developers.

P:\UAT   This would be *common* to all developers.

P:\PRD   This would be *common* to all developers.

 In the preceding case N:\ maps to a directory on a server, for example, USNYSRV8/D\DEV\ALLENP\WIP, and P:\ maps to another directory on a server, for example, USNYSRV8\D\DEV\PROJ.

Then all you would need to do to complete the environment is to carry out these steps:

◆ Two members of the team are designated with the role of library manager (librarian). Only the librarians have the Write privilege to the UAT and PROD libraries. They are responsible for moving the system-tested (quality-assured) objects from the SYS directory to the UAT directory, ready for user acceptance testing. When this is completed satisfactorily, the objects are moved from the UAT directory to the PRD directory, ready for production. The PRD libraries ultimately contain the final versions of the libraries that will be moved out to the production environments.

◆ The librarians create the new libraries on PRD, UAT, and SYS.

◆ The developers create their own work-in-progress libraries and files on N:\ and set up their library search paths.

An example of the development procedures for a PowerBuilder environment in which the object exists already might be:

◆ The developer requests a librarian to copy the object from the relevant PRD library to the SYSWIP.PBL file.

◆ The developer then checks out the object from SYSWIP.PBL to their N:\MYWIP.PBL, makes the necessary changes, and then tests them.

◆ After successful testing, the developer checks in the object back to SYSWIP.PBL.

◆ The system test/quality assurance team then runs the regression test(s) for the areas affected by the change (or better still has an automated testing tool that will run regression tests for the complete application overnight).

If the object is new, then the development procedures for a PowerBuilder environment might be:

◆ The developer creates the object in N:\MYWIP.PBL and then tests it.

- ◆ After successful testing, the developer moves the new object to the SYSWIP.PBL.

- ◆ The system test/quality assurance team then develops an appropriate test or tests for the new object (possibly in conjunction with the developer) and runs the test(s) for the new object (in addition, the test team may want to run regression tests for the complete application overnight).

Once an object is considered complete, that is, it works as expected, the test team notifies a librarian that the object (or a series of objects) is ready to be moved from the SYS library to the UAT library. The object (or series of objects) is ready for testing in accordance with the test plan developed by the user community. The testing will probably take place using an executable to simulate the production environment. Upon successful testing in this environment, the object (or series of objects) is ready for the PRD library. The librarian can then determine which production library the object(s) must be moved to prior to building the executable (and dynamic libraries).

It is important to note that most development tools are not version control systems. The success of these techniques relies, in great part, upon the cooperation of the development team as a whole.

Development tool location

When it comes to installing development software, a couple of questions arise about the environment. The answers determine how you will proceed with the installation:

- ◆ Is this a standalone installation or a network installation?

- ◆ If it's a network installation, should the development environment be installed on each developer workstation or on the network file server?

If this is a stand-alone installation or if the development environment is to be loaded on each developer workstation, then install the product from CD-ROM or floppy disks.

The daily build and test

At Microsoft, at the end of the working day a complete recompile or rebuild of all of the products takes place. Once they are rebuilt, they are tested using standard product regression tests. Project leaders are notified of any problems or issues that occur during the build or regression tests. As a consequence, it is easier to determine which piece of code is causing a problem simply because less code can be changed in a 24-hour period. If you wait a month between builds, you may be left scratching your head trying to sift through the list of modules that have changed, particularly on a project involving a large development team.

You may want to consider carrying out a frequent recompile or rebuild for your application development environment, perhaps on a less-aggressive basis, maybe once a week instead. This technique also requires that you have the test scripts built and available for the parts of the product as they are being implemented. It will probably also require that you invest in one of the many automated test tools that have become an absolute necessity for overnight regression testing on a large scale.

Summary

This chapter has covered the steps required to install or upgrade to SQL Server 7, the databases that are created during the install, and it has also covered the areas that need to be addressed when establishing a development environment. These areas are common skills required on a development project, dividing the work, performing code reviews, acquiring additional development tools, creating and using standards, and creating check-in, check-out, and testing procedures.

Chapter 8

Overview of the Application Development Process

IN THIS CHAPTER

- ◆ Completing prerequisite tasks

- ◆ Designing the database

- ◆ Designing the application

- ◆ Creating a batch interface

- ◆ Creating an interface containing windows, pages, and menus

- ◆ Validating your code

- ◆ Refining your code

"DEVELOPING AN APPLICATION" is one of those catch phrases that can mean different things. For the purposes of this guide, we will focus on the tasks (as well as the relative sequence of the tasks) that make up the average application development life cycle. Each of these steps takes place during the course of development. Some will need to be done more than once. In fact, sometimes a whole group of steps will be performed iteratively. This is not unique to developing with a relational DBMS, such as SQL Server. It is common in most development efforts. Effective planning and hard work can keep these reiterations to a minimum, which will save time, save money, and perhaps maintain the integrity of the objects developed. In any event, this chapter will provide a quick overview and later a basic checklist of the steps involved in SQL Server 7 application development.

Completing Prerequisite Tasks

Before you begin the actual construction portion of the development life cycle, certain prerequisite tasks should be either complete or in an advanced state of preparation. The project team should have a development approach and accompanying plan that includes skilled players to carry it to fruition. They will also need a database logical model and physical manifestation as well as adequate workstation resources. These are the components that provide for successful development.

Logistic prerequisites

The developers must decide on the separation of the application components. The lead developers on a larger project – for example, a team of more than 30 developers – will incorporate an application design based upon either a two-tier (2T) or three-tier (3T) approach. Exactly what a tier is and when it begins and ends can be a somewhat nebulous concept and is largely in the eye of the beholder. In any event, the developers must decide how to break out the functional requirements into logistic tiers that promote a consistent, reusable, and maintainable application system, which performs to the user's satisfaction. The developers must consider how this can be accomplished. There are many aspects of development to consider. They will dictate the type of developers you will staff the effort with, that is, which skills are required to implement the architecture.

Next, what exactly is a 2T or 3T approach? The classic 2T approach implemented ad infinitum uses the CICS/COBOL/MVS client with DB2/MVS server sometimes residing on the same host platform MVS; it includes:

| TIER 1 | Server | Database Server: stores and requests data |
| TIER 2 | Client | Application Objects: receive and present data |

The majority of the application is on the client, including the database access language (SQL3). Another approach is to put the data access (for example, stored procedures) and database on the server and use the client as a presentation tool only. The best implementations are flexible and include the proper mix of client SQL with presentation windows and the use of stored procedures for functions where performance demands are severe. This approach must be made on a case-by-case basis.

To complicate the issue further, the three-tier (3T) development explicitly breaks out everything in the application into a separate layer. The architecture includes the following tiers:

TIER 1	Presentation Logic	Developers build the application tool windows, pages, or menus to provide application presentation and navigation
TIER 2	Business Rules	New wave developers build application servers and handle business rules and processes using nonvisual objects
TIER 3	Database management	DBAs develop database design and access modules, for example, stored procedures

The 3T will require three separate teams of developers and better coordination of effort. It will also break out the types of SQL Server 7 objects developed as well as which external items will have to interface with a GUI presentation tool. For example, the GUI presentation tool objects may call external .DLLs for business logic or message switching.

Depending on the requirements of the application, either the 2T or 3T approach can be useful. The vast majority of client/server systems we have seen, including the ones we have worked on, require an interface into legacy systems (for example, a mainframe-based application). A 2T approach is useful when the legacy system has many integrated business rules and heavy database access, such as mainframe COBOL and CICS programs with embedded SQL to access DB2. Breaking the application into separate components is usually not feasible, so development usually consists of extending or enhancing the current system to include a GUI presentation to the client. For example, this breakout can cause the following connections: PowerBuilder client workstation to access an NT-based SQL Server 7 database server and return the data down the chain to the client for presentation. Figure 8-1 depicts the two-tier architecture, which thus consists of integrated business rules and database access. A 3T approach is useful when the requirements for the application consist of migrating processing requirements from a legacy system onto the client or a middle-layer server.

For example, this breakout can cause the following interactions:

- PowerBuilder client1 workstation to NT SQL Server 7

- The server1/client2 to issue a remote procedure call (RPC) to a SQL Server 7 gateway

- The server2/client3 to access a mainframe CICS transaction to select from a mainframe DB2 database server3 and return the data down the chain to the client for ultimate presentation

The legacy system is viewed mainly as a database server, with the business rules of the application being moved onto an intermediate server, and presentation placed on the end-user client machine. Placing the business rules on the client machine can result in what is physically a 2T system having a 3T architecture, but security and performance concerns have mandated an intermediate server to effect load balancing between database and file servers. The result has been to free up of a lot of expensive mainframe time (database server) and produce a much more efficient system.

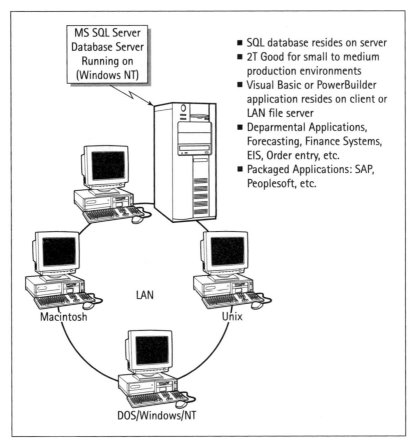

Figure 8-1: Two-tier architecture

Three-tier development is more complex and expensive (see Figure 8-2). It also requires faster network communication to support the increase in messaging between the three tiers. Extensive planning, design, and coordination are also required. The 3T systems we have worked on have all come in well over budget and behind schedule, not only because of a lack of appropriate planning but also because of undereducated and miscast management and developers. Neither approach is *better* than the other, and each should be considered on its own merit and used where appropriate.

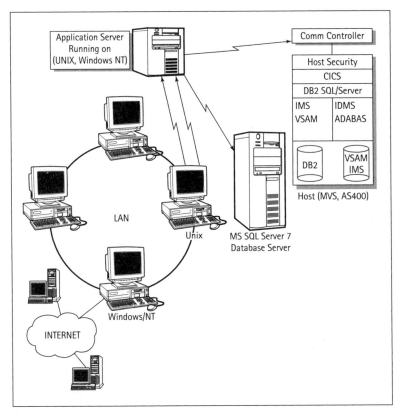

Figure 8-2: Three-tier architecture

Physical prerequisites

Before you begin the physical construction of the application components, certain prerequisite physical items must be in place for use by the development team. Besides an adequate workstation and the appropriate server(s), the project libraries ("GUI presentation tool") accessible to developers should also be available, and the appropriate permissions should be in place. Access to SQL Server 7 with current software maintenance and whatever third-party or in-house class library software is needed should be ready for use from each workstation. Developers should be aware of the guidelines and naming standards the project team has agreed to use to develop the database and the application. These suggestions may seem a bit pedantic, but they will save precious time later in the process. They will also reduce the confusion that accompanies the start of a project. Developers will not hesitate when these conditions are met. They can then be sure that such objects as database tables are named properly, follow suggested guidelines (for example, having a unique index for each table), and are stored in the correct database.

Designing the Database

The design process for the application database is unique to each development environment but will be discussed in general terms here. The specifics of the process may vary from shop to shop. The design process is a critical item, and the degree to which it is completed before commencement of full-scale development is critical to the success of the project.

Determining the application entities

An *entity* is a person, place, object, event, or activity that is relevant to the functionality you are creating. For instance, any noun that can represent information of interest to the organization is an entity. In the logical database design, you try to build an entity-relationship model by identifying the entities and their attributes as well as the relationships between the different entities. The database logical design effort begins as soon as you meet the users. Listen for entities in interviews with the user. If we are developing a database to track employee expenses, the entities will include employee and employee expense detail. Figure 8-3 illustrates a database logical design using a popular tool known as ERwin.

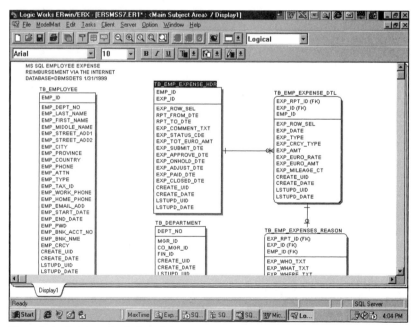

Figure 8-3: Database logical model

The *attributes* of an entity are the things that describe and define it. For example, a television series has a descriptive name, which is an attribute of the series. The date it was originally produced may also be an attribute. Also, listen for relationships in the user interviews. What is a relationship? If an entity cannot exist without a parent, it is dependent, which means it *belongs to* another entity. This is a relationship. Important subsets of an entity with special attributes are subentities. For example, a TV series may be of a type "special" with attributes that only pertain to a "special" series. On the other hand, a dependent entity – for example, an episode – belongs to a series and has a primary key that contains the parent key and an additional key to identify the dependent entity.

Refining each entity and attribute

After you have collected the business entities and attributes from interviews with the user, check the project standards for naming conventions. If applicable, use firm-wide abbreviations to ensure consistent naming. Next, attempt to capture a description and validation criteria for each entity and attribute. Does the project have a data dictionary? If so, then enter the description and validation criteria here. Also check the dictionary to determine if the attribute or entity already exists. SQL Server 7 has its own catalog tables, or extended attributes, which can house descriptions and validation rules. These attributes can be populated from CASE tools like ERwin or PowerDesigner and eventually the SQL Server database diagram. Both of these vendor tools have interfaces to SQL Server 7, which can be used to populate the extended attributes of the GUI tool of choice – for example, PowerBuilder.

Determine the primary key for each entity. The primary key of an entity uniquely identifies entity instances (rows). The primary key of a dependent entity includes the parent key and descriptive column. For example, the primary key for the Episode entity is the `series_code` and `episode_cde` concatenated. Document past or future states are in the description, that is, add `last_update_timestamp`. The primary key will promote database integrity, as you will inhibit table row duplicity and the creation of database orphans, that is, rows in a dependent table with no parent. That is to say that we will not have to worry about having any duplicate rows in the database. Moreover, there will be integrity with respect to any parent-child relationships. No child rows will exist without a parent.

Determining relationships

Again, listen for relationships in interviews with the user. Document the roles of entities in recursive relationships. A series may be a part of another series. Determine the cardinality of the relationship. This will facilitate the choice of keys or indices to access the entity. For example, how many episodes are in a series? Does the identifying key to the relationship have many different values? Decide on a formal name by checking the standards for naming keys. Don't confuse relationships with entities or attributes. Attributes that designate entities are relationships.

If the primary key of an entity consists of other primary keys, it may be a relationship. For example, the TV episode entity would have a primary key consisting of the TV series identifier and the episode identifier. The TV series identifier is the primary key of the series entity.

Creating tables and columns

Typically, when you are using the completed logical design, independent entities are cast as independent tables. Similarly, dependent entities become dependent tables. See Figure 8-4 for an example of a physical design of the logical model that was depicted in Figure 8-3. Before defining the database in the development RDBMS, the designers should verify that tables are in third normal form (3NF), which means that every nonkey column depends on the key, the whole key, and nothing but the key. The designers should attempt to retain normalized subtables unless the cost of application-required table joins is unacceptable.

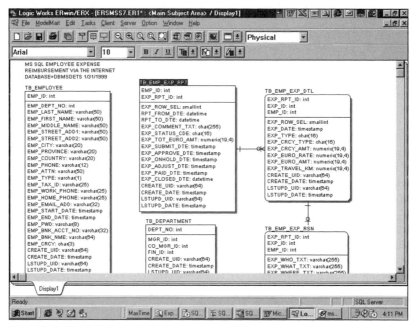

Figure 8-4: Physical database design

Consider merging tables linked by one-to-one relationships. This merger works best if minimum cardinality is also one-to-one, and cardinality is stable. Denormalize for performance as a last resort. You should exhaust physical solutions first, denormalize selectively, and apply updates directly to 3NF tables. Note that when SQL Server has matured in the next year, the need to denormalize will be obviated by the new data types, for example, collections and row types. These upcoming changes will be discussed later in the book.

The attributes of each entity usually become table columns. These table columns should be well-thought-out data types. For instance, do not use a decimal for a number that is always an integer. These table columns should be specified as NOT NULL for required attributes and relationships. You can cause the DBMS to enforce unique attributes/columns by defining them as an index. Attributes of relationships then go with a foreign key. Implement vectors column-wise unless physical size, user access, or number of tables forces row-wise design. Where possible, avoid alternating, encoded, or overlapping columns.

Choosing data types

Data type choices are where SQL Server has had real impact; there are a host of new data types. Suppose in our television series database we want to store more than the fundamental data types, such as numbers, characters, and dates. This application would not have been practical using traditional technology.

Essentially, the SQL-92 data types are:

◆ Integer

◆ Floating-point number

◆ Character string *(fixed or variable length)*

◆ Day-time, time interval

◆ Numeric and decimal

Consider the following additional new wave data as well. Images and large text data types are becoming increasingly popular.

◆ **Geographic locations.** The information for viewer locations, although available, can be efficiently stored or queried in a traditional RDBMS. This type of activity has historically been done in a geographic information system (GIS), but this is a very expensive approach, and the tools don't integrate well.

◆ **Images.** Again, these are at best stored as binary large objects (or BLOBs) within a traditional RDBMS. Technology to search for images *like* another have been available only as a client implementation, and searching an entire image base for *particular* images is just not practical.

Imagine that you want to expand the television series tracking system, and let's say that there are several technical requirements to be met, as follows:

◆ **Image storage and retrieval.** This requirement is for storage and management of series episodes, screening reports, and other images.

♦ **Text search.** Screening reports always contain text descriptions, which have valuable content that is hard to access. Examples include finding similar accidents involving "the commercial did not air properly" – that is, with the words "commercial," "not," and "air" near each other.

♦ **Geospatial analysis.** Consider the issue of finding out which products sell well (for commercial spots) in or near a specific location. Unless both the text information and the geospatial information are in the same server with efficient search optimization, such analysis is impractical.

♦ **Web integration.** The television station Web site is fully dynamic; what you see and interact with must adapt to the type of inquiry.

Creating keys

Besides the primary key and index, secondary keys and indices may be required. In a many-to-one relationship, place the foreign key in the *many*-side table. In a one-to-one relationship, place foreign keys in the table with fewer rows. The many-to-many relationship becomes an associative or junction table. Consider an artificial primary key such as a random number when there are many incoming foreign keys and the natural key is null, not unique, unstable, complex, or not meaningful.

Completing database physical design

Now you have tables and columns and a cluster index, but you are not done yet. To really know if your design will perform, you must list, examine, and explain critical queries and transactions. Critical queries are high-volume, require quick response, or are frequently executed. They are the point of reference for physical design. Create and use critical queries (the SQL used most frequently in the application) for reference and access a clustered index for most if not all tables (usually on the primary key). Occasionally some other column is more important for access and gets the clustered index. Small or temporary tables may have no clustered index.

Create nonclustered indexes (consider foreign key columns) for other columns that are used to search or order the data. Review critical queries after you have assigned a clustered index. Are any of these queries unable to utilize the clustered indices for access? If so, consider nonclustered indexes on column(s) specified in a WHERE clause, particularly join columns. Create a nonclustered index only when the hit ratio is low. Usually, create, at most, three or four indices per table (unless they're read-only). The rest are DBMS-dependent. The DBAs usually determine partitions, locking, granularity, and device assignments. Have whoever is responsible complete the physical design and notify the developers at each significant milestone.

Estimating the size of the database

It is a good practice to know how much volume your database is expected to have for the first years of production. This will help in the physical design of the database and SQL access as well. Toward this end, it is wise to build a spreadsheet to estimate and finalize storage requirements. The steps in this process are as follows:

◆ Estimate the number of tables.

◆ Estimate the length of each row.

◆ Estimate the number of rows for each table (including a year's worth of growth).

◆ Procure additional storage, if needed.

◆ Build a spreadsheet to estimate and finalize access requirements.

◆ Estimate the number of users.

◆ Determine user transaction types (EIS, DSS, or OLTP).

◆ Calculate the cost and frequency of each access.

Setting up the development database environment

It is also good practice to set up your development database to have the first year of production data loaded in a simulated fashion. This will help to certify the physical design of the database and SQL access as well. The steps in this process are as follows:

◆ Create the database, tables, indices, and user permissions.

◆ Use ERwin to generate the database schema.

◆ Use Enterprise Manager to administer and maintain database objects.

◆ Build batch and online procedures to populate and access the database.

◆ Use flat-file extracts to load the initial test bed of data (bcp).

◆ Develop BATCH procedures for periodic mass updates (EMBEDDED SQL/C, C++, or Java).

◆ Develop OLTP using stored procedures and SQL.

◆ Develop techniques for EIS and DSS.

◆ Build database summary tables.

◆ Build ad hoc query tools (dynamic data windows).

◆ Procure warehousing tools (COGNOS, PILOT, and so on).

♦ Use the DBMS EXPLAIN utility for all SQL with problematic performance.

♦ Refine the database physical design.

♦ Add secondary indices to aid access and improve performance.

♦ Repartition and relocate physical components.

Defining the Application

After the development environment has been established, the first step in defining the application is to create the application object. Defining the application not only includes setting up and defining the application object but also establishing the rules of interaction between developers. The developers must buy into the sharing objects they will jointly develop. They should "check in" and "check out" development objects, and use basic teamwork to maximize project productivity.

The application object

The *application object* constitutes the entry point into the application. It is similar to a transaction ID in CICS. The application object names the application and specifies which libraries, or GUI presentation tools, will be used to save the objects and run the application. The library list will also include CLASS libraries used to inherit BASE objects. Finally, it specifies the application-level scripts. The application OPEN event script will usually include a function to set and initialize application variables, test the database connection, and launch or OPEN the application window frame (in an MDI application). Other events in the application object include functionality to handle application events such as IDLE, SYSTEM ERROR, and CLOSE. Application GUI presentation tools are manipulated and default preferences are set for the application development workstation using the respective painter.

The application standards

At this point, you and your developer colleagues should be familiar with certain application defaults. The standard font and size can be set in the application object. The number and names of SQL Server 7 and user interface (UI) libraries should be determined. You can set up libraries and store objects according to application functionality or by object type. Defining an application object is usually done once for an application, but the application object may be copied onto each developer's workstation so that the developer can include his or her own UI presentation tool in the library list (usually first). This is a good technique for setting up a development environment where object sharing is accomplished (library list 2-N contains project-wide UI presentation tools) and developers can test new objects (library list item 1, which contains an individual developer UI presentation tool).

See the remaining chapters in sequence in this part for ideas on developing the user interface.

Creating a Batch Interface

Even a predominantly OLTP system will require some form of BATCH interface. By BATCH interface, we mean jobs and processes consisting of command language (for example, NT command script) that executes a sequential series of utilities and application programs (for example, EMBEDDED SQL/C) to access and manipulate the application database. For example, you might have a GATEWAY data transfer from a mainframe (for example, IBM MVS or AS/400) containing reference data. The flat ASCII reference data, when received, is then loaded into a SQL Server 7 table for use by the OLTP. The LOAD might be followed by a script call to SQL Server 7 to execute a stored procedure to update other tables in accordance with the downloaded data. For example, an ASCII price file is downloaded from an IBM DB2 and used to update the SQL Server 7 price table. The new prices are then used by a SQL Server 7 stored procedure to update client positions in a SQL Server 7 portfolio table.

Initial data loading

Every table has to start drawing content from somewhere. If you have an existing system, you may have a conversion where the old system's data is downloaded and used to seed and populate the new system tables. SQL Server 7 provides a variety of utilities and options to LOAD flat ASCII data into a SQL Server 7 table (for example, bcp). The choice between utilities is based upon speed and flexibility. The utilities and their options are discussed in Chapter 4, "SQL Server 7 Tools and Components."

Creating BASE-class stored procedures and functions

When you have the database designed and you know the set of accesses required by the business functionality, then you can begin to build procedures to access the SQL Server 7 database. A powerful option available with SQL Server 7 is the *stored procedure*. Using stored procedures, you can group SQL statements and control-of-flow stored procedure language (SPL) in one object to improve the performance of SQL Server. Stored procedures are collections of SQL statements and SPL. They are stored in the database, and the SQL is parsed and optimized. An execution plan is prepared and cached when a procedure is run so that subsequent execution is very fast. The SQL is only reoptimized at execution if necessary.

Stored procedures can:

◆ Receive parameters passed by the calling object (for example, PowerBuilder's GUI front end).

- ◆ Call other procedures.

- ◆ Return a status value to a calling procedure or GUI front end to indicate success or failure, and the reason for the failure.

- ◆ Return values of parameters to a calling procedure or GUI front end.

- ◆ Be executed on remote SQL Server 7, that is, as remote procedures calls (RPC).

The capability to use stored procedures greatly enhances the power, efficiency, and flexibility of SQL. Compiled procedures dramatically improve the performance of SQL statements and batches. In addition, stored procedures on other SQL Server 7 servers can be executed if your server and the remote server are both set up to allow remote logins. You can write triggers on your local SQL Server 7 that execute procedures on a remote server whenever certain events, such as deletions, updates, or inserts, take place locally. Stored procedures differ from ordinary SQL statements and from batches of SQL statements in that they are precompiled.

Batching C and Java programs with embedded SQL

Sometimes a table does not require an entire LOAD, because only a small percentage of the table needs to be modified. SQL Server 7 C/Embedded SQL, which is an interface to code embedded SQL (including stored procedures) in a C program, can provide a solution. A small transaction file can be read and selective updating can be applied using a SELECT and UPDATE combination. The choice between using C with embedded SQL and the SQL Server 7 utilities is again based upon speed and flexibility. Embedded SQL and C are discussed in Chapter 17, "C and Java with SQL."

Batching utilities for database tuning and repair

Sometimes a table becomes fragmented and unorganized, degrading your performance, and you would like to know about it as soon as possible. Sometimes a table gets corrupted and you would like to amend it as soon as possible. SQL Server 7 provides a host of utilities to reorganize and repair disorganized and damaged tables. These utilities are discussed in Chapter 4, "SQL Server 7 Tools and Components."

Batching utilities for backup and recovery

Every serious database application should include a scenario for backup and recovery in the case of a system failure – hardware or software that destroys the database. These scenarios range from simple, for an SE-based database on one machine, to extremely involved, where multiple OL databases are arranged in a replicated string across many sites. SQL Server 7 provides various solutions that can support each particular environment.

Creating the Interface

After you have developed the basic presentation/navigation of the application and received user approval, you can build the windows or pages (for the Internet) and menus that present the data. You also develop the menu(s) or navigation pages that allow the user to move from window to window or page to page and perform application tasks. Online Transaction Processing (OLTP) applications should provide easy-to-understand, user-approved data entry characteristics as well as a quick understandable response to each user action.

> The user-approved application presentation and navigation can and should be done at or near the beginning of the development cycle. Make sure the user has seen and used a prototype or example of how the basic system components will look and feel, and make sure the user signs off on the design for that application version.

Choosing an interface style

In the early days of client/server development, OLTP systems would resemble either old dBASE systems or mainframe CICS implementations, or else single-document applications – only one document or sheet open at a time. As software packages like Microsoft Word and Microsoft Excel increased in popularity, their look and feel became the de facto standard. A growing number of users are familiar and accustomed to using Word-like application interfaces. These applications are based upon the so-called multiple document interface (MDI). The MDI consists of a window frame to house the main menu and one or more window sheets that present the application data to the user for update and inquiry. The MDI provides the ability to open more than one window sheet at a time so that work on different parts of an application at the same time can take place. It will also provide a consistent and common interface to all of the operating system features. For example, a SAVE menu item on an application's main menu, once created, will be used by all of the application components, and each user can access the full range of data manipulation features.

Setting up the class library for the interface style

In simple terms, a CLASS library is a collection of application objects (windows, menus, business objects) that have generic functionality that the developer can use by inheriting the CLASS object. For example, you inherit a class object menu that includes the item FILE and subitem PRINT, which triggers an event script to print the current window. Inheriting this class object provides all windows that use this menu with a consistent print interface. Moreover, the interface is only coded once. Each time you inherit it, you save time and money. Eventually, the CLASS library will pay for its cost.

Assuming that we will use the MDI interface, the organization will have either purchased a CLASS library, including an MDI implementation kit, or developed its own CLASS libraries. This will obviate a redo of the application launching objects (window frame and BASE menu) on the part of aggressive developers if the class objects have not been determined. Once the BASE frame, menu, and sheets are created, the developers need only inherit the sheet to be able to create windows, place controls in the windows, and build scripts that specify the processing that will occur when events are triggered.

Building Windows and Pages

Windows are the main interface between the user and SQL Server 7 applications. Windows can display information, request information from a user, and respond to mouse or keyboard actions. There are six types of windows in today's graphical user interface style. Where CLASS libraries are used, the developer will typically be inheriting a MAIN-type window. The MDI FRAME with MICROHELP-type window is usually built once. The other four are used typically to provide information for a MAIN-type window. For example, most GUIs use a CHILD window type when you add a drop-down data window to provide only valid choices for a field on a MAIN window. Most of the windows you develop in an MDI application will be type MAIN.

Each Window object has:

◆ A *style*, which is determined by its attributes. The attributes describe an object, in this case a window. The attributes of a window include but are not limited to whether it is Enabled, its Height, the MenuName if one is associated with the window, the window Title, and, for MDI frames and sheets, Toolbar attributes.

◆ *Events*, which can trigger the execution of scripts. The basic window events include open and close as well as user events that are defined to perform special processing in an MDI application. For example, the BASE menu may have an item SAVE, which has a script to Trigger the event ue_filesave. It will have been defined to contain a user-defined event called ue_filesave. The script associated with this event will be executed.

◆ *Functions*, which are part of the definition of the window and are used in scripts to change the style or behavior of the window, or to obtain information about the window. The window may contain a function wf_update, which contains a script that will perform update processing particular to the current window sheet.

◆ *Structures*, which are part of the definition of the window and are used in scripts to define groups of window-pertinent variables.

Determining the type of window or page

The type of window you use to implement a particular feature of the application is an important decision when you are trying to make your application consistent with other Windows applications. Table 8-1 lists some general considerations.

TABLE 8-1 WINDOW AND PAGE TYPES

Type	Properties
Main	Is a stand-alone window; it has no dependencies
	Has a title bar
	Is independent of other windows (main sheet windows encapsulate functionality); for example, `w_series_sheet` maintains series and `w_episode_sheet` maintains episodes.
	Is sometimes called a parent or overlapped window
	Can be minimized or maximized
	Has its own menu (Is there a standard class-library menu?)
Child	Is always subordinate to its parent window; for example, drop-down Data Access windows
	Is never the active window
	Exists only within the parent window
	May have a title bar
	Automatically closes when its parent window is closed
	Is clipped when you move it beyond the parent window
	Moves with the parent window because its position is always relative to the parent window
	Has no menu

Continued

TABLE 8-1 WINDOW AND PAGE TYPES *(Continued)*

Type	Properties
Pop-up	Has a parent window
	May have a title bar or menu
	Displays inside or outside the parent window
	Never disappears behind its parent window
	Can be minimized; when minimized, it is displayed as an icon at the bottom of the screen
	Minimizes with its parent
Response	Obtains information from and provides information to the user; for example, "The row you are trying to add already exists! Continue? Yes or No"
	Remains the active window until the user responds by clicking a control
	Is application modal, that is, fixed-path menu items are disabled. The user must respond before any other action can be taken.
	When the response window is open, the user cannot go to other windows in the application from which the response window was opened.
	Cannot be minimized but can be moved.

USING MULTIPLE DOCUMENT INTERFACE WINDOWS

You use a main window as the frame and sheets for an MDI application. This is probably the most common window type you will create. The main window suits the open application because you can add user events (ue) that are common to applications. For example, ue_filesave and ue_fileopen include the specific processing in a script behind the event. You can then use the same common main_menu for all the main sheet windows, saving all of the expense of a menu. For example, the menu item SAVE will trigger the event ue_filesave in the current window. Whatever script is embedded in that event will be executed. The script can be different for each window. The basic function; that is to say, the menu item SAVE is the same, but the table updated is different.

Child windows are useful when an application needs to display a variable number of subordinate entities, tables, and data views. If an application's style calls for heavy use of response windows, try to find an open solution using a menu or toolbar item if possible. The downside to response windows is that the approach makes the applications modal or less open. In other words, the user must go down a predefined path to perform a task. There are few options for change. When deciding how to use response windows, look at other Windows applications for some precedents before you commit to an approach. Both child and pop-up windows can have an explicit parent window. If a parent window is not named when the child or pop-up window is opened, the last active main window becomes the parent window.

USING THE BASE OR FRAME WINDOW OF AN MDI APPLICATION

Every Windows application needs a BASE or frame window. This is usually the first window you see when you invoke the application, or after you have supplied login information (in Word, for example, a frame window contains a menu, toolbar(s), and a blank open sheet). The BASE window should be of type main because it is at the highest level in your application hierarchy. It is not subordinate to any other window in the application. This window usually remains on the screen throughout the application session. The MDI frame in an MDI application is a prime example of a BASE window.

USING THE SHEET WINDOWS OF AN MDI APPLICATION

As we mentioned in describing the multiple document interface, sheets are defined as main windows. After the BASE frame is defined, you will build as many sheets as the application requires; for example, one sheet per table for basic maintenance plus as many others as are needed for special functions. Each sheet acts like a main window and follows most of the rules of child windows.

A sheet is always subordinate to its parent window, the MDI frame. A sheet is activated at the same time as the MDI frame. This is one exception to the rules for child windows. A sheet can exist only within the MDI frame. Sheets always have title bars that can be dynamically populated. Sheets are closed automatically when the MDI frame is closed. Sheets move only within the MDI frame because their position is always relative to the MDI frame. They occupy the workspace remaining after the menu and toolbar real estate is established. Sheets can be minimized. When minimized, they display as an icon inside the MDI frame. Sheets can have menus, but developers should attempt to minimize the number of menus. Find the common denominator of menu functionality in your application. Sheets are activated by the user clicking anywhere within the sheet boundary; the menu associated with the sheet also becomes active.

USING THE REST OF THE WINDOWS IN THE MDI

Child windows (for example, the Table windows used in the database painter) are subordinate to the sheets. This nesting can continue. However, MDI does not provide for the nesting of sheets within sheets, and this should not be attempted. Pop-up windows generally are not used in MDI applications because sheets replace the need for pop-up windows.

Response windows, although modal, are used as YIELD or STOP signs to draw the users attention. Although response windows frequently are not invoked directly from the MDI frame, they can be used to open or print application entities, or to perform similar actions. For example, a response window can be used with a data access window's control to search for existing database rows and return the key values to the main window sheet for subsequent retrieval and update. The About box is a response window as well. Response windows are usually used within the context of a sheet, to further refine the definition of an application entity or to specify options for an action. Response windows can also be invoked from other response windows. This is useful when a generic entity interface needs to be invoked or space limitations on the surface of a response window dictate that additional information needs to be gathered elsewhere. Response windows should never be nested more than one level down.

Adding controls to a window or a page

After the window type is chosen, one or more controls are added to enhance the functionality. In the MDI style, the number of controls should be kept to a minimum. The menu and toolbar should be used for carrying out application tasks. The most common control will probably be the data window control. It can provide a good deal of functionality, and it can be used to receive, edit, validate the display of, print, and maintain data. Most of the window controls can be built within a data window. The data window can be associated with a database table or tables, but it does not need to be. For determining an option or value, the external source data access windows can be used. Table 8-2 provides a brief summary of controls.

TABLE **8-2** WINDOW AND PAGE CONTROLS

Control	Determines Option or Value	Notes
CheckBox	Yes	
Button	No	Try to use the menu instead; commonly used on response windows.
Data access, a control that accesses the database to select, insert, update, or delete base or system meta-data	Yes	This *should be* the most common control; you can use it as a better alternative to almost all of the other controls. The data access control includes its own control styles, such as a drop-down list box.

Control	Determines Option or Value	Notes
DropDownListBox	Yes	
Edit mask	No	Display and enter formatted data.
Graph	No	
Group presentation tool box	No	Used to group available selections.
HscrollBar and VscrollBar	No	
ListBox	Yes	
MultiLineEdit	No	Use this control to enter data; try an external data access window instead.
Picture	Yes	This control is cosmetic as well; it's expensive and large.
RadioButton	Yes	
SingleLineEdit	No	Use this control to enter data; try an external (nondatabase) data access window instead.
SpinBox	Yes	
StaticText	No	Use this control to display text information.
User Object	Yes	

The data access window control should be the most common control utilized. Use it with a menu to trigger event processing on the window sheet and the data access window object currently associated with the control.

Creating Menus

Menus in your windows can include a menu bar, drop-down menus, and cascading menus. You can also create pop-up menus in an application. You define the menu items and write scripts that execute when the items are selected. These scripts launch the particular application component. In the MDI application style, menu bars are usually accompanied by toolbars. Toolbar buttons map directly to menu items. Clicking a menu toolbar button is the same as clicking its corresponding menu item (or pressing the accelerator key for that item).

Designing menu interaction

Menu development should be done carefully. Poorly designed menu handling can cause latent problems that may only be detected when the application is used heavily. Menus are expensive – they are one of the larger objects in a SQL Server 7 library – and their misuse can seriously degrade application performance. Poor planning with menus can also cause problems that manifest themselves as inconsistent responses to user actions. These errors are hard to detect, reproduce, and correct.

The menu bar–toolbar combination is the backbone of an MDI application. It provides a common user interface to all of the application components. If you are using a CLASS library, you will probably build menus by inheriting a class object menu and adding your custom items to the existing list of common items – for example, FILE,WINDOW,HELP. Improper handling of menus can make the trivial seem complex. Be aware of the way SQL Server 7 sets the current menu and toolbar. You should follow some basic rules and guidelines for working with menus.

Optimizing menu use

The MDI frame should always have a menu. If the currently active sheet does not have a menu, then the menu and toolbar (if any) associated with the last active sheet remains in place and operative while that previous sheet remains open. So you can see that to avoid unpredictable results, all sheets should have a menu. Another nuance of GUI menu-toolbar workings involves the toolbar. If the currently active sheet has a menu but no toolbar, and the previously active (and still open) sheet has both a menu and a toolbar, then the menu displayed will be the menu associated with the currently active sheet, but the menu toolbar displayed will be the toolbar for the previously active sheet. This will totally confuse a user, and the situation must be avoided.

If you are using toolbars (a virtual give-me in the MDI application), then all sheets should have a menu toolbar. Disabling a menu item will disable its toolbar button as well but will not change the appearance of the button. If you want the button to have the gray look, you must do this programmatically. Hiding a submenu item does not cause its toolbar button to disappear or to be disabled. If you want the button to disappear or be disabled, you must do this programmatically as well. To build a menu, use the MENU painter.

Creating Data Access Objects

Create *data access objects* to retrieve data from the database, format and validate data, analyze data through graphs and crosstabs, create reports, and update the database. A data access object is a window object that enables the user to display and manipulate database information using SQL statements in scripts or stored procedures developed for the particular function. You build a data access object in the data access painter and save it in a library that is available to the application. To build serious data access objects (known as `datawindows` in PowerBuilder) – those that are used for data entry and mission-critical applications – the database design should be in the 90 percent complete zone.

Building data access objects with completed database entities

A good database design will make data access object creation easy. Good design will provide column names that are consistent, data types that are not overly exotic, unique indices that provide uniform data distribution, and primary and foreign keys creating relationships that promote integrity and facilitate "full statement" information joins. When the database is completed, you will probably know all of the accesses required to provide the desired functionality. Now is a good time to create the SQL Server 7 stored procedures and functions to speed up and simplify the processing. These are the database qualities that enable developers to easily build a usable data access object (for example, DataWindow).

If your database has these qualities, then you are ready to proceed. If not, stop here and get out your database design book and read it again carefully. Set up meetings with the database administrators. Take the time to get it right. The lack of a good database design signifies either a lack of business knowledge or a paucity of database administration talent or both. The database design is the most critical component; the presentation can be easily changed and modified, the database cannot. A poor database design can cause integrity as well as performance problems.

At some point, the database design becomes workable and all developers are granted permissions and are ready to build data access objects. To use a data access object in a window, you place a data access control in the window in the window painter and then associate a data access object with the control in the window painter or in a script. During execution, SQL Server 7 creates an instance of the data access object.

Every data access control has:

◆ A *style*, which is determined by its attributes

◆ *Events*, which can trigger the execution of scripts

◆ *Functions*, which are part of the definition of the data access control and are used in scripts to change the style or behavior of the data access control, or to obtain information about the data access control

You may want to customize the data windows and allow for dynamic changes in the BASE data window SQL; SQL Server 7 provides some functions that can help.

PowerBuilder data windows are designed to be intelligent database controls. You can include other objects in a data access control for cosmetic purposes. Data access also enables you to display columns of data in the form of an edit, CheckBox, RadioButton, DropDownListBox, or DropDownData access control. The DropDown data window affords a powerful edit style and can be used to create firm-wide edit capability for code or subject area data.

Advantageous uses of a data access object

The primary strengths of data access controls are as follows:

♦ **Data display.** You do not have to code variables to contain column values, format data, translate data values to display values, or map column values to nontextual display forms (pictures and OLE).

♦ **Data-entry layout.** To define a window with normal controls for data entry, the programmer would need to manage many separate controls collectively. The data access object includes all of the data terms in one control.

♦ **Scrolling.** Data access objects deal with all of the scrolling page formatting issues without any programmer code.

♦ **Reporting.** Data access objects provide extensive reporting capabilities. Calculated columns, formatting, and grouping can all be managed by data access object without any coding.

♦ **Data Validation.** Data can be validated by the data access. This is important for database validity and consistency, especially if you have used the DB painter to create edit styles and validation rules.

♦ **Automatic SQL.** It is not necessary to code the appropriate SQL statements to access the data from the database.

♦ **Performance.** Data entry often requires many different slots for the user to enter or display data. It would require many other controls if you were to implement such an interface without using the data access control. When a data access control displays information, it doesn't use a collection of individual windows controls; it paints the information on the screen as needed. The data access control knows where to activate a particular column by detecting when the user clicks the mouse. The more complicated a data access control is, the greater the performance benefits that are achieved. A data access control with 40 objects on its surface requires nearly the same resources as a data access object with 10 objects, or even only one object, on its surface, because the data access control is actually managed internally by SQL Server, not the Windows environment.

The data access control also provides many other performance advantages. It requires fewer resources. Because Windows paints each control separately and a data access control is only one control, the speed of painting is significantly increased because SQL Server 7 handles it all at once. Because the data window manages many form-oriented tasks internally, you write less code to perform validation and cursor control. Windows considers the data access control as a single control, and therefore, the data access control uses fewer resources compared to multiple standard controls.

◆ **Updates.** One of the most difficult database programming problems is identifying what needs to be updated based on what the user selected and modified. How do you select the appropriate syntax required? The data window object does this for you. The PowerScript UPDATE statement builds the correct SQL based upon the datawindow (DW) settings.

Using data access or standard controls

Some situations call for a data access control, some call for other controls, and some call for use of either a data access control or some other control. In general, most windows will require both data access and standard controls. Data access controls improve performance and reduce programming effort for data access, presentation of data, and data entry. A large percentage of controls within an application will probably be data access controls. Any time you need to access the database (DB), you should use a data access window (DAW). The external DAW with no DB access is also useful as a data entry display object.

Some situations straddle the line between using a data access control and using a standard control. An example of this is a database login window. There is no database information to display; none that originates from a table by use of a SELECT statement. There are no formatting, reporting, or update requirements. On the other hand, there is data entry in that the user is required to enter several pieces of related information into a window and then the information must be collectively processed. This means that you should consider an external data access control. Either way does the job, but the code to accomplish the task will be slightly different depending on the technique you choose.

Adding Scripts or Program Code

Scripts determine the actions that are initiated when an event takes place. For example, when a user runs a SQL Server 7 application, the system opens the application and executes a script in the application for the OPEN event. The application OPEN event might open an application frame window and test the database connection to see if it is active before a user begins processing.

The PowerScript application OPEN might look like this:

```
OPEN (w_appl_frame_window)
CONNECT using SQLCA ;
IF SQLCA.SQLCODE<> O THEN f_db_error(SQLCA)
```

Validating Your Code

You can run your application anytime during development. If you discover problems, you can debug your application by setting breakpoints, stepping through your code statement by statement, and looking at variable and structure values during execution.

Determining when to use the debugger

When you compile a script, the compiler detects obvious errors (such as incompatible data types or a misspelled function name), and the script will not compile until you fix these errors. In addition to compiler errors, you may have errors (such as dividing by zero) that will stop execution of the application or logical errors that may not stop the script from running but produce incorrect results. A debugger helps you find these errors. Debug allows you to suspend the application at selected points in a script (stops) and review the contents of variables used in the application.

Selecting the scripts or code to breakpoint

In Debug mode, you select the script you want to debug, insert stops in the script, and then run or single-step through the script. When a GUI development encounters a stop, it suspends execution of the application and displays the Debug window.
In the Debug window, you can:

♦ Display the objects and user-defined functions in the application, the current values of the objects, the instance variables, and the attributes of the objects.

♦ Display the current values of the global, shared, and local variables.

♦ Edit (add or modify) existing stops.

♦ Select another script to debug.

♦ Modify variable values.

♦ Select the variables you want to watch during the debugging session.

♦ Continue executing the application until the next stop or step until the next executable statement.

When you are using PowerBuilder, the stops remain in the scripts until you remove them or exit the application. When you close Debug, you suspend the Debug session. If you run Debug again during the same session, Debug resumes processing at the point at which you closed Debug. The Debug settings are saved for you in your .INI file so that you can continue an existing debug trail the next time you are ready.

Refining Your Code

At some point in the application development, key developers will see that certain patterns are being repeated frequently within the application. This may mean that certain application functions are being repeated, certain database accesses are being repeated, and certain user tendencies are emerging. The developers must respond and refine those parts of the application so that they perform in an optimal fashion. This is the point in the development cycle that will make or break the new application's acceptance and use.

Things to consider are how you can accomplish:

◆ Code reusability, reducing development time

◆ Code modularity

◆ Reduced maintenance costs

◆ Improved consistency (visual look and feel, nonvisual standards)

◆ Improved performance

You will accomplish these objectives by carrying out the following tasks:

◆ Optimize SQL Server.

◆ Remove redundant classes.

◆ Minimize levels of menus and toolbar inheritance.

◆ Minimize the use of large bitmaps.

◆ Minimize or isolate array processing outside of window open processing.

◆ Minimize the loading of list and drop-down list boxes in the OPEN event (use data access controls or drop-down data access controls instead).

◆ Put inherited GUI presentation tools first in the library search path (in reverse order).

◆ Place the directory that contains the GUI run-time DLLs first in the network search path.

◆ Optimize libraries; for example, if you use Novell, reset the Sharable attribute after optimizing a library.

Creating functions, methods, and structures

To support the refinement effort for your scripts, you probably want to define functions to perform processing that is unique to your application and structures that hold related pieces of data. If you want to be able to reuse components that are placed in windows, define them as user objects and save them in a library. Later, when you build a window, you can simply place a user object instead of having to redefine the components.

Creating an executable

When your client/server application is complete, you prepare an executable version to distribute to your users. Web applications are usually a collection of HTML pages that connect the application components. Before you deliver your application to users, you will need to prepare a standard .EXE file in the application painter.

The .EXE file contains:

♦ A bootstrap routine

♦ The application icon (optional)

♦ The compiled version of each object in the application

PREPARING TO CREATE THE EXECUTABLE

To create an .EXE file, you perform a series of steps that we mention not for the sake of procedure but because each of these items must be fashioned properly long before you reach this point in the development cycle. Make sure that you have considered the placement of the executable library components.

CREATING THE DEPLOYABLE APPLICATION EXECUTABLE

Usually the GUI tool creates the executable, stores it in the specified directory, and closes the Create Executable window. Consider its size and the following questions:

♦ How many libraries must be packaged?

♦ If the application is large, can it be broken up into smaller deliverables?

♦ Is the security in place?

♦ Has the production database been defined with the proper sizing and partitioning?

♦ Is it available for use?

♦ Are the user identifiers in place with the proper permissions?

- ◆ Do the users have connectivity?

- ◆ Has the user-acceptance team been put in place?

- ◆ Are the database support people ready?

These are the types of issues that must be addressed before deploying a production SQL Server 7 application. We will expand upon each of these issues and options throughout the remainder of this book. This iterative style will hopefully minimize the amount of time and effort required to understand how to develop applications in the client/server world.

Summary

This chapter covered the steps required to plan an application development effort for SQL Server 7 and the programming standards that need to be addressed when establishing a development environment. In the next sequence of chapters, we will elaborate on each of the plan components mentioned in this chapter. You are now ready to start designing and constructing the application.

Chapter 9

Defining the Application

IN THIS CHAPTER

- ◆ Types of client/server systems
- ◆ Managing a development project
- ◆ Partitioning an application

WHAT DO WE MEAN when we speak of defining an application? Well, when defining an application, the lead developer typically starts work by attempting to determine the application's technical architecture. This is the definition of all of the interacting software and hardware components that combine to make up the application or system. This is also true for the reengineering of an existing computer system or for the development of a brand new system.

The task of defining an application begins at a very high level and proceeds through various iterations of refinement, which result in a very detailed architecture document that can be updated during the life of a project if, as is often the case, requirements change. At its most simplistic, or highest, level, you can always divide the application into a couple of pieces: the online portion and the batch portion. Even though you have an application that is required to be *available 24 hours a day, 7 days a week, 365 days a year,* you will need to factor in time for tasks such as cleanup processing, which is a batch process. Another task that is often overlooked in a 24 by 7 environment is the scheduling of hardware and software upgrades during the year. Enough of the high-level stuff; this chapter will focus on the design and definition of an object-oriented client/server or Web application.

Web, Client/Server, and Object-Oriented Systems

The terms *Web application, client/server,* and *object-oriented* are now commonplace. The words *architecture* and *application partitioning* are also frequently mixed in with these terms when describing how an application is put together. If these terms are new to you or a little unclear, we are now going to try to define them. Here are the essential concepts that you need to know.

Basic client/server terminology

The client is a consumer of services (see Figure 9-1). It is the process that begins a conversation by issuing a request to be serviced by another process, known as the server process.

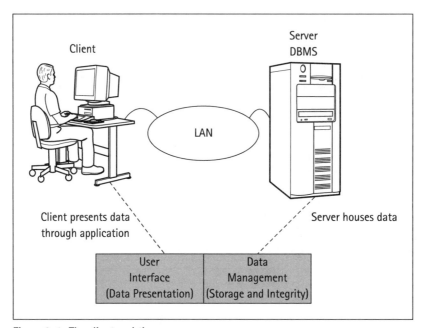

Figure 9-1: The client and the server

The server is a provider of services. It is a process that waits for requests. When it receives a request, it carries out a service and returns a response (or result) to the calling client. A server process is capable of handling requests from several clients' processes and is responsible for the management of responses. This relationship can be likened to a customer (client) placing an order (request for service) to a waiter/waitress (server) in a restaurant.

Object-oriented terminology

Object-oriented languages enable a developer to deliver high-quality products to market more quickly with lower ongoing maintenance costs. Object technology, through the use of modeling, provides the link between the real world and computer technology.

♦ **Object-oriented analysis.** An analyst takes a set of user requirements and reduces them to the business rules.

◆ **Object-oriented design.** A designer will take a set of business rules and design objects that can be implemented with an object-oriented programming language. These objects can be pure business rule objects in addition to user interface and database objects. An object is made up of its data (what it knows) and its methods (what it can do).

◆ **Object-oriented programming.** The programmer takes an object-oriented design, which includes the user interface, business, and database objects, and implements them in the chosen object-oriented programming language. Object-oriented programming languages have become more popular by providing developers with the following object-oriented features, which are also useful in controlling software complexity:

- **Abstraction.** Object-oriented languages release developers from the restriction of fixed data types. Using these new languages, developers can create new data types, known as abstract data types, or *classes*. *Abstraction* is the ability to consider and extract the essential characteristics required and package them into a convenient and compact data type.

- **Encapsulation.** This is closely associated with modularity, or information hiding, which allows ongoing modifications to be made to the internals of an object, provided that these changes do not affect the public interface.

- **Polymorphism.** Meaning "many forms," *polymorphism* allows the developer to define the same named method in different objects in an inheritance tree. The name is the same, but often the method is implemented in a different way. For example, you can define a "Print" method for a wide range of objects. Each object has its own definition of how the "Print" method is implemented.

- **Inheritance.** This enables programmers to define classes by reusing, or inheriting, previously defined classes as the basis for new objects. Some, or all, of the ancestor's methods and data are available for reuse.

Client/server and object-oriented development techniques can provide systems with the following attributes:

◆ **Scalability.** By permitting a more modular architecture, scalability enables you to add hardware power to match demand without rewriting software.

◆ **Usability.** Because client/server and a graphical user interface (GUI) go practically hand in hand these days, applications have become more usable. The GUI is an excellent environment to handle sophisticated user interfaces (Windows, Mac, and Motif, for example) as opposed to the character-based terminals attached to mainframe hosts.

Architecture

Client/server applications can be designed and implemented using one or more levels, or *tiers*. The tiers typically, but not always, correspond to the number of computers involved. These architectures are more commonly known by the following terms:

- **Single-tier.** In the single-tier architecture, the client and server processes are running on the same machine's processor (see Figure 9-2).

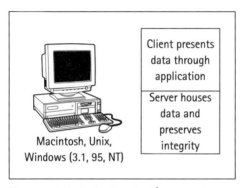

Figure 9-2: A single-tier client/server system

- **Two-tier.** In a two-tier architecture solution, the concept of a network is introduced (see Figure 9-3). A network (for example, TCP/IP or IPX/SPX) connects both the client workstation and the server. The client process running on the client workstation issues its requests via the network to the server process running on a server.

- **Three-tier (or N-tier).** A three-tier (or N-tier) solution is similar to the two-tier solution, in that they are both implemented across a network with the client process running on a client workstation issuing a request to a server process running on a server (see Figure 9-4). However, how the service is carried out is where the third tier (or N-tier) comes in. The server that receives the request from a client can in turn become an additional client to yet another server process.

  There are many possible implementations of this type of architecture. For example, the first client process could be an HTML application running within a Web browser on a workstation. The first server process is a Web server running on a Windows NT machine. The Web server then passes the message to a second server process, which is an application server (for example, SilverStream). The application server finally sends a request to a third server process, which is a database server executing on a UNIX machine.

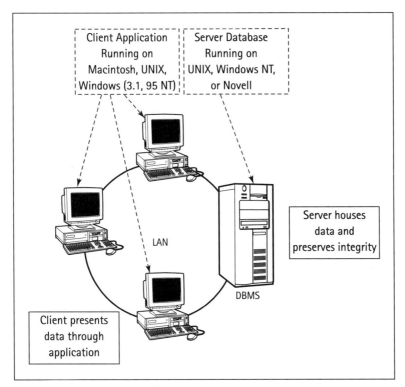

Client Application
Running on
Macintosh, UNIX,
Windows (3.1, 95 NT)

Server Database
Running on
UNIX, Windows NT,
or Novell

Server houses
data and
preserves integrity

LAN

DBMS

Client presents
data through
application

Figure 9-3: A two-tier client/server system

Application partitioning

Client/server implementations can range from slapping a GUI onto an existing application, to completely engineering or reengineering a distributed database application. The client/server strategy is reflected in the distribution of the application processing layers (see Figure 9-5).

The strategies are defined in terms of distributing the layers for presentation, business rules, and data access logic across the client and the server. The presentation layer is responsible for all that is involved with the processing of the user interface, including the formatting of information for display. The business rules layer is responsible for implementing the rules defined for the data. The data access layer handles all processing related to retrieving and maintaining data.

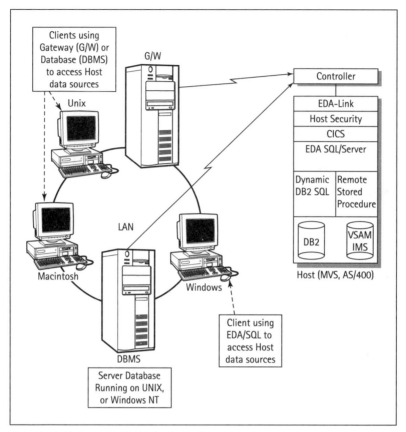

Figure 9-4: A three-tier (or N-tier) client/server system

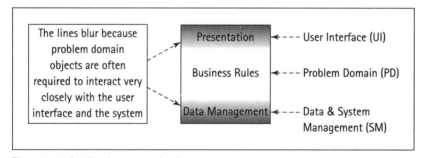

Figure 9-5: Application processing layers

◆ **Distributed presentation strategy (DP).** The distributed presentation is the simplest form of client/server implementation (see Figure 9-6). The presentation layer is present on the client and the server, typically a character-based host mainframe application. Using this strategy, most of the processing takes place on the server, including a large percentage of the presentation component. The remainder of the presentation component runs on the client.

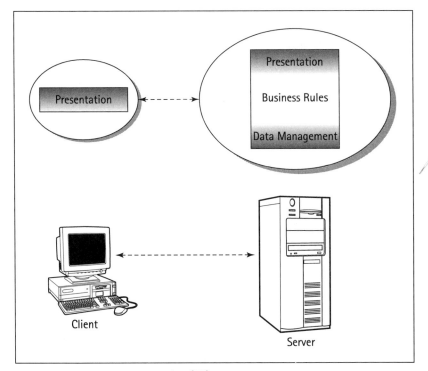

Figure 9-6: Distributed presentation (DP)

◆ **Remote presentation strategy (RP).** The remote presentation strategy places all the presentation logic on the client but leaves the business rules and data access processing on the server (see Figure 9-7).

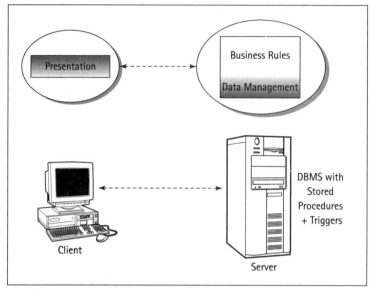

Figure 9-7: Remote presentation (RP)

♦ **Distributed business rules strategy.** The distributed business rules strategy can be complicated by the need to synchronize the business rules processes running on both client and server (see Figure 9-8).

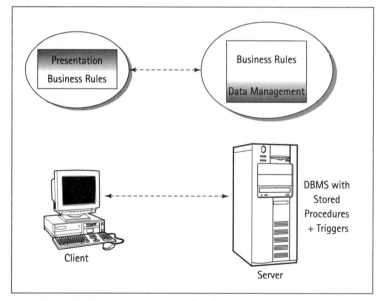

Figure 9-8: Distributed business rules (DBR)

◆ **Remote data management strategy.** The remote data management strategy has all of the application running on the client, but the data remains on the server (see Figure 9-9).

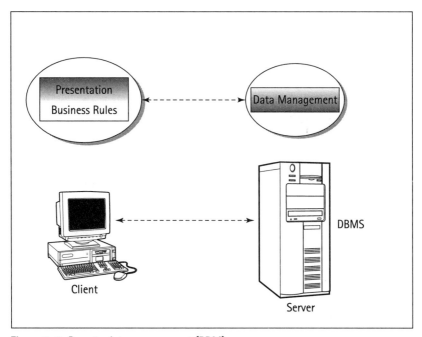

Figure 9-9: Remote data management (RDM)

◆ **Distributed database management strategy.** In the distributed database model, the data is stored on several servers and may be split across the client and the server (see Figure 9-10).

Managing Development Projects

The primary goal of any software development team is to produce high-quality products that fit the business requirements. Here are some essential planning lists.

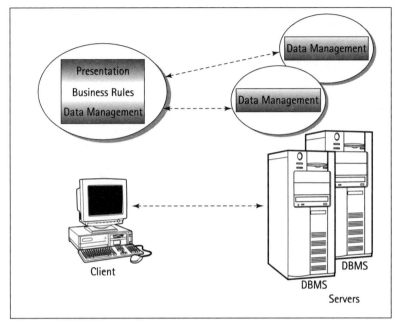

Figure 9-10: Distributed data management (DDM)

Software development goals

All application development projects should have goals or targets. Even if you don't always achieve such targets, your application will certainly benefit from them. Here is a simple list of the goals for an application:

◆ Correct

◆ Robust

◆ Extendible

◆ Reusable

◆ Compatible

Team skills

Development project teams also need a variety of team players. A good balance of disciplines and skills is essential to the success of a project. Here is a list of skills that can be required on a project:

- Project management
- End-user representation
- System architecture and design
- Database administration
- Network administration
- Standards control
- Object management
- Application development
- Documentation
- Multimedia artistry
- Quality assurance

The project life cycle

The *project life cycle* is the name given to the primary steps involved in successfully converting the user requirements into a working application. Repeatedly following a procedure that has been proven to be successful will result in a higher-quality application. Here is a list of the primary and secondary steps for a project:

- Planning
  - Understand the existing system
  - Determine requirements (see Figure 9-11)
  - Technical architecture analysis
  - Hardware evaluations
  - Software
  - Network infrastructure
  - Location strategy (domestic and foreign locations)
  - Migration and transition strategy
  - Operation strategy
  - Support strategy

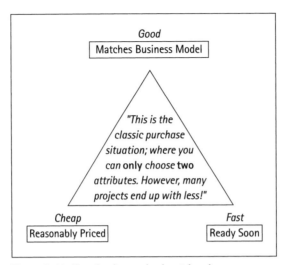

Figure 9-11: The classic purchasing triangle

- ◆ Analysis
  - ■ Interviews
  - ■ Flow charting
  - ■ Entity & object modeling
- ◆ Design
  - ■ Platforms
  - ■ Architecture
  - ■ Subsystems
  - ■ Tools
- ◆ Construction
- ◆ Testing
  - ■ Unit or component level
  - ■ System or integration level
  - ■ User acceptance level
  - ■ Integrity testing (availability, consistency, and resiliency)
  - ■ Performance testing

- ◆ Implementation
  - ■ Backup of existing data and applications
  - ■ Data conversion
  - ■ User documentation and training
  - ■ Software deployment
  - ■ Support
- ◆ Maintenance (repeat it all over again!)

Implementing the project life cycle

Many stages of the system development cycle can be conducted concurrently and/or repeatedly due to the nature and characteristics of objects. This iterative, or spiral, process (see Figure 9-12) differs significantly from a traditional "waterfall" development process (see Figure 9-13).

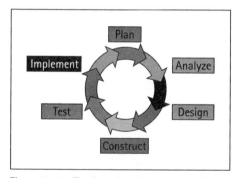

Figure 9-12: The iterative development life cycle

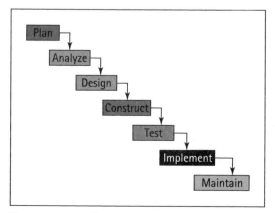

Figure 9-13: The "waterfall" development life cycle

Application Partitioning

Application partitioning is the separation of the application process into three groups, or partitions: the user interface partition, the problem domain partition, and the system management partition (see Table 9-1).

TABLE 9-1 APPLICATION PARTITIONS

Layer	Description
Presentation	User interface or UI
Business rules	Problem domain or PD
Data/system access	Data and system management or DASM

This evolution of application partitioning resembles that of cell division in the natural world (see Figure 9-14).

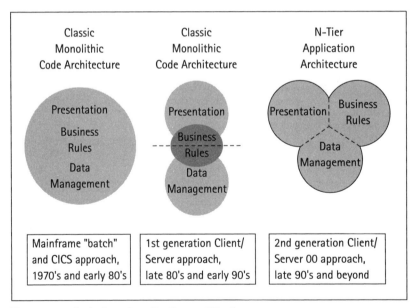

Figure 9-14: Evolution of application partitioning

Once the partitions (or layers) have been defined and documented, they should be formally presented to the whole development team, including any management. This will be good for educational purposes, provide a feeling of technical direction, and establish a forum for feedback from the team.

Partitioning an online application

The online portion of an application, or system, is usually the only part that a user talks about or knows about, if you're lucky. The application will usually break down into one of the following types: either Online Transaction Processing (OLTP) or some form of Decision Support System (DSS). (See Table 9-2 for more information.) DSS may go by the name of Executive Information System (EIS) or Management Information System (MIS). The difference between these types is that OLTP systems capture information from the user for storing in a database, and DSS systems extract information from the database, analyze it, and report it to the user.

TABLE 9-2 TYPES OF DATABASE APPLICATION

Type	Flow of Online Information	Example
OLTP	More data IN than OUT	Transactions capture, or data population
DSS	More data OUT than IN	Analysis, reporting, what if?

Some systems are a combination of both types, but if you try to create a database that is used for capturing many transactions as well as providing extensive query capability, you'll get a very poorly performing system.

User interface (UI)

The *user interface* portion contains all the objects that directly interact with the end user of the application. These include objects such as windows, menus, and toolbars. The user interface objects must not contain any other partition's logic but must delegate the processing by sending a message to the appropriate service in the other partition.

Problem domain (PD)

The *problem domain* contains all the classes and objects that provide specific business-related functionality, also known as *business rules* or *business logic.* Many companies have passed through the *information realization age,* which is the recognition of just how valuable the information that is stored in databases is, extending to how do we keep control over, and keep benefiting from, this increasing amount of information.

Business rules are here, with a positive value for our applications because:

♦ End users can easily relate to them

♦ Data, process, and object-oriented developers can easily relate to them

♦ They focus energy on maintaining data quality

You can measure your organization's acceptance of business rules as valid components of an information system by comparing your situation to each of the following stages:

♦ Stage 1. The organization has no awareness or recognition of business rules as such. The company is aware of only two components of an application, data and process. At best, you might hear that the process component does *something* to process the data.

♦ Stage 2. Some developers appreciate the business rule component, that which is more stable than the process component and less stable than the data component. For example, DBAs implement stored procedures and triggers to protect data by enforcing business rules or logic.

♦ Stage 3. The business rules exist primarily for businesspeople and secondarily for programmers and database designers. However, business rules are ideally represented independently of any programming language or modeling technique.

♦ Stage 4. The business rules move up from the "departmental" level and are considered and discussed at the company-wide or "enterprise" level.

♦ Stage 5. The business rules are considered a business asset, where they are used to shape organizational behavior, instigate change, serve customers, and compete creatively. This level of business rule is the responsibility of companies' leaders and visionaries, and rules can be used to create and reward productivity and prevent ineffective behavior.

Most problem-domain objects relate to "real world" objects, such as an order, a client, or a manufactured component. They are implemented without any visual component, so that they can work independently of the presentation layer.

System management (SM)

The *system management* portion contains the objects used to handle database or system-related services or tasks, such as printing, file access, and security. If one of the system management classes needs to display information to the user or obtain information related to the problem domain, it should send a message to the appropriate class or object in the presentation partition via the problem domain partition.

You can measure your organization's acceptance of data as a valid component of an information system by comparing your situation to each of the following stages:

◆ **Stage 1.** No awareness of data as an asset. A system is considered to be just a process or procedure. The systems process *something,* which just happens to be data.

◆ **Stage 2.** The company formally recognizes two components: the data component as well as the process component. Systems developers see physical data structures as separate from the procedures, or programs, that access and manipulate them.

◆ **Stage 3.** The company is conscious that the business semantics of the data are important, and recognizes a need to present and capture data in the same way across various projects.

◆ **Stage 4.** The company moves its focus from a "departmental" approach to data awareness to a company-wide or "enterprise" level.

◆ **Stage 5.** Data is considered a business asset, where it must be shared and leveraged throughout the enterprise. The quality and availability of the data becomes an enterprise business issue rather than a centralized IS responsibility.

Partitioning the batch portion

Although the *batch portion* of a system is less complex, it still requires some attention with respect to the partitions. You should also consider the following areas of the batch system:

◆ Batch interface (BI)
  ■ Scheduling packages (CRON, NT, 95)
  ■ Program parameters (including input files)
◆ Batch problem domain (BPD)
  ■ Standard business processing modules
  ■ Common file layouts

- ◆ Batch system management (BSM)

  - ■ File/system I/O modules

  - ■ Database processing modules

Understanding Web, N-tier client/server, and object-oriented technology requires some knowledge of the technical details, but it often requires greater appreciation of the way that the use of these technologies impacts the whole organization. Of all these techniques, object reuse has perhaps the greatest impact on the corporate culture, but it also has an impact most likely to result in flexible, reliable, high-quality software with reduced ongoing maintenance costs.

Summary

This chapter covered the design and definition of an object-oriented client/server or Web application. In doing so, it covered some the basic terminology for these applications, including the types of application; object-oriented analysis; design and programming definitions; and the way an application is partitioned into user interface, problem domain, and system management layers. The chapter also looked at how a development project is managed, in terms of goal-setting, putting together a team with the appropriate disciplines and skills, and following a project life cycle in order to deliver a high-quality project on time.

Chapter 10

Designing the Application

IN THIS CHAPTER

◆ The SQL environment

◆ The MS SQL Server defined

◆ Improvements from the last release, 6.5

DESIGNING COMPUTER APPLICATIONS is one of those areas in life where some things change and some things remain the same. The tools and methodologies have changed (they are refined and plentiful), but the problem or opportunity (depending on your viewpoint) is the same: We need to design smart but not necessarily clever business systems to provide accurate and timely information. In this chapter, the SQL environment for designing applications is introduced and product enhancements are itemized.

Designing an Application

Whether one is trying to understand and modify an existing computer-based business system or to create an entirely new one, the biggest obstacle to successful engineering is our inability to analyze and communicate the myriad interacting activities that make up our business process. Conversational languages, such as English, are too ambiguous to be effective, whereas formal languages remain unintelligible to most functional (business) experts. Techniques are needed that structure conversational language in such a way as to eliminate ambiguity and facilitate effective communication and understanding.

To put the current state of business software modeling technology in context at this point in 2000, there is "good news" and "bad news." The good news is that database modeling has come a long way in the last three years. There is a plethora of good tools. This competition moves the techniques along every day. The bad news is that process modeling has not progressed as well. There is a reason for this. Process modeling is more difficult. Database modeling tools cater to the current RDBMS standard SQL. We still have only the beginnings of process models because there is no standard process language. We have 3GLs and 4GLs being used in myriad combinations. We have COBOL, C, and Java programs mixed with PowerBuilder and Visual Basic and Web development tools used in the same shop and sometimes on the same project.

There is hope, however. Many vendors are working to create process-modeling tools that can generate target code for many popular process program languages. Fortunately, this is a book about SQL Server 7, so we will concentrate on database modeling. But be aware that a good database design is not just a nice relational model but also one that supports the business processes with SQL for data manipulation that provides for *fast access* coupled with *integrity*.

Why create a model?

Modeling has been used for centuries. It can be an effective technique for understanding and communicating. In a process model, extraneous detail is eliminated, thus reducing the apparent complexity of the system under study. The remaining detail is structured so as to eliminate ambiguity and highlight important information. Graphics (pictures, lines, arrows, and graphic standards) can be used to provide much of the structure, which is why most people think of process models as pictorial representations. However, well-written definitions of the objects appearing in the model, as well as supporting text, are also critical to the model's serving its role as a communications tool.

In engineering disciplines, it is expected that a model will be constructed before an actual working system is built. In the automotive industry, scale models of cars are constructed for the purpose of extensive testing. In most if not all cases, modeling the target business process is an essential first step in developing any database application. It is an essential road map that will establish the destination. Determining the exact functionality of your target destination is essential. It must be captured and represented in as much detail as possible. A picture can make the objective clear. As the Cheshire cat in *Alice in Wonderland* says: "If you don't know where you are going . . . any road will get you there."

Using a model as a tool

Once a model is developed and available for the developers, refinement of the product can then be accomplished at the logical level. This ensures the likelihood of a successful software product. Architects create blueprints before they actually construct a house. The blueprints are a logical representation of the physical building. There are many advantages to refining the design at the logical level, before the first brick is set. There are tools available to facilitate the construction of the model. Unfortunately, no tool to date can tell you what you want to do. You must determine this yourself. Once you have begun to formulate your requirements, tools can be helpful. Currently available tools such as Visio can be used to create graphical representations of almost anything (see Figure 10-1). They can also be linked with OLE to other tools (for example, Word, Excel, and PowerPoint). You still need to do the *modeling* with the business experts. These tools only help with presentation and control.

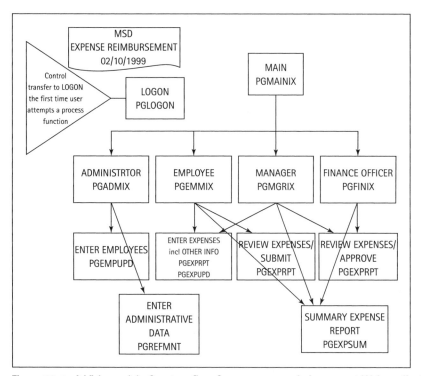

Figure 10-1: A Visio model of system flow for an expense reimbursement Web application

Process modeling enables you to look at a "system of interest" in depth, so that the subtle nuances of your organization can be analyzed, understood, and, perhaps most important, communicated to others. Many reasons might motivate a process-modeling project. Some of the by-products include, but are not limited to, documentation of a multiple step business process. One of the rules of thumb of business is that the longer a document is, the less it will be read. Give a busy person a one- or two-page document with a Visio or PowerPoint diagram, and there is a pretty good chance that person will look it over in a reasonable amount of time. Give that same person a 30-page, single-spaced document, and there is a very good chance that it will sit in the In box for months unread.

Process modeling is a valuable technique to gain consensus on what is being done and to quickly propose alternative new approaches. It costs much less to develop a model than it does to develop a new information system or reorganize a department, only to find out that the new approach has merely created a new set of problems and inefficiencies.

Develop an entity relationship

Once you have a basic model of the business process functionality, you then capture information about the data requirements to support the functionality. Before CASE tools became available, this was a tedious process, and even when they did, CASE was sometimes too large to handle. Thankfully the tools have evolved, and now there are a host of viable alternatives.

CASE Tools "Lite"

So how do you create an entity-relationship diagram in the new world? ERwin and PowerDesigner are generally considered to be the choices of serious developers when it comes to CASE tools. They are similar, and both perform the really important functions. For the purposes of this book, we will use ERwin to illustrate the capabilities of these *new wave* CASE tools. ERwin's stated focus is on quickly creating high-quality robust physical databases. ERwin, sold as a database design tool, does not create processing modeling diagrams, just entity-relationship diagrams (known as ER diagrams, hence the name ERwin).

ERwin's specialization is on the physical side. As of this writing, ERwin 3.5 has been released with support for SQL Server 7 among other database management systems. When you finish modeling the database, you can have ERwin build the data definition language. This is essentially what has been missing from the so-called "upper CASE" tools. Using such tools, ADW or LBMS for example, we have found that, after spending a couple of years designing something, you still don't know that much more about good relational database design . . . and that is critical for client/server success. Tools like ERwin and PowerDesigner show you the physical definition right from the start, not hiding it as "upper CASE" tools do. To build a good database model for physical implementation using SQL Server 7, you have to think like a relational database.

Benefits of new CASE

We can break the benefits of new CASE tools into two categories. First you will notice increased productivity. This is true for those projects that already have an existing database, and also for new projects when we are lucky enough to have a blank slate for a data model.

You will see the second benefit after you create your database. The quality and robustness of the physically generated SQL DDL (data definition language) is unsurpassed by even the largest and most expensive CASE tools on the market. An interesting point to note is the lifespan of ERwin's usefulness on a project. I have found that when tools like ERwin are chosen they are used throughout the entire project, without exception. Where an upper CASE tool is used (LBMS, ADW, and so on), the tool is usually abandoned somewhere during the initial development phase.

We have never seen a project that adopted an upper CASE tool in the middle of development. On many occasions, however, we have seen projects that weren't using any form of CASE tool easily pick up ERwin in midstream and keep with it to the end.

Data modeling using ERwin

ERwin uses a traditional methodology called IDEF1X. Much as with other tools, with ERwin you start creating an ER diagram by placing entities (tables) on your diagram and adding relationships between them. Figure 10-2 shows the ERwin environment, which enables you to do this. SQL Server has its own diagramming tool, but it is immature at this stage and as such unusable.

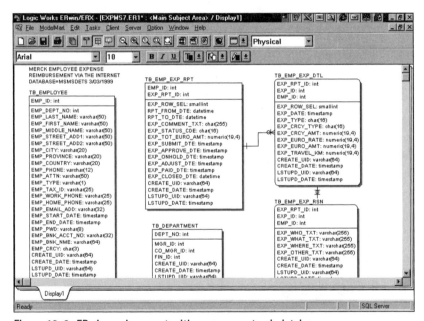

Figure 10-2: ERwin environment with an expense track database

Reverse Engineering

Sometimes the data we will use is contained in a legacy data model or an existing *heritage* data model. Both ERwin and PowerDesigner include the capability to reverse-engineer from any of the supported databases. *Reverse engineering* is the process of examining the previously existing table structure and getting your ERwin data model up to date with what's going on in the real database. In previous versions of ERwin, reverse engineering required you to have the original SQL DDL that was used to create your tables. However, quite often you can find yourself with a DDL that is out of date, or in the worst case, you have no DDL. ERwin solves this problem by providing a *database server suction* in a SERVER/CONNECT/SYNC ERWIN option (see Figure 10-3).

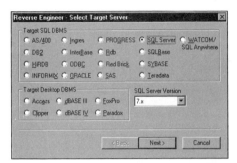

Figure 10-3: Setting the target server as SQL Server

If you prefer, you can still use the traditional approach in the latest version. You are basically using the ERwin OPEN function to read in SQL and create a model. Here are the steps:

1. Start ERwin, which is usually an .exe file; currently it is the modelmart.exe file in the Logic Works directory.

2. From the File menu, select REVERSE ENGINEER.

3. Change the File type to SQL, and specify the SQL file that you wish to reverse-engineer.

4. Specify the DBMS type that the SQL syntax is written for.

In the Reverse Engineer window, you now have several options. You can specify which SQL components you want to capture. You must reverse-engineer tables for obvious reasons, but you can capture foreign keys and indexes as well. You also have the ability to set case conversion options. Last, for the inquisitive, you can display the parse of the SQL as it is happening. When all options are set, press the Reverse-engineer button. Now would be a good time to calculate how much time you are saving by letting ERwin do the reverse engineering as opposed to doing it yourself! Unfortunately, you may not even have time to do that — it's pretty fast. It even runs in the background, so you can press Alt+Tab and go do something else.

ERwin 3.5 has a much better method of reverse engineering than its predecessor. With this capability, ERwin will actually connect to your DBMS and read directly from the system catalogs. This is not a one-time process, but an ongoing synchronization. Basically you connect to the SQL Server 7 database you want to reengineer. Then you choose the SYNC ERWIN with MS SQL SERVER 7 option. The ERwin tool will read the SQL Server 7 system catalog and build the model based on the tables, columns, indices, and so on found in the system catalog (see Figures 10-4 and 10-5). If a developer makes a change directly on the database, it is very easy to pick that up the next time you synchronize. This capability can only strengthen the product's project longevity.

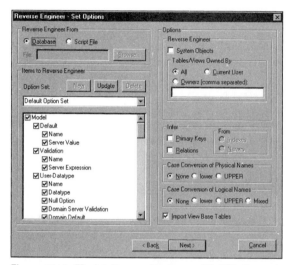

Figure 10-4: ERwin's Reverse Engineer with SQL Server 7

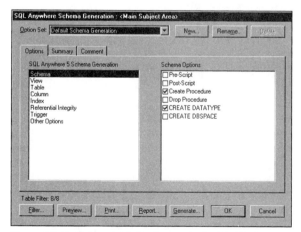

Figure 10-5: Choose tables to be synched with ERwin

Entity Modeling

Whether you are starting from scratch or working with an existing database, there are two types of entities, independent and dependent. *Independent* entities are those that can be uniquely identified without depending on relationships to other entities. Conversely, *dependent* entities cannot be identified uniquely without depending on relationships to other entities. Both types are available within the ERwin environment seen in Figure 10-2. The sharp-cornered entities are independent. The rounded corners represent dependent entities. To add an entity to your diagram, select the appropriate icon from the toolbox and click anywhere in your diagram. ERwin will give your entity a default name. To change the name, you will need to right-click the entity to bring up the list of available editors for that entity.

Invoke the Entity Attribute Editor.

The Entity Attribute Editor shown in Figure 10-6 enables you to enter not only the entity name but the attributes (fields, columns) for the entity. When you enter attributes, you need to decide whether an attribute forms part of the primary key or not, and enter it into the appropriate window. Keep in mind that what we are entering so far are only logical names for attributes and entities. These names can have spaces in them. The logical names will be used to generate default physical names. It might be wise to limit your logical names according to the specifications of your particular database. That way, you may never need to adjust your physical names.

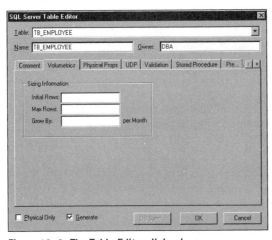

Figure 10-6: The Table Editor dialog box

The Column Editor shown in Figure 10-7 enables you to enter the data type and other physical properties of the particular attribute (table column) within each entity.

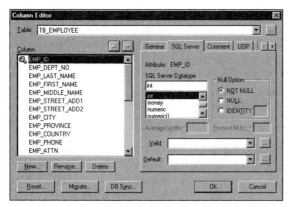

Figure 10-7: The Column Editor dialog box

Relationship Modeling

One of the nicest features of ERwin is its foreign key migration capability. It's a feature you really need to understand before you start adding relationships between entities. The IDEF1X terminology recognizes two types of relationships between entities, identifying and nonidentifying. *Identifying* relationships are used when a child entity is identified through its association with the parent entity. In other words, the foreign key column of the child table is also part of the primary key. *Nonidentifying* relationships indicate that the child entity is not identified by its relationship to the parent entity. Identifying relationships and nonidentifying relationships are represented by solid and dashed lines respectively.

Relationships in ERwin are generally referred to as foreign keys on the physical level. Normally, when you create foreign keys you first define the parent table (with a primary key) and the child table (with some columns in common). Afterward you add a foreign key on the child table's related columns and make that point to the primary key of the parent table. You'll always get an error if the number of columns in the foreign key does not match the number of columns in the primary key of the parent table (or if the data types don't match). This is where the foreign key migration comes into place.

To create a relationship in ERwin, select the appropriate icon (identifying or nonidentifying) from the ERwin toolbox, click the parent table, and then click the child table. ERwin will automatically migrate the primary key attributes of the parent table into the child table. If you draw an identifying relationship (solid line), the primary key attributes of the parent table will migrate into the primary key section of the child entity. Conversely, nonidentifying relationships will migrate the primary key columns of the parent table into the nonkey area of the child entity.

See Figure 10-8 for an example of adding a nonidentifying relationship. Notice that ERwin automatically added the emp_id field in the employee table. The relationship was a nonidentifying one, so the `emp_id` number was automatically inserted in the nonprimary key area of the employee table.

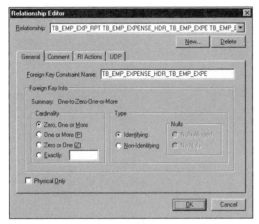

Figure 10-8: Creating a definition in the Relationship Editor dialog box

The best part about this foreign key migration is that it is dynamic. If you change the data type of a primary key column in a parent table, the change is reflected in all child tables. If you add columns to the primary key of a parent table, they are migrated down to the child tables.

Referential integrity

After a relationship has been added between tables, ERwin lets you control the referential integrity between them. To access this feature, you need to right-click the relationship line to bring up the relationship's menu, and select Referential Integrity (see Figure 10-9).

Figure 10-9: The Relationship menu

Once you are in the Referential Integrity Editor, ERwin will display the parent and child table names, as well as the name of the relationship. The first thing you can do is change the verb phrase and the physical name of the relationship. This will be used for the name of the foreign key.

ERwin enables you to control the behavior for an insert, delete, or update on either the parent or the child. Your options for any given action are Restrict, Cascade, Set Null, Set Default, and None.

◆ The Restrict option will cause the database to return an error if the action will violate referential integrity. For example, on a Parent Delete-Restrict setting, if an attempt is made to delete a customer that has orders, the deletion will fail.

◆ The Cascade option will cause the database to trickle any changes between the related entities. A Parent Delete-Cascade setting would cause the attempt to delete a customer with orders to also delete the associated orders. A Parent Update-Cascade setting would result in any attempt to change a customer number (the primary key of the Customer table), also changing the customer number for all orders that belong to this customer.

◆ The Set Null option will cause the database to null out the foreign key columns in the child table during a deletion or an update. For example, a Parent Delete-Set Null option would result in Order records having a null customer number for any orders that once belonged to a deleted customer.

◆ The Set Default is very similar, but instead of setting the foreign key columns to null, it resets them to their original default values.

Not all of the options are available for each action. For example, a Child Update-Set Null setting doesn't make much sense if you think about it for a minute. Also, not all of the options are available for foreign key declaration syntax in your particular DBMS. In fact, most of the options are not supported by the popular DBMSs. However, ERwin provides physical support for all of its options through the use of triggers. If your DBMS supports triggers, you can take advantage of most, if not all, of the options.

ERwin accomplishes this support through a set of trigger templates. These templates are created with a large and feature-filled set of macros. You can customize and even create your own triggers; however, the macro language is poorly documented. This same macro language has now been extended in version 3.5 to support stored procedures and ad hoc scripts. You can create your own stored procedure templates and apply them to tables or to the schema as a whole. This can be powerful for creating the standard select, insert, update, and delete stored procedures to use in your data windows.

Supported Databases

One of ERwin's big strengths is its wide support for various databases. Figure 10-10 shows the Target Server dialog box with all of the supported databases. ERwin doesn't make a big deal out of it, but you can change databases on the fly. ERwin maintains a data type map between databases, so the process of porting from one database to another is only a few clicks away.

Figure 10-10: Supported target databases

It may also be worth mentioning that ERwin/ERX 3.5 supports physical storage parameters for most DBMSs, including SQL Server 7.

Summary

This chapter covered the database design approach for relational databases such as SQL Server 7. We discussed and briefly illustrated the modeling software available. Additionally we used a "reverse engineering" exercise to review how an existing database can be modeled and reengineered using ERwin. We will concentrate on the database environment as well as the process of developing database applications in greater detail as we move on.

Chapter 11

Constructing the Database

IN THIS CHAPTER

◆ The data definition language (DDL) for creating and maintaining an application database

◆ The physical components of an application database

◆ Practical considerations based upon expected volume and component usage

◆ Choosing application component data types

◆ Choosing application index candidates

◆ Using the bulk copy program to populate a newly created table

◆ Creating views

◆ Maintaining the database

◆ SQL Server database utilities

AFTER DESIGN AND ANALYSIS are complete, developers define the physical components of the application database. This chapter describes the data definition language that developers use to create the application database as well as the practical considerations that are incorporated into the definition. This chapter also looks at the processes for creating tables, creating views, and maintaining the database. Finally, we'll take a brief look at utilities that help in redefining and repopulating a database as it is being developed.

Application Database Components

Once we start to get physical, we convert the logical model to a physical SQL Server manifestation. For the purpose of illustration, we will use an employee expense-reporting database as an example (see Figure 11-1). In this example database, we capture employee expense reports and the individual expense items. At the point after the database schema has been defined to our SQL Server database, the application's database will consist of the following components.

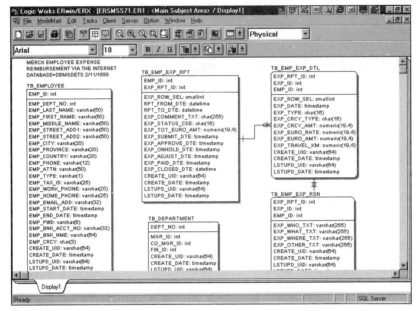

Figure 11-1: An ERwin physical model

- **Tables and columns** are the basic building blocks of a good database. They start off as entities and attributes in the logical model, where they are arranged to satisfy the business processes. See Chapter 6, "Database Administration Using Enterprise Manager," for additional commentary on the physical database components.

- **Indexes** provide a way to search and sometimes control the data rows within a table. One or more columns can be grouped together to form an index. Most tables should have a unique index that can serve not only as a search mechanism but also as a control to avoid duplication.

- **Keys (primary and foreign)** are indexes that provide for database integrity. In the expense-tracking example mentioned previously, the expense report table TB_EMP_EXP_RPT would have a *primary* key of EXP_RPT_ID. The detail table would have a *foreign* key of EXP_RPT_ID to connect the detail to the expense report and also to ensure that an expense report cannot be deleted if any details belonging to the expense report exist.

- **Views** describe their objects' function: to provide a particular view of base tables. Views are vertical tables, made up of columns from one or more tables, usually joined by the same key or keys that they share in common.

Creating a Database

Creating a new database usually happens at two distinct points in a project's life cycle. The first instance of the database is created just before development, and the second instance of the database is created at the point where production is imminent. The first build of the database during development is created without full knowledge of the application; that is, it is still being designed, and hence, it will not typically be configured optimally. The second database build (production) will be based upon all of the knowledge gained in the development phase and will include all of the SQL Server features available for optimizing data access.

So how do you create a new database? First you must be in the *master* database to create a new database. The following syntax for the component definition is then used to provide all that the database server needs to know to account for the new database:

```
CREATE DATABASE database_name
[ON [PRIMARY]
[ <filespec> [,...n] ]
[, <filegroup > [,...n] ]
]
[ LOG ON { <filespec> [,...n]} ]
<filespec> ::=
( [ NAME = logical_file_name, ]
FILENAME = 'os_file_name'
[, SIZE = size]
[, MAXSIZE = { max_size | UNLIMITED } ]
[, FILEGROWTH = growth_increment] ) [,...n]
<filegroup > ::=
FILEGROUP  filegroup _name <filespec> [,...n]
```

The parameters for this component definition are as follows:

- ◆ *database_name* — The name of the new database. Database names must be unique within a server and conform to the rules for identifiers. The *database_name* parameter can be up to 128 characters.

- ◆ ON — Specifies the disk files used to store the data portions of the database (data files) explicitly. The keyword is followed by a comma-delimited list of *<filespec>* items defining the data files for the primary filegroup.

- ◆ PRIMARY — Specifies that the associated *<filespec>* list defines the primary file. The primary filegroup contains all of the database system tables. It also contains all objects not assigned to user filegroups. The first `<filespec>` entry in the primary filegroup becomes the primary file, which is the file containing the logical start of the database and its system tables. A database can have only one primary file. If `PRIMARY` is not specified, the first file listed in the `CREATE DATABASE` statement becomes the primary file.

◆ `n` – A placeholder indicating that multiple files can be specified for the new database.

◆ `LOG ON` – Specifies that the disk files used to store the database log (log files) are explicitly defined. The keyword is followed by a comma-delimited list of `<filespec>` items defining the log files. If `LOG ON` is not specified, a single log file is automatically created with a system-generated name and a size that is 25 percent of the sum of the sizes of all the data files for the database.

◆ `FOR LOAD` – This clause is supported for compatibility with earlier versions of Microsoft SQL Server. The database is created with the database administrator's (DBO's) use only. The database option is turned on, and the status is set to loading. This is not needed in SQL Server version 7 because the `RESTORE` statement can recreate a database as part of the restore operation.

◆ `FOR ATTACH` – Specifies that a database is attached from an existing set of operating system files. There must be a `<filespec>` entry specifying the first primary file. As a practical note, use the `sp_attach_db` system-stored procedure instead of using `CREATE DATABASE FOR ATTACH` directly. Use `CREATE DATABASE FOR ATTACH` only when you must specify more than 16 `<filespec>` items.

◆ `NAME` – Specifies the logical name for the file defined by the `<filespec>`. The `NAME` parameter is not required when `FOR ATTACH` is specified.

◆ `logical_file_name` – The name used to reference the file in any Transact-SQL statements executed after the database is created. The `logical_file_name` parameter must be unique in the database and conform to the rules for identifiers. The name can be a character or Unicode constant, or a regular or delimited identifier.

◆ `FILENAME` – Specifies the operating system filename for the file defined by the `<filespec>`.

◆ `'os_file_name'` – The path and filename used by the operating system when it creates the physical file defined by the `<filespec>`. The path in `os_file_name` must specify a directory on the server in which SQL Server is installed. The `os_file_name` parameter cannot specify a directory in a compressed file system.

♦ SIZE — Specifies the size of the file defined in the ⟨filespec⟩. When a SIZE parameter is not supplied in the ⟨filespec⟩ for a primary file, SQL Server uses the size of the primary file in the model database. When a SIZE parameter is not specified in the ⟨filespec⟩ for a secondary or log file, SQL Server makes the file 1MB.

♦ size — The initial size of the file defined in the ⟨filespec⟩. The KB and MB suffixes can be used to specify kilobytes or megabytes; the default is MB. Specify a whole number; do not include a decimal. The minimum value for size is 512KB. If size is not specified, the default is 1MB. The size specified for the primary file must be at least as large as the primary file of the model database.

♦ MAXSIZE — Specifies the maximum size to which the file defined in the ⟨filespec⟩ can grow.

♦ max_size — The maximum size to which the file defined in the ⟨filespec⟩ can grow. The KB and MB suffixes can be used to specify kilobytes or megabytes; the default is MB. Specify a whole number; do not include a decimal. If max_size is not specified, the file grows until the disk is full.

♦ UNLIMITED — Specifies that the file defined in the ⟨filespec⟩ grows until the disk is full.

♦ FILEGROWTH — Specifies the growth increment of the file defined in the ⟨filespec⟩. The FILEGROWTH setting for a file cannot exceed the MAXSIZE setting.

♦ growth_increment — The amount of space added to the file each time new space is needed. Specify a whole number; do not include a decimal. A value of 0 indicates no growth. The value can be specified in MB, KB, or %. If a number is specified without an MB, KB, or % suffix, the default is MB. When % is specified, the growth increment size is the specified percentage of the size of the file at the time the increment occurs. If FILEGROWTH is not specified, the default value is 10% and the minimum value is 64KB. The size specified is rounded to the nearest 64KB.

Three types of files are used to store a database:

♦ The *primary file* contains the startup information for the database. The primary file is also used to store data. Every database has one primary file.

♦ *Secondary files* hold all of the data that does not fit in the primary data file. Databases need not have any secondary data files if the primary file is large enough to hold all of the data in the database. Other databases may be large enough to need multiple secondary data files, or they may use secondary files on separate disk drives to spread the data across multiple disks.

♦ *Transaction log files* hold the log information used to recover the database. There must be at least one transaction log file for each database, although there may be more than one. The minimum size for a transaction log file is 512KB.

Every database has at least two files, a primary file and a transaction log file. Although *os_file_name* can be any valid operating system filename, the name more clearly reflects the purpose of the file if you use the recommended extensions (see Table 11-1).

TABLE 11-1 RECOMMENDED FILENAME EXTENSIONS

File Type	Extension
Primary data file	.mdf
Secondary data file	.ndf
Transaction log file	.ldf

The *master* database should be backed up after a user database is created. Fractions cannot be specified in the SIZE, MAXSIZE, and FILEGROWTH parameters. To specify a fraction of a megabyte in the size parameters, convert to kilobytes by multiplying the number by 1024. For example, specify 1536KB instead of 1.5MB (1.5 × 1024 = 1536). When a simple CREATE DATABASE *database_name* statement is specified with no additional parameters, the database is made the same size as the model database. All databases have at least a primary filegroup. All system tables are allocated in the primary filegroup. A database can also have user-defined filegroups. If an object is created with an ON *filegroup* clause specifying a user-defined filegroup, then all the pages for the object are allocated from the specified filegroup. The pages for all user objects created without an ON *filegroup* clause, or with an ON DEFAULT clause, are allocated from the default filegroup. When a database is first created, the primary filegroup is the default filegroup.

Preparing to create a database

Before creating a database, the database administrator must determine the database sizing and filegroup placement. To avoid production failures, it is important to accurately specify the amount of space to allocate for it (see Figure 11-2). If you allocate too much space, you waste filegroup space that could be used by other databases. If you allocate too little space, the database may run out of storage space.

However, note that if you don't allocate enough storage space for the database, or if the database later grows to use most or all of its allocated space, you will be able to easily expand the room allocated to the database, as long as there is space available on one or more filegroups. Refer to Chapter 8, "Overview of the Application Development Process," to find a detailed treatment of how to estimate space requirements for SQL Server 7.

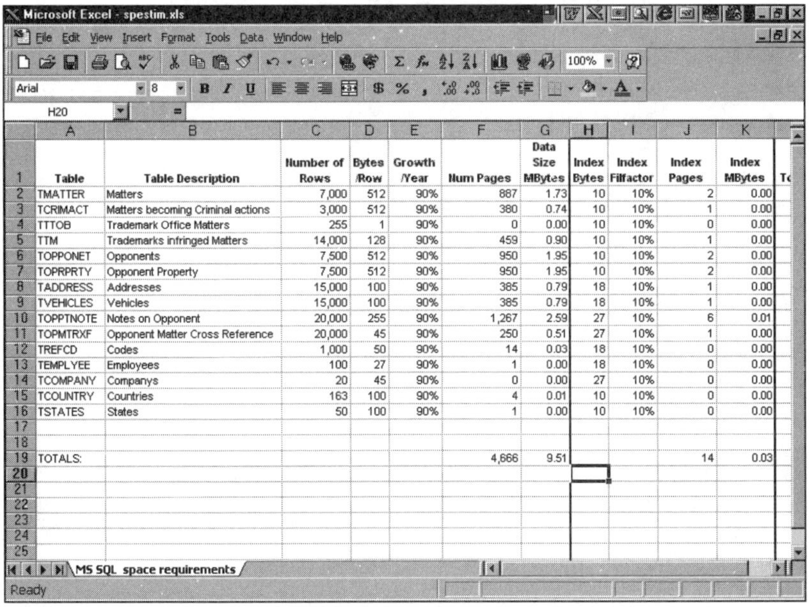

Table	Table Description	Number of Rows	Bytes /Row	Growth /Year	Num Pages	Data Size MBytes	Index Bytes	Index Filfactor	Index Pages	Index MBytes
TMATTER	Matters	7,000	512	90%	887	1.73	10	10%	2	0.00
TCRIMACT	Matters becoming Criminal actions	3,000	512	90%	380	0.74	10	10%	1	0.00
TTTOB	Trademark Office Matters	255	1	90%	0	0.00	10	10%	0	0.00
TTM	Trademarks infringed Matters	14,000	128	90%	459	0.90	10	10%	1	0.00
TOPPONET	Opponents	7,500	512	90%	950	1.95	10	10%	2	0.00
TOPRPRTY	Opponent Property	7,500	512	90%	950	1.95	10	10%	2	0.00
TADDRESS	Addresses	15,000	100	90%	385	0.79	18	10%	1	0.00
TVEHICLES	Vehicles	15,000	100	90%	385	0.79	18	10%	1	0.00
TOPPTNOTE	Notes on Opponent	20,000	255	90%	1,267	2.59	27	10%	6	0.01
TOPMTRXF	Opponent Matter Cross Reference	20,000	45	90%	250	0.51	27	10%	1	0.00
TREFCD	Codes	1,000	50	90%	14	0.03	18	10%	0	0.00
TEMPLYEE	Employees	100	27	90%	1	0.00	18	10%	0	0.00
TCOMPANY	Companys	20	45	90%	0	0.00	27	10%	0	0.00
TCOUNTRY	Countries	163	100	90%	4	0.01	10	10%	0	0.00
TSTATES	States	50	100	90%	1	0.00	10	10%	0	0.00
TOTALS:					4,666	9.51			14	0.03

Figure 11-2: Using an Excel worksheet to estimate space

The SQL Server 7 system catalog

The system catalog is a set of tables that describe the structure of the database (see Figures 11-3, 11-4, and 11-5). It is automatically generated when you create a database. Figure 11-3 lists all of the tables created by SQL Server. Figure 11-4 lists all of the database entries as tracked by the SQL Server system catalog. Figure 11-5 lists all of the objects and their types within each database as tracked by the SQL Server system catalog. Notice the type column in Figure 11-5; V stands for view, and PK identifies a primary key object. Each time a SQL statement is processed, the database server accesses the system catalog for many purposes, including determining system privileges and verifying table and column names. The system catalog tables are not application database tables. They contain data about the application tables. You can, however, select data from these tables using a standard `SELECT` statement.

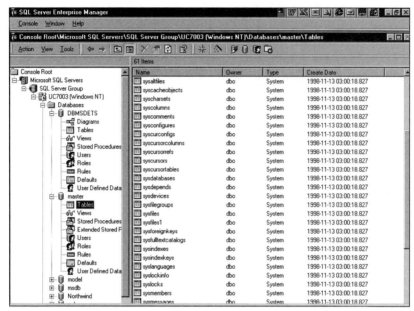

Figure 11-3: A partial list of a system catalog in Enterprise Manager

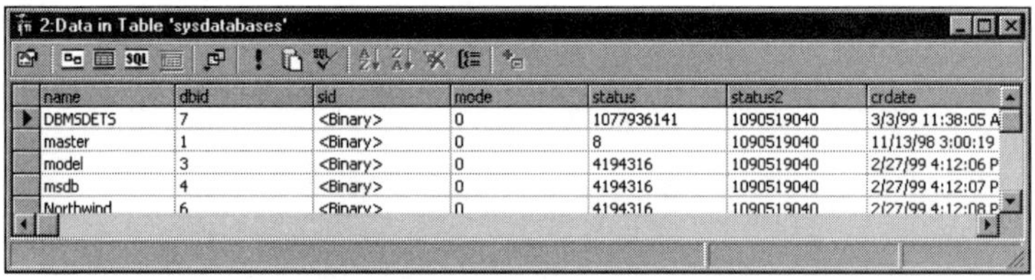

Figure 11-4: A SQL Server system catalog listing objects in the sysdatabases table

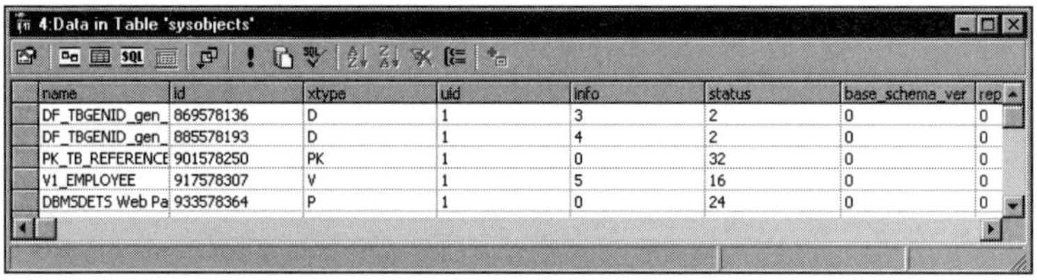

Figure 11-5: System catalog entries for tables, columns, and indices

Databases and filegroups

Using Enterprise Manager, you can specify that a database data and/or log component can be created on a specific filegroup(s). This means for tables and indexes that all the space used by that database – including all system catalogs, the data, and corresponding indexes – will be located in the filegroup or filegroups assigned to that database. Filegroups and their setup is discussed in Chapter 7, "Setting Up the Development Environment." Suffice it to say that generally the data and log portion of that database are stored on separate filegroups for recovery purposes.

Creating Tables

Your organization may use the entity-relationship approach to data analysis. Entity-relationship offers two advantages: It is very close to natural language, and most CASE tools have adopted this approach. In this approach an *entity* is like a noun, a *relationship* is like a verb, and an *attribute* is like a prepositional phrase. This makes it easy to convert information gleaned in an interview with the user into a data model. Learning the entity-relationship approach is good preparation for CASE.

An *entity type* is a set of objects. Expense reports and expense detail items are each different entity types. An *entity instance* is an element of the set. For example, "Expense Report for Writing the SQL Server Book" (the report summary itself) and "buy 5,000 sheets of letter-size paper" (the expense detail item) are instances of entity types. Entity types usually become tables in relational design. Entity instances usually become rows. See Chapter 6, "Database Administration Using Enterprise Manager," for additional information on database table design.

Physically creating a table

The syntax for creating a table in SQL Server is not unlike creating a table in any other DBMS. The CREATE TABLE statement creates new tables and optional integrity constraints within the specified database. The syntax for creating a table and its encapsulated columns is shown in Listing 11-1.

```
CREATE TABLE
[
database_name.[owner].
| owner.
] table_name
```

```
(
{ <column_definition>
| column_name AS computed_column_expression
| <table_constraint>
} [,...n]
)
[ON {filegroup  | DEFAULT} ]
[TEXTIMAGE_ON {filegroup  | DEFAULT} ]
<column_definition> ::= { column_name data_type }
[ [ DEFAULT constant_expression ]
| [ IDENTITY [(seed, increment ) [NOT FOR REPLICATION] ] ]
]
 [ <column_constraint>] [ ...n]
<column_constraint> ::= [CONSTRAINT constraint_name]
{
[ NULL | NOT NULL ]
| [ { PRIMARY KEY | UNIQUE }
[CLUSTERED | NONCLUSTERED]
[WITH FILLFACTOR = fillfactor]
[ON {filegroup  | DEFAULT} ]]
]
| [ [FOREIGN KEY]
REFERENCES ref_table [(ref_column) ]
[NOT FOR REPLICATION]
]
| CHECK [NOT FOR REPLICATION]
(logical_expression)
}
<table_constraint> ::= [CONSTRAINT constraint_name]
{
[ { PRIMARY KEY | UNIQUE }
[ CLUSTERED | NONCLUSTERED]
{ ( column[,...n] ) } }
[ WITH FILLFACTOR = fillfactor]
[ON {filegroup  | DEFAULT} ]
]
| FOREIGN KEY
[(column[,...n])]
REFERENCES ref_table [(ref_column[,...n])]
[NOT FOR REPLICATION]
| CHECK [NOT FOR REPLICATION]
(search_conditions)
}
```

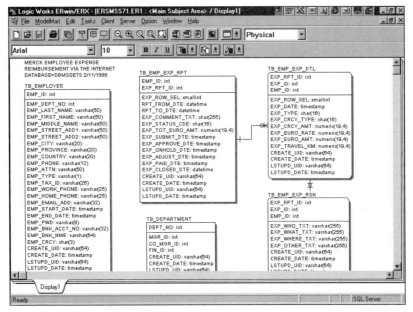

Listing 11-1: The Create Table Syntax

The parameters for this component definition follow.

◆ *database_name* — The name of the database in which the table is created. The *database_name* parameter must specify the name of an existing database. The *database_name* parameter defaults to the current database if it is not specified. The login for the current connection must be associated with an existing user ID in the database specified by *database_name*, and that user ID must have create table privileges.

◆ *owner* — The name of the user ID that owns the new table. The *owner* parameter must be an existing user ID in the database specified by *database_name*. The *owner* parameter defaults to the user ID associated with the login for the current connection in the database specified in *database_name*.

◆ *table name* — The name of the new table. Table names must conform to the rules for identifiers. See Appendix B, "Standards, Guidelines, and Maxims," for some examples of naming standards for this component. The combination of *owner.table_name* must be unique within the database. The *table_name* parameter can contain up to 128 characters, except for local temporary table names (names prefixed with a single number sign [#]) that cannot exceed 116 characters.

- ◆ *column_name* — The name of a column in the table. Column names must conform to the rules for identifiers and must be unique in the table. The *column_name* parameter can be omitted for columns created with a timestamp data type. The name of a timestamp column defaults to timestamp if *column_name* is not specified. See Appendix B, "Standards, Guidelines, and Maxims," for some examples of naming standards for this component.

- ◆ *computed_column_expression* — An expression defining the value of a computed column. A *computed column* is a virtual column not physically stored in the table. It is computed from an expression using other columns in the same table. Computed columns can be used in select lists, WHERE clauses, ORDER BY clauses, or any other locations in which regular expressions can be used, with the following exceptions:

  - A computed column cannot be used as a key column in an index or as part of any PRIMARY KEY, UNIQUE, FOREIGN KEY, or DEFAULT constraint definition.

  - A computed column cannot be the target of an INSERT or UPDATE statement.

- ◆ ON {*filegroup* | DEFAULT} — Specifies the filegroup on which the table is stored. If *filegroup* is specified, the table is stored in the named filegroup. The filegroup must exist within the database. If DEFAULT is specified, or if ON is not specified at all, the table is stored on the default filegroup. The ON {*filegroup* | DEFAULT} can also be specified in a PRIMARY KEY or UNIQUE constraint. These constraints create indexes. If *filegroup* is specified, the index is stored in the named filegroup. If DEFAULT is specified, the index is stored in the default filegroup. If no filegroup is specified in a constraint, the index is stored on the same filegroup as the table. If the PRIMARY KEY or UNIQUE constraint creates a clustered index, the data pages for the table are stored in the same filegroup as the index.

- ◆ TEXTIMAGE_ON — Keywords indicating that the text, ntext, and image columns are stored on the specified filegroup. Obviously, TEXTIMAGE ON is not valid if there are no text, ntext, or image columns in the table. If TEXTIMAGE_ON is not specified, the text, ntext, and image columns are stored in the same filegroup as the table.

- ◆ *data_type* — Specifies the data type of the column. See the section "Data Types" in this chapter for practical considerations. System or user-defined data types are acceptable. User-defined data types are created with the stored procedure sp_addtype before they can be used in a table definition.

- ◆ DEFAULT — Specifies the value provided for the column when a value is not explicitly supplied during an insert. The DEFAULT parameter's definitions can be applied to any columns except those defined as timestamp or those with the IDENTITY property. The timestamp option is set to the current data/time, and IDENTITY is set to the next sequential value in the target table. The DEFAULT parameter's definitions are removed when the table is dropped. Only a constant value, such as a character string; a system function, such as SYSTEM_USER(); or NULL can be used as a default.

◆ *constant_expression* — A constant, NULL, or a system function used as the default value for the column.

◆ IDENTITY — Indicates that the new column is an identity column. When a new row is added to the table, SQL Server provides a unique, incremental value for the column. Identity columns are commonly used in conjunction with PRIMARY KEY constraints to serve as the unique row identifier for the table. (See the subsection "Choosing Index Candidates" later in this chapter for practical considerations. The IDENTITY property can be assigned to tinyint, smallint, int, decimal(p,0), or numeric(p,0) columns. Only one identity column can be created per table. You must specify both the seed and increment or neither. If neither is specified, the default is (1,1).

◆ *seed* — The value that is used for the very first row loaded into the table.

◆ *increment* — The incremental value that is added to the identity value of the previous row that was loaded.

◆ CONSTRAINT — An optional keyword indicating the beginning of a PRIMARY KEY, NOT NULL, UNIQUE, FOREIGN KEY, or CHECK constraint definition. Constraints are special properties that enforce data integrity and create special types of indexes for the table and its columns.

◆ *constraint_name* — The name of a constraint. Constraint names must be unique within a database.

◆ NULL | NOT NULL — Keywords that determine whether null values are allowed in the column. The NULL parameter is not strictly a constraint, but it can be specified in the same manner as NOT NULL.

◆ PRIMARY KEY — A constraint that enforces entity integrity for a given column or columns through a unique index. Only one PRIMARY KEY constraint can be created per table.

◆ UNIQUE — A constraint that provides entity integrity for a given column or columns through a unique index. A table can have multiple UNIQUE constraints.

◆ CLUSTERED | NONCLUSTERED — Keywords to indicate that a clustered or a nonclustered index is created for the PRIMARY KEY or UNIQUE constraint. The PRIMARY KEY constraints default to CLUSTERED, and UNIQUE constraints default to NONCLUSTERED. See the section "Choosing Index Candidates" later in this chapter for practical considerations. You can specify CLUSTERED for only one constraint in a CREATE TABLE statement.

◆ [WITH FILLFACTOR = `fillfactor`] — Specifies how full SQL Server should allocate space on each index page used to store the index data. User-specified `fillfactor` values can be from 1 through 100, with a default of 0. A lower fill factor creates the index with more space available for new index entries, without having to allocate new space. This aids performance when you know a table will experience a good deal of insert activity.

◆ FOREIGN KEY...REFERENCES — A constraint that provides referential integrity for the data in the column or columns. FOREIGN KEY constraints require that each value in the column exists in the corresponding referenced column(s) in the referenced table. The FOREIGN KEY constraints can reference only columns that are PRIMARY KEY or UNIQUE constraints in the referenced table.

◆ `ref_table` — The name of the table referenced by the FOREIGN KEY constraint.

◆ (`ref_column`[,...n]) — A column, or list of columns, from the table referenced by the FOREIGN KEY constraint.

◆ CHECK — A constraint that enforces domain integrity by limiting the possible values that can be entered into a column or columns.

An example of a table CREATE statement is shown in Listing 11-2.

Table	Table Description	Number of Rows	Bytes /Row	Growth /Year	Num Pages	Data Size MBytes	Index Bytes	Index Fillfactor	Index Pages	Index MBytes
TMATTER	Matters	7,000	512	90%	887	1.73	10	10%	2	0.00
TCRIMACT	Matters becoming Criminal actions	3,000	512	90%	380	0.74	10	10%	1	0.00
TTTOB	Trademark Office Matters	255	1	90%	0	0.00	10	10%	0	0.00
TTM	Trademarks infringed Matters	14,000	128	90%	459	0.90	10	10%	1	0.00
TOPPONET	Opponents	7,500	512	90%	950	1.95	10	10%	2	0.00
TOPRPRTY	Opponent Property	7,500	512	90%	950	1.95	10	10%	2	0.00
TADDRESS	Addresses	15,000	100	90%	385	0.79	18	10%	1	0.00
TVEHICLES	Vehicles	15,000	100	90%	385	0.79	18	10%	1	0.00
TOPPTNOTE	Notes on Opponent	20,000	255	90%	1,267	2.59	27	10%	6	0.01
TOPMTRXF	Opponent Matter Cross Reference	20,000	45	90%	250	0.51	27	10%	1	0.00
TREFCD	Codes	1,000	50	90%	14	0.03	18	10%	0	0.00
TEMPLYEE	Employees	100	27	90%	1	0.00	18	10%	0	0.00
TCOMPANY	Companys	20	45	90%	0	0.00	27	10%	0	0.00
TCOUNTRY	Countries	163	100	90%	4	0.01	10	10%	0	0.00
TSTATES	States	50	100	90%	1	0.00	10	10%	0	0.00
TOTALS:					4,666	9.51			14	0.03

Listing 11-2: Create the Expense Detail Table

```
CREATE TABLE TB_EMP_EXP_DTL (
        EXP_RPT_ID              numeric(10) NOT NULL,
        EXP_ID                  numeric(10) NOT NULL,
        EXP_ROW_SEL             numeric(5) NULL,
        EMP_ID                  numeric(10) NOT NULL,
        EXP_TYPE                varchar(16) NULL,
        EXP_CRCY_TYPE           varchar(16) NULL,
        EXP_CRCY_AMT            numeric(19,4) NULL,
        EXP_TRAVEL_KM           numeric(19,4) NULL,
        EXP_DATE                datetime NULL,
        EXP_EURO_RATE           numeric(19,4) NULL,
        EXP_EURO_AMT            numeric(19,4) NULL,
        CREATE_UID              varchar(64) NULL,
        CREATE_DATE             datetime NULL,
        LSTUPD_UID              varchar(64) NULL,
        LSTUPD_DATE             datetime NULL,
        EXP_PAID_BY_MSD         varchar(1) NULL
)
go
```

Creating a temporary table

Sometimes you need a temporary workspace to mix and match result sets from other SQL operations. To solve this problem, you can explicitly create a temporary table that is similar to a permanent table, except that it is only valid for the duration of the program and is not logged. If you close the current database, the temporary table will no longer be valid. There are no entries for the temporary table in the systables or syscolumns system catalog tables. SQL Server supports two types of temporary tables: local and global. A *local* temporary table is visible only to the connection that created it. A *global* temporary table is available to all connections. Local temporary table names (names prefixed with a single number sign [#]) cannot exceed 116 characters. Local temporary tables are automatically dropped at the end of the current session. Global temporary tables are dropped at the end of the last session using the table. (Normally, this is when the session that created the table ends.)

Temporary tables named with # can be created by any user. Once the temporary table is created, the owner of the local table is the only one who can access that table. Permissions cannot be granted on local temporary tables. Once a global temporary table is created, all users can access it; permissions cannot be explicitly revoked. Explicitly creating a temporary table in tempdb (named without a pound sign) can be performed only by those with explicit CREATE TABLE permission in the tempdb database. Permission can be granted to and revoked from these tables.

Because temporary tables are not generally maintained for long (they are automatically dropped by the system), because referenced objects could be dropped (drop dependencies), and because `FOREIGN KEY` constraints are not enforced, a simplified `CREATE TABLE` syntax can be used, as follows:

```
CREATE TABLE #table_name
(column_definition
    [, next_column_definition]...)
```

Table lock modes

The SQL Server locking strategy for tables is comprehensive, especially when compared to other RDBMSs like Sybase. Locks are held on pages that are read or modified during a transaction to prevent problems that might arise from concurrent use of resources by multiple transactions. Minimizing locks increases concurrency, which can improve performance results. Although there are many ways to minimize locks, one method is to commit transactions as soon as you have completed them. If you access related rows, it should always be in the same order or else you will fall into the deadly embrace. The *deadly embrace* is a database term for a locking scenario where two requests block each other from proceeding. For example, process 1 updates table A and then updates table B, and process 2 updates table B and then updates table A. Process 1 locks table A, so process 2 cannot finish; and process 2 locks table B, so process 1 cannot finish (see Figure 11-6).

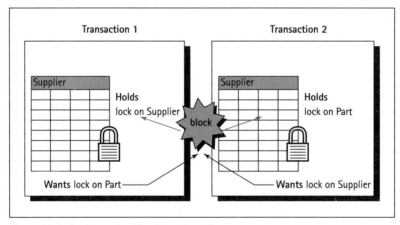

Figure 11-6: Locking: the "deadly embrace"

SQL Server can hold several types of locks. In general, read operations acquire *shared locks,* in which other processes may read the page, and write operations acquire *exclusive locks,* in which other processes may not update the page. Update locks are created at the page level and are acquired during the initial portion of an update operation when the pages are being read or by cursors opened with pessimistic concurrency. Update locks are compatible with shared locks. Later, if the pages are changed, the update locks are promoted to exclusive locks. (See Table 11-2, which describes the three different types of locks that SQL Server uses.) SQL Server locks can be held on a table (table or intent), a page, or an extent. SQL Server tries to satisfy requests with page locks before acquiring table locks. However, if many page locks are held during the course of a transaction, SQL Server upgrades the lock to a table lock (shared or exclusive). This escalation is to avoid all of the lock list checking that can degrade performance. The point at which escalation occurs is configurable with the stored procedure `sp_configure`.

TABLE 11-2 LOCK TYPE DESCRIPTIONS

Lock Type	Description
Shared	SQL Server usually uses shared locks for operations that do not change or update data, such as a `SELECT` statement.
Update	SQL Server uses update locks when it intends to modify a page, and later promotes the update page lock to an exclusive page lock before actually making the changes.
Exclusive	SQL Server uses exclusive locks for the data modification operations `UPDATE`, `INSERT`, or `DELETE`.

SQL Server obtains table locks when it suspects that a transaction might affect an entire table. Table locks provide a way of avoiding lock collisions at the page level. An *intent lock* indicates the intention to acquire a shared or exclusive lock on a data page. (An intent lock prevents another transaction from acquiring an exclusive lock on the table containing that page.) An *extent lock* is held on a group of eight database pages while they are being allocated or freed. Extent locks are set while a `CREATE` or `DROP` statement is running or while an `INSERT` statement that requires new data or index pages is running. In addition, some SQL Server locks are considered *blocking locks*. A blocking lock is a lock that blocks another process that needs to acquire a lock. As soon as the process that is causing the block finishes, the other process can move forward. The different types of items that can be locked by SQL Server are shown in Table 11-3.

TABLE 11-3 **LOCK ITEM DESCRIPTIONS**

Item	Description
Page	A 2KB data page or index page. This is the most common type of lock.
Extent	A contiguous group of eight 2KB data pages or index pages. This lock is only used for allocation.
Table	An entire table, including all data and indexes.
Intent	A special type of table lock to indicate the type of page locks currently placed on the table.

By default, the locking granularity in SQL Server is a page, which can contain several rows depending upon the row size divided into the usable space in a page, typically 2,000 bytes. In SQL Server 7, the lock manager has been enhanced to provide row-level locking (IRL) for most INSERT operations. IRL improves performance in situations where access contention and hotspots, which are areas of unusually high access, occur.

Although row-level locking is not a substitute for a well-designed application, it is especially useful in specific scenarios. Row-level locking is useful when a hotspot develops on a table structured as a sequential file. With SQL Server, hotspots can occur when records are inserted at the end of a table and one of the following conditions exists:

◆ A table does not have an index.

◆ A table has a nonclustered index.

◆ A table has a clustered index with a monotonically increasing key (for example, a clustered index on an identity column).

 If possible, avoid this scenario at design time using a random key generator.

When concurrent users try to insert data into the table's last page and contend for exclusive page access, a hotspot results. To alleviate these performance bottlenecks, enhancements to the lock manager in SQL Server 7 (originally in 6.5) provide row-level concurrency for INSERT operations. Properly implemented IRL increases the speed of multiuser INSERT operations. See the section "Choosing Index Candidates" later in this chapter for practical considerations.

Table 11-4 describes the compatibility of the new types of locks. "Y" means that the requested lock is compatible with the granted lock. "N" means that the requested lock is not compatible with the granted lock. IRL is OFF by default. IRL can be enabled on individual tables or on an entire database by using the sp_tableoption stored procedure. The following example shows how the database owner can turn on the insert row lock option for all tables in the current database:

```
EXECUTE sp_tableoption '%.%', 'insert row lock', 'true'
```

TABLE 11-4 LOCK MODE DESCRIPTIONS

Lock Mode	Description
Insert_page	Multiple transactions can obtain an Insert_page lock on a page while concurrently inserting data. An Insert_page lock is compatible only with other Insert_page locks and is held until the transaction completes.
Link_page	A Link_page lock is obtained by the first transaction that detects that the current page is full and that a new page needs to be allocated and linked to the current page. The transaction's Insert_page lock is upgraded to a Link_page lock. Subsequent requests for Insert_page locks are blocked until the transaction owning the Link_page lock completes.

This next example shows how a user other than the system administrator or database owner can turn off the insert row lock option for the TB_EMP_EXP_DTL table:

```
EXECUTE sp_tableoption 'TB_EMP_EXP_DTL', 'insert row lock', 'false'
```

For recovery purposes, additional information must be logged into the transaction log each time a transaction that uses the IRL concurrency option rolls back. This additional information consists of compensating log records, which are used during recovery to bring the database back to a consistent state. Reducing the locking granularity can result in deadlocks in some applications. *Deadlocks* are caused where locking scenarios prevent processing to continue. It is possible for existing applications to encounter deadlocks if IRL is implemented without adequate testing. For example, consider a transaction that inserts a row on a page and then updates the row within the same transaction.

For the INSERT operation, the transaction must acquire an Insert_page lock, and for the subsequent UPDATE operation, it needs an exclusive page lock. If several such transactions are running concurrently, each transaction can have its own Insert_page lock on the page. When attempting to update the page, each transaction requests an exclusive page lock, which blocks on the Insert_page lock of another transaction and results in a deadlock. To achieve maximum benefit from IRL and to avoid deadlocks, it is recommended that you extensively test existing applications before changing to this new locking level.

Table 11-5 lists whether each type of page lock is compatible with the other. A Yes entry means that these locks are compatible; a No entry means that these locks are incompatible. While a particular type of lock is held on a specific page, only compatible lock types can be placed on that same page. For example, while an exclusive lock is held, no other transaction can acquire a lock of any kind (shared, update, or exclusive) on that item until the exclusive lock is released at the end of the first transaction. If a shared lock has been applied to an item, other transactions can also acquire a shared lock or an update lock on that item, even if the first transaction hasn't completed. However, other transactions cannot acquire an exclusive lock until the shared lock has been released.

TABLE 11-5 LOCK COMPATIBILITY DESCRIPTIONS

	Shared	Update	Exclusive
Shared	Yes	Yes	No
Update	Yes	No	No
Exclusive	No	No	No

Data Types

SQL Server's data type system handles the interaction with the data types. A *data type* is a descriptor that is assigned to a variable or column and that indicates the type of data that the variable or column can hold. It also determines which database methods will be used to access, display, and update the data.

SQL Server uses a data type to determine the following information:

◆ The layout or internal structure the database server can use to store the data type values on disk.

◆ Which operations (such as multiplication or string concatenation) the database server can apply to values of a particular data type. An operation must be defined on the values of a particular data type; otherwise, the database server does not allow the operation to be performed.

◆ Which access methods the database server can use for values in columns of this data type. An access method defines how to handle storage and retrieval of a particular data type in a table.

Fundamental data types

Defining data types amounts to specifying the type of information, size, and storage format of columns, stored procedure parameters, and local variables. In the context of SQL Server, the scope of possible data types is virtually unlimited and will be driven by market requirements. We will discuss traditional data types — numbers, characters, and dates — and then we will delve into the expanded data typing soon to be available with SQL Server. Table 11-6 lists the system-supplied data types provided for various types of information, as well as the synonyms recognized by SQL Server.

TABLE 11-6 SYSTEM-SUPPLIED DATA TYPES BY TYPE

Type	Data Type	Description
Integer	Bit	Integer data with either a 1 or 0 value
	Int	Integer (whole number) data from -2^{31} ($-2,147,483,648$) through $2^{31} - 1$ ($2,147,483,647$)
	Smallint	Integer data from -2^{15} ($-32,768$) through $2^{15} - 1$ ($32,767$)
	Tinyint	Integer data from 0 through 255
Decimal and numeric	Decimal	Fixed-precision and scale numeric data from $-10^{38} -1$ through $10^{38} -1$
	Numeric	A synonym for decimal
	Money	Monetary data values from -2^{63} ($-922,337,203$, $685,477.5808$) through $2^{63} - 1$ ($+922,337,203$, $685,477.5807$), with accuracy to a ten-thousandth of a monetary unit

Continued

TABLE 11-6 SYSTEM-SUPPLIED DATA TYPES BY TYPE *(continued)*

Type	Data Type	Description
Decimal and numeric *(continued)*	Smallmoney	Monetary data values from –214,748.3648 through +214,748.3647, with accuracy to a ten-thousandth of a monetary unit
	Float	Floating precision number data from $-1.79E + 308$ through $1.79E + 308$
	Real	Floating precision number data from $-3.40E + 38$ through $3.40E + 38$
Datetime and smalldatetime	Datetime	Date and time data from January 1, 1753, to December 31, 9999, with an accuracy of three-hundredths of a second, or 3.33 milliseconds
	Smalldatetime	Date and time data from January 1, 1900, through June 6, 2079, with an accuracy of one minute
Character	Char	Fixed-length non-Unicode character data with a maximum length of 8,000 characters
	Varchar	Variable-length non-Unicode data with a maximum of 8,000 characters
	Text	Variable-length non-Unicode data with a maximum length of $2^{31} - 1$ (2,147,483,647) characters
	Nchar	Fixed-length Unicode data with a maximum length of 4,000 characters
	Nvarchar	Variable-length Unicode data with a maximum length of 4,000 characters. The sysname data type is a system-supplied user-defined data type that is a synonym for nvarchar(128) and is used to reference database object names
	Ntext	Variable-length Unicode data with a maximum length of $2^{30} - 1$ (1,073,741,823) characters
	Binary	Fixed-length binary data with a maximum length of 8,000 bytes
	Varbinary	Variable-length binary data with a maximum length of 8,000 bytes

Type	Data Type	Description
Character (continued)	Image	Variable-length binary data with a maximum length of $2^{31} - 1$ (2,147,483,647) bytes

For simplicity, system data types are printed in lowercase characters, although SQL Server allows you to enter them in either upper- or lowercase. Most SQL Server-supplied data types are not reserved words and can be used to name other objects. In SQL Server, each column, local variable, expression, and parameter has a data type. User-defined data types, which are aliases for system-supplied data types, can also be defined.

Data type synonyms, which are listed in Table 11-7, are included for SQL-92 compatibility.

TABLE 11-7 DATA TYPE SYNONYMS

Synonym	Mapped to System Data Type
binary varying	Varbinary
char varying	Varchar
Character	Char
Character	char(1)
character(*n*)	char(n)
character varying(*n*)	varchar(n)
Dec	Decimal
double precision	Float
float[(*n*)] for *n* = 1–7	Real
float[(*n*)] for *n* = 8–15	Float
Integer	Int
national character(*n*)	nchar(n)
national char(*n*)	nchar(n)
national character varying(*n*)	nvarchar(n)

Continued

TABLE 11-7 DATA TYPE SYNONYMS *(continued)*

Synonym	Mapped to System Data Type
national char varying(*n*)	`nvarchar(n)`
national text	`Ntext`
Numeric	`Decimal`

INTEGERS

SQL Server provides two data types, `smallint` and `integer`, to store integers (whole numbers). These types are exact numeric types; they preserve their accuracy during arithmetic operations. Choose among the integer types based on the expected size of the numbers to be stored. Internal storage size varies by type between two and four bytes.

DECIMAL NUMBERS

SQL Server provides numeric types like decimal and float for numbers that include decimal points. Data stored in decimal columns is packed to conserve disk space and preserves its accuracy to the least significant digit after arithmetic operations. The decimal types accept two optional parameters, precision and scale, enclosed within parentheses and separated by a comma:

```
decimal [(precision [, scale])]
```

SQL Server treats each combination of precision and scale as a distinct data type. The precision and scale determine the range of values that can be stored in a decimal or numeric column. The precision specifies the maximum number of decimal digits that can be stored in the column. It includes all digits to the right and left of the decimal point. You can specify a precision of 1 to 16 digits or use the default precision of 16 digits. The scale specifies the maximum number of digits that can be stored to the right of the decimal point. Note that the scale must be less than or equal to the precision. You can specify a scale of 0 to 16 digits, or use the default scale of 0 digits. Exact numeric types with a scale of 0 are displayed without a decimal point. If you enter a value that exceeds either the precision or scale for the column, SQL Server returns an error message.

The storage size for a numeric or decimal column depends on its precision. The minimum storage requirement is two bytes for a one- or two-digit column. Storage size increases by one byte for each additional two digits of precision, up to a maximum of nine bytes. The approximate numeric types are especially suited to data that covers a wide range of values.

The real and double-precision types are built on types supplied by the operating system. The range and storage precision for all three types are machine-dependent. You enter approximate numeric data as a mantissa followed by an optional exponent. The mantissa is a signed or unsigned number, with or without a decimal point. The column's binary precision determines the maximum number of binary digits allowed in the mantissa. The exponent, which begins with the character "e" or "E," must be a whole number. The value represented by the entry is the following product:

mantissa × 10 exponent

For example, 2.4E3 represents the value 2.4 times 10^3, or 2,400.

NUMERIC DATA TYPES

To reiterate and summarize, there are five numeric data types: INTEGER, SMALLINT, FLOAT, SMALLFLOAT, and DECIMAL.

- ◆ INTEGER — Whole numbers –2,147,483 647 to +2,147,483,647

- ◆ SMALLINT — Whole number –32,767 to +32,767

- ◆ FLOAT — Binary floating-point numbers, double precision

- ◆ SMALLFLOAT — Binary floating-point numbers, single precision up to 8 significant digits

- ◆ DECIMAL — Precision and scale designation up to 32 significant digits

An INTEGER uses four bytes, and a SMALLINT uses two bytes of disk space. The two-byte savings is probably not significant in small tables, but it can make a substantial difference in large tables. You can always convert a SMALLINT to an INTEGER without loss of data. The FLOAT and SMALLFLOAT values store binary floating-point numbers. The number of significant digits can vary from machine to machine. FLOAT can store twice as many digits as SMALLFLOAT data types. The FLOAT data type's columns do not necessarily store larger numbers; they store numbers with greater precision. A FLOAT uses eight bytes, and a SMALLFLOAT uses four bytes of disk space.

The DECIMAL and MONEY values store numbers with the number of digits specified by the user. You can specify up to 32 significant digits. The range of numbers that you can store is 10×10^{-128} to 10×10^{128}. However, only 32 digits are significant. The DECIMAL data type numbers can be formatted with a given precision and scale. Precision is the total number of digits. Scale is the number of digits to the right of the decimal point.

A DECIMAL column with a definition (5,2) would store a five-digit number with three digits before the decimal point and two digits after the decimal point. However, specifying precision and scale is optional.

- ◆ No Precision DECIMAL is treated as DECIMAL (16), a floating decimal with a precision of 16.

◆ No Scale DECIMAL is treated as a floating-point decimal.

The number of bytes it takes to store a DECIMAL value can be calculated by taking the precision of a DECIMAL column, dividing it by two, and adding one. (If the precision is odd, add one to it, and then divide by two.) For example, a DECIMAL value with a precision of 16 would take nine bytes to store:
Precision / 2 + 1 = 16 / 2 + 1 + 9
The advantages of using the DECIMAL data type over the FLOAT data type are:

◆ The DECIMAL data type allows greater precision (32) over the FLOAT (7 OR 14) and the ability to round a number. It requires some amount of processing to convert.

◆ The available precision of FLOAT may differ from machine to machine, which may have some significance when transferring data across a network. The FLOAT data type is less CPU-intensive when it comes to conversion and processing.

CHARACTER DATA TYPES

The character types store strings consisting of letters, numbers, and symbols. Use the fixed-length type, char(n), and the variable-length type, varchar(n), for single-byte character sets such as English. Possibly consider the use of the text type for strings longer than 255 characters. Character literals are treated as variable-length types. You can use the like keyword to search character strings for particular characters, and the built-in string functions to manipulate their contents. Strings consisting of numbers can be converted to exact and approximate numeric types with the convert function and then used for arithmetic.

Use n to specify the length in characters for the fixed-length types, char(n). Entries shorter than the assigned length are blank-padded; entries longer than the assigned length are truncated without warning. Fixed-length columns that allow nulls are internally converted to variable-length columns. Use n to specify the maximum length in characters for the variable-length types, varchar(n) and nvarchar(n). Data in variable-length columns is stripped of trailing blanks; storage size is the actual length of the data entered. Data in variable-length variables and parameters retains all trailing blanks but is not padded to the fully defined length. Fixed-length columns tend to take more storage space than variable-length columns but are accessed somewhat faster.

The CHAR columns (character) store any combination of letters, numbers, and symbols. Tabs and spaces can be included. No other nonprintable characters are allowed. The maximum length of a CHAR column is 32,767 bytes. The CHAR columns are of fixed length. If a character column is defined with a width of 400 bytes, data for that column will take up that amount of space on disk even if the data is less than 400 bytes.

The VARCHAR columns store variable-length character data. The primary benefit of using the VARCHAR data type is that, when used correctly, it can increase the number of rows per page of storage on disk. The VARCHAR data type is most effectively used when the majority of rows need only a small amount of space, and some rows require significantly more. For example, a comments column may not be used in 80 percent of the rows in a table. However, when it is populated, VARCHARS can increase performance on sequential reads of tables and reduce disk storage waste when compared to the same data stored in CHAR data type fields. The VARCHAR data type columns may store between 0 and 8,000 bytes of character data. When specifying a VARCHAR data type, a maximum length is included in the syntax of the column definition.

The max-size parameter sets the upper limit on the length of the characters allowed within the data item. The min-size parameter sets a minimum amount of disk space that will always be reserved for data within the data item. When a row is written, SQL Server sets aside either the number of bytes needed to store the data or the number of bytes specified in min-size for the column (whichever is greater). If the column later grows to a size greater than the space available in the row, the row may have to be moved to another place on a page or part of the row may be moved to another page. You can see why it is important to specify an accurate, average min-size when the table is created. Besides the actual contents of the VARCHAR column, a one-byte length indicator is stored at the beginning of the column.

The bottom line in choosing between VAR and VARCHAR is as follows:

◆ CHAR — Use this data type if the content of the column is predictable or fixed (for example, for street address or area code data). The CHAR and INTEGER data types are common to all RDBMSs and will probably be the most frequent types of data used.

◆ VARCHAR — Use this data type if the majority of the rows use a small amount of space and the maximum size of the column is the exception. Use it when space saving is compelling (for example, when there are a large number of table rows).

Character strings must be enclosed in single or double quotes. If you have set quoted_identifier on, use single quotes for character strings, or SQL Server treats them as identifiers. Strings that include the double-quote character should be surrounded by single quotes. Strings that include the single-quote character should be surrounded by double quotes.

Other data types

Relational database management systems (RDBMS's) introduced special data types that were done in inconsistent ways in the older database management architectures. SQL Server includes special data types for generating sequential numbers and for storing dates, times, and large objects.

Columns that have the IDENTITY property contain system-generated values that uniquely identify each row within a table. You can use this feature to generate sequential numbers (for example, employee identification numbers). When inserting values into a table with an identity column, SQL Server automatically generates the next identifier on the basis of the last-used identity value (incremented by adding rows) and the increment value specified during column creation. There is no need to remember which column has the IDENTITY property; simply use the IDENTITYCOL keyword instead. When referencing data in a table, use the keyword IDENTITYCOL in place of the identity column name. It can be qualified with a table name if necessary. The IDENTITYCOL keyword can be used in SELECT, INSERT, UPDATE, and DELETE statements to reference an identity column.

Two system functions return identity information for an object containing an identity column. The IDENT_SEED function returns the seed value specified during the creation of an identity column. The IDENT_INCR function returns the increment value specified during the creation of an identity column.

MANIPULATING DATA IN IDENTITY COLUMNS

Data inserted into the table should not include a value for an identity column in the INSERT statement; instead, use the DEFAULT VALUES option (which is available with the INSERT statement).

By default, data cannot be inserted directly into an identity column; however, if a row was accidentally deleted, an identity value can be recreated and reconstructed. To get the last identity value, use the @@IDENTITY global variable. This variable is accurate after an insert into a table with an identity column; however, this value is reset after an insert occurs into a table without an identity column. To allow an insert with a specific identity value, see the SET statement for the IDENTITY_INSERT option in the upcoming example. When explicitly inserting values into the identity column, SQL Server does not validate uniqueness or the possibility of a gap based on the explicitly entered value. To ensure that this value is unique, use a UNIQUE or PRIMARY KEY constraint, or create a unique index on the identity column.

If an IDENTITY column exists for a table with frequent deletions, gaps can occur between IDENTITY values. If this is a concern, do not use the IDENTITY property. However, to ensure that no gaps have been created or to fill an existing gap, evaluate the existing identity values before explicitly entering one with the IDENTITY_INSERT option ON.

If you are reusing a removed identity value, use the following sample code to check for the next available identity value. Replace tablename, column_type, and max(column_type) with your table name, identity column data type, and numeric value of the maximum allowable value (for that data type).

```
SET IDENTITY_INSERT tablename ON

Go
```

```
DECLARE @nextidentval column_type
SELECT @nextidentval = MIN(IDENTITYCOL) IDENT_INCR(tablename)
FROM tablename t1
WHERE IDENTITYCOL BETWEEN IDENT_SEED(tablename) AND
max(column_type) - 1
AND NOT EXISTS (SELECT * FROM tablename t2
               WHERE t2.IDENTITYCOL = t1.IDENTITYCOL
               IDENT_INCR(tablename))
go
SET IDENTITY_INSERT tablename OFF
```

USING THE IDENTITY PROPERTY

Ordinarily, when you are including an existing identity column into a new table or view, the new column inherits the identity property. If one of the following conditions is true, the new column does not inherit the identity property:

- ◆ The SELECT statement contains a union, join, group by, or aggregate function.

- ◆ The identity column is selected more than once.

- ◆ The identity column is part of an expression.

If one of these conditions is true, the column is created NOT NULL instead of inheriting the identity property. Because this column does not have the identity property, a column value must be explicitly specified when inserting a row into the new table. If none of these conditions is true, the new table will inherit the identity column. All rules and restrictions for the identity columns apply to the new table.

USING THE DATE, DATETIME, AND INTERVAL DATA TYPES

Relational database systems introduced special data types that were done in inconsistent ways before RDBMS. People would store a date as a six-character field (*MMDDYY*), an eight-character field (*MMDDYYYY*), a decimal number, or an integer. This created a need for special programs and functions to calculate and compare dates. Relational databases including SQL Server provide a consistent way of storing, calculating, and comparing dates. SQL Server includes special data types for storing dates and times. Date and time data consist of alphanumeric data representing a date and time of day. The default display format for dates is "Mon(char(3)) *dd yyyy hh:mm*AM" (or PM), such as "Dec 31 1999 11:59PM". When time data is entered, the order of time components is significant: hours; minutes; seconds; milliseconds; AM, am, PM, or pm (12AM is midnight, 12PM is noon). To be recognized as a time, a value must contain either a colon (:) or an AM/PM signifier.

SQL Server recognizes the date portion and the time portion of the data separately, so the time can precede or follow the date. Use date functions with the

CONVERT function to display seconds and milliseconds and to get other date styles and date part orderings by converting datetime data to char. The date and time data types are included here.

DATETIME   The datetime data type is stored in eight bytes of two four-byte integers: four bytes for the number of days before or after the base date of January 1, 1900, and four bytes for the number of milliseconds after midnight. The date segments of datetime values representing dates prior to the base date are stored as negative values.

Data values for datetime range from January 1, 1753, to December 31, 9999, to an accuracy of one three-hundredth second, or 3.33 milliseconds. SQL Server rejects all values it cannot recognize as dates between 1753 and 9999. You can omit either portion, but if you omit both, datetime defaults to January 1, 1900, 12:00:00:000AM. If you omit the time portion of a datetime value, the default (12:00:00:000AM) is supplied. If you omit the date portion, the default (Jan 1 1900) is supplied. For example, an empty string or missing date is interpreted as the base date, January 1, 1900. A time value without a date, for example 4:33, is interpreted as January 1, 1900, 4:33AM.

SMALLDATETIME   The smalldatetime date and time data type is less precise than datetime. This parameter's storage size is four bytes, consisting of one small integer for the number of days after January 1, 1900, and one small integer for the number of minutes past midnight. Data values for smalldatetime range from January 1, 1900, through June 6, 2079, with accuracy to the minute.

DATE FORMATS

SQL Server recognizes the following formats (alphabetic, numeric, and unseparated string) for date data. Enclose each format with single quotation marks (').

ALPHABETIC FORMAT   The month can be the full name or the abbreviation given in the current language; commas are optional and capitalization (case) is ignored. If you specify only the last two digits of the year, values less than 50 are interpreted as 20yy, and values greater than or equal to 50 are interpreted as 19yy. For example, if you specify 3, the result is 2003. If you specify 82, the result is 1982. You must type the century when the day is omitted or when you need a century other than the default. If the day is missing, the first day of the month is supplied. The DATEFORMAT session setting is not applied when you specify the month in alphabetic form. For an example, see the SET statement in the code example in the section "Manipulating data in identity columns."

NUMERIC FORMAT   You must specify the month, day, and year in a string with slashes (/), hyphens (-), or periods (.) as separators. The setting for DATEFORMAT determines how date values are interpreted. If the order doesn't match the setting, the values are not interpreted as dates (because they are out of range), or the values are misinterpreted. For example, 12/10/08 can be interpreted as one of six dates, depending on the DATEFORMAT setting. For an example, see the SET statement in the previous code example.

TIME FORMATS   SQL Server recognizes several formats for time data. Enclose each format with single quotation marks ('). The hour can refer to 12-hour or 24-hour time. Capitalization (case) for AM or PM is ignored. Milliseconds can be preceded by either a colon (:) or a period (.). If preceded by a colon, the number means thousandths of a second. If preceded by a period, a single digit means tenths of a second, two digits mean hundredths of a second, and three digits mean thousandths of a second. For example, "12:30:20:1" means twenty and one-thousandth seconds past 12:30; "12:30:20.1" means twenty and one-tenth seconds past 12:30.

USING DATA AND TIME DATA TYPES

You can perform some arithmetic calculations on datetime data with the built-in date functions. Be exact here because searching for datetime values with an equal sign (=) and the month, day, and year returns only those time values that are precisely 12:00:00:000 AM (the default). If you use the keyword LIKE with datetime values, SQL Server first converts the dates to datetime format and then to varchar. Because the standard display formats don't include seconds or milliseconds, you cannot search for them with LIKE and a matching pattern, unless you use the CONVERT function with the *style* parameter set to 9 or 109. However, LIKE works well when searching for datetime values that contain a variety of date parts. For example, if you insert the value 9:20 into a column named arrival_time, the clause WHERE arrival_time = '9:20' does not find the value, because SQL Server converts the entry into Jan 1 1900 9:20AM. However, the clause WHERE arrival_time LIKE '%9:20%' does find the value.

BINARY LARGE OBJECTS

Binary Large Objects, or BLOBs, are streams of bytes of arbitrary value and length. A BLOB can be any arbitrary collection of bytes for any purpose. Anything that you can store in a file system of a computer can be stored in a BLOB. SQL Server allows BLOBs to be stored as columns within a database. The theoretical limit to their size is over 2.1 billion bytes; this size is based on the highest value that can be held in a four-byte signed integer. Internally SQL Server uses 56 bytes of reserved space within the row for general BLOB information. The BLOB itself is stored in pages separate from the rest of the row. There are two types of BLOB data types: BYTE and TEXT. They are described as follows:

TEXT	Large amounts of data containing ASCII values
BYTE	Large amounts of unstructured data with unpredictable contents

A data object of type TEXT is restricted to a combination of printable ASCII text (and a few specific control characters) such as: word processing files, manual chapters, engineering specifications, or program source code files. The text field stores a pointer to another page. The additional page stores the actual text. The BYTE data type can store any type of binary data such as spreadsheets; program modules; and digitized images, for example, photographs and drawings or voice patterns. The BYTE data type is an undifferentiated byte stream. SQL Server knows only the length of the BLOB and storage location on the disk. Other programs can be called to display the BLOB information.

Determining column types

The database administrator should analyze the potential column contents and the way a column will be accessed before deciding the data type of every column. This step is important in deciding whether a column should be INTEGER or, DECIMAL or INTEGER, and so on. For character columns, the administrator must choose between VARCHAR, CHAR, and TEXT. The maximum size of a character column may disqualify the use of VARCHAR (which has a maximum size of 255). If the administrator determines that a column is usually empty except for a small percentage of rows, then VARCHAR may be the best choice.

Determine also how data will be accessed. For example, if a zip code is not involved in arithmetic operations, perhaps it should be created as a character column. Another example of a difficult choice is a comments column. Should a comments column be VARCHAR, CHAR, or TEXT? If queries do not involve the character column in a filter, and the comments column may be vary large, perhaps it should be a TEXT column, so that it can be stored apart from the row itself.

Creating indices and keys

Data in tables has both a relational order and a physical one. The relational order of values is the usual arithmetic sequence for numbers, or dictionary sequence for character data. The physical order of rows in a table is the combination of the sequence of pages on the disk drive, and the sequence of rows within each page. Of course, disk drives are not serial filegroups, and pages are spread across tracks and around sectors.

A table is *clustered* on a column when the physical order of rows matches the relational order of values in the column. For example, the table TB_EMP_EXP_DTL is clustered on EXP_RPT_ID, EXP_ID. In some database systems, clustering can be imperfect — a table is considered clustered even when some rows are on the wrong page. MVS/DB2 maintains a cluster ratio or the percent of rows that are clustered. An index on a column is a list of column values, with pointers to the location of the row containing each value. A composite index is defined over several columns. A *clustering* index, sometimes called a primary index, is defined on a clustering column, that is, a column ideally with a uniform distribution of values with which to group rows together for common/fast access.

A *nonclustering* index, sometimes called a secondary index, is not defined on a clustering column. A *dense* index contains one entry for each row of the table. A *nondense* index contains one entry for each page of the table with the low and high value index values. Nondense indexes are possible only on clustered columns. Nondense indexes have a great advantage over dense indexes – they have far fewer entries, and therefore occupy fewer pages. As a result, they are more efficient.

How does this structure handle insertions and updates? SQL Server places a new row on the correct page based on its clustering column. If this page is full, it splits in two to create free space, and a new entry is inserted at the bottom level of the index. If this index page is full, it splits in two to create more space, and a new entry is necessary in the bottom level of the index. If this index page is full, it splits to create more space, and another entry is necessary at the next higher level of the index. In the worst case, these splits propagate all the way through the top of the index, and a new level is created. Because the new level is created at the top of the index, all branches of the index tree are always the same length. Consequently, this kind of index is often called a B-tree – the "B" stands for "balanced." In theory, the system could reverse the process when rows are deleted, merging pages and reducing the index. However, this is not supported by SQL Server and other vendors, in that deletions are less frequent than insertions.

Occasionally a table will not have a clustered index. In this case, new rows are always inserted at the end of the table. When a row is deleted, the empty slot is not reused until the table is physically reorganized. Because there is no clustered index, rows remain in order of initial load or insertion. Because no meaningful order is maintained, this structure has limited utility. It is useful for tables of five pages or less; after all, if a table is small, the system can scan it quickly without an index. It is also useful for archival or temporary tables.

A table can have only one clustered index but any number of nonclustered indexes. Nonclustered indexes are necessarily dense. When and how can nonclustered indexes accelerate queries? A critical factor is percentage of rows selected by a query, variously known as *hit ratio,* filter factor, or selectivity. When the hit ratio is high, nonclustering indexes are useless. For example, suppose we set up a nonclustered index on a holiday column within a TV EPISODE table. The holiday column contains a code that lets us know which episodes have a holiday theme (for example, Halloween). Suppose we select all episodes not associated with a holiday. The hit ratio is quite high; most or all pages contain qualifying rows because most days are not holidays, that is to say, there are 12–20 holidays out of 365 days in a year. It is faster to ignore the index and scan the entire table. In contrast, if we select all episodes associated with Halloween, the *hit ratio* is low. Less than five percent of episodes qualify. A nonclustered index on HOLIDAY quickly locates the few pages of interest.

THE CREATE INDEX STATEMENT

Use the CREATE INDEX statement to create a unique or duplicate index, and optionally to cluster the physical table in the order of the index. The CREATE INDEX statement creates an index on a given table that either changes the physical ordering of the table or provides the optimizer with a logical ordering of the table to increase efficiency for queries. When creating an index for the primary key, use the table- and column-level PRIMARY KEY constraint provided with the CREATE TABLE statement. Only the table owner can create indexes on that table. The owner of a table can create an index at any time, whether or not there is data in the table. Indexes can be created on tables in another database by specifying a qualified database name.

The syntax for this component definition is:

```
CREATE [UNIQUE] [CLUSTERED | NONCLUSTERED]
INDEX index_name ON table (column [,...n])
[WITH
[PAD_INDEX]
[[,] FILLFACTOR = fillfactor]
[[,] IGNORE_DUP_KEY]
[[,] DROP_EXISTING]
[[,] STATISTICS_NORECOMPUTE]
]
[ON filegroup ]
```

The parameters for this component definition are:

◆ UNIQUE — The UNIQUE parameter creates a unique index (one in which no two rows are permitted to have the same index value). SQL Server checks for duplicate values when the index is created (if data already exists) and checks each time data is added with an INSERT or UPDATE statement. If duplicate key values exist, the CREATE INDEX statement is canceled and an error message giving the first duplicate is returned. A unique index cannot be created on a single column or multiple columns (composite index) in which the complete key (all columns of that key) is NULL in more than one row; these are treated as duplicate values for indexing purposes.

When a unique index exists, UPDATE or INSERT statements that would generate duplicate key values are rolled back, and SQL Server displays an error message. This is true even if the UPDATE or INSERT statement changes many rows but causes only one duplicate. If an attempt is made to enter data for which there is a unique index and the IGNORE_DUP_KEY clause is specified, only the rows violating the UNIQUE index fail. When processing an UPDATE statement, IGNORE_DUP_KEY has no effect. (For more information, see the IGNORE_DUP_KEY item later in this section.)

SQL Server does not allow the creation of a unique index on columns that already include duplicate values, whether IGNORE_DUP_KEY is set. If that is attempted, SQL Server displays an error message; duplicates must be eliminated before a unique index can be created on the column(s).

♦ CLUSTERED — The CLUSTERED parameter creates an object where the physical order of rows is the same as the indexed order of the rows, and the bottom (leaf) level of the clustered index contains the actual data rows. Because nonclustered indexes are rebuilt when a clustered index is created, create the clustered index before creating any nonclustered indexes. If CLUSTERED is not specified, a nonclustered index is created.

♦ NONCLUSTERED — The NONCLUSTERED parameter creates an object that specifies the logical ordering of a table. With a nonclustered index, the physical order of the rows is not the same as their indexed order. The leaf level of a nonclustered index contains index rows. Each index row contains the nonclustered key value and one or more row locators that point to the row that contains the value. If the table does not have a clustered index, the row locator is the row's disk address. If the table does have a clustered index, the row locator is the clustered index key for the row.

Each table can have as many as 249 nonclustered indexes (regardless of how they are created, implicitly with PRIMARY KEY and UNIQUE constraints or explicitly with CREATE INDEX). Each index can provide access to the data in a different sort order.

♦ index_name — The index_name parameter specifies the name of the index. Index names must be unique within a table but need not be unique within a database. Index names must follow the rules of identifiers. See Appendix B, "Standards, Guidelines, and Maxims," for suggested naming standards for indices.

♦ table — The table parameter specifies the table that contains the column or columns to be indexed. Specifying the database and table owner names is optional.

♦ column — The column parameter specifies the column or columns to which the index applies. Specify two or more column names to create a composite index on the combined values in the specified columns. List the columns to be included in the composite index (in sort and search priority order) inside the parentheses after table. Composite indexes are used when two or more columns are best searched as a unit or if many queries reference only the columns that are specified in the index. As many as 16 columns can be combined into a single composite index. All the columns in a composite index must be in the same table. The maximum allowable size of the combined index values is 900 bytes. (That is, the sum of the lengths of the columns that make up the composite index cannot exceed 900 bytes.)

♦ n — The n parameter is a placeholder indicating that multiple columns can be specified for any particular index.

♦ PAD_INDEX — The PAD_INDEX parameter specifies the space to leave open on each page (node) in the intermediate levels of the index. The PAD_INDEX option is useful only when FILLFACTOR is specified, because PAD_INDEX uses the percentage specified by FILLFACTOR. By default, SQL Server ensures that each index page has enough empty space to accommodate at least one row of the maximum size the index can have, given the set of keys on the intermediate pages. If the percentage specified for FILLFACTOR is not large enough to accommodate one row, SQL Server internally overrides the percentage to allow the minimum.

♦ FILLFACTOR = fillfactor — The FILLFACTOR = fillfactor parameter specifies a percentage that indicates how full SQL Server should make the leaf level of each index page during index creation. When an index page fills up, SQL Server must take time to split the index page to make room for new rows, which is quite expensive. For update-intensive tables, a properly chosen FILLFACTOR value yields better update performance than an improper FILLFACTOR value. The value of the original FILLFACTOR is stored with the index in sysindexes.

User-specified FILLFACTOR values can be from 1 through 100. If no value is specified, the default value is 0. When FILLFACTOR is set to 0, only the leaf pages are filled. Space is left in nonleaf pages for at least one row. You can change the default FILLFACTOR setting by executing the stored procedure sp_configure. Use a FILLFACTOR of 100 only if no INSERT or UPDATE statements will occur, such as with a read-only table. If FILLFACTOR is 100, SQL Server creates indexes with leaf pages 100 percent full. An INSERT or UPDATE made after the creation of an index with a 100 percent FILLFACTOR causes page splits for each INSERT and possibly each UPDATE.

When FILLFACTOR is set to any value other than 0 or 100, space is left in nonleaf pages for one row (two for nonunique clustered indexes). Space is left in leaf pages so that no leaf page is more full than the percentage specified by FILLFACTOR, as shown in Table 11-8.

TABLE 11-8 FILLFACTOR DESCRIPTIONS

FILLFACTOR	Internal Page	Leaf Page
0%	One free slot*	100% full
1–99%	One free slot*	<= FILLFACTOR % full
100%	100% full	100% full

◆ IGNORE_DUP_KEY — The IGNORE_DUP_KEY parameter controls what happens when you attempt to enter a duplicate key in a unique clustered index. It is meaningful only when the UPDATE or INSERT statement affects multiple rows. SQL Server issues a warning and does not insert the row containing the duplicate. If IGNORE_DUP_KEY is set and you issue an UPDATE or INSERT statement that creates duplicate keys, the row that causes the duplicates is ignored. In the case of UPDATE, the row is discarded. Other changes to the database caused by the UPDATE or INSERT attempt (for example, changes to index pages) are also backed out. However, if the UPDATE or INSERT attempt affects multiple rows, the other rows are added or changed as usual. If IGNORE_DUP_KEY is not specified, no rows will be inserted by the UPDATE or INSERT statement.

You cannot create a unique index on a column that already includes duplicate values, whether IGNORE_DUP_KEY is set or not. If you attempt to do so, SQL Server displays an error message and lists the duplicate values. You must use SQL data manipulation language statements such as SELECT and UPDATE in combination to eliminate duplicates before you can create a unique index on the column. Reorganizing the data is a good idea when a table becomes fragmented. To determine whether a table is contiguous, use the database consistency check utility DBCC statement SHOW_CONTIG.

◆ IGNORE_DUP_ROW and ALLOW_DUP_ROW — The IGNORE_DUP_ROW and ALLOW_DUP_ROW parameters are options for creating a nonunique clustered index; they are mutually exclusive. When creating a nonunique, nonclustered index, these options are irrelevant because SQL Server attaches a unique row identification number internally; it never checks for duplicate rows or for identical data values.

The IGNORE_DUP_KEY, IGNORE_DUP_ROW, and ALLOW_DUP_ROW index options control what happens when a duplicate key or duplicate row is created with the INSERT or UPDATE statement. Table 11-9 shows when these options can be used.

TABLE 11-9 DUP ROW OPTIONS

Index Type	Options
Clustered	IGNORE_DUP_ROW or ALLOW_DUP_ROW
Unique clustered	IGNORE_DUP_KEY
Nonclustered	None
Unique nonclustered	IGNORE_DUP_KEY

Table 11-9 illustrates how ALLOW_DUP_ROW and IGNORE_DUP_ROW affect attempts to create a nonunique clustered index on a table that includes duplicate rows and attempts to enter duplicate rows into a table.

♦ ON *filegroup* — The ON *filegroup* specifies the database filegroup on which the index is to be created. A nonclustered index can be created on a different filegroup from the data pages. Before creating an index on a segment, verify which segments you can use. Certain segments can be allocated to specific tables or indexes for performance reasons or for other considerations. The ON *filegroup* clause can affect the placement of the data portion and the index portions of a table:

- Creating a nonclustered index on a specified *filegroup* ensures that index pages (current and future) will be placed on that filegroup. All data pages will continue to be allocated from the original filegroup on which the table was created.

- Creating a clustered index with SORTED_DATA_REORG on a specified *filegroup* causes the entire table to be moved to that filegroup.

- Creating a clustered index with SORTED_DATA on a specified *filegroup* causes all future data pages to be allocated from the new *filegroup* only. The index pages (the B-tree) are created on the new *seqment_name* only. Current page allocations will not be affected.

Space is allocated to tables and indexes in increments of one extent (eight 2KB pages) at a time. Each time an extent is filled, another is allocated. For a report on the amount of space allocated and used by an index, use the system-stored procedure sp_spaceused or the Enterprise Manager. Creating a clustered index requires space available in your database equal to approximately 1.2 times the size of the data. This is space in addition to the space used by the existing table; the data is duplicated (unless SORTED_DATA is specified) to create the clustered index, and the old, nonindexed data is deleted when the index is complete.

If there is no data in the table when an index is created, run the UPDATE STATISTICS statement after data is added. To check when the statistics were last updated, use DBCC SHOW_STATISTICS. A composite index, like any other index, is represented by one row in the sysindexes table.

The following simple index example creates an index on the EMP_ID column of the TB_EMPLOYEE table:

```
CREATE INDEX XO_ EMPLOYEE  ON TB_EMPLOYEE (EMP_ID)
```

The following unique clustered index example creates an index on the EMP_ID column of the TB_EMPLOYEE table that enforces uniqueness. This index will physically order the data on disk because the CLUSTERED option is specified:

```
CREATE UNIQUE CLUSTERED INDEX XO_ EMPLOYEE  ON TB_EMPLOYEE (EMP_ID)
```

The following simple composite index example creates an index on the EXP_RPT_ID and EXP_ID columns of the TB_EMP_EXP_DTL table:

```
CREATE UNIQUE CLUSTERED INDEX XPKTB_EMP_EXP_DTL ON TB_EMP_EXP_DTL
(
        EXP_RPT_ID,
        EXP_ID
)
```

CHOOSING INDEX CANDIDATES

An index is used to find a row quickly, similar to the way an index is used in a book. Indexes are organized in a binary tree of pages containing encoded data. That is to say, the binary tree (B+ tree) is a set of nodes that contain keys and pointers that are arranged in a hierarchy. The B+ tree is organized into levels. Level 0 contains a pointer, or address, to the actual data. The other levels contain pointers to nodes on different levels that contain keys that are less than or equal to the key in the higher level. When you access a row through an index, you read the B+ tree starting at the root node and follow the nodes down to level 0, which contains the pointer to the data. It is important to keep key size to a minimum for two reasons:

- One page in memory will hold more key values, therefore, potentially reducing the number of read operations to look up several rows.

- A smaller key size may cause fewer B+ tree levels to be used. This is very important from a performance standpoint. An index with a four-level tree will require one more read per row than an index with a three-level tree. If 100,000 rows are read in an hour, this means there will be 100,000 less reads to get the same data.

In SQL Server, the size of a node is the size of one page, typically 2KB (2,048 bytes).

B+TREE SPLITS

The binary tree responds to growth in a set way. When a node gets full, it must be split into two nodes. B+ trees grow toward the root. Attempting to add a key into a full node forces a split into two nodes and promotion of the middle key value into a node at a higher level. If the key value that causes the split is greater than the other keys in the node, it is put into a node by itself during the split. The promotion of a key to the next higher level can also cause a split in the higher-level node. If the full node at this higher level is the root, it also splits. When the root splits, the tree grows by one level and a new root node is created. Using this method, it is impossible for a B+ tree to be unbalanced (having different levels in different parts of the tree).

UNIQUE AND DUPLICATE INDICES

Four characteristics are associated with indexes: unique, duplicate, composite, and clustered. An index must be either unique or duplicate. In addition, it may or may not be composite, and it may or may not be clustered. A unique index allows no more than one occurrence of a value in the indexed column. Therefore, a unique index prohibits users from entering duplicate data into the indexed column. For column(s) serving as a table's primary key, a unique index ensures the uniqueness of every row. As a general rule, a unique index should be chosen for each table. The choice of a unique key for a table should be carefully considered. A duplicate index allows identical values in different rows of an indexed column.

COMPOSITE INDEX

An index on two or more columns is a *composite index*. The principal functions of a composite index are to:

♦ Facilitate multiple column joins (for example, expense details by expense report and date)

♦ Increase uniqueness of indexed values (for example, expense report and sequence number for details within an expense report)

Composite indexes can be very helpful for improving performance on a query. SQL Server allows up to sixteen columns in a composite index, with a maximum key size of 255 bytes.

CLUSTERED INDEXES

Information stored in a database is extracted from the hard disk in blocks (sections of disk space). Through *clustering,* you can cause the physical placement of data on the disk to be in an indexed order. This can increase the efficiency of data retrievals when the retrievals are in a similar order as the index. In the previous example, if a clustered index is put on lname, the data row would be ordered physically by lname. A SELECT statement retrieving many rows in the customer table in order by lname will be more efficient, especially if the table is large.

The clustered index physically alters the placement of data stored on the disk. Only one clustered index can exist per table. Clustered indexes are not updated when rows are added to the table or data is updated. Therefore, clustered indexes are most effectively used on often-queried static tables and are less effective on dynamic tables.

A *clustered index* is one in which the physical order of rows is the same as the indexed order of rows. The bottom, or leaf, level of a clustered index contains the actual data pages. As mentioned, you can have only a single clustered index per table, so use this index wisely. The UPDATE and DELETE operations are often accelerated by clustered indexes, since these operations require much reading. Typically, for a table that has at least one index, you should make one of those indexes a clustered index.

When a significant number of rows are being inserted into a table, avoid putting a clustered index on a monotonically increasing column, such as an identity column, of that table. Insert performance can be degraded if you do this, because each inserted row must go at the end of the table, on the last data page of the table. While one row is being inserted into the last data page (thus locking the data page), all other inserted rows must wait in a queue until the current insert is complete. The leaf-level pages of a clustered index are actual data pages, and the data pages are physically ordered on the hard disk using the logical order of the clustered index.

DROPPING AN INDEX

The DROP INDEX statement does not apply to indexes created by PRIMARY KEY or UNIQUE constraints. For details about dropping constraints, see the ALTER TABLE statement later in this chapter.

The syntax for this component definition is:

```
DROP INDEX [owner.]table_name.index_name
  [, [owner.]table_name.index_name...]
Where
```

The parameters for this component definition are:

♦ *table_name* – Specifies the table where the indexed column is located. If DROP INDEX is used by the DBO or SA, then the owner name can be included to drop an index not owned by the DBO.

♦ *index_name* – Specifies the index to be dropped.

The following example removes the index XPKTB_EMP_EXP_DTL on the expense detail TB_EMP_EXP_DTL table.

```
DROP INDEX TB_EMP_EXP_DTL.XPKTB_EMP_EXP_DTL
```

Benefits of indexing

Several performance benefits are associated with the indexing of database tables. Performance improves when indexes are applied to the following columns:

♦ Columns that are used to join two tables

♦ Columns applied as filters to a query

♦ Columns in an ORDER BY or GROUP BY

In these cases, using the index to find the desired rows greatly reduces the time needed to find the row. Without an index, table(s) are accessed by sequentially reading each row until the WHERE condition is satisfied. An index can reduce that

I/O considerably. An index on a column or columns can be used to retrieve data in a sorted order. When you perform an indexed read (a read of the table via an index), rows returned will automatically be in sorted order. This prevents the database server from having to sort the output data. You can create an index on a column with the UNIQUE keyword, that is, only one row in the table can have a column with that value. You still need to perform any uniqueness checking through the application program and return the appropriate response, but you are assured that the table contains no duplication. Also, when all columns listed in the SELECT clause are part of the same index, SQL Server does not read the data rows, as all the data is already available via the index. This can greatly reduce the amount of I/O needed to process such a query.

Costs of indexing

The first cost associated with an index is one of disk space. An index contains a copy of every unique data value in the indexed column(s) plus a four-byte pointer for every row in the table and a one-byte delete flag. This can add many blocks or pages to the space requirements of the table. It is not unusual to have as much disk space dedicated to index data as to row data.

The second cost is one of time while the table is modified. Before a row is inserted, updated, or deleted, the index key must be looked up in the B+ tree first. Assume an average of two I/Os is needed to locate an index entry. Some index nodes may be in shared memory, though other indexes that need modification may have to be read from disk. Under these assumptions, index maintenance adds time to different kinds of modifications as follows:

◆ When a row is deleted from a table, the related entries are deleted from all indexes. Null values are entered in the row in the data file. When a row is inserted, the related entries are inserted in all indexes. The node for the inserted row's entry is found and rewritten for each index.

◆ When a row is updated, the related entries are looked up in each index that applies to a column that was altered. The index entry is rewritten to eliminate the old entry; then the new column value is located in the same index and a new entry made.

Many insert and delete operations can also cause a major restructuring of the index (as they are implemented using B+trees), requiring more I/O activity.

Some basic guidelines for choosing an index candidate are as follows:

◆ Add an index for columns that are involved in JOINS

◆ Add an index for columns that are used as selective filters and have a large range of values (>25)

♦ Add an index for columns that are frequently used for ordering or sorting (for example, popular reports)

♦ Avoid highly duplicative indexes (for example, gender)

LIMITING INDICES

Limit the number of indices to those that give you the most bang for the buck; that is, do not index everything. Choose columns that are commonly used to search (for example, identifiers like name). There should be an index on at least one column named in any join expression. If there is no index, the database server will either build a temporary index before the join, perform a sort merge join or nested loop join, or sequentially scan the table and then perform a hash join.

When there is an index on both columns in a join expression, the optimizer has more options when it constructs the query plan. As a general rule in OLTP environments, you should place an index on any foreign key column, and on any other column that is frequently used in a join expression. If, however, only one of the tables in a join is chosen to be indexed, give preference to the table with unique values for the key corresponding to the join column(s). A unique index is preferable to a duplicate index for implementing joins. As a general rule, in DDS environments where large amounts of data are read and sequential table scans are performed, indexes may not play an optimal role in implementing joins because hash joins are the preferred method.

If a column is often used to filter the rows of a large table, consider placing an index on it. The optimizer can use the index to pick out the desired rows, avoiding a sequential scan of the entire table. An example is a table containing a large mailing list. If you find that a `zipcode` column is often used to filter out a subset of rows, consider putting an index on it even though it is not used in joins.

This strategy will yield a net savings of time only when the selectivity of the column is high, that is, only when there are not a lot of duplicate values in that column. Nonsequential access through an index takes more disk I/O operations to retrieve many rows than sequential access, so if a filter expression will cause a large percentage of the table to be returned, the database server might as well read the table sequentially.

Generally, indexing a filter column will save time when the column is used in filter expressions in many queries or in queries of a large table or a table where there are relatively few duplicate values.

USING INDEXES JUDICIOUSLY

When a large quantity of rows has to be ordered or grouped, the database server has to put the rows in order. The database server will sort the selected rows via a sort package before returning them to the front-end application. If, however, there is an index on the ordering column(s), the optimizer will sometimes plan to read the rows in sorted order through the index, avoiding the final sort. Whether the index is used depends upon the complexity of the query.

Because the keys in an index are in sorted sequence, the index really represents the result of sorting the table. By placing an index on the ordering column(s), you can eliminate many sorts during queries.

When duplicate keys are permitted in an index, the entries that have any single value are grouped in a list. When the selectivity of the column is high, these lists will be short. But when there are only a few unique values, the lists become quite long. For example, in an index on a column whose only two values are male and female, all the index entries are contained in just two lists of duplicates. Such an index is not very useful.

When an entry has to be deleted from a list of duplicates, the server has to read the whole list and rewrite some part of it. When adding an entry, the database server puts the new row at the end of the list. Neither operation is a problem until the number of duplicate values becomes very high. The server is forced to perform many I/O operations to read all the entries, in order to find the end of the list. When it deletes an entry, it will typically have to update and rewrite half of the entries in the list.

When such an index is used for querying, performance can also degrade, because the rows addressed by a key value may be spread out over the disk. Imagine an index addressing rows whose location alternates from one part of the disk to the other. As the database server tries to access each row via the index, it must perform one I/O for every row read. It will probably be better off reading the table sequentially, and applying the filter to each row in turn.

If it is important to index a column with a large number of duplicated values, you may consider forming a composite key with another column that has few duplicate values.

Because of the extra reads that must occur when indexes are updated, some degradation will occur when there are many indexes on a table that is being updated frequently. An extremely volatile table should probably not be heavily indexed unless you feel that the amount of querying on a table outweighs the overhead of maintaining the index file. Indexes can be dropped and recreated. During periods of heavy querying (for example, reports), you can improve performance by creating an index on the appropriate column. Creating indexes for a large table, however, can be a time-consuming process. Also, while the index is being created, the table will be exclusively locked, preventing other users from accessing it.

Because an index can require a substantial amount of disk space to maintain, it is best to keep the size of the index small relative to the row size. This is because of the way key values are stored in the index: the larger the key value, the fewer the keys that will fit in a node of the B+ tree. More nodes require more I/O operations to access the rows indexed.

When the rows are short or the key values are long, it may be more efficient to just read the table sequentially. There is, of course, a certain break-even point between the size of a key and the efficiency of using that index, though this will vary according to the number of rows in the table.

An exception to this is the key-only select. This type of select occurs if all of the columns selected in the query are in the index. The table data will not be read, thus increasing the efficiency of using such an index.

As mentioned, composite indexes are indexes created on more than one column. They facilitate joining tables on multiple columns and can increase the uniqueness of indexed values. When you create a composite index to help improve query performance, some of the component columns can also take advantage of this index. A composite index on three columns, say a, b, and c, can be used for queries on the two columns a and b or just on column a. You would not need to create additional indexes on these columns. This is known as a *partial key search*. This index would not be used for a search on columns b and c, or column c alone.

If several columns of one table join with several columns in another table, create a composite index on the columns of the table with many duplicate values. Adding a unique (or more nearly unique) column to a column that has many duplicate values will increase the uniqueness mentioned. The query will be able to perform a partial key search using the first (highly duplicative) field, which will be faster than searching the duplicate lists. When a table is commonly sorted on several columns, a composite index corresponding to those columns can sometimes be used to implement the ordering.

REDUCING DISK ACCESSES

One of the primary performance objectives in database management is to reduce the number of disk accesses. SQL Server uses a unit of I/O, that is, the page. Having as many rows as possible physically on the same block (or page) and in the same order as an index increases the efficiency of an indexed retrieval. By placing rows that are frequently used together in close physical proximity, you can substantially reduce disk access time. Clustering data files in index order puts logically related rows in the same disk block (or page). Clustering is most useful for relatively static tables.

Clustering and reclustering takes a lot of space and time. You can avoid some clustering by loading data into the table in the desired order in the first place. The physical order of rows is their insertion order, so if the table is initially loaded with ordered data, no clustering is needed.

In some applications, the majority of table updates can be confined to a single time period. Perhaps all updates are applied overnight or on specified dates (the end of the month, for example). When this is the case, consider dropping all nonunique indexes while the updates are being performed, and then creating new indexes afterward. This can have two positive effects:

◆ First, because there are fewer indexes to update, the updating program is likely to run faster. It is often the case that the total time to drop the indexes, update without them, and recreate them afterward will be less than the time to update with the indexes in place.

◆ Second, newly made indexes are the most efficient ones. Frequent updates tend to dilute the index structure, causing it to contain many partly filled index nodes. This reduces the effectiveness of an index, as well as wasting disk space.

Another timesaving measure is making sure that a batch-updating program calls for rows in the sequence defined by the primary key index. That will cause the pages of the primary key index to be read in order and only one time each.

Creating Views

A *view* is an alternative way of looking at the data in one or more tables. Views are virtual tables made up of columns from one or more tables, usually joined by the same key or keys that they share in common.

Why use a view?

Views facilitate access to the data. They can provide a measure of security as well. For example, you may restrict the selection of employee column data such as salary. The CREATE statement will build a virtual table that represents an alternative way of looking at the data in one or more tables. You can use views as security mechanisms by granting permission on a view but not on underlying tables.

The syntax for this component definition is:

```
CREATE VIEW [owner.]view_name
[(column_name [, column_name]...)]
AS select_statement [WITH CHECK OPTION]
```

The parameters for this component definition follow:

◆ view_name — The view_name parameter specifies the name of the view. View names must follow the rules for identifiers.

◆ column_name — The column_name parameter specifies the name to be used for a column in a view. Naming a column in CREATE VIEW is always legal but only necessary when a column is derived from an arithmetic expression, a function, or a constant. Naming is also necessary when two or more columns could otherwise have the same name (usually because of a join); or when you want to give a column in a view a name different from the column from which it is derived. Column names can also be assigned in the SELECT statement. If column_name is not specified, the view columns acquire the same names as the columns in the SELECT statement.

♦ AS `select_statement` — The AS `select_statement` parameter is the SELECT statement that defines the view. It can use more than one table and other views. You must have permission to select from the objects referenced in the SELECT clause of a view you are creating.

♦ WITH CHECK OPTION — The WITH CHECK OPTION forces all data modification statements executed against the view to adhere to the criteria set within the `select_statement` defining the view. When a row is modified through a view, the WITH CHECK OPTION guarantees that the data will remain visible through the view after the modification has been committed.

A view need not be a simple subset of the rows and columns of one particular table. You can create a view using more than one table and/or other views with a SELECT clause of any complexity. There are, however, a few restrictions on the SELECT clauses in a view definition:

♦ You cannot include ORDER BY, COMPUTE, or COMPUTE BY clauses.

♦ You cannot include the INTO keyword.

♦ You cannot reference a temporary table.

You can create a view only in the current database. A view can reference a maximum of 250 columns. In a view defined with a SELECT * clause (don't do this), if you alter the structure of its underlying table(s) by adding columns, the new columns do not appear in the view unless the view is first deleted and redefined. The asterisk shorthand is interpreted and expanded when the view is first created. When you query through a view, SQL Server checks to make sure that all the database objects referenced anywhere in the statement exist, that they are valid in the context of the statement, and that data modification statements do not violate any data integrity rules. A check that fails returns an error message. A successful check translates the action into an action against the underlying table(s).

Modifying data through views

Although views are useful for querying the database, they are much more restrictive when it comes to updating the underlying tables. For example, Delete statements are not allowed on multitable views. Moreover, you cannot insert a row through a view that includes a computed column. Insert statements are not allowed on join views created with the distinct or with the check option. Update statements are allowed on join views with the check option. The update fails if any of the affected columns appears in the WHERE clause, in an expression that includes columns from more than one table. If you insert or update a row through a join view, all affected columns must belong to the same base table.

Maintaining the Database

Creating the physical database objects is an iterative process in the development stage of any project. Your administrator will need to back up the database or selected objects, such as tables, and then amend the object and restore. SQL Server provides a fair amount of help toward making these amendments.

Modifying DDL statements

A table can be altered in most cases without having to unload and reload the data. If the ALTER TABLE statement causes columns to be physically changed, a complete copy of the table is made with the changes specified. When the statement has completed, the old copy is deleted, and the new copy of the table is used. This means that you must have enough space in your FILEGROUP to hold two copies of the table being altered.

The syntax for this component definition is as follows:

```
ALTER TABLE [database.[owner].]table_name
[WITH NOCHECK]
[ADD
    {col_name column_properties [column_constraints]
    | [[,] table_constraint]}
        [, {next_col_name | next_table_constraint}]...]
|
[DROP [CONSTRAINT]
    constraint_name [, constraint_name2]...]
```

The parameters for this component definition follow:

◆ *table_name* – Specifies which table to alter. You can include local or global temporary tables, but FOREIGN KEY constraints are not enforced on temporary tables.

◆ WITH NOCHECK – The WITH NOCHECK parameter allows CHECK or FOREIGN KEY constraints to be added to a table without verifying existing data for constraint violations. PRIMARY, KEY, and UNIQUE constraints are always checked. When this option is not specified (the default), any added constraints will be validated against existing data. If there are any constraint violations, the ALTER TABLE statement fails and a message is returned, stating the type of constraint and name that caused the violation. Use this option with extreme caution. This option is useful when you know your data already meets the new constraints or when a business rule requires the constraint to be enforced only from this point forward.

- ◆ `ADD` — The `ADD` parameter allows a column- or table-level constraint to be added to an existing table.

- ◆ *col_name* — The *col_name* parameter is a new column for the table. Column names must conform to the rules for identifiers and must be unique in the table.

  - ■ *column_properties* =

  - ■ *datatype* [NULL | IDENTITY[(*seed, increment*)]]

- ◆ *datatype* — Specifies the data type of the column. System or user-defined data types are acceptable. Columns added to a table must be defined as `NULL`. When a column is added, the initial value for the column will be set to `NULL`. This restriction forces the `ALTER TABLE` statement to fail if the `bit` or `timestamp` data types are used.

- ◆ `IDENTITY[(seed, increment)]` — The `IDENTITY [(seed, increment)]` statement generates values for existing rows based on the *seed* and *increment* parameters. If used, the *seed* value will be assigned to the first row in the table and each subsequent row will receive the next identity value, equal to the last identity plus the *increment* value. If neither argument is given, both default to 1. The `IDENTITY` property cannot be added to an existing column; it can be added only to a new column. See the Create Table syntax for additional details.

Following is an example that uses `ALTER` to add a `PRIMARY KEY` constraint. The `TB_EMPLOYEE` table in SQL Server 7 includes a `PRIMARY KEY` constraint on the `EMP_ID` column. This example shows how to add only this constraint (with an explicit name):

```
ALTER TABLE TB_EMPLOYEE
ADD
CONSTRAINT UPKCL_auidind PRIMARY KEY CLUSTERED (EMP_ID)
```

Following is an example that uses `ALTER` to add a `CHECK` constraint. The `TB_EMPLOYEE` table has a *zip* column where a five-digit character string is required. This example adds a `CHECK` constraint to guarantee that only numbers are entered.

```
ALTER TABLE TB_EMPLOYEE
ADD
CONSTRAINT CK_zip CHECK (zip LIKE '[0-9][0-9][0-9][0-9][0-9]')
```

Data space reclamation

Once an extent has been allocated to a table, that extent will never be freed up for reuse by other tables. If an extent should become empty (due to massive deletes from the table), the extent will remain part of the `tblspace`. The space will be reused, however, when additional rows are inserted into the same table in the future.

If you want to reclaim the space in empty extents and make it available to the `FILEGROUP` to use for other tables, you can use the `ALTER TABLE` command to achieve such a compression. Be aware, however, that `ALTER TABLE` will only physically restructure the table if it is necessary. Thus, running an `ALTER TABLE` statement that does not actually change the table (for example, altering a column to be the same as it already is) will not result in a restructuring of the table. The best way to force a restructuring of the table is to alter one of the table's indexes to `CLUSTER`; this will always physically restructure the table, even if the index is currently clustered. An example follows:

```
ALTER INDEX x1_order TO CLUSTER;
```

This statement will physically restructure the table on which the index `x1_order` is created. This restructuring will pack the table, freeing up space used by the empty extents. For more information about a clustered index, refer to the Indexing Strategy section, "Creating indices and keys."

The `DROP TABLE` command will free up space that was allocated for the table to be used for other purposes. The data will no longer be accessible. The `DROP DATABASE` command frees up space that was allocated for all the tables in the database. The system catalog tables are dropped.

SQL Server Database Utilities

When developing applications, changes occur frequently. The picture and content of the database as it is forming must be redefined and repopulated to allow development to proceed. SQL Server 7 provides utilities to facilitate the requirements.

Generating a database schema

The Enterprise Manager, the DMO utility, or third-party tools such as ERwin can be used to produce a SQL command file that contains the `CREATE TABLE`, `CREATE INDEX`, `GRANT`, `CREATE SYNONYM`, and `CREATE VIEW` statements required to replicate an entire database or a selected table. The resulting script can be saved as a text file and used to quickly recreate the database and its components within a different server. For example, when migrating a database from the development server to the quality-assurance server, the script can be used to quickly port selected development objects.

Populating a database

During application database development phase, one of the most frequent requirements is loading tables from flat file extracts from other systems. For example, downloads from a mainframe MVS or AS400 legacy or "heritage" systems are commonly used to create the content of a SQL Server table. SQL Server provides various options for loading a table but a few notes about the target table definition. The presence of indices in the target table slows down the population of tables. Drop the indices and then load the table. Create the indices after the table load is complete. Loading a table that has no indexes at all is a very quick process (little more than a disk-to-disk sequential copy). But updating indexes adds a great deal of overhead.

After you've created tables, you'll want to put data into the tables and work with the data. You can change data, remove data, or add more data. You can also import and export data to and from other applications. In SQL Server, you work with data by using data modification statements. You add data using the INSERT statement; change data using the UPDATE, WRITETEXT, or UPDATETEXT statements; and remove data using the DELETE or TRUNCATE TABLE statements. Each SQL Server statement is by default a transaction. You can process transactions individually or collectively. For example, to add five rows to a table, you can issue five INSERT statements separately, or you can group them into a single transaction.

There are utilities to either unload data from a database or to load data into a database. The bcp or the bulk copy program copies a database table to or from an operating system file in a user-specified format.

The syntax for this utility is:

```
bcp [[database_name.]owner.]table_name {in | out} datafile
[/m maxerrors] [/f formatfile] [/e errfile]
[/F firstrow] [/L lastrow] [/b batchsize]
[/n] [/c] [/E]
[/t field_term] [/r row_term]
[/i inputfile] [/o outputfile]
/U login_id [/P password] [/S servername] [/v] [/a packet_size]
```

The parameters for this utility are as follows:

◆ *database_name* — The *database_name* parameter specifies the database. If the table being copied is in your default database, this parameter is optional.

◆ *owner* — The *owner* parameter is the owner's name. This name is optional if you own the table being copied. If no owner is specified and you do not own a table of that name, the program will not execute.

◆ *table_name* — The *table_name* parameter specifies which database table to copy.

♦ in | out — The in | out parameter specifies the direction of the copy. The in option copies from a file into the database table; the out option copies to a file from the database table.

♦ datafile — The datafile parameter is the full path of an operating system file when copying a table to or from a hard-disk file or a single floppy disk. The path can have from 1 to 255 characters. When copying a table to or from multiple floppy disks, *datafile* is a drive specifier only (such as A:).

♦ /m maxerrors — The /m maxerrors parameter is the maximum number of errors that can occur before the copy is canceled. Each row that cannot be rebuilt by bcp is ignored and counted as one error. If this option is not included, the default is 10.

♦ /f formatfile — The /f formatfile parameter is the full path of a file with stored responses from a previous use of bcp on the same table; creation of the format file is optional. Use this option when you have already created a format file that you want to use when copying in or out. After you answer format questions, bcp asks whether you want to save your answers in a format file. The default filename is bcp.fmt. The bcp utility can refer to a format file when copying data so that you do not have to duplicate your previous format responses interactively. If this option is not used, bcp queries you for format information.

♦ /e errfile — The /e errfile parameter is the full path of an error file where bcp stores any rows that it was unable to transfer from the file to the database. Error messages from the bcp utility go to the user's workstation. If this option is not used, no error file is created.

♦ /F firstrow — The /F firstrow parameter specifies the number of the first row to copy (the default is the first row).

♦ /L lastrow — The /L lastrow parameter specifies the number of the last row to copy (the default is the last row).

♦ /b batchsize — The /b batchsize parameter specifies the number of rows per batch of data copied (the default copies all the rows in one batch).

♦ /n — The /n option performs the copy operation using the data's native (database) data types as the default. This option does not prompt for each field; it uses the default values.

♦ /c — The /c option performs the copy operation with a character data type as the default. This option does not prompt for each field; it uses char as the default storage type, no prefixes, \t (tab) as the default field separator, and \n (newline) as the default row terminator.

◆ /E — The /E option is used when identity values are present within the table to be imported. When importing data, an identity column is temporarily assigned an identity value of 0. As the rows are inserted into the table, SQL Server assigns unique values based on the seed and increment values specified during table creation. Use the /E flag when identity values already exist in the file. If SQL Server–generated identity values are preferred, place only nonidentity columns in the file.

◆ /t field_term — The /t field_term parameter is the default field terminator.

◆ /r row_term — The /r row_term parameter is the default row terminator.

◆ /i inputfile — The /I inputfile parameter is the name of a file that redirects input to bcp.

◆ /o outputfile — The /o outputfile parameter is the name of a file that receives output redirected from bcp.

◆ /U login_id — The /U login_id parameter is a login ID.

◆ /P password — The /P password parameter is a user-specified password. If this option is not used, bcp prompts for a password. If this option is used at the end of the command line without any password, bcp uses the default password (NULL).

◆ /S servername — The /S servername parameter specifies which SQL Server to connect to. The servername is the name of the server computer on the network. This option is required when you are executing bcp from a remote computer on the network.

◆ /v The /v option reports the current DB-Library version number.

◆ /a packet_size — The /a packet_size parameter is the number of bytes, per network packet, sent to and from the server. A server configuration option can be set using SQL Enterprise Manager (or the sp_configure system stored procedure). However, this option can be overridden on an individual basis with the bcp /a option. The valid values for packet_size are 512 through 65535. The server default is 4096; the default value for the Windows NT–based version of bcp is 4096. The default value for MS-DOS is 512, although larger sizes can be requested. Increased packet size may enhance performance on bulk copy operations. Microsoft testing indicates that 4096 to 8192 is typically the fastest setting for bulk copy operations. If a larger packet is requested but cannot be granted, the client will default to 512. The performance statistics generated at the end of a bcp run will show the actual packet size used.

Following is an example SQL Server bulk copy (bcp) execution:

```
D:\MSSQL\BINN>bcp ADVANI2..IND_INDIVIDUAL_PROFILE
in c:\advani\profile1.txt /c / t ,  /U jbesq7 /P jbesq7
Starting copy...
DB-LIBRARY error:
    Attempt to convert data stopped by syntax error in source field.
DB-LIBRARY error:
    Attempt to bulk-copy an oversized row to the SQL Server.
2002 rows copied.
Network packet size (bytes): 4096
Clock Time (ms.): total =     30 Avg =      15 (66.67 rows per sec.)
```

In this example we have loaded 2,002 rows with two errors.

Summary

This chapter covered application database definitions. See Chapter 6, "Database Administration Using the Enterprise Manager," for working on specific day-to-day changes to your database using a database administrator–friendly GUI. More likely, at the conclusion of your design and the creation of the DDL you will use ISQL (see Chapter 4, "SQL Server 7 Tools and Components") or a batch-oriented tool to execute a batch of DDL. The larger tasks, those that involve changes to many or most of the database tables, are usually scripted and performed in a bulk/batch fashion. You can execute multiple SQL statements as a batch, interactively, or in a file.

Chapter 12

Manipulating Data

IN THIS CHAPTER

- ◆ Basic data manipulation language
- ◆ Database transactions
- ◆ Database searching
- ◆ Database operations and data manipulation

THE BUSINESS LOGIC ENCAPSULATED in the typical application involves database manipulation. A sometimes gray area in the application design is the database transaction that consists of data manipulation (DML). Where does it start and where does it end? After you use DML for a while, you will begin to ask questions like "Should we use stored procedures, or do we use embedded SQL to access and update the database?" Stored procedures afford you the advantage of being independent of the front-end GUI, but they neutralize some of the benefits developers can derive from developing native SQL. When developing the application with native SQL, the prudent developer must consider how to manage database transactions and database access during application execution.

There are a number of things to consider. How to manage database-specific logical units of work is critical to database integrity. How to control and avoid potentially expensive database operations is critical to database performance. How and when to use techniques for dynamically modifying the database is critical to database performance and integrity. Finally, how to control and provide viable and concurrent access by multiple users is critical to database performance, integrity, and making the user happy. This chapter describes how you can select and maintain the database using SQL manipulation statements.

Basic Data Manipulation Language

The Structured Query Language, or SQL, as it is commonly known, is an English-like language that enables you to create, manage, and use databases. The SQL provided with SQL Server 7 products is an enhanced version of the industry-standard query language that was originally developed by IBM. Data manipulation is a special subset of SQL that includes:

◆ Data definition statements – Create a database and define its structure.

◆ Data manipulation statements – Select, insert, update, or delete data in a database.

◆ Cursor manipulation statements – Work with cursors (open, fetch, or close a cursor).

◆ Dynamic management statements – Dynamically manage resources at run time.

◆ Data access statements – Determine how data can be accessed (often referred to as Data Control (DCL) statements).

◆ Data integrity statements – Preserve data integrity.

◆ Query optimization information statements – Obtain information regarding the execution of a query.

◆ Stored procedure statements – Execute and debug stored procedures.

In this chapter, we will concentrate on data manipulation statements, which in the instance of the SQL Server 7 relational model include:

◆ SELECT – Allows you to select a set of data (one or more rows) from the database.

◆ INSERT – Allows you to insert a set of data (one or more rows) into the database.

◆ UPDATE – Allows you to update a set of data (one or more rows) already in the database.

◆ DELETE – Allows you to delete a set of data (one or more rows) already in the database.

Connecting to the database

In most contemporary GUI front-end software, such as PowerBuilder, all database connections are managed using a transaction object typically known as a SQL control area or SQLCA for relational database systems. Additionally, Web- and Java-based front-end software, such as SilverStream, also makes use of a JDBC control object to manage connections. This JDBC connection object will be discussed later in Chapter 17, "C and Java with SQL."

When you are using a client/server enterprise tool like PowerBuilder, the contents of pertinent SQL Server 7 SQLCA fields, SQLCODE, are transferred to the

PowerBuilder SQLCA so that the application can examine the content and determine what to do next. The SQLCA contains all of the fields used to manage the database access – for example, user login, database return codes, and so on. The default transaction object SQLCA is created when the application is invoked and is destroyed when the application terminates. It is important to note that Microsoft products such as Visual Basic and Visual C++ also use an SQLCA to communicate with the SQL Server.

You can prime SQLCA, that is, set up the connect to a database, using one or more of the following techniques:

♦ Loading values from an application .ini file or the NT Registry (static servername, database name, and specifics)

♦ Prompting the user for values using a login screen (user id and password)

♦ Coding the values in a script (varying between servers based upon availability)

A database CONNECT is generally an expensive operation and should be managed carefully. Try to optimize their invocation. Sometimes they are unavoidable.

USING A TRANSACTION OBJECT

In a GUI front end like PowerBuilder, all database connections are managed using a transaction object. The default transaction object, SQLCA, is created when the application is invoked and is destroyed when the application terminates. Table 12-1 describes the attributes for SQLCA.

TABLE 12-1 SQLCA ATTRIBUTES

SQLCA Attributes	Description
DBMS	Which relational database engine will be used (SQL 7)
Database	The name of the database where system catalog tables will be built
UserID	Database user ID
DBPass	Database passwords
Lock	Type of locking
LogID	User ID
LogPass	User password

Continued

TABLE 12-1 SQLCA ATTRIBUTES *(Continued)*

SQLCA Attributes	Description
ServerName	The name of the server (the name of the NT machine where SQL resides)
DBParm	Database parameters specific to SQL 7
SQLCode	Return code from the last SQL access; *always* check this after each access

PRIMING TRANSACTION OBJECTS

Before connecting to a database, an application must prime the transaction object (SQLCA or user-defined) with the attribute values required by the target database. Review the particular attribute settings for each DBMS to ensure the proper connection.

These are the basic SQLCA parameters. The ideal technique is to read most of these values from an application .ini file and prompt the user for LOGINID and PASSWORD. You can use one, two, or a combination of all three methods depending on the requirements of your site.

MANAGING DATABASE CONNECTIONS

At various times within the course of development, for example, embedded SQL development, when you invoke the database from within an application execution, a GUI front end like PowerBuilder connects to the database. The connection takes place when the CONNECT verb is executed or a DML statement coded by the programmer is executed.

MANAGING LOGICAL UNITS OF WORK

Once connected, you will need to manage the database transactions also known as logical units of work. A logical unit of work is a set of database operations that must be completed or rejected together, meaning debiting one account and crediting another. For example, in a banking application, the SQL might look like this:

```
UPDATE tb_acct   SET balance_qty = balance_qty + 1000
          WHERE acct_no = 12345;
   IF Sql_code <> 0 .quit transaction ; return to caller
UPDATE tb_acct   SET balance_qty = balance_qty - 1000
          WHERE acct_no = 67890;
IF Sql_code <> 0
```

```
    ROLLBACK
ELSE
    COMMIT;
```

The developer needs to recognize a logical unit of work within the context of the application to guarantee the integrity of the data. For instance, in our expense-reporting example, if we are deleting a report, we must delete all of its detail items first before we can delete the expense report; otherwise, we will have orphaned detail items, that is, details that have no parent reports. When several users can access the same data at the same time, you must take precautions to prevent any collisions.

Concurrency is a database issue rather than a GUI front-end issue, but that does not relieve the developer from understanding the implications of the SQL that is generated. The prudent developer must be aware of the various types of concurrent transactions: retrieve only, single-row retrieval with single-row update, multiple-row retrieval with single-row (or limited) update, and multiple-row retrieval with multiple-row update. Each of these will have an effect on how you will manage the logical unit of work. A well-placed stored procedure or a well-constructed user object with embedded SQL script can overcome shortcomings or semantic front-end snafus.

Using the SELECT statement

The most popular DML statement is SELECT. The SELECT statement is used for retrieving a resulting set of data from the tables in a database. Finally the Venn diagrams we studied in elementary school can pay some dividends. That is to say that "set theory" is useful in understanding and constructing good SQL SELECT statements. The SELECT statement's WHERE clause will describe the contents of the set or set intersection using logical connectors such as AND. The basic SELECT is made up of the clauses listed here:

```
SELECT [ALL | DISTINCT] select_list
    [INTO [new_table_name]]
[FROM {table_name | view_name}[(optimizer_hints)]
    [[, {table_name2 | view_name2}[(optimizer_hints)]
    [..., {table_name16 | view_name16}[(optimizer_hints)]]]]
[WHERE clause]
[GROUP BY clause]
[HAVING clause]
[ORDER BY clause]
[COMPUTE clause]
[FOR BROWSE]
```

The clauses in a SELECT statement must be used in the order shown here. (For example, if the statement includes a GROUP BY clause and an ORDER BY clause, the GROUP BY clause must precede the ORDER BY clause.)

The names of database objects must be qualified if ambiguity exists about which object is being referred to. You can uniquely identify a table or column by specifying other names that qualify it: the database name, the owner's name, and the table name or view name for a column. Each of these qualifiers is separated from the next by a period, as shown here:

```
database.owner.table_name.column_name
```

Only the SELECT clause and the FROM clause are required. These clauses specify the tables and columns to be retrieved. The remaining clauses are optional. When you are writing a SELECT statement, keywords, database names, column names, and table names are not case-sensitive unless the server is set up as a "case-sensitive" server. This is not recommended.

You can use the SELECT statement to look at one, several, or all rows in a table. Unless you specify otherwise by including a WHERE clause, all rows will be retrieved. The select-list, which immediately follows the word SELECT, determines which columns the SELECT statement will retrieve. An asterisk (*) is shorthand for saying that you want to retrieve all columns in the table. You can use the asterisk (*) whenever you want all of the columns in a table in their defined order. The FROM keyword, which is required, is followed by the name of the table(s) or view(s) that contains the data you want. In the following example DML, all rows and columns are retrieved from the orders table.

```
SELECT  * from orders
```

You can specify which columns you want the SELECT statement to find by including them in the select-list immediately after the keyword SELECT. Any number of columns can be specified, and only those columns will appear in the output. The order of the columns in the select-list determines the order of the columns in the output.

```
SELECT sku, description, retail_price  from sku_master
```

You can suppress duplicate rows of data from being retrieved by including the keyword DISTINCT, or its synonym UNIQUE, in your SELECT statement at the start of the select-list.

```
SELECT DISTINCT sku, quantity  from ship_history
```

You can select part of the value of a column that is of the character data type by including a substring in your select-list. For example, if you wanted to find the geographical distribution of your customers according to their zip codes, you could use the following SELECT statement to retrieve only the first three characters of each customer's zip code.

```
SELECT zip_cde(1,3)  from customers
```

THE WHERE CLAUSE

Probably the most important clause in the SELECT statement from an impact point of view is the WHERE clause. This is where the game is won or lost in terms of performance and accuracy of data retrieval.

The WHERE clause specifies comparison conditions that define the search criteria for the rows you want to retrieve. You are literally saying, "fFind me the set of rows where . . . ." The WHERE clause is like the Venn diagrams of our childhood days. It creates an intersection of qualities to limit the resulting set. See Figure 12-1, which illustrates this point. SQL includes special keywords that can be used in comparison conditions. See Table 12-2.

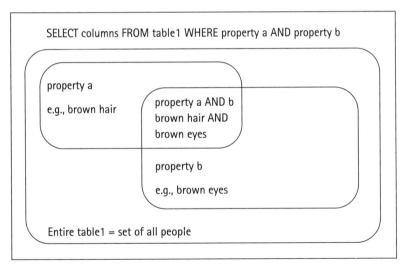

Figure 12-1: The WHERE clause

TABLE 12-2 WHERE KEYWORDS USED IN COMPARISON CONDITIONS

Keyword	Description
BETWEEN	Finds a range of values between x and y
IN	Finds a subset of values in x where x is one or more values

Continued

TABLE **12-2** WHERE KEYWORDS USED IN COMPARISON CONDITIONS *(Continued)*

Keyword	Description
LIKE	Performs variable text searches
IS NULL	Identifies NULL values
NOT	Used with any of the preceding keywords to specify the opposite condition
AND	Finds the intersection of two WHERE conditions
OR	Finds the union of two WHERE conditions

Consider the following example:

```
SELECT select-list
FROM table-name
[WHERE condition]
```

The WHERE clause is used for two distinct purposes:

♦ To specify search criteria for selecting specific rows

♦ To create join conditions among multiple tables

You can also use relational operators in place of a keyword to test for equality (see Table 12-3).

TABLE **12-3** RELATIONAL OPERATORS

Operator	Meaning
=	Equals
!=or<>	Does not equal
>	Is greater than
>=	Is greater than or equal to
<=,	Is less than or equal to
<	Is less than

So how do you include or exclude rows? The examples demonstrate how the WHERE clause can be used to include or exclude values when selecting rows from a database table.

The first example uses the equals operator (=) to find all rows in which the column equals one particular case. The second example uses the not equals operator (!= or <>) to find all rows except those in which the column equals the target case. As a practical matter, columns used frequently in the WHERE clause of your SELECT statements should be indexed if and only if they have a range of uniformly distributed values whose number exceeds 20 or more. For example, a customer's gender code, male or female, should not be indexed, as there are only two possible values. The keywords BETWEEN and AND can be used to find rows with values in a specified range. The example that follows finds all rows with a unit price between $20.00 and $30.00. The same results may be obtained using the greater than or equal to (>=) and less than or equal to (<=) relational operators, as shown here:

```
select   stock num, manu code, description, unit price
         from stock
         where unit price = 20.00

select   stock num, manu code, description, unit price
         from stock
         where unit price <> 20.00

select   stock num, manu code, description, unit price
         from stock
         where unit price BETWEEN 20.00 and 30.00

select   stock num, manu code, description, unit price
         from stock
         where unit price >= 20.00 AND unit price <= 30.00
```

The following example finds all customers who live in the states of New Jersey, New York, or Massachusetts:

```
select * from    customer    where state IN ('NJ', 'NY', 'MA')
```

The IN keyword of a WHERE clause can be used as shorthand for the OR keyword. The preceding example could also have been written as follows:

```
select *     from customer
where state = 'NJ' OR  state = 'NY' OR  state = 'MA'
```

Both statements return the same information, but when you use OR, the state column name must be repeated for every value that you wish to check. The SELECT statement, shown in the previous example, could be modified to retrieve all rows except rows where the state is equal to NJ, NY, or MA by inserting the NOT keyword prior to the IN keyword.

```
select * from    customer    where state NOT IN ('NJ', 'NY', 'MA')
```

THE ORDER BY CLAUSE

The ORDER BY clause enables you to sort the query results by the values contained in one or more columns. Including the keyword ASC following a column name in the ORDER BY clause specifies that the results should be sorted in ascending order, which is the default. DESC specifies that the results should be sorted in descending order. You might need both if scrolling is required. The NULL values are evaluated as less than non-null values when ordering result rows. The ORDER BY column must be in the select-list. The column listed first in the ORDER BY clause takes precedence over the second column, which takes precedence over the third column, and so on.

```
SELECT select-list
    FROM table-name
    [WHERE condition]
    [GROUP BY column-list]
    [HAVING condition]
    [ORDER BY column-name]
```

Make sure that if the expected result set is large, the ORDER BY column is an index. This will avoid sorting the data and thereby improve performance.

If there is no index on the ORDER BY column, then TEMPDB will be used to hold the sorted result set.

AGGREGATE FUNCTIONS

In addition to column names and operators, an expression can include one or more functions. There are many aggregate functions that can be used. Here are some of the more commonly used functions:

◆ COUNT (*) — Counts the number of rows that satisfy the conditions of the SELECT statement.

◆ SUM (column/expression) — Sums the values in the given numeric column or expression.

- ◆ AVG (column/expression) – Finds the arithmetic mean of the values in the given numeric column or expression.

- ◆ MAX (column/expression) – Finds the maximum value in the given column or expression.

- ◆ MIN(column/expression) – Finds the minimum value in the given column or expression.

Some of these functions can also be used with the DISTINCT keyword, as follows:

- ◆ COUNT (DISTINCT column-name) – Counts the distinct value in a particular column.

- ◆ SUM(DISTINCT column-name) – Sums the distinct values in a particular numeric column.

- ◆ AVG (DISTINCT column-name) – Finds the arithmetic mean of the distinct values in a particular numeric column.

The COUNT (*) function counts the total number of rows in the result set. When the DISTINCT keyword is included with a column name, the COUNT (DISTINCT description) function counts only the distinct values in the description column.

The SUM (total price) function sums all of the values in the total price column of the result set and presents the total. When the DISTINCT keyword is included with a column name, the SUM (DISTINCT total price) function adds up the distinct values in the total price column.

ALGEBRAIC AND TRIGONOMETRIC FUNCTIONS

There are many algebraic and trigonometric functions that can be used. Here is a list of some of the more commonly used functions.

- ◆ ROUND(expression) – Returns the rounded value of a an expression.

- ◆ TAN(expression) – Returns the tangent of a radicand expression.

- ◆ ABS(expression) – Returns the absolute value of an expression.

STATISTICAL FUNCTIONS

The following statistical functions are included in SQL Server 7.x:

- ◆ Standard deviation – The stdev() function returns the standard deviation of the selected rows and is computed using the formula for the standard deviation of a sample of a population. The standard deviation is the square root of the variance.

♦ Variance – The `var()` function returns the sample variance of the selected rows. This function uses the following formula: (sum(X**2) – sum(X)**2 / N) / (N – 1). The X represents each value in the selected column, and the N represents the total number of values in the column.

TIME FUNCTIONS

You can use the time functions in either the `SELECT` clause or the `WHERE` clause of a query. These functions return a value that corresponds to the expression(s) or argument(s) that you use to call the function. The time functions are described as follows:

♦ `DAY (date/datetime expression)` – Returns an integer that represents the day.

♦ `MONTH (date/datetime expression)` – Returns an integer that represents the month.

♦ `DATEPART (WEEKDAY , date/datetime expression)` – Returns an integer that represents the day of the week (1 through 7, where Sunday is 1).

♦ `YEAR (date/datetime expression)` – Returns a four-digit integer that represents the year.

♦ `GETDATE()` – Returns a `datetime` value with the date and time of day of the current instant.

A date/datetime expression is an expression that evaluates to a `DATE` or `DATETIME` value.

THE GROUP BY CLAUSE

The `GROUP BY` clause produces a single row of results for each *group* of rows having the same value in a given column. It sorts the data into groups and then compresses all the rows in each group with like values into a single row. The number of groups depends on the number of distinct values within the column in the table.

```
select customer_number , SUM(order_quantity) from orders
        GROUP BY customer_number
```

In the preceding example, the `SELECT` statement with the `GROUP BY` clause returns only one row for each distinct customer number in the `orders` table.

THE GROUP BY CLAUSE AND AGGREGATES

The GROUP BY clause is used with aggregate calculation functions to provide summary information for a group. The SELECT statement shown in the previous subsection groups all rows in the orders table together with the same customer number. After the groups are formed, the SUM function is applied within each group. The result is a list of customer numbers and the sum total quantity of orders for each customer. You will get an error if all nonaggregate columns in the SELECT clause are not listed in the GROUP BY clause. For example, the following SELECT statement will generate an error message:

```
select city, state, count(*)
      from customer
      group by city
```

You can use an aggregate function to avoid this. For example, use the MAX function with the state column. This will work properly as all the rows with the same city should be in the same state. The SQL is as follows:

```
select city, MAX(state) , count (*)
      from customer
      group by city
```

ORDERING GROUPED DATA

The GROUP BY clause does not order data. You should include an ORDER BY clause after your GROUP BY clause if you want to sort the rows returned into a particular order. You can use an integer in an ORDER BY clause or GROUP BY clause to indicate the position of column names in the group list or order list.

 Null values are grouped together and will appear first in an ascending sort.

```
select city, state , count (*)
from customer
group by 1 , state
order by city , 2
```

The HAVING clause can be used in conjunction with the GROUP BY clause to apply one or more qualifying conditions to groups after they are formed. The HAVING clause provides a filter for grouped results, in the same way that a WHERE clause is used to filter individual row results.

```
select customer_num , sum(order_price)
from orders
group by 1
having count(*) > 10
```

> The HAVING clause does not require a GROUP BY clause, although it is almost always used with one. If the HAVING clause is used without a GROUP BY clause, the HAVING condition applies to all rows that satisfy the search condition. In other words, all rows that satisfy the search condition make up a single group.

JOINS AND THE FROM CLAUSE

Given the average relational database, it will not be long before a business query will require information from more than one table. For example, you may want to see a customer and all of his or her orders. Typically, the customer and orders tables have a one-to-many relationship. For every entry in the customer table, there could be one or more entries in the orders table. To view a customer and all of his or her orders, you would need to find the customer number in the customer table and then find all occurrences of that customer number in the orders table.

In order to access data from two tables, you must enter some additional information into the SELECT, FROM, and WHERE clauses of your SELECT statement.

```
select customer_name, Order_num
from customer, order
where customer.Customer_num = order.Customer_num
```

Within the FROM clause, you must list the tables from which you are selecting the columns entered in the SELECT statement. Within the WHERE clause, you must list the columns to be matched to join the two tables together. For this example, they would be the customer.customer_num and orders.customer_num columns.

> Because both tables being selected from include the column customer_num, you must specify which particular class of customer_num you want to reference. This is accomplished using the table_name.column syntax.

In this query, multiple rows are returned for customers with more than one order. No rows are returned for customers who have not placed orders. Because NULL values represent unknowns, they will not participate in the join.

> When you join large tables, check to determine that the columns in the join condition are indexed; otherwise, performance may not meet user expectations.

If you get an ambiguous column error, look at the column in parentheses and find it in your SELECT statement. This column must have a table prefix everywhere it occurs in the SELECT statement. Because both tables include the column customer_num, you must state which customer_num you want to see. In the case of a join column, it does not matter which one you choose.

When you perform a multiple table query without specifying a join condition, the result is the dreaded "Cartesian product." A Cartesian product consists of every possible combination of rows from the tables you are querying. This is usually a very large result that contains inaccurate data. Beware of this. Desk-check your SQL to avoid this; otherwise, you will be contacting Operations to cancel your session before the machine explodes.

EQUI-JOINS AND NATURAL JOINS

An *equi-join* is a join based on matching values in the WHERE clause of a SELECT statement using the equals(=) operator. In an equi-join, the select-list contains all columns from both tables, so the column(s) in common appears twice in the result.

Natural joins are simply equi-joins with the duplicate column eliminated from the output by means of a more explicit select list. This is the most common type of join.

> All joins are associative. The order of the joining terms in the WHERE clause does not affect the meaning of the join. The optimizer will resolve this and choose the best path to the data.

THE SIMPLE OUTER JOIN

In an outer join, the tables are treated asymmetrically. One of the tables is dominant (also called preserved); the other is subservient. All of the rows of the dominant table are retrieved whether or not there are corresponding rows in the subservient table. The subservient table follows the keyword OUTER. If the subservient table has no rows satisfying the condition, the columns from the subservient table will have

NULL values. If an OUTER join is specified, a join condition must exist in the WHERE clause.

In the outer join example that follows, the orders table is subservient to the customer table because it follows the keyword OUTER. The simple join query shown on the previous page fetches only customers who have placed an order. The outer join query, on the other hand, fetches all customers, whether or not they have placed an order. This is because the customer table is the dominant table, and therefore, the rows of the customer table that would have been discarded in a simple join are preserved. The outer join example that follows queries only two tables. You can in fact, use outer joins to query any number of tables.

```
select customer_name, Order_num
from customer, outer order
where customer.Customer_num = order.Customer_num
```

The outer join query shown here is an example of a nested simple join. It produces a list of all customers with supplemental information (order number). The outer join then combines the customer table with the order information.

SELF JOINS

A join does not always have to involve more than one table. You can join a table to itself, creating a *self join*. A self join is useful when you want to compare values in a column to other values in the same column. You can think of a self join as a join between two tables that are in fact the same table. To resolve column name ambiguities in the select-list and in the WHERE clause, both references to the table must be given an alias in the FROM clause.

 When you want to join one or more columns in the same table, using a self join is more efficient than creating a temporary table. A self join can result in faster execution and less disk usage.

Self joins are also useful for recursive relationships. A recursive relationship is one in which a row of one table is related to one or more rows of the same table. A more complete view of the SELECT statement syntax is shown in Listing 12-1.

Listing 12-1: The SELECT statement syntax

```
SELECT [ ALL | DISTINCT ]
[ TOP n [PERCENT] [ WITH TIES] ] <select_list>
[ INTO new_table ]
[ FROM <table_sources> ]
[ WHERE <search_conditions> ]
[ [ GROUP BY [ALL] group_by_expression [,...n]]
```

```
[HAVING <search_conditions> ]
[ WITH { CUBE | ROLLUP } ]]
[ ORDER BY { column_name [ ASC | DESC ] } [,...n] ]
```

The extra SELECT clauses you can use include:

```
[ COMPUTE { { AVG | COUNT | MAX | MIN | SUM } (expression) }
[,...n]]

[ FOR BROWSE ]

[ OPTION (<query_hints>) ]

<select_list> :: = { [ { <table_or_view> | table_alias }.]* |
{ column_name | expression | IDENTITYCOL | ROWGUIDCOL }
[ [AS] column_alias ] |
 new_column_name = IDENTITY(data_type, seed, increment)
 | GROUPING (column_name)| { table_name | table_alias}
.RANK| column_alias = expression | expression column_name} [,...n]

<table_sources> :: ={ <table_or_view>| (select_statement)
[AS] table_alias [ (column_alias ...[,...m]) ]| <table_or_view>
CROSS JOIN <table_or_view>|
<table_or_view>{ { INNER | { FULL | LEFT | RIGHT } OUTER ]
[ <join_hints> ] [ JOIN ]} <table_or_view> ON <join_condition>|
<rowset_function>}[,...n]

<table_or_view> :: ={ table_name [ [AS] table_alias ]
[ WITH (<table_hints> [...n]) ]| view_name
[ [AS] table_alias ]}<table_hints> ::=
{ INDEX(index_name | index_id [,...n])
| FASTFIRSTROW| HOLDLOCK| NOLOCK|
PAGLOCK| READCOMMITTED| READPAST|
READUNCOMMITTED| REPEATABLEREAD|

ROWLOCK| SERIALIZABLE| TABLOCK  TABLOCKX | UPDLOCK}

<join_hints> ::={ HASH | LOOP | MERGE }

<query_hints> :: ={ { HASH | ORDER } GROUP | { CONCAT | HASH |
MERGE } UNION| FAST number_rows| FORCE ORDER| MAXDOP number|
 ROBUST PLAN}
```

```
<join_condition> :: ={ table_name | table_alias | view_name
}.column_name <logical_operator> { table_name | table_alias |
 view_name }.column_name

<logical_operator>:: ={ = | > | < | >= | <= | <> | != | !< | !> }

<rowset_function> :: ={ CONTAINSTABLE [ [ AS] table_alias]( table,
 { column | *}, '<contains_search_condition>' )|
FREETEXTTABLE [ [ AS] table_alias]
( table, {column | * }, 'freetext_string')| OPENQUERY
(linked_server, 'query')| OPENROWSET( 'provider_name',
{'datasource';'user_id';'password' | 'provider_string'},
{[catalog.][schema.]object_name | 'query'})
<search_conditions> ::={ [ NOT ] <predicate>
 [ { AND | OR } [ NOT ] <predicate> ]
| CONTAINS( {column | * },
'<contains_search_condition>' )|
FREETEXT({column | * }, 'freetext_string')
| fulltext_table.fulltext_key_column = fulltext_table.[KEY]} [,...n]

<predicate> ::={expression { = | <> | != | > | >= | !> | < | <= |
!< } expression| string_expression
[NOT] LIKE string_expression
[ESCAPE 'escape_character']| expression
[NOT] BETWEEN expression AND expression
| expression IS [NOT] NULL| expression
 [NOT] IN (subquery | expression [,...n])
| expression { = | <> | != | > | >= | !>
| < | <= | !< }{ALL | SOME | ANY} (subquery)| EXISTS (subquery)}
```

Now that is quite an impressive set of additional features that you can use in your SQL Server 7 SELECT statement. We have included some information about all of the features. Whole manuscripts have been written just to cover the SQL SELECT statement. Please seek out particular examples in the SQL material that comes with the product before using some of the more exotic expressions. Also be wary that these features may not translate to other relational DBMS syntax. So if there is a possible DBMS switch in store for your application, then keep the SQL simpler.

SELECT STATEMENT ARGUMENTS
Let's turn to arguments for the SELECT statement. Their context within the syntax is described in the following list.

◆ ALL – Specifies that duplicate rows can appear in the result set. Duplicate rows appear only if the ALL keyword is specified immediately following the SELECT keyword.

◆ DISTINCT — Specifies that only unique rows can appear in the result set. Null values are considered equal for the purposes of the DISTINCT keyword.

◆ TOP n — Specifies that only the first n rows are to be output from the query result set. When the query includes an ORDER BY clause, this causes the first n rows ordered by the ORDER BY clause to be output. When the query has no ORDER BY clause, then the n number of rows is arbitrary.

◆ PERCENT — Specifies that only the first n % of the rows (rounded to the next integer value, if the percentage yields a fractional row) be output from the query result set. When the query includes an ORDER BY clause, this causes the first n % rows ordered by the ORDER BY clause to be output. When the query has no ORDER BY clause, then the n % of rows is arbitrary.

◆ WITH TIES — When used with TOP n or PERCENT, specifies that additional rows be returned from the base result set with the same value in the ORDER BY columns appearing as the last of the TOP n (PERCENT) rows. The TOP WITH TIES argument can only be specified when an ORDER BY clause exists.

◆ ⟨select_list⟩ — Specifies the list of columns, expressions, and/or keywords to select.

◆ ⟨table_or_view⟩ — Specifies the name of the table or view.

◆ table_name — The name(s) of the table(s), or joined table, used in the SELECT statement. Up to 256 tables can be used in a DELETE, INSERT, UPDATE, or SELECT statement.

◆ table_alias — The name of the table (specified as an alias) used in the SELECT statement.

◆ ⟨table_hints⟩ — Specifies a table scan, one or more indexes to be used by the optimizer, or a locking method to be used by the optimizer with this table and for this SELECT statement. Although this is an option, the optimizer can usually pick the best optimization method without hints being specified. Commas between ⟨table_hints⟩ are optional but are supported for backward compatibility. If a table (including system tables) contains computed columns and the computed columns are computed by expressions or functions accessing columns in other tables, then the table hints are not used on those tables (the table hints are not propagated). For example, a NOLOCK table hint is specified on a table in the query. This table has computed columns that are computed by a combination of expressions and functions (accessing columns in another table). The tables referenced by the expressions and functions will not use the NOLOCK table hint when accessed.

◆ INDEX(`index_name` | `index_id`) – Specifies the name or ID of the index to be used by SQL Server when processing the statement. Only one index hint per table can only be specified. The alternative INDEX = `syntax` (which specifies a single index hint) is supported only for backward compatibility. If a clustered index exists, INDEX = 0 forces a clustered index scan and INDEX = 1 forces a clustered index scan or seek. If no clustered index exists, INDEX = 0 forces a table scan and INDEX = 1 is interpreted as an error. Any index hints specified for a view are ignored, and SQL Server returns an error message. SQL Server does not allow more than one table hint from each of the following groups:

- Granularity hints: PAGLOCK, NOLOCK, ROWLOCK, TABLOCK, or TABLOCKX

- Isolation level hints: HOLDLOCK, NOLOCK, READCOMMITTED, REPEATABLEREAD, SERIALIZABLE

In addition, the NOLOCK and READPAST `<table_hints>` are only allowed in SELECT statements and not in DELETE, INSERT, or UPDATE statements.

◆ *m* – A placeholder indicating that multiple `<table_hints>` can be specified.

◆ *n* – A placeholder indicating that any of the preceding item(s) can be repeated multiple times. The maximum number of indexes in the `<table_hints>` is 250 nonclustered indexes.

◆ FASTFIRSTROW – Equivalent to OPTION (FAST 1); for details, see the discussion of FAST in the `<query_hint>` item.

◆ HOLDLOCK – Equivalent to SERIALIZABLE, the HOLDLOCK option applies only to the table or view for which it is specified and only for the duration of the transaction defined by the statement in which it is used. The HOLDLOCK option cannot be used in a SELECT statement including the FOR BROWSE option.

◆ NOLOCK – Allows dirty reads, which means that no shared locks are issued and no exclusive locks are honored. This can result in higher concurrency, but at the cost of lower consistency. If this option is specified, it is possible to read an uncommitted transaction or to read a set of pages rolled back in the middle of the read, so error messages might result. If you receive error message 605, 606, 624, or 625 when NOLOCK is specified, resolve them as you would a deadlock error (1205) and retry your statement.

◆ PAGLOCK – Takes shared page locks where a single shared table lock is normally taken.

◆ READCOMMITTED — Performs a scan with the same locking semantics as a transaction running at READ COMMITTED isolation level.

◆ READPAST — Reads past locked rows and basically skips them. For example, assume table T1 contains a single integer column with the values of 1, 2, 3, 4, and 5. If transaction A changes the value of 3 to 8 but has not yet committed, a SELECT * FROM T1 (READPAST) yields values 1, 2, 4, and 5. The READPAST argument only applies to transactions operating at READ COMMITTED isolation and only reads past row-level locks. This lock hint is primarily used to implement a work queue on a SQL Server table.

◆ READUNCOMMITTED — Equivalent to NOLOCK.

◆ REPEATABLEREAD — Performs a scan with the same locking semantics as a transaction running at REPEATABLE READ isolation level.

◆ ROWLOCK — Takes a shared row lock where a single shared page or table lock is normally taken.

◆ RIALIZABLE — Equivalent to HOLDLOCK, makes shared locks more restrictive by holding them until the completion of a transaction (instead of releasing the shared lock as soon as the required table or data page is no longer needed, whether the transaction has been completed). The scan is performed with the same semantics as a transaction running at the SERIALIZABLE isolation level.

◆ BLOCK — Takes a shared table lock on the table held until the end-of-statement. If HOLDLOCK is also specified, the shared table lock is held until the end of the transaction.

◆ BLOCKX — Takes an exclusive table lock on the table held until the end-of-statement or end-of-transaction.

◆ UPDLOCK — Takes update locks instead of shared locks while reading the table and holds them until the end-of-statement or end-of-transaction.

◆ view_name –The name(s) of the view(s) used in the SELECT statement.

  *asterisk (*) — Specifies that all columns, in the order in which they were specified in the CREATE TABLE statement, should be retrieved. Using * in the <select_list> affects all tables in the SELECT statement's FROM clause. Be careful with * and tables that have been altered with additional columns. It may cause old applications to fail.

◆ column_name — The name of the column to retrieve. To SELECT multiple column names, separate the names with commas. When used with the optional COMPUTE clause, column_name is the column used by the row aggregate function.

◆ *expression* – A column name, constant, function, any combination of column names, constants, and functions connected by an operator(s), or a subquery. Only expressions of the numeric data type category can be used with SUM and AVG. When used with SELECT INTO, the expression can be used to set up an identity column by using the IDENTITY() function with SELECT INTO – for example, ID = IDENTITY(int,1,1). When using an expression with a COMPUTE clause, remember the following: When used as a row aggregate function, an expression is usually the name of a column. One COMPUTE clause can apply the same function to several columns or several functions to one column.

◆ *column_alias* – A user-defined, temporary heading to replace the default column heading (the column name). For more information about column aliases, see the FROM argument, later in this list.

◆ *new_column_name* – A new column name (of the integer data type category except for the bit data type, or decimal data type) that does not allow null values.

◆ IDENTITY – Specifies that the specified column in the new table should use the IDENTITY property.

◆ *data_type* – The data type of the IDENTITY column. Valid data types for an IDENTITY column are any data types of the integer data type category (except for the bit data type), or decimal data type.

◆ *seed* – The value to be assigned to the first row in the table. Each subsequent row is assigned the next identity value, which is equal to the last IDENTITY value plus the *increment* value. If neither *seed* nor *increment* is specified, both default to 1.

◆ *Increment* – The increment to add to the *seed* value for successive rows in the table.

◆ GROUPING – Causes an additional column to be output with a value of 1, when the row is added by either the CUBE or ROLLUP operator, or 0, which distinguishes those null values appearing in summary rows from the null values appearing in a GROUP BY column. The GROUPING function is applied to a *column_name* in <select_list>. The *column_name* must be one of the columns appearing in the GROUP BY clause. A value of 1 is returned when a NULL is returned in the result set for the *column_name* when it appears in a summary row. A value of 0 is returned when a NULL is returned in the result set for the *column_name*. This function is allowed only with a GROUP BY clause and either the CUBE or ROLLUP operator.

◆ RANK – Specifies that the ranking value for each row returned by a full-text query is to be displayed. Use with a table that has been registered as enabled for full-text querying.

◆ INTO *new_table_name* — The name of a new table to be created based on the columns specified in the `<select_list>` and the rows chosen in the WHERE clause. To SELECT into a permanent table, execute sp_dboption to turn on the SELECT into/bulkcopy option. By default, the SELECT into/bulkcopy option is off in newly created databases. The *new_table_name* option must follow the same rules as *table* (which is described later) with the following exceptions:

   ■ If SELECT into/bulkcopy is on in the database where the table is to be created, a permanent table is created. The table name must be unique in the database and conform to the rules for identifiers.

   ■ If SELECT into/bulkcopy is not on in the database where the table is to be created, permanent tables cannot be created using SELECT INTO; only local or global temporary tables can be created. To create a temporary table, the table name must begin with a number sign (#). For details on temporary tables, see the CREATE TABLE statement.

   ■ SELECT INTO is a two-step operation. The first step creates the table. The user executing the statement must have CREATE TABLE permission in the destination database. The second step inserts the specified rows into the new table.

   ■ You can use SELECT INTO to create an identical table definition (different table name) with no data by having a false condition in the WHERE clause. When you are selecting an existing identity column into a new table, the new column inherits the IDENTITY property unless one of the following conditions is true:

   The SELECT statement contains a join, GROUP BY clause, or aggregate function.

   Multiple SELECT statements are joined with UNION.

   The IDENTITY column is listed more than once in the `<select_list>`.

   The IDENTITY column is part of an expression.

   If any of these conditions is true, the column is created NOT NULL instead of inheriting the IDENTITY property. If none of the conditions is true, the new table will inherit the identity column. All rules and restrictions for the identity columns apply to the new table. Computed columns referenced in a SELECT . . . INTO statement will no longer be computed columns in *new_table_name;* they will be regular, noncomputed columns.

◆ FROM `<table_sources>` — Specifies the table(s) from which to retrieve information.

◆ CROSS JOIN — Specifies the cross-product of two tables. Returns the same rows as if no WHERE clause was specified in an old-style, non-SQL-92-style join.

◆ INNER — Specifies that all matching pairs of rows be returned and discards unmatched rows from both tables. This is the default if no join type is specified.

◆ LEFT [OUTER] — Specifies that all rows from the left table not meeting the condition specified be included in the result set, and output columns from the other table be set to NULL in addition to all rows returned by the INNER JOIN.

◆ RIGHT [OUTER] — Specifies that all rows from the right table not meeting the condition specified be included in the result set, and output columns corresponding to the other table be set to NULL in addition to all rows returned by the INNER JOIN.

◆ FULL [OUTER] — If a row from either the left or right table does not match the selection criteria, specifies that the row be included in the result set, and output columns that correspond to the other table be set to NULL. This is in addition to all rows normally returned by INNER JOIN.

Earlier versions of SQL Server joins (using the *= and =* syntax in the WHERE clause) cannot be used within the same statement as SQL-92-style joins.

◆ <join_hints> — Specifies one <join hint> or *execution algorithm* per join in the query's FROM clause. If a <join_hint> is specified for any two tables, the query optimizer automatically enforces the join order for all joined tables in the query, based on the position of the ON keywords. In the case of FULL OUTER JOINS, when the ON clauses are not used, parentheses can be used to indicate the desired join order.

◆ {LOOP | HASH | MERGE} — Specifies that the join in the query should use looping, hashing, or merging. Using LOOP | HASH | MERGE JOIN in the FROM clause, with SQL-92-style join syntax, enforces a particular join between two tables.

◆ JOIN — Indicates that the specified join operation should take place between the given tables or views.

◆ ON <join_condition> — Specifies the criteria that must match for the specified JOIN to be performed. As part of the <join_condition>, specifies a common column_name from each table in the join. A <join_condition> also specifies a <logical_operator>.

◆ `<logical_operator>` – Specifies the condition that rows to be returned must meet.

◆ `<rowset_function>` – Specifies that one of the `rowset` functions is to be used.

◆ *n* – A placeholder indicating that any of the preceding item(s) can be repeated multiple times.

◆ `WHERE` – Specifies that a `WHERE` clause is used to restrict the rows returned.

◆ `<search_conditions>` – Specifies the restricting condition(s) for the rows returned in the result set. There is no limit to the number of `<search_conditions>` that can be included in a SQL statement. When a `WHERE` clause is used, the `<search_conditions>` restrict the rows included in the calculation of the aggregate function but do not restrict the rows returned by the query.

◆ `GROUP BY` – Specifies the groups into which the table is partitioned and, if aggregate functions are included in the `<select_list>`, finds a summary value for each group. The groups are formed by collecting rows having the same value for the expressions in the `GROUP BY` clause, into a group. You can refer to the new summary columns in the `HAVING` clause. The `text`, `image`, and `bit` data types cannot be used in a `GROUP BY` clause. When a `GROUP BY` clause is used, each item in `<select_list>` must produce a single value for each group. A table can be grouped by any combination of columns; however, you cannot group by a column heading. You must use a column name or an expression. In Transact-SQL, any valid expression is allowed in the `GROUP BY` clause as long as it does not involve aggregate functions (although not with column headings).

Any column referenced in the `<select_list>` must also be referenced in the `GROUP BY` clause unless the column is being used in an aggregate function. Null values in the `GROUP BY` column are put into a single group when the `GROUP BY` column is also contained in `<select_list>`. You cannot group by an alias. You can list more than one column in the `GROUP BY` clause to nest groups; that is, you can group a table by any combination of columns. You can use a `WHERE` clause in a query containing a `GROUP BY` clause. Rows that do not satisfy the conditions in the `WHERE` clause are eliminated before any grouping is done. A maximum of 10 grouping expressions is permitted in a `GROUP BY` clause when `CUBE` or `ROLLUP` is specified. Otherwise, the number of grouping expressions is limited in accordance with the `GROUP BY` column sizes, the aggregated columns, and the aggregate values involved in the query. This limit originates from the limit of 8,060 bytes on the intermediate worktable needed for holding intermediate query results.

- *group_by_expresssion* — The expression upon which to perform the GROUP BY operation.

- ALL — Includes all groups and result sets, even those that do not have any rows that meet the `<search_conditions>` specified in the WHERE clause. If ALL is specified, null values are returned for summary columns for groups that do not meet the `<search_conditions>`.

- CUBE — Specifies that, in addition to the usual aggregate rows provided by GROUP BY, *super-aggregate* rows are introduced into the result set. A super-aggregate row is a summary row generated by grouping on a subset of the *expressions* in the GROUP BY clause. Result sets with the super-aggregate rows are typically used for reports.

- Columns included in the GROUP BY clause are cross-referenced to produce a superset of groups. The aggregate function specified in the `<select_list>` is applied to these groups to produce summary values for the additional super-aggregate rows. The number of extra groups in the result set is determined by the number of columns included in the GROUP BY clause. Each operand (column) in the GROUP BY clause is bound under the null value, and grouping is applied to all other operands (columns). The null value in this case represents all the values in a particular column.

- ROLLUP — Specifies that a subset of super-aggregates is computed along with the usual aggregate rows for elements within a GROUP BY clause. This is useful when you have sets within sets.

- HAVING `<search_conditions>` — Specifies the conditions for aggregate functions in `<select_list>`; the `<search_conditions>` restrict the rows returned by the query but do not affect the calculations of the aggregate function(s). The HAVING clause sets conditions for the GROUP BY clause similar to the way that WHERE sets conditions for the SELECT statement. Because the HAVING clause is used to restrict groups, it is recommended that HAVING always be specified with a GROUP BY clause. However, if HAVING is specified without a GROUP BY clause, then a single group is produced and HAVING limits the data returned. When multiple conditions are included in the HAVING clause, they are combined with AND, OR, or NOT. For more information about `<search_conditions>`, refer to the preceding section of this chapter and Figure 12-1.

♦ ORDER BY — Specifies the sort order used on columns returned. Either specify a `column_name` (which can be qualified by the table or view name), or specify a nonnegative integer representing the position of the column name, column heading, alias, or expression in the `<select_list>`. If the result set is sorted by the column number, the columns to which the ORDER BY clause refers must be included in the <select_list>. There is no limit on the number of items in the ORDER BY clause. However, there is a limit of 8,060 bytes for the row size of intermediate work tables needed for sort operations. This limits the total size of columns specified in an ORDER BY clause and the SELECT list. In Transact-SQL, the ORDER BY clause can include items not appearing in the <select_list>. You can sort by a column name, a column heading (or alias), an expression, or the select_list_number. The <select_list> can be a single asterisk (*). If you use COMPUTE BY, you must also specify an ORDER BY clause. If SELECT DISTINCT is specified, the ORDER BY items must appear in the <select_list>.

♦ ASC – Specifies that the sorted result set should be returned in ascending order, from the smallest value to the largest value.

♦ DESC – Specifies that the sorted result set should be returned in descending order, from the largest value to the smallest value.

♦ COMPUTE – Generates summary values that appear as additional rows in the query results for row aggregate functions (unlike the aggregate function results, which appear as new columns in a SELECT statement). The COMPUTE clause cannot be used with INTO and cannot contain aliases for column names, although aliases can be used in the <select_list>. The columns in the COMPUTE clause must appear in the SELECT list. You cannot use COMPUTE in a SELECT INTO statement because statements including COMPUTE generate tables and their summary results are not stored in the database. Therefore, any calculations produced by COMPUTE do not appear in the new table created with the SELECT INTO statement.

♦ BY – Specifies that the values for row-aggregate functions be calculated for subgroups. When the values of BY items change, row aggregate function values are generated. If you use BY, you must also use an ORDER BY clause. Listing more than one item after BY breaks a group into subgroups and applies the aggregate function at each level of grouping. The columns listed after a COMPUTE clause must be identical to, or a subset of, those listed after an ORDER BY clause. They also must be in the same left-to-right order, start with the same expression, and not skip any expression – for example, if the ORDER BY clause is: ORDER BY a, b, c.

Using the UPDATE statement

The UPDATE DML statement functions to change data in existing rows, either by adding data to previously NULL columns or by modifying existing data currently stored in a column. That is to say that the UPDATE statement is used to change the content of one or more columns in one or more existing rows of the table. The WHERE clause of the UPDATE statement is used to specify precisely which rows are to be updated. Without the WHERE clause, all rows in the table will be updated. If you want to ensure that you will UPDATE only one row, specify the primary key columns(s) in the WHERE clause. The basic UPDATE is made up of the clauses listed here:

```
UPDATE [[database.]owner.]{table_name | view_name}
SET [[[database.]owner.]{table_name.|view_name.}]
column_name1 ={expression1|NULL|(select_statement)}
 [, column_name2 =      {expression2|NULL|(select_statement)}]...
 [FROM [[database.]owner.]{table_name | view_name}
 [,[[database.]owner.]{table_name|view_name}]...]
[WHERE search_conditions] [where current of cursor_name]
```

The UPDATE arguments and their context within the syntax are listed here:

- ◆ SET — Specifies the column name and assigns the new value. The value can be an expression or a NULL. When more than one column name and value pair is listed, they must be separated by commas.

- ◆ FROM — Uses data from other tables or views to modify rows in the table or view you are updating.

- ◆ WHERE — A standard WHERE clause. (See the section, "The WHERE clause" earlier in this chapter.)

- ◆ WHERE CURRENT OF — Causes SQL Server 7 to update the row of the table or view indicated by the current cursor position for cursor_name.

Use UPDATE to change values in rows that have already been inserted. Use INSERT to add new rows. SQL Server 7 does not prevent you from issuing an UPDATE statement that updates a single row more than once in a given transaction. However, because of the way the update is processed, updates from a single statement do not accumulate. That is, if an UPDATE statement modifies the same row twice, the second UPDATE is based not on the new values from the first UPDATE but on the original values. The results are unpredictable because they depend on the order of processing.

Updating variable-length character data or text columns with the empty string ("") inserts a single space. Fixed-length character columns are padded to the defined length. All trailing spaces are removed from variable-length column data, except in the case of a string that contains only spaces. Strings that contain only spaces are truncated to a single space.

UPDATE PERMISSIONS

The UPDATE permissions default to the table owner, who can transfer them to other users. The SELECT permissions are also required for the table being updated if the

UPDATE statement contains a WHERE clause, or if an expression in the SET clause uses a column in the table.

 The UPDATE statement can be used to change existing rows in one or more tables and does not return any rows of data. To load new rows into a table, use INSERT and the INTO option of the SELECT statement. To return rows of data, use SELECT, and to delete rows, use the DELETE or the TRUNCATE TABLE command. See the section "Using the DELETE statement" later in this chapter.

UPDATE AND CURSORS

There are two forms of UPDATE based on what is specified in the WHERE clause:

◆ Searched UPDATES specify <search_conditions> to qualify the rows to delete. The <search_conditions> options specifies the restricting conditions upon which the join is based or for the rows to be updated. There is no limit to the number of <search_conditions> that can be included in a SQL statement.

◆ Positioned updates use the CURRENT OF clause to specify a cursor; the delete operation occurs at the current position of the cursor. The CURRENT OF clause specifies that the update is performed at the current position of the specified cursor.

To update a row using a cursor, first define the cursor with DECLARE CURSOR, and then open it. Any update to the cursor result set also affects the base table row that the cursor row is derived from. The table_name or view_name specified with an UPDATE . . . WHERE CURRENT OF must be the table or view specified in the first FROM clause of the select statement that defines the cursor. If that FROM clause references more than one table or view (using a join), you can specify only the table or view actually being updated. After the update, the cursor position remains unchanged. You can continue to update the row at that cursor position as long as another SQL statement does not move the position of that cursor. SQL Server 7 enables you to update columns that are not specified in the list of columns of the cursor's SELECT, but that are part of the tables specified in the select_statement. However, when you specify a column_name_list with FOR UPDATE when declaring the cursor, you can only update those specific columns.

UPDATING IDENTITY COLUMNS

A column with the IDENTITY property cannot be updated, either through its base table or through a view. To determine whether a column was defined with the IDENTITY property, use the SQL Enterprise Manager to review the base table.

THE COMPLETE SYNTAX FOR THE UPDATE STATEMENT

The complete syntax for the UPDATE statement is included in Listing 12-2.

Listing 12-2: Complete Syntax of the UPDATE statement

```
UPDATE {<table_or_view>}
SET {column_name = {expression | DEFAULT}|
 @variable = expression} [,...n]
[FROM{<table_or_view>
| (select_statement) [AS] table_alias [ (column_alias [,...m]) ]
| <table_or_view> CROSS JOIN <table_or_view>
| INNER [<join_hints>] JOIN <table_or_view> ON <join_condition>
| <rowset_function>}[, ...n]]
[WHERE <search_conditions>
| CURRENT OF { { [GLOBAL] cursor_name } | cursor_variable_name} }
][OPTION (<query_hints>, [,...n] )]

<table_or_view> :: ={ table_name [ [AS] table_alias ]
 [ WITH (<table_hints> [...m]) ]
| view_name [ [AS] table_alias ]
 }<table_hints> ::={ INDEX(index_name | index_id )
| FASTFIRSTROW| HOLDLOCK| PAGLOCK|
READCOMMITTED| REPEATABLEREAD| ROWLOCK| SERIALIZABLE| TABLOCK |
TABLOCKX}

<join_hints> ::={ HASH | LOOP | MERGE }

<query_hints> :: ={ { HASH | ORDER } GROUP |
 { CONCAT | HASH | MERGE } UNION| FAST number_rows|
FORCE ORDER| ROBUST PLAN}

<join_condition> :: ={ table_name |
 table_alias | view_name }.column_name
<logical_operator> { table_name | table_alias
| view_name }.column_name

<logical_operator>:: ={ = | > | < | >= | <= | <> | != | !< | !> }

<rowset_function> :: = { OPENQUERY (linked_server, 'query')|
 OPENROWSET( 'provider_name', {'datasource';'user_id';'password' |
 'provider_string'},{[catalog.][schema.]object_name
| 'query'})}
```

```
<search_conditions> ::={ [ NOT ] <predicate> [ { AND | OR } [ NOT ]
<predicate> ] } [, ...n]

<predicate> ::={ expression { = | <> | != | > | >= | !> | < | <= |
!< } expression| string_expression [NOT] LIKE string_expression
[ESCAPE 'escape_character']| expression [NOT] BETWEEN expression
AND expression
| expression IS [NOT] NULL| expression
[NOT] IN (subquery | expression [,...n])
| expression { = | <> | != | > | >= | !> | < | <= | !< }
{ALL | SOME | ANY} (subquery)
| EXISTS (subquery)
}
```

The UPDATE arguments and their context within the syntax are described in the
following list in greater detail:

- ◆ `<table_or_view>` — Is the name of the table or view that is used to
  provide criteria for the UPDATE operation.

- ◆ `table_name | view_name` — Is name of the table or view in which data is
  updated. The name can be qualified with the linked server, database,
  and/or owner name if the object is not in the current server or database,
  or is not owned by the current user. If *view_name* refers to multiple tables,
  only one of the tables can be updated.

- ◆ `table_alias` — Is the name of an alias. Each table or view can be given
  an alias, either for convenience or to distinguish a table or view in a self-
  join or a subquery.

- ◆ `column_alias` — Is a user-defined, temporary heading to replace the
  default column heading (the column name). For more information about
  column aliases, see FROM.

- ◆ `<table_hints>` — Specifies a table scan, one or more indexes to be used
  by the optimizer, or a locking method to be used by the optimizer with
  this table and for this SELECT. Although this is an option, the optimizer
  can usually pick the best optimization method without hints being specified. Commas between `<table_hints>` are optional but are supported for
  backward compatibility.

- INDEX(*index_name* | *index_id*) – Specifies the name or ID of the index to be used by SQL Server when processing the statement. Only one index hint per table can only be specified. The alternative INDEX = *syntax* (which specifies a single INDEX hint) is supported only for backward compatibility. Any INDEX hints specified for a view are ignored, and SQL Server returns an error message. SQL Server does not allow more than one table hint from each of the following groups:

  - Granularity hints: PAGLOCK, NOLOCK, ROWLOCK, TABLOCK, or TABLOCKX

  - Isolation level hints: HOLDLOCK, NOLOCK, READCOMMITTED, REPEATABLEREAD, SERIALIZABLE

  In addition, the NOLOCK and READPAST <table_hints> are only allowed in SELECT statements and not in DELETE, INSERT, or UPDATE statements.

- *m* – A placeholder indicating that multiple <table_hints> can be specified.

- *m* – A placeholder indicating that more than one *column_alias* can be specified.

- <*rowset_function*> – Specifies that one of the rowset functions is to be used.

- OPENQUERY – Executes the specified pass-through query.

- OPENROWSET – Includes all connection information necessary to access remote data from a data source.

- SET – Introduces the list of column or variable names to be updated.

- *column_name* – A column in the updated table that will be changed. When multiple columns are to be updated in *table_name*, each should be separated by commas.

- *expression* – A variable, literal value, expression, or a parenthetical subSELECT statement that returns a single value. The value returned by expression replaces the existing value(s) in column or @*variable*.

- DEFAULT – Indicates that the default defined for the column will replace the existing values in the column. This can also be used to change the column to NULL if the column has no default and is defined to allow NULL values.

- @*variable* – A declared variable that is set to the value returned by expression.

- *n* – A placeholder to indicate that the preceding item can be specified multiple times.

♦ FROM – Specifies that another table is used to provide criteria values for the UPDATE operation. Is the name of the table to provide criteria values for the UPDATE operation.

♦ *view_name* – The name of the view to provide criteria values for the UDPATE operation.

♦ CROSS JOIN – Specifies the cross-product of two tables. Returns the same rows as if no WHERE clause was specified in an old-style, non-SQL-92-style join.

♦ INNER – Specifies that all matching pairs of rows are returned and discards unmatched rows from both tables. This is the default if no join type is specified.

♦ *<join_hints>* – Specifies that SQL Server's query optimizer use one *<join_hints>*, or execution algorithm, per join specified in the query's FROM clause.

♦ ON *<join_condition>* – Specifies the conditions upon which the join is based.

♦ WHERE – Specifies the conditions used to limit the number of rows that are updated. There are two forms of update based on what is specified in the WHERE clause:

  ▪ Searched updates specify *<search_conditions>* to qualify the rows to delete.

  ▪ Positioned updates use the CURRENT OF clause to specify a cursor, the delete operation occurs at the current position of the cursor.

♦ GLOBAL – Specifies that *cursor_name* refers to a global cursor.

♦ *cursor_name* – The name of the open cursor from which the fetch should be made. If both a global and a local cursor exist with *cursor_name* as their name, then *cursor_name* refers to the global cursor if GLOBAL is specified. If GLOBAL is not specified, *cursor_name* refers to the local cursor. The cursor must allow updates.

♦ *cursor_variable_name* – The name of a cursor variable. The cursor variable must reference a cursor that allows updates.

♦ OPTION (*<query_hints>*, [,...*n*]) – Keywords to indicate that optimizer hints are used to customize SQL Server's processing of the statement.

♦ {HASH | ORDER} GROUP – Specifies that the aggregations specified in the GROUP BY or COMPUTE clause of the query should use hashing or ordering.

- ◆ {MERGE | HASH | CONCAT} UNION — Specifies that all UNION operations should be performed by merging, hashing, or concatenating UNION sets. If more than one UNION hint is specified, the optimizer will select the least expensive strategy from those hints specified.

- ◆ FAST number_rows — Specifies that the query is optimized for fast retrieval of the first number_rows (a nonnegative integer). After the first number_rows are returned, the query continues execution and produces its full result set.

- ◆ FORCE ORDER — Specifies that the join order indicated by the query syntax should be preserved during query optimization.

- ◆ ROBUST PLAN — Forces the query optimizer to attempt a plan that works for the maximum potential row size at the expense of performance. If no such plan is possible, the optimizer returns an error rather than deferring error detection to query execution. Rows may contain variable-length columns; SQL Server allows rows to be defined whose maximum potential size is beyond the capability of SQL Server to process them. Normally, despite the maximum potential size, an application stores rows whose actual size is within the limits that SQL Server can process. If SQL Server encounters a row that is too long, an execution error is returned.

  A positioned UPDATE using a WHERE CURRENT OF clause updates the single row at the current position of the cursor. This can be more accurate than a searched UPDATE that uses a WHERE search_conditions clause to qualify the rows to be updated. A searched UPDATE updates multiple rows if the search_conditions do not uniquely identify a single row.

When updating rows, these rules apply:

- ◆ Identity columns cannot be updated.

- ◆ All char and nchar columns are right-padded to the defined length.

- ◆ If ANSI_PADDING is set OFF, all trailing spaces are removed from data inserted into varchar and nvarchar columns, except in strings containing only spaces. These strings are truncated to an empty string. If ANSI_PADDING is set ON, trailing spaces are inserted. The Microsoft SQL Server ODBC driver and SQL Server OLE DB provider automatically SET ANSI_PADDING ON for each connection. This can be configured in ODBC data sources or by setting connection attributes or properties.

- ◆ If an update to a record violates a constraint or rule, if it violates the NULL setting for the column, or if the new value is an incompatible data type, the statement is cancelled, an error is returned, and no records will be updated.

◆ When an UPDATE statement encounters an arithmetic error (overflow, divide by zero, or a domain error) during expression evaluation, the UPDATE is not performed. The remainder of the batch is not executed, and an error message is returned.

Using the INSERT statement

The INSERT DML statement functions to add a new row or group of rows to a table. It can be used to create a single new row using column values you supply. The values listed in the VALUES clause have one-to-one correspondence with the columns in the table. Notice also that the order of the values is exactly the order of the columns in the table. These are key requirements when writing an INSERT statement.

Another key requirement is that the values supplied in the VALUES clause of an INSERT statement must be constants, not expressions. If you attempt to insert a value that is not allowed into a column (for example, a NULL value into a column that does not allow nulls), your INSERT statement will fail. Because data is case sensitive, be careful to enter data in the format you want.

If you are entering every column in a table, the column-list can be omitted. There was one value in the value-list for each column of the table. If you do not have values in your value-list for all of the columns in the table, you must specify which columns you want the data inserted into by including a column-list. You must list the data in the value-list in the same order as you list the columns in the column-list. The columns not included in the column-list will receive null or default values. Therefore, they must be defined to allow null values or the INSERT statement will fail. As a practical matter, always insert values for the primary key column(s) of the table.

If the table contains a column with IDENTITY data type, use a zero as a placeholder for the IDENTITY column *customer_num,* and a NULL is used as a placeholder for the nullable columns that you do not have data for. These placeholders are necessary for a one-to-one correspondence between the values in the value-list and the columns in the table. Using a zero as a placeholder for an IDENTITY column will cause the server to generate the next actual value in sequence before inserting the new row into the database.

The basic INSERT is made up of the clauses listed that follow:

```
INSERT [into][database.[owner.]]{table_name|view_name}
(column_list)]
{VALUES (expression [, expression]...)  |select_statement }
INTO .
```

The INSERT arguments and their context within the syntax are listed as follows:

◆ *column_list* — Is a list of one or more columns to which data is to be added. Enclose the list in parentheses. The columns can be listed in any order, but the incoming data (whether in a values clause or a select clause) must be in the same order. The column list is necessary when some, but not all, of the columns in the table are to receive data. If no column list is given, the insert is assumed to affect all of the columns in the receiving table (in create table order).

◆ VALUES — Is a keyword that introduces a list of expressions.

◆ *expression* — Specifies constant expressions, variables, parameters, or null values for the indicated columns. The values list must be enclosed in parentheses and must match the explicit or implicit column list. Enclose character and datetime constants in single or double quotes. See Chapter 11, "Constructing the Database," for more information about data entry rules.

◆ *select_statement* — Is a standard select statement used to retrieve the values to be inserted.

COLUMN LIST

The column list determines the order in which values are entered. You can leave out items in the column list and values list as long as the omitted columns allow null values. The INSERT statement interacts with the options set with the CREATE INDEX command. A rule or check constraint can restrict the domain of legal values that can be entered into a column. A default value is supplied if a user does not explicitly enter one. If an INSERT statement violates domain or integrity rules or if it is the wrong data type, the statement fails and SQL Server 7 displays an error message.

Inserting an empty string ("") into a variable character type or text column inserts a single space. The char columns are padded to the defined length. All trailing spaces are removed from data inserted into varchar columns, except in the case of a string that contains only spaces. Strings that contain only spaces are truncated to a single space. Strings longer than the specified length of a char, nchar, varchar, or nvarchar column are silently truncated. You can define a trigger that takes a specified action when an insert command is issued on a specified table. You can select rows from a table and insert them into the same table in a single statement. To insert data with SELECT from a table that has null values in some fields into a table that does not allow null values, you must provide a substitute value for any NULL entries in the original table. Two tables may be identically structured but differ in whether null values are permitted in some fields.

IDENTITY COLUMNS

When inserting a row into a table, do not include the name of the IDENTITY column in the column list, or its value in the values list. If the table consists of only one column, an IDENTITY column, omit the column list and leave the values list empty as follows:

```
insert id_table values()
```

The first time you insert a row into a table, SQL Server 7 assigns the IDENTITY column a value of 1. Each new row gets a column value one higher than the last. Server failures can create gaps in IDENTITY column values. The maximum size of the gap depends on the setting of the IDENTITY burning set configuration variable. Gaps can also result from manual insertion of data into the IDENTITY column, deletion of rows, and transaction rollbacks.

Using the DELETE statement

The DELETE DML statement functions to removes rows from a table. The DELETE statement specifies a table and usually contains a WHERE clause that designates the row or rows that are to be removed from the table. If the WHERE clause is not included, all rows in the table will be deleted. Without the WHERE clause in the example, all of the data in a table would be deleted.

The basic DELETE statement is made up of the clauses listed here:

```
DELETE [from] [[database.]owner.]{table_name|view_name}
[WHERE search_conditions]
```

The DELETE arguments and their context within the syntax are listed as follows:

◆ FROM – An optional keyword used for compatibility with other versions of SQL. Follow it with the name of the table or view from which you want to remove rows.

◆ WHERE – A standard WHERE clause.

◆ WHERE CURRENT OF cursor_name – Causes SQL Server 7 to delete the row of the table or view indicated by the current cursor position for cursor_name.

RESTRICTIONS ON THE USE OF DELETE

You cannot use DELETE with a multitable view (one whose FROM clause names more than one table) even though you may be able to use UPDATE or INSERT on that same view. When you delete a row through a view you change multiple tables, which is not permitted. The INSERT and UPDATE statements that affect only one base table of the view are permitted.

DELETING ALL ROWS FROM A TABLE

If you don't use a WHERE clause, all rows in the table named after DELETE [FROM] are removed. The table, though empty of data, continues to exist until you issue a drop table command.

DELETE AND TRANSACTIONS

You can define a trigger that will take a specified action when a DELETE command is issued on a specified table. Use the clause where current of with cursors. Before deleting rows using the WHERE CURRENT OF clause, you must first define the cursor with DECLARE CURSOR and open it using the OPEN statement. Position the cursor on the row you want to delete using one or more FETCH statements. The cursor name cannot be an SPL parameter or local variable. The cursor must be an updatable cursor or SQL Server 7 returns an error. Any deletion to the cursor result set also affects the base table row from which the cursor row is derived. You can delete only one row at a time using the cursor.

You cannot delete rows in a cursor result set if the cursor's SELECT statement contains a JOIN clause, even though the cursor is considered updatable. The table_name or view_name specified with a DELETE . . . WHERE CURRENT OF must be the table or view specified in the first FROM clause of the SELECT statement that defines the cursor. After the deletion of a row from the cursor's result set, the position of the cursor points before the next row in the cursor's result set. You must still use FETCH to access the next row. If the deleted row is the last row of the cursor result set, the cursor points after the last row of the result set. If a client deletes a row (using another cursor or a regular delete) and that row represents the current cursor position of other opened cursors owned by the same client, the position of each affected cursor is implicitly set to before the next available row. However, it is not possible for one client to delete a row representing the current cursor position of another client's cursor. If a client deletes a row that represents the current cursor position of another cursor defined by a join operation and is owned by the same client, SQL Server 7 still accepts the DELETE statement. However, it implicitly closes the cursor defined by the join.

Using the Data Manipulation Statements

Now that we have examined the syntax of the SQL data manipulation language, we will review some practical techniques that should be used in conjunction with the manipulation language to affect the data while maintaining its integrity.

Validating the user-entered data

A typical GUI front end validates the data as it moves it from the edit control into the underlying item(s) in the buffer. Validation begins when the user modifies data in the edit control and one of these conditions occurs:

◆ The SUBMIT key or its equivalent has been activated.

◆ The user moves (changes focus) to a different item (field) in the visual control – for example, an HTML page.

During the validation procedure, the values in the item buffer and the edit control may be different. The edit control receives the user-entered data and holds it until the data is validated. The information in the item comes from the database and is updated only after the new data in the edit field has passed all levels of validation. As each column passes a data validation test, it continues to the next test until it passes all levels. When the contents of the edit control pass all validation levels, the item and its status are updated, but the database does not change, because no SQL has been submitted for execution. This is just one approach to data validation. There are a number of ways to update the table data. You can perform updates individually or in a batch using a shadow file to contain the amendments.

DID THE ITEM CHANGE?

In the first validation test, examine the content of the edit control to determine if they have changed from the item in the buffer. When the contents of the edit control are different, this condition is satisfied and additional edit checks and validation are performed depending on the data type. When you use the Tab key or the mouse to move away from a field, the control determines that there has been no change and the validation stops. If the value has changed, the validation continues to the next level.

IS THE ENTERED DATA OF THE CORRECT DATA TYPE?

In the second validation test, a GUI front end checks to see if the data type of the entry in the edit control matches the data type of the item. For example, if a numeric column of type integer contains 123 and the user attempts to enter non-numeric characters into the edit control, this action passes the first-level validation (something changed) but does not pass the second-level validation because "ABC" is not a valid integer.

IF DATA TYPE VALIDATION FAILS, THEN WHAT HAPPENS?

When the data type validation fails, an ItemError event occurs. You can let a GUI front end handle the error, or you can develop a script to handle the error and perform additional processing. When you let a GUI front end handle the validation error, the user receives a standard message that the entry did not pass the validation rules.

VALIDATION RULES: BEYOND JUST DATA TYPE

The third validation test checks for any validation rules you defined for a column in the window or visual data control. These validation rules can be set for the database column using the extended attributes, that is, a GUI front-end system's catalog tables. They can be populated in a number of ways, including the use of CASE design tools such as ERwin. You can also use window or visual data control (for example, HTML page object) validation rules for anything that is appropriate.

- Range validation: column1 > 10000 and column1 < 100000

- Cross-column validation: If column1 is 1, then column2 must be greater than 1

- Specific value checks: column1 must be A or B or C

When a column fails a window or visual data control validation rule, an `ItemError` event occurs.

VALIDATING DATA WITH REFERENCE TABLES

Reference tables provide a good technique for validating data in a window or visual data control. Reference tables compare what the user enters in a column against a list of valid values for that column. If the data does not pass validation when entered, an error status message box is displayed, or the `ItemError` event is triggered (if a script is coded).

Sometimes verifying data values with a reference table is impractical – for example, if a coded number needs to fall in some range, but the range is very large (1 to 3000), a drop-down list or choice box would be impractical. Although it is possible to prime the reference table with the valid values, it is impractical for performance reasons. For such situations, window or visual data control validation rules can often be used to achieve the same result.

Validation rules are simple expressions that result in a Boolean (TRUE or FALSE) value. When you build a rule, form the expression so that it will validate the data while resulting in a Boolean value. You can think of a validation rule as an IF statement:

```
if validation rule (returns TRUE)
  then let the data pass
  else issue an error message
or ItemError event occurs
```

Validation rules are typically triggered for a modified column when:

- The ENTER or SUBMIT key interrupt is invoked.

- Focus leaves the column when a user presses Tab or an arrow key.

♦ Focus leaves when the user clicks in another window or visual data control.

What Is a Transaction?

A *transaction* is a set of actions that are executed as a group. If any of the actions cannot be completed, all other actions must be undone. A transaction always has a beginning and an end. The database server guarantees either that operations done within the bounds of a transaction will be completely and perfectly committed to disk or, if that is not possible, that the database will be restored to the state it was in before the transaction started. Let's take for example a transaction that everyone knows, such as transferring money from your savings account to your checking account. The actions involved with this transaction are:

♦ Update savings to show a withdrawal.

♦ Update checking to show a deposit.

These actions must both be completed successfully before the transfer is complete. If anything goes wrong with either of these two actions, the transaction fails. For example, if you tried to transfer more money into your checking account than you had in your savings account, the transfer would not occur, and your account balances would remain as they were before you attempted the transfer.

THE TRANSACTION LOG

Many things, such as a hardware or software failure, can make a transaction fail. Because of this, the database server must have a way to track all of the changes made during a transaction. This is done in the transaction log. The server uses the transaction log to record each change that it makes to the database during a transaction. If for any reason the transaction cannot be completed, the server automatically uses the data in the transaction log to reverse the changes.

Databases do not have transaction logging automatically. The database administrator must decide whether to make a database with transaction logging. If a database does not have logging, transactions are not available.

SPECIFYING TRANSACTIONS

SQL statements are used to specify the boundaries of a transaction. You use the `BEGIN TRANSACTION` statement to specify the start of a multiple-statement transaction, and the `COMMIT TRANSACTION` statement to specify the end of a transaction.

When the database server reaches a COMMIT TRANSACTION statement, it makes sure that all modifications have been completed properly and committed to disk. If any external failure prevents the transaction from being completed, the partial transaction will be rolled back when the system is restarted. In ANSI databases, you do not need to mark the beginning of a transaction with the BEGIN TRANSACTION statement. A transaction is always in effect, and you only need to indicate the end of each transaction with the COMMIT TRANSACTION statement.

ROLLBACK TRANSACTION
In some cases, you will want to have your program cancel a transaction deliberately if certain circumstances occur. Use the ROLLBACK TRANSACTION statement to do this. The ROLLBACK TRANSACTION statement causes the database server to cancel the current transaction and undo any changes that have been made.

READ CONCURRENCY
In a fashion similar to other relational DBMSs, SQL Server 7 provides four levels of isolation for reading by implementing a *locking* mechanism:

- Dirty read

- Committed read

- Cursor stability

- Repeatable read

SQL Server 7 uses shared locks. Shared locks let other processes read rows but not update them.

DIRTY READS   At the isolation level of DIRTY READ, your process is not isolated at all. You get no locks whatsoever, and the process does not check for the existence of any locks before reading a row. During retrieval you can look at any row, even those containing uncommitted changes. Such rows are referred to as "dirty data." Rows containing dirty data may be phantoms. A *phantom row* is a row that has been inserted with a transaction, which is later rolled back before the transaction completes. Although the phantom row never existed in a permanent sense, it would have been visible to a process using an isolation level of DIRTY READ. The DIRTY READ levels of isolation can be useful, though, when the table is static or 100 percent accuracy is not as important as speed and freedom from contention or you cannot wait for locks to be released.

COMMITTED READS   A COMMITTED READ attempts to acquire a shared lock on a row before trying to read it. It does not actually try to place the lock; rather, it sees if it could acquire the lock. If it can, it is guaranteed that the row exists and is not being updated by another process while it is being read. Remember, a shared lock cannot be acquired on a row that is locked exclusively, which is always the case when a row is being updated. With COMMITTED READ, you have low-level isolation. During retrieval, you will not be looking at any phantoms or dirty data. You know that the current row was committed (at lease when your process read it). After your process has read the row, though, other processes can change it. The COMMITTED READ levels can be useful for lookups, queries, and reports yielding general information. For example, COMMITTED READs are useful for summary-type reports such as month-ending sales analyses.

CURSOR STABILITY   With CURSOR STABILITY, a shared lock is acquired on each row as it is read via a cursor. This shared lock is held until the next row is retrieved. If data is retrieved using a cursor, the shared lock is held until the next FETCH is executed. At this level, not only can you look at committed rows, but you are also assured the row will continue to exit while you are looking at it. No other process can change (UPDATE or DELETE) that row while you are looking at it. SELECT statements using an isolation level of CURSOR STABILITY can be used for lookups, queries, and reports yielding operational data. For example, SELECT statements using CURSOR STABILITY are useful for detail-type reports like price quotation or job-tracking systems. If the isolation level of CURSOR STABILITY is set and a cursor is not used, CURSOR STABILITY behaves in the same manner as COMMITTED READ (the shared lock is never actually placed).

REPEATABLE READS   The REPEATABLE READ isolation level places a shared lock on all the rows examined by the database server; all these locks are held until the transaction is committed. With REPEATABLE reads, you have high-level isolation. In explicit transactions, you are assured the row will continue to exist not only while you are looking at it, but also when you reread it later. No other process can change (UPDATE or DELETE) that row until you COMMIT your transaction. The REPEATABLE READs (RR) are useful when you must treat all rows read as a unit or to guarantee that a value will not change. For example, critical, aggregate arithmetic (for example, account balancing) or coordinated lookups from several tables (for example, reservation systems) are good candidates for RR.

It is important to note that with REPEATABLE READs all the rows examined are locked; this includes rows that do not meet the select criteria but had to be read in order to determine their ineligibility. For example, if you use the REPEATABLE READ isolation on a query that requires a table to be read sequentially (if no indexes are available, for instance), all the rows in the table are locked, and those locks are held for the duration of the transaction. Additionally, to ensure the integrity of the data set (that is, to ensure that new rows matching the criteria are not added), the corresponding index keys are also locked.

SETTING THE LEVEL OF ISOLATION   To make use of process isolation, your database must use logging. To pick an isolation level, use the SET ISOLATION statements. If logging is not turned on, all reads are DIRTY READs and the isolation level cannot be set. Each database server process can set its own isolation level.

Following is an example of a SET ISOLATION statement:

```
SET ISOLATION to Cursor stability;
```

SET TRANSACTION   The SET TRANSACTION statement complies with ANSI SQL-92. This statement is similar to the SQL Server 7 SET ISOLATION statement; however, the SET ISOLATION statement is not ANSI-compliant and does not provide access modes. The isolation levels that you can set with the SET TRANSACTION statement are almost parallel to the isolation levels that you can set with the SET ISOLATION statement, as shown in the preceding example.

Another difference between the SET TRANSACTION and SET ISOLATION statements is the behavior of the isolation levels within transactions. The SET TRANSACTION statement can be issued only once for a transaction. With the SET ISOLATION statement, after a transaction is started, you can change the isolation level more than once within a transaction. Following is an example of SET TRANSACTION statement:

```
SET TRANSACTION to Repeatable Read;
```

Controlling the cost of the transaction

The basic language of the relational database management system (RDMS) is SQL. SQL uses only four verbs — SELECT, INSERT, DELETE, and UPDATE — to perform data manipulation (DML). SQL is a set-oriented language rather than a record-oriented language. In record-oriented systems, such as IBM's VSAM or QSAM, the programmer control file access gets the first record, gets the next record, and so on. In most cases, the programmer also knows how many records may be traversed in a transaction and, therefore, can identify potentially expensive operations. These operations can then be stopped before they start, or the user can be warned that a particular operation may take time to complete.

When the program issues a SQL data manipulation statement (SELECT, INSERT, DELETE, or UPDATE), the programmer usually doesn't know how many rows will be returned and how long the statement will take to complete. In addition, RDMS databases, in general, don't provide a way to estimate the cost of execution or determine how many rows will be affected. Some RDMSs, such as DB2/MVS, do work with EXPLAIN, or as it is known in SQL Server, SET SHOWPLAN performance utilities, which provide this information in accordance with the current state of the database objects to be accessed.

USING UNIQUE KEYS

You can control the nonretrieval SQL (for example, UPDATE) verbs by including a unique primary key in the WHERE clause for the target table.

```
UPDATE series
WHERE series_cde  ='LEAVE IT TO BEAVER'
```

For example, deleting SERIES rows according to a single SERIES_CDE guarantees that at most only one row will be accessed to complete the statement. Retrieving a SERIES row by SERIES_CDE will have the same limiting effect as in the nonretrieval case, for example:

```
SELECT * FROM EPISODE
WHERE SERIES_CDE = "LUCY" AND EPISODE_CDE= "225".
```

However, most retrieval situations don't fit into this category. Frequently, the search criteria are supplied entirely by the user in an ad hoc fashion. It is the programmer's responsibility to provide governing mechanisms to prevent a user from executing a potentially expensive retrieval.

For example, the query SELECT * FROM episode will retrieve all rows in the episode table. If the table is large, this query could degrade system performance significantly.

LIMITING THE USER TO A SPECIFIC WHERE CLAUSE

Limiting the user to a specific WHERE requires that the programmer prevent the user from executing any query that might result in retrieving a large number of rows. You need to include some form of WHERE criteria in the SELECT regardless of what options the user is able to specify. Because the programmer is in control during development, the programmer can make a reasonable estimate of the data to be returned.

For example, instead of allowing a user to retrieve information for all episodes in all series, the application would allow the user to retrieve only episodes that reside in a particular television series. This option has a disadvantage. It limits the flexibility for the user. In many situations, it is difficult for the programmer to anticipate how the user will want to use the application. For example, some users may be happy viewing episodes one series at a time, but others may want to view them based on a holiday or associated genre. In addition, this option doesn't consider growth. It is possible that even limiting the user to accessing episodes by series would eventually return a large amount of data.

PERFORMING A COUNT(*) CALCULATION

To provide flexibility for the user while limiting the number of rows retrieved, you can query the database server to determine how many rows will be retrieved. This provides an accurate count of the rows that will be sent to the client requester once the completed query is processed.

For example, if you provide users with the capability of retrieving episode rows completely ad hoc, they may end up executing a wide range of queries:

```
SELECT episode_name, series_name, episode_holiday
FROM episode
WHERE series_cde LIKE "L%";
```

It would by difficult to estimate the number of rows that might be retrieved for any of these queries. If, however, the query is executed with a COUNT (*) and no other columns, the single value returned will determine the total number of rows that meet the criteria and should provide you with an accurate estimate of the expense of the query:

```
SELECT count(*) FROM series WHERE series_CDE="LUCY"
```

Because there are no columns in the column list, the database can process the request without sending a lot of data to the client. Once the count is known, you or the educated consumer can decide that any query resulting in more than a certain number of rows will be disallowed. This technique is not always the answer; depending on the volume of data and configuration of the database, the COUNT(*) request can be costly in terms of server time and, therefore, may not be feasible. For example, the WHERE predicate column, especially in the querymode example, may not be an index, and a table scan might be needed to determine the COUNT. In addition, if the retrieval is subsequently issued, the server must obtain the rows that meet the WHERE criteria again.

USING A CURSOR

To have complete control over the retrieval and be able to resume the retrieval after determining that the user wants more rows, you can access the data directly from a SQL cursor. By defining a cursor and issuing each FETCH explicitly, you can count the number or rows and determine when to prompt the user. For example, if you want to prompt the user after the first 100 rows, you suspend FETCHes from the server by popping up a message box to the user with the buttons Continue, Yes, and No. If the user responds Yes, the FETCH loop continues until the next point at which you want to ask if the retrieval should continue. If the user responds No, the cursor is closed and no more rows are sent to the requesting transaction window. You are not only in complete control of the number of rows retrieved, but you can also periodically prompt the user to determine whether to continue. See Listing 12-3 for an example of this technique.

Listing 12-3: Using a Cursor with the PowerBuilder Script Language

```
// DECLARE THE CURSOR
DECLARE C1 CURSOR FOR
  SELECT epsseg.series_cde,epsseg.episode_cde,
  epsseg.eps_seg_num,epsseg.eps_seg_len
  FROM  epsseg
  WHERE episode_cde = :ls_episode_cde AND
series_cde = :ls_series_cde ;
//
// check the return code to verify
//whether the cursor was successfully created.
```

```
// If not successful display error message
IF sqlca.sqlcode <>  0 THEN f_db_error( sqlca," in CURSOR build ")
SetPointer(HourGlass!)
li_counter = 0
// OPEN THE CURSOR: POINT AT THE FIRST ROW
OPEN C1;
IF sqlca.sqlcode <  0 THEN f_db_error( sqlca," epsseg CURSOR OPEN ")
// Set the values in the data entry window with the values retrieved
// from the database. Pass through the loop while the FETCH
// is successful
// FETCH result ends with sqlcode = 100
li_sqlcode = 0
DO WHILE li_sqlcode = 0
// FETCH THE NEXT ROW IN CURSOR
FETCH C1 INTO :ls_series_cde,
:ls_episode_cde, :li_seg_num,
:li_seg_len ;
// ARE WE PAST THE LAST ROW IN THE CURSOR
IF sqlca.sqlcode <> 0  and sqlca.sqlcode <> 100
THEN f_db_error( sqlca," epsseg FETCH error ")
IF sqlca.sqlcode = 100 THEN li_sqlcode = sqlca.sqlcode
IF sqlca.sqlcode <> 100 THEN li_counter = li_counter + 1
IF sqlca.sqlcode <>   100 AND li_counter > 64
THEN MessageBox ( this.title , "This select will caused " + &
String( li_counter ) + " rows to be returned.~r~nDo you want to
continue?" & ,question! , okcancel! , 2 ) = 2 then li_counter = 0
LOOP
// CLOSE THE CURSOR
CLOSE  C1;
```

Using a cursor in a conversational mode can be very expensive due to the additional overhead on the client. Processing queries through a cursor, retrieving the values into local variables, and then setting controls in a window or page takes up valuable resources. Also, the cursor remains open while you are prompting the user whether to continue. This not only ties up resources on the server but may also cause locks on the retrieved records. This can interfere with other users' database access.

EXPLAINING THE SQL
After you get the desired result – the data returned is the correct result – then use the EXPLAIN, or as it is also known, the SET SHOWPLAN SQL tool to examine the SQL. The SET SHOWPLAN SQL tool displays information about the path that SQL Server 7 will use to access the data. Sometimes there is more than one way to code a SQL statement to obtain the desired result. The SET SHOWPLAN SQL tool can help you

select the more efficient method. This is most useful when you are retrieving or updating data in an indexed column or using multiple tables.

In many cases, the majority of the work done in an application, in terms of processing time, is that done by the SQL queries used by that application. The most difficult SQL should be identified at an early stage and monitored. In fact the application should be "tuned" regularly, especially in the early stages of production. In tuning applications, the first area that should be examined for optimization possibilities is the SQL queries themselves. Some obvious ways to make SQL faster are to change the SQL query so that it accesses specific data. You can have it read fewer rows, or you can limit the need to sort results.

The way to achieve these ends, however, is not always obvious. The specific methods depend very strongly on the details of the application and the database design. The ideas in this section suggest a general approach and include some techniques that apply in limited circumstances. There may be some SQL queries that are "needed" and just inherently slower than others, and not much can be done to improve their performance.

OPTIMIZING YOUR SQL-DML

Before you begin working to optimize your queries, be sure to run the UPDATE STATISTICS statement to ensure that the data in the system catalog tables is current. The optimizer uses this data to determine the fastest way to retrieve the requested data. The database server does not update this data automatically. The UPDATE STATISTICS command should be executed regularly in any event, as it improves overall system performance. If SET SHOWPLAN does not help, then test the problem SQL. First, select a single query that you think is running slowly. Then set up an environment in which you can take predictable, repeatable timings of that query.

CONSISTENT SYSTEM LOAD   If you are using a multiuser system or network on which the system load varies widely from hour to hour, you may need to perform your experiments at the same time each day to get repeatable results. You may even need to work at off-peak hours. There are tools that can create varying loads of simulated data traffic. Performix uses a neat transaction generator that can simulate *n* users by sending traffic from, let's say, NT1 (transaction generator) to NT2 (system under test), which contains the database.

A SCALED-DOWN DATABASE   If the real query takes many minutes or hours to complete, it might be a good idea to prepare a scaled-down database to run tests more quickly. This can be helpful, but you must be aware of potential problems. The optimizer may make different choices in a small database than in a large one, even when the relative sizes of the tables are the same. Execution time is rarely a linear function of table size. Sorting time, for example, increases faster than table size, as does the cost of indexed access when an index goes from two to three levels. What appears to be a big improvement in the scaled-down environment may be less significant with the full database. Any conclusion you reach as a result of tests in the model database must be considered tentative until verified in the large database.

ML SELECT

hieve the same result with less effort. This section includes some
ations on how to reduce the effort required by a query.

IFY SORTS   Avoid sorting by placing your data in a temporary
rts by sorting on fewer or narrower columns. A sort is not neces-
g. The sort algorithm of the database server is highly tuned and
ent. It is certainly as fast or faster than any external sort program
y to the same data. As long as the sort is being done only occasion-
latively small number of output rows, there is no need to avoid it.
should try to avoid or simplify repeated sorts of large tables. Using a
ble is one way to avoid sorts. If a sort is necessary, look for ways to
ie sort will generally be quicker if you can sort on fewer or narrower

AVOID CORRELATED SUBQUERIES   A *correlated subquery* is one in which a column label appears in both the SELECT list of the main query and the WHERE clause
of the subquery. Because the result of the subquery might be different for each row
that the database server examines, the subquery will be executed anew for every
row. This can be extremely time-consuming. Unfortunately, there are some queries
that cannot be stated in SQL without the use of a correlated subquery.

When you see a subquery in a time-consuming SELECT statement, look to see if
it is correlated. If this is the case, try to rewrite the query to avoid this correlation.
If the correlation cannot be avoided, look for ways to reduce the number of rows
that are examined. For instance, you may be able to reduce the number of rows by
adding other filter expressions to the WHERE clause, or by selecting a subset of
records into a temporary table and searching only these records.

AVOID DIFFICULT REGULAR EXPRESSIONS   The LIKE keyword supports wildcard
matches, also referred to as regular expressions. Some regular expressions are more
difficult than others for the server to process. A wildcard in the initial position, for
example, will force the database server to examine every value in the column
because the index cannot be used.

Regular expression tests on an indexed column with wildcards only in the middle or at the end do not force every value to be examined. However, the query can
still be slow to execute. Depending on the data in the column, some expressions
can be rewritten more simply. If a difficult regular expression test is essential, avoid
combining it with a join. First process the single table, applying the regular expression condition to select the desired rows. Save the result in a temporary table, and
join that table to the others.

AVOID NONINITIAL SUBSTRINGS   A filter based on a noninitial substring of a column also requires every value in the column to be tested. Even if an index exists, it
will not be used to evaluate this type of filter. If possible, rewrite your query to

avoid noninitial substrings. However, in some cases, a noninitial substring may be the only way to find the data you need.

AVOID JOINING ON LONG CHARACTER STRINGS   Operations that are applied to character strings are relatively slow because character strings are only compared two bytes at a time. When long strings are used as join columns, the situation is even worse because of the number of characters that have to be compared. Whenever possible, join two tables on a numeric column such as `integer`, `smallint`, or `IDENTITY`.

USE A TEMPORARY TABLE TO SPEED QUERIES   In some cases, the use of temporary tables can result in more efficient processing of queries, even when the overhead of the temporary table is taken into account. Temporary tables can be useful for conducting multiple queries on the same subset of data. You can `SELECT` the desired subset of data `INTO` a temporary table and then direct your queries against the temporary table. Any changes made to the primary table after the temporary table has been created will not be reflected in the output.

Stored procedures versus embedded SQL

Embedded SQL requires that you create your own SQL statements. You will use embedded SQL whenever you want something you cannot easily do with a GUI tool, for example, the PowerBuilder Data window. In general, you will use embedded SQL when the data is brought in to be manipulated rather than displayed. When using embedded SQL, you must always check the SQLCode attribute from the transaction object to determine whether the SQL statement executed successfully or not. Embedded SQL can take several forms:

◆ Static SQL, including cursors

◆ Stored procedures

◆ Dynamic SQL

EMBEDDED STATIC SQL
Use *embedded static SQL* when the components of the SQL statement do not change; only the values passed as arguments to the `WHERE` clause change. Consider the following example:

```
SELECT series_cde , series_name
FROM dbo.series  WHERE series_cde = :ls_series_cde
```

Host variables are prefixed with a colon and must be declared before being referenced in SQL statements. It is not necessary to use the "&" character to continue the line when the SQL statement wraps across multiple lines. Always check the SQLCode attribute of your transaction object after executing the SQL statement to verify success or failure. If you do not prefix a table with the owner name, a GUI front end assumes that the owner of the table is whatever was specified in your `logon_id` or `userid`. It is a good idea always to use the `USING` clause, even when the transaction object is SQLCA.

STORED PROCEDURES

Stored procedures are named precompiled sets of modal SQL, such as Transact SQL. Stored procedures hit the ground running. Unlike dynamic SQL, which must be parsed, validated, optimized, and compiled before the request can be executed, stored procedures enable you to define procedural SQL statements in the database for use by all applications. Using stored procedures to perform database updates enables you to enhance database security, integrity, and performance. Because stored procedures provide for conditional execution, you can also use them to enforce additional business rules.

Locking

A *lock* is an object used by software to indicate that a user has some dependency on a resource. The software does not allow other users to perform operations on the resource that would adversely affect the dependencies of the user owning the lock. Locks are managed internally by system software and are acquired and released in response to actions taken by the user.

LOCKING GRANULARITY

Locking granularity refers to the size of the object being locked. Granularity ranges through five levels, from coarse to fine. This range enables you to make trade-offs between currency and locking overhead. SQL Server 7 provides different levels of locking granularity. The coarsest level is database-level locking; the finest level is row-level locking. Key-level locking is performed on index entries.

DATABASE-LEVEL LOCKING

It is occasionally necessary or advantageous to prevent other users from accessing any part of the database for some period of time. This may be the case if you are a database administrator and you're using a utility or program that is:

- ◆ Executing a large number of updates involving many tables

- ◆ Archiving the database files for backups

- ◆ Altering the structure of the database

To facilitate these DBA-type requirements, you would like to eliminate contention from other users who have database permissions. The entire database can be locked by starting SQL Server in *single-user mode*. When you start SQL Server in single-user mode, only a single user can connect, and the CHECKPOINT process is not started. The CHECKPOINT process guarantees that completed transactions are regularly written from the disk cache to the database device. To allow other users access to the database, you must execute the CLOSE DATABASE statement and then reopen the database.

TABLE-LEVEL LOCKING

Sometimes you want exclusive control over a table to perform some special updates. You want to eliminate contention from other batch or OLTP users who have access and update permissions on the subject table(s). SQL Server 7 provides *table-level locking,* which can be used to prevent other users from modifying the database. It is prudent to use table-level locking to avoid conflict with other users during batch operations that affect most or all of the rows of a table. It is also prudent to use table-level locking to prevent users from updating a table for a period of time and prevent access to a table while altering its structure or creating indexes. Use table-level locking only when making major changes to a table in a multiuser environment, and when simultaneous interaction by another user would interfere. Only one lock can apply to a table at any given time. That is, if a user locks a table, no other user can lock that table until the first user has unlocked it. You cannot lock the system catalog tables.

If your database has transactions, tables can only be locked within transactions. Therefore, be sure that you have executed BEGIN TRANSACTION (unless you are using a MODE ANSI database) before attempting to lock a table. The table will be unlocked when the transaction is completed.

If you want to give other users read access to the table but prevent them from modifying any of the data that it contains, then you should use the TABLOCK parameter in the various statements with the option (for example, SELECT or perhaps bcp). When a table is locked in SHARE mode, other users are able to SELECT data from the table, but they are not able to INSERT, DELETE, or UPDATE rows in the table or ALTER the table.

It should be noted that locking a table in SHARE mode does not prevent row locks from being placed for updates by your process. If you wish to avoid exclusive row locks in addition to the share lock on the table, you must lock the table in EXCLUSIVE mode.

If you want to prevent other users from having any access to the table, then you should lock it in EXCLUSIVE mode. In EXCLUSIVE mode, other users will be unable to SELECT (unless dirty read isolation is used), INSERT, DELETE, or UPDATE rows in the table until you unlock the table. Only one lock is used to lock the table, regardless of the number of rows that are updated within a transaction.

PAGE- AND ROW-LEVEL LOCKING

Page-level locking causes an entire data page to be locked whenever a single row locked on that page needs to be locked. *Row-level locking* causes only the row in question to be locked.

Page locks are useful when, in a transaction, you process rows in the same order as the table's clustered index or process rows in physically sequential order. Row locks are useful when, in a transaction, you process rows in an arbitrary order. When the number of locked rows becomes large, you run the risk of the number of available locks becoming exhausted or the overhead for lock management becoming significant.

There is a trade-off between these two levels of locking. Page-level locking requires fewer resources than does row-level locking, but it also reduces concurrency. If a page lock is placed on a page containing many rows, other processes needing other data from that same page could be denied access to that data.

Summary

This chapter covered application data manipulation and considerations revolving around data integrity and performance. The DML statements covered here will be discussed and used in the remaining chapters, especially the programming section that includes Java and SQL Server stored procedures. See Chapter 17, "C and Java with SQL."

Chapter 13

Developing the User Interface

IN THIS CHAPTER

◆ The converging of Web and client/server systems

◆ The user interface (UI) as the focal point

◆ Typical UI features

THE USER INTERFACE, or presentation layer, is what will sell your application to the end user. Be assured that if the user interface is awkward or difficult to grasp, then the end user will, wherever possible, avoid using it. This could happen even though the product was the most functional application that you ever built. In case you haven't quite got it yet, it's really important to have a great user interface. Well, how does one build a great user interface? The answer is practice, practice, and more practice. However, because you never have enough time to do this, we are going to give you some items to bear in mind when you are building a user interface.

Let's start with a basic understanding of what things can put the user interface into effect. Certainly the interface is affected by the visual metaphor; in other words it is affected by the interaction of menus, toolbars, icons, frames, framesets, and windows. The multimedia aspects such as images, sound, and motion also affect it. The coupling of these elements and aspects makes the user interface one of the most important aspects and, therefore, one of the biggest challenges, when building an application. This chapter discusses the design considerations for building a good user interface. It covers the various features of the user interface including a help feature for your application.

Converging Web and Client/Server Systems

The emergence of the Internet, the World Wide Web, and browsers (specifically Netscape Navigator and Microsoft Internet Explorer) is changing the landscape of application development. Although there is still an air of doubt about the security of Internet applications, many companies are now shifting their development projects to the Web. This environment is basically a merging of two types of computing: mainframe and client/server. In effect, we've kept the graphical user interface, adopted the object-oriented/event-driven programming models, and moved the business rules back onto a server. Which, if oversimplified, could be made to sound like we've come full-circle and ended up slapping a GUI on top of CICS!

One thing that is happening is that the Web and client/server applications have converged (or at the very least are beginning to converge), as shown in Figure 13-1. Practically all companies need to provide up-to-date information to the general public. This means that building static content on Web pages will not suffice. Many companies would like to provide their existing customers, or their field salespeople, with access to information stored within the internal client/server systems. However, remote connection to these systems is too complicated or expensive to establish. So companies are tackling these issues from one or both ends. That is, client/server applications, or at least their data sources, are being enabled for the Internet, and Web applications are being connected to databases. The lines between these efforts have now blurred.

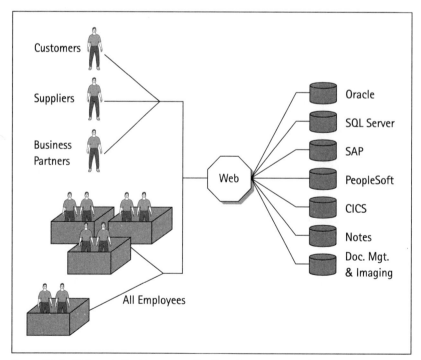

Figure 13-1: Web and client/server applications have converged

Some early Online Transaction Processing (OLTP) applications circa 1972 were run on IBM's CICS, a transaction-processing program environment. It became the most popular mainframe OLTP development environment. As graphic-capable front-end environments have become more popular, character-based systems developed using CICS have become nonexistent. Character-based systems have data entry and presentation limitations; you are limited to a small set of keyboard-based controls and you can only display in character form. The GUI enables you to dictate actions like SAVE and to perform actions by pointing the mouse pointer and clicking symbols, icons, or data as well as using accelerator keys via the keyboard. The older OLTP equivalent was the program function key ("PF Key"), whose meanings also had to be standardized to promote ease of use and end-user acceptance.

The typical GUI window is navigable by way of a menu bar and toolbar running along the top of the window. The menu bar contains items such as File, Edit, Window, and Help. When the user clicks a menu item or its toolbar counterpart (a picture or symbol), the application will respond in kind (for example, opening a new window). Within an enterprise, developing standards of presentation and user appeal for this new GUI interaction is important. We can look at other popular GUI applications, such as Microsoft Word or Microsoft Excel. They give us some ideas about the look and feel of the GUI, and they both conform to a standard. They are both developed in the Multiple Document Interface style (MDI).

The limitations of a character-based system like CICS fostered the need to develop applications using graphical user interface (GUI) front-end tools like Visual Basic and PowerBuilder. CICS did teach us some important lessons about large-scale OLTP development. OLTP applications should have a consistent look and feel across an enterprise. The framesets, frames, windows, menus, and controls should look and function consistently. The obvious prerequisite to accomplishing consistency would be that OLTP development should be standardized within an organization. Developing firm-wide standards and guidelines for OLTP and building firm-wide class objects, functions, and database interfaces will be both practical and cost effective as well as promote consistency. An organization does not evolve to that level after one project, but strategy and appropriate initiatives should be deployed early enough to facilitate the transition.

To the extent that it is possible, an organization should try to create a *technology governance and application development support group*. Its purpose would be to meet regularly to discuss various technologies and development issues such as: adoption of any new tool, recommended development strategy, and developing standards and guidelines. If all of this information were placed on an intranet site, it would quickly become the logical focal point for information interchange. Included in these discussions could be individuals who have in-depth knowledge of the company's existing systems.

The Focal Point

The reason the graphical user interface (GUI) has been a success is that its attention is focused on the user and the user's task in hand. The user interface is an essential part of most client/server systems. The appeal of the user interface is typically constrained by three things: first, the presentation system, for example, an HTML or Java or Windows GUI application; second, the development tool used, for example, SilverStream, PowerBuilder, or Visual Basic; and last, but not least, the visual painting skills of the developer. Please note, however, that the development tool may not be completely able to exploit the presentation system. Similarly, an inexperienced designer will not get the best from the tool.

A good user interface is something that should make an application easy to learn, satisfying to use, effective for the task, and consistent in appearance and interaction, with the same look and feel as many existing popular user interfaces. Other interface features should help prevent the user from making errors, put the user in control, and above all be intuitive. An ugly user interface will make a product much harder to sell and less pleasurable to use. Other considerations for user interface design are:

- Accommodation of unskilled or infrequent users
- Aesthetics
- Careful use of color
- Descriptive and helpful messages
- Feedback
- Allowance of reversible actions
- Proportion
- Typography
- Use of suitable images and visual metaphors (icons and toolbars)

For further reading on graphical user interface design see:

- *The Windows Interface Guidelines for Software Design,* Microsoft Press, 1995, ISBN 1556156790
- Weinschenk, Jamar, and Yeo, *GUI Design Essentials,* John Wiley & Sons, 1997, ISBN 0471175498

Giving control to the user

An important principle of contemporary application design is that users must always feel as if they are in control of the computer, rather the contrary. The user plays an active, instead of reactive, role where even if the situation is extensively automated the application should still be implemented in a way that allows the user to maintain overall control. In a GUI application, there is nothing more frustrating than an hourglass without a clue as to how much longer a task will take and no means of canceling the process. Users will typically tolerate only a few seconds of an unresponsive interface. If the interface can support it (that is, not HTML), it is better to show (or simulate) the progress of the task (see Figure 13-2).

Figure 13-2: Provide a progress indicator for a lengthy process.

Another suggestion for a GUI application is that it should accommodate the widely varying skills and individual preferences of the end user. For example, Microsoft Windows provides the user with the ability to change system default properties, such as colors, screen size, and fonts. A well-constructed application should take these settings into account and adjust appropriately.

Being consistent

Consistency enables users to transfer existing knowledge to new applications, learn new tasks quickly, and focus on the results, because they need not spend time trying to remember how to interact with specific parts of a system. Consistency provides a sense of stability, because it makes the interface familiar and therefore more predictable. See Figure 13-3, which shows the now-familiar File, Window, and Help menu structure.

Figure 13-3: Use generally accepted standards.

Consistency should play a part of all aspects of the interface, including names of commands, visual presentation of information, and operational behavior. To design consistency into software, you must consider several aspects:

◆ **Application consistency.** Present common operations using a consistent set of commands and interfaces. For example, a print command that immediately carries out the operation in one situation but in another presents a dialog box that requires user input should be avoided.

♦ **Operating system consistency.** Be consistent with the interaction and interface conventions provided by Windows. The application will then benefit from the users' ability to apply already learned skills.

♦ **Metaphor consistency.** If a particular behavior is more characteristic of a different object than its metaphor implies, the user may have difficulty learning to associate that behavior with an object. For example, the wastebasket icon conveys an element of recoverability for objects thrown into it.

Exhibiting directness

Design your software so that a user can manipulate data directly. Users should immediately see on the screen the result of their actions on the objects. The information that is displayed coupled with the choice of next-possible actions should help to guide the user through the application.

A visual metaphor will help support user recognition rather than recollection. Many users will recognize functionality represented by an icon more easily than they can recall a command line syntax equivalent (see Figure 13-4).

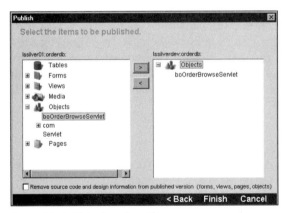

Figure 13-4: Metaphors in action

Providing feedback

Always provide feedback for a user's actions as close to the point of the user's interaction as possible, which is usually immediately. Visual and audible cues can be used to confirm that the application is responding to the user's input and also to communicate details that characterize the action. When the application is processing a particularly lengthy task, it is a good practice to provide the user with information regarding the progress of the process and, if possible, to provide the ability to cancel the task. An example of feedback for a simple task might be mouse pointer changes or a status bar message; whereas feedback for a complex process might involve the display of a dialog box indicating the task's progression (refer to Figure 13-2).

Allowing undo

People can explore and learn how to use a new application by trial and error. A good user interface displays appropriate sets of choices and warns about potential situations where previous versions of data will be overwritten, or unrecoverable (see Figure 13-5).

Figure 13-5: Try to warn the user before data is lost or overwritten.

However, the best intentions of any user can still result in mistakes. How many times have you pressed the No button when you really needed to press Yes? For this reason, consider building a form of undo capability into your application, as shown in Figure 13-6. This probably will involve a log file that preserves the prior version of the data concerned, so that if users so choose, they can scroll back to a prior copy of the data.

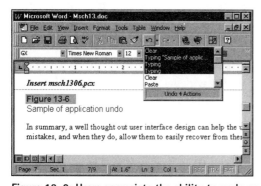

Figure 13-6: Users appreciate the ability to undo an action.

In summary, a well-thought-out user interface design can help the user avoid making mistakes, and when they do, allow them to easily recover from them.

Keeping it simple

Visual controls should communicate helpful impressions and important cues to the required interaction of objects. Every visual control competes for the user's attention, so it pays to keep an interface as simple, easy to learn, and easy to use as possible. This is not to be confused with "simplistic," because it is the user interface that must provide access to all functionality provided by an application. It is the balance between simplicity and functionality that will lead to a very pleasing application. An example of simplification would be to use concise descriptions for commands and messages.

Other Interface Features

There are other features that Windows provides for client/server applications that can either help a user navigate the application or provide various forms of assistance.

Providing accelerator keys

In Windows applications, you can define accelerator keys for your controls to enable users to change focus to the control by pressing Alt + an accelerator key. How you do it depends on whether the type of control has display text associated with it. Be aware that these accelerators will only work if they do not clash with the accelerators attached to the menu. If you assign an accelerator key to a control that is already used as an accelerator for a menu, then the menu will take preference.

Equipping an HTML application with help

If you're developing a Web-based HTML application, the choices for providing help on the same page are limited, so you'll probably develop an HTML-based help system. See Figure 13-7 for an example of HTML frames being used to provide help for the SilverStream Web Application development tool.

HTML image tag help

If you have images on an HTML page, there is a way to produce help that is like the tool tip help provided in other client/server development tools (see Figure 13-8).

By using the ALT HTML tag you can add some tool tip-style help to your HTML pages.

Figure 13-7: A help page for an HTML application

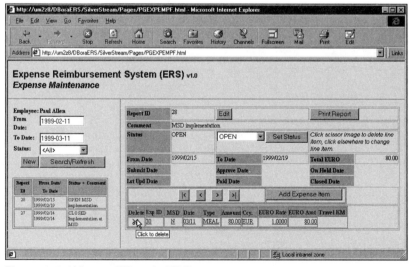

Figure 13-8: Using an ALT tag in HTML

Equipping your client/server application with help

Client/server applications (typically developed for Microsoft Windows) provide many ways to provide the user with assistance. Here is a list of the types of help techniques and styles that are available to you:

- ◆ Standard, or Reference
- ◆ Context sensitive
- ◆ Tool tip
- ◆ Status bar
- ◆ Task oriented
- ◆ Wizard

However, not all development tools can make use of or display each type. Check with your development tool documentation for details.

BUILDING STANDARD HELP

Standard help, also known as Reference help, is really your complete online documentation. This is where the features of your application are described using a combination of text and images. See Figure 13-9 for an example.

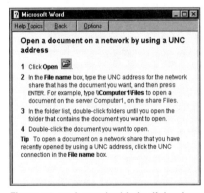

Figure 13-9: A standard help dialog box

SHOWING CONTEXT-SENSITIVE HELP

Context-sensitive help is usually a pop-up-style window that provides help for the specific control that is in focus, as shown in Figure 13-10.

Because of its narrow focus, context-sensitive help is one of the more useful approaches to providing help in your application.

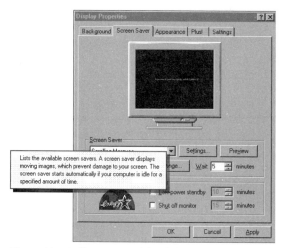

Figure 13-10: Context-sensitive help

USING TOOL TIP HELP

Tool tip, or "bubble," help is basically a form of context-sensitive help that displays when the user positions the mouse over a toolbar icon (see Figure 13-11). With tool tip help in place, your application can then allow the user to turn off the toolbar icon text, which shrinks the toolbar considerably. The smaller toolbar will let the user reclaim valuable screen real estate for the more important data hopefully being provided by your application.

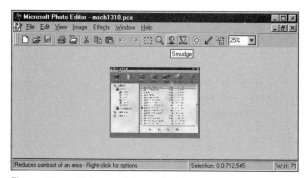

Figure 13-11: Using tool tip or "bubble" help

SHOWING HELP ON THE STATUS BAR

The status bar is useful when you need to display a small amount of context-sensitive help in an application, as shown in Figure 13-12. Because of the limited amount of information that can be displayed in this area, don't leave it as the only source of help for your users.

Figure 13-12: Displaying help on the status bar

Remember to remove status bar help when it no longer applies to the control that is in focus.

BUILDING TASK-ORIENTED HELP

Sometimes a task may take several steps to complete. In this case you may want to put together a help page that describes these steps in detail, as shown in Figure 13-13.

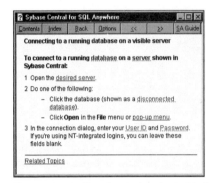

Figure 13-13: Showing task-oriented help

USING A WIZARD TO HELP

The wizard approach is a very useful way of helping the user to complete a more complex or new task by stepping them through the process in smaller chucks (see Figure 13-14). This is especially useful for tasks that require the user to input larger amounts of data that can be grouped into sections and presented separately.

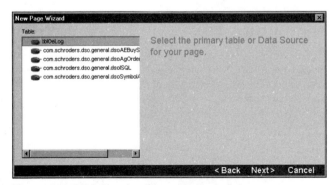

Figure 13-14: Using a wizard to guide the end user

If users become very familiar with the complex task being stepped through by a wizard, they may have outgrown its usefulness. If so, you could also build in another way to complete the task outside of a wizard approach. In other words, a single input dialog box or form instead of the many simpler forms being presented by the wizard.

Summary

This chapter covered the development of the user interface. We discussed the design considerations for building a good user interface, these being control, consistency, directness, feedback, and simplicity. We also covered the various features of the user interface, including a help feature for your application.

Chapter 14

Tuning Your Environment

THIS CHAPTER WILL COVER as much of the tuning arena as possible and hopefully uncover some of the gems that we, as developers, have found on our travels. Although the primary focus will be on the performance and tuning aspects of SQL Server, we will also provide some coverage of the hardware and operating system issues. If you are looking for very detailed information regarding the hardware and operating system software, you should consult the respective vendor. Some of the specific details and best information on tuning are usually provided in the courses that are typically offered by these vendors. This chapter will guide you through the various areas that may be affecting the performance of the MS-SQL Server environment, hopefully enabling you to resolve any problems as soon as possible. We will focus on tuning an application with respect to performance.

Performance and Tuning

The performance of an application may be affected by a large list of factors. A performance problem usually stems from one or more of the following areas:

- Application code
- Database system software
- Hardware
- Operating system
- User expectations

369

The user expectations are mentioned because users may be looking for a split-second response to a "what-if" type of query that requires the database to search, sift through, and join a massive amount of data. This is unrealistic, and it is important to try to ease users' expectations into a more realistic view.

Here's a scenario that you may already be familiar with. You've developed the application and you're ready to implement it, or you've already distributed your application to a pilot group performing a *user acceptance test (UAT),* which is a common testing phase performed by the user community before they accept any application into their production environment. Or better still, you've rolled out the shiny new application to the complete user environment. So you either a) make plans for a well-deserved vacation or b) start a new project to make use of the current development momentum. Then the difficulties begin, slowly at first, with just a trickle of complaints about how long it is taking to open a window, save a transaction, or run a report. The complaints escalate until finally the system crashes or the administrator is forced to shut it down and restart it because it is no longer responding. You've then got to deal with angry users who cannot understand how this has happened.

You are now going to start an investigation. However, because of the number of interconnected products, layers, and possibilities involved in a client/server application, this task is similar to finding a needle in a haystack, in that it will take a considerable amount of time and effort to diagnose the symptoms, determine where the problems are, and then implement the appropriate solution. Welcome to the world of performance and tuning – a nightmare if ever there was one. But it need not be, with the right amount of *planning* and *execution.*

Performance tuning usually begins with an issue that needs to be addressed. The issue can arise from a complaint from users, or a decision about application or database design, hardware, and software acquisitions, or some other capacity of planning concern. Before your project gets started down the road to potential trouble, take the steps necessary to help quickly address these issues and solve these problems. You can do this by laying down the foundations of a support structure for capturing and tracking incidents and problems and any additional data that can help you to tune the performance of an application.

Preparing for performance tuning

Before you get down to the task of using any tools to measure the performance of any application, you will need to gather some basic information about your environments and then establish a way to keep track of problems or incidents as they arise.

DOCUMENTING YOUR ENVIRONMENT

It is important to standardize and document the hardware and software environments that the application is being tested on. These include the developer workstations, the testing workstations, and ultimately the end-user workstations that the application will run on. In the case of a commercial product, you will have difficulty representing the myriad of hardware and software combinations that are potentially available. But it will still make sense to at least try the product out on a multitude of configurations ranging from low end to high end. If the product is being developed for in-house use, you probably will be able to control the environment issues a little more easily. Many companies standardize on a small number of hardware vendors and very specific configurations of hard disk, memory, and processor. This standard is usually fixed for between one and three years, and you should be able to research, define, and publish the configuration settings that work with your application.

TRACKING INCIDENTS AND PROBLEMS

An essential tool for the support of an application and its performance is some sort of central log (preferably a database table or spreadsheet) that can be used to track any incidents or unexpected behavior or problems with the application. This database should contain general information describing the incident as well as any other information that may be useful when analyzing the success of the application. Some ideas for the type of information that you should consider tracking are listed in Table 14-1.

TABLE 14-1 INFORMATION YOU CAN TRACK

Attribute	Description
Number	Incremental number allocated to a new problem or incident
Description	Details of the problem or incident to be investigated
Priority	For example, 1=high, 5=low
Severity	For example, 1=high, 5=low
Status	Current status (OPEN, CLOSED)
Occurrence	Number of times the problem or incident has been reported
Symptom	Predefined characteristics attached to the problem
Keyword	Predefined attributes that you attach to the problem or incident
Environment	Predefined code representing hardware/software definition
Notes	Additional notes

You should also set up a supplement to this log to track any changes to the status of an existing problem or incident. The kinds of things that need to be logged are shown in Table 14-2.

TABLE 14-2 TRACKING CHANGES IN STATUS

Attribute	Description
Date	Date of action
Time	Time of action
Build	Build version number
Cycle	Cycle in which the action took place
By	Person taking the action
Action	Action taken (opened, closed, and pending)
To	Person affected by the action
Status	Status after action

These logs should help you to analyze and determine when, where, and under what conditions the system is failing or its performance is less than adequate. These incidents must record as much information as possible about the environment, the time of day of the incident, and any possible parameters used that lead to the error or unacceptable response.

UNDERSTANDING TYPES OF PERFORMANCE DATA

Performance data typically comes in two types:

◆ Short-term, or *snapshot,* data is returned by monitoring tools that show information while the activity is still in progress – a quick picture if you like. Snapshot data is useful when you try to evaluate and react to a current performance issue.

◆ Long-term data is useful for proactive planning or strategy. Monitoring tools usually provide the capability for performance data to be logged to disk. This logged data can then be used to produce reports that can be compared to previous instances. This will help identify where significant changes have occurred in the system's use over a longer period of time. These changes can help predict future system use and allow you to plan accordingly.

Diagnosing and curing problems

What follows is a step-by-step approach to problem solving or diagnosing the problem and some examples of ways to speed up your system if it is already exhibiting performance problems.

When a performance problem is encountered, the first and most important step is to ensure that the correct problem is resolved. Many hours and countless amounts of money can be spent solving the wrong problem. An example of this mistake might be to upgrade to a faster CPU and then to find out that the real problem was an insufficient amount of, or badly configured, memory resources. Here are the steps to take to correctly diagnose a performance problem:

1. **Investigate.** The first step is to adequately define the problem. This begins with the capture of as much of the pertinent information as possible. This can include performance measures of the components being used. Use as many of the SQL Server tools as necessary to gather performance data at the lowest component levels.

2. **Assess.** Compare the component performance data to established standards, or an estimate of what seems reasonable. Highlight the exceptions and consider them first for tuning.

3. **Tune.** Focus on making changes to one resource at a time. This is so that you can determine exactly how successful, or unsuccessful, the change is.

4. **Re-evaluate.** Compare the new results to the previously problematic one. Even if the problem appears to be resolved, it makes sense that you regression-test the remaining parts of your system to ensure that you haven't transferred the problem elsewhere.

Prior release issues

If you are currently using SQL Server 6.*x*, note that many of the problems you may encounter have been addressed in SQL Server 7.0 (see Table 14-3 for more details).

TABLE 14-3 PROBLEMS IN 6.X THAT HAVE BEEN RESOLVED IN 7.0

SQL 6.x Problem	SQL Server 7.0 Resolution
Costly B-tree page splitting overhead	A revised storage structure has significantly reduced this problem.

Continued

TABLE 14-3 PROBLEMS IN 6.X THAT HAVE BEEN RESOLVED IN 7.0 *(Continued)*

SQL 6.x Problem	SQL Server 7.0 Resolution
Frequent tuning of lazy writer	Now the product automatically configures and tunes the lazy writer. You don't need to manually tune `free buffer` and `max lazywrite IO`.
Frequent tuning of checkpoint	Now the product automatically monitors and tunes the recovery interval when the recovery interval option is set to 0.
Difficult to easily spread a table across disks	Now there is an easy way to spread data across disk drives through the files and filegroups that replace the device/segment model.
Too many configuration tuning options.	Now the product is largely self-configuring, self-tuning, and self-managing. The `max async IO` option is the only option that may need configuring for large amounts of storage.
Mixing of the log pages with data pages in the cache.	Now the log manager has its own cache. Separation has enhanced performance for both components.

The `max async IO` option should be reviewed and adjusted if necessary during your initial configuration of SQL Server 7.0. The `max async IO` option default of 32 is sufficient for low-end disk subsystems. If you have a high-end RAID storage subsystem that is capable of high disk I/O transfer rates attached to a database server, you can adjust the setting higher to issue more simultaneous disk transfer requests. If the SQL Server write activity also dictates the need for more disk transfer capability, the `max async IO` option should be set higher. Here is an example of how to change this setting:

```
sp_configure 'max async io', 64
```

A quick rule of thumb for SQL Servers running on large disk subsystems is to set the max async IO value to two or three times the number of physical drives available for simultaneous I/O. Use the Performance Monitor to look for signs of disk activity or queuing issues. If you set this value too high, the checkpoint process will hog disk subsystem bandwidth, denying other I/O operations such as reads.

To set the max async IO option value, execute this command in SQL Server Query Analyzer where *value* is expressed as the number of simultaneous disk I/O requests that SQL Server system can submit to the Windows operating system during a checkpoint operation, which in turn submits the requests to the physical disk subsystem.

Server Considerations

The areas that affect database server performance are obviously limited to the hardware being used and, less obviously, to the configuration of the operating system and database management system software. The latter is largely affected by parameters that can be changed or *tuned*. This sections deal with the server's various hardware components and software settings that affect performance.

What affects database performance?

To improve performance, you must first understand what server resources are used and how they collectively affect server performance. In trying to measure the response time for a database access within an application, focus on the time that it takes for a query to be sent from the client to the database server, execute the necessary query, and return the result to the client. If you ignore, or discount, the time that it takes for the message to be formatted, sent, and carried over the network, and focus on the time that is being consumed with processing on the database server, we can summarize the major resources that affect server performance into the following list (see Figure 14-1):

- ◆ Central processing unit (CPU)
- ◆ Volatile storage (memory)
- ◆ Persistent storage (disk)

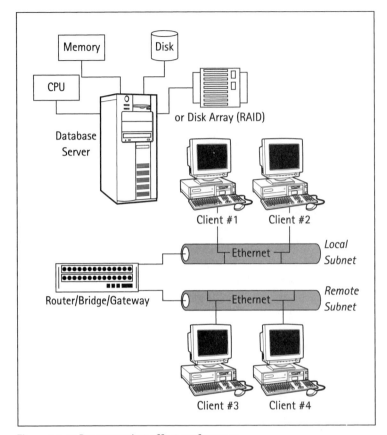

Figure 14-1: Resources that affect performance

VOLATILE STORAGE (MEMORY)

Memory is only a factor if a) your system does not have enough of it or b) it is dedicated to an unused type of processing. In both cases, if you limit the amount of memory that a process within a system has, performance will be directly affected. With the relatively low cost-to-benefit ratio of memory, making that extra investment in more memory up front will pay great dividends in the future.

CENTRAL PROCESSING UNIT (CPU)

The CPU component controls the entire application process. The CPU processing speed greatly affects all performance. There are many standard measures of relative CPU speed. The two most common are millions of instructions per second (MIPS) and millions of floating operations per second (MFLOPS). These measurements are quite narrow in focus and may be of little use when determining the type and amount of CPU resources that your product will require.

PERSISTENT STORAGE (DISK)

Disk storage is ultimately where all database information, or data, will reside; disks usually consist of one or more magnetic plates, or *platters*. These platters are accessed by one or more read/write heads. In the case of multiple head and platter devices, the data is stored across the magnetic surfaces in what is commonly known as a *cylinder* (see Figure 14-2).

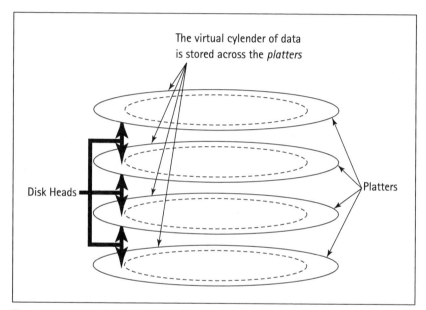

Figure 14-2: Typical disk configuration

When required, the disk read/write head traverses back and forth across the magnetic surface, in a motion that is known as *seeking*. The time that it takes to move to the required cylinder is known as *seek time*. The disk rotates at a very high speed, and the device waits until the required area is in position under the head before reading or writing; this waiting time is known as *latency time*. The *transfer time* is the speed that a specified amount of data can be transferred to or from the disk. A typical disk measurement is *access time,* which is usually calculated as follows:

access time = seek time + latency time + transfer time

Disk manufacturers provide these disk statistics for side-by-side comparison.

OTHER COMPONENTS THAT USE SERVER RESOURCES

There are additional parts, or components, of SQL Server that consume resources. These components will have an effect on the performance of your SQL Server queries, so you should take them into account when assessing the performance of your server.

CHECKPOINT   The checkpoint process writes out dirty pages to the SQL Server data files. A *dirty page* is a page that has been modified since being brought into the buffer cache. A buffer written to disk by checkpoint still contains the page, and users can read or update it without rereading it from disk. You can adjust the checkpoint behavior by using the `sp_configure` option `max async IO`, which sets the number of 8KB cache flushes that can be simultaneously submitted to the operating system and consequently to the disk subsystem. If this option is set too high and excessive disk queuing is occurring, you should decrease this option or add more disks to the disk subsystem.

LAZY WRITER   The lazy writer's job is to free up cache buffers. These are 8KB data pages in the cache that contain no data. Each freed-up page is marked so that it can be used by other data. Lazy writer produces free buffers during periods of low disk I/O, so disk I/O resources are readily available for use, and there is minimal impact on other SQL Server operations. SQL Server automatically configures and manages the level of free buffers.

You can also adjust the lazy writer behavior by using the `sp_configure` option `max async IO`, which sets the number of 8KB cache flushes that can be simultaneously submitted to the operating system and consequently to the disk subsystem. Again, if this option is set too high, it will cause excessive disk queuing.

LOG MANAGER   All write activity (inserts, updates, and deletes) performed on the database is logged to help recoverability in the event that the server crashes. Before any transaction can be completed, the Log Manager must receive notification from the disk I/O subsystem that the transaction has been written successfully to the log file. This guarantees that the SQL Server databases can be recovered by reading and applying what is in the transaction log when the server is restarted.

READ AHEAD MANAGER   The Read Ahead Manager process is integrated with the query processor operations. When the query processor identifies a situation that will benefit from doing read-ahead scans (reading consecutive pages of data), it tells the Read Ahead Manager. Large table scans, large index range scans, and probes into clustered and nonclustered index B-trees are situations that would benefit from a read-ahead.

WORKER THREADS   SQL Server maintains a pool of *worker threads* (at the operating system level) to take care of batches of commands submitted to the server. The maximum number of these threads is set using the `sp_configure` option `max worker threads`. The worker threads will be shared among connections if the number of connections submitting batches exceeds the maximum number of worker threads.

Partitioning tables

Partitioning a database can improve performance. When you split a large table into smaller, individual tables, queries accessing only a fraction of the data will run faster. Also note that maintenance tasks, such as index rebuilds or back, will execute quicker.

You can also partition your database by placing a table on one physical drive and related tables on a separate drive. SQL Server filegroups can be used to specify on which disks to place the tables. Let's look at specific kinds of partitioning.

HARDWARE PARTITIONING

Hardware partitioning designs the database to take advantage of the available hardware architecture. Examples of hardware partitioning include:

- Multiprocessors that allow multiple threads of execution, permitting many queries to execute at the same time. Alternatively, a single query may be able to run faster on multiple processors by parallelizing. For example, each table referenced in the query can be scanned at the same time by a different thread.

- RAID (Redundant Array of Independent Disks) devices that allow data to be striped across multiple disk drives, permitting faster access to the data because more read/write heads read data at the same time. A table striped across multiple drives can typically be scanned faster than the same table stored on one drive. Alternatively, storing tables on separate drives from related tables can significantly improve the performance of queries joining those tables.

HORIZONTAL PARTITIONING

Horizontal partitioning segments a table into multiple tables, each containing the same number of columns but obviously fewer rows. Partitioning data horizontally on the basis of age/use is common. For example, a table may contain data for the last three years, but only data from the current year is regularly accessed. In this case, you could divide the data into three tables, with each table containing data from a single year.

VERTICAL PARTITIONING

Vertical partitioning segments a table into multiple tables containing fewer columns. There are two types of vertical partitioning: normalization and row splitting. *Normalization* is the process of removing redundant columns from a table and placing them in secondary tables. By eliminating as many columns as possible from the frequently accessed tables, you will reduce I/O and increase performance. *Row splitting* divides the original table vertically into tables with fewer columns. Each logical row in a split table matches the same logical row in the others. For example, joining the hundredth row from each split table reconstructs the original row.

Tuning input/output

SQL Server 7.0 has been significantly reengineered for optimum performance. Keep the following in mind if you decide to perform any tuning:

◆ Don't consume all RAM with unneeded columns.

◆ Create an appropriate number of indexes; too few or too many hurt performance. Use the Profiler and Index Tuning Wizard to help in the analysis.

◆ Ensure the disk I/O subsystem is the right match.

◆ Examine and tune all of your application queries. Use the graphical Showplan and Query Analyzer to help in the analysis.

◆ Use Performance Monitor to help with analysis.

RAID

When scaling databases more than a few gigabytes (GB), you should have at least a basic understanding of RAID (Redundant Array of Inexpensive Disks) technology and how it relates to database performance. Figure 14-3 depicts the same amount of user data configured for the most typically used RAID levels.

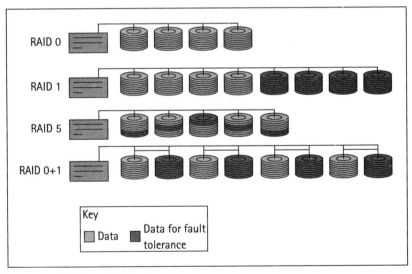

Figure 14-3: Typical RAID levels

RAID 1 and RAID 0+1 offer the best data protection and best performance among RAID levels but cost more because of the extra disks required. RAID 5 provides fault tolerance at the lowest cost but takes twice as long as RAID 1 and 0+1 on disk writes because of the additional I/O for the parity information. RAID 5 is not as fault tolerant as RAID 1 and 0+1. RAID 0 (disk striping with no fault-tolerance protection) gives the best disk I/O performance because it has no fault-tolerance overhead. RAID 0 is very good for development environments and also is suitable for testing environments that do not need to give an indication of the production performance.

Implementing indexes

Typically all database vendor indexing methods are implemented through what is known as a *B+ tree,* which is a set of nodes, or pages, that contain index keys and pointers that are arranged in a hierarchy.

SQL Server data and index pages are each 8KB. The data pages contain all of the data associated with rows of a table, except text and image data. For text and image data, the data page contains a pointer to a B-tree structure of one or more 8KB pages. The index pages contain only data from columns that make up a particular index. So if a query is selecting rows from a table that has a WHERE clause on an indexed column equal to a set of values, then the database server will read the index pages for that column and match them to the specified set of values.

The matched index key rows contain the pointer to the data rows that the server can then access and return in the result set. The indexes are built upon B-tree structures, with the upper parts of B-tree being referred to as the *nonleaf* (or root) levels of the index and the lower parts being referred to as the *leaf* levels. In a nonclustered index, the leaf levels contain the data for the index. In the nonclustered index leaf levels, index rows contain pointers to the actual row data on the associated data page. Figure 14-4 shows a diagram depicting these differences.

Your choice of indexes will significantly affect the performance of your queries. A nonclustered index is suitable for queries that retrieve a small number of rows or rows that are spread throughout the table's data pages. Clustered indexes are better for queries that return ranges of data. For example, a query that returned all employees with an emp_type = 'P' would be better serviced by a nonclustered index on the emp_type column. A query that returned all employees with a emp_id between 10000 and 25000 would be better serviced by a clustered index on emp_id.

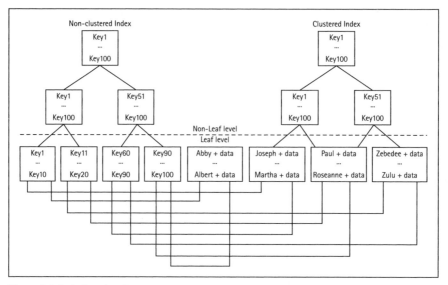

Figure 14-4: Index structure

Using the FILLFACTOR and PAD_INDEX options

If a table has a considerable amount of insert activity, then it is a good candidate for the performance problems associated with page splitting. A page split occurs when the page is full and yet, because of the logical ordering of data defined for this page, a new row has to be inserted into this page. So SQL Server splits the page (hence the name) in two by moving half of the data to a new page, leaving each page with open space. This takes time and system resources to carry out. You can help to avoid this overhead by providing and maintaining the open space on pages before it becomes an issue.

The FILLFACTOR option on the CREATE INDEX and DBCC DBREINDEX statements provides a way to specify the percentage of open space to leave on pages. The PAD_INDEX option on the CREATE INDEX statement applies what has been specified for FILLFACTOR to the nonleaf level (root) index pages. Without the PAD_INDEX option, FILLFACTOR largely affects the leaf-level index pages of clustered indexes.

To monitor for excessive page splits, you can use the Performance Monitor and watch the SQL Server: Access Methods - Page Splits object counter. If a value greater than zero appears during periods of high insert activity, then this indicates excessive page splitting. (You can also use the DBCC SHOWCONTIG command to view the *scan density,* which should be as close to 100 percent as possible.) If you choose to rebuild a clustered index, do it with the DROP_EXISTING option. This will enable you to recreate the index faster than if you chose to explicitly drop the index and then recreate it.

Running a query in parallel

SQL Server can run on single or multiple CPU systems. On the multiple CPU, or Symmetric Multiprocessing (SMP), systems, the processors share the system resources, that is, disk, memory, and bus. The operating system is responsible for spreading the workload among the CPU's processors, such that as processors are added, the performance is typically improved. This ability is also known as *scalability*. The advantage of an SMP system is that it can execute tasks simultaneously, one task for each processor. This scalability varies among the various hardware and operating system vendors. Most, if not all, systems have a limit of the number of CPUs that they can utilize, after which no additional performance advantage is perceived.

Nonetheless, a single task will still not run any faster on an SMP system than it will on a single CPU system, assuming that both systems had the same model CPU and other resources were similarly matched. This is because the single task can only run on one processor, while all other processors execute other tasks or remain idle.

However, many vendors have come up with a way of utilizing the extra CPUs and completing the task in a shorter amount of time by dividing a task into smaller subtasks, or *threads*. Each subtask is able to execute, in parallel, on its own CPU. Microsoft has engineered the SQL Server product for this type of parallel processing. The SQL Server product can execute the following subtasks in parallel:

◆ Aggregation

◆ Grouping

◆ Index building

◆ Recovery

◆ Scanning

◆ Sorting

By performing a query in parallel using several operating system threads, SQL Server can complete complex queries quicker. During query optimization, SQL Server looks for queries that might benefit from parallel execution. For these queries, SQL Server inserts exchange operators into the query execution plan to prepare the query for parallel execution. An *exchange operator* is an operator in a query execution plan that provides process management, data redistribution, and flow control. After exchange operators are inserted, the result is a *parallel query execution plan*. A parallel query execution plan can use more than one thread, whereas a serial execution plan, used by a nonparallel query, uses only a single thread for its execution. The actual number of threads used by a parallel query is determined at query plan execution initialization and is called the degree of parallelism.

SQL Server automatically detects the best degree of parallelism for each instance of a parallel query execution by considering the following:

♦ Is this a computer with several processors? Only computers with more than one processor can take advantage of parallel queries.

♦ What number of concurrent users are active? SQL Server monitors CPU use and adjusts the degree of parallelism at the query startup time. It will lower the degree of parallelism if the system's CPUs are already very busy.

♦ Is enough memory available? A parallel query requires more memory to execute than a nonparallel query. If not enough memory is available for a given degree of parallelism, SQL Server either decreases the degree of parallelism or abandons the parallel plan for the query and executes a serial plan.

♦ What type of query is being executed? Queries that heavily utilize the CPU cycles are the best candidates for parallel optimization. So the best candidates are queries with joins of large tables, substantial aggregations (for example, SUM and COUNT), and sorting (for example, ORDER BY) of large result sets. SQL Server compares the estimated cost of executing the query with the "cost threshold for parallelism" server setting to determine if a query will benefit from parallelization. The cost threshold for parallelism option is, by default, set to 5. It can be changed to any value from 0 through 32767 using the sp_configure command.

♦ Are we dealing with a large number of rows? If the optimizer determines that the number of rows is too low, it does not create a parallel plan.

Additional Considerations

Having tuned the database server, you can also take a look at a few other areas for performance improvement.

Deadlocking

If you have several transactions, or functions, that update two or more of the same tables, there is the potential for a deadlock. For example, we have two transactions. Both transactions update the same three tables.

Transaction 1

```
BEGIN TRANACTION ONE
UPDATE TABLEA ...//remainder of the update statement
UPDATE TABLEB ...//remainder of the update statement
```

```
UPDATE TABLEC ...//remainder of the update statement
COMMIT TRANSACTION ONE
```

   Transaction 2

```
BEGIN TRANSACTION TWO
UPDATE TABLEC ...//remainder of the update statement
UPDATE TABLEB ...//remainder of the update statement
UPDATE TABLEA ...//remainder of the update statement
COMMIT TRANSACTION TWO
```

If these two transactions are executing at the same time, then Transaction 1 has updated (and therefore locked) TABLEA and TABLEB, and it is about to obtain a lock on TABLEC. At the same time, Transaction 2 has updated (and therefore locked) TABLEC and is now about to obtain a lock on TABLEB. At this point both transactions will be unable to proceed because the resource that each transaction requires is being locked by the other, hence the term *deadly embrace* or *deadlock*. To avoid this situation, make sure that the updates of the tables occur in the same order for both transactions.

Syntax to avoid

Using the "not equals" operators in queries will force the server to perform a table scan to calculate the inequalities. This will result in excessive I/O if this query is performed on a large table. For example, look at the following query:

```
SELECT * FROM TB_EXP_HIST
WHERE EXP_STATUS_CDE != "ABC"  // != can also be <>
```

This query can be rewritten to avoid the inequality test, thus:

```
SELECT * FROM TB_EXP_HIST
WHERE (EXP_STATUS_CDE < "ABC"
OR EXP_STATUS_CDE > "ABC")
```

The query will then be able to use an index (ideally a clustered one) because you have specified a range instead.

Network capacity

On systems with a large number of clients accessing a database server, the administrator is duty bound to examine and monitor the network closely, making adjustments to the database server where necessary. When a network is overloaded, systems will most likely try to send packets over the network at the same time, causing collisions. If the network software detects a collision, it will resend the packet. This duplication of work will delay messages passed back and forth between the application and the database. A certain number of collisions within a network are normal. However, if your network is experiencing collisions for a prolonged period of time, it will probably mean that the network should be either upgraded or reconfigured.

Some obvious network-configurable parameters that you may consider altering are:

♦ **Window Size.** The number of messages sent before an acknowledgment. This is typically a 1:1 ratio; you may see better utilization by increasing the size to 5.

♦ **Packet Size.** The number of bytes per message. A large number is better suited to DSS, and a smaller size is potentially (depending on the size of the message) better suited to OLTP.

Reducing network traffic

An obvious way to avoid congestion on a network is to reduce the amount of traffic or move some of it elsewhere. Most corporate networks are collections of subnetworks interconnected by one or more routers. If the client workstations are on a different subnetwork than the database server, then any traffic is *hopping* from one subnetwork to the other. If the subnetworks are configured with multiple routers in between, then this hopping, or hop count, will possibly delay the messaging, and you may consider connecting the database server to the same subnetwork as the majority of the clients. This will allow the simultaneous database connection to multiple subnetworks rather than letting the traffic flow through, and become delayed by, a combination of routers.

Look for opportunities to reduce the size of the result set by eliminating columns in the select list that do not have to be returned, or by returning only the required rows. This reduces I/O and CPU consumption.

There are some programming techniques that can reduce the amount of network traffic. For example, you can use stored procedures for tasks that have groups of SQL statements, because they reduce the number and size of messages. In other words, you'll be sending one message containing the call to the stored procedure in place of several messages, each containing individual SQL transactions. Additionally, ensuring that the database takes care of referential integrity, instead of coding it in the application, will also reduce unnecessary traffic. Your application should request the smallest amount of data necessary to support the application. For example, do not construct your application so that it retrieves more rows and/or columns than it needs in order to provide the required functionality. Equally, your application should not retrieve data that it does not display to the user.

SQL Server Monitoring and Tuning Tools

Database issues will regularly require you to use the monitoring and tuning tools that are provided with SQL Server 7. These tools enable you to look at internal data that is maintained by the database server (see Figure 14-5).

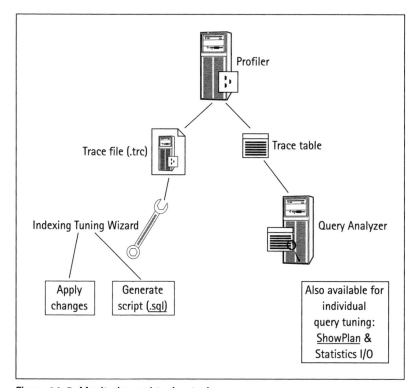

Figure 14-5: Monitoring and tuning tools

The tools that you can use for monitoring and subsequent tuning are:

◆ Profiler

◆ Index Tuning Wizard

◆ Query Analyzer (including Statistics I/O and Showplan)

◆ Performance Monitor (See Chapter 15, "Debugging," for details.)

The Profiler (called SQL Trace in SQL Server 6.*x*) can be configured to record and save information about server activity. This information includes, but is not limited to, I/O and CPU statistics, locking requests, Transact-SQL and RPC statistics, index and table scans, warnings and errors raised, stored procedure operations, and cursor operations.

Using the Profiler and the Index Tuning Wizard

The Profiler can record resource consumption information in a trace (.trc) file. The Index Tuning Wizard can read and evaluate the trace file and provide recommendations for indexes that should be created (or dropped).

To feed the Index Tuning Wizard:

1. Start SQL Server Profiler.

2. On the File menu, point to New, and then click Trace.

3. Type a name for the trace.

4. Check the Capture to File check box and enter the name of the trace (.trc) file.

5. Run the query for which you want to determine the appropriate indexes.

6. On the File menu, click Stop Traces.

7. In the Stop Selected Traces dialog box, choose to stop the trace that you created in Step 3.

Index Tuning Wizard can either automatically create the proper indexes for the database by scheduling the automatic index creation or generate a Transact-SQL script that can be reviewed and executed later.

These are the steps for analyzing a query load:

1. Choose Index Tuning Wizard on the Tools menu of Profiler.

2. Select the database and click Next.

3. Choose I have a saved workload file and click Next.

4. Choose My workload file, locate and enter the trace filename, click OK, and then click Next.

5. In Select Tables to Tune, choose the tables and click Next.

6. In Index Recommendations, choose the indexes you want to create and click Next.

7. In Schedule Index Update Job, either choose to apply the changes now or at a specified time, or choose to save the index DDL to a script file. Click Next, and finally click Finish.

The Profiler and Index Tuning Wizard are powerful tools that you should run frequently to see if queries on rapidly changing tables have changed to the extent that they require a different set of indexes to deliver the maximum performance.

Using the Profiler and the Query Analyzer

The Profiler can also record trace information in a database table. This table can then be used by Query Analyzer to determine if specific queries are using excessive amounts of resources.

To feed the Query Analyzer:

1. Start SQL Server Profiler.

2. On the File menu, point to New, and then click Trace.

3. Type a name for the trace.

4. Check the Capture to Table check box and enter the name of the table.

5. Run the query for which you want to determine the appropriate indexes.

6. On the File menu, click Stop Traces.

7. In the Stop Selected Traces dialog box, choose to stop the trace that you created in Step 3.

After the information is recorded into the SQL Server table (Table 14-4 shows the list and description of the columns in a trace table), you can write your own queries in the Query Analyzer to determine which queries on the system are consuming the most resources. For example:

```
select top 10
    convert(varchar(50),textdata) Operation,
    duration,
    cpu,
    reads,
    writes
from mytracetable
order by cpu desc
```

The preceding query displays the top ten consumers of CPU resources on the server. It also displays the Duration, Read, and Write I/O information.

TABLE 14-4 TRACE TABLE COLUMNS

Column	Description
EventClass	See Table 14-5 for more on event classes
TextData	(Dependent on context)
ConnectionID	Database connection ID
NTUserName	Windows NT login name
ApplicationName	Application generating the workload
SQLUserName	SQL login name
SPID	Server Process ID
Duration	Amount of time for the duration of this event (milliseconds)
StartTime	Date and time the trace started
Reads	Number of I/O reads
Writes	Number of I/O writes
CPU	Amount of CPU usage

If you run an analysis query on a significantly large trace table and it is taking a long time, you can consider creating indexes on the trace table to speed the analysis. Table 14-5 provides a list of event classes that appear in a trace table.

TABLE 14-5 EVENT CLASSES

Value	Event Class	Description
0	TraceStart	Trace has started.
1	TracePause	Trace has paused.
2	TraceRestart	Trace has restarted.
3	TraceAutoPause	Trace is in automatic pause state.
4	TraceAutoRestart	Trace is in automatic restart state.
5	TraceStop	Trace has stopped.

Value	Event Class	Description
6	EventRequired	Trace is in events to trace changed state.
7	FilterChanged	Trace is in a filter changed state.
8		Reserved.
9		Reserved.
10	RPC:Completed	Remote procedure call (RPC) is completed.
11	RPC:Starting	RPC has started.
12	SQL:BatchCompleted	Transact-SQL batch is completed.
13	SQL:BatchStarting	Transact-SQL batch is starting.
14	Connect	Client requested a connection to a server.
15	Disconnect –	Client issued a disconnect command.
16	Attention	Client-interrupt request or broken client connection.
17	ExistingConnection	User that was logged in before trace started.
18	ServiceControl	Server control events, such as pause or restart.
19	DTCTransaction	MS DTC cross database coordinated transactions.
20	LoginFailed	Login attempt to SQL Server from a client failed.
21	EventLog	Event logged to the NT application log.
22	ErrorLog	Event logged to the SQL Server error log.
23	Lock:Released	Resource has been released from a lock.
24	Lock:Acquired	A resource has been locked.

Continued

TABLE 14-5 EVENT CLASSES *(Continued)*

Value	Event Class	Description
25	Lock:Deadlock	Two transactions are trying at the same time to obtain locks on resources the other transaction owns, causing a deadly embrace.
26	Lock:Cancel	Lock acquisition on a resource has been canceled (possible due to deadlocking).
27	Lock:Timeout –	Lock acquisition has timed out. Time-out is determined by the @@LOCK_TIMEOUT function and can be set with the SET LOCK_TIMEOUT statement.
28	Insert	Just before an INSERT statement.
29	Update	Just before an UPDATE statement.
30	Delete	Just before a DELETE statement.
31	Select	Just before a SELECT statement.
32	ConnectionBeingKilled	Connection is being killed.
33	Exception	An exception has occurred in SQL Server.
34	SP:CacheMiss	A stored procedure is not found in the procedure cache.
35	SP:CacheInsert	An item is inserted into the procedure cache.
36	SP:CacheRemove	An item is removed from the procedure cache.
37	SP:Recompile	Stored procedure is recompiling.
38	SP:CacheHit	Stored procedure is found in the procedure cache.
39	SP:ExecContextHit	Execution version of a stored procedure has been found in the procedure cache.

Value	Event Class	Description
40	SQL:StmtStarting	Transact-SQL statement is starting.
41	SQL:StmtCompleted	Transact-SQL statement has completed.
42	SP:Starting	Stored procedure has started.
43	SP:Completed	Stored procedure has completed.
44	SP:StmtStarting	Statement within a stored procedure is starting.
45	SP:StmtCompleted	Statement within a stored procedure has completed.
46	Object:Created	Object has been created, for example, via CREATE INDEX, CREATE TABLE, and CREATE DATABASE.
47	Object:Deleted	Object has been deleted, for example, via DROP INDEX or DROP TABLE.
48	Object:Opened	Object has been accessed, for example, via SELECT, INSERT, or DELETE.
49	Object:Closed	Object has been closed, for example, after SELECT, INSERT, or DELETE.
50	SQLTransaction	Occurs on BEGIN, COMMIT, SAVE, and ROLLBACK TRANSACTION.
51	Scan:Started	A table or index scan has started.
52	Scan:Stopped	A table or index scan has stopped.
53	CursorOpen	A cursor has been opened on a table by ODBC or DB-Library.
54	TransactionLog	A transaction is written to the transaction log.

Continued

Table **14–5 EVENT CLASSES** *(Continued)*

Value	Event Class	Description
55	HashWarning	A hashing operation (for example, a hash join, hash aggregate, hash union, or hash distinct) that is not processing on a buffer partition has reverted to an alternate plan. This can occur because of recursion depth, data skew, trace flags, or bit counting.
56		Reserved.
57		Reserved.
58	Auto-UpdateStats	An automatic updating of index statistics event.
59	Lock:Deadlock Chain	Event leading up to a deadlock.
60	Lock:Escalation	Lock level has increased (for example, row lock escalated to page lock).
61	OLEDB Errors	OLE DB error has occurred.
62	Replay Error	Error returned by ODBC.
63	Replay Internal Error	Internal replay error.
64	Replay Result Set	Beginning of a result set returned by a query.
65	Replay Result Row	Each row returned from a replay result set.
66		Reserved.
67	Execution Warnings	Warnings that occurred during the execution of a SQL Server statement or stored procedure.
68	Execution Plan	Displays the plan tree of the statement being executed.
69	Sort Warnings	Indicates sort operations that do not fit into memory, i.e., very big ones.

Value	Event Class	Description
70	CursorPrepare	Cursor has been prepared on a statement by ODBC or DB-Library.
71	Prepare SQL	ODBC, OLE DB, or DB-Library has prepared a statement.
72	Exec Prepared SQL	ODBC, OLE DB, or DB-Library has executed a prepared statement.
73	Unprepare SQL	ODBC, OLE DB, or DB-Library has unprepared (deleted) a prepared statement.
74	CursorExecute	Prepared cursor is executed.
75	CursorRecompile	Cursor has been recompiled either directly or due to a schema change.
76	CursorImplicitConversion	Cursor converted from one type to another.
77	CursorUnprepare	Cursor is unprepared (deleted).
78	CursorClose	Previously opened cursor is closed.
79	Missing Column Statistics	Possibly useful column statistics are not available to the query optimizer.
80	Missing Join Predicate	Multiple table query is being executed without join predicate (potentially long running!).
81	Server Memory Change	SQL Server memory usage has increased or decreased by either 1MB or 5 percent of the maximum server memory, whichever is greater.
82	UserConfigurable:1	User configurable event.
83	UserConfigurable:2	User configurable event.
84	UserConfigurable:3	User configurable event.
85	UserConfigurable:4	User configurable event.
86	UserConfigurable:5	User configurable event.

Using the Query Analyzer alone

If you choose to analyze queries without using the Profiler to capture trace information, there are a couple of features that can help in determining inefficiencies. They are called Showplan and Statistics I/O.

STATISTICS INPUT/OUTPUT

You can obtain information regarding disk activity generated for each table referenced in a query statement. This option is a helpful way to monitor the effect of query tuning. To show this information along with the results, go to the Current Connections Options dialog box. The General tab contains a check box for Show stats I/O.

```
Table 'Winery'. Scan count 176, logical reads 378, physical reads 1,
read-ahead reads 0.
Table 'Wine'. Scan count 1, logical reads 4, physical reads 0, read-
ahead reads 0.
```

The preceding example output shows the result of a query that joins two tables. The information shown includes the name of the table being used, the number of scans performed, the number of pages read from the data cache and the disk, and the number of pages placed into the cache for the query.

SHOWPLAN

A query Showplan displays information about what the query optimizer is doing. There are two types of Showplan, a character-based version and a graphical version. To enable the character-based version, enter SET SHOWPLAN_ALL ON before your query. To enable the graphical Showplan, press the Ctrl and L keys simultaneously in the Query Analyzer window. The various icons represent the operations that the query optimizer will perform when the query is executed. The details of each operation are displayed when you hold the mouse pointer over the operation icon. The arrows designate the flow of data from each operation.

Summary

This chapter covered the area of performance and tuning, including the tools and the attitude that are required to succeed at it. We looked at what affects performance, and how the hardware and operating system configurations will have an effect. We looked at the monitoring and tuning tools that come with SQL Server and Windows NT. We've shown you how to tune and configure SQL Server. We also looked at how to tune your SQL code. You are now armed and ready to enhance your application and your SQL to measure the performance and hopefully improve it.

Chapter 15

Debugging

IN THIS CHAPTER

- ◆ Debugging issues
- ◆ What is a bug?
- ◆ Psychology of debugging
- ◆ Locating and correcting errors
- ◆ The debugging toolkit

DEBUGGING CONSIDERATIONS include problem determination and resolution. This chapter will discuss the fundamentals of debugging, including items to consider when attempting to locate a problem, and some of the tools that are available for the debugging process.

Debugging Issues

Debugging is the technique used to identify and resolve a problem within program code. It is typically a task that is created as a result of your testing process, for this is where you should detect as many of the errors as possible. On occasion, debugging may require as much as 50 percent of the time taken to develop your application, and it is often considered to be the toughest part of programming.

Debugging can be viewed in several ways. First, there are bugs known as syntax errors, which can most often be found visually or with the compiler. Then there are bugs that occur at execution time, such as a program not handling data exceptions — for example, alphabetic data where numeric data is expected. Finally, there is another kind of bug that is not really a bug per se. It's that the user encounters a result that is not anticipated, perhaps because the user is unfamiliar with the application. In any case, all of these bugs create feedback that will aid in improving the application.

In general, debugging is the means by which the programmer must determine what is or is not a problem. We may call our problems "bugs" because some programmers once traced a circuit malfunction to a large moth that had found its way into a computer. Most problems that we will experience, however, are not traceable to large moths. The truth of the matter is that these are errors within our code, and sooner or later the programmer will be called upon to resolve the problem.

Quality control through debugging

Although debugging should not be the only path to creating a high-quality application, it is your major tool in determining and ensuring the continued reliability of your application. Quality should be considered in the early design phase, and debugging is your tool to ensure that it is error free. Good coding practices, careful analysis, and superior design are all part of ensuring a quality application. Debugging is only a tool to assist you on your way.

Variations in debugging performance

Why talk about debugging? Doesn't everyone know how to debug? No, not everyone knows how to debug. Studies of experienced programmers have found that there is roughly a 20-to-1 range in the time it takes experienced programmers to find the same set of errors. Moreover, some programmers find more errors and make corrections more accurately. Table 15-1 shows the results of one study that examined how effectively professional programmers with at least four years of experience debugged a program with 12 errors.

TABLE 15-1 PROFICIENCY OF DEBUGGING

Measurement	Three Fastest Coders	Three Slowest Coders
Average debug time	5 minutes	14.1 minutes
Average number of errors not found	0.7	1.7
Average number of errors made correcting errors	3	7.7

Source: J.D. Gould, "Some Psychological Evidence on How People Debug Computer Programs," International Journal of Man-Machine Studies, Vol. 7, No. 2, 1975, pp. 151–182.

The three programmers who were best at debugging were able to find the defects in about one-third the time and made only about two-fifths as many errors as the three who were the worst. The best programmer found all the defects and didn't make any errors in correcting them. The worst missed 4 of the 12 defects and made 11 errors in correcting the 8 defects he found. This wide variation has been confirmed by other studies.

In addition to providing insight into debugging, the evidence supports the General Principle of Software Quality: Improving quality reduces development costs. The best programmers found the most errors, found the errors most quickly, and made correct modifications most often. You don't have to choose between quality, cost, and time; they all go hand in hand.

Using errors as opportunities

What does having an error mean? Assuming that you don't want the program to have errors, it means that you don't fully understand what the program does. The idea of not understanding what the program does is unsettling. After all, if you created the program, it should do your bidding. If you don't know exactly what you're telling the computer to do, you're merely trying different things until something seems to work. If you're programming by trial and error, errors are guaranteed. You don't need to learn how to fix errors; you need to learn how to avoid them in the first place.

Most people are somewhat fallible, however, and you might be an excellent programmer who has simply made a modest oversight. If this is the case, an error in your program represents a powerful opportunity. You can:

◆ **Learn about the program you're working on.** You have something to learn about the program because if you already knew it perfectly, it wouldn't have an error. You would have corrected it already.

◆ **Discover the kinds of mistakes that you made.** If you wrote the program, then it's you that have coded the error. It's not every day that you have an opportunity to learn about your mistakes. Once you find the mistake, ask why did you make it? How could you have found it more quickly? How could you have prevented it? Does the code have other mistakes that are the same or similar? Can you correct them now, before they cause problems?

◆ **Determine how readable your code is.** Somebody will have to read your code to find the error. This is an opportunity to look critically at the quality of your code. Is it easy to read? Can it be improved? Use what you have learned to make your future programs even better.

◆ **Find out how to solve problems.** Do you have confidence in your approach when attempting to debug your code? Does your approach work? Do you find errors quickly? Or are your debugging skills weak? Do you feel anguish and frustration? Do you guess randomly? Do you need to improve? Considering the amount of time spent debugging many projects, you definitely won't waste time if you observe how you debug. Take some time to analyze and change the way you debug; this might be the quickest way to decrease the total amount of time it takes you to develop a program.

◆ **Find the best way to correct errors.** In addition to learning how to locate your errors, you can learn how to fix them correctly. Do you make the simplest correction, by adding a `goto` statement or a simple workaround that doesn't completely eliminate the whole problem? Or do you systematically review, diagnose, and correct the problem?

All things considered, debugging is a valuable skill that needs to be developed and occasionally resharpened, allowing you to always improve an application. Debugging truly begins with the application creation process, for it is the readability, design, code quality, and so forth that allow us to build in the reliability, availability, and service-ability that all applications require. If the code is good to begin with, there is less time consumed in the debugging stage.

Taking an "ineffective" approach

Unfortunately, programming classes in colleges and universities hardly ever offer instruction in debugging. If you studied programming in college, you might have had a lecture devoted to debugging. Although our computer-science education was excellent, the extent of the debugging advice typically received was to "put print statements in the program to find the error." This is not adequate. If other programmers' educational experiences are like ours, then they are being forced to reinvent debugging concepts on their own. What a waste!

A Guide to Ineffective Debugging

Here's a simple, and all too common, guide to debugging:

◆ **Create a trail.** To locate an error, add print statements in many of the obvious areas throughout your program. Examine the output to determine where the error is. If you can't locate the error with print statements, try changing things in the program until something seems to work. Always keep a backup copy of the original program. Use a secondary copy for modifications; so you will be free to make whatever changes you deem necessary. Keep a record of the changes that you make; build a trail. Stock up on coffee and cake because you're in for a long night in front of your workstation.

◆ **Don't waste time trying to understand the problem.** It's likely that the problem is trivial, and you don't need to understand it completely to fix it. Simply finding it may be enough.

◆ **Correct the error with the most obvious fix.** It's usually good just to fix the specific problem you see, rather than wasting a lot of time making some big, ambitious correction that's going to affect the whole program. This is a perfect example:

```
x = Compute( y )
if ( y = 23 ) then x = 22.10
/* Compute()doesn't work for y = 23,so fix it */
```

In the preceding example, there is no need to look into the code for the Compute() function to correct an obscure problem with the value of 23 when you can just write a special case for it in the obvious place. How many times have you taken this approach?

Leaving your ego at home

If you have a problem with a program you've written, it's your fault. It's not the computer's fault, and it's not the compiler's fault. The program doesn't do something different every time. It didn't write itself; you wrote it, so take responsibility for it.

Even if an error appears not to be your fault, it's strongly in your interest to assume that it is. This assumption helps you to debug. It's hard enough to locate an error in your code when you're looking for it; the task only becomes even more formidable when you assume that your code is error-free. It also improves your credibility because when you do claim that an error arose in someone else's code, other programmers will believe that you have examined the problem carefully. Assuming the error is your fault also saves you the embarrassment of claiming that an error is someone else's fault and then having to recant publicly later when you find out that it was your error after all.

The psychology of debugging

Debugging is as intellectually demanding as any other software-development activity. Your ego tells you that your code is good and doesn't have an error, even when you have a problem in front of you. You have to be methodical, form a hypothesis, collect data, analyze the hypothesis, and methodically reject successive hypotheses with a formality that's unnatural to many people. If you're both building code and debugging it, you have to switch quickly between the process of creative thinking for the design and the critical thinking that goes with debugging. As you read your code, you must fight with the code's familiarity and guard against seeing what you expect to see.

DEBUGGING BLINDNESS

Your frame of mind contributes to debugging blindness. For instance, when you see a token in a program that says *int,* what do you see? Do you see a misspelling of the word "integrate"? Or do you see the abbreviation for "integer"? Most likely, you see the abbreviation for "integer." This is an integral part of your mindset. Are you seeing what is expected? Take the following into consideration:

- ◆ All programs do not operate in the same fashion; each programmer usually has a different style. Some use top-down programming techniques and *gotos,* whereas others refuse to use *gotos* and will only use functions or program calls. When they see code that contains *gotos,* for instance, they should not expect the *gotos* to be utilized as they would, but instead the code should be examined from point to point to see how the *gotos* are being used.

- ◆ When learning about *while* loops, we often expect the condition of the loop to be continuously evaluated until it is false and at that point the loop ends. However, it is important to remind ourselves that that the condition is only evaluated at the top or bottom of the while loop, not in the middle.

♦ Perhaps the most difficult errors to resolve are data movement errors, when we try to either convert data from one type to another, or just move data from one variable to another. Sometimes programmers are unable to determine what the data looked like before the error occurred, or how it got into our program in the first place. Often programmers look for off-by-one errors and side effects but overlook problems in simple statements, or perhaps erroneous data.

♦ Sometimes the problem can be very simple; for instance, let's say that two variables defined as VAR01 and VAR1 are being utilized within the same program. One might tend to believe that both are actually the same, and never take notice until unexpected results are produced from the program.

Why is our mindset so important when we have to debug some code? To begin with, if we think about debugging hard enough, we help reinforce good programming practices. We begin to appreciate the formatting style and insertion of meaningful comments. We realize the significance of naming conventions for our variables and functions within our programs. Finally, we design our programs so that they have a straightforward flow, which makes it easier and faster for us to pinpoint the area that is at fault.

Once we can focus on a specific area that we believe to be at fault, we feel a sense of accomplishment, which encourages us to delve further. All of these practices are contributing factors that make us better, more efficient programmers. At times, you may find that you have mistakenly chosen the wrong piece of code as the suspect code. This will happen, but life goes on, and you will once again realize that you are not superhuman. If you find yourself on the debugging treadmill, then just step off for a minute and come back with a different approach. Perhaps even discuss it with one of your peers, even if you must put your ego on the shelf for a short time.

If you find yourself taking an inordinate amount of time within a small section of code, you may decide that you have chosen the wrong section. If this is the case, you may want to review how you are locating the offending code. Perhaps you haven't chosen the correct area to debug.

STEPPING BACK

Sometimes the problem will be staring right at you, but you have been searching so hard that you feel it must be some super-sophisticated algorithm embedded in there somewhere. It's times like this when you may wish to step away for a moment and come back with a fresh perspective. For example, after taking a second look, you determine that you have two variables that you mistakenly thought of as one – for instance, you thought that VAR01 and VAR01 were the same when in fact they were not. At other times you may have already convinced yourself that the suspect code is within, let's say, three lines, never looking back to see how the variables used within those lines were populated. If this should happen to you, don't become discouraged; just think of it as part of the learning process. It will make you a better programmer for the long term.

Locating and Correcting Errors

Debugging consists of locating an error and correcting it. Locating an error (and understanding it) is typically 90 percent of the work. Fortunately, there is an approach to debugging that's better than random guessing. Debugging by thinking about the problem is much more effective and interesting than debugging via guesswork. Think of yourself as a detective, trying to solve a crime. Which approach would be more effective: going door to door throughout the country, or examining the scene, searching for clues, and determining the criminal's identity? Most people would rather deduce the person's identity by examining the clues, and most programmers find the intellectual approach to debugging more satisfying. Even better, an effective programmer who debugs in one-twentieth the time of an ineffective programmer isn't randomly guessing about how to correct the program. That programmer is using the scientific method.

Adding science to the art of debugging

Here are the steps you go through when you use the scientific method:

1. Gather data through repeatable experiments.

2. Form a hypothesis that accounts for as much of the relevant data as possible.

3. Design an experiment to prove or disprove the hypothesis.

4. Prove or disprove the hypothesis.

5. Repeat as needed.

This process has many parallels in debugging. Here's an effective approach for locating an error:

1. Stabilize the error.

2. Locate the source of the error.

3. Correct the error.

4. Test your program.

5. Look for similar errors.

The first step is similar to the scientific method's first step in that it relies on repeatability. The defect is easier to diagnose if you can make it occur reliably. The second step uses all the steps of the scientific method. You gather the test data that divulged the error, analyze the data that has been produced, and form a hypothesis about the source of the error. You design a test case or an inspection to evaluate the hypothesis and then declare success or renew your efforts, as appropriate.

Let's look at each of the steps in conjunction with an example. Assume that you have a product database program that has an intermittent error. The program is supposed to print a list of products with pricing information in alphabetical order. Here is part of the output:

Ear_Cleaners	$5.29
Napkins	$1.66
Nail_Polish_Remover	$3.29
Staples	$2.20
Toothpaste	$2.59
Window_Cleaner	$2.79

The error reported is that the output is not being displayed in ascending product name sequence. In other words, "Nail_Polish_Remover" and "Napkins" are being displayed in the wrong sequence.

Stabilizing the error

If a defect doesn't occur reliably, it's almost impossible to diagnose. Making an intermittent defect occur predictably is one of the most challenging tasks in debugging.

An error that doesn't occur predictably is usually an initialization error or a dangling-pointer problem. If the calculation of a sum is correct sometimes and wrong sometimes, a variable involved in the calculation probably isn't being initialized properly; most of the time it just happens to start at 0. If the problem is a strange and unpredictable phenomenon and you're using pointers, you almost certainly have a pointer that was not initialized or are using a pointer to an area of memory has been freed up.

Stabilizing an error usually requires more than finding a test case that produces the error. It includes narrowing the test case down to its simplest form that still produces the error. If you work in an organization that has an independent test team, sometimes it's the team's job to make the test cases simple. Most of the time, it's your job.

To simplify the test case, you bring the scientific method into play again. Suppose you have 10 factors that, if used in combination, produce the error. Form a hypothesis about which factors used in combination produce the error. Form a hypothesis about which factors were irrelevant to producing the error. Change the supposedly irrelevant factors, and rerun the test case. If you still get the error, you can eliminate those factors and you've simplified the test. Then you can try to simplify the test further. If you don't get the error, you've disproved that specific hypothesis and you know more than you did before. It might be that some subtle change would still produce the error, but you know at least one specific change that does not.

In the product example, when the program is run initially, "Nail_Polish_Remover" is listed after "Napkins." When the program is run a second time, however, the list is fine:

Ear_Cleaners	$5.29
Nail_Polish_Remover	$3.29
Napkins	$1.66
Toothpaste	$2.59
Staples	$2.20
Window_Cleaner	$2.79

It isn't until "Potato_Chips" has been entered into the database and subsequently shows up in an incorrect position that you recall that "Nail_Polish_Remover" had also just been entered before it showed up in the wrong spot. What's odd about both cases is that they were entered singly. Usually, products are entered in groups. You hypothesize: The problem has something to do with entering a single new product.

If this is true, then running the program again should place "Potato_Chips" in the right position. Here are the results of a second run:

Ear_Cleaners	$5.29
Nail_Polish_Remover	$3.29
Napkins	$1.66
Potato_Chips	$1.89
Toothpaste	$2.59
Staples	$2.20
Window_Cleaner	$2.79

This successful run supports the hypothesis. To confirm it, you want to try adding a few new products, one at a time, to see whether they show up in the wrong order and whether the order changes after a second run.

Locating the source of the error

The goal of simplifying the test case is to make it so simple that changing any aspect of it changes the behavior of the error. Then, by changing the test case carefully and watching the program's behavior under controlled conditions, you can diagnose the problem.

Locating the source of an error also calls for using the scientific method. You might suspect that the defect is the result of a specific problem, an "off-by-one" error. You could then vary the parameter that you suspect is causing the problem: one below the boundary, one on the boundary, and one above the boundary. Then you can determine whether your hypothesis is correct.

In the product example, the source of the problem could be an off-by-one error that occurs when you add one new product but not when you add two or more products. Examining the code, you don't find an obvious off-by-one error. Resorting to Plan B, you run a test case with a single new product to see whether this is truly the problem. You add "Hangers" as a single product and hypothesize that this record will be out of order. Here's what you find:

Ear_Cleaners	$5.29
Hangers	$3.79
Nail_Polish_Remover	$3.29
Napkins	$1.66
Potato_Chips	$1.89
Toothpaste	$2.59
Staples	$2.20
Window_Cleaner	$2.79

The line for "Hangers" is exactly where it should be, which means that your first hypothesis is false. Simply adding one product at a time doesn't cause the problem. It's either a more complicated problem or something completely different.

Examining the test-run output again, you notice that "Nail_Polish_Remover," "Window_Cleaner," "Potato_Chips," and "Ear_Cleaners" are the only names containing underscores. "Nail_Polish_Remover" was out of order when it was first entered, but "Ear_Cleaners" and "Window_Washer" weren't, or were they? Although you don't have a printout from the original entry, in the original error "Napkins" appeared to be out of order, but this item was next to "Nail_Polish_Remover." Maybe "Nail_Polish_Remover" was out of order and "Napkins" was all right.

You hypothesize: The problem arises from product names with underscores, not products that are entered singly.

But how does that account for the fact that the problem shows up only the first time a product is entered? You look at the code and find that two different sorting routines are used. One is used when a product is entered, and the other is used when the data is saved. A closer look at the routine used when a new product is entered shows that it isn't supposed to sort the data completely. It only puts the data in approximate order to speed up the save routine's sorting process. Thus, the problem is that the data is printed before it's sorted. The problem with underscores in product names arises because the rough-sort routine doesn't handle niceties such as underscore characters. Now, you can refine the hypothesis even further.

You hypothesize: Names with underscores aren't sorted correctly until they're saved. You later confirm this hypothesis with additional test cases.

Tips for tracking down errors

Once you have stabilized an error and refined the test case that produces it, finding its source can be either trivial or challenging, depending on how well you have written your code. If you are having a hard time finding an error, it's probably because the code wasn't well written. You might not want to hear that, but it's true. If you're having trouble, consider these tips:

♦ **Use all available data in your analysis.** When analyzing the source, try to locate your error by accounting for as much of the data as you can in your analysis. In the previous products example, you might have noticed that "Nail_Polish_Remover" was out of order and so created a hypothesis that names beginning with an "N" are sorted incorrectly. That's a poor hypothesis because it doesn't account for the fact that "Potato_Chips" was out of order or that those product names are sorted correctly the second time around. If the data doesn't fit the hypothesis, don't discard the data; ask why it doesn't fit, and create a new hypothesis. The second hypothesis in the same example – that the problem arises from product names with underscores, not product names that are entered singly – also seemed at first to fail to account for the fact that product names were sorted correctly the second time around. In this case, however, although the second hypothesis doesn't account for all of the data at first, it can be refined to do so.

♦ **Modify the test cases that cause the error.** If you can't find the source of an error, try modifying the test cases further than you already have. You might be able to vary one parameter more than you had assumed, and focusing on one of the parameters might provide the crucial breakthrough.

♦ **Recreate the error several different ways.** Sometimes trying cases that are similar to the error-producing case, but not exactly the same, is instructive. Think of this approach as triangulating the error. If you can get a fix on it from one point and a fix on it from another, you can determine exactly where it is. Reproducing the error several different ways aids in the diagnosis of the error. Once you think you've identified the error, run a case that's close to the cases that produce errors but that should not produce an error itself. If it does produce an error, you don't completely understand the problem yet. Errors often arise from combinations of factors, and trying to diagnose the problem with only one test case sometimes doesn't diagnose the root problem.

◆ **Introduce more data to generate more hypotheses.** Choose test cases that are different from the test cases you already know to be erroneous or correct. Run them to create more data, and use the new data to add to your list of possible hypotheses.

◆ **Use the results of negative tests.** Suppose you create a hypothesis and run a test case to prove it. Next, suppose the test case disproves the hypothesis, so that you still don't know the source of the error. You still know something you didn't before, such as, the error is not in the area in which you thought it was. This narrows your search field and the set of possible hypotheses.

◆ **Brainstorm for possible hypotheses.** Rather than limiting yourself to the first hypothesis you think of, try to come up with several. Don't analyze them at first; just come up with as many as you can in a few minutes. Then look at each hypothesis and think about test cases that would prove or disprove it. This mental exercise is helpful in breaking the debugging logjam that results from concentrating too hard on a single line of reasoning.

◆ **Narrow the suspicious region of the code.** If you've been testing the whole program, or a whole module or routine, test a smaller part instead. Systematically remove parts of the program, and see whether the error still occurs. If it doesn't, you know it's in the part you took away. If it does, you know it's in the part you've kept. Rather than removing regions haphazardly, divide and conquer. Use a binary search algorithm to focus your search. Try to remove about half the code the first time. Determine the half the error is in, and then divide that section. Again, determine which half contains the error, and again, chop that section in half. Continue until you find the error. If you use many small routines, you'll be able to chop out sections of code simply by commenting out calls to the routines. Otherwise, you can use comments or preprocessor commands to remove code. If you are using a debugger, you don't necessarily have to remove pieces of code. You can set breakpoints part of the way through the program and check for the error that way instead. If your debugger allows you to skip call routines, eliminate suspicious code by skipping the execution of certain routines and seeing whether the error still occurs. The process with a debugger is otherwise similar to the one in which pieces of a program are physically removed.

◆ **Be suspicious of routines that have had errors before.** Routines that have had errors before are likely to continue to have errors. A routine that has been troublesome in the past is more likely to contain a new error than a routine that has been error-free. Reexamine error-prone routines.

◆ **Examine code that has changed recently.** If you have a new error that's hard to diagnose, it's usually related to code that's changed recently. It could be in completely new code or in changes to old code. If you can't locate an error, run an old version of the program to see whether the error occurs. If it doesn't, you know the error is in the new version or is caused by an interaction with the new version. Scrutinize the differences between the old and new versions.

◆ **Expand the suspicious region of the code.** It's easy to focus on a small section of code, if you are relatively sure that "the error *must* be in this section." If you don't find it in the suspect section, consider the possibility that the error isn't in that section. Expand the area of code you suspect, and then focus on pieces of it using the binary search technique described previously.

◆ **Integrate incrementally.** Debugging is easy if you add pieces to a system one at a time. If you add a piece to a system and encounter a new error, remove the piece and test it separately. Strap on a test harness and exercise the routine by itself to determine what's wrong.

◆ **Force the issue.** If you've used incremental integration and a new error raises its ugly head, you'll have a small section of code in which to check for the error. It is sometimes tempting to run the integrated code to locate the error rather than taking the code and checking the new routine by itself. Running a test case through the integrated system, however, might require a few minutes, whereas running one through the specific code you're integrating takes only a few seconds. If you don't find the error the first or second time you run the whole system, bite the bullet, isolate the code, and debug the new code separately.

◆ **Set a time limit for quick and dirty debugging.** It's always tempting to try for a quick fix rather than systematically testing the code and giving the error no place to hide. The risk taker in each of us would rather try an approach that might find the error in five minutes than the surefire approach that will find the error in half an hour. The risk is that if the five-minute approach doesn't work, you get stubborn. Finding the error the "easy" way becomes a matter of principle, and hours pass unproductively. When you decide to go for the quick victory, set a maximum time limit for trying the quick way. If you go past the time limit, resign yourself to the idea that the error is going to be harder to diagnose than you originally thought, and flush it out the hard way. This approach allows you to get the easy errors right away and the hard errors after a bit longer.

♦ **Check for common errors.** Use code-quality checklists to stimulate your thinking about possible errors. Focus on the elements that are part of the error, the data types involved, the specific area of code where the error occurs, and other modules or functions that are entered or exited at the time of error. If you keep a history of past problems that may have occurred in your environment, review them. Create a checklist, and follow it through.

♦ **Review the problem with someone else.** Sometimes you just have to bite the bullet and tell someone else about your problem. You often discover your own error in the act of explaining it to another person. This result is typical, and this approach is perhaps your most potent tool for solving difficult errors.

♦ **Give the problem a rest.** Sometimes you concentrate so hard you can't think. How many times have you paused for a cup of coffee and figured out the problem on your way to the coffee machine? Or in the middle of lunch? Or on the way home? If you're debugging and making no progress, once you've tried all the options, let it rest. Go for a walk. Work on something else. Let your subconscious mind tease a solution out of the problem. The auxiliary benefit of giving up temporarily is that it reduces the anxiety associated with debugging. The onset of anxiety is a clear sign that it's time to take a break.

Syntax errors

Syntax errors are slowly going away. As compilers improve, they provide better diagnostic messages, and the days when you had to spend two hours finding a misplaced semicolon in a C listing are almost gone. Here is a list of guidelines you can use to speed your way to the elimination of syntax errors:

♦ **Don't trust line numbers in compiler messages.** When your compiler reports a mysterious syntax error, look immediately before and immediately after the error. The compiler could have misunderstood the problem or simply have poor diagnostic capabilities. Once you find the real error, try to determine the reason the compiler put the message on the wrong statement. Understanding your compiler better can help you find future errors.

♦ **Don't trust compiler messages.** Compilers try to tell you exactly what's wrong, but compilers aren't always clear, and you often have to read between the lines to know what one really means. For example, in UNIX C you can get a message that says "floating exception" for an integer divide-by-0. You can probably come up with many examples of your own.

♦ **Resolve your errors in the order of occurrence.** Some compilers are good at detecting multiple errors. Some compilers get so excited after detecting the first error that they continue to roll out dozens of error messages that don't mean anything. Other compilers are more levelheaded, and although they must feel a sense of accomplishment when they detect an error, they refrain from spewing out inaccurate messages. If you can't quickly find the source of the second or third error message, don't worry about it. Fix the first one and recompile it.

♦ **Divide and conquer.** The idea of dividing the program into sections to help detect errors works especially well for syntax errors. If you have a troublesome syntax error, remove part of the code and compile again. You'll get no error (because the errors were in the part you removed), get the same error (meaning you need to remove a different part), or get a different error (because you have tricked the compiler into producing a message that makes more sense).

♦ **Find extra comments and quotation marks.** If your code is tripping up the compiler because it contains an extra quotation mark or beginning comment somewhere, insert the following sequence systematically into your code to help locate the error:

```
for the c language      /*"/**/
```

Correcting an error

Once you have found the error, correcting the error is normally the easy part. However, as with many easy tasks, the fact that it's easy makes it especially error-prone. The attempt to apply a quick fix after locating the error may only lead to a defective correction. In fact, the quick fix is known to be defective 50 percent of the time. Here are a few guidelines for reducing the chance of error:

♦ **Understand the problem before you fix it.** The best way to make your life difficult and corrode the quality of your program is to fix problems without really understanding them. Before you fix a problem, make sure you understand it to the core. Triangulate the error both with cases that should reproduce the error and with cases that shouldn't reproduce the error. Keep at it until you understand the problem well enough to predict its occurrence correctly every time.

◆ **Understand the program, not just the problem.** If you understand the context in which a problem occurs, you're more likely to solve the problem completely rather than only one aspect of it. A study done with short programs found that programmers who achieve a global understanding of program behavior have a better chance of modifying the program successfully than programmers who focus on local behavior, learning about the program only as they need to (Littman, D., Pinto, J., Letovsky, S., & Soloway, E., *Mental Models and Software Maintenance, Empirical Studies of Programmers*, pp. 80-98, 1986.). Because the program in this study was small (280 lines), it doesn't prove that you should try to understand a 50,000-line program completely before you fix a defect. It does suggest that you should understand at least the code in the vicinity of the error correction – the "vicinity" being not a few lines but a few hundred.

◆ **Confirm the error diagnosis.** Before you rush to fix an error, make sure that you have diagnosed the problem correctly. Take the time to run test cases that prove your hypothesis and disprove competing hypotheses. If you've proved only that the error could be the result of one of several causes, you don't yet have enough evidence to work on the one cause, rule out the others first.

◆ **Relax.** Hurrying to solve a problem is one of the most time-ineffective things you can do. It leads to rushed judgments, incomplete error diagnoses, and incomplete corrections. Wishful thinking can lead you to see solutions where there are none. The pressure, often self-imposed, encourages haphazard trial-and-error solutions, sometimes assuming that a solution works without verifying that it does. Relax long enough to make sure your solution is the right one. Don't be tempted to take short cuts. It may take more time, but it'll probably take less. If nothing else, you'll fix the problem correctly and your manager won't call you back from your vacation.

◆ **Save the original source code.** Before you begin fixing the error, be sure to make a backup copy of the code that you can return to later. It's easy to forget which change in a group of changes is the significant one. If you have the original source code, at least you can compare the old and the new files and see where the changes are.

◆ **Correct the problem, not the symptom.** Although resolving the symptom is important, the focus should be on correcting the underlying problem rather than performing some cosmetic fix that is only good for a specific case. If you don't thoroughly understand the problem, you're not fixing the code. You're fixing the symptom and making the code worse. Suppose you have this C program example of code that needs to be fixed:

```
int sku;
int prodnum;
double total, price;
for (sku = 1; sku <= prodnum; sku++)
```

```
   total += price;
   printf ("%10.2f %10.2f \n", total, price);
return 0;
```

Given that when `prodnum` equals 25, `total` turns out to be wrong by $9.99, here's an example of "patching," the wrong way to fix the problem:

```
int sku;
int prodnum;
double total, price;
for (sku = 1; sku <= prodnum; sku++)
   total += price;
if (sku == 25)              /*  HERE IS MY FIX  */
   total += 9.99            /*  I solved this problem  */
   printf("%10.2f %10.2f \n", total, price);
return 0;
```

Now suppose that when `prodnum` equals 49, the total turns out to be off by $3.27. Here's a C program example of making the code worse by "patching" it (phase two):

```
int sku;
int prodnum;
double total, price;
for (sku = 1; sku <= prodnum; sku++)
   total += price;
if (sku == 25)              /*  HERE IS MY FIX  */
   total += 9.99            /*  I solved this problem  */
if (sku == 49)              /*  HERE IS MY SECOND FIX  */
   total += 3.27            /*  Solved another problem  */
   printf("%10.2f %10.2f \n", total, price);
return 0;
```

If we allow this to go on any longer, and increase our supply of products, we may end up with one giant program containing two lines of code for each new product. This is by no means a fix; perhaps it is more likely to be the birth of a monster. It would be impossible to list all the problems that could be created by this type of coding. More important, we should review what might be the root cause of a majority of problems. Here are three key items to consider:

- These fixes won't work most of the time. The problems look as though they're the result of initialization errors. Initialization errors are, by definition, unpredictable, so the fact that the total for `prodnum` (25) is off by $9.99 today doesn't tell you anything about tomorrow. It could be off by $1,000,000.00, or it could be correct. That's the nature of initialization errors.

- Such code is a nightmare to maintain. When code is special-cased to work around errors, the special cases become the code's most prominent feature. The $9.99 won't always be $9.99; the price will change and another error will show up later. The code will be modified again to handle the new special case, and the special case for $9.99 won't be removed. The code will become increasingly entangled with special cases. Eventually the code will be unable to be supported, and it will come back to haunt you when you least expect it.

- Use a calculator, not a computer, to make corrections. Computers are good at predictable, systematic calculations, but humans are better at fudging data creatively. You'd be wiser to treat the output with correcting fluid and a typewriter than to mess with the code.

♦ **Change your code, when you have a good reason to.** As we analyze the symptoms of a problem, this technique requires us to change our code at random until it appears to work. A typical line of reasoning would be: "There appears to be an error in our loop. Perhaps it's an off-by-one error, so let's insert a −1 here and try it. Done. That didn't work, let's try a +1 in instead. Done. It's working. It must be fixed." Although this practice is popular, it isn't the most effective. Changing code randomly without truly understanding the problem is most often considered the Band-Aid approach where we don't really know if the problem is resolved. This method teaches you nothing, and if your problem is not corrected, then you've just wasted your time.

When you change your program randomly, you're actually admitting that you don't understand what the problem is and you're just hoping that it works. Don't change code randomly. The more modifications you make to it without understanding it, the less confidence you'll have that it works correctly. Before you make a change, be confident that it will work. Being wrong about a change should leave you astonished. It should cause self-doubt, personal reevaluation, and deep soul-searching; thus, it should happen rarely.

♦ **Control your changes.** Making changes should not be considered a trivial task, and changes should be implemented one at a time so that you can be confident about your modifications. When you perform two or more changes at a time, they can introduce subtle errors that look like the original errors. This places you in the position of not knowing whether (1) you didn't correct the error, (2) you corrected the error but introduced a new one that looks similar, or (3) you didn't correct the error and you introduced a similar new error. Keep it simple: Make just one change at a time.

- ◆ **Test your fix.** Test the program yourself, have someone else test it for you, or walk through it with someone else. Run the same test cases you used to diagnose the problem to ensure that all aspects of the problem have been resolved. If you've solved only part of the problem, you'll find out that you still have work to do. Rerun the whole program and look for side effects of your changes. The easiest and most effective way to test for side effects is to run the program through an automated suite of regression tests.

- ◆ **Look for similar errors.** When you find one error, look for others that are similar. Errors tend to occur in bunches, and one of the values of paying attention to the kinds of errors you make is that you can correct all the errors of that kind. Looking for similar errors requires you to have a thorough understanding of the problem. Watch for the warning sign: If you can't figure out how to look for similar errors, that's a sign that you don't completely understand the problem.

The Debugging Toolkit

As you work on your debugging skills, you will begin to find that you are not out there alone, and although far from perfect, there are some debugging tools that you will find available.

Source code control

In general, the key features of all source control management tools are a controlled backup of your original code and a synchronized update process, which ensures that only one copy of the file – be it a program, script, or data file – is being modified at any given time. Typically a developer retrieves the latest copy of code by a process commonly known as issuing a "check-out." The source code can only be checked out by a single developer, so at this point other developers are prevented from making any changes to the same program. Once the developer has finished making changes, the code can be saved back into the source control management tool by issuing a "check-in."

Comparing your source

After you have made multiple changes to your source, you may find that you no longer know what was original, and what you recently modified. If you are using source control management software, then you can retrieve a copy of the source before you made any modifications to it; if not, hopefully you have made a backup prior to making any changes.

Compiler messages

You will find that one of the best debugging tools that you have is your compiler. The messages can be very helpful in the creation of quality code. Three rules to aid in your development efforts are:

- ◆ **Make the compiler show all messages and warnings.** When you do this, try not to ignore any of the warning messages if at all possible. Worse yet, don't turn them off as a means of fixing them. If you think this will do any good, you are mistaken. After receiving warning messages, don't ignore them. Understand what the compiler is telling you, and correct as many of them as possible.

- ◆ **Consider that each warning is a potential error.** Various compilers allow you to treat warnings as errors. You should make use of this feature, because it will heighten the importance of a warning. This will actually improve the quality of code over time, as well as ease the transition between different versions of compilers (C 1.0 to C 2.0). Sometimes later releases of compilers treat certain warnings as errors, so if you get rid of all warnings to begin with, it will pay dividends later.

- ◆ **Decide on compiler option standards for application development.** This is an often overlooked, but key item that must be considered when developing new applications. If not everyone is working with the same standards, you may find that when it comes time to integrate the various modules to create a system, a brand new set of error messages appears.

The Debugger

Debuggers are typically a more efficient means of analyzing your program than utilizing print statements scattered randomly throughout your program. The decision of which tool to use should be based upon where the failure occurred. Did the failure occur when you entered a SQL statement or when you executed a statement within your C program. Both kinds of debugger should be utilized whenever necessary. Additionally, contact your systems administrator to determine if any other commercially available debuggers have been installed at your site.

A good debugger will enable you to set breakpoints; you can break when execution reaches a specific line, or on the nth iteration of a specific line, or when a global variable changes, or when a variable is assigned a specific value. For example, you want the debugger to break execution when an integer liCount has a value of 42. Good debuggers enable you to step through code line by line and return to the point where an error originated. Additionally, a good debugger will enable you to log the execution of specific statements, similar to spreading print statements throughout your program. The debugger should also enable you to examine your data, monitoring it as it is read and after you modify it. A good debugger will enable you to monitor dynamically allocated data fields as well. In addition to providing you the capability to perform ad hoc queries of your data, your debugger should allow you to modify your data and restart your program. To be perfectly honest, we have yet to find the debugger that provides all of these capabilities on any platform.

In summation, I would have to say that perhaps the best debugging tool is your own train of thought. If you experience a problem within your code, you should understand what your program is supposed to do, read your code and play computer, and if all else fails, use your debugger to focus on the offending area within your program.

The Debugging Checklist

Following is a checklist of items that will assist you in your debugging efforts.

Search for clues that may have caused the error by doing the following:

◆ Examine all of the available data before you form a hypothesis.

◆ Modify the test cases that produce the error.

◆ Recreate your error in multiple ways.

◆ Create more data to see if it affects your hypothesis.

◆ Examine cases that may negate your hypothesis.

◆ Don't allow your ego to hold you back; review your problem with others.

◆ Isolate the area of code that appears to be the problem.

◆ Review recent changes to your program.

◆ Modify the offending code incrementally.

◆ Be wary of routines that have caused problems in the past.

◆ Don't spend too much time on quick-and-dirty debugging.

◆ Look for common errors.

◆ Walk away and come back later with fresh thoughts.

Use the following error correction techniques:

◆ Understand the cause and effect of the problem.

◆ Get to know the program as well as the problem.

◆ Find a means to confirm your diagnosis.

◆ Don't panic.

Continued

The Debugging Checklist *(Continued)*

◆ Make backups of your original code.

◆ Correct the problem, not just the symptom.

◆ Understand the changes you are making and why.

◆ Limit the number of changes that you make with each new test.

◆ After making changes, perform multiple tests.

◆ Test for other possible errors.

Assume the debugging mindset by doing the following:

◆ View debugging as an opportunity to learn more about your program, enabling you to reduce your mistakes and improve the overall quality of your code, as well as a means to enhance your problem-solving capabilities.

◆ Don't spend too much time with the trial-and-error approach, as this may just prove to be a waste of time.

◆ Always assume that the problem is yours, until you have had a chance to diagnose further.

◆ Take a methodical approach to each problem; this will make you a better programmer as well as a better debugger.

◆ Utilize all available tools to locate your errors.

◆ Upon your initial diagnosis, keep an open mind by examining all possible causes of the problem.

◆ Thoroughly test your fix to ensure that it is correct.

◆ Review all messages; they may provide some hidden clues.

◆ Check your system logs during the time of execution.

Debugging stored procedures and triggers

The Enterprise Edition of Visual InterDev includes a SQL debugger that you can use to debug SQL Server stored procedures and triggers.

SQL debugging requires the following:

◆ You must have the Enterprise Edition of Visual Studio.

♦ Your workstation must be running Windows 95, Windows 98, or Windows NT 4.0, or later.

♦ Make sure that you have installed SQL debugging components on your SQL Server.

♦ Establish a Windows NT user who has administration privileges on the server computer where SQL Server is running.

♦ Configure Distributed COM (DCOM) on the server for SQL debugging.

♦ Make sure the DCOM configuration on the client supports SQL debugging (Windows 95 or Windows 98 only).

To install SQL Server Debugging Components:

1. On the SQL Server computer, start the Visual Studio, Enterprise Edition Setup program.

2. The Installation Wizard presents slightly different choices, depending on whether you have previously installed server components on the computer.

   ■ If certain (or any) components are already installed, under Add/Remove Options, choose Server Applications and Tools.

   ■ If no other components have been installed, proceed through the wizard until you reach Enterprise Setup Options. Choose Server Applications.

3. Select Launch BackOffice Installation Wizard, and then choose Install.

4. When the BackOffice Business Solutions Wizard is displayed, choose Custom and then Next.

5. Proceed until you see the page offering a list of components to install. Clear the check boxes on all components except the following:

   ■ SQL Server Debugging

   ■ MS Data Access Components

   ■ Visual InterDev Server

6. Proceed with the installation.

To use SQL debugging, you must be able to provide the name and password of a Windows NT user who has administration privileges on the server computer where SQL Server is running. To establish this user:

1. In Windows Control Panel on the server, choose Services.

2. Select MSSQLServer, and then choose Startup.

3. Check the Log On As settings. If the option is set to System Account, change it to This Account, enter the valid domain and user account (format domain\account) of a user with administration privileges, and then enter the password (see Figure 15-1).

4. If you have changed the setting, restart SQL Server.

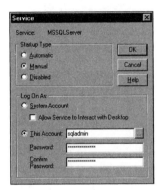

Figure 15-1: Setting a new user account for SQL Server

CONFIGURING DCOM FOR SQL DEBUGGING

If you can house a local copy of the database in question on your local machine, then you won't need to configure DCOM to do cross-machine debugging. However, if you cannot store a local copy, then you must configure DCOM to allow a remote user to attach the debugger to a process on the server. By default, the correct DCOM settings are in place when SQL Server is installed on the server. However, given security considerations for the computer running SQL Server, you might want to restrict access to debugging. Use the following as a general procedure for setting up DCOM for the SQL Server computer.

To configure DCOM on the server for SQL debugging:

1. From the Windows Start menu on the server, choose Run, and then in the Open box, type **dcomcnfg.exe** at the prompt.

2. In the Distributed COM Configuration Properties window, choose the Default Security tab. Under Default Access Permissions, choose Edit Default.

3. If the group Everyone does not already have permissions, choose Add, and then add the domain and user account (in the form domain\account) of a user with administration privileges.

4. After adding the account, check for SYSTEM. If it is not already on the list, add it by choosing it from the list of users in the Add Names and Groups dialog box.

5. If you have changed any of the settings described in this procedure, restart SQL Server.

 If you added your account to the remote server but the current account on the remote server has not been added, that account cannot debug even if a user with that account name is running Visual InterDev on the server computer.

RUNNING THE T-SQL DEBUGGER

The only way to debug stored procedures or triggers is through the T-SQL Debugger add-in. From the Add-Ins menu of Microsoft Visual Basic editor, click T-SQL Debugger and the T-SQL Debugger setup dialog will appear (see Figure 15-2).

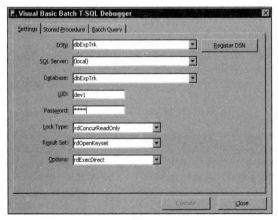

Figure 15-2: The T-SQL Debugger setup dialog box

From the Settings tab of the T-SQL Debugger setup dialog, you should choose the DSN, choose the SQL Server, and enter the UID (userid) and password. If you've entered the connection data correctly, the Stored Procedure tab will become enabled. Click the Stored Procedure tab and select the stored procedure to be debugged. The dialog box will then display and give you an opportunity to enter values for the selected stored procedure's parameters (see Figure 15-3).

When you are ready to debug the procedure, click Execute in the T-SQL Debugger setup dialog and the T-SQL Debugger will appear, displaying the text of the selected stored procedure (see Figure 15-4).

Within the T-SQL Debugger you can set breakpoints and step through the procedure. You can view the values of variables and passed parameters in the Local Variables window (see Figure 15-5). The results of SQL PRINT statements are displayed in the Output window.

If you are working with simple SELECT statements – ones that return only a single value – the return value is in a variable that you can inspect in the Local Variables window. However, if the SELECT statement returns a result set, it is not displayed in the debugger. You can view the result set in the Output window.

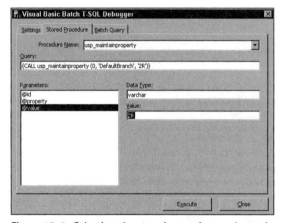

Figure 15-3: Selecting the stored procedure and entering its parameters

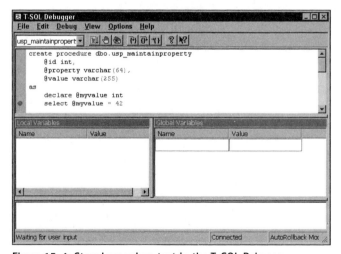

Figure 15-4: Stored procedure text in the T-SQL Debugger

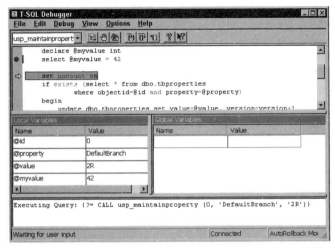

Figure 15-5: Setting breakpoints and displaying values in the T-SQL Debugger

Using Performance Monitor

Although you might not think of a performance monitor as a debugging tool, you may want to consider the following items before releasing a new application. Did you ever wonder why your new application is consuming a large amount of memory or is taking too long to execute? These are very costly issues that will adversely affect not only this application but also any other applications on the system. See Table 15-2 for a list of the essential objects and counters required for performance tuning.

TABLE 15-2 ESSENTIAL PERFORMANCE MONITOR OBJECTS AND COUNTERS

Object: Counter	Recommendation/Explanation
LogicalDisk Current Disk Queue PhysicalDisk: Current Disk Queue LogicalDisk: Average Disk Queue PhysicalDisk: Average Disk Queue	Excessive disk queuing (greater than two requests in a queue) will slow performance because subsequent disk queue) will slow performance because subsequent disk I/O requests are not being serviced quickly enough. The "Average Disk Queue" is the average queue length for the Update Time Interval. Divide this value by the number of physical hard disk drives in the array to determine the queue for each physical disk in a RAID configuration.

Continued

TABLE **15-2 ESSENTIAL PERFORMANCE MONITOR OBJECTS AND COUNTERS**
(Continued)

Object: Counter	Recommendation/Explanation
System: Processor Queue Length	Excessive processor queuing (greater than two requests for a single CPU) will slow the performance of query execution. You may want to add more CPUs or else tune your queries by dropping existing indexes or creating new indexes.
Memory: Pages/Sec Memory: Page Reads/Sec Memory: Page Faults/Sec	Excessive paging will slow performance because Windows is either going to disk (hard page fault: "Pages/Sec" greater than 0, "Page Reads/Sec" greater than 5) or to RAM outside of the application's Working Set (soft page fault: "Page Faults/Sec" > 2) to resolve memory references. Add more RAM.
Processor: Processor Time % System:Processor Queue	Excessive CPU usage ("Processor Time %" > 95) or system queuing ("Processor Queue" > 2 per CPU) will slow performance because they indicate that the CPU is saturated with work. Add more CPUs or reduce the workload by tuning the queries.

The Performance Monitor provides the ability to log (or interactively view in chart mode) available Windows NT and SQL Server performance monitor objects and counters (see Figure 15-6).

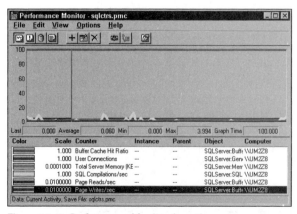

Figure 15-6: Performance Monitor in action

Be aware that the Performance Monitor uses some CPU and disk resources. If you're monitoring in graph mode and the machine doesn't have enough CPU and disk resources to spare, you can monitor them from a second machine on the network. When sampling to a log file, it is better to run the Performance Monitor on the same machine you are monitoring and to use a sampling interval of 60 seconds or more. This will be more efficient as well as prevent the log file from quickly becoming too big. You can choose to sample with smaller intervals, and if you do, don't forget you're doing it; and be sure that you have enough free disk space for the log file.

You'll need to run `diskperf -y` from a command window and then reboot the machine to be able to monitor disk counters with Performance Monitor. This does consume resources on the machine and will affect the performance of the machine, but it is worth it because you will be able to diagnose and see any disk I/O and queuing issues. To turn off the disk monitoring objects and counters, run `diskperf -n` from a command window and then reboot the machine.

Summary

This chapter covered the area of debugging, including the tools and the attitude that is required to succeed at it. We covered the issues surrounding debugging, including quality control, the psychology of debugging, and effective and ineffective approaches. We also looked at ways to locate and correct errors by adding a little science to the art of debugging. Additionally, we looked at what is available in terms of a toolkit for debugging. We hope that we gave you enough so that you are now armed and ready to weed out those bugs from your code.

For more information on how to use SQL Server's monitoring and tuning tools, see Chapter 14, "Tuning Your Environment."

Part IV

Programming Languages and Tools

Chapter 16

Stored Procedures

IN THIS CHAPTER

- Executing stored procedures
- Defining triggers
- Stored procedure improvements from SQL Server 6.5

YOU CAN GROUP SQL statements and control-of-flow procedure language (Transact-SQL) in a stored procedure to execute multiple SQL statements in one invocation to improve the performance of SQL Server. Stored procedures are collections of SQL statements and Transact-SQL. They are stored in the database, and the SQL is parsed and optimized. An execution plan is prepared and cached when a procedure is run, so that subsequent execution is very fast. The SQL is only reoptimized at execution if it is so specified. In this chapter, we will discuss the use of stored procedures, triggers, and the enhancements to stored procedures that SQL Server 7 provides over SQL Server 6.5. In addition, we will introduce the database procedure by using a real example to illustrate Transact-SQL statements and their integration.

Using Stored Procedures

The ability to write stored procedures greatly enhances the power, efficiency, and flexibility of SQL. Compiled procedures dramatically improve the performance of SQL statements and batches. In addition, stored procedures on other servers running SQL Server can be executed if your server and the remote server are both set up to allow remote logins. You can write triggers on your local SQL Server that execute procedures on a remote server whenever certain events, such as deletions, updates, or inserts, take place locally. Stored procedures can:

- Receive parameters passed by the calling object (for example, PowerBuilder's GUI front end)
- Call other procedures
- Return a status value to a calling procedure or GUI front end to indicate success or failure, and, in the event of a failure, the reason for failure

- ◆ Return values of parameters to a calling procedure or GUI front end

- ◆ Be executed on remote SQL Server, that is, as remote procedure calls (RPCs)

Stored procedures differ from ordinary SQL statements and from batches of SQL statements in that they are precompiled. When you create a procedure, SQL Server's query processor analyzes it and prepares an execution plan that is ultimately stored in system tables. Subsequently, the procedure is executed according to the stored plan. Because most of the query processing work has already been performed, stored procedures execute almost instantaneously.

To fast-track you through most of the important Transact-SQL statements, we will use a real example (see Listing 16-1). The important statements are commented and documented to give you an integrated flavor and to illustrate stored procedure construction.

Listing 16-1: A Sample Stored Procedure

```
/** THIS IS AN EXAMPLE STORED PROCEDURE THAT ILLUSTRATES *****/
/** A GOOD DEAL OF THE FUNCTIONALITY POSSIBLE ***************/

/** THIS EXAMPLE IS RUN FROM ISQL TO CREATE THE PROCEDURE   *****/
/** IT IS TANTAMOUNT TO SOURCE CODE   *************************/


/** This procedure will load some data using the Bulk *****/
/** Copy Program (BCP) **********************************/

/** Object:  Stored Procedure dbo.usp_load_rms *****/
/** Script Date: 1/8/99 2:28PM ********************/

/** SEE THE COMMENT LIKE THIS ONE BELOW TO SEE EACH *****/
/** STATEMENT'S PURPOSE *********************************/
/** let's do some stored procedure functionality *****/

/** Does the Procedure exist, if so then DROP it *****/
if exists (select * from sysobjects where id =
object_id('dbo.usp_load_rms') and sysstat & 0xf = 4)
    drop procedure dbo.usp_load_rms
GO

/** Now let's create a stored procedure *****/

CREATE PROC usp_load_rms AS
```

```
/** let's declare some variables and their data types *****/

    declare
        @err             int,
        @success         integer,
        @table        varchar(100),
        @infile        varchar(150),
        @fmtfile        varchar(100),
        @path            varchar(100),
        @database        varchar(50),
        @server        varchar(20),
        @msg            varchar(100),
        @current_fiscal     varchar(6),
        @start_pos_fiscal        integer,
        @length_fiscal_string integer,
        @idx_name        varchar(100),
        @idx_clust        tinyint,
        @idx_unique        tinyint,
        @idx_allowduprow        tinyint,
        @idx_keys        varchar(255),
        @idx_cmd        varchar(255)
/** let's set some values; see also the SET *****/
    select @success = 0
    select @length_fiscal_string = 8

/** let's execute another stored procedure that logs *****/
/** our progress ************************************/

    exec usp_delete_procedure_log 'load_rms'
    exec usp_insert_procedure_log 'load_rms', 'Started RMS EOM
Load'

/** let's SELECT some data from various tables *****/

    /* Select new fiscal period */
    select @current_fiscal = char_data
        from config_general
        where var_name = 'current_fiscal'

    select @msg = 'Current fiscal is ' + @current_fiscal
    exec usp_insert_procedure_log 'load_rms', @msg

    /*********************/
```

```
/* Set BCP constants */
/*********************/
select @path = var_val
    from config_bcp
    where var_name = "RMS PATH"

select @database = var_val
    from config_bcp
    where var_name = "DATABASE"

select @server = var_val
    from config_bcp
    where var_name = "SERVER"
```

```
/** let's CREATE a temporary table *****/
/***************************/
/* Create table for indexes */
/***************************/
create table #t_indexes (
    table_name          varchar(100),
    index_name          varchar(100),
    is_unique           tinyint,
    is_clustered    tinyint,
    is_allowduprow     tinyint,
    keys                varchar(255)
    )
```

```
/***************************************************/
/* Save indexes, truncate tables, and drop indexes */
/***************************************************/
/** let's DECLARE a cursor *****/
    declare rms_tables cursor
    for select distinct table_name
        from config_rms_input_files
        order by table_name
```

```
/** let's OPEN a cursor *****/

    open rms_tables
```

```
/** let's FETCH the next row in an open cursor *****/

    fetch next from rms_tables into @table
```

```
/** let's use the WHILE flow statement to loop thru code *****/

    while @@fetch_status = 0

/** let's BEGIN a statement block to be executed as a unit *****/

    BEGIN

/** let's INSERT a row into a temp table selected from *****/
/** another table ****************************************/

        insert into #t_indexes
            select
                table_name,
                index_name,
                is_unique,
                is_clustered,
                is_allowduprow,
                keys
            from table_indexes
            where table_name = @table

        exec usp_drop_table_indexes @table

/** let's truncate a table in an inline fashion  *****/


        exec ('truncate table ' + @table)

/** let's publish the fact that we truncated a table  *****/

        select @msg = 'Truncated ' + @table
        exec usp_insert_procedure_log 'load_rms', @msg

        fetch next from rms_tables into @table

/** let's END a block of code *****/

    END
/** let's CLOSE and DEALLOCATE an open cursor *****/

    close rms_tables
    deallocate rms_tables
```

```
/****************************************************/
/* BCP Files                                        */
/****************************************************/
declare rms_input_files cursor
for select table_name, dbcode + '.' + input_file, format_file
    from dbcodes, config_rms_input_files
    order by table_name

open rms_input_files

fetch next from rms_input_files
    into @table, @infile, @fmtfile

while @@fetch_status = 0
BEGIN

    /* Replace string <fiscal> with the current fiscal period */
    /* First find the first position of the string <fiscal> ***/
/*                                & then replace it */
    select @start_pos_fiscal = charindex('<fiscal>',@infile)
    select @infile = CASE
        WHEN @start_pos_fiscal > 0 THEN
stuff(@infile,@start_pos_fiscal,@length_fiscal_string,@current_fisca
l)
        ELSE @infile
        END

/** let's EXECUTE the BCP program inline with an @err *****/
/** as a return ***********************************/


    exec @err = usp_bcp
     @server, @database, @table, @path, 'in', @infile,
@fmtfile, null, 0

/** let's test the result *****/

    if @err != @success
        insert into bcp_error_log
            values ('usp_load_rms', @table, getdate(), @err)

    select @msg = 'Loaded ' + @table + ' from ' + @infile +
```

```
'. Error Code: ' + str(@err)
    exec usp_insert_procedure_log 'load_rms', @msg

    fetch next from rms_input_files
        into @table, @infile, @fmtfile

END

close rms_input_files
deallocate rms_input_files


/*********************************************************/
/* Recreate indexes                                     */
/*********************************************************/
declare IDXS cursor
for select *
    from #t_indexes

open IDXS

fetch next from IDXS
    into @table, @idx_name, @idx_unique, @idx_clust,
        @idx_allowduprow, @idx_keys

while @@fetch_status = 0
BEGIN
    select @idx_cmd =
        'create ' +
/** let's use a CASE statement (see better example later *****/
        CASE WHEN @idx_unique = 1 THEN ' unique ' ELSE NULL
END +
        CASE WHEN @idx_clust = 1 THEN ' clustered ' ELSE NULL
END +
        ' index ' +
        rtrim(@idx_name) +
        ' on ' +
        rtrim(@table) +
        ' (' + rtrim(@idx_keys) + ') ' +
        ' WITH FILLFACTOR = 100' +
        CASE WHEN @idx_allowduprow = 1 THEN ', ALLOW_DUP_ROW
' ELSE NULL END

    exec (@idx_cmd)
```

```
          select @msg = 'Indexed ' + @table + '.' + @idx_name + '.
Error Code: ' + str(@@error)
          exec usp_insert_procedure_log 'load_rms', @msg

          exec ('sp_recompile ' + @table)

          fetch next from IDXS
               into @table, @idx_name, @idx_unique, @idx_clust,
                    @idx_allowduprow, @idx_keys


     END
     close IDXS
     deallocate IDXS

     drop table #t_indexes

     exec usp_insert_procedure_log 'load_rms', 'Completed'

     /************************/
     /* Update last load date */
     /************************/
     delete from config_bcp
          where var_name = 'LAST_RMS_LOAD_DATE'

     insert into config_bcp
          SELECT 'LAST_RMS_LOAD_DATE', convert(varchar, getdate())


     /**************************/
     /* Display Success Message */
     /**************************/

     Select 'usp_load_rms process completed normally'

/** let's GO and CREATE the procedure *****/

GO
```

As we mentioned, a stored procedure is a saved collection of Transact-SQL statements that can take and/or return user-supplied parameters. Procedures can be created for permanent use or for temporary use within a user's session (local

temporary procedure) or for temporary use within all users' sessions (global temporary procedure). Stored procedures can also control access and update databases
by executing business logic between the user request and the actual database
statement(s).

The syntax to create a stored procedure is as follows:

```
CREATE PROC[EDURE] procedure_name{@parameter data_type}  [= default]
[OUTPUT][,...n]
[WITH {RECOMPILE | ENCRYPTION | RECOMPILE, ENCRYPTION}]
[FOR REPLICATION]
AS sql_statement [...n]
```

The parameters and their semantics are discussed in the following list:

◆ *procedure_name* — The name of the new stored procedure. Procedure
   names must conform to the rules for identifiers and must be unique
   within the database and its owner. The complete name cannot exceed
   128 characters.

◆ *@parameter* — A parameter in the procedure. One or more parameters can
   optionally be declared in a CREATE PROCEDURE statement. The user must
   supply the value of each declared parameter when the procedure is
   executed (unless a default for the parameter has been defined). A stored
   procedure can have a maximum of 1,024 parameters. Specify a parameter
   name with the at sign (@). However, the first character of a parameter
   name must be the at sign (@) and conform to the rules for identifiers.
   Parameters are local to the procedure; the same parameter names can be
   used in other procedures.

◆ *data_type* — The data type of the parameter. All data types, including
   text and image, may be used as a parameter for a stored procedure.

◆ *default* — A default value for the parameter. If a *default* is defined,
   a user can execute the procedure without specifying a value for that
   parameter. The default must be a constant. It can include wildcard
   characters (%, _, [], and [^]) if the procedure uses the parameter with the
   LIKE keyword. The default can be NULL. The procedure definition can
   specify that some action be taken if the parameter value is NULL.

◆ OUTPUT — Indicates that the parameter is a return parameter. The value of
   this option can be returned to EXEC[UTE]. Use return parameters to return
   information to the calling procedure. Text parameters cannot be used as
   OUTPUT parameters. An output parameter using the OUTPUT keyword can
   be a cursor placeholder.

◆ *n* — A placeholder indicating that up to 1,024 parameters may be specified.

◆ {RECOMPILE | ENCRYPTION | RECOMPILE, ENCRYPTION} — The RECOMPILE statement indicates that SQL Server does not cache a plan for this procedure and the procedure is recompiled each time it is executed. When created, a stored procedure is resolved, which allows the procedure to be associated with a particular table. When that table is dropped at a later date, then all stored procedures associated with that table should be dropped and recreated to be resolved again. The WITH RECOMPILE option does not perform the resolution process; therefore, using WITH RECOMPILE with new tables after the procedure was originally created is not useful. Executing the WITH RECOMPILE option allows SQL Server to rebuild the query plan that SQL Server uses each time the procedure is executed. The ENCRYPTION statement indicates that SQL Server encrypts the syscomments table entry containing the text of the CREATE PROCEDURE statement.

◆ FOR REPLICATION — This option is mutually exclusive of the WITH RECOMPILE option. It specifies that stored procedures created for replication cannot be executed on the subscribing server and is used when creating a filter stored procedure that is executed only by replication.

◆ AS — Specifies the actions the procedure is to take.

◆ sql_statement — Any number and type of Transact-SQL statements to be included in the procedure. Some limitations do apply.

◆ n — A placeholder indicating that multiple Transact-SQL statements may be included in this procedure.

When you are creating procedures using the CREATE PROCEDURE statement, the maximum size of a stored procedure is 128KB. When you are defining a user-defined stored procedure, a stored procedure can be created only in the current database (except for temporary procedures, which are always created in tempdb). The CREATE PROCEDURE statement cannot be combined with other Transact-SQL statements in a single batch.

A user-defined stored procedure may exist in any database, including master or any user-defined database. However, when a user-defined stored procedure that exists in the master database is owned by a member of the db_owner fixed database role, and starts with sp_ as the first three characters of the procedure name, then this user-defined stored procedure is more correctly identified as a user-defined system stored procedure.

If the first three characters of the procedure name are `sp_`, SQL Server searches the `master` database for the procedure. If no qualified procedure name is provided, SQL Server searches for the procedure as if the owner name were `dbo`. To resolve the stored procedure name as a user-defined stored procedure with the same name as a system stored procedure, provide the fully qualified procedure name.

Getting information about stored procedures

To display the text used to create the procedure, execute `sp_helptext` (in the database where the procedure exists) with the procedure name as the parameter. For a report on the objects referenced by a procedure, use `sp_depends`. To rename a procedure, use `sp_rename`.

Executing stored procedures

When a `CREATE PROCEDURE` statement is successfully executed, the procedure's name is stored in the `sysobjects` system table, and the text of the `CREATE PROCE-DURE` statement is stored in the system catalog table known as `syscomments`. When executed for the first time, the procedure is compiled to determine an optimal access plan to retrieve the data.

A stored procedure can be run by issuing the `EXECUTE` statement along with the procedure's name and any parameters. When specifying parameters with the `EXECUTE` statement, parameters supplied in the format of `@parameter = value` can be supplied in any order; however, if one parameter is supplied in the form `@parameter = value`, all subsequent parameters must also be supplied in this way. If parameters are not supplied in the form `@parameter = value`, the parameters must be supplied in the order given in the `CREATE PROCEDURE` statement.

Executing stored procedures automatically

One or more stored procedures can execute automatically when SQL Server starts. The stored procedures must be created by the SA and executes under the SA account as a background process. The procedure(s) cannot have any input parameters.

There is no limit to the number of startup procedures you can have, but be aware that each consumes one connection while executing. If you need to execute multiple procedures at startup but you don't need to execute them in parallel, you can make one procedure the startup procedure and have that procedure call the other procedures. This uses only one connection.

Execution of the stored procedures starts when the last database has been recovered at startup. To skip launching these stored procedures, you can specify trace flag `4022` as a startup parameter. If you start SQL Server with minimal configuration (using the `-f` flag), the startup stored procedures are not executed.

To create a startup stored procedure, you must be logged in as the SA and create the stored procedure in the `master` database. Use `sp_procoption` to either:

- ◆ Make an existing stored procedure a startup procedure
- ◆ Stop a procedure from executing at SQL Server startup
- ◆ View a list of all procedures that execute at SQL Server startup

Nesting stored procedures

Stored procedures can use nesting (one stored procedure calling another). The nesting level is incremented when the called procedure starts execution, and it is decremented when the called procedure finishes execution. Exceeding the maximum levels of nesting causes the whole calling procedure chain to fail. The current nesting level is stored in the `@@nestlevel` function. To estimate the size of a compiled stored procedure, use the database consistency feature `DBCC MEMUSAGE`.

Recognizing SQL limits within a procedure

Any `SET` statement can be specified inside a stored procedure except `SET SHOW-PLAN_TEXT` and `SET SHOWPLAN_ALL`, which must be the only statements in the batch. The `SET` option chosen remains in effect during the execution of the stored procedure and then reverts to its former setting.

Inside a stored procedure, object names used with certain statements (the utility statements) must be qualified with the name of the object owner if other users are to use the stored procedure. The utility statements are: `ALTER TABLE`, `CREATE INDEX`, `CREATE TABLE`, all `DBCC` statements, `DROP TABLE`, `DROP INDEX`, `TRUNCATE TABLE`, and `UPDATE STATISTICS`.

Creating permissions

Permissions for the `CREATE PROCEDURE` statement default to the members of the `db_owner` and `db_ddladmin` fixed database roles. Members of the `db_owner` fixed database role members of the `sysadmin` fixed database role can transfer `CREATE PROCEDURE` permissions to other users. Permissions to execute a stored procedure are given to the procedure owner, who can grant execution permission on it to other database users.

Responding by executing a stored procedure

Stored procedures are executed in response to a program or script invocation. To execute stored procedure `pr_table1`, use the `execute` procedure or `call` command invoked within the caller, for example, an embedded SQL C program or a GUI front end (PowerBuilder).

```
execute procedure pr_table1
```

The EXECUTE statement is used to invoke a system procedure, a user-defined stored procedure, or an extended stored procedure. Use the following syntax to execute a stored procedure:

```
[[EXEC[UTE]] {[@return_status =]{procedure_name [;number] |
@procedure_name_var}[[@parameter =] {value | @variable [OUTPUT] |
[DEFAULT]] [,...n][WITH RECOMPILE]
```

The parameters for this stored procedure follow:

◆ *@return_status* — An optional integer variable that stores the return status of a stored procedure. This variable must be declared in the batch or stored procedure before it is used in an EXECUTE statement.

◆ *procedure_name* — The fully qualified or non-fully qualified name of the stored procedure to call. Procedure names must conform to the rules for identifiers. A procedure that has been created in another database can be executed if the user executing the procedure owns the procedure or has the appropriate permission to execute it in that database. A procedure can be executed on another server running SQL Server if the user executing the procedure has the appropriate permission to use that server (remote access) and to execute the procedure in that database. If a server name is specified but no database name is specified, SQL Server looks for the procedure in the user's default database.

◆ *@parameter* — The parameter for a procedure, as defined in the CREATE PROCEDURE statement. Parameter names must be preceded by the at sign (@). When used with the *@parameter_name = value* form, parameter names and constants do not have to be supplied in the order in which they are defined in the CREATE PROCEDURE statement. However, if the *@parameter_name = value* form is used for any parameter, it must be used for all subsequent parameters.

◆ *value* — The value of the parameter to the procedure. If parameter names are not specified, parameter values must be supplied in the order defined in the CREATE PROCEDURE statement. If the value of a parameter is an object name, is a character string, or is qualified by a database name or owner name, the entire name must be enclosed in single quotation marks. If the value of a parameter is a keyword, the keyword must be enclosed in double quotation marks.

◆ *@variable* — The variable that stores a parameter or a return parameter.

◆ OUTPUT — Specifies that the stored procedure returns a parameter. The matching parameter in the stored procedure must also have been created with the keyword OUTPUT. If OUTPUT parameters are being used and the intent is to use the return values in other statements within the calling batch or procedure, the value of the parameter must be passed as a variable (that is, @parameter = @variable). You cannot execute a procedure specifying OUTPUT for a parameter that is not defined as an OUTPUT parameter in the CREATE PROCEDURE statement. Constants cannot be passed to stored procedures using OUTPUT; the return parameter requires a variable name. The variable's data type must be declared and a value assigned before executing the procedure. Return parameters can be of any data type except text or image.

◆ DEFAULT — Supplies the default value of the parameter as defined in the procedure. When the procedure expects a value for a parameter that does not have a defined default and either a parameter is missing or the DEFAULT keyword is specified, an error occurs.

◆ WITH RECOMPILE — Forces a new plan to be compiled. Use this option if the parameter you are supplying is atypical or if the data has significantly changed. The changed plan is used in subsequent executions.

◆ @string_variable — The name of a local variable. The @string_variable variable can be of char, varchar, nchar, or nvarchar data type with a maximum value of the server's available memory. If the string is greater than 4,000 characters, concatenate multiple local variables to use for the EXECUTE string.

◆ Permissions — The EXECUTE statement permissions for a stored procedure default to the owner of the stored procedure, who can transfer them to other users. Permissions to use the statement(s) within the EXECUTE string are checked at the time EXECUTE is encountered, even if the EXECUTE statement is included within a stored procedure. When a stored procedure is run that executes a string, permissions are checked in the context of the user who executes the procedure, not in the context of the user who created the procedure. However, if a user owns two stored procedures in which the first procedure calls the second, then EXECUTE permission checking is not performed for the second stored procedure.

Improving procedure performance

As a database is changed by such events as adding indexes, the original query plans used to access its tables should be optimized again by recompiling them. This optimization happens automatically the first time that a procedure is run after SQL Server is restarted. It also happens if an underlying table used by the procedure changes. But if a new index is added that the procedure might benefit from,

optimization does not automatically happen (until, for example, the next time SQL
Server is restarted and the procedure is run). The sp_recompile system procedure
forces a recompile of a procedure the next time it's run. Additionally, before recompiling it is a good idea to execute, that is, run, the UPDATE STATISTICS utility. The
UPDATE STATISTICS utility updates information about the distribution of key values for one or more statistics groups (collections) in the specified table.

SQL Server keeps statistics about the distribution of the key values in each index
and uses these statistics to determine which index(es) to use in query processing.
Query optimization depends on the accuracy of the distribution steps. If there is
significant change in the key values in the index, rerun UPDATE STATISTICS on that
index. If a large amount of data in an indexed column has been added, changed, or
removed (that is, if the distribution of key values has changed), or the table has
been truncated using the TRUNCATE TABLE statement and then repopulated, use
UPDATE STATISTICS. To see when the statistics were last updated, use the STATS_
DATE function.

Passing data to a stored procedure

You can pass variables or parameters into a stored procedure at run time. Note that
the CREATE PROCEDURE statement must declare every value being passed in. The
variables must be declared inside of the parentheses. You may give default values
to variables that are passed into procedures. The number of parameters in the EXE-
CUTE statement should be less than or equal to the number of parameters in the
CREATE PROCEDURE statement. Any parameters that are not passed in will be given
their default values or else will be undefined. The assignment of values is from left
to right.

You can also execute the procedure by tagging each value with its respective
variable name (as defined in the stored procedure). Parameters are used to exchange
data between stored procedures and whatever called the stored procedure. Input
parameters allow the caller to pass a data value to the stored procedure. Output
parameters allow the stored procedure to pass a data value back to the caller. Every
stored procedure returns an integer return code to the caller. If the stored procedure
does not explicitly set a value for the return code, the return code is 0. The sample
stored procedure shown in Listing 16-2 illustrates the use of an input parameter, an
output parameter, and a return code.

Listing 16-2: Stored Procedure with Input and Output Parameters

```
USE DBPGA001
GO
-- Create a procedure that takes one input parameter
-- and returns one output parameter and a return code.
CREATE PROCEDURE Pr_sample @Ai_InputParm INT,
@Ai_OutputParm INT OUTPUT
AS
-- Declare and initialize a variable to hold @@ERROR.
```

```
DECLARE @ErrorSave INT
SET @ErrorSave = 0
-- Do a SELECT using the input parameter.
SELECT FirstName, LastName, Title
FROM TB_Employees
WHERE EmployeeID = @Ai_InputParm
-- Save any nonzero @@ERROR value.
IF (@@ERROR <> 0)
SET @ErrorSave = @@ERROR
-- Set a value in the output parameter.
SELECT @Ai_OutputParm = MAX(Quantity)
FROM TB_ORDER
IF (@@ERROR <> 0)
SET @ErrorSave = @@ERROR
-- Returns 0 if all went well, otherwise return the last error.
RETURN @ErrorSave
GO
```

When a stored procedure is executed, input parameters can either have their value set to a constant or use the value of a variable. Output parameters and return codes must return their values into a variable. Parameters and return codes can exchange data values with either Transact-SQL variables or application variables.

If a stored procedure is called from a batch or a script, the parameters and return code values can use Transact-SQL variables defined in the same batch. The example shown in Listing 16-3 is a batch that executes the procedure created in Listing 16-2. The input parameter is specified as a constant, and the output parameter and return code place their values in Transact-SQL variables.

Listing 16-3: Executing a Stored Procedure within a Batch Script

```
-- Declare the variables for the return code and output parameter.
DECLARE @ReturnCode INT
DECLARE @MaxQtyVariable INT
-- Execute the stored procedure and specify which variables
-- are to receive the output parameter and return code values.
EXEC @ReturnCode = Pr_sample @Ai_InputParm = 9,
@Ai_OutputParm = @MaxQtyVariable OUTPUT
-- Show the values returned.
PRINT ' '
PRINT 'Return code = ' + CAST(@ReturnCode AS CHAR(10))
PRINT 'Maximum Quantity = ' + CAST(@MaxQtyVariable AS CHAR(10))
GO
```

An application can use parameter markers bound to program variables to exchange data between application variables, parameters, and return codes.

Returning values from a stored procedure

As we illustrated in the preceding example, you can return one or more values from a stored procedure. Typically in an update you are sending a row image, the key, or a set of columns, and you are receiving back a return code and perhaps a row count. Depending upon which front end you use, you will need to determine and set up a command set for executing SQL Server stored procedures for initiating, sending data to, and receiving data from the procedure. There are a host of tools — SilverStream, PowerBuilder, Delphi, and Visual Basic as well as the SQL Server tools — that we will discuss shortly. The application tool receives returned values from a stored procedure similarly to the way it receives returned values from a SELECT statement.

Stored procedures return a status value that indicates that they completed successfully or states the reasons for failure. This value can be stored in a variable when a procedure is called and used in future Transact-SQL statements. SQL Server–defined return status values for failure range from 1 through 99; users can define their own return status values outside this range. Stored procedures can also return information to the caller through return parameters. Parameters designated as return parameters in the CREATE PROCEDURE and EXECUTE statements return the parameter values back to the calling procedure. The caller can then use conditional statements to check the returned value.

Return status values and return parameters allow you to *modularize* your stored procedures. A set of SQL statements used by several stored procedures can be created as a single procedure that returns its execution status or the values of its parameters to the calling procedure. For example, many of the SQL Server–supplied system procedures execute a procedure that verifies that certain parameters are valid identifiers. Remote procedure calls (stored procedures run on a remote SQL server) also return both types of information. All of the following examples in this section could be executed remotely if the syntax of the EXECUTE statement included the server, database, and owner names as well as the procedure name.

Stored procedures can return an integer value called a *return status*. This status can indicate that the procedure completed successfully, or it can indicate the reason for failure. SQL Server has a defined set of return values; users can also define their own values. When a CREATE PROCEDURE statement and an EXECUTE statement both include the OUTPUT option with a parameter name, the procedure can use a variable to return the value of that parameter to the caller. By use of the OUTPUT keyword, any changes to the parameter that result from the execution of the procedure are retained even after the procedure finishes executing, and the variable can subsequently be used in additional SQL statements in the batch or calling procedure. This is often referred to as a "pass-by-reference capability." If the OUTPUT keyword is not used, changes to the parameter are not retained after the procedure finishes executing. In addition, a value can be returned directly ("pass-by value") using the RETURN statement.

A single stored procedure can use any or all of these capabilities to return:

♦ One or more results sets

♦ An explicit return value (using the RETURN statement)

♦ An output parameter

The values passed in the parameters must be passed in this form:

```
@parameter = @variable [OUTPUT]
```

If you specify output while you're executing a procedure and the parameter is not defined using OUTPUT in the stored procedure, you'll get an error message. It is not wrong to call a procedure that includes return value specifications without requesting the return values with OUTPUT; you just won't get the return values.

The examples in Listing 16-4 illustrate how some SQL Server application interfaces execute stored procedures. Notes on the front-end procedure interfaces follow. It is prudent to check with each vendor to ensure that your GUI-to-SQL Server interface is set up properly and is optimized for integrity and performance.

Listing 16-4: Invoking a Stored Procedure

```
POWERBUILDER
DECLARE logical_procedure_name PROCEDURE FOR
    SQL SERVER_procedure_name
    ({:arg1,:arg2 , ...})
    {USING transaction_object};

create procedure sp_delete_order (:p_sku_num) into
    :p_sku_num, :p_item_count as .....
end procedure

declare del_order_proc procedure for sp_delete_order(:p_sku_num)
into    :p_sku_num, :p_item_count using sqlca;

execute del_order_proc (1001);
```

PowerBuilder requires a declarative statement to identify the database-stored procedure that is being used and to specify a logical name. The logical name is used to reference the procedure in subsequent SQL statements. The general syntax for declaring a procedure is:

```
DECLARE logical_procedure_name PROCEDURE FOR
    SQL SERVER_procedure_name
    ({:arg1,:arg2 , ...})
    {USING transaction_object};
```

where *logical_procedure_name* can be any valid PowerBuilder identifier and SQL SERVER_procedure_name is the name of the stored procedure in the SQL SERVER database. The parentheses after SQL SERVER_procedure_name are required even if the procedure has no parameters. You can create a stored procedure within PowerBuilder by changing the Terminator Character value in Database preferences to something other than a semicolon (;), for example, the | character (obtained on some keyboards by pressing Shift+Backslash). You need to do this because SQL SERVER uses semicolons in its internal syntax. You can then create stored procedures in the Database Administration painter. The parameter references can take the form of any valid parameter string that SQL SERVER accepts. PowerBuilder does not inspect the parameter list format except for purposes of variable substitution. The USING clause is required only if you are using a transaction object other than the default transaction object (SQLCA).

You specify the EXECUTE statement the same way regardless of whether a stored procedure takes arguments. The arguments used in the DECLARE statement get passed automatically, without you having to state them in the EXECUTE statement.

Using a RETURN statement

When a RETURN is executed, control is returned to the calling routine (either another stored procedure or the application), and all variables are reset to undefined. The next time the procedure is called, it is started over. That is to say that the RETURN exits unconditionally from a query or procedure. The RETURN statement is immediate and complete and can be used at any point to exit from a procedure, batch, or statement block. Statements following RETURN are not executed. In this statement

```
RETURN [(integer_expression)]
```

the *integer_expression* is the integer value returned. Stored procedures can return an integer value to a calling procedure or an application. Unless documented otherwise, all system-stored procedures return a value of 0, which indicates success; a nonzero value indicates failure. A RETURN statement cannot return a null value. If a procedure attempts to return a null value (for example, using RETURN @status and @status is NULL), a warning message is generated and a value from 0 through –14 is returned. The return status value can be included in subsequent Transact-SQL statements in the batch or procedure that executed the current procedure, but it must be entered in the following form:

```
EXECUTE @return_status = procedure_name
```

As mentioned previously, a zero (0) indicates a successful return and negative values from –1 through –99 indicate different reasons for failure. If more than one error occurs during execution, the status with the highest absolute value is returned. User-defined return values always take precedence over those supplied by

SQL Server. User-defined return status values should not conflict with those reserved by SQL Server. If no user-defined return value is provided, the SQL Server value is used. The values 0 through –14 are currently used.

Batches and Control-of-Flow Language

Up to this point, most of the examples in the chapter have consisted pretty much of individual statements. You obviously can submit individual statements to SQL Server one at a time, entering statements and receiving results interactively à la ISQL. SQL Server can also process multiple statements submitted as a batch, either interactively or from a file. A batch of SQL statements is terminated by an end-of-batch signal that instructs SQL Server to go ahead and execute the statements. Technically speaking, a single SQL statement can constitute a batch, but it is more common to think of a batch as containing multiple statements.

Frequently, a batch of statements is written to an operating system file before being submitted to ISQL. Within a stored procedure this is also possible. Transact SQL provides special constructs called *control-of-flow language* that allow the user to control the flow of execution of statements. Control-of-flow language can be used in single statements, batches, stored procedures, and triggers. Without control-of-flow language, separate SQL statements are performed sequentially, as they occur. Control-of-flow language permits statements to connect and to relate to each other using programming-like constructs. Control-of-flow language constructs are illustrated in Listing 16-5.

Listing 16-5: Control-of-Flow Constructs

```
IF Boolean_expression
{sql_statement | statement_block}
[ELSE
{sql_statement | statement_block}] for conditional performance of
commands
Example IF@proc_name = NULL
        delete from procedure_log
      ELSE
        delete from procedure_log
        where log_proc = @proc_name
WHILE Boolean_expression
{sql_statement | statement_block}
[BREAK]
{sql_statement | statement_block}
[CONTINUE]
Example WHILE (@@fetch_status = 0)
    BEGIN
```

```
            select @key_cnt = count(*) from cust_credit_hist
            where dbcode = @dbcode and cust_no = @cust_no
            IF @key_cnt > 1 BEGIN
                  insert into log_duplicates (dbcode, cust_no, dup_cnt)
                        values(@dbcode, @cust_no, @key_cnt)
                            END
            fetch next from SELECT_FILE into @dbcode, @cust_no
      END
CASE input_expression
WHEN when_expression THEN result_expression
[,...n]
[ELSE else_result_expression]
END
Example CASE
WHEN @idx_allowduprow = 1 THEN ', ALLOW_DUP_ROW '
ELSE NULL
END
```

Declaring variables

All variables used in a stored procedure must be defined in the stored procedure.

```
DECLARE @local_variable
```

Variables are declared in the body of a batch or procedure with the DECLARE statement and given or assigned values with either a SET or SELECT statement. Cursor variables can be declared with this statement and used with other cursor-related statements. After declaration, all variables are initialized as NULL.

The syntax for this construct is as follows:

```
DECLARE
{{@local_variable data_type}|
{cursor_variable_name CURSOR}} [, ...n]
```

The parameters for this construct are described in the following list:

- ◆ @local_variable — The name of a variable. Variable names must begin with an at sign (@). Local variable names must conform to the rules for identifiers.

- ◆ data_type — Any system-supplied or user-defined data type. A variable cannot be of the text, ntext, or image data type. For more information on system data types, see Chapter 11, "Constructing the Database." For more information about user-defined data types, see the SQL internal documentation on the system stored procedure sp_addtype.

- ◆ *cursor_variable_name* — The name of a cursor variable. A cursor name cannot be the same name as a variable of any type (the name cannot start with @. The *cursor_variable_name* parameter must conform to the naming specifications of *@local_variable*.

- ◆ CURSOR — Specifies that the variable is a local, cursor variable.

- ◆ *n* — A placeholder indicating that multiple variables can be specified and assigned values.

Variables are often used in a batch or procedure as counters for WHILE, LOOP, or for an IF . . . ELSE block. Variables can be used only in expressions, not in place of object names or keywords. To construct dynamic SQL statements, use EXECUTE. The scope of a local variable is the batch, stored procedure, or statement block in which it is declared. For more information about using local variables in statement blocks, see the BEGIN . . . END block construct described later in this chapter.

A cursor variable that currently has a cursor assigned to it can be referenced as a source in any of the following statements:

CLOSE

DEALLOCATE

FETCH

OPEN

Positioned DELETE or UPDATE

SET CURSOR variable (on the right side)

In all these statements, SQL Server raises an error if a referenced cursor variable exists but does not have a cursor currently allocated to it. If a referenced cursor variable does not exist, SQL Server raises the same error raised for an undeclared variable of another type.

A cursor variable can be the target of a cursor type or another cursor variable can be referenced as a target in an EXECUTE statement if the cursor variable does not have a cursor currently assigned to it and should be regarded as a pointer to the cursor. (For more information, see the Transact SQL statement SET *@local_variable* in the SQL Server online documentation.)

Variables passed into a program must be defined in the CREATE PROCEDURE statement. Variables can have the same names as columns. If there is a variable with the same name as a column used in a SQL statement, the procedure will assume that the variable name is being referenced, not the column name. To reference the column, qualify the column name with the table name.

Assigning values to variables

If variables are not assigned a value, they have an undefined value. The undefined value is treated very differently than a NULL value. Any attempts to use those variables will result in an error. It is best to assign a value to a variable before it is used, using a SET statement. The SET keyword is required. The right-hand side of the SET statement can contain any SQL expression that can be used in a WHERE clause except an aggregate expression. You may assign values to more than one variable at a time. When a value is assigned to a variable in a stored procedure, the procedure will attempt to convert the value to the data type supplied. The SET statement will fail if it cannot convert the value.

The SET @local_variable statement sets the specified local variable, previously created with the DECLARE @local_variable statement, to the given value.

The syntax for this construct is as follows:

```
SET {{@local_variable = expression}| { @cursor_variable = {
@cursor_variable
| cursor_name| { CURSOR[FORWARD_ONLY | SCROLL] [STATIC | KEYSET |
DYNAMIC][READ_ONLY | SCROLL_LOCKS | OPTIMISTIC]
FOR select_statement
[FOR {READ ONLY | UPDATE [OF column_list] } ]
}}}}
```

The parameters for this construct are discussed in the following list:

♦ @local_variable – The name of a variable of any type except cursor. Variable names must begin with only one at sign (@). Variable names must conform to the rules for identifiers. The variable must have been previously declared with a DECLARE @local_variable statement.

♦ expression – Any valid Microsoft SQL Server expression.

♦ cursor_variable – The name of a cursor variable. If the target cursor variable previously referenced a different cursor, that previous reference is removed.

♦ cursor_name – The name of the a cursor declared using the DECLARE CURSOR statement.

♦ CURSOR – Specifies that the SET statement contains a declaration of a cursor.

♦ SCROLL – Specifies that the cursor supports all fetch options (FIRST, LAST, NEXT, PRIOR, RELATIVE, and ABSOLUTE).

◆ FORWARD_ONLY – Specifies that the cursor only supports the FETCH NEXT option. The cursor can only be retrieved in one direction, from the first to the last row. If FORWARD_ONLY is specified without the STATIC, KEYSET, or DYNAMIC keyword, the cursor is implemented as DYNAMIC. When neither FORWARD_ONLY nor SCROLL are specified, FORWARD_ONLY is the default unless the keywords STATIC, KEYSET, or DYNAMIC are specified. STATIC, KEYSET, and DYNAMIC cursors default to SCROLL.

◆ STATIC – Defines a cursor that makes a temporary copy of the data to be used by the cursor. All requests to the cursor are answered from this temporary table in tempdb; therefore, modifications made to base tables are not reflected in the data returned by fetches made to this cursor, and this cursor does not allow modifications.

◆ KEYSET – Specifies that the membership and order of rows in the cursor are fixed when the cursor is opened. The set of keys that uniquely identify the rows is built into a table in tempdb known as the keyset. Changes to nonkey values in the base tables, either made by the cursor owner or committed by other users, are visible as the owner scrolls around the cursor. Inserts made by other users are not visible (inserts cannot be made through a Transact-SQL Server cursor). If a row is deleted, an attempt to fetch the row returns an @@FETCH_STATUS of –2. Updates of key values from outside the cursor resemble a delete of the old row followed by an insert of the new row. The row with the new values is not visible, and attempts to fetch the row with the old values return an @@FETCH_STATUS of –2. The new values are visible if the update is done through the cursor by specifying the WHERE CURRENT OF clause.

◆ DYNAMIC – Defines a cursor that reflects all data changes made to the rows in its result set as you scroll around the cursor. The data values, order, and membership of the rows can change on each fetch. The absolute and relative fetch options are not supported with dynamic cursors.

◆ READ_ONLY – Prevents updates from being made through this cursor. The cursor cannot be referenced in a WHERE CURRENT OF clause in an UPDATE or DELETE statement. This option overrides the default capability of a cursor to be updated.

◆ SCROLL LOCKS – Specifies that positioned updates or deletes made through the cursor are guaranteed to succeed. SQL Server locks the rows as they are read into the cursor to ensure their availability for later modifications.

◆ OPTIMISTIC – Specifies that positioned updates or deletes made through the cursor do not succeed if the row has been updated since it was read into the cursor. SQL Server does not lock rows as they are read into the cursor. It instead uses comparisons of timestamp column values, or a checksum value if the table has no timestamp column, to determine if the row was modified after it was read into the cursor. If the row was modified, the attempted positioned update or delete fails.

◆ FOR *select_statement* — A standard SELECT statement that defines the result set of the cursor. The keywords COMPUTE, COMPUTE BY, FOR BROWSE, and INTO are not allowed within the *select_statement* of a cursor declaration. If DISTINCT, UNION, GROUP BY, and/or HAVING are used, or an aggregate expression is included in the *select_list,* the cursor will be created as STATIC. If each of the underlying tables does not have a unique index and a SQL-92 SCROLL cursor or a Transact-SQL KEYSET cursor is requested, it will automatically be a STATIC cursor. If the *select_statement* contains an ORDER BY where the columns are not unique row identifiers, a DYNAMIC cursor is converted to a KEYSET cursor or to a STATIC cursor if a KEYSET cursor cannot be opened. This also happens for a cursor defined using SQL-92. The syntax for this construct is ": " but without the STATIC keyword.

◆ READ ONLY — Prevents updates from being made through this cursor. The cursor cannot be referenced in a WHERE CURRENT OF clause in an UPDATE or DELETE statement. This option overrides the default capability of a cursor to be updated. This keyword varies from the previous READ_ONLY by having a space instead of an underscore between READ and ONLY.

◆ UPDATE [OF *column_list*] — Defines updatable columns within the cursor. If OF *column_list* is supplied, only the columns listed will allow modifications. If no list is supplied, all columns can be updated unless the cursor has been defined as READ_ONLY. After declaration, all variables are initialized to NULL. Use the SET statement to assign a value that is not NULL to a declared variable. The SET statement that assigns a value to the variable returns a single value. When initializing multiple variables, use a separate SET statement for each local variable. Variables can be used only in expressions, not in place of object names or keywords. To construct dynamic SQL statements, use EXECUTE.

Using statement blocks

Every stored procedure has at least one statement block, which is a group of Transact-SQL and SQL statements. There is an implicit statement block that begins after the CREATE PROCEDURE statement and continues to the end of the procedure. You can define explicit statement blocks by using the BEGIN and END statements.

Explicit statement blocks enable you to do the following:

◆ Define variables to be used only within a statement block

◆ Handle exceptions differently within that statement block

A variable is valid within a statement block, and any statement block nested within that statement block, unless it is redefined. In the preceding example, variable_1 is defined in the outer statement block and in the nested statement block. This means there are two different, independent variables called variable_1, and variable_1 takes on a value of 2 only within the nested statement block. The value that gets returned a different variable_1 is 1. Don't try this at home.

Using the IF . . . THEN . . . ELSE statement

The IF . . . ELSE statement imposes conditions on the execution of a Transact-SQL statement. The Transact-SQL statement following an IF keyword and its condition is executed if the condition is satisfied (when the Boolean expression returns TRUE). The optional ELSE keyword introduces an alternate Transact-SQL statement that is executed when the IF condition is not satisfied (when the Boolean expression returns FALSE).

The syntax for this construct is as follows:

```
IF Boolean_expression
{sql_statement | statement_block}
[ELSE
{sql_statement | statement_block}]
```

The parameters for this construct are discussed in the following list:

- ◆ Boolean_expression – An expression that returns TRUE or FALSE. If the Boolean expression contains a SELECT statement, the SELECT statement must be enclosed in parentheses.

- ◆ {sql_statement | statement_block} – Any Transact-SQL statement or statement grouping as defined with a statement block. The IF or ELSE condition can affect the performance of only one Transact-SQL statement, unless a statement block is used.

IF . . . ELSE constructs can be used in batches, in stored procedures, and in ad hoc queries. The IF keyword tests can be nested, either after another IF or following an ELSE. There is no limit to the number of nested levels. Following is an example:

```
if @num_months_prior =  0
    select @amt_1  = @monthly_amount + @amt_1
else if @num_months_prior =  1
    select @amt_2  = @monthly_amount + @amt_2
```

Using the BEGIN . . . END statement

The BEGIN . . . END statement encloses a series of Transact-SQL statements so that a group of Transact-SQL statements can be executed. The BEGIN . . . END statement blocks can be nested.

The syntax for this construct is as follows:

```
BEGIN
{sql_statement | statement_block}
END
```

The parameter for this construct, {sql_statement | statement_block} is any valid Transact-SQL statement or statement grouping as defined with a statement block. To define a statement block, use the control-of-flow language keywords BEGIN and END. Following is an example:

```
BEGIN
    select @idx_cmd =
    'create ' +CASE WHEN @idx_unique = 1 THEN ' unique ' ELSE NULL
END
```

Using the WHILE loop

The WHILE loop sets a condition for the repeated execution of a sql_statement or statement block. The statements are executed repeatedly as long as the specified condition is true. The execution of statements in the WHILE loop can be controlled from inside the loop with the BREAK and CONTINUE keywords.

The syntax for this construct is as follows:

```
WHILE Boolean_expression
{sql_statement | statement_block}
[BREAK]
{sql_statement | statement_block}
[CONTINUE]
```

The parameters for this construct are discussed in the following list:

♦ Boolean_expression — An expression that returns TRUE or FALSE. If the Boolean expression contains a SELECT statement, the SELECT statement must be enclosed in parentheses.

♦ {sql_statement | statement_block} — Any Transact-SQL statement or statement grouping as defined with a statement block.

- BREAK — Causes an exit from the innermost WHILE loop. Any statements appearing after the END keyword, marking the end of the loop, are executed.

- CONTINUE — Causes the WHILE loop to restart, ignoring any statements after the CONTINUE keyword.

If two or more WHILE loops are nested, the inner BREAK exits to the next outermost loop. First, all the statements after the end of the inner loop run, and then the next outermost loop restarts.

Using the CASE function

The CASE function evaluates a list of conditions and returns one of multiple possible result expressions. The CASE function has two formats: The simple CASE function compares an expression to a set of simple expressions to determine the result. The searched CASE function evaluates a set of Boolean expressions to determine the result. Both formats support an optional ELSE. The syntax for a simple CASE function is as follows:

```
CASE input_expression
WHEN when_expression THEN result_expression [,...n]
[ELSE else_result_expression]
END
```

The syntax for a searched CASE function is as follows:

```
CASE
WHEN Boolean_expression THEN result_expression [,...n]
[ELSE else_result_expression]
END
```

The parameters for this construct are discussed in the following list:

- input_expression — The expression that is evaluated when using the simple CASE format. The input_expression is any valid Microsoft SQL Server expression.

- WHEN when_expression — A simple expression to which input_expression is compared when using the simple CASE format. The when_expression is any valid SQL Server expression. The data types of input_expression and each when_expression must be either the same or must be an implicit conversion.

♦ *n* – A placeholder indicating that multiple WHEN *when_expression* and THEN *result_expression* clauses, or multiple WHEN *Boolean_expression* and THEN *result_expression* clauses can be used.

♦ THEN *result_expression* – The expression that is returned when *input_expression* evaluates to TRUE, or *Boolean_expression* evaluates to true. The *result_expression* is any valid SQL Server expression.

♦ ELSE *else_result_expression* – The expression that is returned if no comparison operation evaluates to TRUE. If this is omitted and no comparison operation evaluates to TRUE, CASE returns NULL. The *else_result_expression* is any valid SQL Server expression. The data types of *else_result_expression* and any *result_expression* must either be the same or be an implicit conversion.

♦ WHEN *Boolean_expression* – The Boolean expression that is evaluated when using the searched CASE format. The *Boolean_expression* is any valid Boolean expression.

♦ Result Types – Returns the highest precedence type from the set of types in *result_expression* and the optional *else_result_expression*.

♦ Result Values – For the simple CASE function, this parameter evaluates *input_expression*, and then, in the order specified, evaluates *input_ expression* = *when_expression* for each WHEN clause. It returns the *result_expression* of the first (*input_expression* = *when_expression*) that evaluates to TRUE. If no *input_expression* = *when_expression* evaluates to TRUE, SQL Server returns the *else_result_expression* if an ELSE clause is specified, or a NULL value if no ELSE clause is specified.

For the searched CASE function, this parameter evaluates, in the order specified, *Boolean_expression* for each WHEN clause. It returns *result_ expression* of the first *Boolean_expression* that evaluates to TRUE. If no *Boolean_expression* evaluates to TRUE, SQL Server returns the *else_result_expression* if an ELSE clause is specified, or a NULL value if no ELSE clause is specified.

Using an update cursor

An update cursor puts an update lock on a row so that no other process can update the row until either the next row is fetched (if it was only read) or an update or delete has occurred and the transaction has ended. An update cursor is useful if you do not want other users to change the row between the moment it is fetched into your procedure and the moment it is changed.

```
while (SQLCODE == 0)
BEGIN
```

```
EXEC SQL FETCH C1 INTO :fname,:lname;
if (SQLCODE == 0)
UPDATE TB_PGA SET pga_lname=:lname
WHERE CURRENT OF C1;
END
```

Using operating system commands

The isql utility enables you to enter Transact-SQL statements, system procedures, and script files; it uses DB-Library to communicate with Microsoft SQL Server.

 DB-Library remains at the SQL Server version 6.5 level of functionality. DB-Library applications such as isql do not support some SQL Server 7.0 features. For example, they cannot retrieve Unicode ntext data. The osql utility has a user interface modeled on isql and supports the full set of SQL Server 7 features.

The syntax for the isql utility is as follows:

```
isql -U login_id [-e] [-E] [-p] [-n] [-d db_name] [-q "query"] [-Q
"query"]
[-c cmd_end] [-h headers] [-w column_width] [-s col_separator]
[-t time_out] [-m error_level] [-L] [-?] [-r {0 | 1}]
[-H wksta_name] [-P password]
[-S server_name] [-i input_file] [-o output_file] [-a packet_size]
[-b] [-O] [-l time_out] [-x max_text_size]
```

The parameters are discussed in the following list:

◆ -U login_id – The user login ID. Login IDs are case-sensitive.

◆ -e – Echoes input.

◆ -E – Uses a trusted connection instead of requesting a password.

◆ -p – Prints performance statistics.

◆ -n – Removes numbering and the prompt symbol (>) from input lines.

◆ -d db_name (Issues a USE db_name statement when isql is started.

◆ -q "query" – Executes a query when isql starts. (Note that the query statement should not include GO). Use double, straight quotation marks around the query and single quotation marks around anything embedded in the query.

♦ -Q "*query*" — Executes a query and immediately exits isql. Use double quotation marks around the query and single quotation marks around anything embedded in the query.

♦ -c *cmd_end* — Specifies the command terminator. By default, commands are terminated and sent to SQL Server by entering GO on a line by itself. When you reset the command terminator, do not use SQL reserved words or characters that have special meaning to the operating system, whether preceded by a backslash or not.

♦ -h *headers* — Specifies the number of rows to print between column headings. The default is to print headings one time for each set of query results. Use –1 to specify that no headers will be printed. If using –1, there must be no space between the parameter and the setting (-h-1, not -h -1).

♦ -w *column_width* — Allows the user to set the screen width for output. The default is 80 characters. When an output line has reached its maximum screen width, it is broken into multiple lines.

♦ -s *col_separator* — Specifies the column-separator character, which is a blank space by default. To use characters that have special meaning to the operating system (for example, | ; & < >), enclose the character in double quotation marks (" ").

♦ -t *time_out* — Specifies the number of seconds before a command times out. If no *time_out* value is specified, a command runs indefinitely; the default time out for logging into isql is eight seconds.

♦ -m *error_level* — Customizes the display of error messages. The message number, state, and error level are displayed for errors of the specified severity level or higher. Nothing is displayed for errors of severity levels lower than the specified level. Use –1 to specify that all headers are returned with messages, even informational messages. If using –1, there must be no space between the parameter and the setting (-m-1, not -m -1).

♦ -L — Lists the locally configured servers and the names of the servers broadcasting on the network.

♦ -? — Displays the syntax as follows: summary of isql switches.

♦ -r {0 | 1} — Redirects message output to the screen (stderr). If you don't specify a parameter, or if you specify 0, only error messages with severity 17 or higher are redirected. If you specify 1, all message output (including "print") is redirected.

♦ -H *wksta_name* — A workstation name. The workstation name is stored in *sysprocesses.hostname* and is displayed by sp_who. If it is not specified, the current computer name is assumed.

◆ -P *password* — A user-specified password. If the -P option is not used, isql prompts for a password. If the -P option is used at the end of the command prompt without any password, isql uses the default password (NULL). Passwords are case sensitive.

◆ -S *server_name* — Specifies which SQL Server to connect to. The *server_name* is the name of the server computer on the network. This option is required if you are executing isql from a remote computer.

◆ -i *input_file* — Identifies the file that contains a batch of SQL statements or stored procedures. The less than (<) comparison operator can be used in place of -i.

◆ -o *output_file* — Identifies the file that receives output from isql. The greater than (>) comparison operator can be used in place of -o.

◆ -a *packet_size* — Allows you to request a different-sized packet. The valid values for *packet_size* are 512 through 65535. The default value for the Microsoft Windows NT–based versions of isql is 8192; otherwise, the default value is 512 for MS-DOS, although larger sizes can be requested with that version as well. Increased packet size can enhance performance on larger script execution where the number of SQL statements between GO statements is substantial. Microsoft testing indicates that 8192 is typically the fastest setting for bulk copy operations. A larger packet size can be requested, but isql defaults to 512 if the request cannot be granted.

◆ -b — Specifies that isql exits and returns a DOS ERRORLEVEL value when an error occurs. The value returned to the DOS ERRORLEVEL variable is 1 when the SQL Server error message has a severity of 10 or greater; otherwise, the value returned is 0. MS-DOS batch files can test the value of DOS ERRORLEVEL and handle the error appropriately.

◆ -0 — Specifies that isql reverts to the behavior of earlier versions. These features are deactivated:

  ■ EOF batch processing

  ■ Automatic console width scaling

  ■ Wide messages

  It also sets the default DOS ERRORLEVEL value to -1.

◆ -l *time_out* — Specifies the number of seconds before an isql login times out. If no *time_out* value is specified, a command runs indefinitely. The default time out for login to isql is eight seconds.

◆ -x *max_text_size* — Specifies, in bytes, the maximum length of text data to return. Text values longer than *max_text_size* are truncated. If *max_text_size* is not specified, text data is truncated at 4,096 bytes.

Practical notes on developing SQL scripts and stored procedures

All DB-Library applications, such as isql, work as SQL Server 6.5-level clients when connected to SQL Server 7. They do not support some of the new SQL Server 7 features. The osql utility is based on ODBC and does support all new SQL Server 7 features. Use osql to run scripts that isql cannot run.

The SQL Server Query Analyzer default is to save SQL scripts as Unicode files. The isql utility does not support Unicode input files. Attempting to specify one of these files in the -i switch results in a 170 error:

```
Incorrect The Syntax is as follows:  near ' '.
```

Use the osql utility to run these Unicode files. An alternative is to specify ANSI instead of Unicode in the File format list of the SQL Server Query Analyzer File → Save As dialog box.

The isql utility is started directly from the operating system with the case-sensitive options listed here. After starting, isql accepts Transact-SQL statements and sends them to SQL Server interactively. The results are formatted and printed on the standard output device (the screen). Use QUIT or EXIT to exit from isql.

If you do not specify a username when you start isql, SQL Server checks for the environment variables and uses those. For example, isqluser=(user) or isqlserver=(server). If no environment variables are set, the workstation username is used. If you do not specify a server, the name of the workstation is used.

If neither the -U or -P option is used, SQL Server attempts to connect using Windows NT Authentication Mode. Authentication is based on the Windows NT account of the user running isql.

In addition to using Transact-SQL statements within isql, these commands are also available.

The command terminators GO (by default), RESET, ED, !!, EXIT, QUIT, and Ctrl+C are recognized only if they appear at the beginning of a line, immediately following the isql prompt. Anything entered on the same line after these keywords is disregarded by isql.

The GO command signals both the end of a batch and the execution of any cached Transact-SQL statements. When you press Enter at the end of each input line, isql caches the statements on that line. When you press Enter after typing GO, all of the currently cached statements are sent as a batch to SQL Server.

The current isql utility works as if there is an implied GO at the end of any script executed so all statements in the script execute. Some earlier versions of isql would not send any statements to the server unless there was at least one GO in an input script. Any statements after the last GO would not be executed. Earlier versions of the isql utility may require that GO be at the start of a line, without any blanks preceding it.

End a command by typing a line beginning with a command terminator. The results are printed once, at the end of execution. With `isql`, there is a limit of 1,000 characters per line. Large statements should be spread across multiple lines.

Operating system commands

Operating system commands can also be executed by starting a line with two exclamation points (`!!`) followed by the command. The command recall facilities of `DOSKEY` can be used to recall and modify previously entered `isql` statements on a computer running Windows NT. The existing query buffer can be cleared by typing `RESET`.

When running stored procedures, `isql` prints a blank line between each set of results in a batch. In addition, the "0 rows affected" message does not appear when it doesn't apply to the statement executed.

Semicolons (`;`) should be placed after every statement in a stored procedure, including the `FOR`, `FOREACH`, and `WHILE` statements and after the `END FOR`, `END FOREACH`, and `END WHILE` statements. The rules are similar with the `IF` and `ON EXCEPTION` statements.

If you have a `RETURNING` clause in the `CREATE PROCEDURE` statement, use a semicolon after the `RETURNING CLAUSE`.

What Is a Trigger?

A *trigger* is a special kind of stored procedure that goes into effect when you insert, delete, or update data in a specified table. Triggers can help maintain the referential integrity of your data by maintaining consistency among logically related data in different tables. Referential integrity means that primary key values and corresponding foreign key values must match exactly.

The main advantage of triggers is that they are automatic; they work no matter what caused the data modification — a clerk's data entry or an application action. A trigger is specific to one or more of the data modification operations, update, insert, or delete. The trigger is executed once per SQL statement; it fires immediately after the data modification statements are completed. The trigger and the statement that *fires* it are treated as a single transaction that can be rolled back from within the trigger. If a severe error is detected, the entire transaction rolls back.

In which situations are triggers most useful?

Triggers can *cascade* changes through related tables in the database. Triggers can disallow or *roll back* changes that would violate referential integrity, canceling the attempted data modification transaction. Such a trigger might go into effect when you try to insert a foreign key that does not match its primary key. Triggers can enforce restrictions much more complex than those defined with rules. Unlike rules, triggers can reference columns or database objects.

Triggers can perform simple what-if analyses. For example, a trigger can compare the state of a table before and after a data modification and take actions based on that comparison.

As an alternative to using triggers, you can use the referential integrity constraint of the CREATE TABLE statement to enforce referential integrity across tables in the database. However, referential integrity constraints differ from triggers in that they cannot perform the following tasks:

◆ Cascade changes through related tables in the database.

◆ Enforce complex restrictions by referencing other columns or database objects.

◆ Perform what-if analyses.

In addition, referential integrity constraints do not roll back the current transaction as a result of enforcing data integrity. With triggers, you can have the transaction roll back or continue depending on how you handle referential integrity. If your application requires one of the preceding tasks, you should use triggers. Otherwise, referential integrity constraints offer a simpler way to enforce data integrity.

 SQL Server checks referential integrity constraints before any triggers, so a data modification statement that violates the constraint does not also fire the trigger.

Creating triggers

A trigger is a database mechanism that will execute a SQL statement automatically when a certain event occurs. The event that can trigger an action can be an INSERT, UPDATE, or DELETE statement on a specific table. The UPDATE statement that triggers an action can specify either a table or one or more columns within the table. The table that the trigger event operates on is called the *triggering table*. When the trigger event occurs, the trigger action will be executed. The action can be any combination of one or more INSERT, UPDATE, DELETE, or EXECUTE PROCEDURE statements.

Triggers are a feature of the database server, so the type of application tool used to access the database is irrelevant in the execution of a trigger. By invoking triggers from the database, a DBA can ensure that data is treated consistently across application tools and programs. A trigger is a database object. When you create a trigger, you specify the table and the data modification commands that should fire or activate the trigger. Then you specify the action or actions the trigger is to take.

Triggers are used to maintain referential integrity, which assures that vital data in your database, such as the unique identifier for a given piece of data, remains

accurate and can be used as the database changes. Referential integrity is coordinated through the use of primary and foreign keys. The primary key is the column
or combination of columns that uniquely identifies a row. It cannot be null and it
must have a unique index. A table with a primary key is eligible for joins with foreign keys in other tables. The primary key table can be thought of as the master
table in a master-detail relationship. The foreign key is a column or combination of
columns whose values match the primary key. A foreign key doesn't have to be
unique. They are often in a many-to-one relationship with a primary key. Foreign
key values should be copies of the primary key values; no value in the foreign
key should ever exist unless the same value exists in the primary key. A foreign key
may be null. If any part of a composite foreign key is null, the entire foreign
key must be null.

Tables with foreign keys are often called *detail* or *dependent* tables to the master
table. Referential integrity triggers keep the values of foreign keys in line with
those in primary keys. When a data modification affects a key column, triggers
compare the new column values to related keys by using temporary work tables
containing the table column deltas or changes. When you write your triggers, you
base your comparisons on the data that is temporarily stored in the trigger test
tables. When you insert a new foreign key row, you want to make sure the foreign
key matches a primary key. The trigger should check for joins between the inserted
row or rows and the rows in the primary key table, and then roll back any inserts
of foreign keys that do not match a key in the primary key table.

When you delete a primary key row, you should delete corresponding foreign
key rows in dependent tables. This preserves referential integrity by ensuring that
detail rows are removed when their master row is deleted. If this were not done, you
could end up with a database that had detail rows that could not be retrieved or
identified. A trigger that performs a cascading delete is required.

In actual practice, you may find that you want to keep some of the detail rows.
This may be either for historical purposes (to check how many sales were made on
discontinued titles while they were active) or because transactions on the detail
rows are not yet complete. A well-written trigger should take these factors into
consideration.

Because a primary key is the unique identifier for its row and for foreign key
rows in other tables, an attempt to update a primary key should be taken very seriously. In this case, you want to protect referential integrity by rolling back the
update unless specified conditions are met.

Generally speaking, it's best to prohibit any editing changes to a primary key, for
example, by revoking all permissions on that column. But if you did want to prohibit updates only under certain circumstances, use a trigger.

More on creating a trigger

A trigger is a database object. You can create a trigger by specifying the current
table and the data modification statements that activate the trigger, and then

specifying the action or actions the trigger is to take. Only the owner of the table has CREATE TRIGGER and DROP TRIGGER permissions for the table. These permissions cannot be transferred to others.

A table can have multiple triggers of a given type providing they have different names, and each trigger can perform numerous functions. However, each trigger can apply to only one table, although a single trigger can apply to all three user actions (UPDATE, INSERT, and DELETE).

You cannot create a trigger on a view or on a temporary table, although triggers can reference views or temporary tables. You can use the SET statement inside a trigger. Any SET option you invoke remains in effect during the execution of the trigger and then reverts to its former setting.

The syntax for the CREATE TRIGGER statement

The CREATE TRIGGER statement creates a trigger that is a special kind of stored procedure that is automatically executed when a user attempts the specified data-modification statement on the specified table. If either primary or foreign key constraints are violated, the trigger is not executed (fired). SQL Server 7 allows the creation of multiple triggers for any given INSERT, UPDATE, or DELETE statement.

```
CREATE TRIGGER trigger_name ON table
[WITH ENCRYPTION] { {FOR {[,] [DELETE] [,] [INSERT] [,] [UPDATE] }
[WITH APPEND]
[NOT FOR REPLICATION]
AS
sql_statement [ ...n]} | {FOR {[,] [INSERT] [,] [UPDATE]}
[WITH APPEND] [NOT FOR REPLICATION]
AS
{ IF UPDATE (column)[{AND | OR} UPDATE (column)] [ ...n]
| IF (COLUMNS_UPDATED() {bitwise_operator} updated_bitmask) {
comparison_operator} column_bitmask [...n] }
 sql_statement [ ...n]
}}
```

The parameters and their semantics are discussed in the following list:

♦ trigger_name — The name of the trigger. A trigger name must conform to the rules for identifiers and must be unique within the database. Providing the trigger owner name is optional.

♦ table — The table on which the trigger is executed; it is sometimes called the trigger table. Providing the owner name of the table is optional. Views cannot be specified.

♦ WITH ENCRYPTION — Encrypts the syscomments entries that contain the text of CREATE TRIGGER.

♦ {[,] [DELETE] [,] [INSERT] [,] [UPDATE] } | {[,] [INSERT] [,]
[UPDATE]} — Keywords that specify which data modification statements,
when attempted against this table, activate the trigger. At least one option
must be specified. Any combination of these in any order is allowed in the
trigger definition. If more than one option is specified, separate the
options with commas.

♦ WITH APPEND — Specifies that an additional trigger of an existing type
should be added. Use of this optional clause is needed only when
sp_dbcmptlevel sets the compatibility level setting less than or equal
to 65. If sp_dbcmptlevel sets the compatibility level setting greater
than or equal to 70, then the WITH APPEND optional clause is not needed
to add an additional trigger of an existing type.

♦ NOT FOR REPLICATION — Indicates that the trigger should not be executed
when a replication process modifies the table involved in the trigger.

♦ AS — The actions the trigger is to take.

♦ sql_statement — The trigger condition(s) and action(s). Trigger conditions
specify additional criteria that determine whether the attempted DELETE,
INSERT, or UPDATE statements can cause the trigger action(s) to be carried
out. The trigger actions specified in the Transact-SQL statements go into
effect when the user action (DELETE, INSERT, or UPDATE) is attempted.
Triggers can include any number and kind of Transact-SQL statements but
should not include the SELECT statement. A trigger is designed to check or
change data based on a data modification statement; it should not return
data to the user. The Transact-SQL statements in a trigger often include
control-of-flow language. A few special tables are used in CREATE
TRIGGER statements.

The deleted and inserted tables are logical (conceptual) tables. They are
structurally similar to the table on which the trigger is defined (that is, the
table on which the user action is attempted) and hold the old values or
new values of the rows that may be changed by the user action. For
example, to retrieve all values in the deleted table, use the following:

SELECT * FROM deleted

In a DELETE, INSERT, or UPDATE trigger, SQL Server does not allow text,
ntext, or image column references in the inserted and deleted tables
if the compatibility level of sp_dbcmptlevel is equal to 70. The text,
ntext, and image values in the inserted and deleted tables cannot be
accessed. To retrieve the new value in either an INSERT or UPDATE trigger,
join the inserted table with original update table.

♦ n — A placeholder indicating that multiple Transact-SQL statements can be
included in the trigger. For the IF UPDATE (column) statement, multiple
columns can be included by repeating the UPDATE (column) clause.

◆ IF UPDATE (*column*) — Tests for an INSERT or UPDATE action to a specified column and is not used with DELETE operations. More than one column can be specified. Because the table name is specified in the ON clause, do not include the table name before the column name in an IF UPDATE clause. To test for an INSERT or UPDATE action for more than one column, specify a separate UPDATE(*column*) clause following the first one.

The IF UPDATE (*column*) clause functions identically to a regular IF, IF . . . ELSE, or WHILE statement and can use the BEGIN . . . END block.

◆ *column* — The name of the column to test for either an INSERT or UPDATE action. This column can be of any data type supported by SQL Server. For more information, see Chapter 11, "Constructing the Database," specifically the sections on data types.

◆ IF (COLUMNS_UPDATED()) — Tests to see, in an INSERT or UPDATE trigger only, if the mentioned column or columns were inserted or updated.

◆ *bitwise_operator* — The bitwise operator to use in the comparison.

◆ *updated_bitmask* — The integer bitmask of those columns actually updated or inserted. For example, table t1 contains columns C1, C2, C3, C4, and C5. To check if columns C2, C3, and C4 were all updated (with table t1 having an UPDATE trigger), specify a value of 14 (2 + 4 + 8). To check if only column C2 was updated, specify a value of 2.

◆ *comparison_operator* — The comparison operator. Use the equal sign (=) to check if all columns specified in updated_bitmask were actually updated. Use the greater than symbol (>) to check if any or not all columns specified in updated_bitmask were updated.

◆ *column_bitmask* — The integer bitmask of those columns to check if they were updated or inserted.

SQL Server provides declarative referential integrity (DRI) through the table creation statements (ALTER TABLE and CREATE TABLE); however, DRI does not provide cross-database referential integrity. To enforce referential integrity (rules about the relationships between the primary and foreign keys of tables), use primary and foreign key constraints (the PRIMARY KEY and FOREIGN KEY keywords of ALTER TABLE and CREATE TABLE).

Trigger limitations

The CREATE TRIGGER statement must be the first statement in the batch and can apply to only one table. A trigger is created only in the current database; however, a trigger can reference objects outside the current database. If the trigger owner name is specified (to qualify the trigger), qualify the table name in the same way. The same trigger action can be defined for more than one user action (for example, INSERT and UPDATE) in the same CREATE TRIGGER statement. Any SET statement can be specified inside a trigger. The SET option chosen remains in effect during the execution of the trigger and then reverts to its former setting.

When a trigger fires, results are returned to the calling application, just like stored procedures. To eliminate having results returned to an application due to a trigger firing, do not include either SELECT statements that return results or statements that perform variable assignment in a trigger. It is also recommended that a trigger not include SELECT statements that return results to the user, since special handling for these returned results would have to be written into every application in which modifications to the trigger table are allowed. If variable assignment must occur in a trigger, use a SET NOCOUNT statement at the beginning of the trigger to eliminate the return of any result sets.

A trigger cannot be created on a view. A TRUNCATE TABLE statement is not caught by a DELETE trigger. Although a TRUNCATE TABLE statement is, in effect, like a DELETE without a WHERE clause (it removes all rows), it is not logged and thus cannot execute a trigger. Because permission for the TRUNCATE TABLE statement defaults to the table owner and is not transferable, only the table owner should be concerned about inadvertently circumventing a DELETE trigger with a TRUNCATE TABLE statement. The WRITETEXT statement, whether logged or unlogged, does not activate a trigger.

The Transact-SQL statements depicted in Table 16-1 are not allowed in a trigger.

TABLE 16-1 TRANSACT-SQL STATEMENTS NOT ALLOWED IN A TRIGGER

ALTER DATABASE	CREATE TRIGGER	DROP VIEW
ALTER PROCEDURE	CREATE VIEW	GRANT
ALTER TABLE	DENY	LOAD DATABASE
ALTER TRIGGER	DISK INIT	LOAD LOG
ALTER VIEW	DISK RESIZE	RESTORE DATABASE
CREATE DATABASE	DROP DATABASE	RESTORE LOG
CREATE DEFAULT	DROP DEFAULT	REVOKE

CREATE INDEX	DROP INDEX	RECONFIGURE
CREATE PROCEDURE	DROP PROCEDURE	TRUNCATE TABLE
CREATE RULE	DROP RULE	UPDATE STATISTICS
CREATE SCHEMA	DROP TABLE	
CREATE TABLE	DROP TRIGGER	

Determining when a trigger fires

When you create a trigger, you can define it to be fired under three different actions: during inserts, updates, and deletes to the table on which the trigger is defined. You can use the FOR option to designate INSERT, UPDATE, and/or DELETE. For example, if you create a trigger with the FOR INSERT option, the statements in the body of the trigger will be executed whenever an insert statement loads a row of data into the table. The same is true for DELETE triggers.

Although a TRUNCATE TABLE statement is, in effect, like a DELETE statement without a WHERE clause (it deletes all rows), it cannot activate a trigger because the TRUNCATE TABLE statement is not logged. When you use the FOR UPDATE option, you can use the IF UPDATE OF *colname* control-of-flow structure to customize the actions of the trigger for updates to selected columns in the table. If you need the trigger to perform special activities for each type of action (INSERT, UPDATE, and DELETE), you can either create a single trigger with the Transact-SQL code to perform all the activities, or you can define three separate triggers, one for each type of action.

Using the special inserted and deleted tables

Two special tables are used in trigger statements: the deleted table and the inserted table. These temporary tables are used in trigger tests. Use these tables to test the effects of certain data modifications and to set conditions for trigger actions. You cannot directly alter the data in the trigger test tables, but you can use the tables in SELECT statements to determine whether the trigger was fired by an INSERT, UPDATE, or DELETE statement.

The deleted table stores copies of the affected rows during DELETE and UPDATE statements. During the execution of a DELETE or UPDATE statement, rows are deleted from the trigger table and transferred to the deleted table. The deleted table and the trigger table ordinarily have no rows in common.

The inserted table stores copies of the affected rows during INSERT and UPDATE statements. During an INSERT or an UPDATE transaction, new rows are added to the inserted table and the trigger table at the same time. The rows in the inserted table are copies of the new rows in the trigger table.

An UPDATE transaction is, conceptually, a delete followed by an insert; the old rows are copied to the deleted table first, and then the new rows are copied to the trigger table and to the inserted table.

When setting trigger conditions, use the inserted and deleted tables as appropriate for the action that fired the trigger. Although it is not wrong to reference deleted while testing an INSERT, or inserted while testing a DELETE, these trigger test tables will not contain any rows in these cases.

The @@ROWCOUNT variable, which stores the number of rows affected by the most recent data modification operation, tests for a multirow insert, delete, or update. If any other SELECT statement precedes the test on @@ROWCOUNT within the trigger, you should use local variables to store the value for later examination. (All Transact-SQL statements that don't return values reset @@ROWCOUNT to 0).

When triggers that include ROLLBACK TRANSACTION statements are executed from a batch, they cancel the entire batch. In the following example, if the INSERT statement fires a trigger that includes a ROLLBACK TRANSACTION, the DELETE statement is not executed because the batch is canceled:

```
INSERT employee VALUES ()
DELETE employee WHERE...
```

For triggers that include ROLLBACK TRANSACTION, sometimes SQL statements are fired from within a user-defined transaction; the ROLLBACK TRANSACTION rolls back the entire transaction. In this example, if the INSERT statement fires a trigger that includes a ROLLBACK TRANSACTION, the UPDATE statement is also rolled back.

```
BEGIN TRAN
UPDATE employee SET....
INSERT employee VALUES (.....)
END TRAN
```

Trigger Enhancements in SQL Server 7

SQL Server has enhanced triggers that can be recursive. Moreover, you can now have multiple triggers per INSERT, UPDATE, or DELETE statement. You can now append multiple triggers of the same type to a single table. For example, a single table can have one delete trigger, three insert triggers, and two update triggers. This enhancement enables you to put different business rules into different triggers. A database option allows triggers to call themselves recursively.

Updating a foreign key

A change or update to a foreign key by itself is probably an error. A foreign key is just a copy of the primary key; the two should never be independent. If for some reason you want to allow updates of a foreign key, you might want to protect integrity by creating a trigger that checks updates against the master table and rolls them back if they don't match the primary key. Multirow considerations are particularly important when the function of a trigger is to automatically recalculate summary values, that is, ongoing tallies. Triggers used to maintain summary values should contain group-by-clause triggers using group-by clauses, or subqueries that perform implicit grouping to create summary values when more than one row is being inserted, updated, or deleted.

Before an INSERT, UPDATE, or DELETE statement is executed by the database server, the dictionary in the database server memory is scanned for a trigger that exists for the table and type of SQL statement that is being executed. If a trigger exists, it is retrieved, optimized, and executed by the database server at the appropriate time.

Determining when to use triggers

Triggers can restrict how data is manipulated in a database. Without some enforcement of these restrictions, the programmer or SQL user is free to manipulate data in any way (assuming that he/she has permission to do so). Some examples of how triggers can be used are:

- **Business rules.** The term *business rules* refers to the way a business uses data. Triggers can be used to enforce business rules for data within a database. An example of a business rule may be: If inventory for an item reaches a certain level, automatically place an order to restock the item.

- **Derived values.** In some cases, it may be necessary to store a derived value, such as an account balance, in a database. Using triggers to do this will force the derived value to be synchronized with the values from which it is derived.

- **Table replication.** Triggers can be used to replicate changes to a table automatically. Three triggers would be needed: one for inserted rows, one for updated rows, and one for deleted rows. The duplicate table could reside in the same database, or in a different database on another machine.

- **Audit trials.** An organization may have a need to record certain transactions in an audit table. Triggers will assure that all of the specified transactions will be recorded. For example, if an employee's salary gets changed, an audit record can be added to the audit table, specifying the change made and the login of the person who made the change.

◆ **Cascading deletes.** If a row in a table gets deleted, corresponding information in another table can automatically be deleted at the same time with triggers. For example, if an order is deleted, the corresponding items for an order can also be deleted. Although cascading deletes are part of referential integrity starting with version 6.0 of database servers, earlier versions of the database server can use triggers to perform the same function.

◆ **Security authorization.** Triggers can be used to augment database security that already exists. For example, triggers can be used to check for a date before authorizing a change, or to allow only certain people to create orders greater than $1,000.

Summary

This chapter covered the MS SQL Server 7 stored procedures and triggers. They are a sound way to increase performance and enforce business rules and data integrity. They require the careful coding of an intermediate-to-advanced application developer or database administrator to ensure that they are properly developed.

Chapter 17

C and Java with SQL

IN THIS CHAPTER

◆ The SQL database programming environment

◆ Introducing C and SQL Server programming

◆ Introducing Java and SQL Server programming

TODAY'S PROCESSING SOMETIMES requires background batch utilities to run and either produce reports or massage data on a scheduled basis. These batch or background procedures are the mechanism by which data from one part of the organization is consumed and refined by another for their specific requirement. For example, in a brokerage environment, newly entered trades may be posted to a SQL 7–based data warehouse application database that tracks inventory updates. Developers need a tool that can use common programming languages – for example, C and Java – that have the capability to access relational databases. This chapter will compare and contrast the two languages and their embedded SQL functionality.

Running SQL in the Background

Most conventional DBMS systems provide tools that have the capability of accessing relational databases. When using SQL Server–Embedded SQL for C (ESQL/C), you can embed SQL statements directly into your C programs. Correspondingly, when using Java and SQL 7, developers use the JDBC interface to access SQL 7 data. JDBC is a Java API for executing SQL statements. (As a point of interest, JDBC is a trademarked name and is not an acronym; nevertheless, JDBC is often thought of as standing for Java Database Connectivity.) It consists of a set of classes and interfaces written in the Java programming language. JDBC provides a standard API for tool and database developers and makes it possible to write database applications using a pure Java API.

Using JDBC and SQL Server 7

Using JDBC, it is easy to send SQL statements to virtually any relational database, including SQL Server 7. In other words, with the JDBC API, it isn't necessary to write one program to access a SQL Server database, another program to access an Oracle database, another program to access an Informix database, and so on. One can write a single program using the JDBC API, and the program will be able to send SQL statements to the appropriate database. And, with an application written in the Java programming language, one also doesn't have to worry about writing different applications to run on different platforms.

Combining Java and JDBC

The combination of Java and JDBC lets a programmer write an application once and run it anywhere. Java, being robust, secure, easy to use, easy to understand, and automatically downloadable on a network, is an excellent language basis for database applications. What is needed is a way for Java applications to talk to a variety of different databases. JDBC is the mechanism for doing this. JDBC extends what can be done in Java. For example, with Java and the JDBC API, it is possible to publish a Web page containing an applet that uses information obtained from a remote database. Or an enterprise can use JDBC to connect all its employees (even if they are using a conglomeration of Windows, Macintosh, and UNIX machines) to one or more internal databases via an intranet.

With more and more programmers using the Java programming language, the need for easy database access from Java is continuing to grow. MIS managers like the combination of Java and JDBC because it makes disseminating information easy and economical. Businesses can continue to use their installed databases and access information easily even if it is stored on different database management systems. Development time for new applications is short. Installation and version control are greatly simplified. A programmer can write an application or an update once, put it on the server, and everybody has access to the latest version. And for businesses selling information services, Java and JDBC offer a better way of getting out information updates to external customers. Simply put, JDBC makes it possible to do the following three steps:

1. Establish a connection with a database.

2. Send SQL statements.

3. Process the results.

The code fragment in Listing 17-1 gives a basic example of these three steps.

Listing 17-1: Establishing a Connection, Executing SQL, and Processing the Results

```
// establish the connection
Connection con = DriverManager.getConnection (
  "jdbc:odbc:JBDCdatabase", "login", "password");
 Statement stmt = con.createStatement();
// execute the SQL
```

```
ResultSet rs = stmt.executeQuery("SELECT a, b, c FROM Table1");
// process the results
while (rs.next()) {
int x = getInt("a");
String s = getString("b");
float f = getFloat("c");
}
```

Using Java and SQL

SQL is the standard language for accessing relational databases. Unfortunately, SQL is not yet as standard as we would like it to be. One area of difficulty is that data types used by different DBMSs sometimes vary, and the variations can be significant. JDBC deals with this by defining a set of generic SQL type identifiers in the class java.sql.Types. Note that, as used in this book, the terms JDBC SQL type, JDBC type, and SQL type are interchangeable and refer to the generic SQL type identifiers defined in java.sql.Types.

Another area of difficulty with SQL conformance is that although most DBMSs use a standard form of SQL for basic functionality, they do not conform to the more recently defined standard SQL syntax or semantics for more advanced functionality. For example, not all databases support stored procedures or outer joins, and those that do are not consistent with each other. It is hoped that the portion of SQL that is truly standard will expand to include more and more functionality. In the meantime, however, the JDBC API must support SQL as it is. One way the JDBC API deals with this problem is to allow any query string to be passed through to an underlying DBMS driver. This means that an application is free to use as much SQL functionality as desired, but it runs the risk of receiving an error on some DBMSs. Most prudent developers will use an interactive SQL facility to test the expected results before using the JDBC interface.

In fact, an application query need not even be SQL, or it may be a specialized derivative of SQL designed for specific DBMSs (for document or image queries, for example). A second way JDBC deals with problems of SQL conformance is to provide ODBC-style escape clauses. The escape syntax provides a standard JDBC syntax for several of the more common areas of SQL divergence. For example, there are escapes for date literals and for stored procedure calls. For complex applications, JDBC deals with SQL conformance in a third way. It provides descriptive information about the DBMS by means of the interface DatabaseMetaData so that applications can adapt to the requirements and capabilities of each DBMS.

Because the JDBC API will be used as a base API for developing higher-level database access tools and APIs, it also has to address the problem of conformance for anything built on it. The designation JDBC Compliant was created to set a standard level of JDBC functionality on which users can rely. To use this designation, a driver must support at least ANSI SQL-2 Entry Level. (ANSI SQL-2 refers to the standards adopted by the American National Standards Institute in 1992. Entry Level refers to a specific list of SQL capabilities.)

Driver developers can ascertain that their drivers meet these standards by using the test suite available with the JDBC API. The JDBC Compliant designation indicates that a vendor's JDBC implementation has passed the conformance tests provided by JavaSoft. These conformance tests check for the existence of all of the classes and methods defined in the JDBC API, and check as much as possible that the SQL Entry Level functionality is available. Such tests are not exhaustive, of course, and JavaSoft is not currently branding vendor implementations, but this compliance definition provides some degree of confidence in a JDBC implementation. With wider and wider acceptance of the JDBC API by database vendors, connectivity vendors, Internet service vendors, and application writers, JDBC is quickly becoming the standard for Java database access.

The JDBC API

JDBC is a low-level interface, which means that it is used to invoke (or call) SQL commands directly. It works very well in this capacity and is easier to use than other database connectivity APIs, but it was designed also to be a base upon which to build higher-level interfaces and tools. A higher-level interface is user-friendly, using a more understandable or more convenient API that is translated behind the scenes into a low-level interface such as JDBC.

JDBC requires that the SQL statements be passed as strings to Java methods. An embedded SQL preprocessor enables a programmer to instead mix SQL statements directly with Java; for example, a Java variable can be used in a SQL statement to receive or provide SQL values. The embedded SQL preprocessor then translates this Java/SQL mix into Java with JDBC and calls a direct mapping of relational database tables to Java classes. JavaSoft and others have announced plans to implement this. In this object/relational mapping, each row of the table becomes an instance of that class, and each column value corresponds to an attribute of that instance. Programmers can then operate directly on Java objects; the required SQL calls to fetch and store data are automatically generated beneath the covers.

More sophisticated mappings are also provided – for example, where rows of multiple tables are combined in a Java class. As interest in JDBC has grown, more developers have been working on JDBC-based tools to make building programs easier as well. Programmers have also been writing applications that make accessing a database easier for the end user. For example, an application might present a menu of database tasks from which to choose. After a task is selected, the application presents prompts and blanks for filling in information needed to carry out the selected task. With the requested input typed in, the application then automatically invokes the necessary SQL commands. With the help of such an application, users can perform database tasks even when they have little or no knowledge of SQL syntax.

JDBC and ODBC

At this point, Microsoft's ODBC API is probably the most widely used programming interface for accessing relational databases. It offers the capability to connect to almost all databases on almost all platforms. So why not just use ODBC from Java? The answer is that you can use ODBC from Java, but this is best done with the help of JDBC in the form of the JDBC-ODBC bridge. The question now becomes, why do you need JDBC? There are several answers to this question. ODBC is not appropriate for direct use from Java, because it uses a C interface. Calls from Java to native C code have a number of drawbacks in the security, implementation, robustness, and automatic portability of applications. A literal translation of the ODBC C API into a Java API would not be desirable. For example, Java has no pointers, and ODBC makes copious use of them. You can think of JDBC as ODBC translated into an object-oriented interface that is natural for Java programmers.

ODBC is hard to learn. It mixes simple and advanced features together, and it has complex options even for simple queries. JDBC, on the other hand, was designed to keep simple things simple while allowing more advanced capabilities where required. A Java API like JDBC is needed to enable a pure Java solution. When ODBC is used, the ODBC driver manager and drivers must be manually installed on every client machine. When the JDBC driver is written completely in Java, however, JDBC code is automatically installable, portable, and secure on all Java platforms from network computers to mainframes.

In summary, the JDBC API is a natural Java interface to the basic SQL abstractions and concepts. It builds on ODBC rather than starting from scratch, so programmers familiar with ODBC will find it very easy to learn JDBC. JDBC retains the basic design features of ODBC; in fact, both interfaces are based on the X/Open SQL Call Level Interface (CLI). The big difference is that JDBC builds on and reinforces the style and virtues of Java, and, of course, it is easy to use.

More recently, Microsoft has introduced new APIs beyond ODBC: data access objects such as RDO, ADO, DAO, and OLE DB. These designs move in the same direction as JDBC in many ways. For example, they're object-oriented interfaces to databases based on classes that can be implemented on ODBC. However, we did not see functionality in any of these interfaces that is compelling enough to make them an alternative basis to ODBC, especially with the ODBC driver market well established. Mostly they represent a thin veneer on ODBC. This is not to say that JDBC does not need to evolve. However, we feel that most new functionality belongs in higher-level APIs such as the object-relational mappings and embedded SQL discussed earlier.

JDBC for two-tier and three-tier applications

The JDBC API supports both two-tier and three-tier models for database access. In the two-tier model, a Java applet or application talks directly to the database. This requires a JDBC driver that can communicate with the particular DBMS being accessed. A user's SQL statements are delivered to the database, and the results of those statements are sent back to the user. The database may be located on another machine to which the user is connected via a network. This is referred to as a client/server configuration, with the user's machine as the client, and the machine housing the database as the server. The network can be an intranet, which, for example, connects employees within a corporation, or it can be the Internet.

In the three-tier model, commands are sent to a middle tier of services, which then send SQL statements to the database. The database processes the SQL statements and sends the results back to the middle tier, which then sends them to the user. MIS directors find the three-tier model very attractive because the middle tier makes it possible to maintain control over access and the kinds of updates that can be made to corporate data. Another advantage is that when there is a middle tier, the user can employ an easy-to-use higher-level API that is translated by the middle tier into the appropriate low-level calls.

Finally, in many cases, the three-tier architecture can provide performance advantages. Until now, the middle tier has typically been written in languages such as C or C++, which offer fast performance. However, with the introduction of optimizing compilers that translate Java bytecode into efficient machine-specific code, it is becoming practical to implement the middle tier in Java. This is a big plus, making it possible to take advantage of Java's robustness, multithreading, and security features. Of course, JDBC is important in allowing database access from a Java middle tier.

JDBC Components

The JDBC API is a natural choice for Java developers because it offers easy database access for Java applications and applets. Consult the JDBC Web page for the latest information. It can be found at the following URL: http://java.sun.com/products/jdbc. JavaSoft provides three JDBC product components:

- JDBC driver manager – included as part of the Java Development Kit (JDK)

- JDBC driver test suite (available from the JDBC Web site)

- JDBC-ODBC bridge (included in the Solaris and Windows versions of the JDK)

The JDBC driver manager is the backbone of the JDBC architecture. It is actually quite small and simple; its primary function is to connect Java applications to the correct JDBC driver and then get out of the way. The JDBC driver test suite provides some confidence that JDBC drivers will run your program. Only drivers that pass the JDBC driver test suite can be designated JDBC Compliant. The JDBC-ODBC bridge allows ODBC drivers to be used as JDBC drivers. It was implemented as a way to get JDBC off the ground quickly, and in the long term will provide a way to access some of the less popular DBMSs if JDBC drivers are not implemented for them. The JDBC drivers fit into one of four categories:

◆ **JDBC-ODBC bridge plus ODBC driver.** The JavaSoft bridge product provides JDBC access via ODBC drivers. Note that ODBC binary code, and in many cases database client code, must be loaded on each client machine that uses this driver. As a result, this kind of driver is most appropriate on a corporate network where client installations are not a major problem, or for application server code written in Java in a three-tier architecture.

◆ **Native-API partly-Java driver.** This kind of driver converts JDBC calls into calls on the client API for Oracle, Sybase, Informix, DB2, or other DBMSs. Note that, like the bridge driver, this style of driver requires that some binary code be loaded on each client machine.

◆ **JDBC-Net pure Java driver.** This driver translates JDBC calls into a DBMS-independent net protocol that is then translated to a DBMS protocol by a server. This net server middleware is able to connect its pure Java clients to many different databases. The specific protocol used depends on the vendor. In general, this is the most flexible JDBC alternative. It is likely that all vendors of this solution will provide products suitable for intranet use. For these products to also support Internet access, they must handle the additional requirements for security, access through firewalls, and so forth that the Web imposes.

◆ **Native-protocol pure Java driver.** This kind of driver converts JDBC calls into the network protocol used by DBMSs directly. This allows a direct call from the client machine to the DBMS server and is an excellent solution for intranet access. Because many of these protocols are proprietary, the database vendors themselves will be the primary source. Several database vendors have these in progress. The expectation is that eventually driver categories 3 and 4 will be the preferred way to access databases from JDBC. Driver categories 1 and 2 are interim solutions where direct pure Java drivers are not yet available. There are possible variations on categories 1 and 2 (not shown in the list that follows) that require a connector, but these are generally less-desirable solutions. Categories 3 and 4 offer all the advantages of Java, including automatic installation (for example, downloading the JDBC driver with an applet that uses it).

The following companies provide third-party JDBC drivers for SQL Server:

◆ Connect Software – http://www.connectsw.com/

◆ IBM – http://www.ibm.com

◆ Intersolv – http://www.intersolv.com/

- ◆ I-Kinetics — http://www.i-kinetics.com/

- ◆ KonaSoft — http://www.konasoft.com/

- ◆ Oracle — http://www.oracle.com/

- ◆ Sybase — http://www.sybase.com/

- ◆ Visigenic — http://www.visigenic.com/

- ◆ WebLogic — http://www.weblogic.com/

The rest of the chapter will predominantly discuss C with ESQL. Where appropriate, we will discuss Java and JDBC. This embedded SQL technique, especially ESQL/C, is similar to the embedded SQL interface available with IBM DB2 used with either COBOL or C. Within SQL Server ESQL/C you will find libraries, header files, and a preprocessor. The library of routines will help your work with all SQL data types and enhance your ability to interpret status messages and work with SQL Server-spawned processes. Within the JDBC interface there are Java methods similar in functionality.

What Is Embedded SQL?

SQL Server–ESQL/C is an application development tool that provides a C programmer with the capability to create batch or scheduled applications that can interface with a SQL Server database. For simplification we will refer to SQL Server–ESQL/C as ESQL/C. With Java and JDBC, you can compile (javac) and run (java) programs to create batch or scheduled applications that can interface with a SQL Server database.

Embedded SQL method

Embedded SQL programs with C require preprocessing by a precompiler. The embedded SQL precompiler converts embedded SQL statements in the program (not valid C code) into C function calls that can be accepted by a C compiler. The embedded SQL statements are converted to comments and passed to the next compile step. The C compiler can then compile the resulting source code into an executable program. With Java and JDBC, you can compile (javac) the program and be sure to import the Java JDBC classes to connect to the JDBC driver for SQL Server 7.

To get right to it, these example programs follow: a C program that uses embedded SQL and a Java program with embedded SQL in the form of JDBC. As mentioned previously, embedded SQL enables programmers to connect to a database and include SQL code right in the program, so that their programs can use, manipulate, and process data from a database. This example C Program (using embedded SQL) will print a report. The Java example uses the SQL Server 7 sample database,

Northwind, with the JDBC-ODBC bridge and Microsoft's 32-bit ODBC driver under Microsoft Windows 95, 98, or NT.

An Embedded SQL and C program

Embedded SQL is great for creating batch programs to perform scheduled reporting or utility work. Consider the following example:

```
/*START of ESQL/C EXAMPLE PROGRAM*****************/
 /***********************************************/
#include <stdio.h>
```

This section declares the host variables; these will be the variables your program uses. Additionally, these variables will be used by SQL Server to store values in or retrieve values from. We will declare an integer BuyerID and char fields for names and items:

```
EXEC SQL BEGIN DECLARE SECTION;
int BuyerID;
char FirstName[100], LastName[100], Item[100];
EXEC SQL END DECLARE SECTION;
```

This next code snippet causes the inclusion of the SQLCA variable, so that some error checking can be done. SQL Server uses the SQL communications area (SQLCA) data structure to trap and report run-time errors to your embedded SQL applications. Your application can check the error fields and status indicators of the SQLCA data structure to determine the success or failure of an embedded SQL statement. The precompiler automatically inserts the following statement that includes the SQLCA data structure in embedded SQL applications:

```
EXEC SQL INCLUDE SQLCA;
```

Each embedded SQL statement starts with the introductory expression EXEC SQL. This expression tells the precompiler that the code entered between EXEC SQL and the semicolon (;) contains embedded SQL statements.

```
main()
{
/* This is a login to the database */
EXEC SQL CONNECT TO pga.routedw AS dw1 USER sa;
```

This code either says that you are connected or checks if an error code was generated, meaning the login was incorrect or not possible.

```
if(sqlca.sqlcode != 0)
{
printf(Printer, "Error connecting to database server.\n");
exit();
}
printf("Connected to database server.\n");
```

This next code snippet declares a cursor. A *cursor* is a commonly occurring SQL construct. It is used when a query returns more than one row and an operation is to be performed on each row resulting from the query. With each row returned by this query, we will extrapolate some data and use it in the report. For each row in the result set, Fetch will be used to get or fetch each row that satisfies the declared SELECT, one row at a time. To establish a start for the query, the Open cursor statement is used. The Declare cursor does not actually execute anything; it just establishes the query:

```
EXEC SQL DECLARE ItemCursor CURSOR FOR
  SELECT ITEM, BUYERID
       FROM ANTIQUES
ORDER BY ITEM;
EXEC SQL OPEN ItemCursor;
if(sqlca.sqlcode != 0)
{
printf(Printer, "Error opening the cursor server.\n");
exit();
};
```

Fetch puts the values of the next row of the query in the host variables, respectively. However, a priming fetch (programming technique) must first be done. When the cursor is out of data, a sqlcode will be generated allowing us to leave the loop. Notice that, for simplicity's sake, the loop will leave on any sqlcode, even if it is an error code. Otherwise, specific code checking must be performed.

```
EXEC SQL FETCH ItemCursor INTO :Item, :BuyerID;
while(sqlca.sqlcode == 0)
{
```

With each row, we will also do a couple of things. First, bump the price up by 15 percent (a dealer's fee) and get the buyer's name to put in the report (see Listing 17-2). To do this, we'll use an UPDATE and a SELECT, before printing the line on the screen. The update assumes, however, that a given buyer has only bought one of any given item, or else the price will be increased many times. Note the colons before host variable names when used inside of SQL statements.

Listing 17-2: Using an UPDATE and SELECT

```
EXEC SQL UPDATE ANTIQUES
SET PRICE = PRICE * 1.15
        WHERE ITEM = :Item AND BUYERID = :BuyerID;

EXEC SQL SELECT OWNERFIRSTNAME, OWNERLASTNAME
INTO :FirstName, :LastName FROM ANTIQUEOWNERS
WHERE BUYERID = :BuyerID;

printf("%25s %25s %25s", FirstName, LastName, Item);
/* -for example purposes only! Get the next row. */

EXEC SQL FETCH ItemCursor
INTO :Item, :BuyerID;
}

/* Close the cursor, commit the changes (see below),
 and exit the program. */
EXEC SQL CLOSE ItemCursor;

/* This is a commit i.e. guarantee your changes
 are made to the database */
EXEC SQL COMMIT RELEASE;

/* This is a logoff from the database */
EXEC SQL DISCONNECT dw1;

 exit();
}
```

A JDBC and Java program

The program shown in Listing 17-3 demonstrates the use of JDBC within a stand-alone Java application. This is an alternative to using a C program with embedded SQL. This example uses the SQL Server 7 sample database, Northwind, with the JDBC-ODBC bridge and Microsoft's 32-bit ODBC driver under Windows 95, 98, or NT.

- ◆ To compile this program, we'll use: `javac SQL7JDBC.java`
- ◆ To run this program, we'll use: `java SQL7JDBC`

The code (we will name it SQL7JDBC.java) in Listing 17-3 illustrates an example of the JDBC and the SQL Server 7 DBMS. As Java is becoming more popular and displaces C, there will be more batch programs written using this interface.

Listing 17-3: A Java and JDBC Example

```java
import java.sql.*;
class SQL7JDBC {
    static Connection con; // database connection object
    /** Main routine : invoked methods are coded below*/
    public static void main(String args[]) throws Exception {
        // Load the JDBC-ODBC bridge driver
        Class.forName ("sun.jdbc.odbc.JdbcOdbcDriver");
// invoke method to
// Open the database and display all
//rows in a table
        open();
        select();

// invoke method:Add a new row show result insert();
        select("WHERE EmployeeId = 100");

// invoke method to Update a row and commit the result
        update(true);
        select("WHERE EmployeeId = 100");

// invoke method to Update a row and rollback the result
        update(false);
        select("WHERE EmployeeId = 100");
// invoke method to Delete a row and show the result
        delete();
        select("WHERE EmployeeId = 100");

// invoke method to Close the database
        close();

    }

    /** Method to Open a database connection */
    static void open() throws SQLException {

// point at the MS SQL 7.x ODBC data source name
        String dsn = "jdbc:odbc:Northwind";
        String user = "nsc";
        String password = "area47";
        // Connect to the database
        con = DriverManager.getConnection(dsn, user, password);
        // Shut off autocommit
        con.setAutoCommit(false);
```

```
    }

    /** Commit all pending transactions and close the database
connection */
    static void close() throws SQLException {
        con.commit();
        con.close();
    }

    /** Issue a SQL query with a WHERE clause */
    static void select(String whereClause)
            throws SQLException {
        Statement stmt; // SQL statement object
        String query;   // SQL SELECT string
        ResultSet rs;   // SQL query result set
        boolean more;   // "more rows found" switch
// set up the Select statement ; there are some
// restrictions on which DML parameters can be used
query = "SELECT EmployeeID, LastName, FirstName, Title "
            + "FROM Employees "
            + whereClause;
// build the SQL and execute it
        stmt = con.createStatement();
        rs = stmt.executeQuery(query);
// did we find anything
        // Check to see if any rows were read
        more = rs.next();
        if (!more) {
            System.out.println("No employee rows found.");
            return;
        }
        // Loop through the rows retrieved from the query
while (more) {
 System.out.println("ID: " + rs.getInt("EmployeeId"));
 System.out.println("Name: " + rs.getString("FirstName") + " " +
rs.getString("LastName"));
 System.out.println("Title: " + rs.getString("Title"));
 System.out.println("");
 more = rs.next();
        }
// close the result set
        rs.close();
        stmt.close();
    }
```

```java
/** Issue a SQL query without a WHERE clause */
static void select() throws SQLException {
    select("");
}
/** Insert a new row */
static void insert() throws SQLException {
    Statement stmt; // SQL statement object
    String sql;     // SQL insert command
    int rows;       // Number of rows inserted

    sql = "INSERT INTO Employees "
        + "VALUES (100, 'Clinton', 'William', 'Manager', "
        + "NULL, NULL, NULL, NULL, NULL, "
        + "NULL, NULL, NULL, NULL, NULL, "
        + "NULL, NULL, NULL)";

    stmt = con.createStatement();
    rows = stmt.executeUpdate(sql);
    con.commit();
    stmt.close();
    System.out.println(rows + " row(s) added");
}

/** Update a new row */
static void update(boolean commit) throws SQLException {
    Statement stmt; // SQL statement object
    String sql;     // SQL UPDATE command
    int rows;       // Number of rows inserted
    String title;   // New title for the update

    if (commit)
        title = "Goober";
    else
        title = "President";

    sql = "UPDATE Employees "
        + "SET Title='" + title + "' "
        + "WHERE EmployeeId = 100";

    stmt = con.createStatement();
    rows = stmt.executeUpdate(sql);
```

```
    if (commit)
       con.commit();
    else
       con.rollback();

    stmt.close();
    System.out.println(rows + " row(s) updated");

}

/** Delete a row */
static void delete() throws SQLException {
    Statement stmt; // SQL statement object
    String sql;     // SQL delete command
    int rows;       // Number of rows inserted
    sql = "DELETE FROM Employees "
       + "WHERE EmployeeId = 100";
    stmt = con.createStatement();
    rows = stmt.executeUpdate(sql);
    con.commit();
    stmt.close();
    System.out.println(rows + " row(s) deleted");
}
}

/* END OF Java Example*/
```

Whether we use C or Java, the embedded SQL approach using programming statements similar to Transact-SQL is more concise than the call-level method approach and is tightly coupled to the existing database structure. Moreover, it is a lot simpler and requires less development effort to convert meta-data about columns and data types into a working utility. Note that Java JDBC contains classes and methods that can access the SQL Server 7 meta-data. Using this meta-data, the Java program can be coded to respond to changes in the database environment.

The embedded SQL is simpler to code and easier to maintain, and a basic C or Java programmer can easily code a program; however, there are limitations. Because the SQL statements are directly included in the C or Java source code, embedded SQL programs are usually special-purpose applications. Embedded SQL is well suited for environments where the C or Java programmer is also in control of the database structure. However, embedded SQL is less flexible in environments where the database structure is changing or is not predictable.

Embedded SQL for C files

The Setup program installs the groups of files required to develop using Embedded SQL and C. These files include precompilers and other services for the developer. For a complete list see Table 17-1.

TABLE 17-1 C AND SQL PRECOMPILERS AND RUNTIME SERVICES

Directory	File	Description
C:\Program Files\Microsoft SQL Server\ MSSQL$instancename \Binn	Nsqlprep.exe	Precompiler for Windows NT and Windows 95
	Sqlaiw32.dll	Precompiler services for Windows NT and Windows 95
	Sqlakw32.dll	Run-time services for Windows NT and Windows 95
C:\Program Files\Microsoft SQL Server\ MSSQL$instancename \Include	Sqlca.h	SQLCA header
	Sqlda.h	SQLDA header
C:\Program Files\Microsoft SQL Server\ MSSQL$instancename \Lib	Caw32.lib	SQLCA library for Windows NT and Windows 95
	Sqlakw32.lib	Run-time services import library for Windows NT and Windows 95
C:\Program Files\Microsoft SQL Server\ MSSQL$instancename \Samples\Esqlc	*.*	C samples

Embedded SQL programming

As displayed in the examples within the preceding section, embedded SQL programs incorporate Transact-SQL statements into C or Java source code. Embedded SQL programming is a multistep development process that converts your original embedded SQL source code into a SQL Server application that is an executable file compiled for the appropriate operating system.

Embedded SQL steps for C

To produce an executable, the program must be compiled in a more comprehensive fashion than the normal C program. Because we are interfacing with a database, the required API stubs must be embedded within the executable. That is to say that all SQL statements are commented out and replaced with program calls to the embedded SQL API. The following steps compose the C compile. Embedded SQL programming operates as follows:

♦ At a command prompt, the name of the embedded SQL source file and the appropriate build parameters are submitted to `nsqlprep`, which is the embedded SQL precompiler for Windows NT, Windows 95, and later operating systems. The precompiler parses the submitted file, finds the embedded SQL statements included in the code, and processes the statements.

♦ The precompiler produces a C source-code file with the embedded SQL statements removed and, if appropriate, a bind file is added. The embedded SQL statements are replaced by calls to the run-time library. The run-time library calls DB-Library to access SQL Servers across a network.

♦ The C source code file is compiled with a supported C compiler to produce an object code file.

The object code file and library routines are linked together with a supported linker to produce an executable file.

Embedded SQL steps for Java and JDBC

To begin, you will need to install the JDBC and the JDBC-ODBC bridge. (They can be obtained at `http://splash.javasoft.com/jdbc`.). If you are using any version of the JDK newer than version 1.1, both JDBC and the JDBC-ODBC bridge are included.

Make the changes to your Java `CLASSPATH` variable specified in the installation instructions for JDBC and JDBC-ODBC. (No changes are needed to the `CLASSPATH` if you're using any JDK newer than 1.1.) Here's an example of what should be included in the `CLASSPATH` for Windows NT:

```
.;%SystemRoot%\java\lib\classes.zip;%SystemRoot%\java\Jdbc\jdbc\classes\;
%SystemRoot%\java\Jdbc\jdbc-odbc\classes\;
```

With Windows NT, you can reset the CLASSPATH variable by opening the Control Panel, double-clicking System, and then clicking the Environment tab. You can always set the variables by placing a SET CLASSPATH command in your autoexec.bat file. You can also temporarily set the CLASSPATH by typing **SET CLASSPATH <...>** at the command prompt in an MS-DOS window. This setting only applies to that particular MS-DOS window and thus is less convenient to use.

Changes in the autoexec.bat file don't become effective until you restart the machine. Changing environmental variables in Windows NT does not require restarting the machine. However, with NT, setting any environment variable from the Control Panel has no effect on any open MS-DOS windows, so open a new MS-DOS window to see the effects of your CLASSPATH changes.

Next, install the Microsoft Desktop Database drivers on your Web server. These may not be included in a normal Windows NT or 98 installation. Thus, you might need to do a custom installation. The drivers should be under some section of the installation dealing with ODBC. Also install anything that relates to enabling ODBC.

Next, create your database (use the SQL Server 7.*x* Enterprise Manager), or you can use the Northwind database that comes with the SQL Server 7.*x* software. Register the database as an ODBC database. To do this, go into the Control Panel, double-click ODBC, click Add, click Microsoft SQL 7 Driver, then type in the name of your database, and click Select to browse for your database. That's all you should need to do. Note that if you want your database to be available regardless of who is logged onto your machine, you must register the database as a System DSN. Click the appropriate tab on the ODBC Control Panel to add a System DSN. If your machine has only one user, a User DSN is fine, provided you remain logged in as that user.

The jdbc:odbc: part that is the variable String dsn = "jdbc:odbc:Northwind" from our example in the previous section indicates that you intend to use the JDBC-ODBC bridge to open the database called Northwind. If you have created your own database, then change the name of the database to the database you plan to use. The name of the database should exactly match the name you gave to the database when you registered it in the ODBC step. Once you've amended the sample program, save it, and compile it with the following commands:

♦ To compile this program use: javac SQL7JDBC.java

♦ To run this program use: java SQL7JDBC

Embedded SQL statements for C and Java

As mentioned previously, to distinguish embedded SQL statements from C source code, each embedded SQL statement must begin with the introductory keyword EXEC SQL and end with a semicolon (;). This convention was actually established by IBM in its call interface to DB2 and CICS. This proved to be a very productive style. In the 1980s, the mainframe development using these tools was greatly enhanced using the *embedded* API call interface. SQL Server has wisely adopted this style. Experience shows that this will enhance development efforts involving SQL Server.

Additional syntax rules for the EXEC interface provide for a backslash (\) to continue SQL strings across more than one line of source code. A single quote must precede the first character of the SQL string on the first line of source code, and a single quote must appear after the last character of the SQL string on the last line of source code. For example:

```
EXEC SQL INSERT INTO TBTEST VALUES ('THIS IS THE TEST FOR THE R\
ULE OF THE CONTINUATION OF LINES FROM ONE LINE TO THE NEXT LINE.');
```

You can also include embedded SQL variable declaration sections in C language code where it is valid to declare variables. Use the BEGIN DECLARE SECTION and END DECLARE SECTION statements. Executing a Java program with embedded SQL statements is also, for the most part, a two-step process:

- ◆ Create a *Statement* object.

- ◆ Execute the SQL command through the *Statement* object.

If you're comfortable with SQL, this is a very easy process. Our SQL INSERT statements are also pretty simple. Here's an example of how we create our *Statement* object and then insert a record for a person named William Jones, a manager.

```
sql = "INSERT INTO Employees " + "VALUES (100, 'Jones', 'William', 'Manager')";
stmt = con.createStatement();
rows = stmt.executeUpdate(sql);
```

As you can see, you just 1) create a *Statement* object, and 2) run your SQL INSERT statement using the *Statement* object's executeUpdate() method.

Connecting to a database using ESQL/C

The first thing one would do in a database program is establish that the database is active and establish a connection. Use a CONNECT TO statement in your application to specify the SQL Server name, the database name, the login ID, and the password for the connection. Use the SET OPTION statement to change the connection time-out. It is also prudent to provide some error checking using the SQLCA control data to alert Operations so that the database can be made active or so that other steps may be taken to correct the failure.

Connecting to a database using Java and JDBC

Before you start working with JDBC, you'll need a copy of the Java JDK. If you don't have it already, you can get the JDK for free at Java's Web site (http://www.java.sun.com), or it will also be included with many IDEs that you can purchase, such as Visual Cafe. Once you have the JDK, the next thing you need to do is to get the correct JDBC driver for your database. Establishing a connection is a two-step process. Once you have the correct JDBC driver installed, establishing a connection from your Java programs to your SQL database is fairly simple. Load the JDBC driver and the URL. The syntax of the DriverManager.getConnection() method is:

```
DriverManager.getConnection(String url, String username, String password);
```

The username and password are the normal names you use to log into your database. The URL you use will again vary with the database you use. In Listing 17-4, we're establishing a connection to a database named Northwind. If you stick with standard SQL commands, it can be very easy to switch from one database server to another. The process is nearly identical for all SQL databases, and the only real differences are 1) the driver name, and 2) the URL used to connect to the database.

Listing 17-4: Establishing a Connection to the Northwind Database

```
//Establish a connection to an MS SQL 7 example
// "Northwind"database using JDBC.
import java.sql.*;
class SQL7JDBC {
public static void main (String[] args) {
try { // Step 1: Load the JDBC driver.
Class.forName("sun.jdbc.odbc.JdbcOdbcDriver ");
// Step 2: Establish the connection to the database.
String url = "jdbc:odbc:Northwind ";
Connection conn = DriverManager.getConnection(url,"nsc","area47");
} catch (Exception e) {
System.err.println("Got an exception! ");
System.err.println(e.getMessage());
}
}
```

Using host variables in a C program

You can set up storage for SQL predicates and computation as well as manage input and output for embedded SQL statements by using host variables. *Host variables* are standard C-program variables that are declared in an embedded SQL declare section by using the BEGIN DECLARE SECTION and END DECLARE SECTION statements. A data buffer is created for the block of storage defined between this Declare bracket. Use host variables when the number of items and their data types are known at compile time.

You can use host variables in static SQL statements to specify input values or to receive output values. You can also use host variables together to specify input values or to receive the output of a dynamically prepared cursor. A familiar convention provides that when a host variable name is used in an embedded SQL statement, the variable name begins with a colon (:). This colon enables the compiler to distinguish between host variables and tables or columns that might have the same name.

Using the JDBC classes and methods to embed SQL

The first thing to do is to import the packages or classes you will be using in the new Java program or class. The classes in our example use the java.sql package (the JDBC API), which is made available when the following line of code precedes the class definition:

```
import java.sql.*;
```

The asterisk (*) indicates that all of the classes in the package, java.sql, are to be imported. Importing a class makes it visible and means that you do not have to write out the fully qualified name when you use a method or field from that class. If you do not include import java.sql.*; in your code, you will have to write java.sql. and the class name in front of all the JDBC fields or methods you use every time you use them. Note that you can import individual classes selectively rather than a whole package. Java does not require that you import classes or packages, but doing so makes writing code a lot more convenient.

Using Cursors

When you write code for a transaction that retrieves a single row of results, you can use a SELECT INTO statement. This is called a *singleton select statement*. More often than not, you will have to write code for a transaction where the result set includes several rows of data. You may want to walk the set of database rows for employees from department 100 and give them a 15 percent raise. To do this, you would have to select that subset of employees and then update the salary for each one by 15 percent. If we wanted to report on this activity, we would also select certain row columns and send them to a print device.

Declaring a Cursor

To accomplish the salary update as mentioned, you must declare and use a cursor. For example, if you write code that includes a SELECT statement or stored procedure that returns multiple rows, you must declare a cursor and associate it with the SELECT statement. Then, as we saw in our example earlier in the chapter, by using the FETCH statement, you can retrieve one row at a time from the result set.

Using a Cursor

So a cursor is a mechanism you can use to fetch rows one at a time. You can also use cursors to perform operations within a result set. These operations are known as *positioned update* and *positioned delete*. Embedded SQL includes standard cursor types and browse cursor types. A *standard cursor* is used to retrieve one row of data at a time; it shares the same connection to SQL Server as the main program. Standard cursors require a unique index in SQL Server version 6.0 and earlier. To set standard cursors, use the SET CURSORTYPE CUR_STANDARD statement or the DECLARE CURSOR statement with the FOR UPDATE option. A *browse cursor* is used to retrieve one row of data at a time; it requires a separate connection to SQL Server. To set browse cursors, use the SET CURSORTYPE CUR_BROWSE statement.

Standard and browse cursors are declared and used (including FETCH and positioned update or delete operations) in the same way. Standard cursors allow multiple cursor operations to share the same connection to SQL Server; each browse cursor requires a separate connection. For most applications, standard cursors are recommended and are the default because a shared single connection avoids potential locking conflicts between cursors. Standard cursors also use the cursor functions of DB-Library, so embedded SQL applications that use standard cursors can automatically take advantage of any future performance enhancements in DB-Library cursors. DB-Library cursors have several options for controlling row membership, locking, and performance characteristics.

These options are available to embedded SQL programs through the SET ANSI_DEFAULTS, SET CURSOR_CLOSE_ON_COMMIT, SET SCROLLOPTION, SET CONCURRENCY, and SET FETCHBUFFER statements. A SET option remains in effect for all cursor operations within an embedded SQL program until that option is changed by another SET statement.

If positioned UPDATE or DELETE statements are used on a browse cursor, the SELECT statement used in the cursor declaration must include the FOR BROWSE option. However, because each browse cursor uses a separate database connection, SQL Server treats each cursor as a separate user. This can result in locking conflicts between different cursors in the same program.

Managing Transactions

Critical to every database operation that causes an update is the ability to define the transaction. Embedded SQL provides a pair of statements that bracket the transaction. The COMMIT TRANSACTION statement marks the end of a user-defined transaction initiated by a BEGIN TRANSACTION statement. The COMMIT statement makes changes to the transaction's database permanent and visible to other users. It frees up the log records that were retained to provide rollback to the before image if a failure occurs before the data is committed. It also removes all locks from the affected data so that other users can access the data.

As with other SQL Server applications, statements not bound by BEGIN TRANSACTION and COMMIT are automatically committed when the statement executes without an error. That is to say, there is an implied transaction bracket. When updating a large number of rows it is important to COMMIT periodically to avoid exhausting the log space and to obviate a long ROLLBACK period, should the application fail. As the name implies, the ROLLBACK statement reverses the effects of a user-specified transaction to the beginning of the OPEN TRANSACTION. After a transaction is committed, it cannot be rolled back.

Note that by default, a COMMIT or ROLLBACK statement does not close cursors and applies only to the current connection if multiple connections are active. This is a good default, as it avoids the need to close and reopen and reposition the cursor when a positioned update takes place. You can use the SET CURSOR_CLOSE_ON_ COMMIT statement to automatically close all cursors on a connection when a COMMIT TRANSACTION or a ROLLBACK TRANSACTION statement is issued.

In the case of Java and the JDBC, if a connection is in autocommit mode (for example, setAutoCommit(True)); then all its SQL statements will be executed and committed as individual transactions. Otherwise, its SQL statements are grouped into transactions that are terminated by either commit() or rollback(). By default, new connections are in autocommit mode. The commit occurs when the statement completes or the next execute occurs, whichever comes first. In the case of statements returning a ResultSet, the statement completes when the last row of the ResultSet has been retrieved or the ResultSet has been closed. In advanced cases, a single statement may return multiple results as well as output parameter values. Here the commit occurs when all results and output parameter values have been retrieved.

Using the SQLCA data structure

In a similar fashion to DB2 and Sybase SQL Server, Microsoft SQL Server uses the SQL communications area (SQLCA) data structure to collect and report data about run-time errors to your embedded SQL applications. Your application can check the error fields and status indicators of the SQLCA data structure to determine the success or failure of an embedded SQL statement.

As mentioned previously, the precompiler automatically includes the SQLCA data structure in embedded SQL applications. The SQLCA contains descriptive data pertaining to each access as it happens. It is typically examined after each access to ensure that the desired result has been achieved. In an enterprise situation, the database group should provide model error-handling code to facilitate and enforce error checking in production database procedures. You can include routines in your application to test the SQLCODE, SQLWARN, SQLERRM, SQLERRD, and SQLSTATE fields of the SQLCA data structure and to provide follow-up procedures according to the status returned.

◆ The SQLCODE field contains the negative SQL Server error code (the embedded SQL standard requires that error codes be negative).

◆ The SQLWARN flags are set if certain exceptions, such as data truncation, occur.

◆ The SQLERRM field contains the text of the error message.

◆ The SQLERRD1 field contains the error number.

◆ The SQLERRD3 array indicates the number of rows affected.

◆ The SQLSTATE field contains run-time errors that generate ANSI-standard SQLSTATE codes.

Because the character fields of SQLCA (such as SQLWARN and SQLERRMC) are FAR pointers in Windows, you must use the %Fs format specifier for them when using printf and similar functions.

Handling errors with Java and JDBC

Java requires that when a method throws an exception, there must be some mechanism to handle it. Generally a catch block will catch the exception and specify what happens (which you may choose to be nothing). The first try block contains the method Class.forName, from the java.lang package. This method throws a ClassNotFoundException, so the catch block immediately following it deals with that exception. The second try block contains JDBC methods, which all throw SQLException objects, so one catch block at the end of the application can handle all of the rest of the exceptions that might be thrown because they will all be SQLException objects.

JDBC lets you see the warnings and exceptions generated by your DBMS and by the Java compiler. To see exceptions, you can have a catch block print them out. For example, the two catch blocks from the sample code in Listing 17-5 print out a message explaining the exception.

Listing 17-5: Catch Blocks for Printing Messages about the Exception

```
try {
    // Code that could generate an exception goes here.
    // If an exception is generated, the catch block below
    // will print out information about it.
} catch(SQLException ex) {
    System.err.println("SQLException: " + ex.getMessage());
}
try {
    Class.forName("myDriverClassName");
} catch(java.lang.ClassNotFoundException e) {
    System.err.print("ClassNotFoundException: ");
    System.err.println(e.getMessage());
}
```

There are actually three components, however, and to be complete, you can print them all out. The following code fragment shows a catch block that is complete in two ways. First, it prints out all three parts of a SQLException object: the message (a string that describes the error), the SQL state, and the vendor error code (a number that is the driver vendor's error-code number). The SQLException object ex is caught, and its three components are accessed with the methods getMessage, getSQLState, and getErrorCode.

The second way the following catch block is complete is that it gets all of the exceptions that might have been thrown. If there is a second exception, it will be chained to ex, so ex.getNextException is called to see if there is another exception. If there is, the while loop continues and prints out the next exception's message, SQLState, and vendor error code. This continues until there are no more exceptions (see Listing 17-6).

Listing 17-6: Calling to See if There's Another Exception

```
try {
    // Code that could generate an exception goes here.
    // If an exception is generated, the catch block below
    // will print out information about it.
} catch(SQLException ex) {
    System.out.println("\n--- SQLException caught ---\n");
    while (ex != null) {
        System.out.println("Message:   " + ex.getMessage ());
        System.out.println("SQLState:  " + ex.getSQLState ());
        System.out.println("ErrorCode: " + ex.getErrorCode ());
        ex = ex.getNextException();
        System.out.println("");
    }
}
```

SQLWarning objects are a subclass of SQLException that deal with database access warnings. Warnings do not stop the execution of an application, as exceptions do; they simply alert the user that something did not happen as planned. For example, a warning might let you know that a privilege you attempted to revoke was not revoked. Or a warning might tell you that an error occurred during a requested disconnection.

A warning can be reported on a Connection object, a Statement object (including PreparedStatement and CallableStatement objects), or a ResultSet object. Each of these classes has a getWarnings method, which you must invoke to see the first warning reported on the calling object. If getWarnings returns a warning, you can call the SQLWarning method getNextWarning on it to get any additional warnings. Executing a statement automatically clears the warnings from a previous statement, so they do not build up. This means, however, that if you want to retrieve warnings reported on a statement, you must do so before you execute another statement.

An Embedded SQL for C Reference

Because we are working within the confines of a 3GL-programming environment, there are certain constraints on the use of the embedded SQL. Embedded SQL statements work somewhat differently from, or are in addition to, standard Transact-SQL statements. The maximum size of a single embedded SQL statement is 8,191 characters for 16-bit Microsoft Windows and 19,999 characters for Microsoft Windows NT.

Embedded SQL keywords and statements are not case-sensitive, because they are to be converted to comments by the precompiler. However, the names specified for embedded SQL names, such as cursors, prepared statements, and connections, are case-sensitive. The same case must be used to declare and use these names. Note that hyphens (-) are not permitted in Transact-SQL identifiers, such as table and column names.

This section includes some of the most frequently used statements and their syntax, organized by use. In the heat of the development struggle, you would like to find all statements that relate to the CURSOR construct close to each other. Moreover, things typically come in pairs, and so we have avoided the dreaded alphabetical sort order but adopted a pure relational approach.

The DECLARE SECTION statement

We will typically require some host variables to store data during the process. The BEGIN DECLARE SECTION statement marks the beginning of a C host-variable declaration section. Correspondingly, the END DECLARE SECTION statement marks the end of a declaration section for host variables. Everything in between is a host variable. This data area is buffered by the call interface and kept separate from the normal C variable storage. This is to ensure integrity of data that may be used to update the database. The syntax follows:

```
BEGIN DECLARE SECTION & END DECLARE SECTION
```

The BEGIN DECLARE SECTION statement can be included anywhere C permits declaring variables, and where host variables that are declared follow the normal rules for scoping in C. Use END DECLARE SECTION to identify the end of a C declaration section. The embedded BEGIN DECLARE SECTION statement must follow the EXEC SQL introductory keyword. The Declare sections cannot be nested.

Use the following rules for declaring host variables:

♦ Host variables must be declared in C, not in Transact-SQL.

♦ Host variables referenced by SQL statements must be included in a declaration section that appears before the SQL statement.

Following is an example:

```
EXEC SQL BEGIN DECLARE SECTION;
int id;
char name[30];
EXEC SQL END DECLARE SECTION;
```

The CONNECT TO and DISCONNECT statements

The first and perhaps the last things you do involve database connections. The first task that should be performed in the program is to get a database connection. Always include error checking using the SQLCA after attempts to connect to the database. CONNECT TO will connect to a specific database using the supplied username and password. Following is the syntax:

```
CONNECT TO {[server_name.]database_name} [AS connection_name] USER
    [login[.password] | $integrated]
```

The parameters for this syntax are discussed in the following list:

♦ *server_name* — The server running Microsoft SQL Server. If you omit *server_name*, the local server is assumed.

♦ *database_name* — The database.

♦ *connection_name* — A name for the connection. Connection names can have as many as 30 characters and can include alphanumeric characters and any symbols that are legal in filenames. Hyphens (-) are not permitted. The first character must be a letter.

♦ *login* — The user's login ID.

♦ *password* — The user's password.

♦ $integrated — Specifies that forced integrated security is used for run-time or compile-time applications instead of the login and password.

The options can include character literals or host variables. If you use only one connection, you do not need to supply a name for the connection. When you use more than one connection, you must specify a name for each connection.

Correspondingly, DISCONNECT disconnects one or all database connections. The syntax follows:

```
DISCONNECT [connection_name | ALL | CURRENT]
```

The parameters for the syntax are discussed in the following list:

♦ *connection_name* — The connection to be disconnected.

♦ ALL — Specifies disconnecting all connections. This option must be used before you can exit the program.

♦ CURRENT — Specifies disconnecting the current connection. The current connection is either the most recent connection established by a CONNECT TO statement or a subsequent connection set by a SET CONNECTION statement.

As you would expect, when a connection is disconnected, all cursors opened for that connection are automatically closed.

To ensure a clean exit, an embedded SQL program must issue a DISCONNECT ALL statement before it exits the main application.

The WHENEVER statement

Similar to DB2 embedded SQL and like a Java JDBC try/catch, the WHENEVER construct does not cause anything to happen at the point it is encountered in the code. Instead, WHENEVER specifies the action (CONTINUE, GOTO, or CALL) to be taken when one of three possible SQLCODE conditions is met following the execution of an embedded SQL statement. The syntax follows:

```
WHENEVER {SQLWARNING | SQLERROR | NOT FOUND} {CONTINUE | GOTO
stmt_label | CALL function()}
```

The parameters for the syntax are discussed in the following list:

♦ SQLWARNING — Specifies that an embedded SQL warning occurred and was stored in the SQLCA data structure.

◆ SQLERROR – Specifies that a Microsoft SQL Server message was received and stored in the SQLCA data structure.

◆ NOT FOUND – Specifies that no rows were returned from a valid and properly executed SELECT statement or that a FETCH statement returned no more rows, and that SQLCODE was set to 100 in the SQLCA data structure.

◆ CONTINUE (default) – Specifies running the next physically sequential statement in the source program.

◆ stmt_label – The place in the program where control is assumed.

◆ function() – A function in your application. Parentheses (( )) are required following the function name (function()). If parentheses are omitted, the function is not called. The function can include parameters.

For SQLCODE conditions and values, see Table 17-2.

TABLE 17-2 SQLCODE VALUES

Condition	Value	Description
No error	0	
NOT FOUND	100	End of result set
SQLWARNING	+1	Data truncation on output
SQLERROR	< 0 (negative)	Constraint violation

The WHENEVER statement's actions are related to the position of statements in the source code, not in the run sequence. The default is CONTINUE for all conditions. Following are some examples:

```
EXEC SQL WHENEVER sqlerror GOTO displayca;
EXEC SQL WHENEVER sqlerror CALL error_funct(param);
```

The SELECT, UPDATE, and DELETE statements

Now let's briefly review SQL statements that can be used to select, update, and delete database rows. The syntax should be used based upon the settings of the Whenever statement used to handle processing exceptions.

USING THE SELECT INTO STATEMENT

The SELECT INTO statement retrieves one row of results. The SELECT INTO statement is also known as a *singleton select statement*. Refer to the Chapter 12, "Constructing the Database," to find detailed syntax for the SELECT statement. Note that there are certain restrictions on the select capability within the embedded SQL interface. Following is the syntax:

```
SELECT [select_list] INTO {:hvar [,...]} select_options
```

The parameters for the syntax are discussed in the following list:

- *select_list* — The list of items (table columns, expressions) to retrieve data from.

- *hvar* — One or more host variables to receive the *select_list* items.

- *select_options* — One or more statements or other options that can be used with the Transact-SQL SELECT statement (for example, a FROM or WHERE clause). The GROUP BY, HAVING, COMPUTE, CUBE, and ROLLUP clauses are not supported.

The SELECT INTO statement retrieves one row of results and assigns the values of the items in *select_list* to the host variables specified in the INTO list. If more columns are selected than the number of receiving host variables, then the value of SQLWARN3 is set to W. The data type and length of the host variable must be compatible with the value assigned to it. If data is truncated, the value of SQLWARN3 is set to W.

The embedded SQL SELECT INTO statement is compatible with the Transact-SQL SELECT INTO statement. The embedded SQL SELECT INTO statement is used only when results are retrieved for substitution in the application. The Transact-SQL SELECT INTO statement does not return results to the application and must be issued by using the embedded SQL EXECUTE statement.

If more than one row is returned, SQLCODE is set to +1, which indicates an exception. Following is an example:

```
EXEC SQL SELECT msd_lname INTO :name FROM msd_employee WHERE
emp_id=:id;
```

USING THE UPDATE (SEARCHED) STATEMENT

The UPDATE (SEARCHED) statement changes data in existing rows of a table. The UPDATE (SEARCHED) statement is a standard Transact-SQL statement. This form is used when you are outside of a cursor. When using the UPDATE statement, a developer needs to be sure how many and which rows will be effected. Code to check the SQLCA should be included after the update. Following is the syntax:

```
UPDATE {table_name | view_name}
SET [table_name. | view_name.] {column_name={expression | NULL |
```

```
(select_statement)}[,...]}
[FROM {table_name | view_name}[,...]]
[WHERE search_condition]
```

The parameters for the syntax are discussed in the following list:

- ◆ *table_name* — The table to be updated.

- ◆ *view_name* — The view to be updated.

- ◆ *column_name* — The column to be updated.

- ◆ *expression* — The value of a particular column. This value must be an expression.

- ◆ *select_statement* — A valid SELECT statement that returns a single row with a single column of data.

- ◆ *search_condition* — Any expression that can legally follow the standard Transact-SQL WHERE clause.

Updating a varchar or text column with the empty string (' ') inserts a single space. All char columns are padded to the defined length. All trailing spaces are removed from varchar column data. Strings that contain only spaces are truncated to a single space.

The SQL batch size of 128K limits the maximum amount of data that you can alter with UPDATE. Because some memory is required for the query's execution plan, the actual amount of data you can include in an UPDATE statement is somewhat less than 128K. For example, you can update one column of about 125K or two columns of about 60K each. Following is an example:

```
UPDATE msd_employee SET msd_fname = 'Fred' WHERE msd_lname = 'White'
```

USING THE DELETE (SEARCHED) STATEMENT

The DELETE (SEARCHED) removes table rows that meet the search criteria. The DELETE statement is a standard Transact-SQL statement. This form is used when you are outside of a cursor. When using the UPDATE statement, a developer needs to be sure how many and which rows will be effected. Code to check the SQLCA should be included after the delete. Following is the syntax:

```
DELETE [FROM] {table_name | view_name}
[WHERE search_conditions]
```

The parameters for the syntax are discussed in the following list:

- ◆ FROM — An optional keyword included for compatibility with other versions of SQL.

◆ `table_name` — The table to remove rows from.

◆ `view_name` — The view to remove rows from.

◆ `search_conditions` — Any expression that can legally follow the standard Transact-SQL `WHERE` clause.

If you do not use a `WHERE` clause, all rows in the table specified in the `DELETE` statement are removed. The table, although it no longer contains data, exists until you use a `DROP TABLE` statement.

You cannot use `DELETE` with a view that has a `FROM` clause that specifies more than one table. This would change several tables and is not supported. However, `UPDATE` and `INSERT` statements that affect only one base table of the view are supported. Following is an example:

```
EXEC SQL DELETE FROM msd_employee WHERE msd_lname = 'White'
```

The CURSOR statements

The `DECLARE CURSOR` statement defines a cursor for row-at-a-time data retrieval. This statement does not cause any access to take place; it merely initializes interface control areas with information about the select statement. Following is the syntax:

```
DECLARE cursor_name [INSENSITIVE] [SCROLL]
CURSOR FOR {select_stmt | prepared_stmt_name} [FOR { READ ONLY |
UPDATE [ OF column_list ] } ]
```

The parameters for the syntax are discussed in the following list:

◆ `cursor_name` — The cursor name in subsequent statements. Cursor names can have as many as 30 characters and can include alphanumeric characters and any symbols that are legal in filenames. Hyphens (-) are not permitted. The first character must be a letter. Optionally, the `cursor_name` parameter can be enclosed in quotation marks (' ').

◆ `INSENSITIVE` — Specifies creating a standard-mode, read-only cursor that is a snapshot of the cursor result set at open time. It is equivalent to the `INSENSITIVE` option of the Transact-SQL `DECLARE CURSOR` statement.

◆ `SCROLL` — Specifies allowing first, last, and backward fetch operations. It is equivalent to issuing the `SET CURSORTYPE CUR_STANDARD` and `SET SCROLLOPTION KEYSET` statements.

◆ `select_stmt` — Any valid Transact-SQL `SELECT` statement. Browse cursors can also use a stored procedure that contains a `SELECT` statement. This `SELECT` statement must not contain any aggregates.

◆ *prepared_stmt_name* — The name of a prepared SQL SELECT statement.

◆ FOR READ ONLY — Specifies the use of standard DB-Library read-only cursors. This is equivalent to issuing both the SET CONCURRENCY READONLY and the SET CURSORTYPE CUR_STANDARD statements. Using the FOR READ ONLY option overrides the SET CONCURRENCY statement.

◆ FOR UPDATE — Specifies that cursors are updatable by default; therefore, the DECLARE statement does not require a FOR UPDATE option. However, if the DECLARE statement contains the FOR UPDATE option, the effect is equivalent to issuing both the SET CONCURRENCY LOCKCC and the SET CURSORTYPE CUR_STANDARD statements. Using the FOR UPDATE option overrides the SET CONCURRENCY statement.

The DECLARE CURSOR statement associates the cursor name with the specified SELECT statement and enables you to retrieve rows of data by using the FETCH statement. Cursor names are global within a program module (source code file). Cursors cannot be shared by separately compiled programs that are linked into a single executable module or by a program and dynamic-link libraries that run in a single process.

The DECLARE CURSOR statement must appear before the first reference of the cursor. The SELECT statement runs when the cursor is opened. The following rules apply to the SELECT statement:

◆ It cannot contain an INTO clause or parameter markers (?).

◆ It can contain input host variables that were previously identified in a host variable declaration section.

◆ It must include a HOLDLOCK option to enable repeatable reads. Additionally, standard cursors require that an explicit user-defined transaction is open (opened by using BEGIN TRANSACTION).

For a standard cursor, use the SET CURSORTYPE CUR_STANDARD if you do not use the FOR UPDATE option.

For a browse cursor, include the FOR BROWSE option and use the SET CURSORTYPE CUR_BROWSE statement if positioned updates or deletions will be performed on a browse cursor. If the SET CURSORTYPE statement is not used, the FOR BROWSE option makes the cursor read-only. Do not use the FOR UPDATE option.

You must declare a dynamic cursor by using the DECLARE CURSOR statement before you prepare a SELECT statement. Following are some examples:

```
EXEC SQL DECLARE C1 CURSOR FOR
SELECT msd_fname, msd_lname FROM msd_employee FOR BROWSE;
```

USING THE OPEN STATEMENT

The OPEN statement begins row-at-a-time data retrieval for a specified cursor. Following is the syntax:

```
OPEN cursor_name [USING DESCRIPTOR :sqlda | USING :hvar [,...]]
```

The parameters for the syntax are discussed in the following list:

◆ cursor_name — A previously declared, opened, and fetched cursor.

◆ sqlda — An input SQLDA data structure that was previously constructed by the application. The SQLDA data structure contains the address, data type, and length of each input parameter. This option is used only with cursors that are declared by dynamically prepared SQL statements.

◆ hvar — One or more input host variables that correspond to parameter markers in the SELECT statement. This option is used only with cursors that are declared by dynamically prepared SQL statements.

The OPEN statement runs the SELECT statement specified in the corresponding DECLARE CURSOR statement to produce a result set, which is accessed one row at a time by the FETCH statement.

If the cursor is declared with a static SELECT statement (that is, a statement that was not prepared), the SELECT statement can contain host variables (hvar) but not parameter markers (?). Host variables can only be used in place of constants. They cannot be used in place of the names of tables, columns, other database objects, or keywords. The current values of the host variables are substituted when the OPEN statement runs. Because the OPEN statement is for a statically declared cursor, it cannot contain the USING :hvar and USING DESCRIPTOR :sqlda options.

If the cursor is declared by using a dynamic SELECT statement (that is, a statement that was prepared), the SELECT statement can contain parameter markers but not host variables. Parameter markers can be used in place of column names in the SELECT statement. If the SELECT statement has parameter markers, the OPEN statement must include either the USING :hvar option with the same number of host variables as in the SELECT statement or the USING DESCRIPTOR :sqlda option that identifies the SQLDA data structure already populated by the application.

With the USING DESCRIPTOR :sqlda option, the values of the program variables are substituted for parameter markers in the SELECT statement. The program variables are addressed by corresponding sqldata entries in the SQLDA data structure. A separate database connection is used for each open browse cursor. Each connection counts toward the total number of user connections configured on Microsoft SQL Server. If an attempt to make a new connection when opening a browse cursor fails, or if a valid current connection is not made when opening a standard cursor, run-time error –19521, "Open cursor failure," usually occurs. Following are some examples:

```
EXEC SQL DECLARE C1 CURSOR FOR
SELECT msd_fname,msd_lname FROM msd_employee FOR browse;
EXEC SQL OPEN C1;
while (SQLCODE == 0)
{
EXEC SQL FETCH C1 INTO :fname,:lname;
}
```

USING THE FETCH STATEMENT

The FETCH statement retrieves a specific row from the cursor. Following is the syntax:

```
FETCH [ [ NEXT | PRIOR | FIRST | LAST ] FROM ] cursor_name [USING
DESCRIPTOR :sqlda_struct | INTO :hvar [,...]]
```

The parameters for the syntax are discussed in the following list:

◆ NEXT – Specifies returning the first row of the result set if this FETCH statement is the first FETCH against the cursor; otherwise, specifies moving the cursor one row in the result set. The NEXT statement is the default method used to move through a result set.

◆ PRIOR – Specifies returning the previous row in the result set.

◆ FIRST – Specifies moving the cursor to the first row in the result set and returning the first row.

◆ LAST – Specifies moving the cursor to the last row in the result set and returning the last row.

◆ cursor_name – A previously declared and opened cursor.

◆ sqlda_struct – An output SQLDA data structure that was previously populated by the DESCRIBE statement and that contains output value addresses. This option is used only with a cursor that is declared by prepared SELECT statements. (SELECT statements are prepared by using the PREPARE statement.)

◆ hvar – One or more host variables to receive the data.

If the NEXT, PRIOR, FIRST, or LAST options are not specified, the FETCH statement retrieves the next n rows from the result set produced by the OPEN statement for this cursor. The FETCH statement then writes the values of the columns in those rows to the corresponding host variables or to addresses specified in the SQLDA data structure.

An OPEN *cursor_name* statement must precede a FETCH statement, and the cursor must be open while FETCH runs. Also, the data type of the host variable must be compatible with the data type of the corresponding database column.

If the number of columns is less than the number of host variables, the value of SQLWARN3 is set to W. If an error occurs, no further columns are processed. (Processed columns are not undone.) The SQLCODE value of 100 indicates that no more rows exist in the result set.

The USING DESCRIPTOR :*sqlda_struct* option can be used only with a dynamically defined cursor. The INTO :*hvar* option can be used with either a dynamic or static cursor. Some examples follow:

```
EXEC SQL DECLARE C1 CURSOR FOR
select msd_fname, msd_lname from msd_employee for browse;
EXEC SQL OPEN C1;
while (SQLCODE == 0)
{
EXEC SQL FETCH C1 INTO :fname, :lname;
}
```

USING THE UPDATE (POSITIONED) STATEMENT

The UPDATE (POSITIONED) statement changes data in the row where the cursor is currently positioned. The syntax follows:

```
UPDATE {table_name | view_name} SET {column=expression[,...]} WHERE
CURRENT OF cursor_name
```

The parameters for the syntax are discussed in the following list:

- ◆ *table_name* — The table to be updated.

- ◆ *view_name* — The view to be updated.

- ◆ *column* — The column to be updated.

- ◆ *expression* — The value of a particular column name. This value can be an expression or a null value.

- ◆ *cursor_name* — A previously declared, opened, and fetched cursor.

In addition to having the *searched* update functionality of the Transact-SQL UPDATE statement, the embedded SQL UPDATE statement includes functionality that is known as a *positioned update*. A positioned update changes the row most recently fetched by a cursor.

In a positioned update, the WHERE CURRENT OF option is used in place of a search condition clause. The WHERE CURRENT OF option cannot be used in a PREPARE statement.

In a positioned update that uses a browse cursor, the SELECT statement used to open the cursor must include a FOR BROWSE clause, and the base table(s) must include a timestamp column. If an error prevents any row found by the search condition WHERE CURRENT OF from being deleted, no changes are made to the database.

When using a browse cursor, or a standard cursor with optimistic concurrency control (SET CONCURRENCY with the OPTCC or OPTCCVAL option), and the row has been changed since the last FETCH statement, no changes are made to the database. The value of SQLCODE is set to –532, which means that a positioned UPDATE or DELETE statement failed because of a conflict with another user. Also, the SQLERRD3 field in the SQLCA data structure shows no rows processed. Some examples follow:

```
while (SQLCODE == 0)
{
EXEC SQL FETCH c1 INTO :fname,:lname;
if (SQLCODE == 0)
{
printf("%s %s", fname, lname);
printf("Update? ");
scanf("%c", &reply);
if (reply == 'y')
{
printf("New last name? ");
scanf("%s", &lname);
EXEC SQL
UPDATE msd_employee SET msd_lname=:lname
WHERE CURRENT OF c1;
printf("update sqlcode= %s", SQLCODE);
}
}
}
```

USING THE DELETE (POSITIONED) STATEMENT

The DELETE (POSITIONED) statement removes the row where the cursor is currently positioned. Following is the syntax:

```
DELETE [FROM] {table_name | view_name} WHERE CURRENT OF cursor_name
```

The parameters for the syntax are discussed in the following list:

◆ FROM — An optional keyword included for compatibility with other versions of SQL.

◆ *table_name* — The same table used in the SELECT statement portion of the DECLARE CURSOR STATEMENT.

◆ *view_name* — The same view used in the SELECT statement portion of the DECLARE CURSOR statement.

◆ *cursor_name* — A previously declared, opened, and fetched cursor. Cursor names can have as many as 30 characters, and can include alphanumeric characters and any symbols that are legal in filenames. Hyphens (-) are not permitted. The first character must be a letter.

In addition to having the functionality of the Transact-SQL DELETE statement, the embedded SQL DELETE statement includes functionality known as *positioned delete,* which deletes the row most recently fetched by a cursor. The DELETE statement used in standard Transact-SQL statements is known as a *searched delete.*

Note that a positioned delete has no search condition. The WHERE CURRENT OF option is used in place of a search condition clause. The WHERE CURRENT OF option cannot be used in a PREPARE statement.

In a positioned delete that uses a browse cursor, the SELECT statement used to OPEN the cursor must include a FOR BROWSE clause. The base table(s) must include a timestamp column. If an error prevents any row found by the search condition from being deleted, no changes are made to the database.

When using a browse cursor, or a standard cursor with optimistic concurrency control (SET CONCURRENCY with the OPTCC or OPTCCVAL option), if the row has been changed since the last FETCH statement, no changes are made to the database and the value of SQLCODE is set to -532. Also, the SQLERRD3 field in the SQLCA data structure shows that no rows were processed. Some examples follow:

```
EXEC SQL DECLARE C1 CURSOR FOR
select msd_fname, msd_lname from msd_employee for browse;
EXEC SQL OPEN C1;
while (SQLCODE == 0)
{
EXEC SQL FETCH C1 INTO :fname, :lname;
if (SQLCODE == 0)
{
printf("%12s %12s\n", fname, lname);
printf("Delete? ");
scanf("%c", &reply);
if (reply == 'y')
{
```

```
EXEC SQL DELETE FROM MSD_EMPLOYEE WHERE CURRENT OF C1;
printf("delete sqlcode= %d\n", SQLCODE(ca));
}
```

USING THE CLOSE STATEMENT

The CLOSE statement ends row-at-a-time data retrieval initiated by the OPEN statement for a specified cursor, and closes the cursor connection. The syntax follows:

```
CLOSE cursor_name
```

The cursor_name parameter is a previously declared and opened cursor. Cursor names can have as many as 30 characters, and can include alphanumeric characters and any symbols that are legal in filenames. Hyphens (-) are not permitted. The first character of a cursor name must be a letter.

The CLOSE statement discards unprocessed rows and frees any locks held by the cursor. The cursor must be declared and opened before it can be closed. All open cursors are closed automatically at the end of the program. Some examples follow:

```
EXEC SQL DECLARE C1 CURSOR FOR
SELECT ID, NAME, DEPT, JOB, YEARS, SALARY, COMM FROM MSD_EMPLOYEE;
EXEC SQL OPEN C1;
while (SQLCODE == 0)
{
/* SQLCODE will be zero if data successfully fetched */
EXEC SQL
FETCH C1 INTO :id, :name, :dept, :job, :years, :salary, :comm;
if (SQLCODE == 0)
printf("%4d %12s %10d %10s %2d %8d %8d",id, name, dept, job, years,
salary, comm);
}
EXEC SQL CLOSE C1;
```

Summary

This chapter provided an introduction to the SQL Server 7 programming interface for C and Java. There are many other tools that also provide a programmed interface to SQL 7.x. For example, Web development tools such as SilverStream can be set up to access SQL Server 7 database data using Java and classes that extend the JDBC access.

Appendix A

Third-party Tools

THIS APPENDIX CONTAINS details for a number of product areas that combine with Microsoft SQL Server to provide a feature-rich application development environment with connectivity to enterprise-wide server systems. The need for these products in a development project depends on a number of factors, including the size and functionality of the application and time and budget constraints.

Modeling Tools

A modeling tool is the most important tool when designing a database. Although SQL Server 7 comes equipped with a diagramming tool, it is not yet mature enough. You are much better off purchasing one or more of the products in this section.

ER/Studio

Embarcadero Technologies, Inc.
400 Montgomery Street, Suite 300
San Francisco, CA 94104 USA
Tel: +1 415.834.3131 Fax: +1 415.434.1721
http://www.embarcadero.com

ER/Studio is a database design tool that enables users to create logical data models and to transform them into any number of physical database designs. It has a merge utility that displays any differences between logical and physical models and can initiate bidirectional synchronization between them. The product also features automatic database and schema generation, accurate reverse-engineering of databases, and documentation and reporting facilities.

ERwin

PLATINUM Technology, Inc.
1815 S. Meyers Rd.
Oakbrook Terrace, IL 60181-5241 USA
Tel: 800.378.7528 or +1 708-620-5000 Fax: +1 708.691.0710
http://www.platinum.com

ERwin is a database design tool that helps you design, generate, and maintain high-quality, high-performance database applications. From a logical model of

513

your information requirements and business rules that define your database, to a physical model optimized for the specific characteristics of your target database, ERwin lets you visualize the proper structure, key elements, and optimized design of your database. ERwin automatically generates tables and thousands of lines of stored procedure and trigger code for leading databases. Its "complete-compare" technology enables iterative development so that your model is always synchronized with your database. By integrating with some of the leading development environments – for example, Visual Basic and PowerBuilder – ERwin also speeds the creation of data-centric applications.

ERwin scales across the enterprise by integrating with PLATINUM ModelMart, a model management system that enables database designers, application developers, and end users to share ERwin model information.

HOW

Riverton Software, Inc.
One New England Executive Park
Burlington, MA 01803 USA
Tel: +1 781.229.0070 Fax: +1 781.229.1138
http://www.riverton.com

HOW is a component-based modeling tool and deployment framework expressly designed for building N-tier business applications. Developers design and generate complete, framework-based partitioned applications that feature separate presentation, business logic, and data-access layers. The analysis, design, and application production tools are integrated through a repository. The product generates application code for use with PowerBuilder, Visual Basic, and Java.

PowerDesigner

Sybase, Inc.
6475 Christie Avenue
Emeryville, CA 94608 USA
Tel: 800.8.SYBASE or +1 510-922-3555
http://www.sybase.com

Sybase's PowerDesigner product family offers a comprehensive modeling solution that business and systems analysts, designers, DBAs, and developers can tailor to meet their specific needs. Its modular structure offers affordability and expandability, so organizations can apply the tools they need according to the size and scope of their projects. The analysis and design features enable a structured approach to creating a database or data warehouse without demanding strict adherence to a specific methodology. It provides intuitive notations to ease database creation, standardize communication within the project team, and simplifies the presentation of database and application design to nontechnical audiences.

Rational Rose

Rational Software, Inc.
20 Maguire Road
Lexington, MA 02421-3104 USA
Tel 800-728-1212 or +1-781-676-2400 Fax +1-781-676-2410
http://www.rational.com

Rational Rose is a visual modeling tool that allows developers to define and communicate software architecture. The tool allows communication among various team members which leads to accelerated development. It enables mapping business processes to software architecture and helps you to make design decisions visually.

System Architect 2001

Popkin Software
Corporate Headquarters
11 Park Place
New York, NY 10007-2801 USA
Tel: 800.REAL.CASE or +1 212.571.3434 Fax: +1 212.571.3436
http://www.popkin.com

System Architect 2001 integrates the many aspects of modeling, including business process modeling, object-oriented and component modeling with UML, relational data modeling, and structured analysis and design. All functionality is harnessed within System Architect's repository with native support for Microsoft VBA.

Database Administration Tools

The SQL Enterprise Manager is a superb tool for managing SQL Server databases. But just in case, you can consider some other tools described in this section.

DBArtisan

DBArtisan, from Embarcadero Technologies, Inc., enables the DBA to concurrently manage multiple databases from a single graphical console. It provides facilities for schema and data migration, visual schema management, change management, storage management, security management, and server configuration and optimization. (See the preceding section, "Modeling Tools," for contact information for Embarcadero Technologies, Inc.)

Desktop DBA/Enterprise DBA

Desktop DBA/Enterprise DBA, from PLATINUM Technology, Inc., is the DBA utility for SQL database servers. It allows the management of multiple databases/servers simultaneously, and it permits users to drag-and-drop copy databases from server to server or database objects from database to database. (For contact information for PLATINUM Technology, Inc., see the preceding section, "Modeling Tools.")

DELTAR

SOFTRA, Inc.
2287 Paseo Noche
Camarillo, CA 93012
Tel: 800.388.1177
http://www.softra.com

DELTAR manages the issues of change control between different versions of a database. A project typically has many versions of the same database, ranging from the development version to production – encompassing unit, integration, system, and quality assurance stages in between. This tool automates managing the different versions. DELTAR can be considered to be a tool that highlights the differences between two ODBC-compliant databases.

Fast Unload and Fast Load

Fast Unload and Fast Load, from PLATINUM Technology, Inc., quickly and efficiently load and unload large amounts of data into and out of database tables, respectively. Because data is unavailable to users during data load and unload processes, it is important to have utilities that reduce this window of data inaccessibility.

SQL-Archive

SQL-Archive from PLATINUM Technology, Inc., automates both logical and physical backups. You can schedule, execute, monitor, and verify backups for multiple Microsoft SQL Server databases from a single GUI-based console. These are the product's three key features:

- ◆ Capability to manage backup tasks from any network node, providing DBAs with greater flexibility in managing backups across an enterprise

- ◆ Off-line verification of backup integrity, virtually eliminating any impact on normal processing

♦ A graphical interface that enables a DBA to perform all backup management tasks with the ease of point-and-click computing, increasing user productivity

Logical backups are ideal for data archiving because they allow data to be used in the future with different Microsoft SQL Server versions, or on different hardware platforms. Physical backups are ideal for securing data on a day-to-day basis.

Help and Web Authoring Tools

Your client/server applications will definitely require a help system, and if you're going to build a Web front end, then you may need to go beyond the Microsoft toolset. Following are some tools for you to consider.

Doc-To-Help

WexTech Systems, Inc.
400 Columbus Avenue
Valhalla, New York 10595 USA
Tel: 800.939.8324 or +1 914.741.9700 Fax: +1 914.741.9768
http://www.wextech.com

Doc-To-Help is an add-on to Microsoft Word that enables users to create tailored online help systems in the Windows environment by converting documents (.doc) to help files (.hlp).

FrontPage and Visual InterDev

Microsoft Corporation
One Microsoft Way
Redmond, WA 98052-6399 USA
Tel: +1 206.882.8080
http://www.microsoft.com

FrontPage has easy-to-use features that enable you to create professional Web sites without programming. Comprehensive management tools enable you to quickly build and maintain well-organized Web sites. Good integration with existing content and with desktop applications you already have help to increase productivity. Visual InterDev is a tool specifically designed for developers (as opposed to nonprogrammers), who want to build sophisticated, dynamic Web applications. Visual InterDev supports team-based development and fully interoperates with FrontPage.

HyperHelp

Bristol Technology Inc.
39 Old Ridgebury Road
Danbury, CT 06810-5113 USA
Tel: +1 203 798.1007 Fax: +1 203.798.1008
http://www.bristol.com

HyperHelp provides the same capability as the help compiler (hc.exe) for Microsoft Windows. It uses the same rich text format (.rtf), project (.hpj), and bitmap (.bmp) files, and compiles an online help file for use on UNIX platforms that run Motif applications. HyperHelp enables you to maintain a single source for your help system across Windows and UNIX platforms.

RoboHELP

Blue Sky Software
7777 Fay Avenue
La Jolla, CA 92037
Tel: 800.793.0364 or +1 619.459.6365 Fax: +1 619.459.6366
http://www.blue-sky.com

RoboHELP is a help authoring tool that offers bidirectional Microsoft Word document (.doc)–to–help file (.hlp) conversion. RoboHELP designs, tests, and generates context-sensitive help systems.

SilverStream

SilverStream Software, Inc.
One Burlington Woods
Burlington, MA 01803 USA
Tel: +1 781.238.5400 Fax: +1 781.238.5499
http://www.silverstream.com

SilverStream is an enterprise application server that enables corporations to build and deploy complex Java and HTML applications on which they can run their businesses. It is designed and optimized for the Internet, intranets, and extranets, and it delivers both client- and server-side Java and client-side HTML. SilverStream is one of the first enterprise application servers to tightly integrate business logic, extensive database access, content creation, publishing, collaboration, and communications, in one solution. The comprehensive solution is designed to make developers productive with its tightly integrated design tools that lets them build secure enterprise Web applications that utilize the power of a database to store, retrieve, and manipulate content.

Version Control Tools

While building and deploying applications, you'll need to consider how you'll manage the source code. This is particularly true if there is more than one developer on the project. Following are some tools for you to consider.

PVCS Version Manager

Merant Corporation
735 SW 158th Avenue
Beaverton, OR 97006
Tel: +1 503.645.1150 or 800.547.7827 Fax +1 503.629.0186
http://www.merant.com/pvcs

PVCS (originally Polytron Version Control System) Version Manager organizes, manages, and protects software assets, supporting effective software configuration management (SCM) across your entire enterprise. The intuitive graphical user interface, based on Windows Explorer concepts, is easy to use and encourages team members to apply SCM practices consistently and effectively. PVCS Version Manager Plus adds the power of PVCS VM Server, enabling distributed teams and remote developers to work collaboratively via the Web, while sharing protected and centrally managed software archives.

SourceSafe

SourceSafe, from Microsoft Corporation, is a version control system for managing software and Web-site development. Fully integrated with the Visual Basic, Visual C++, Visual J++, Visual InterDev, and Visual FoxPro development environments, as well as with Microsoft Office applications, it provides project-oriented version control. Visual SourceSafe works with any type of file produced by any development language, authoring tool, or application. The project-oriented features of Visual SourceSafe make managing the day-to-day tasks associated with team-based application and Web-site development more efficient. (See the preceding section, "Help and Web Authoring Tools," for Microsoft's contact information.)

Source Integrity/Web Integrity

Mortice Kern Systems, Inc.
185 Columbia Street West
Waterloo, Ontario, N2L 5Z5 Canada
Tel: 800.265.2797 or +1 519.884.2251 Fax: +1 519.884.8861
http://www.mks.com

Source Integrity/Web Integrity is a software configuration management tool for protecting your source code. It tracks changes to source code as it is created, tested, and revised by programmers. Source Integrity/Web Integrity includes configuration and document management, encryption, visual difference locking, branching, merging, locking, a menu-driven interface, and support for binary and text files. It provides formal processes and engineering methodologies for all development projects. You can monitor and manage all facets of the entire development lifecycle, minimize risk, speed time to market, and guarantee the overall integrity of mission-critical business applications.

Testing Tools

Whatever you've built will need to be tested. This section describes some tools used for testing for you to consider.

EMPOWER/CS

Performix, Inc.
8200 Greensboro Drive
Suite 1475, McLean, VA 22102 USA
Tel: +1 703.448.6606 Fax: +1 703.893.1939

EMPOWER/CS permits multiuser load testing without the need for a PC for each emulated user. It uses the C language for scripts for flexibility, its global variable and synchronization capability aids in emulating complex workloads, and the interactive monitoring feature enables control and debugging of scripts during testing.

Silk

Segue Software, Inc.
201 Spring St.
Lexington, MA 02421 USA
Tel: 800.287.1329 or +1 781.402.1000 Fax 781.402.1099
http://www.segue.com

The Silk product family delivers Web and client/server management and testing products to help you address the risks and complexities that can affect the reliability and quality of your mission-critical system. The Silk product family includes SilkTest for automated functional and regression testing; SilkDeveloper for code coverage and unit testing; SilkPerformer for load and performance testing; SilkControl for enterprise Web-site management; SilkMeter for CORBA-based access control and usage metering; SilkPilot for unit testing of CORBA objects; SilkObserver for end-to-end transaction management and monitoring; SilkRealizer for scenario testing and system modeling; and SilkRadar for automated defect tracking. The Silk products offer proven technologies and methodologies to help you accelerate your QA and development process, and to ensure the continued quality and reliability of your e-business application.

TeamTest

TeamTest, from Rational Software, Inc., is a testing tool that provides integrated functional testing of Web, ERP, and client/server applications. Built on a scalable, integrated server-based test repository, Rational TeamTest combines leading-edge testing power and comprehensive management tools to set the standard for automated testing of Web, ERP, and client/server applications. Rational TeamTest consists of the following component products: Rational Robot, a test recording tool; Rational ClearQuest/TT Edition, a defect-tracking tool; Rational SiteCheck, a Website management tool; TestManager WebEntry, a Web-based defect-entry tool; and TestManager, a test planning, management, and analysis tool. (See the earlier section "Modeling Tools" for contact information for Rational Software, Inc.)

Visual Test

Visual Test, from Rational Software, Inc., is an automated testing tool that brings new levels of productivity to developers and testers, and makes it easier for organizations to deploy mission-critical applications for the Microsoft Windows 95 and Windows NT operating systems and for the World Wide Web. Visual Test helps developers create tests for applications created with any Windows development tool. Visual Test is integrated with Microsoft Developer Studio, a desktop-development environment, and has extensive integration with Microsoft Visual C++. (See the earlier section, "Modeling Tools" for contact information for Rational Software, Inc.)

WinRunner/LoadRunner

Mercury Interactive Corporation
1325 Borregas Ave.
Sunnyvale, CA. 94089 USA
Tel: 800.TEST.911 or +1 408.822.5200 Fax: +1 408.822.5300
http://www.merc-int.com

WinRunner/LoadRunner is an enterprise functional testing tool that verifies applications work as expected. By capturing and replaying user interactions automatically, WinRunner identifies defects and ensures that applications work flawlessly the first time, and remain reliable. LoadRunner/PC tests system functionality and response under stress load conditions by replicating heavy use of a system by distributing applications across the network. This enables you to find critical failures and unacceptable performance issues before going to production.

Software Distribution Tools

Once your application is built and tested, you'll need to deploy it. This section describes some tools for you to consider deploying to your applications.

InstallShield

InstallShield Software Corporation
900 National Parkway, Suite 125
Schamburg, IL 60173-5108 USA
Tel: 800-374-4353 or +1 (847) 240-9111, Fax: +1 (847) 240-9120
http://www.installshield.com

InstallShield enables you to drag-and-drop your application files and logically group them into file groups and application components. The MediaBuild Wizard lets you create any sizes of media from the same installation project. With just a few steps of the MediaBuild Wizard, you can create installations for floppy disks, CD-ROMs, or Internet distribution.

Tivoli Software Distribution

Tivoli Systems, Inc.
9442 Capital of Texas Hwy. N.
Plaza I, Suite 500
Austin, TX 78759 USA
Tel: 800-2-TIVOLI or +1 512.436.8000
http://www.tivoli.com

Tivoli Software Distribution allows system managers to automatically distribute software updates. It identifies any applications package or collection of files, indicates machines that subscribe to the software, and automatically distributes new modules to these computers.

WinInstall

Seagate Software
920 Disc Drive
Scotts Valley, CA 95067 USA
Tel: +1 408.438.6550 Fax: +1 408.438.7612
http://www.seagate.com

WinInstall automates software distribution, making quick work of deploying software to desktops across your enterprise. It creates distribution packages quickly using a Discover Wizard that captures changes made by any installation procedure. It is a network operating system and protocol-independent, so it is a good choice for heterogeneous environments.

Appendix B

Standards, Guidelines, and Maxims

THE PURPOSE OF THIS appendix is to suggest model standards and guidelines, as well as to provide designers with maxims that can aid in the development of applications for the Internet, intranet, or extranet environments using MS SQL Server 7 as the development tool. This appendix is targeted at the lead designers and developers who are responsible for establishing the development environment.

Standards and Development Guidelines

The kinds of standards and guidelines that should be in place at the start of the development include:

- ◆ User-interface guidelines

- ◆ Naming standards

- ◆ Programming guidelines

- ◆ Documentation standards

- ◆ Standard error and status routines

If you're working on a project team, one or more team members are commonly responsible for maintaining and/or enforcing particular sets of standards and guidelines. For example, a database administrator (DBA) might handle standards related to database implementation, whereas an object manager might oversee most of the application development standards.

If you're working solo, you still have plenty of reasons to come up with standards and guidelines to follow. They promote consistency and order, especially on projects that involve many components and whose development life cycles extend over long periods of time. Enforced standards and guidelines are especially valuable later in the cycle, as they make it easier for you to maintain or enhance an application when the original development team is not directly available.

General Design Guidelines

The development team should presume that at least some users have no experience with client/server environments, or expertise with intranets or the Internet. The team should therefore design the interface to be as foolproof as possible. A good design will allow for varying operating preferences and levels by providing menus with both keyboard and mouse-access capabilities. A good design will provide for visual and operational consistency within the application – and to the extent possible – it should be consistent with other commercially available client/server or intranet- or Internet-based applications. Consistency will provide several advantages, including but not limited to the following development environment objectives. It will

- Help in migrating from one application to another with ease and speed

- Facilitate the learning process; that is, in terms of what is expected of each developer

- Minimize training requirements for additional applications that the team will develop

- Increase overall productivity and harmony

- Minimize user confusion and the time it takes a new user to become confident

- Provide users with a sense of stability, thereby increasing their confidence in the reliability of the application(s) you provide

Remember to design the application as a tool for those who wish to use it. Try to make it self-explanatory and, if possible, intuitive. Prototype the product through consultation with representatives of the user community early in the development process. (This is sometimes referred to as JAD or joint application development.) Try to keep any user messages polite and friendly, and avoid computer jargon. Get to know the users' business and use labels for data that are familiar to the users. These measures will enable the user to be in control of the application, not the reverse.

A good, open design will provide the ability to get from any point in the application to any other appropriate point in the application directly, without having to return through application navigation levels in a modal fashion. This applies to Internet, intranet, and extranet applications. If the user must wait for processing to complete, the fact should be made obvious visually; for example, the pointer should change to an hourglass. The user should receive timely and tangible feedback for his or her actions. For example, if a user selects an object, visual feedback that the object has been selected should be provided; this can be in the form of graphical, textual, or even auditory feedback.

Accommodate user mistakes without pain or penalty. A good design will minimize opportunities for error, and when the inevitable occurs, the application should handle errors consistently in a soft-fail fashion. The application should provide error messages that state the problem objectively and, when possible, offer viable solutions.

Provide the appropriate tools or utilities within the application to aid the user. The application should provide methods rather than expect the user to remember or calculate information offline (for example, the day of the week corresponding to a certain date). The application should present choices explicitly rather than expecting users to recall an involved set of options or commands.

Build into the early phases of the development process iterations of design review with the users and, if required, a rework of the interface design. In designing and testing an interface, be certain to consider the larger context within which the application will be used initially and, to the extent known or predictable, in the future. For example:

- Will the distributed software be used in a stand-alone environment or on a network?

- Will the application be used alone or with other applications?

- Is this a custom application with different components for each user?

- Will the application be used with other commercially available applications or software?

Reflect and facilitate any required integration with other applications by providing data-exchange techniques that are consistent across the applications. It is recommended that any common methods be identified and named during the design phase, thus allowing method development to be assigned as a separate project task, such that, for instance, other developers can avoid having to develop these method calls during Java event-handler development. They will then only need to mark a place in the application where the method call and arguments will be inserted later.

Web UI development tools like SilverStream provide a wide variety of components and options that you can use to construct the user interface of your application. Although this gives you a great deal of flexibility, it also requires you to make choices about what is appropriate for your project. By making these choices early on and establishing them as conventions, you can make the application more consistent, attractive, and usable while also saving yourself from a lot of clean-up work later.

To gather intelligent user-interface conventions, you must either learn something about good graphical design or draw upon the expertise of someone who does. Here are some suggestions for doing both. Find some good examples. You can find a lot of good ideas for your user-interface conventions by looking at existing Web applications, especially some of the more popular commercial sites (for instance, Amazon.com). You probably already use several of these sites and know which aspects of their user interfaces you like, and which you don't. If the intended users of your application work frequently with a particular site, you might even consider adopting a similar user interface to take advantage of their experience and lower the learning curve.

Adopting commonly used conventions

You might consider adopting several commonly used conventions for the user interfaces you design and build. In Chapter 13, "Developing the User Interface," you learned that an application can employ different user-interface styles for the user interface: SDI (Single Document Interface), Frameset (Multiple Document Interface, or MDI), or a combination. MDI was a popular choice in client/server environments because of the flexibility it gives the user, and all of the built-in services it provides. In Web-based development it may not be the *de facto* default any longer. SDI may be appropriate if your application is very simple, especially if it deals with only one kind of data and the user needs to perform only one operation at a time. A combination interface may be useful in an application that performs very diverse operations, but you must design it with great care to avoid confusing the user.

Internet page conventions you might apply to the applications developed on the Internet, intranet, or extranet include those listed in Table B-1.

Table B-1 INTERNET PAGE CONVENTIONS

Internet, Intranet, or Extranet Page Area	Possible Convention
Kinds of controls	To keep the interface intuitive, use an appropriate kind of control for each feature you want to implement on an Internet, intranet, or extranet page. For instance, don't use a RadioButton to initiate a command; use a CommandButton or PictureButton instead.
Number of controls	Limit the number of controls you place in an extranet, intranet, or Internet page to avoid overwhelming the user. Use multiple pages instead of trying to cram too many controls into one.
Spacing of controls	Leave enough white space on an Internet, intranet, or extranet page. Don't crowd controls together.
Borders of controls	To make other controls stand out, display them (such as StaticText) without any borders.
Availability of controls	Gray out (disable) a control when it is not available to the user.

Internet, Intranet, or Extranet Page Area	Possible Convention
Length of list controls	Limit the number of items in a `ListBox` or `Choice` control to prevent it from becoming too long to scroll through. You'll usually want to keep the number of items well under 50.
Keyboard support	Provide keyboard access to every control on an Internet, intranet, or extranet page.
Colors	Use color judiciously. It is most effective for bringing out those portions of a page that you want the user to see most readily. When possible, use color defaults so that the user's settings (from the Internet, intranet, or extranet paging system) can take effect.
Fonts	Limit the number of fonts to one or two (and make sure that users will have those fonts installed on their computers). Keep font size large enough to be legible and use a very limited number of different font sizes.
Modality	Try to use nonmodal page flow whenever possible to give the user maximum control over the interface. Use modal (response) page flow only when the application must focus the user's attention.
Toggles	If a menu item serves as a toggle between one state and another (such as on or off), indicate the current state to the user either by displaying a check mark (for example, ✓ On) or by switching the menu item name (such as from On to Off).
Help	Make sure that every menu bar provides menu items that display your application's help system and information about the application.
Keyboard support	Provide keyboard access to every menu item.
Frameset and client/server or intranet/Internet page	In an Internet, intranet, or extranet application, provide a menu for the frame (which displays when no Internet, intranet, or extranet pages are open) and a separate menu for each kind of Internet, intranet, or extranet page (which displays when a page of that kind is active).

Table B-2 presents some commonly used conventions for page and form style standards, and the fonts and colors for them.

TABLE B-2 PAGE AND FORM STYLE STANDARDS

Item	Standard
Banner	As attached (top or left aligned)
Background	White
Application name	Helvetica 28 Bold (left aligned)
Screen name	Helvetica 18 Bold Italic (left aligned)
Labels	TimesRoman 14 Bold
Buttons	Standard Gray Helvetica 12
Links	Helvetica 18 Normal
View titles	Times Roman 14 (or 12) Bold
View text	Times Roman 14 (or 12) Normal

If your users may have small-sized monitors, make sure you design your application for them and not just for large, high-resolution monitors, such as those that developers might have.

The choice of some user-interface conventions will depend on the particular platform on which your application is to be deployed. For example, certain conventions that may be appropriate for Microsoft Internet Explorer users might not make sense for Netscape users. Make sure you are familiar enough with your target platform to choose conventions that suit it. If you're planning to deploy an application on multiple platforms, your user-interface conventions should take any platform differences into account and specify how to handle them.

Designing the development environment

A good development environment is a prerequisite to successful application development. The new developer should be able to hit the ground running when he or she receives a userid. Standards, guidelines, and the like should be available and up to date. Global methods and so on should be placed in a specific JAR file (such as methods.jar).

A development environment should be established consisting of libraries in directories for various levels of development, and support activities including:

♦ A "development" directory for work in progress shared among developers

◆ "Personal" libraries for each developer working on a new or existing version of an application component; existing versions should be "checked out"

◆ A "staging" directory for production-ready code and rollout support

◆ A "production" directory for released code (fully rolled out)

◆ "Backup" libraries that are copies of "production" libraries (optional)

Using directories and databases

The "development" databases should be used for development of the application and any, or all, major enhancements to the application. It should also be used as the starting point for preparing any, or all, releases of the application, frozen at a point in time. It should only be frozen temporarily, long enough to capture and migrate to the "staging" directory or databases. It will probably always be active until the entire application is complete, which means it will last forever. It should be fully accessible to all developers.

The "staging" databases and libraries are used for rollout preparation. They should be used for support during rollout, which means they will contain the source code corresponding to the application executable being rolled out. They will be emptied (by the administrator) after rollout is complete, that is, at the conclusion of migrating to "production." They should be accessible to all developers, but only be used on rare occasions.

 Care must be taken that any changes made in these databases and libraries also are reflected in the "development" libraries for future releases of the application.

The "production" databases and libraries should be used for reference. They will contain the source code corresponding to an application executable that has been fully released. They should be used as the starting point of source code for fixes after rollout is complete and new development has begun. They should be accessible to all developers on a *read-only basis*. They should only be fully accessible by the administrator for capturing the source code corresponding to an application executable that has been fully rolled out by migrating from the "staging" directory of libraries.

Naming Standards

While developing your application, you'll create a lot of different components and have to specify names for them too. These components include database objects such as tables and indices, and application objects such as forms, pages, objects, and controls that go into your SQL Server database. To keep those names straight, you should devise a set of naming conventions and follow them faithfully throughout your project. This is critical when you're working on a team (to enforce consistency and enable others to understand your code), but it's even important if you work on your own (so that you can easily read your own code).

Most component names in SQL Server can be up to 128 characters long. Developers should not abuse this maxim, and names should follow conventions. For example, a good practice is to use the first few characters to specify a prefix that identifies the kind of component it is. An underscore (_) character comes next, followed by a string of characters that uniquely describes this particular component.

Using the relational database object naming convention

Future releases of relational databases could cause modifications or additions to this appendix. All names for relational database objects will be in lowercase. The standards suggested in this appendix provide various naming standard formats. One format should be chosen for the application and followed for all objects. Any text marked in italics represents a placeholder for which an appropriate value may be substituted in the application. The data definition language for database objects named throughout this document should be stored in the DDL subdirectory in the application file structure.

DATABASE AND TABLE NAMING

Today, it is not uncommon to be migrating from mainframe DB2 to a server-based DBMS. If this is the case, then there are several reasons to use the DB2 naming standards for relational database objects. For a database that may be ported to DB2 from SQL Server, the DB2 naming standards should be followed so that names do not have to be changed for DB2. For a database that will be used in conjunction with a DB2 database, the DB2 standards are recommended for the relational database. This will provide a consistent standard for the cross-platform databases. For a database ported from DB2 where the DB2 database will not be retained, the DB2 standards are optional. However, use of these standards may ease the transition for developers familiar with the DB2 database. It is important to note that if you are using the DB2 standard, you should limit database and table names to 8 characters and columns to 18 characters. Tables B-3 and B-4 provide standards for database and table names.

Table B-3 DATABASE NAMING STANDARDS

Standard	Description
Database name	This object name describes an application database.
Format	DB_AAA_DATABASE NAME
	Where:
	db is a two-character constant (required)
	_ (an underscore) is optional
	aaa is a three-character application ID (optional)
	_ (an underscore) is optional
	database name (required) is the name that describes the objects contained within the database. The maximum length of this name can range from 14 to 18 characters depending on the optional parts chosen.
Max length	128 characters
Example	DB_ABC_EXPTRK
	DBEXPTRK

Table B-4 TABLE NAMING STANDARDS

Standard	Description
Table name	This object name describes a table contained within a database.
Format	TB_AAA_TABLE NAME
	Where:
	tb is a two-character constant (required)
	_ (an underscore) is optional
	aaa is a three-character application ID (optional)
	_ (an underscore) is optional

Continued

TABLE B-4 TABLE NAMING STANDARDS *(Continued)*

Standard	Description
	table name (required) is the name that describes the contents of a table. The maximum length of this name can range from 20 to 24 characters depending on the optional parts chosen.
Max length	128 characters (limited length because of view, index, and trigger names)
Example	TB_ABC_EXPENSE
	TBEXPENSE

TABLE COLUMN NAMES

A table column name describes a column associated with a table. It is strongly recommended that the business names be used with some abbreviation list to construct the column names.

The column name should be created from an appropriate business name by applying an abbreviations list to each component word in the business name. Abbreviations for words and phrases should be maintained in the organization's central dictionary. If a word used in the business name is not found in the abbreviations list, it should be added to the list, or suggestions for an alternative from among available words or phrases should be sought. A maximum of 18 characters is permitted for each standard abbreviated name, including separators. This is to ensure compatibility with SQL requirements (see Table B-5 for column naming standards).

TABLE B-5 COLUMN NAMING STANDARDS

Standard	Description
Column name	This object name describes a column contained within a table.
Format	*descname_classname*
	Where:
	descname is a 14-character descriptive name (required)
	amt is for a numeric field
	txt is for a character text field

Standard	Description
	nme is for a character text name field
	adr is for a character text address field
	cde is for a character text code field
	id is for an integer numeric
	dte is for datetime
Max length	128 characters (limited length because of view, index, and trigger names)
Example	user_ID

VIEWS

Views are templates that can be used to encapsulate a SQL query (see Table B-6 for view naming standards).

TABLE B-6 VIEW NAMING STANDARDS

Standard	Description
Ordinary view name	This object name describes any view on a table. A view can consist of columns from one or more tables
Format	VW_AAA_VIEW NAME
	Where:
	vw is a two-character constant (required)
	_ (an underscore) is optional
	aaa is a three-character application ID (optional)
	_ (an underscore) is optional
	view name (required) is the name that describes the contents of the view. The maximum length of this name can range from 24 to 28 characters depending on the optional parts chosen.
Max length	128 characters

Continued

TABLE **B-6** VIEW NAMING STANDARDS *(Continued)*

Standard	Description
Example	VW_ABC_SERIES
	VWSERIES

THE BASE VIEW NAME

The base view name describes a view based on a single table. In addition, this view will always contain the same number, order, and name of the columns in the table from which the view is based.

INDEX NAMING

Index naming standards are depicted in Table B-7.

TABLE **B-7** INDEX NAMING STANDARDS

Standard	Description
Index name	This object name describes an index defined on a table.
Format	XN_TABLE NAME
	Where:
	x is a one-character constant
	n is a one-digit number from 0 through 9 and will be used to sequence multiple indexes defined on a table (required). The number '0' should be used for the clustering index, and the numbers 1–9 should be used for nonclustering indexes.
	aaa is a three-character application ID (optional)
	_ (an underscore) is optional
	table name (required) is the name that should be the same as the table on which it is defined excluding the table prefix (tb) and applid, if used.
	Max length 128 characters

Standard	Description
Examples	Clustering:
	X0_ABC_SERIES
	X0SERIES
	Nonclustering
	X1_ABC_SERIES
	X1SERIES

STORED PROCEDURE NAMING

The stored procedure name describes stored procedures that consist of a collection of SQL and program control language statements bound into an executable plan. Table B-8 lists naming standards for stored procedures.

TABLE B-8 STORED PROCEDURE NAMING STANDARDS

Standard	Description
Stored procedure name	This object name describes any stored procedure.
Format	PR_AAA_PROCEDURE NAME
	Where:
	pr is a two-character constant (required)
	aaa is a three-character application ID (optional)
	_ (an underscore) is optional
	procedure name (required) is the name that describes the purpose of the stored procedure. The maximum length of this name can range from 23 to 27 characters depending on the optional parts chosen.
Max length	128 characters
Example	PR_ABC_SERIES

TRIGGER NAMING

The trigger naming object describes a stored procedure that will be executed when an INSERT, UPDATE, or DELETE is performed on a specified table (see Table B-9).

TABLE **B-9** TRIGGER NAMING STANDARDS

Standard	Description
Trigger	This object name describes any trigger.
Format	T TYPE_TABLE NAME
	Where:
	t is a one-character constant (required)
	type is a one-character constant indicating the SQL operation that will cause the trigger. The allowable values are 'i', 'u', and 'd' for INSERT, UPDATE, and DELETE (required).
	_ (an underscore) is optional
	table name (required) is the name that should be the same as the table on which it is defined, excluding the table prefix (tb) and applid, if used.
Max length	128 characters
Example	TU_ABC_SERIES
	TUSERIES

RELATIONAL OBJECT NAME FORMAT SUMMARY

Table B-10 summarizes all of the standards into one example.

TABLE **B-10** NAMING STANDARDS SUMMARY

Object Type	Format
Database	DB_AAA_DATABASE NAME
Table	TB_AAA_TABLE NAME
View	VW_AAA_VIEW NAME

Object Type	Format
Base view	*VB_AAA_VIEW NAME*
Index	*XN_TABLE NAME*
Stored procedure (application)	*PR_AAA_PROCEDURE NAME*
Stored procedure (system)	*SP_PROCEDURE NAME*
Trigger	*T TYPE_TABLE NAME*

NAMING STANDARDS FOR OTHER OBJECTS

The naming of objects like pages, forms, and data-source objects is important both for recognition and for logically grouping the objects together. For these objects to be grouped in the application's libraries, the names must all begin with the same prefix. This grouping of objects will be helpful in the migration and library-management activities.

The object name can begin with a one- or two-letter abbreviation indicating the object type, followed by an underscore and a descriptive name (the descriptive name may start with a one- to three-letter abbreviation designating a portion of the application, such as a subsystem or conversation group). Short, descriptive abbreviations are recommended. All letters should be lowercase (see Table B-11).

TABLE **B-11 OBJECT NAMING STANDARDS**

Type	Abbreviation	Example
Form	frm_	frm_main
Internet page	pg_	pg_customer_maint
Data SourceObject	dso_	dso_customer_display

Naming variables

When working with or using variables in programs, please refer to this section for guidelines and standards for naming, declaration, and use of variables. The concepts regarding scope of access can be loosely applied to structure and method declarations, and use. Please keep this in mind while reading this section. Development languages typically support variables with varying scope; for example, the Web-development tool SilverStream supports Global, Instance, and Local variables. Each type of variable has a different life expectancy, a different scope of access, and a different level of overhead.

In the case of Web-development tools like SilverStream, Global and Instance variables are all considered to be static because they are declared at design time, are loaded into memory once, and remain in memory even while no code is being executed. Local variables, on the other hand, are loaded into memory when the Java is executed, and disappear when the Java event handler completes. Choosing the right scope of declaration for a variable is extremely important in good Web development. The following sections describe the behavior of each variable type. As a general rule, when choosing the scope (type) of a variable, consider what code is going to have to access this variable. The whole application? A particular Internet page? A specific Java event handler? The answer to this question will steer you toward the right choice for the type of variable required.

The following naming convention should be used when declaring variables:

st_b

Each abbreviation in this example is described in the following list:

♦ The *s* is the scope abbreviation, e.g., g for global.

♦ The *t_* is the data type abbreviation (for example, c for character).

♦ The *b* is the name relevant to the business or application.

The scope information is critical because it gives developers an instant understanding of where the variable has been declared and, therefore, what its life expectancy is and what objects have access to it. The data type is also a very important part of the variable name because it indicates, without one's having to refer to the declaration of the variable, what the data type is.

The business or application name tells the developer what the significance of the variable is, thus giving it meaning outside of a particular code context. For example, scope abbreviations used for Web-development tools like SilverStream should be prefaced with an indicator to indicate the variable's context or scope (see Table B-12).

TABLE B-12 SCOPED VARIABLE NAMING STANDARDS

Abbreviation	Scope
g_	Global
i_	Instance
l_	Local (Java event handler–defined)

For example, data-type abbreviations for Web-development tools like SilverStream should be prefaced with a data-type indicator (see Table B-13).

TABLE B-13 DATA TYPE VARIABLE NAMING STANDARDS

Abbreviation	Data Type
bl	Blob
be	Boolean
ch	Character
dt	Date
i	Integer

The business or application portion of the name should indicate the type of information that is contained in the variable and should comply with the application-specific abbreviation standards of your project. If the name is a conglomerate of a multiword description, the various words should have their first letters capitalized. If the name contains an abbreviation or word commonly displayed as all uppercase, it should be named consistently (see Table B-14).

TABLE B-14 BUSINESS VARIABLE NAMING STANDARDS

Variable	Description
gc_version	Global character containing the application version number
li_acctnum	Local integer representing an account number
ib_winmod	Instance Boolean to keep track of a whether an Internet page has been modified
li_counter	Local integer used for counting in a loop

Headers and comments

Commenting code acts as in-line documentation for the benefit of other developers. The application specifications are essential to understanding where the localized logic has probably been placed in an event-driven application component. There are two forms of comments that are common to most, if not all, development languages:

♦ Comment header

♦ In-line comment

INCLUDING A COMMENT HEADER

Listing B-1 provides an example of a comment header block that should be placed at the beginning of *all* Java event handlers.

Listing B-1: Placing a Comment Header Block in a Java Event Handler

```
/***********************************
[METHOD]
        Put method name here in mixed case.
        (EXAMPLE)
        f_GetConnectInfo( )

[DESCRIPTION]
        Write a description of the method that says only what the
        method does, not how it does it or in what order.
        This method description should be
        used for verification.

[ACCESS]
        Public, Private, Protected.

[INPUTS]
        Put a description of all inputs to the methods.
        This includes PARAMETERS,
        TABLES, EXTERNAL METHODS, FILES, GLOBAL VARIABLES, etc.

        (EXAMPLE)
        PARAMETERS:
        AV_sINIFile - A string variable containing
        the name of an INI file.
        [ASSUMPTIONS]
        List here any assumptions that the program makes
        or dependencies that exist.
        For example, the method may required the existence
        of certain global variables
        or files.  List these assumptions below.
```

```
[RETURNS]
        Describe all possible return values of the method
        in the following format.

        (EXAMPLE)
        POSSIBLE VALUES:
        0          =          Method completed successfully
        -1         =          file not found
        -2         =          section not defined
        -3         =          etc...

[CHANGE LOG]
        NAME        DATE            CHANGE DESCRIPTION
        PRA         9/20/99         original method
        JJB         10/25/99        added error checking code



*******************************/
// VARIABLE DECLARATIONS
int        L_iRetVal

// BEGIN JAVA EVENT HANDLER
//
//        !!!!!! METHOD BODY GOES HERE !!!!!!
//
Return L_iRetVal
//*************** END JAVA EVENT HANDLER
```

USING IN-LINE COMMENTS

In-line comments should be used to explain particular lines or sections of code. A comment should consist of a description of a change and a reason for the change, followed by developer name and date:

```
//Description of change.  Made by JSMITH 10/09/98.
```

This is especially important if you comment something out:

```
//The following line was commented out because the logic is no

longer needed.  ALLENPA 10/25/99.
```

Use the block comment (/* ... */) for large multiline comments. Comments are placed at the beginning of Java event handlers that are complex or difficult to follow.

Comments at the beginning of methods should describe the valid values for parameters and what the possible return codes are.

ADDING SPACING

Single spaces should be placed:

- ◆ Before and after all operators, including the assignment operator (=)
- ◆ After the comma of each argument in method parameter lists
- ◆ Before a close parenthesis, if there are nested parentheses
- ◆ Before the THEN clause of an IF...THEN statement.

Do not put spaces before the open parenthesis (for example, "(") of a method call. Tabs should be used to generally improve readability. Use tabs to align assignment statements for greater readability.

Tips and Techniques

This section presents a mix of tips and techniques that refine the application from a technical point of view. These techniques include providing documentation, error handling, and standard error and status routines.

User documentation and error handling

In addition to comments and online help, you may want to address printed documentation in your standards as well. For instance, you might consider requiring one or more of the following manuscript types:

- ◆ **Developer manuals.** Would it be useful to have someone write one or more internal documents that developers could then reference for information on application components? If so, you need to specify what is to be described as well as how it is to be organized and formatted.

- ◆ **End-user manuals.** Do users need training or reference documents to assist them as they run your application? If so, you should indicate what these documents should cover as well as how they are to be organized and formatted.

Standard error and status routines

Housekeeping chores such as error and status checking are often good candidates for standardization. This is because you'll usually want to handle them the same way across many applications and because you'll want to minimize the chance of accidentally omitting a particular test. For example, you might consider standardizing the way you check for:

◆ Network connection errors

◆ Database access errors

◆ Data entry errors

Fortunately, the object-oriented features of many development languages make it easy to standardize and implement common chores like these. For example, in a Web-development tool like SilverStream, you will want the page controls in your Internet, intranet, or extranet to check for various data-entry and database-access errors. The hard way to accomplish this is to write the appropriate Java event handlers in each individual page control. The easy, object-oriented way is to:

◆ Create your own version of a generic page control by defining a business object for it.

◆ Write your error-processing Java event handlers in this business-object page control.

◆ Inherit the page controls you want to place in Internet, intranet, or extranet pages from your business-object page control. These inherited controls will automatically be able to perform your error processing.

Interesting Facts and Maxims

The following sections contain SQL Server maxims, which are the limits for objects defined and used in SQL Server. These are important to review at the beginning of the project to ensure that the design does not breach any of them. A breach would require redesign and perhaps reprogramming if the discovery is made late in the development cycle.

Maximum capacity specifications

Table B-15 specifies the maximum sizes and numbers of various objects defined in SQL Server 7 databases, or referenced in Transact-SQL statements.

TABLE B-15 CAPACITY SPECIFICATIONS

Object	Maximum Sizes/Numbers SQL Server 6.5	SQL Server 7
Batch size	128KB	65,536* Network Packet Size
Bytes per short string column	255	8,000
Bytes per text, ntext, or image column	2GB – 2	2GB – 2
Bytes per GROUP BY, ORDER BY	900	8,060
Bytes per index	900	900
Bytes per foreign key	900	900
Bytes per primary key	900	900
Bytes per row	1,962	8,060
Bytes in source text of a stored procedure	65,025	Lesser of batch size or 250MB
Clustered indexes per table	1	1
Columns in GROUP BY, ORDER BY	16	Limited only by number of bytes
Columns or expressions in a GROUP BY WITH CUBE or WITH ROLLUP statement	10	10
Columns per index	16	16
Columns per foreign key	16	16
Columns per primary key	16	16
Columns per base table	250	1,024
Columns per SELECT statement	4,096	4,096
Columns per INSERT statement	250	1,024
Connections per client	Max. value of configured connections	Max. value of configured connections
Database size	1TB	1,048,516TB
Databases per server	32,767	32,767
Filegroups per database	N/A	256

Object	Maximum Sizes/Numbers	
	SQL Server 6.5	SQL Server 7
Files per database	32	32,767
File size (data)	32GB	32TB
File size (log)	32GB	4TB
Foreign key table references per table	16	253
Identifier length (in characters)	30	128
Locks per connection	Max. locks per server	Max. locks per server
Locks per server	2,147,483,647	2,147,483,647 (static) 40% of SQL Server memory (dynamic)
Nested stored procedure levels	16	32
Nested subqueries	16	32
Nested trigger levels	16	32
Nonclustered indexes per table	249	249
Objects concurrently open in a server*	2 billion	2,147,483,647
Objects in a database*	2 billion	2,147,483,647
Parameters per stored procedure	255	1,024
REFERENCES per table	31	63
Rows per table	Limited by available storage	Limited by available storage
SQL string length (batch size)	128KB	128 * TDS packet size
Tables per database	2 billion	Limited by number of objects in a database
Tables per SELECT statement	16	256
Triggers per table	3	Limited by number of objects in a database
UNIQUE indexes or constraints per table	249	249 nonclustered and 1 clustered

* Database objects include all tables, views, stored procedures, extended stored procedures, triggers, rules, defaults, and constraints. The sum of the number of all these objects in a database cannot exceed 2,147,483,647.

Data types and their limitations

In SQL Server, each column, local variable, expression, and parameter has a data type. The set of system-supplied data types is shown in Table B-16. User-defined data types, which are aliases for system-supplied data types, can also be defined.

TABLE B-16 DATA TYPES

Type	Description
Integers	
bit	Integer data with either a 1 or 0 value
int	Integer (whole number) data from -2^31 (-2,147,483,648) through $2^31 - 1$ (2,147,483,647)
smallint	Integer data from 2^15 (-32,768) through $2^15 - 1$ (32,767)
bigint	Specifies an eight-byte integer that supports whole numbers in the range from -2^63 to $2^63 -1$. The bigint data type can be specified in all places that a tinyint, smallint, or int data type can be specified.
tinyint	Integer data from 0 through 255
Decimal and numeric	
decimal	Fixed precision and scale numeric data from $-10^38 -1$ through $10^38 -1$
numeric	A synonym for decimal
money	Monetary data values from -2^63 (-922,337,203,685,477.5808) through $2^63 - 1$ (+922,337,203,685,477.5807), with accuracy to a ten-thousandth of a monetary unit
smallmoney	Monetary data values from -214,748.3648 through +214,748.3647, with accuracy to a ten-thousandth of a monetary unit
float	Floating precision number data from -1.79E + 308 through 1.79E + 308
real	Floating precision number data from -3.40E + 38 through 3.40E + 38

Type	Description

datetime and smalldatetime

| datetime | Date and time data from January 1, 1753, to December 31, 9999, with an accuracy of three-hundredths of a second, or 3.33 milliseconds |
| smalldatetime | Date and time data from January 1, 1900, through June 6, 2079, with an accuracy of one minute |

Character Strings

char	Fixed-length non-Unicode character data with a maximum length of 8,000 characters
varchar	Variable-length non-Unicode data with a maximum of 8,000 characters
text	Variable-length non-Unicode data with a maximum length of 2^31 − 1 (2,147,483,647) characters
nchar	Fixed-length Unicode data with a maximum length of 4,000 characters
nvarchar	Variable-length Unicode data with a maximum length of 4,000 characters. sysname is a system-supplied user-defined data type that is a synonym for nvarchar(128) and is used to reference database object names.
ntext	Variable-length Unicode data with a maximum length of 2^30 − 1 (1,073,741,823) characters
binary	Fixed-length binary data with a maximum length of 8,000 bytes
varbinary	Variable-length binary data with a maximum length of 8,000 bytes
image	Variable-length binary data with a maximum length of 2^31 − 1 (2,147,483,647) bytes
sql_variant	Allows a single column, variable, or parameter to support values of various data types. For example, a column defined as sql_variant can store int, binary, and char values. The only types of values that cannot be stored using sql_variant are text, ntext, image, timestamp, and sql_variant.

Continued

TABLE **B-16** **DATA TYPES** *(Continued)*

Type	Description
Character Strings	
table	Allows applications to temporarily store result sets for later use. The data type also allows user-defined functions to return result sets as their output. The table data type can be specified only in variables, or as the data type returned by user-defined functions.

Synonyms

Data-type synonyms are included for SQL-92 compatibility (see Table B-17).

TABLE **B-17** **SYNONYMS**

Synonym	Mapped to System Data Type
binary varying	Varbinary
char varying	Varchar
character	Char
character	char(1)
character(n)	char(n)
character varying(n)	varchar(n)
dec	Decimal
double precision	Float
float[(n)] for n = 1-7	real
float[(n)] for n = 8-15	float
integer	int
national character(n)	nchar(n)
national char(n)	nchar(n)
national character varying(n)	nvarchar(n)

Synonym	Mapped to System Data Type
national char varying(*n*)	nvarchar(*n*)
national text	ntext
numeric	decimal

Specifications and limits

You should always review the limits of any tool you employ (see Table B-18).

TABLE B-18 LIMITATIONS

Item	Specification
Dimensions in a database	65,535 maximum, regardless of the number of cubes or whether dimensions are shared or private
Levels in a database	65,535 maximum
Cubes in a virtual cube	32 maximum
Measures in a cube	127 maximum
Dimensions in a cube	63 maximum
Levels in a cube	128 maximum
Levels in a dimension	64 maximum
Members in a virtual dimension	760 maximum
Members in a parent	64,000 maximum
Calculated members (server-defined) in a cube	65,535 maximum
Calculated members in a parent measure in session context	32,700 maximum
Calculated members in a parent measure in query context	32,700 maximum
Calculated members in a parent dimension member in session context	760 maximum

Continued

TABLE B-18 LIMITATIONS *(Continued)*

Item	Specification
Calculated members in a parent dimension member in query context	760 maximum
Aggregations per partition	65,535 maximum
Cells returned by a query	$2^{\wedge}31 - 1 = 2{,}147{,}483{,}647$ cells maximum
	Although cubes can be larger than this limit, a query that requests more than $2^{\wedge}31 - 1$ cells from a cube will fail.
Record size for source database table	64 kilobytes (KB) maximum
Length of object name (except dimension name)	50 characters maximum when using the OLAP Manager
using PivotTable Service	24 characters maximum when
Length of dimension name	24 characters maximum
Length of aggregation prefix	22 characters maximum

SOURCE COLUMN DATA TYPES

The data type of the source column for a measure must be numeric except when the COUNT function is used. The data type of the source column for a dimension level must be string or numeric (except currency).

EXTERNAL LIMITATIONS

Limitations imposed by other technologies, such as the RDBMS being used, may limit some features of SQL Server OLAP Services. For example, when merging two partitions containing a large number (> 100) of aggregations, you may receive an error message indicating that the maximum number of ODBC Access 97 File Sharing lock counts has been exceeded. This number is controlled by the Access 97 MaxLocksPerFile Registry entry, not by any configuration parameter in OLAP Services. Other such external limitations may apply as well.

SQL Server editions

SQL Server 7.5 comes in three editions: Standard, Enterprise, and Small Business Server (SBS). In addition, users covered by a per-seat license from any of these three editions can install a Desktop SQL Server installation on their client computer. Table B-19 compares the capabilities of the Standard, Enterprise, and SBS editions.

TABLE B-19 COMPARISON OF SQL SERVER EDITIONS

Feature	SBS	Standard	Enterprise
Runs on Microsoft BackOffice Small Business Server	Yes	Yes	No
Runs on Microsoft Windows NT 4 Server	No	Yes	No
Runs on Windows NT Server, Enterprise Edition	No	Yes	Yes
Maximum database size	10GB	Unlimited	Unlimited
Number of SMP CPUs	4	4	32
Extended memory support	No	No	Yes
SQL Server Failover Support	No	No	Yes
Supports Microsoft Search Service, full-text catalogs, and full-text indexes	Yes	Yes	Yes
Supports Microsoft SQL Server OLAP Services	No	Yes (No user-defined cube partitions)	Yes (Includes user-defined cube partitions)

The performance of the Small Business Server Edition is limited to the throughput typical of 50 concurrent users, although individual SBS installations may be licensed for fewer than 50 users. The performance of the Standard and Enterprise editions is limited only by the hardware and operating systems on which they run.

Although the Desktop edition can accept remote connections, it is intended for SQL Server clients that have the following characteristics:

♦ Clients that operate in a mobile environment where they are sometimes not connected to their SBS, Standard, or Enterprise edition of SQL Server and need a local database to store data while disconnected.

♦ Clients that store most of their SQL-based data in an SBS, Standard, or Enterprise edition of SQL Server, but that occasionally run applications that need local database storage

SQL SERVER AND THE YEAR 2000

As of the date that SQL Server 7.5 was shipped, it contained fixes for known year-2000 issues. For the most current year 2000-compliance information on SQL Server 7, please visit `www.microsoft.com/year2000`.

CONVERTING DATA TYPES FROM ORACLE TO SQL SERVER

SQL Server 7 has a larger selection of data types than Oracle. There are many possible conversions between the Oracle and SQL Server data types (see Table B-20).

TABLE B-20 ORACLE AND SQL SERVER DATA TYPES CONVERSIONS

Oracle	SQL Server
CHAR	char is recommended. char type columns are accessed faster than varchar columns because they use a fixed storage length.
VARCHAR2 and VARCHAR	varchar.
LONG	varchar or text. (If the length of the data values in your Oracle column is 8,000 bytes or less, use varchar; otherwise, use text.)
CLOB	text. Oracle CLOB columns can store up to 4GB of data. SQL Server text columns are limited to 2GB.
NCHAR	nchar is recommended. SQL Server nchar columns contain values from the Unicode standard, not a particular national character set.

Oracle	SQL Server
NVARCHAR2	nvarchar is recommended. SQL Server nvarchar columns contain values from the Unicode standard, not a particular national character set.
NCLOB	ntext. Oracle NCLOB columns can store up to 4GB of data. SQL Server ntext columns are limited to 2GB.
RAW	varbinary.
LONG RAW	varbinary or image. (If the length of the data values in your Oracle column is 8,000 bytes or less, use varbinary; otherwise, use image.)
BLOB	image. Oracle BLOB columns can store up to 4GB of data. SQL Server image columns are limited to 2GB.
BFILE	SQL Server does not support the use of external data sources in the same way as an Oracle BFILE column. External data sources can be accessed by SQL Server but are not mapped to a column.
NUMBER	If the integer is from 1 through 255, use tinyint.
	If the integer is from –32768 through 32767, use smallint.
	If the integer is from –2,147,483,648 through 2,147,483,647, use int.
	If you require a number with decimal places, use decimal. Do not use float or real, because rounding may occur (Oracle NUMBER and SQL Server decimal do not round).
	If you are not sure, use decimal; it most closely resembles Oracle NUMBER data type.
DATE	datetime or timestamp.
ROWID	Use the identity column type.
MLSLABEL	MLSLABEL is used only for backward compatibility with earlier versions of Oracle using Trusted Oracle. MLSLABEL columns are not needed in SQL Server.

TIMESTAMP COLUMNS   A `timestamp` column enables `BROWSE`-mode updates and makes cursor-update operations more efficient. A `timestamp` column is updated automatically every time a row is inserted or updated.

DATETIME COLUMNS   Use the function `GETDATE()` in place of the Oracle `SYSDATE` function to get the current system date and time.

SEQUENCES AND THE IDENTITY PROPERTY   If your Oracle application currently uses sequences to generate sequential numeric values, it can be altered to take advantage of the SQL Server `IDENTITY` property. The primary difference between SQL Server and Oracle is that the `IDENTITY` property is actually part of the column, whereas a sequence is independent of any tables or columns.

Index

SYMBOLS

my2cents.idgbooks.com

Register This Book — And Win!

Visit **http://my2cents.idgbooks.com** to register this book and we'll automatically enter you in our fantastic monthly prize giveaway. It's also your opportunity to give us feedback: let us know what you thought of this book and how you would like to see other topics covered.

Discover IDG Books Online!

The IDG Books Online Web site is your online resource for tackling technology — at home and at the office. Frequently updated, the IDG Books Online Web site features exclusive software, insider information, online books, and live events!

10 Productive & Career-Enhancing Things You Can Do at www.idgbooks.com

- Nab source code for your own programming projects.

- Download software.

- Read Web exclusives: special articles and book excerpts by IDG Books Worldwide authors.

- Take advantage of resources to help you advance your career as a Novell or Microsoft professional.

- Buy IDG Books Worldwide titles or find a convenient bookstore that carries them.

- Register your book and win a prize.

- Chat live online with authors.

- Sign up for regular e-mail updates about our latest books.

- Suggest a book you'd like to read or write.

- Give us your 2¢ about our books and about our Web site.

You say you're not on the Web yet? It's easy to get started with IDG Books' *Discover the Internet*, available at local retailers everywhere.